£50

2 vol set

H aid

Models of Capitalism: Debating Strengths and Weaknesses
Volume III

Wherever possible, the articles in these volumes have been reproduced as originally published using facsimile reproduction, inclusive of footnotes and pagination to facilitate ease of reference.

For a list of all Edward Elgar published titles visit our site on the World Wide Web at
http://www.e-elgar.co.uk

Models of Capitalism: Debating Strengths and Weaknesses Volume III

The Ascendancy of Liberal Capitalism

Edited by

David Coates

Worrell Professor of Anglo-American Studies
Wake Forest University, USA

An Elgar Reference Collection
Cheltenham, UK • Northampton, MA, USA

Published by
Edward Elgar Publishing Limited
Glensanda House
Montpellier Parade
Cheltenham
Glos GL50 1UA
UK

Edward Elgar Publishing, Inc.
136 West Street
Suite 202
Northampton
Massachusetts 01060
USA

A catalogue record for this book is available from the British Library.

Library of Congress Cataloguing in Publication Data

Models of capitalism : debating strengths and weaknesses / edited by David Coates.
    p. cm. — (Elgar mini series)
    Selections of articles from various sources.
    Includes bibliographical references and indexes.
    Contents: v. 1-2. Capitalist models under challenge – v. 3. The ascendancy of liberal capitalism.
    1. Capitalism. I. Coates, David. II. Series.

HB501 .M692 2002
330.12'2—dc21   2002070655

ISBN   1 84064 440 0 (3 volume set)

Printed and bound in Great Britain by MPG Books Ltd, Bodmin, Cornwall

Contents

Acknowledgements

The editor and publishers wish to thank the authors and the following publishers who have kindly given permission for the use of copyright material.

American Economic Association for table 4 included in excerpt: Moses Abramovitz and Paul A. David (1996), 'Convergence and Deferred Catch-up: Productivity Leadership and the Waning of American Exceptionalism', in Ralph Landau, Timothy Taylor and Gavin Wright (eds), *The Mosaic of Economic Growth*, 21–62, 425–32.

Blackwell Publishing Ltd for article: David Coates (1999), 'Models of Capitalism in the New World Order: The UK Case', *Political Studies*, **47** (4), September, 643–60.

Cambridge University Press for excerpts: David M. Gordon (1994), 'Chickens Home to Roost: From Prosperity to Stagnation in the Postwar U.S. Economy', in Michael A. Bernstein and David E. Adler (eds), *Understanding American Economic Decline*, Chapter 2, 34–76; J. Rogers Hollingsworth (1997), 'Continuities and Changes in Social Systems of Production: The Cases of Japan, Germany, and the United States', in J. Rogers Hollingsworth and Robert Boyer (eds), *Contemporary Capitalism: The Embeddedness of Institutions*, Chapter 9, 265–310.

Canadian Public Policy – Analyse de Politiques for article: Richard B. Freeman (2000), 'The US Economic Model at Y2K: Lodestar for Advanced Capitalism?', *Canadian Public Policy – Analyse de Politiques*, **XXVI** (1), July, S187–S200.

Frank Cass & Co. Ltd for article: Julie Froud, Colin Haslam, Sukhdev Johal, Jean Shaoul and Karel Williams (1996), 'Sinking Ships? Liberal Theorists on the American Economy', *Asia Pacific Business Review*, **3** (1), Autumn, 54–72.

Economic History Association and Cambridge University Press for article: Bernard Elbaum and William Lazonick (1984), 'The Decline of the British Economy: An Institutional Perspective', *Journal of Economic History*, **XLIV** (2), June, 567–83.

William Lazonick and Mary O'Sullivan for their own articles: (1997), 'Finance and Industrial Development. Part I: The United States and the United Kingdom', *Financial History Review*, **4**, 7–29; (1997), 'Finance and Industrial Development. Part II: Japan and Germany', *Financial History Review*, **4**, 117–38.

New Left Review for articles: Robert Brenner (2000), 'The Boom and the Bubble', *New Left Review*, **6**, November/December, 5–43; Ronald Dore (2000), 'Will Global Capitalism be Anglo-Saxon Capitalism?', *New Left Review*, **6**, November/December, 101–19.

In addition the publishers wish to thank the Marshall Library of Economics, Cambridge University, the Library of the University of Warwick and the Library of Indiana University at Bloomington, USA for their assistance in obtaining these articles.

Introduction

David Coates

The current favourite in the race between varieties of capitalism is definitely 'liberal capitalism'. In much of the contemporary popular and academic debate on the strengths and weaknesses of various national systems of capital accumulation, the predominant model (and certainly that to which most commentators trained in neo-classical economics seem inexorably to drift) is that exemplified by the United States (and, from 1979, by the United Kingdom too). The two economies are not organized in exactly the same way. The UK retains a significantly larger publicly funded welfare system than does the US. In both economies, however, defining elements of the liberal capitalist model prevail. Private companies control their own investment decisions and their own access to open capital markets. Unions are weak, wages are fixed in only lightly regulated labour markets, and direct state involvement in the economy is restricted to the management of the broad monetary and fiscal conditions within which labour and capital make their own private contracts and individual market decisions. In liberal capitalisms, the state is less active than in the East Asian capitalisms discussed in Volume II. Social compacts play a less central role than they do in the coordinated market capitalisms of the Western European kind also discussed in that second volume. In liberal capitalisms, that is, unregulated market forces play a central role, nowhere more so than in the contemporary United States. The defining characteristics of the American economic system, and the depth to which those defining characteristics are socially and politically embedded, are well captured in the first extract here: J. Rogers Hollingsworth's 'The Institutional Embeddedness of American Capitalism'.

That liberal capitalism of the US variety would emerge again as the dominant model in the global order was not always so evident. It was particularly not evident in the 1980s and early 1990s when the attractiveness of Japanese-made cars and consumer electronics to even American consumers began to threaten core US jobs and industries. In that decade and a half, the central concern of much of the relevant academic literature was not the superiority of the US economic model. On the contrary, US economic decline, and the need for US structural economic reform, was the key issue of the day. The resulting US 'declinist' literature was comprehensively and accurately surveyed in the essay by Stephen Cohen reproduced here as Extract 2. For some of the analysts involved in that debate, the 'waning of American exceptionalism' was a perfectly intelligible consequence of 'catch up and convergence' by other advanced capitalisms (Extract 3; also Baumol et al., 1994). For others, the narrowing of the gap between US productivity levels and those in Western Europe and Japan was best understood as the long-term consequence of structural contradictions buried deep in the social settlements that had underpinned US economic dominance in global capitalism's brief post-war 'golden age' (Extract 4; also Bowles et al., 1990). For yet others, the waning of US economic leadership was indicative of the extent to which US industry had settled into patterns of organization and behaviour which, though effective once, were now increasingly outmoded. Lazonick's advocacy of Japanese cooperative capitalism (Volume I, Extract 4) was written from that perspective (also Lazonick and O'Sullivan, 1995), as were arguments by, among others, Reich (1983) and Dertouzos, Lester and Solow (1989) surveyed in Extract 5. But, of course, within a decade many of those arguments had been weakened by the unexpected scale and longevity of the US economic revival. As the new century begins, the central issues surrounding US liberal capitalism have changed. Scholars are asking once more whether US ways of organizing national economic activity now constitute the *only* successful way forward for advanced capitalist economies as a whole; and they are exploring whether the 1990s US growth spurt was built on solid or on fragile foundations. Richard Freeman's widely cited paper on the first of those more recent questions is reproduced here as Extract 6. Robert Brenner's more critical response to the second recent question is reproduced as Extract 7.

Yet even if liberal capitalism is now being canvassed as *the* way forward for successful economies in the new millennium, it is not the case that all liberal capitalisms have been, or are, equally successful, or that liberal capitalisms that have been dominant in the past have always managed to retain their dominance. The UK economy certainly has not, and in its long twentieth-century slippage from world leadership to its current position – around fourteenth/ fifteenth in most global league tables – it has triggered a huge amount of academic interest in its decline (for surveys, see Coates, 1994; Cox, Lee and Sanderson, 1997; English and Kenny, 2000). Fierce disagreements run through the UK decline literature: on the character and contribution (if any) to long-term UK economic under-performance of the militancy of the UK labour movement, the character of UK management and systems of finance-generation, the quality of UK systems of education and training, UK cultural networks and UK state policies. The interlocking nature of those weaknesses, and their capacity to create a downward spiral of performance, is well captured in the widely cited essay by Elbaum and Lazonick reproduced here as Extract 8. The resulting post-war emergence of a low skill–low wage equilibrium in UK labour markets is well documented in the equally widely cited essay by Finegold and Soskice reproduced here as Extract 9, and the resulting dynamic of under-performance is splendidly captured in Jill Rubery's analysis of the British production system reproduced as Extract 10. But labour has never been the only target of academic attention in the decline literature. Features of UK business organization and industrial finance have figured large too, with UK business practices often compared unfavourably to those prevalent in Germany (Extract 11; also Whitley, 1992) and with City–industry linkages in the UK compared adversely to industry–finance links in both Japan and Germany (Extract 12; also Dimsdale and Prevezer, 1994; Porter, 1995). The capacity of large UK companies (both industrial and financial) to move capital abroad, with resulting and self-sustaining weaknesses in the UK manufacturing sector is well documented by the essay by Karel Williams and colleagues reproduced as Extract 13, and the resulting UK model is described and analysed in mutually supporting presentations by Radice and Coates (Extracts 14 and 15 respectively).

This three-volume collection closes with a set of important articles drawn from the rapidly growing comparative literature on capitalist models (see also Berger and Dore, 1996; Crouch and Streeck, 1998; Hall and Soskice, 2001; Hollingsworth and Boyer, 1997; Whitley, 1999). J. Rogers Hollingsworth's comparative essay on Germany, Japan and the United States (Extract 16) is an outstanding example of this comparative material. William Lazonick and Mary O'Sullivan's comparative work on different financial systems extends that comparative framework, and is reproduced here as Extracts 17 and 18. The very mapping of different models in this fashion implicitly challenges the dominant conventional view on convergence and liberal capitalist superiority that now shapes public policy in the advanced capitalist world, and the collection closes with two studies that make that challenge in more explicit form. Buchele and Christiansen's research challenges the conventional view that liberal capitalisms are better engines of job creation than are welfare capitalisms of the Western European kind (see also Buchele and Christiansen, 1992; Cooke and Noble, 1998; Coates, 2000). Ronald Dore challenges the view that institutional congruity with US practices will be the order of the day in Germany and Japan. His is an appropriate voice on which to conclude, for he leaves open the question that many other commentators wish now to close. He questions whether global capitalism will inevitably be Anglo-Saxon in form. For the many social groups and political forces – from Western European trade unionists and Third World workers to environmentalists and women's groups – all of whom would suffer a serious loss of resource and power if the world took that shape, it is to be hoped that he and others are right when they answer that it need not necessarily be so.

References

Baumol, W.J., R.R. Nelson and E.N. Wolff (1994), *Convergence of Productivity: cross-national Studies and Historical Evidence*, Oxford: Oxford University Press.

Berger, S. and R. Dore (eds) (1996), *National Diversity and Global Capitalism*, Ithaca: Cornell University Press.

Bowles, S., D. Gordon and T. Weisskopf (1990), *After the Wasteland: A Democratic Economics for the Year 2000*, New York: M.E. Sharpe.

Buchele R. and J. Christensen (1992), 'Industrial relations and productivity growth: a comparative perspective', *International Contributions to Labour Studies*, 2, 77–97.

Coates, D. (1994), *The Question of UK Decline*, Hemel Hempstead: Harvester Wheatsheaf.

Coates, D. (2000), *Models of Capitalism: Growth and Stagnation in the Modern Era*, Cambridge, UK: Polity Press.

Cooke, N. and D.S. Noble (1998), 'Industrial relations systems and US foreign direct investment abroad', *British Journal of Industrial Relations*, 36 (4), 581–609.

Cox, A., S. Lee and J. Sanderson (1997), *The Political Economy of Modern Britain*, Cheltenham, UK: Edward Elgar.

Crouch, C. and W. Streeck (eds) (1997), *Political Economy of Modern Capitalism*, London: Sage.

Dertouzos, M.L., R.K. Lester and R.M. Solow (1989), *Made in America: Regaining the Productive Edge*, Boston, MA: MIT Press.

Dimsdale, N. and M. Prevezer (eds) (1994), *Capital Markets and Corporate Governance*, Oxford: Clarendon Press.

English, R. and M. Kenny (2000), *Rethinking British Decline*, London: Macmillan.

Hall P. and D. Soskice (2001), *Varieties of Capitalism: The Institutional Foundations of Comparative Advantage*, Oxford: Oxford University Press.

Hollingsworth, J.R. and R. Boyer (eds) (1997), *Contemporary Capitalism: The Embeddedness of Institutions*, Cambridge, UK: Cambridge University Press.

Lazonick, W. and M. O'Sullivan (1995), 'Organization, Finance and International Competition', *Industrial and Corporate Change*, 5 (1), 1996, 1–49.

Porter, M. (1995), 'Capital Disadvantage: America's Failing Capital Investment System', in K. Ohmae (ed.), *The Evolving Global Economy*, Cambridge, MA: Harvard Business Review Books, pp. 33–66.

Reich, R. (1983), *The Next American Frontier*, Harmondsworth: Penguin Books.

Whitley, R. (ed.) (1992), *European Business Systems: Firms and Markets in their National Context,* London: Sage.

Whitley, R. (1999), *Divergent Capitalisms: The Social Structuring and Change of Business Systems,* Oxford: Oxford University Press.

Part I
Liberal Capitalism: USA

[1]

THE INSTITUTIONAL EMBEDDEDNESS OF AMERICAN CAPITALISM

J. Rogers Hollingsworth

This chapter makes several arguments: that contemporary American capitalism must be comprehended in terms of global economic changes; that the distinctive configuration of American capitalism has evolved over a long period and has a logic to its institutional evolution; that the dominant forms of governance of the American economy have been private hierarchies, markets, and the state, with associations being very weak; that variation in governance forms has made for varying performance of industrial sectors over time; that American economic institutions are part of a larger institutional context, and therefore are unlikely to converge with the configuration of capitalism elsewhere; and that the dynamism of American capitalism, with its heavy emphasis on a market mentality and widespread inequality in income distribution, threatens to erode the institutions which have, historically, shaped it.

Capitalism is contradictory, undermining the institutions essential for its continuation. Historically, a variety of social and political institutions have contained the destructive forces of capitalism, keeping firms in harmony with society, but the weakening of existing modes of regulation has recently created serious problems in American capitalism. In order to understand American capitalism, it is important to understand it as part of a social system of production which is characterized by the following:

1 an emphasis on short-term horizons in decisions;
2 a low capacity in most industrial sectors for making high-quality products, but high adaptiveness in some sectors to new product development;
3 a weak commitment to collective governance in the private sector but high reliance on the state as a regulatory agent;
4 a strong commitment to continuous economic change;
5 a weak commitment to economic equality.

134   POLITICAL ECONOMY OF MODERN CAPITALISM

The logic of development of American capitalism

Long-term historical factors explain why the market mentality became so pervasive in the USA, why Americans have a weakly developed civil society and have championed individualism over collective responsibility, and why they have historically preferred mass standardized products over customized and specialized ones. In the USA, there were no 'ancient' religious, aristocratic, or political authorities to overthrow, as the Americans attained democratic and modern institutions without a democratic revolution. Modernization developed without a modern state, and unlike most other advanced capitalist societies, Americans have had a decentralized state with diffused power and little policy coherence. This has resulted in the development of a conservative American political culture. In some European countries, socialist and social democratic parties gained strength by fighting for basic political rights. But not in the USA. Because working men in the USA early on enjoyed political and civil rights, there were fewer incentives for organizing along class lines.

Unlike nations with aristocratic traditions, Americans have historically highly valued entrepreneurship. American Puritanism provided spiritual legitimation for the virtues of enterprise, which, combined with the weakness of traditional communities, partly explains why Americans have historically had a weakly developed civil society. By the end of the eighteenth century, the ease of accumulating land and wealth stimulated a materialistic culture. In the absence of an aristocracy, this produced a class of merchants and manufacturers with a craving for material wealth. An egalitarian political culture, combined with Puritan traditions emphasizing hard work and achievement, reinforced the belief in the USA that one could 'get ahead' by hard work and individual initiative.

These social norms eventually became associated with the American system of standardized mass production, known as early as the 1850s as the 'American system of manufacturing'. That system came into existence before the development of a transcontinental railway system, before the accumulation of the great American fortunes, before availability of low-cost Mesabi range ores and cheap oil, and before the development of a large national market. Part of the reason for the early development of the 'American system' was the high costs of labour and the shortage of skills. But also of great importance were the norms and habits, the lack of sharp class distinctions, and the homogenized tastes of Americans. They tended to place a monetary value on almost everything and supported a market mentality more pervasive than in any other capitalist society.

As communication and transportation revolutions led to declining transportation rates, firms in numerous industries after the Civil War were able to extend product markets, increase output, utilize economies of scale and scope, and undersell smaller and less efficient firms. But after a few decades of expanding markets and impressive profits, they were faced with the classic problems of intense price competition, 'saturated'

INSTITUTIONAL EMBEDDEDNESS OF AMERICAN CAPITALISM   135

markets, idle plants, accumulating inventories, severe price declines, and the threat of bankruptcy. Efforts to cope with these problems resulted in a fundamental transformation of the American economy during the late nineteenth and early twentieth centuries.

Firms in many industries attempted to limit output and stabilize prices by resorting to ineffective informal agreements. Formal arrangements such as trade associations emerged, so that by 1900, associative behaviour had become quite common in a variety of industrial sectors. Trade associations, however, generally failed to stabilize output and prices, because the strong tradition of individualism sanctioned the freedom of American firms to behave as they wished. Also important was the large size of the country, with attendant large numbers of firms and diversity of interests among firms in the same industry. Business associations in the USA have been less developed and therefore have tended to have less autonomy, fewer resources, and less capacity to govern their members than in smaller countries. Moreover, American courts and legislatures declared cartel arrangements and many other forms of collective behaviour illegal, and in 1890 Congress passed the Sherman Anti-Trust Act.

Anti-trust law had the unintended consequence of accelerating the development of large corporate hierarchies. The courts ruled that 'loose combinations' (for example, 'gentlemen's' agreements, pools and other types of cartels) were illegal under the Sherman Anti-Trust Act, but that firms could not be held to be in violation of the law simply because of their size and market share. Before the courts would rule that 'tight combinations' were illegal, there had to be convincing evidence that the firm had engaged in abusive, restrictive, or predatory behaviour, that a company had acted with the 'intent to restrain trade', and that as a result of this 'intent', it had already succeeded or would succeed in the future in obtaining monopoly power. By acting reasonably toward competitors, firms were permitted to do things within a 'tight combination' that were illegal under a 'loose combination'. The Sherman Act encouraged firms to forsake practices of restraining competitors through loose combination, and to pursue internal strategies (for example, hierarchical arrangements) to enhance their market position and stabilize their industries. A long-term consequence of the Act was to enhance concentration of the American economy.

Horizontal and vertical mergers

There was an extensive merger movement in the late nineteenth and early twentieth centuries, with the USA having more mergers than any other country – both in absolute numbers and in proportion to the number of firms in the country. Horizontal mergers occurred with greater frequency in industries which were capital intensive, had undergone rapid expansion prior to the depression of the 1890s, and experienced severe price

136   POLITICAL ECONOMY OF MODERN CAPITALISM

competition. Consolidations succeeded only when tight integration resulted in economies of scale and lower labour costs, or raised barriers to entry; in industries with high volume, large batch or continuous-process production; in industries with high energy consumption; and in those that had large markets. These included food processing, oil, chemicals, primary metals, paper, and consumer durables (for example, sewing machines, agricultural machinery, electrical equipment, elevators).

Firms in a number of other industries believed they obtained cost advantages over competitors by becoming vertically integrated. There were several motives for American firms to integrate vertically. The first was to reduce uncertainty about availability of raw materials and transport facilities by backward integration, and to attain outlets for products by forward integration. The second was to enhance market share by erecting barriers to new competition. In general, firms resorted to vertical integration because of distrust of actors on whom they were heavily dependent. Indeed, low trust among transacting partners has historically been a distinctive trait of the American economy.

Backward integration occurred when processors had few sources of supply; when it was difficult to write contracts for supply far into the future; the production technology was relatively stable; and the product was in a mature stage of the life cycle. Thus, the food processing and tobacco industries did not engage in backward integration, for they had large numbers of suppliers. But backward vertical integration was quite common in oil refining, steel, aluminium and copper, where processing firms believed sources of supply might be cut off, or supplies might become very expensive. Similarly, when firms were engaged in recurring transactions of highly specific assets, vertical integration was used to avoid monopolistic pricing (Williamson, 1975, 1985; Chandler, 1977; Lamoreaux, 1985).

There was also often an offensive strategy to backward vertical integration. Firms in some industries bought up raw materials in order to limit competitors' access. In the steel, copper, aluminium, and newsprint industries, a small number of firms gradually gained control of vital ore deposits and timber. Research and development also were increasingly vertically integrated, for it was exceedingly difficult for firms to write satisfactory contracts specifying research on new products. Firms feared that by contracting out research and development, they might lose their proprietary interests to opportunistic contractors. Firms such as American Telephone and Telegraph, General Electric, and Westinghouse used in-house research and patents to restrict competition and enhance market share.

The logic of networks in the American economy

Even after corporate hierarchies were established by horizontal and vertical integration, it was possible for firms to engage in ruinous price

INSTITUTIONAL EMBEDDEDNESS OF AMERICAN CAPITALISM   137

competition. Many first therefore looked for some form of industry-wide or collective stabilization of prices. Although it was illegal to fix prices through cartels, firms frequently employed price leadership (the dominant firm strategy) as an alternative way of collective price setting, with the price of a good being announced by one firm and the rest of the industry then adopting the same price.

The sectors in which price leadership occurred most frequently were steel, autos, copper, petroleum, agricultural implements, anthracite coal, newsprint, industrial alcohol, and the refining of sugar and corn products. While dominant firm pricing tended to stabilize prices in the short term, in the long run the leader's market share invariably declined, differences in firm size diminished, and leadership tended to decay as a result of competition. Because price leadership stabilized the industry in the short term, firms had few incentives to innovate or adopt new technologies. Hence, firms adopting price leadership as a strategy tended to decline in efficiency. While some American industries used dominant firm pricing to their advantage prior to and after World War II, Japanese firms in the same industries found themselves in fierce competition with one another for domestic market share, which helped them to be efficient and successful once they entered American markets. The Japanese pattern suggests that intensive price competitiveness without price leadership may lead to high efficiency over the long run.

To understand the importance of sources of capital for the coordination of American industrial sectors, one needs to think comparatively. In Japan and Germany, where industrialization occurred somewhat late and where mass markets were much smaller than in the USA, large firms before World War II were dependent for capital on outside financiers – the large banks in Germany and the major financial groups (*Zaibatsu*) in Japan. Historically it was common for Japanese and German firms to rely on one or two major banks for capital. Not only did those banks closely monitor the firms' operations, but they often held equity in them. In Japan there was also extensive cross-company stock ownership. These are important reasons why Japanese and German firms were able to forsake short-term profit maximization in favour of long-term goals.

In the USA, where equity markets are more developed, large firms have been much less dependent on commercial banks for financing. Indeed, during the last 35 years, the proportion of American industrial funds from commercial bank loans has been among the lowest among highly industrialized countries. Equity markets developed earlier and became more important in capital intensive industries in the USA because the country industrialized early. Substantial profits generated from textiles and sailing ships were available for investment purposes in the late nineteenth century. Specifically, investment banking houses in the USA served by the end of the nineteenth century as intermediaries between those needing and those having capital, and without this intermediary to monitor investments and corporate practices, many large firms could not have emerged.

138   POLITICAL ECONOMY OF MODERN CAPITALISM

The role of a few investment banks was so important in transforming and regulating the American railroad industry that they could determine which areas of the country would have railroad expansion, and how many railroads would be established between major cities.

After 1914, state policy was the most important reason for the declining role of investment banking in the coordination of the American economy. The Clayton Anti-Trust Act of 1914 made interlocking directorships among large banks and trusts illegal, and forbade a corporation from acquiring the stock of another if the acquisition reduced competition in the industry. In addition, in 1933 the American government forced a sharp separation between commercial and investment banking. From that point on, investment banks lost much of their access to capital and had diminished capacity to regulate or govern non-financial corporations. The net result was that both types of banks came to have little control over the modern American corporation.

American non-financial corporations thus became dependent on liquid financial markets for raising capital, on the whims of stockholders, who in turn have pressured the federal government to become involved in regulating the behaviour of the equity markets. When owners of American securities think their investments are not properly managed, they sell their assets. Since American management during the past half century has been evaluated more and more by the current selling price of the stocks and bonds of the company it manages, the American corporate structure has increasingly become embedded in an institutional arrangement placing strong incentives on short-term considerations and heavy regulation by the American state.

As a result of this short termism, shareholders in America have relatively little loyalty to the firms in which they are part owners. Individuals invest in companies for appreciation in the value of shares, and the boards of directors of American firms know that their primary responsibility is to assist shareholders in maximizing their returns or risk being removed, or worse, sued. Thus, American management is preoccupied with boosting stock prices (Garten, 1992: 122–4).

Industrial relations in hierarchically coordinated firms

During the late nineteenth century, mass production became the undisputed means of enhancing industrial efficiency in numerous sectors of the American economy, and the basic strategy for expanding markets and minimizing costs. Those firms that engaged in mass production followed a distinctive logic. Mass producers took seriously Adam Smith's prescription that the most efficient way of organizing a factory was to routinize and differentiate workers' tasks down to the smallest detail. The key to breaking manufacturing into ever more detailed operations was to employ specific purpose machinery for each task along an assembly line.

INSTITUTIONAL EMBEDDEDNESS OF AMERICAN CAPITALISM 139

Employment was viewed as an impersonal economic exchange relationship, with machines easily substituted for workers when profitable. Whatever labour was needed to work on assembly lines could be hired or dismissed at short notice. As machinery became more and more specialized, the skill and autonomy of workers declined, and management had little incentive to engage in long-term contracts with workers or to invest in their skills.

Prior to 1960, American mass production strategies were dominant among:

1 producers of low priced, semi-perishable packaged products, with large batch, continuous process technology (for example, cigarettes, breakfast cereals);
2 processors of perishable products for regional and national markets (for example, meat packing and processing firms);
3 manufacturers of consumer durables produced with continuous process technology (for example, sewing machines, automobiles, office equipment);
4 makers of high margin production goods that were technologically complex but standardized (for example, elevators and pumps);
5 other industries which were capital intensive, energy consuming and reliant on continuous production technology (for example, chemicals, oil refining, rubber products).

In the USA, there has been considerable variation in the way that labour–management relations have been coordinated, over time and in different sectors of the economy. Despite the dominance of the standardized mass production paradigm for a number of decades, some industries were always organized differently. Indeed standardized mass production itself demanded the existence of industries organized along opposite principles as special purpose machines necessary for mass production cannot be mass-produced but have to be custom-made. In other words, industrial dualism was a logical necessity even when standardized production was the dominant technology (Piore, 1980).

Mass production was also inappropriate in industries where production was labour intensive and low in energy consumption, and where product markets were heterogeneous. Examples included lumber products, printing and publishing, and residential construction firms. These were industries where each product was relatively unique and required considerable worker autonomy. Such activities took place in settings involving long-term stable relationships among craftsmen.

Still, by 1950 numerous manufacturing sectors of the American economy were tightly integrated into a system of mass production, which was dependent on very large stable markets for products low in technological complexity and slow in their rate of technological change. American management tended to believe that hierarchically organized firms were particularly well suited for mass production and distribution. The

140   POLITICAL ECONOMY OF MODERN CAPITALISM

system was complemented and supported by public sector mass education which provided a labour force with basic training in reading, writing, and discipline to work on assembly lines. American students decided voluntarily how much to invest in their own education. Over time, this voluntarism meant that the level of human capital investment was lower in the USA than in countries with apprenticeship training mandated for specific occupations. Comparing American and German workers, Hansen (1991) points out that American manufacturing workers received virtually no formal training on the job. Of the monies which American firms invested in human capital, most went to managers, technicians and supervisors. American systematic training of rank-and-file employees historically was brief, narrow, and job specific. And through the 1950s, this system struck most American managers as being quite effective.

Challenges from abroad: the postwar period

Many of the USA's industrial firms succeeded with a hierarchical form of coordination because the barriers to entry were too high for effective competition from other firms, both domestic and foreign. But the day of reckoning was to come. By 1960, various European and Japanese manufacturers were adopting some of the latest technology, at a time when transportation costs were declining and markets for high quality consumer goods were expanding. Moreover, manufacturers in Japan, Germany and several other countries had never been as committed to the hierarchical form of standardized mass production as the Americans. Indeed, those countries had very different ways of coordinating manufacturing sectors – geared more to flexible production, to strategic alliances instead of hierarchies based on vertical integration, and to collective forms of governance.

In Japan, Germany and other countries where industrialization occurred later and markets were smaller, modes of coordination which were less hierarchical and more network-like had long been common. They proved more effective once markets became unstable and consumers demanded products based on complex and changing technologies. Hierarchical coordination, by comparison, is effective when markets are stable, consumer tastes are homogeneous, and technology is not highly complex and slow to change.

Following the first world oil crisis in the 1970s, many American manufacturers producing standardized goods found themselves with products for which there was little demand, and with rigid systems of production that had little capacity to adjust. Many American firms responded to market saturation and decline in profits simply by trying to reduce costs. Some froze or rolled back their employees' wages. Others took advantage of the declining costs of transportation and communication to shift

INSTITUTIONAL EMBEDDEDNESS OF AMERICAN CAPITALISM   141

production to low-wage areas. Because of the pervasiveness of the market mentality and the widespread view of labour as a commodity, thousands of firms reduced labour forces and introduced automated equipment. Many firms and their trade associations – especially in the shoe, textile, steel and automobile industries – pressured the government for protection against foreign competitors. Despite these expedients, it became evident that standardized systems of production were incompatible with volatile and unstable markets. Even when the market demand for certain goods remained relatively stable, less developed countries with lower wage rates were able to copy standardized products and sell them in the USA at lower prices. Hence, American mass producers increasingly faced severe price competition and losses.

Eventually, it became obvious that a different coordinating strategy was needed in many manufacturing sectors. The question was whether industries in the USA, historically coordinated predominantly by corporate hierarchies, could shift to the more flexible coordinating strategies employed by their foreign competitors, to overcome their slow response time, their inability to develop in-house components with complex technologies, and their high production costs.

Some American firms adopted certain aspects of Japanese management (for example, just-in-time production, self-managing teams, quality circles and 'statistical process control'). But this was not sufficient to transform the American economy. A nation's financial markets, educational and industrial relations systems and other socio-political factors influence sectoral and national economic performance. And the American economy cannot mimic the Japanese economy simply by adopting some of the Japanese management and work practices.

Importance of multilateral and collective behaviour in advanced capitalist societies

The dominant social system of production in American society was historically coordinated by markets and corporate hierarchies, with firms embedded in a weakly developed civil society. At the same time, there has been, for some years, an emerging subordinate system, one in which economic coordination takes place, not within firms, but within networks of cooperating actors who have developed flexible long-term relations with one another. These networks exist in the absence of highly developed associative institutions like trade unions, business associations or training institutes organized by capital or labour.

Some of the most effective American networks involve cooperative relations among university-based firms with a strong knowledge base and state and federal governments. Where such networks have been successful, much of the leadership has come from the state. Significantly, the American state has rarely sought to develop coordinating networks among

142   POLITICAL ECONOMY OF MODERN CAPITALISM

manufacturing firms in more traditional industries. Rather, it has been active during the past half century in developing networks for manufacturing firms in relatively new industries addressing military and health-related needs of society. The following are products and technologies coordinated by networks firmly embedded in environments involving cooperative relations with university-based scientists and engineers, the state (especially the military), and other firms, both suppliers and competitors: aircraft, semiconductors, integrated circuits, computers, nuclear power, microwave telecommunications, new materials such as high strength steel alloys, fibre-reinforced plastics, titanium, and metal fabrication such as numerical-controlled machine tools. Without such networks, these technologies and products could not have developed in the USA.[1]

One important feature of networks is their linking together organizations with different knowledge bases. This kind of coordination is not possible within a hierarchy, as no single firm has the knowledge and resources to develop any of the technologies and products listed above. Nor could a single firm linked with suppliers develop such products. They could be developed only because firms were engaged in established, cooperative, long-term relationships with other organizations. Networks have been vital in linking experts in industry, government laboratories and land grant universities with knowledge in many different areas.

Industries in which American manufacturing is strong are those in which knowledge is constantly changing at a rapid rate and in unpredictable directions, and in which the strategies of firms are ambiguous and rapidly evolving. Because the relationship of such firms with their suppliers of capital and knowledge is also changing, they can flourish only in an institutional environment that is extraordinarily flexible, one in which scientists, engineers and venture capital are highly mobile. Such firms are born and disappear with great rapidity, just as engineers and scientists are ever shifting from one product and industry to another.

Many Americans are socialized in their educational system to be highly individualistic and to excel in entrepreneurship. Because of the pervasiveness of the market mentality, the strong tradition of entrepreneurship, the flexibility of external labour markets and the presence of venture capital markets, it has been relatively easy for American researchers and engineers to set up their own firms to commercialize new products, especially when the federal government has blessed such ventures with research and development funds and immunity from anti-trust concerns. This has been especially common in information-based industries in and around Silicon Valley, as well as in the biomedical, biochemical, artificial intelligence, and defence-related industries. With a cross-national perspective, it is apparent that network arrangements have performed extremely well in American society in advancing knowledge at the frontiers of science and in developing new products from basic science.

The American R&D system has been less successful in improving upon older products for commercial markets. The Japanese system of research

INSTITUTIONAL EMBEDDEDNESS OF AMERICAN CAPITALISM   143

and development offers a contrast in styles. Although the Japanese are much weaker in basic science, have been somewhat less successful in developing radically new products, and may be somewhat deficient in entrepreneurial leadership, they have established close communication among researchers, engineers, and production and marketing personnel involved in existing product technologies. Japanese firms tend to be rather successful in linking scientists and engineers within established production facilities. In the USA, research and development tends to involve production personnel only in a very limited manner (Aoki, 1988; Powell, 1990; Powell and Brantley, 1992).

Because of the flexible external labour market in the USA, it is very difficult for American firms to keep knowledge proprietary. Movement of personnel from one organization to another undoubtedly facilitates communication, creativity, and development of new products. But because knowledge is so easily siphoned from American firms, they are limited in their ability to focus their talents on long-term development, whereas the less flexible internal labour market in Japan permits firms there to focus more energy on the improvement and refinement of products.

Differences in the underlying institutional structure in capitalist societies have led to substantial variation in their network structures. In the USA, networks are either state led or private–contractual in nature. In Japan, networks are socially or communally based, while in Germany they are quasi-public or associationally constructed.[2]

American-style capitalism and distributional issues

The relevance of this for the USA in the 1990s is that a number of major innovations during the past forty years has had a Schumpeterian clustering effect – innovations and discoveries in biotechnology, electronics, computers, communication, instrumentation, and new materials (synthetic and otherwise). Most of these innovations are occurring in industries in which product lives are short. The American social system of production with its institutional arrangements facilitating creativity, individualism, 'short termism' and flexible labour and capital markets fosters the development of totally new industries. Moreover, the same institutional environment has facilitated the rise of the USA to world leadership in the entertainment and publishing industries, sectors which place a great deal of emphasis on the development of new products with short lives.

There is considerable evidence that the American economy is becoming more concentrated without becoming more centralized. Large firms are becoming leaner and cutting back their in-house operations to essential 'core competencies', delegating other work to outside suppliers. While some scholars have speculated that dual labour markets would disappear in advanced industrial societies, there is increased evidence that they are becoming even more institutionalized in America. Ultimately, economic power and control is becoming not less but more concentrated within multinational manufacturing corporations and financial institutions (Harrison, 1994). While many who discuss the increasing flexibility of the American economy focus on small firms with good jobs and trained workers, there has been a tendency to ignore the low-wage, superexploitative character of many firms on the periphery that support the entire system by suppressing labour costs. For example, in Silicon Valley, an area associated with creativity, high skills, and high pay, nearly one-half of the workers perform production and maintenance tasks and are officially classified as semi-skilled and unskilled. For them, pay is extremely low and benefits are non-existent (Harrison, 1994: 115). In the meantime, the decline of the old industries, such as, steel, textiles, and construction has led to a workforce increasingly polarized between management and other highly skilled workers on the one hand, and low-skilled workers with little capacity to change their skill levels on the other. Viewing the American economy as a whole, the number of people that is highly trained is increasing, but skilled jobs are supported by a very large segment of the population with very low skills.

As American firms in both manufacturing and services engage in vertical disintegration, downsizing, outsourcing and network building across sectors and national borders, there has been a steady decline in union membership which in turn has contributed to increased wage inequality. The dramatic increase in immigration has also contributed to declining union density and rising inequality of wages (Borjas et al., 1992; Freeman, 1993). Indeed, since 1979 there has been a sharp acceleration in the growth of earnings inequality, especially among males (Levy and Murnane, 1992).

During the past decade, Americans had a larger number of new jobs than any other highly industrialized society, but a substantial proportion of these have been involuntary part-time positions with low wages and few fringe benefits, resulting in frequent job turnover. Since 1982, temporary employment in the USA has been gaining three times more rapidly than employment as a whole. Throughout the American economy, workers on average take home 7 to 12 per cent less income than in 1970 (Callaghan and Hartmann, 1991; Levy and Murnane, 1992; Karoly, 1993; Mishel and Bernstein, 1993).

Increasingly, more and more Americans have slowly been moving to the political right in response to promises of tax cuts and reductions in welfare spending. As Keynesian policies are discredited, politicians increasingly articulate political–economic views resembling those of the 1920s: there should be less state and social regulation of the economy, tight monetary and fiscal policies, and more economic coordination by the market. Although much of the American economic recovery is being driven by the expansion of new industries, these industries are embedded in an institutional framework and a political culture that are unlikely to be able to sustain the recovery.

INSTITUTIONAL EMBEDDEDNESS OF AMERICAN CAPITALISM   145

Concluding observations

In assessing the relative roles of corporate hierarchies and networks in the USA, several points should be noted. First, since stable, homogeneous markets continue to exist for many products of low technological complexity, hierarchical coordination remains dominant in many industries. 'Dis-integration' may be occurring in other sectors, but hierarchical coordination is still widespread in American manufacturing, especially in market segments where there are relatively homogeneous tastes for inexpensive products, such as paper products, breakfast cereals, soft drinks, bug sprays, floor wax, deodorants, soaps, and shaving cream. Mass markets for these products are stable and far from saturated, and remain ready for products manufactured by semi-skilled workers and distributed by general purpose firms.

Second, the ability of the USA to produce high quality products in more traditional industries is drastically limited by the rules, norms, and arrangements which influence practices of industrial relations. An industrial relations system that facilitates diversified high quality production is one in which workers have broad skills and some form of assurance that they will not be dismissed. Indeed, job security tends to be necessary for employers as well to have incentives to make investments in worker skills. This type of incentive and skill system has become much more widespread in Japan and West Germany than in the USA, where downsizing of firms and 'sweating' of labour are more pervasive.

Third, the associational system of a country influences both its industrial relations system and its ability to engage in diversified quality production (Streeck, 1991). Where there is a well-developed civil society and associational system, firms have a greater capacity to enter into collective agreements with their competitors not to poach one another's workers. This encourages firms to develop more flexible internal labour markets, and to invest in the skills of their workforces. One consequence of the highly fragmented American associational system is a very flexible external job market combined with rigid internal labour markets, conditions which limit the development of a highly trained labour force in more traditional industries.

Fourth, capital markets in the USA have also placed constraints on the development of broad worker skills. American capital markets have encouraged firms to engage in short-term profit maximization. By comparison, firms in Japan and Germany have relied more on bank loans and cross-firm ownership as a source of capital. The short-term profit horizon of many American corporations has been due to their dependency on liquid equity markets, combined with the fact that American banks have been disinclined to provide long-term interest loans.

Fifth, as technology becomes more complex, changes more rapidly and becomes more expensive, firms are finding that various types of networks are an effective form of coordinating transactions, even in rather traditional industries. But to maximize their effectiveness as governance arrangements in more traditional industries, networks need to be embedded in a rich institutional environment involving various forms of collective behaviour. American firms with networks as a major form of coordination are very weakly embedded in institutional arrangements of a collective nature.

The social environment plays an important role in shaping the behaviour of firms, their types of products and their production strategies. If firms are embedded in an institutional environment rich in collective goods, flexible systems of production in more traditional industries are likely to be dominant. But in a society where there is a lack of such an environment, the market mentality becomes more important, and the collective goods necessary for the flexible production of high quality products and for international competitiveness in more traditional industries are lacking. On the other hand, precisely because American firms are not embedded in a rich institutional environment, they are extraordinarily adaptable, which has given them a distinct advantage in newer sectors that emphasize individualism and creativity and that have a need for well-developed venture capital markets. At the same time, underneath all the glamour of the new industries in the American economy, the institutional underpinnings requisite for sustaining a vibrant economy and a high degree of civility remain extremely weak. The long-term prognosis for American capitalism is therefore problematic, with two competing visions.

Those sharing a neo-Polanyian view (Hollingsworth, 1994) believe that effective civility and governance at the local level are in crisis, with law and order breaking down, social pathologies widespread, and boundaries among ethnic and racial groups becoming more rigid. In this view, the power to govern the states and metropolitan districts has now shifted to suburban areas. As a consequence, schools in large cities remain underfunded and become increasingly unsafe, and urban violence and despair are becoming more widespread. The gap between the life chances of minorities and those of white Americans is widening, and labour market opportunities for minorities are declining. Every American census since 1940 has demonstrated that the metropolitan areas of the country have become increasingly more segregated along lines of race and ethnicity, with middle-class whites moving to suburbia, and central cities populated by African-Americans, Hispanics, and other low-income Americans. In 1990, 60 per cent of Chicago's population consisted of ethnic minorities, while surrounding suburbs were 80 per cent white. As a result, monetary resources for coping with problems of inner American cities are in decline. The tax base of American cities has continued to diminish, while federal government spending on urban problems has declined from 18 per cent of the federal budget in 1980 to 6.4 per cent in 1990.

The implications of these trends for the next generation are threatening. If the USA is to adjust to the economic requirements of an advanced industrial democratic society during the twenty-first century, it must either

INSTITUTIONAL EMBEDDEDNESS OF AMERICAN CAPITALISM   147

rebuild or construct new institutions at the local level. If it fails in this endeavour, order and civility may well break down, and the USA would then lack the capacity to develop at local–regional levels the social institutions necessary for the governance of the economy in an advanced industrial society.

The alternative view is articulated by some centrist and conservative political leaders in the USA and is somewhat more optimistic about the nation's future. With low taxes, an inegalitarian income distribution, high immigration of both cheap manual labour and well-trained Asian engineers, the USA may be able to continue to be innovative in industrial sectors with short product lives. Also, as a result of American military power, the country can continue to offer incentives to the economic and political elites of other countries to be supportive of the American political economy, despite huge trade deficits and a falling dollar. In short, the social infrastructure of American society may be disintegrating, and crime and other social pathologies may be spreading among the surplus population, but the upper third of American society may be able to live extremely well, feasting on the social infrastructures of other countries and on the world market.[3] How long the band can continue to play on in such a world cannot be predicted with accuracy, and depends on the course of events both within and outside the USA.

Notes

1   American agriculture owes much of its success to the fact that agricultural producers have been embedded in a rich institutional environment, with cooperative activity among agricultural producers under an anti-trust exemption; dissemination by the state of university-based knowledge to agricultural scientists; and financial assistance from a number of public and quasi-public institutions.

2   I am indebted to Wolfgang Streeck for these insights.

3   These views were developed after extensive conversations with Colin Crouch and Wolfgang Streeck.

Vol. III, Ch. 1, p. 18

BIBLIOGRAPHY

Aoki, M. (1988) *Information, Incentives and Bargaining in the Japanese Economy*. Cambridge: Cambridge University Press.

Borjas, G., Freeman, R.B. and Katz, L. (1992) 'On the labor market effects of immigration and trade', in R.B. Freeman and G. Borjas, *Immigration and the Work Force: Economic Consequences for the United States and Source Areas*. Chicago: University of Chicago Press. pp. 213–44.

Callaghan, P. and Hartmann, H. (1991) *Contingent Work: A Case Book on Part-Time and Temporary Employment*. Washington, DC: Economic Policy Institute, for the Institute for Women's Policy Research.

Chandler, A.D. (1977) *The Visible Hand: The Managerial Revolution in American Business*. Cambridge: Harvard University Press.

Freeman, R.B. (1993) 'How much has de-unionization contributed to the rise in male earnings inequality', in S. Danziger and P. Gottschalk (eds), *Uneven Tides: Rising Inequality in America*. New York: Russell Sage.

Garten, J.E. (1992) *A Cold Peace: America, Japan, and Germany, and the Struggle for Supremacy*. New York: Twentieth Century Fund.

Hansen, H. (1991) *Manufacturing Skills: Institutionalizing Vocational Education and Training in the United States and Germany, 1870–1918*. Madison: Department of History, University of Wisconsin.

Harrison, B. (1994) *Lean and Mean. The Changing Landscape of Corporate Power in the Age of Flexibility*. New York: Basic Books.

Hollingsworth, J.R. (1994) 'Re-thinking democratic theory in advanced capitalist societies'. Annual Meeting of American Sociological Association, Los Angeles, 5–9 August.

Karoly, L.A. (1993) 'The trend in inequality among families, individuals and workers in the United States: a twenty-five year prospective', in S. Danziger and P. Gottschalk (eds), *Uneven Tides: Rising Inequality in America*. New York: Russell Sage. pp. 19–97.

Lamoreaux, N. (1985) *The Great Merger Movement in American Business 1885–1904*. New York: Cambridge University Press.

Levy, F. and Murnane, R. (1992) 'U.S. earnings levels and earnings inequality: a review of recent trends and proposed explanations', *Journal of Economic Literature*, 30: 1333–81.

Mishel, L. and Bernstein, J. (1993) *The State of Working America, 1992*. Armonk: Sharpe.

Piore, M.J. (1980) 'Dualism as a response to flux and uncertainty. The technological foundations of dualism and discontinuity', in S. Berger and M.J. Piore (eds), *Dualism and Discontinuity in Industrial Societies*. Cambridge: Cambridge University Press. pp. 13–81.

Powell, W.W. (1990) 'Neither market nor hierarchy: network forms of organization', in L.L. Cummings and B. Staw (eds), *Research in Organizational Behavior*. Greenwich: JAI Press. pp. 295–336.

Powell, W.W. and Brantley, P. (1992) 'Competitive cooperation in biotechnology: learning through networks', in N. Nohria and R. Eccles (eds), *Networks and Organizations*. Boston: Harvard Business School Press. pp. 366–94.

Streeck, W. (1991) 'On the institutional conditions of diversified quality production', in E. Matzner and W. Streeck (eds), *Beyond Keynesianism: The Socio-Economics of Production and Unemployment*. Aldershot: Elgar. pp. 21–61.

Williamson, O.E. (1975) *Markets and Hierarchies: Analysis and Anti-Trust Implications*. New York: Free Press.

Williamson, O.E. (1985) *The Economic Institutions of Capitalism*. New York: Free Press.

[2]

Stephen D. Cohen

Does the United States Have an International Competitiveness Problem?

A growing service industry has formed in the United States around the contentious, multidimensional debate on the state of this country's international competitiveness problem—specifically, whether it truly exists and, if so, its causes, significance, magnitude, costs, and cure. In an increasingly crowded, highly competitive field, countless academics, executive branch officials, congressional committees, think tanks, and advocacy councils have produced a proliferating body of books, reports, monographs, essays, articles, newsletters, and conferences. Each entry offers diagnosis and prescription or some combination thereof, but there are many inconsistencies and little common ground when the literature is considered as a whole.

These circumstances make it difficult, if not impossible, for the uninformed observer to attain a clear understanding of the competitiveness issue simply by combining an open mind with a voracious reading appetite. The literature is inadequate in that it fails even to agree on a common methodology for defining and measuring the problem. The proliferation of studies and opinions has produced relatively little that might serve as the basis for consensus on matters of either method or substance; instead, the published works have produced a welter of conflicting assertions. To paraphrase (now Labor Secretary) Robert Reich, speaking before the U.S. Senate Appropriations Committee (1988), the subject of competitiveness in the United States shifted fairly quickly from the status of obscurity to one of contentious ambiguity, with no intervening period of coherence.

The central thesis advanced in this chapter is that the abundance of conflicting arguments, along with the lack of rigorous methodological standards to sort them out, have created a situation in which the vast bulk of the literature is so contradictory that it collectively cancels itself out as a contributor of definitive insights or as a major step toward consensus. At best, the literature might be viewed as a metaphor for the unusual complexity and numerous imponderables of the subject. At worst, the widespread failure to acknowledge the difficult necessity of trying to assess, weight, and integrate

21

22   *Stephen D. Cohen*

the range of operational definitions of competitiveness suggests either inattention to the scientific method or the prevalence of ideological arguments. Indeed, it is fair to characterize the debate among scholars and policymakers as a manifestation of a deeply rooted argument between those with an ambitious agenda for major changes in government policies and corporate practices and those preferring the status quo.

While appreciating the complexity of the competitiveness issue, this study is nonetheless critical of the overall body of literature that has been produced. A critique of published efforts since the mid-1980s to assess the extent of the U.S. competitiveness problem risks incorporating the author's own biases.[1] The purpose of this chapter, however, is not to reach conclusions on the substantive nature of the problem, but rather to demonstrate that an unjustifiably wide gap exists between the seemingly endless nuances and complexities involved in assessing competitiveness and the immodest rush to judgment on causes and prescriptions found in much of the literature.

Because of this study's limited scope and length, it will address competitiveness only in the economic sense of the term. Related questions such as decline in the overall U.S. position in the international political economy, the merits of and need for a U.S. industrial policy, and other recommended remedial courses of action are not addressed here. The focus instead is on the more specific question of whether and why the United States is suffering a significant decline in its ability to compete effectively in the *industrial* sector against its major trading partners. The balance of this chapter first surveys the main operational measures that have been adduced as indicators of U.S. competitiveness. It then turns to discussion of seven different positions arranged along a continuum of concern about the competitiveness issue.

ALTERNATIVE MEASURES OF COMPETITIVENESS

Most analysts have accepted the definition of competitiveness offered in the 1985 Report of the President's Commission on Industrial Competitiveness (1985) as the "industry standard": "the degree to which a nation can, under free and fair market conditions, produce goods and services that meet the test of international markets while simultaneously maintaining or expanding the real incomes of its citizens." Beyond this conceptually sound definition, disagreements quickly arise, particularly over how to determine the precise means to measure the degree to which the United States is passing or failing the competitiveness test. In consequence, conflicting technical definitions, ambiguous statistics, and multiple interpretations of data plague measurement of the competitiveness concept. Even if we were certain about how to measure competitiveness, we would still be left with the question of whether the United States has lost a significant measure of it. Unfortunately, few analysts seem to acknowledge the methodological and substantive problem posed by Scott (1985: 16):

> The challenge for the analyst is to fit together the various measurements
> into a theory that not only gives a sound appraisal of past performance, but
> also sheds some light on future prospects. . . . Some closing of the gap by
> other countries was explicitly sought by the United States [after 1945] and
> is not a sign of loss of competitiveness. At what point, and with what cri-
> teria is one to conclude that the closing of the gap has already—or soon
> will have—gone too far to be consistent with U.S. interests? The answer
> can only be relative.

Absent satisfactory answers to the question Scott poses, it is not surprising
that a wide array of conflicting and overlapping evidence has been assembled by those alleging or denying a serious decline in U.S. competitiveness.

For virtually every major quantitative indicator of the state of U.S. competitiveness, there is at least one contradictory interpretation, or at least one
competing statistical measure. There is no self-evident, incontrovertible
piece of datum that is not discounted or ignored by other participants in the
debate. What follows is a critical survey of the principal measures used as
barometers of U.S. competitiveness: trade balances, world market shares,
productivity growth, research and development (R&D) efforts, and the cost
of capital.

Trade Balances

Perhaps the most commonly cited quantitative indicator of the U.S. competitiveness problem is its large multilateral trade deficit. This deficit peaked at
$152 billion in 1987, then dipped to a still mammoth $67 billion in 1991; by
1993, it was again well above $100 billion, and climbing. The validity of
trade deficits as a measure of competitiveness is arguable, however, even
assuming acceptance in principle (which is not universal) that a net excess
of imports per se is evidence of a significant competitive problem. For example, trade balances are often a simple reflection of business cycles. Given the
possibility that inclusion of raw materials such as oil and labor-intensive
goods such as apparel can distort overall trade figures, some international
economists prefer to measure U.S. industrial competitiveness through the
more specific, but largely ignored U.S. trade balance in high-technology
goods. By utilizing the high-tech trade balances produced by the Commerce
Department's International Trade Administration, a slightly more positive
trade outlook is suggested. If one prefers a significantly more upbeat statistical series also focused on high tech, one could cite the numbers produced
elsewhere in the Commerce Department (using different definitions) that
show a steadier, larger trade surplus in high-tech goods.[2]

Some economists have argued that all variations of trade balances
should be disregarded as accurate measures of competitiveness on the
grounds that they do not consider an increasingly critical indicator of the

ability of U.S. companies to sell in foreign markets: foreign direct investment. Commerce Department data show sales abroad by foreign subsidiaries
of U.S. multinational corporations to be enormous. A total sales figure of
$1.2 trillion can be used for the analyst seeking to make the case that things
are really better than they appear; alternatively, the more honest and relevant
number of $620 billion for subsidiaries' sales of manufactured goods alone
should be cited in an objective analysis of U.S. industrial competitiveness.[3]
In any event, adding foreign sales of manufactured goods by U.S.-affiliated
companies overseas to exports would provide a fuller measure of international competitiveness. Indeed, the combination of these two forms of sales
to foreigners would produce a significant surplus in a revised balance of
U.S. merchandise transactions with the rest of the world and, in turn, a much
rosier measure of U.S. competitiveness (even after adjusting for sales within the U.S. by foreign-controlled companies). Similarly, a study of trade patterns during the 1966–1977 period found that U.S. companies with overseas
production experienced an increased market share in world exports of manufactured goods, thereby far outdistancing the declining performance of
companies without overseas production (Lipsey, 1985/1986).

Shares of World Markets

Choosing particular base years, or beginning points, is often used to make a
data series appear to support one or another argument. By manipulating
selection of base years, arguments are easily supported that there is, may be,
or is not a clear and present U.S. competitiveness problem. Believers of the
existence of a serious problem will measure current U.S. shares of world
trade and world GNP against a base year centered in the early 1950s. For
example, between 1950 and 1980, the U.S. share of world GNP dropped
from 40 percent to 21.5 percent, and its portion of world trade declined from
20 percent to 11 percent (Scott, 1985: 18). In the atypical, immediate
post–World War II period, the U.S. share of world manufacturing was close
to one-half, a "proportion never before or since attained by a single nation"
(Kennedy, 1987a: 29). The validity of utilizing such an artifactual base year
to demonstrate a long-term U.S. economic decline is dubious.

   Adherents of the optimistic view of U.S. competitiveness usually use
the 1970s as a base period. This choice is a kind of damage control insofar
as there is no way (or no base year) that allows denial of the fact that there
was some decline in the United States' global share of manufactured exports
between 1950 and the late 1980s. Optimists with up-to-date statistics can
argue that the unusually strong U.S. export growth after 1989 signals a
major recovery in competitiveness that stems at least in part from the depreciation in the dollar's exchange rate. Finally, advocates of the argument that
the U.S. competitiveness problem is focused on Japan can point to data
showing that virtually all of the decline in U.S. shares of world trade in high-

tech goods between 1970 and 1986 is accounted for by that one country; Western European shares were basically stagnant (National Science Foundation, 1988: 92).

Productivity Growth

The ability of a country to raise its standard of living and to increase real wages is closely tied to productivity growth, which thus serves as another barometer of a country's ability to compete internationally. Indeed, some analysts contend that the competitiveness concept connotes nothing more than productivity increases (e.g., Krugman, 1994a). The United States' rate of productivity growth has lagged relative to most other industrial countries over the past thirty years, but the bewildering array of different base years and different statistical sources presented in the competitiveness literature gives a highly uneven picture of just how bad and how permanent the United States' relative productivity performance has actually been. More optimistic economists ignore such numbers entirely and point to the statistical truism that the United States remains the most productive country in the world, measured in terms of either output per capita or output per employed worker (e.g., Balk, 1990: 1). The pessimists seem to ignore the principal rebuttal to this measure: by measuring all economic output, i.e., goods and services, it is biased upward by the relatively efficient U.S. services sector. The total output figure therefore exaggerates the ability of any particular U.S. industrial sector to compete in the internationally traded goods sector.

In point of fact, no consistent or definitive data exist to measure comparative national productivity levels in manufacturing as a whole or by particular industry. In contrast to optimistic results suggesting that the United States is still ahead (e.g., Lawrence, 1984: 33), there is the troubling finding that between 1973 and 1985, in thirteen major industries, U.S. productivity growth trailed Japan and Germany in all of the thirteen industries studied. During this period, Japan's average annual productivity increases in the electrical machinery, transportation equipment, chemicals, and scientific instruments sectors were at least triple U.S. increases (Neef, 1988: Table 6).

Research and Development

Data on outlays for research and development also provide an especially fertile field for ambiguity and disagreement. First, the good news: the United States spends far more on R&D efforts than any other country, outspending (in inflation-adjusted dollars) Japan, Germany, France, and the United Kingdom combined (National Science Foundation, 1990b: 15). In addition, the U.S. ratio of R&D outlays to GNP compares favorably with all other major industrialized countries. Next, the bad news: a closer look at the statistics shows that a disproportionately large percentage of U.S. R&D has gone into defense-related efforts that contribute little or nothing to enhance-

26   *Stephen D. Cohen*

ment of commercial competitiveness. The ratio of nondefense R&D to GNP for the United States in 1988 of 2.0 percent compares unfavorably with the 2.9 and 2.6 percent ratios of Japan and Germany, respectively (National Science Foundation, 1990b: 15). On the one hand, in absolute terms, the United States is still spending more on nondefense R&D than either of these countries because of a larger GNP. On the other hand, much of this category of spending in the United States goes into the space, health, and energy sectors, which do not necessarily have a direct effect on competitiveness in internationally traded industrial goods.

Finally, there is the ambiguous news. First, no data on expenditures (either absolute amounts or as a percentage of GNP) can provide an accurate measure of the *effectiveness* of R&D efforts, i.e., the relationship between money spent and results secured. Smaller R&D expenditures in one country conceivably could generate disproportionate success relative to another less "R&D efficient" country. Second, a more precise estimate of the probable contribution of national R&D outlays to competitiveness awaits the collection and dissemination of internationally comparable data measuring R&D outlays for the specific kinds of commercial and manufacturing technology used in the civilian industrial sector. Third, there is the question of what exchange rate to use when converting foreign R&D outlays into dollars. In addition to differences arising from the choice of exchange rate measure (e.g., purchasing power parity exchange rates), occasionally rapid exchange rate movements distort estimates of R&D efforts.

Cost of Capital

The cost of capital is an important indicator of competitiveness because it affects corporate investment and pricing decisions. The lower the borrowing costs, the longer a company can wait to recoup the costs of its capital investments. With quicker amortization of costs, a company can implement a patient, long-term, growth-oriented strategy more easily than a short-term, profit-oriented strategy that seeks to quickly recoup investment costs. It is widely assumed that the lower cost of capital enjoyed until recently by Japanese industrial concerns has been a major source of competitive strength. The problem is that no two studies find the same difference, owing to the inherent difficulties of defining and measuring these costs over time. Hence, the exact magnitude of the relative U.S. disadvantage in this important criterion of competitiveness is unknown (for a survey of these studies, see Ostrom in U.S. Congress, Joint Economic Committee, 1990).

It is clear that no measure of competitiveness is adequate by itself. Each is subject to differing interpretations, and we do not know how to weight or combine multiple indicators to form a composite measure. We now look at the competitiveness question from a different perspective—the range of different positions arrayed according to how each assesses the competitive status of the United States.

A CONTINUUM OF POSITIONS
ON THE COMPETITIVENESS ISSUE

Methodological problems are also inherent to the task of finding ways to summarize the various viewpoints, or positions, in the competitiveness debate. One method would be to classify the different schools of thought by specific substantive argument, e.g., the competitive implications of the trade deficit or of the shift to services based on information and communication technologies. Given the large number of such arguments, as well as the considerable overlap among them, this approach is not ideal for a short but inclusive survey. Another way to classify the literature would be to slice it into the main levels of economic and policy activity most frequently claimed to be the source or location of competitiveness problems (e.g., macroeconomic, sectoral, microeconomic, the external sector), but this too would likely prove too cumbersome for the task at hand.

This critique first differentiates the various schools of thought according to how they assess the big issues, and then focuses on the shades of difference that often prevail among scholars sharing the same general outlook. The simplest, clearest, most complete taxonomy for the distinctive schools of thought appearing in the competitiveness literature is based on a "continuum of concern" about the severity of the situation. What follows is a description of seven principal positions along this continuum, from the most pessimistic to the most optimistic, to those who do not think competitiveness is a meaningful concept.

The "Cassandras," the first of seven principal approaches identified, is probably the most widely subscribed position: a deeply rooted, multifaceted competitiveness problem exists, one posing a clear and present economic danger (though there are differences within this school of thought as to major causes and preferred remedies). A second approach is based on the belief that the decline in U.S. international competitiveness is real, but not global in scope; deterioration in U.S. industrial capabilities is seen as resulting primarily from the extraordinary competitive strength, and occasionally unfair trading tactics, of Japan. A third school of thought argues that while there is currently a problem, it is a macroeconomic problem that can be corrected by means of reduction of the federal budget deficit and sufficient dollar depreciation (although the latter course would seem to be exhausted by mid-1994).

The "middle ground" spans two additional schools of thought. The first acknowledges that U.S. industrial competitiveness has been declining, but regards this is as a natural evolutionary trend to which U.S. society needs to adapt rather than resist. The other "moderate" school of thought, herein dubbed the "pragmatists," holds that continuation of certain negative trends eventually would create a serious problem. Improvements and reforms are advisable now in order to ensure that this contingency does not materialize.

The "Pollyannas," the sixth school of thought identified in this study, occupies the more positive, optimistic side of the continuum. Adherents to the variants of this position believe that no significant competitiveness problem exists; perhaps the principal worry here is that any effort to fix what does not need fixing will only damage an acceptable economic status quo. Finally, there are those who argue that competitiveness is not a meaningful operational term, either because of inherent conceptual difficulties or because ongoing changes in the world economic order—from international to transnational—make impossible a definitive judgment on the question of U.S. competitiveness. We now turn to more detailed explication of these different positions.

Cassandras

The school of thought that seems to attract the most popular attention puts forth unambiguous statements that the United States has serious and immediate competitiveness problems. The President's Commission on Industrial Competitiveness (1985: 1, 5) concluded that U.S. "ability to compete in world markets is eroding," and that there is "compelling evidence of a relative decline in our competitive performance." Five years later, Congress's Office of Technology Assessment (1990: 1) opened a report with the somber assessment that "American manufacturing has never been in more trouble than it is now." A branch of the National Academy of Sciences concluded that "recent economic data and the experiences of specific industries suggest that a strong case can be made that U.S. manufacturers, with the exception of a handful of enlightened companies, are not responding adequately or entirely appropriately to new competitive challenges" (National Research Council, 1986: 22). That "U.S. national competitiveness has been declining for two decades" is a central conclusion of the private, nonpartisan National Planning Association (Morici, 1988: 26).

Similarly, pessimistic conclusions have been reached in the academic community: "The United States has a serious international competitive problem and that problem is largely one of competitiveness in manufacturing . . . [which] has indeed performed poorly relative to foreign competition." It is an "unassailable fact that the position of the United States in the world economy is weakening" (Krugman and Hatsopoulos, 1987: 28, 18). According to the present chair of the Council of Economic Advisers, Laura D. Tyson (1988: 96), while some narrowing of the international competitive gap, thanks to post–World War II reconstruction, was inevitable, "the pace and extent of the catch-up—or to put it differently, the pace and extent of the decline in the U.S. position—were not inevitable."

Concerns about the apparent decline in the United States' technological position and about American illusions that "all is well" inspired the Council on Competitiveness to debunk what it dubbed the "five myths of U.S. leadership in technology": (1) the United States retains overall technological dominance; (2) U.S. industries are still ahead in leading-edge technologies; (3) foreign competitors cannot innovate on their own and must copy U.S. innovations; (4) the United States has the world's premier technology infrastructure, as evidenced by the awards and accomplishments of U.S. scientists; and (5) once the U.S. government realizes the severity of the problem, it will initiate post-Sputnik-like corrective action (testimony in U.S. Senate Committee on Commerce, Science, and Transportation, 1989: 144–152).

This sampling is indicative of widespread public and private concerns about U.S. competitiveness. The Cassandras can be divided, for present purposes, into those focusing on the causes of the alleged decline in U.S. competitiveness and those more concerned with consequences (though, of course, the two sets of concerns are far from independent). Among those emphasizing causes, some offer long laundry lists of causal factors, while others concentrate on a single, primary cause. Among the most frequently cited factors are sagging productivity; inadequate savings translating into inadequate investment in new plant and equipment; damaging U.S. government policies (e.g., the budget deficit, trade policy, excessive antitrust enforcement); inadequate or misguided R&D expenditures; and infrastructural problems, mainly in education and transportation.

The National Association of Manufacturers' senior vice president offered no fewer than seventeen causal factors of U.S. industrial deterioration, grouped into four categories: business cycle volatility, international competitiveness (including such factors as the dollar's overvaluation, productivity, and inflation), long-term structural problems, and corporate factors (testimony in U.S. Congress, Joint Economic Committee, 1983: 288). The falling-competitiveness diagnosis of the Berkeley Roundtable on the International Economy (an academic group) focused on five factors: trade balances, market shares, technological capability, productivity growth, and real wage trends (testimony in U.S. Senate, Committee on Governmental Affairs, 1987: 307–327).

Others tend to be more select in their specification of causes of declining competitiveness. A frequently mentioned culprit has been shortcomings in the organization and business practices of U.S. firms (see Chapter 3). One highly influential work in this category is *Made in America,* a report by the interdisciplinary MIT Commission on Industrial Productivity that found weaknesses in the way Americans "cooperate, manage, and organize themselves, as well as the ways they use technology, learn a new job, and interact with government." In addition, the MIT Commission concluded

> that the setbacks many firms suffered are not merely random events or part of the normal process by which firms constantly come and go; they are symptoms of more systematic and pervasive ills. We believe the situation

will not be remedied simply by trying harder to do the same things that have failed to work in the past. The international business environment has changed irrevocably, and the United States must adapt its practices to this new world. (Dertouzos et al., 1989: 8, 42)

Similarly, Cohen and Zysman (1988: 98) contend that the United States' "basic problem is not our technology or our workers, but how our corporations organize production and use people in the manufacturing process, how they set automation strategies and goals for product innovation. U.S. industry has contributed massively to its own undoing."

The alleged weakness of U.S. industry in commercializing new technology is one of the more specialized causal factors cited. There is a special irony here in that the United States remains strong in basic science but has trailed Japan, at least until the early 1990s, in quickly developing commercial applications for new inventions and technologies. "Considerable evidence suggests that America is failing to commercialize the kinds and quality of technology that the market demands" (Council on Competitiveness, n.d.: 13). Inman (1990) spells out the implications of this failure for the competitiveness of U.S. firms: "In one industry after another, foreign companies have captured market share—or in some cases, entire industries—because they have done a superior job of developing and commercializing new technologies, many of them American in origin."

The second subgroup of Cassandras focuses on the allegedly costly consequences of declining U.S. competitiveness. One important manifestation of the problem involves the ways that U.S. industry has trimmed the costs of declining competitiveness: had it not been for a decline in U.S. real wage rates and an exchange rate–induced reduction in terms of trade, the ability of U.S. firms to sell goods in foreign markets and to fend off foreign-made goods in the domestic market would have been further diminished in the late 1980s and early 1990s. These two declines represent a costly, undesirable combination that inevitably produces a reduction in the country's living standards. A depreciating exchange rate contributes to a decline in a country's terms of trade, which can be defined as the ratio between the prices of a country's total exports to its total imports (or as the quantities of exports needed to pay for a given quantity of imports). Even when petroleum is excluded from consideration, the long-term trend since the early 1970s has been a deterioration in the U.S. terms of trade (Bosworth and Lawrence, 1989).

Economic data provide a convincing case that for many years the U.S. industrial sector has utilized a falling exchange rate and falling real wages as ways to minimize, or compensate for, its decline in competitiveness. "To accept a falling dollar as a solution to America's competitiveness problem is to accept an economy that competes on the basis of low wages and not higher productivity," and that gradually shifts toward manufacture of labor-intensive, low-technology, low-productivity products (Thurow, 1985: 101).

Expressed in real terms, current wages at present are lower than, and total compensation barely equal to, comparable levels at their peak in 1973 (R. Reich, 1991b; see also the annual reports of the President's Council of Economic Advisers; and Business Roundtable, 1987). A further deterioration in the level of real wages is foreseen by those who have calculated that jobs lost in the U.S. manufacturing sector (because of competitiveness problems) pay better on average than the newly generated jobs in the service sector (Tyson, 1988: 102). As Hatsopoulos, Krugman, and Summers (1988: 300) point out: "If the United States had maintained its one-time advantage over Japan in productivity, technology, and product quality, the fall in U.S. relative wages would have given U.S. manufacturers a huge advantage over their Japanese rivals. Obviously, this did not happen."

One industry that has received a lot of attention from those alarmed about U.S. competitiveness problems has been electronics, an enormous, critically important growth industry that encompasses such key products as computers, telecommunications equipment, consumer electronics, and components (principally semiconductors). Its extraordinary importance prompted Craig Fields, formerly director of the Defense Advanced Research Projects Agency, to assert: "If you control microelectronics and computers, you control the world" (quoted in *Business Week,* July 23, 1990: 31). One U.S. government study concluded that "U.S. leadership in electronics is under serious challenge and may very well be eclipsed." Unless broad remedial measures are taken, it warned, "the long-term competitiveness of the U.S. electronics industries could be placed at unnecessary risk" (U.S. Department of Commerce, 1990b: x, xii).

The competitiveness problems of the U.S. electronics industry, excepting consumer electronics, seem to have been alleviated by late 1993. Prior to this reversal, it was widely thought that electronics might well be part of a larger syndrome in which Japan appeared to be moving into the dominant position in many sectors of high technology (see the following section) . Using a number of criteria of success (including R&D, product introduction, existing level of technology, and product manufacturing/engineering), specialized studies conducted by official agencies in both countries showed that a majority of performance indicators in numerous important emerging technologies had shifted in favor of Japan (see, for example, Japan Society and Council on Competitiveness, 1990: 15; U.S. Department of Commerce, 1990c: 13; and National Science Foundation data cited in S. D. Cohen, 1991: 245). Assessments of Japan's technological ascendancy, and now of a "comeback" on the part of some U.S. industries, are blurred by the fact that no totally uniform or precise measure of high-tech competitiveness across countries exists.

An important offshoot of these warnings of alleged sectoral problems and technological deficiencies is national security–related anxieties in the U.S. Department of Defense. The Pentagon has stated that it shares the U.S.

public's concern about the U.S. industrial sector's "downhill course to second-class status. . . . Many basic industries of importance to defense production have declined. . . . Left unchecked, such erosion could rob the
United States of industrial capabilities critical to national security" (U.S.
Department of Defense, 1988: 1). Another Pentagon report warned that the
"continued deterioration of the industrial and technology base diminishes
the credibility of our deterrent. It is a national problem" (Defense Science
Board, 1988: 2).

The potential significance of this linkage of competitiveness to national security is that it takes the issues involved beyond concerns with welfare.
Were U.S. security widely seen to be compromised by competitiveness
problems, the linkage could be used to justify more drastic corrective measures than the economic situation alone would warrant (see Chapter 9).

Competitiveness as a Problem Only in Relation to Japan

Belief in these sectoral problems and the overall competitive deficiencies of
U.S. high-tech industry leads to a second, more specialized school of
thought, one that argues that there definitely is a competitiveness problem,
but not in relation to all major competitors. Instead, it takes the form of
Japan surpassing the United States in one industrial sector after another (at
least until quite recently, when Japan's prolonged recession combined with
what seems to be a resurgence of many U.S. industries). By one account,
"the United States is being gradually but pervasively eclipsed by Japan . . .
[and] the long-term structural patterns of U.S. interaction in finance and
high technology imply a future of U.S. decline and dependence on Japan."
A more effective U.S. response to "Japan's technocratic Prussianism" is
urgently needed (Ferguson, 1989: 123, 125). Similarly, the United States
"does not appear to have a serious competitive problem with its . . .
European rivals." Japan is a "special case," a country with the "most aggressive" trading pattern of any major industrial country, a situation reflecting
the close relationship of trade policy to that country's industrial development strategy (Scott, 1985: 69). There is also the fact that Japan, until quite
recently, has been investing on a per capita basis almost 2.5 times as much
per annum as the United States for new plant and equipment, a trend that
suggests a momentum is building further favoring Japan's relative competitiveness (Courtis, 1990: 19).

Suffice it to say, however, that unanimity does not prevail with regard to
the Japanese challenge. At one extreme, Scott (1989: 118) has suggested that
competing with Japan is like joining a poker game "where the other players
cooperate to drive you out." In contrast, Nye (1988: 118) has likened stiff
Japanese competition to a positive-sum game in which the United States
benefits by having its industry kept on its toes and its citizens provided with
desirable products. By 1993, the U.S. public's anxieties about Japan's com-

petitive strength had been alleviated, at least temporarily, by awareness of that county's prolonged economic and political difficulties.

Competitiveness as a Macroeconomic Problem

A third school of thought, one based on qualified pessimism, sees not so much an inability of the U.S. economy to compete internationally, but rather a worrisome structural macroeconomic disequilibrium that effectively perpetuates an excess of imports over exports. With the dollar no longer overvalued as it was throughout the first half of the 1980s, the cause of and cure for the international disequilibrium is easily linked to this internal disequilibrium. All adherents to this school of thought point to the same accounting identity: a shortfall in private and governmental savings (mainly from the federal budget deficit) relative to investment will invariably produce a deficit in the goods and services component of a country's balance of payments. Simply put, the United States has been consuming more goods than it is producing, thereby making a trade deficit inevitable. The emergence of relatively large federal budget deficits and sluggish rates of savings in the early 1980s led to an ongoing situation that some call the "twin deficits," others a "consumption binge." "By cushioning the United States from the consequences of its savings collapse, the willingness of foreigners to finance our trade deficit has created a false sense that the situation is acceptable" (Hatsopoulos, Krugman, and Summers, 1988: 306).

A simple, direct way to increase U.S. exports relative to imports is for U.S. citizens to rid themselves of dependence on capital inflows by autonomously increasing their rate of savings (thereby reducing consumption) and/or for the federal government to reduce its budget deficit through some combination of reduced spending and increased revenue. Two Brookings Institution economists downplay entirely the notion that the United States can blame the rest of the world for its economic problems, which "primarily reflect failings in U.S. domestic policies," specifically the need for increased national savings and productivity growth (Bosworth and Lawrence, 1989: 15).

Declining U.S. Competitiveness as a Natural Development

In the center position along the continuum of concern, between the Cassandras on the one hand, and the Pollyannas on the other, are several moderate positions. The first of these construes declining U.S. competitiveness as a long-term evolutionary trend of the world economy. From this perspective, sustainable U.S. shares of global production and exports of manufactured goods are understandably on lower levels than the artificial highs of the immediate post–World War II period. The transition in the U.S. economy from a manufacturing-oriented to a postindustrial, services-based economy leads some to view the natural diffusion of manufacturing capacity as less than alarming. The shift to "third-wave" service activities is seen by some as an entirely healthy, desirable ascent to a higher plane of economic development, one long on knowledge-intensive data analysis and information transmission services and short on traditional, polluting industries.

Pessimists deny that this would necessarily be "progress," asserting instead that "manufacturing matters. The wealth and power of the United States depends upon maintaining mastery and control of production" (Cohen and Zysman, 1987a: 261). John Alic of the Congressional Office of Technology Assessment has argued that "services and manufacturing complement and depend on one another. Loss of the U.S. manufacturing base would harm our industries" (U.S. Congress, House Committee on Science, Space, and Technology, 1987: 19). Other warnings about a further withering of manufacturing include doubts that services exports could ever be sufficient to pay for the $400 billion-plus that the United States spends annually on imported goods.

A variant of the evolutionary approach stresses the historical inevitability of relative U.S. competitive decline inasmuch as the rise of U.S. manufacturing earlier in the century was largely a result of the country's dominant share of the world's supplies of critical industrial materials and fuels. The conditions that made the United States uniquely suited to industrial success faded as modern exploration and transportation methods evened out the access of other countries to raw materials, and as electronics-based high-tech industries, with relatively little absorption of raw materials, became increasingly important (Wright, 1990). The upshot of this argument is that for the United States there is no easy or automatic means of restoring its historically bounded industrial preeminence.

Pragmatists

The "pragmatists" represent another moderate position between the optimists and pessimists. Analysts in this school see some potentially troubling development in the U.S. economy, but they are not yet ready to declare a clear and present danger. Some of the pragmatists acknowledge that there may be a problem, depending on the terms of reference employed. This perspective leads to concern among the pragmatists with the adequacy of current private and public efforts to respond to the competitiveness challenge. For example, Nye (1990: 207) argues:

> The problem for the [United States] is not so much economic sclerosis or domestic decay but complacency in the face of new external challenges. Even if there has been little decline from the long-run American standards of the past, those standards are not good enough for the future. Current levels of savings, quality of education, and patterns of research, development, and manufacturing will not meet the rising standards of the third industrial revolution, in which knowledge and information play the critical role.

Another approach within the pragmatists school assumes that relative rates of productivity increases are critical determinants of long-term competitiveness, but concludes only that a problem *could* develop:

> The overall conclusion . . . is that there is no basis for either of the extreme interpretations that can be given to postwar developments in productivity growth. On the one side, the data offer no clear basis for a conclusion that the long-run growth rate of productivity in the United States has fallen below its historical level, or that it is about to do so. The available statistics also are not inconsistent with the possibility that the recent superiority in growth rates of other industrialized countries will turn out to have been a temporary affair, representing a period of catch-up during which the others were learning industrial techniques from us. Thus, the longer-run data constitute no grounds for hysteria or recourse to ill-considered measures that are grasped at in a mood of desperation. (Baumol, Blackman, and Wolff, 1989: 6)

In sum, there is no unequivocal optimism to be derived from the assumption that most of the relatively poor U.S. productivity performance beginning in the 1960s probably was due to above-average (and likely unsustainable) improvements in other countries' productivity growth rather than an absolute decline in U.S. performance. The sobering side of this explanation is that it is not so different from the British experience before World War I, when that country embarked on its long decline (Baumol, Blackman, and Wolff, 1989: 108). Another study concluded that while "the data reviewed in this article do not show that all U.S. industries are flourishing, they also reveal no evidence of profound economic ills" (McUsic, 1987: 15).

A variant of the hedged position is to point to the wide margin of error, or room for additional ruin, in the U.S. industrial sector:

> U.S. policy could continue more or less on its current course for many years without any crisis. The reason is simply that the U.S. economy is so huge, and the sins of economic policy so comparatively venal, that we can afford to be irresponsible for a long time. (*Washington Post*, Mar 25, 1990: C 1)

After presenting a long list of U.S. internal and external ills, the continuation of which would bring eventual damage to U.S. wealth and strength, another author quickly added that there are no grounds for concluding that the "*causes* of such trends are irreversible and inevitable" (Kennedy, 1988: 27).

Pollyannas

The sixth school of thought flatly denies that the United States has a competitiveness problem of any significance. It advances unabashed optimism about current and future U.S. economic strength as well as incredulity over the "decline-speak" of the Cassandras. The United States' constant and unjustified obsession with decline, says one optimist, reveals a narcissism, a lack of self-knowledge, and "a skewed perspective only marginally related to who we are" (Balk, 1990: 111). A supply-side economist (Roberts, 1989: 30) categorically stated that the United States "has a trade deficit because the Reagan tax-rate reductions made the U.S. a good place to invest money. . . . Today a trade deficit can be a sign of investors' confidence and serve as a leading success indicator." Furthermore, some hypothesize that the critical importance of a society's ability to renew itself means that the United States "is less likely to decline than any other major country. . . . Its engines of renewal are competition, mobility and immigration" (Huntington, 1988/1989: 89).

According to D. Allan Bromley, former director of the White House's Office of Science and Technology, the United States still has "the strongest science and technology base the world has ever seen" (quoted in Council on Competitiveness, 1991: 8). There is no basic disagreement with this assessment in the private sector (see, for example, Dertouzos, Lester, and Solow 1989: 67). In another forum, Bromley argued that the United States has

> a culture that prizes innovation, a university system superior to all others, an open and hospitable society that attracts the best scientific minds and inventive talents of the world, a business climate that encourages innovative enterprises, and a financial system that provides the opportunity for such new enterprises to grow quickly into major businesses. (U.S. Senate, Committee on Commerce, Science, and Transportation, 1990: 66)

There are numerous macroeconomic analyses that attempt to discredit the claim of widespread economic decay. In a widely quoted article criticizing advocacy of an industrial policy, Schultze (1983: 10) found "no evidence that in periods of reasonably normal prosperity American labor and capital are incapable of making the gradual transitions" from older industries to newer, more technologically advanced ones, as is "always required in a dynamic economy." What to some appears to be a competitiveness problem is merely the process of adjustment to a new international competitive environment in which the United States now is merely first among equals. A related line of argument claims that the United States "has not lost its comparative advantage in manufacturing as a whole," but only in labor-intensive and those capital-intensive products manufactured with standardized technologies (such as televisions). In sum, the optimists see a healthy situation in which U.S. comparative advantage is increasing in high-tech and resource-intensive products.

Competitiveness as a Meaningless Concept

A final school of thought contends that the concept of national competitiveness is at best obsolete and meaningless or, in the worst case, dangerous. The concept is dismissed as obsolete on the grounds that the identity, planning, ownership, and production facilities of big manufacturing corporations have evolved so far toward a global, and away from a national, orientation. Changes in the contemporary international economy have altered traditional concepts to such an extent that the standards and terminology used in the debate over U.S. *national* competitiveness no longer have clear meaning.

One variant of this argument contends that the concept of U.S. corporate ownership is less relevant than the existence of companies within the United States engaged in research and development, worker training, etc., regardless of the owners' nationality. "So who is us? The answer is, the American work force, the American people, but not particularly the American corporation," the end result being that U.S. competitiveness will be at least partially a function of foreign investors favoring the United States (R. Reich, 1990: 54). The gist of recent writings by a noted Japanese management consultant (Ohmae, 1990) suggests that the emergence of the "interlinked" world economy has greatly reduced the significance of traditional national borders, with the result that global competition today is something occurring less between countries than between globalized, "nationalityless" corporations.

More recently, Krugman (1994: 30) has forcefully argued that "it is simply not the case that the world's leading nations are to any important degree in economic competition with one another, or that any of their major economic problems can be attributed to failures to compete in world markets." Krugman (1994a: 41–44) goes on to contend that the "obsession" with competitiveness poses real dangers insofar as it could lead to serious misallocation of resources, result in protectionism and heighten international trade conflict, and debase the quality of public discourse on economic policy and thus the quality of public policy itself.

CONCLUSIONS

Taken as a whole, the collective literature on the existence and severity of the U.S. international competitiveness problem remains far from conclusive—for good reasons and bad. Part of the problem is the inherent complexity and nuances of a multidimensional subject about which honorable people can disagree. Furthermore, a country's global competitiveness is not static; any analysis thus reflects conditions and trends that may well prove to be fleeting. But another part of the problem is that advocacy and selectively chosen data continue to frame the debate. Regrettably, too many claims on all sides of the argument share the characteristics of overconfidence and underdocumentation. Some of the literature is deliberately brief, designed to develop a single theme rather than to illuminate the entire breadth of the topic. Other works seem to aim to defend ideologies or existing institutional agendas rather than to achieve status as solid academic work. It may be that only academic reviewers are favorably disposed to studies that are carefully hedged in their conclusions or suggest that existing data are not adequate to allow definitive conclusions. Moreover, economic theory seldom mixes well with sensitive public policy debates dominated by politicians and business people.

Given the sharp contrast between the pessimists and optimists, it is important to avoid thinking that one side of the contentious debate must be correct and the other wrong. In one of the better commentaries on the divergence between doomsday forecasts of the impending erosion of the U.S. industrial base and more optimistic interpretations, it was suggested that

> both sides are right and both sides are wrong. The [pessimists] are right in asserting that something is amiss with the competitive [performance of U.S. manufacturing], but wrong in believing that this can lead to a collapse of our manufacturing sector. The [optimists] are right in arguing that deindustrialization is not an issue, but wrong in dismissing worries over U.S. manufacturing performance. (Krugman and Hatsopoulis, 1987: 18)

Even if one accepts that there are long-term problems with the competitiveness of U.S. firms, it seems clear that many pessimists have exaggerated the short-term urgency of the problem. Rather as Lenz (1991: 195) suggests, the decline in U.S. competitiveness is analogous to the country suffering from hardening of the arteries rather than a heart attack.

By 1993, U.S. firms—especially in information-related fields—seem to have strengthened their competitive position in the world economy. Their apparent turnaround stems largely from the enhanced efforts of these firms, but it is also due to the ongoing appreciation of the Japanese yen vis-à-vis the U.S. dollar. Given the prevalent interpretation of trade (im)balances as indices of national competitiveness, there is a danger that the U.S. government will try to promote further dollar depreciation as a solution to perceived competitiveness problems. This solution is "easy" politically insofar as it poses few serious costs on U.S. constituencies in the short term. But since the accepted definition of competitiveness connotes rising living standards and an upgraded work force, such a course of action would be a classic case of the cure being worse than the disease. Similarly, enhancing U.S. exports by a continued stagnation in the real wages of blue collar workers does not meet the economist's definition of competitiveness.

The single most important question here is whether current data and emerging trends unequivocally suggest that U.S. industry can generate strong, sustained increases in exports of high-tech, high-value-added, high-profit margin goods made by efficient, well-paid workers. The changing arithmetic of the U.S. trade balance is less important than changes in the product composition of imports and exports. The desired changes in product composition should not be the result of the rest of the world coming to fear

The United States & International Competitiveness 39

the "deplorable and unfair competition of the underpaid labor of the United States" (Baumol, Blackman, and Wolff, 1989: 7), nor should they be anticipated through wishful thinking that our main foreign competition, Japan, has succumbed to economic malaise.

The desirable turnaround in the product composition of U.S. exports should come about because of greater efficiency in the U.S. industrial sector generated by at least four factors: high relative increases in productivity, better management strategies, more supportive government policies, and a better trained and educated work force that will enable U.S. firms to outperform their increasingly skillful competition in Europe and Asia. Probably the single most relevant determinant of whether the United States has a competitiveness problem is the extent to which the observer believes that all or many of these four improvements are currently and sufficiently under way.

NOTES

1. For the record, I believe that a moderately severe problem currently exists.
2. The above is derived from a U.S. Census Bureau press release dated March 19, 1990.
3. The source for these data is the U.S. Commerce Department's *Survey of Current Business*, June 1990.

Vol. III, Ch. 1, pp. 37–9

REFERENCES

Balk, A. (1990) *The Myth of American Eclipse*. New Brunswick, N.J.: Transaction.
Baumol, W. J., S. A. B. Blackman, and E. N. Wolff (1989) *Productivity and American Leadership: The Long View*. Cambridge: MIT Press.
Bosworth, B. P., and R. Lawrence (1989) "America's Global Role: From Dominance to Interdependence." In J. Steinbruner, ed., *Restructuring American Foreign Policy*. Washington, D.C.: Brookings Institution.
Business Roundtable (1987) *American Excellence in a World Economy*. New York: Business Roundtable.
Cohen, S. D. (1991) *Cowboys and Samurai: Why the United States Is Losing the Battle with the Japanese, and Why It Matters*. New York: HarperCollins.
Cohen, S. S., and J. Zysman (1986) "Can America Compete?" *Challenge* (May/June): 56–64.
——— (1987a) *Manufacturing Matters: The Myth of the Post-Industrial Economy*. New York: Basic Books.
——— (1988) "Puncture the Myths That Keep American Managers from Competing." *Harvard Business Review* (November/December): 98–102.
Council on Competitiveness (n.d.) *Picking Up the Pace: The Commercial Challenge to American Innovation*. Washington, D.C.: Council on Competitiveness.
——— (1991) *Challenges*. Washington, D.C.: Council on Competitiveness.
Courtis, K. S. (1990) "Strategic Challenge." *JAMA Forum* (November): 18–23.
Defense Science Board (1988) "The Defense Industrial and Technology Bases." Washington, D.C.: Office of the Undersecretary of Defense for Research and Engineering.

Dertouzos, M. L., R. K. Lester, and R. W. Solow (1989) *Made in America: Regaining the Productive Edge.* Cambridge: MIT Press.

Ferguson, C. H. (1988) "Obsolete Arms Production, Obsolescent Military." *New York Times,* April: A19.

────── (1989) "America's High-Tech Decline." *Foreign Policy* (Spring): 123–144.

Hatsopoulos, G. N., P. Krugman, and L. H. Summers (1988) "U.S. Competitiveness: Beyond the Trade Deficit." *Science,* July 15: 299–307.

Huntington, S. P. (1988/1989) "The U.S.: Decline or Renewal?" *Foreign Affairs* (Winter): 76–96.

Inman, B. R. (1990) "Why We're Slipping—and What's to Be Done." *Washington Post,* Oct. 3, 1988, p. A11.

Japan Society and Council on Competitiveness (1990) "Technology and Competitiveness: New Frontiers for the United States and Japan."

Kennedy, P. (1987a) "The (Relative) Decline of America." *Atlantic Monthly,* August: 29–38.

────── (1988) "A Guide to Misinterpreters." *New York Times,* April 17: IV 27.

Krugman, P. R., ed. (1986) *Strategic Trade Policy and the New International Economics.* Cambridge: MIT Press.

────── (1994a) "Competitiveness: A Dangerous Obsession." *Foreign Affairs* 73, 2: 28–44.

Krugman, P. R., and G. N. Hatsopoulos (1987) "The Problem of U.S. Competitiveness in Manufacturing." *New England Economic Review* (January/February): 18–28.

Lawrence, R. Z. (1984) *Can America Compete?* Washington, D.C.: Brookings Institution.

Lenz, A. J. (1987) "Overview of the U.S. Competitiveness Position Today." In C. E. Barfield and J. H. Makin, eds., *Trade Policy and U.S. Competitiveness,* pp. 27–35.

────── (1991) *Beyond Blue Economic Horizons: U.S. Trade Performance and International Competitiveness in the 1990s.* New York: Praeger.

Lipsey, R. E. (1985/1986) "The International Competitiveness of U.S. Firms." *NBER Reporter* (Winter): 18–21.

McUsic, M. (1987) "U.S. Manufacturing: Any Cause for Alarm?" *New England Economic Review* (January/February): 3–16.

Morici, P. (1988) *Reassessing American Competitiveness.* Washington, D.C.: National Planning Association.

National Research Council (1986) *Toward a New Era in U.S. Manufacturing: The Need for a National Vision,* Washington, D.C.: National Academy Press.

National Science Foundation (NSF) (1988) "International Science and Technology Data Update: 1988." Washington, D.C.: NSF.

────── (1990b) "Research and Development in Industry: 1988." Washington, D.C.: NSF.

Neef, A. (1988) "An International Comparison of Manufacturing Productivity and Unit Labor Cost Trends." Presentation to the Social Science Research Council Conference, October 28–30.

Nye, J. S. (1988) "Understanding U.S. Strength." *Foreign Policy* (Fall): 105–129.

────── (1990) *Bound to Lead: The Changing Nature of American Power.* New York: Basic Books.

Ohmae, K. (1990) *The Borderless World.* New York: HarperCollins.

President's Commission on Industrial Competitiveness (1985) *Global Competition: The New Reality.* Washington, D.C.: U.S. Government Printing Office.

Reich, R. (1987) "The Rise of Techno-Nationalism." *Atlantic Monthly,* May: 63–69.

────── (1990) "Who Is Us?" *Harvard Business Review* (January/February): 53–59.

────── (1991b) "A More Perfect State of the Union Message." *Wall Street Journal,* January 30: A10.

Roberts, P. C. (1989) "Time to Trade in Our Old Notions About Deficits." *Business Week*, November 13: 30.

Schultze, C. L. (1983) "Industrial Policy: A Dissent." *Brookings Review* (Fall): 3–12.

Scott, B. R., ed. (1985) *U.S. Competitiveness in the World Economy*. Boston: Harvard Business School Press.

———— (1989) "Competitiveness: Self-Help for a Worsening Problem." *Harvard Business Review* (July/August): 115–120.

Thurow, L. C. (1985) *The Zero-Sum Solution*. New York: Simon & Schuster.

Tyson, L. (1988) "Competitiveness: An Analysis of the Problem and a Perspective on Future Policy." In M. K. Starr, ed., *Global Competitiveness: Getting the U.S. Back on Track*. New York: W. W. Norton.

U.S. Congress, House Committee on Science, Space, and Technology (1987) *Technology and Economics in a Shrinking World*. Washington, D.C.: U.S. Government Printing Office.

U.S. Congress, Joint Economic Committee (1983) *Industrial Policy, Economic Growth, and the Competitiveness of U.S. Industry*. Washington, D.C.: U.S. Government Printing Office.

———— (1990) *Japan's Economic Challenge*. Washington, D.C.: U.S. Government Printing Office.

U.S. Congress, Office of Technology Assessment (1990) *Making Things Better: Competing in Manufacturing*. Washington, D.C.: U.S. Government Printing Office.

U.S. Department of Commerce (1987) "Improving U.S. Competitiveness," proceedings of a conference, September 22.

———— (1990b) "The Competitive Status of the U.S. Electronics Sector from Materials to Systems."

———— (1990c) "Emerging Technologies: A Survey of Technical and Economic Opportunities.

U.S. Department of Defense (1988) "Bolstering Defense Industrial Competitiveness."

U.S. Senate, Committee on Commerce, Science, and Transportation (1989) *National Science and Technology Policy*. Washington, D.C.: U.S. Government Printing Office.

———— (1990) *Competitiveness Challenge Facing the U.S. Industry*. Washington, D.C.: U.S. Government Printing Office.

U.S. Senate, Committee on Governmental Affairs (1987) *Government's Role in Economic Competitiveness*. Washington, D.C.: U.S. Government Printing Office.

Wright, G. (1990) "Where America's Industrial Monopoly Went." *Wall Street Journal*, December 20: A16.

[3]

Convergence and Deferred Catch-up: Productivity Leadership and the Waning of American Exceptionalism

MOSES ABRAMOVITZ AND PAUL A. DAVID

> There are two lines of agency visibly at work shaping the habits of thought of [a] people in the complex movements of readjustment and rehabilitation [required by industrialization]. These are the received scheme of use and wont and the new state of the industrial arts; and it is not difficult to see that it is the latter that makes for readjustment; nor should it be any more difficult to see that the readjustment is necessarily made under the surveillance of the received scheme of use and wont.
>
> —Thorstein Veblen (1915)

The comparative productivity experience of nations is commonly viewed as a race. But there is a difference between a runners' race and a productivity race between nations. In a track race, if one runner gets off to a fast start, there is no reason why, on that account alone, her rivals should then be able to run faster than she. A productivity race is different: under certain conditions, being behind gives a productivity laggard the ability to grow faster than the early leader. That is the main contention of the "convergence hypothesis." The most striking example of the convergence to which this hypothesis refers was the experience since World War II, when America's large lead eroded and the productivity levels of the other technologically advanced countries converged.

The convergence hypothesis stands on four sturdy pillars—which in turn float on one large assumption. The assumption is that the countries in the productivity race differ only in their initial levels of productivity but are

We acknowledge with thanks the comments and suggestions of colleagues who read previous drafts of this paper: William J. Baumol, Avner Greif, Alex Inkeles, Dale Jorgenson, R. C. O. Matthews, William N. Parker, Melvin Reder, Bart Verspargen, Herman van de Wee, and Gavin Wright. In preparing this version for publication we have had the additional benefit of Timothy Taylor's extraordinary editorial skills. Deficiencies that have outlasted all this remedial attention are solely ours.

22   ABRAMOVITZ AND DAVID

otherwise similar. The four pillars are the four advantages in growth potential that a laggard nation enjoys just because it is behind.

First, when a leader's capital stock is replaced or expands, the improvement in technology embodied in the new plant and equipment is limited by such advances in the efficiency of capital goods as may have been made during the life of a representative asset. In a laggard country, however, the tangible capital is likely to be technologically obsolete. After all, that is one reason the laggard is behind. When such equipment is replaced, the new equipment can embody state-of-the-art technology; so, on that account, the laggard can realize larger improvements in the average efficiency of its productive facilities than are available to the leader. An analogous argument applies to a laggard's potential advance in disembodied technology, that is, in the forms of industrial organization; routines of purchasing, production, and merchandising; and managerial practice generally.

Second, laggard countries tend to suffer from low levels of capital per worker. That condition, especially in view of the chance to modernize capital stock, tends to make marginal returns to capital high and so to encourage rapid rates of capital accumulation.

Third, laggard countries often maintain relatively large numbers of redundant workers in farming and petty trade; so productivity growth can occur by shifting labor from farms to nonfarm jobs and from self-employment and family shops to larger-scale enterprises, even allowing for the cost of the additional capital that might be needed to maintain productivity levels in the new jobs.

Fourth, the relatively rapid growth from the first three sources makes for rapid growth in aggregate output and, therefore, in the scale of markets. This encourages the sort of technical progress which is dependent on larger-scale production.

These, then, are the components of the convergence hypothesis in its elemental form.[1] And if national characteristics were, indeed, to conform

---

1. Whether the formulation offered here is more or less "elemental" than the neoclassical growth models patterned on Solow's (1956) seminal paper is a matter of taste. In Solow-style models, there exists a unique and globally stable growth path to which the level of labor productivity (and per capita output) will converge, and along which the rate of advance is fixed (exogenously) by the rate of technological progress. A large crop of mutant models of aggregate growth has flowered since the mid-1980s. These have diverged from the pure neoclassical strain of growth theory by rejecting, in one way or another, the assumption that all forms of capital accumulation eventually run into diminishing marginal returns. Consequently, they contest the Solow model's global convergence implications. See Lucas (1988) and Romer (1986, 1990) for seminal contributions in this vein, and the useful recent surveys by Van de Klundert and Smulders (1992),

to the underlying assumption of similarity, we would expect that any national differences in productivity levels which might appear would be eliminated sooner or later, because of the growth advantages inherent in being behind.

The assumption of similarity calls for some explanation here. By it we mean that there are no *persistent* differences in national characteristics that would inhibit a laggard country from exploiting the advantages that being behind would otherwise present. In actual experience, productivity differences among countries stem from both persistent and transient causes. Persistent causes include poverty of natural resources; small scale of domestic markets, coupled with barriers to foreign trade; forms of economic organization or systems of taxation that reduce the rewards for effort, enterprise, or investment; or deeper elements of national culture that limit the responses of people to economic opportunities. Transient causes are occurrences like natural or military disasters, or dysfunctional forms of economic organization and public policy that may have ruled in the past but that have been effectively reformed.[2] The strength of the long-run tendency to convergence depends on a balance of forces: on one side, the advantages in growth potential that are inherent in being behind, and on the other side, the limitations inherent in those persistent causes of backwardness that may originally have caused a country to become a productivity laggard. Therefore, in the limiting case envisaged by the model of unconditional convergence, where differences in productivity levels arise solely from transient "shocks," productivity growth rates in any period would be found to vary inversely with their respective initial levels, so that laggards would tend to catch up with the leaders and differences in levels eventually would be eliminated.

Verspargen (1992), and Amable (1994). Harris (1993) and Dosi and Fabiani (1994) essay thoroughly non-neoclassical approaches to modeling convergence and divergence phenomena.

2. It would be convenient to be able to treat recovery from the effects of war-related destruction and disruption on the productivity of surviving resources as an unambiguous short-run, "rebound" process, in other words, as being clearly distinguishable from the phenomenon of long-run convergence. But in actual experience, the two may be difficult to disentangle. Such is the case when reconstruction provides an opportunity for widespread introduction of structures, capital equipment, and organizational forms that are of much more recent vintage than the economically obsolete facilities that had been destroyed. Dumke (1990), for example, argues that much of western Europe's "supergrowth" after 1948 is attributable to postwar reconstruction; using the ratio of 1948 GDP to 1938 GDP as a measure of the war-related supply shock a country had sustained, he finds from regression analysis that this variable continued to affect growth rates into the 1960s.

For a quarter-century following World War II, as was noted, the growth record of the presently advanced countries was strikingly consistent with this simple formulation of the convergence hypothesis. But not all of the historical experience of economic growth, even for this same group of countries, fits the hypothesis. From 1870 to about 1950, America not only maintained but actually widened its lead over other countries in terms of real GDP per capita and labor productivity. Britain, the world's first industrial nation, had held the lead during the century before that, and the Netherlands did so at a still earlier time when it was a great mercantile power.

The insistent question, therefore, is how to reconcile the convergence hypothesis with the experience of persistent leadership. This involves asking what differences among countries impose limitations on the abilities of laggard countries to profit from the advantages of being backward. We must then ask how and why these limitations changed so as to become less constraining and thus led to the great boom in catch-up and convergence that has marked the era since World War II.[3]

To sharpen the focus of this inquiry, we confine ourselves to a comparison between the United States and a group of presently advanced capitalist countries since 1870. The group consists of sixteen presently industrialized countries of western Europe and North America together with Japan and Australia. (The list of countries appears in the note to Table 1.) They are the countries for which Angus Maddison (1991, p. 196) has compiled estimates of man-hour productivity rendered comparable over time by standard methods of price deflation and across countries by the purchasing-power-parity ratios prepared by Eurostat and the OECD. The next section reviews the broad features of the growth experience of these countries from 1870 to 1990. This is followed by a section in which we

---

3. In the recent literature on the subject of convergence (discussed at greater length below), the term "catch-up" often has been used interchangeably with "convergence." An effort has been made here to eschew that practice. "Catch-up" refers to the long-run process· by which productivity laggards close the proportional gaps that separate them from the productivity leader (as reflected in the average measures presented here in Table 1). "Convergence," in our usage, refers to a reduction of a measure of dispersion in the relative productivity levels of the array of countries under examination. Our idea of convergence is associated with the concept that Barro and Sala-i-Martin (1992) have labeled "σ-convergence." This refers to a narrowing of the dispersion within the international cross section of productivity levels over time—as measured by the standard deviation of the logarithm of productivity, or, equivalently here, by the coefficient of variation of the productivity relatives (presented in Table 2). Since it is "quasi-global" σ-convergence, measured for the entire group of advanced countries (including the United States), that we have in mind when speaking simply of "convergence," it is entirely possible for this to occur in the absence of any general catch-up.

identify the kinds of factors other than a low productivity level that may give one or more countries an advantage in growth and, by the same token, operate as limitations on the ability of others to catch up. We then go on to sketch the particular forces that, during the last 120 years, first supported a strong American advantage and inhibited the forces of convergence, and later undermined the basis of that leadership advantage and lent impetus to the catch-up movement among the other industrially developed economies.

The nub of our argument is that in the closing decades of the nineteenth century, the U.S. economy had moved into the position of global productivity leadership, which was to hold for a remarkably long period thereafter, through a fortunate concordance between America's own exceptional economic and social characteristics and the nature of the dominant path of technological progress and labor productivity advances. During the late nineteenth and early twentieth centuries, that path was natural resource–intensive, tangible capital–using, and scale-dependent in its elaboration of mass-production and high-throughput technologies and modes of business organization. Although this trajectory can be traced back to technological and industrial initiatives in both Britain and the United States earlier in the nineteenth century, it found fullest development in the environment provided by the North American continent. And so, during the course of the nineteenth century, it came to provide the United States with a strong productivity leadership advantage. This was so because the historical circumstances of contemporaneously developing economies, particularly those conditions affecting what we refer to as "technological congruence" and their "social capability," imposed limitations on the abilities of the productivity laggards of western Europe and Japan to derive a strong potential for rapid growth simply on the basis of being behind the United States.

Yet America's distinctive advantages did not retain their initially great importance throughout the first half of the twentieth century. The advantage conferred by America's rapid development of its rich endowment of mineral resources gradually dissipated. Some of the peculiar benefits that its industries derived from the larger scale and greater homogeneity of its domestic markets were eroded, partly by the growth of both domestic and foreign markets elsewhere, and partly by a gradual shift of the nature and direction of technological progress. In its global impacts, the course of innovation became less biased towards the ever more intense application of tangible capital and natural resource inputs and, instead, came to favor greater emphasis on intangible capital formation through investments in education and R&D. For these and still other reasons, we contend that the waning of American exceptionalism and the changing trajectory in the development of internationally available technology had the effect of reducing the *comparative* handicaps under which other countries seeking rapid productivity increases formerly were obliged to operate.

With the erosion of these American advantages, the ground was prepared for other countries with broadly similar economic and social institutions to participate in the interconnected processes of "catch-up investment" and "productivity convergence." As we shall see, however, the realization by the laggards among the industrialized countries of that potentiality for differentially faster productivity growth, after having been deferred by the circumstances of the Great Depression of the 1930s and World War II, was fostered by a number of special conditions that obtained internationally during the postwar decades.

The Comparative Productivity Record

In 1870, levels of aggregate labor productivity in the United States and the United Kingdom were apparently quite similar. Maddison's estimates (1991, table 3.4) put the United Kingdom ahead by 4 percent, but given the uncertainties of such calculations, so small a difference can hardly be thought significant. The statistics, however, speak much more clearly about two other matters. First, both the United Kingdom and the United States enjoyed large leads over the other countries that had begun to industrialize by 1870. Second, between 1870 and 1913, the United States established a large lead over the United Kingdom (28 percent) and increased its already large lead over the generality of the other industrializing countries (as shown in Table 1).

Over the course of this long period of general peace and development, there is no sign of a catch-up with the new front-runner by the laggard countries. Among the fifteen advanced countries other than the United States, only America's northern neighbor, Canada, improved its relative productivity position, and only one European country, Germany, was able to maintain its 1870 relative level—which was but half as high as that of the leader. The average level of the fifteen countries other than the United States fell from 62 percent of the American level in 1870 to 54 percent in 1913.[4]

---

4. As the text below points out, however, the speed of convergence within the group of sixteen countries (including the United States) in this period was very slow compared with its pace after 1950, but also compared with the speed of convergence among the

TABLE I

*Mean Labor Productivity Levels in Fifteen Advanced Countries Relative
to United States and in Nine Western European Countries Relative
to United Kingdom and Measures of Rates of Catch-up*

Fifteen advanced countries[a]				Nine western European countries[b]			
Mean level (U.S. = 100)		Rate of catch-up[c] (% per annum)		Mean level (U.K. = 100)		Rate of catch-up[c] (% per annum)	
1870	62	1873–1913	−0.35	1870	57	1870–1913	+0.35
1913	54	1913–1938	−0.30	1913	66	1913–1938	+0.80
1938	50	1938–1950	−1.15	1938	81	1938–1950	−0.67
1950	43	1950–1973	+1.82	1950	74	1950–1973	+1.34
1960	49	1950–1960	+1.28	1960	88	1950–1960	+1.66
1973	66	1960–1973	+2.24	1973	101	1960–1973	+1.09
1987	79	1973–1987	+1.31	1987	103	1973–1987	+0.10

SOURCE: Maddison (1991, Table C-11).
    [a] The fifteen advanced countries include the nine western European countries in the following note plus Australia, Austria, Canada, Finland, Japan, and the United Kingdom.
    [b] The nine western European countries are Belgium, Denmark, France, Germany, Italy, Netherlands, Norway, Sweden, and Switzerland.
    [c] The rate of catch-up is the change per annum in the log of the mean level of productivity relative to that of the United States (or the United Kingdom) times 100.

On the other hand, virtually all the countries of western Europe were closing the proportionate gaps that separated them from Britain, the former productivity leader.[5] This would seem to be quite consistent with the view that in the spread of industrialization during the later nineteenth century, the successful western European "followers" were looking toward Britain, rather than the United States, as the technological and economic leader that it was most relevant for them to attempt to emulate.[6] If that

western European countries. In a recent paper, Taylor and Williamson (1994) estimate that the large population movements during 1870–1913 should have tended to raise the relatively low levels of productivity in Europe and to reduce the relatively high levels in the immigrant-receiving countries, among which the United States was the largest. If one accepts their calculations, the widening relative gap in labor productivity between western European countries and the United States during this same period is even more remarkable: the fall in the ratio of the nine-country western European mean level (see notes to Table 1) vis-à-vis the U.S. level of productivity was from .65 to .53, even more pronounced than the drop shown for the full fifteen-country sample.

5. In describing Britain as "the former productivity leader," we have abstracted from the anomalously high relative level of productivity recorded for Australia in the early twentieth century. Australia's lead at the time rested only on its huge supply of land relative to labor in an economy almost entirely devoted to agriculture and animal ranching.

6. Interestingly enough, Alexander Gerschenkron's classic paper "Economic Backwardness in Historical Perspective"—first published in 1955 and reprinted in Gerschenkron (1962, chap. 3)—took the proposition of British leadership as virtually self-evident, basing it on much less firm empirical foundations than subsequently have been put in place. It now appears that the erosion of British productivity leadership vis-à-vis

view is correct, it suggests another way to frame the central question we are addressing in the present essay: Why did not the industrial latecomers of the European continent follow the lead of America, whose economy was giving visible indications of forging ahead of Britain's?

Between 1913 and 1938, the laggard countries held back by World War I and by the financial disturbances of the 1920s fell back still further. And World War II, which was a great stimulus to U.S. growth as its economy returned to high levels of capacity utilization, was a severe setback to the relative positions of the European countries and Japan. By 1950, after recovery from the most severe aftereffects of the wartime destruction and dislocation, the average relative productivity levels of the other countries had sunk from 54 to 43 percent of the American level.[7]

There then followed the great "catch-up boom" from 1950 to the present.[8] The movement proceeded in two stages. During the first, from 1950 to 1973, the pace of catch-up was relatively fast: the laggards rose toward the American level at a rate of 1.8 percent a year, so that their average

the Continental followers was almost universal; over the 1870–1913 interval, the United Kingdom was able to maintain parity in the growth of real GDP per man-hour only against Belgium (Maddison, 1991, Table 3.4). It would be of interest to try to gauge the extent to which the intra-European convergence observed over the period 1870–1913 was promoted by differentially heavier overseas emigration from the Continent as a whole (vis-à-vis the British Isles), and especially from the Continent's peripheral regions—first Scandinavia, and subsequently southern and eastern Europe. Although Taylor and Williamson (1994) discuss the role of international labor migration in convergence phenomena, their work focuses attention on the potential for altering productivity relationships between sending and receiving regions, not on productivity relationships among the regions that differed in rates of net emigration.

7. The western European productivity catch-up relative to the United Kingdom continued between 1913 and 1938 while losing ground to the United States. All the Continental countries grew at a faster rate than Britain, and their average productivity level rose from 66 to 81 percent of the U.K. level. World War II, however, hit the Continental countries harder than it did the United Kingdom. Only Sweden and Switzerland, the two neutrals, continued their relative rise, and the western European average fell back to 74 percent of Britain's level (Maddison, 1991, Table C.11).

8. In speaking of a "catch-up" movement, we are referring to the rise in the mean of the followers' productivity relatives vis-à-vis the productivity leader, which in this instance is the United States. Throughout the following text, as was forecast in note 3, a distinction is maintained between "catch-up" and "convergence." In the recent macroeconomics literature, reference is often made to a different concept of catch-up that was called "β-convergence" by Barro and Sala-i-Martin (1991, 1992). It is essentially the coefficient on a negative correlation between productivity growth rates and initial levels of productivity (often with additional explanatory variables inserted). However, this kind of catch-up can easily confuse short-run, disequilibrium processes (like recovering from war-related destruction) with long-term convergence. Just as our preferred measures of "catch-up" and of "convergence" can diverge in their movements, σ-convergence is not implied by β-convergence: even though the lower-productivity member of a pair is experiencing faster growth, the size of the absolute gap between them (the dispersion) may nonetheless be widening.

TABLE 2

Measures of Dispersion of Labor Productivity Levels in Sixteen Advanced Countries and in Western Europe, and Rates of Convergence

Sixteen advanced countries[a]				Ten western European countries[b]			
Dispersion $(\sigma/\bar{x})$		Rate of convergence (% per annum)		Dispersion $(\sigma/\bar{x})$		Rate of convergence (% per annum)	
1870	.44	1870–1913	0.36	1870	.31	1870–1913	0.75
1913	.37	1913–1938	0.46	1913	.22	1913–1938	1.73
1938	.33	1938–1950	−2.10	1938	.14	1938–1950	−2.56
1950	.43	1950–1973	4.00	1950	.20	1950–1973	4.51
1960	.34	1950–1960	2.24	1960	.12	1950–1960	4.78
1973	.17	1960–1973	5.35	1973	.07	1960–1973	4.30
1987	.13	1973–1987	1.74	1987	.10	1973–1987	2.88

SOURCE: Maddison (1991, Table C-11).

NOTE: Dispersion is measured by the coefficient of variation $(\sigma/\bar{x})$. The rate of convergence is the negative of the change per annum in the log of $\sigma/\bar{x}$ times 100. Rates of convergence were calculated from unrounded numbers and therefore are not precisely consistent with the rounded measures of dispersion shown above.

[a] The sixteen advanced countries are those listed in note *a* to Table 1, plus the United States.

[b] The ten western European countries are those listed in note *b* to Table 1, plus the United Kingdom.

relative level, which was 43 in 1950, reached 66 in 1973. During this stage, the catch-up was achieved in spite of rapid American productivity growth, which was at least as fast as, and may have been even faster than, in any previous period of comparable duration (Maddison, 1991, Table 3.3). Since 1973, catch-up has been distinctly slower—only 1.3 percent a year—in spite of the severe slowdown in the United States. Growth rates in Europe and Japan fell even more (in percentage points) than in the United States.

There was no general catch-up to the United States before 1950, but it is worth recording that from 1870 to 1938, there was a substantial decline in the dispersion of productivity levels among the laggards, as can be seen from the figures for the western European countries in Table 2. Although for the full sample of sixteen countries the trend rate of convergence was a weak 0.42 percent per annum, the corresponding downward drift of the coefficient of variation among the western European countries including the United Kingdom proceeded at an average rate of 1.11 percent per annum over this 68-year period.[9] Thus, over this long period be-

9. In their study of convergence in real GDP per capita levels in Europe during 1850–1990, based on an augmented and revised version of Maddison's (1991) data, Prados de la Escosura, Dabán, and Oliva (1993, p. 11) present the standard deviation of the logs measure of dispersion for the eight countries of the western European core (Belgium, Denmark, France, Germany, Netherlands, Sweden, Switzerland, and the United Kingdom). This shows the same trend rate of decline (1.1 percentage points per annum) over the interval 1860–1938, with a faster rate of convergence during 1860–1913 being interrupted by a sharp rise in the dispersion in the 1913–20 interval.

fore World War II there was "convergence among the followers," without the occurrence of "catch-up" vis-à-vis the newly emerged productivity leader.

During the wartime decade of the 1940s, however, the international dispersion of productivity levels increased markedly; in 1950 the coefficient of variation was larger than its 1938 value by almost two-thirds. From 1950 to 1973 the great "postwar catch-up and convergence movement" proceeded very systematically: the inverse rank-order correlation between countries' initial levels of productivity in 1950 and their subsequent growth rates between 1950 and 1973 was almost perfect—the lower was a country's productivity level in 1950, the higher was its subsequent rate of growth.[10] In company with this, the process of convergence resumed at a pace that was historically unprecedented; the coefficient of variation declined at an average annual rate almost ten times as fast as its pre–World War II trend. Eventually, in the period after 1973, when the postwar growth boom had passed into history and the rate of catch-up vis-à-vis the United States had slowed down appreciably, convergence also became substantially slower.

The general features of the postwar experience of the advanced capitalist economies is consistent with the predictions of a simple convergence hypothesis. Between 1950 and 1973, the gaps separating the productivity levels in the laggard countries from that in the United States were rapidly reduced, and the dispersion of relative levels within this group of econo-

---

10. The Spearman rank correlation coefficient was −0.96, as calculated from the data in Maddison (1989). See also Baumol, Blackman, and Wolff (1989, chap. 5). Prados de la Escosura, Dabán, and Oliva (1993, Table 4) present regression results for the fit of the unconditional convergence specification to real GDP per capita for sixteen European countries over the entire period 1950–90: the estimated regression coefficient on the logarithm of past per capita GDP is highly significant and implies a β-convergence rate of 1.7 percent per annum. Such statistical results, however, are not unproblematic. Abramovitz (1986) pointed out that the measures of inverse rank correlation which he reported and, by the same token, the (β-convergence) results from linear regression analysis of the sort presented by Baumol (1986) would tend to overstate the strength of the negative relationship. DeLong (1988) developed a related point of criticism, noting that inasmuch as the estimates of initial productivity levels were constructed by methods that involved extrapolating backward from later benchmark data, measurement errors in the growth rates would be (negatively) correlated with those in the initial productivity levels. Friedman (1992) presents a systematic treatment of the same classic problem of regression bias due to errors in variables. All the foregoing, it should be noted, do not question the validity of the regression specification of the relationship as being linear in the logarithms of the countries' respective productivity levels, as does Verspargen (1991), for example, to cite a notable exception in the literature. Therefore, whether or not the use of β-convergence-type measures results in the overstatement of the strength of the "true" convergence process post-1950 in comparison with that for the period pre-1938, or pre-1913, is not a matter that has been resolved.

mies declined swiftly. There was catch-up as well as convergence. Since 1973, with productivity gaps reduced, the rate of catch-up has slowed down and the process of convergence has weakened. So far, so good.

But why was there no general catch-up (and only modest convergence) throughout the eight decades from 1870 to 1950? For the period from 1913 to 1950, one may well think (correctly, in our view) that the forces making for catch-up and convergence were overwhelmed by two general wars, by the territorial, political, and financial disturbances that followed, and by the variant impacts of the Great Depression on different countries.[11] Still, what circumstances inhibited catch-up vis-à-vis the United States for more than four decades of peaceful development between 1870 and 1913? And what occurred to release the forces of convergence and catch-up after the Second World War? The next section outlines a framework for study and discussion of these questions.

The Elements of Catch-up Potential and Its Realization

The conditions that govern the abilities of countries to achieve relatively rapid rates of productivity growth may be grouped into two broad classes: those that govern the potential of different countries to raise their productivity levels, and those that influence their abilities to realize that potential.

The convergence hypothesis tells us that one element governing countries' relative growth potentials is the size of the productivity differentials that separate them from the leader. Manifestly, however, the record of growth does not conform consistently to the predictions of the unconditional convergence hypothesis. The assumption that countries are "otherwise similar" is not fulfilled. There are often persistent conditions that have restricted countries' past growth and that continue to limit their ability to

---

11. Actually, the effects of World War I and the Great Depression do not appear to have been sufficient to do more than temporarily interrupt the slow secular reduction of the dispersion in productivity levels that was taking place *within* the core group of western European countries. For compelling evidence on this point, see the study of Prados de la Escosura, Dabán, and Oliva (1993) on the convergence in real GDP per capita levels in Europe from 1850 to 1990. Focusing just on the 1929–1938 interval, we calculate from Maddison's (1991) comparative GDP per man-hour estimates that the coefficient of variation within the group of ten Western European economies (see Table 1) declined by almost 40 percent of its 1929 magnitude. Yet the same measure computed for the entire sample of sixteen advanced countries declined by only some 10 percent. Thus, the Great Depression decade had more of an effect in deferring the convergence of the western European group toward the higher productivity of the United States and other regions of recent settlement than it had in delaying the process at work within the western European "convergence club" itself.

make the technological and organizational leaps that the convergence hypothesis envisages. We divide constraints on the potentials of countries into two categories.

One consists of the limitations of "technological congruence." Such limitations arise because the frontiers of technology do not advance evenly in all dimensions; that is, with equi-proportional impact on the productivities of labor, capital, and natural resource endowments, and with equal effect on the demands for the several factors of production and on the effectiveness of different scales of output. They advance, rather, in an unbalanced, biased fashion, reflecting the direct influence of past science and technology on the evolution of practical knowledge and the complex adaptation of that evolution to factor availabilities, as well as to the scale of markets, consumer demands, and technical capabilities of those relatively advanced countries operating at or near the frontiers of technology.[12]

It can easily occur that the resource availabilities, factor supplies, technical capabilities, market scales, and consumer demands in laggard countries may not conform well to those required by the technologies and organizational arrangements that have emerged in the leading country or countries. Although technological choices do adapt to changes in the economic environment, there are strong forces making for persistence in the effects of past choices and for path-dependence in the evolution of technological and organizational systems. These may render it extremely difficult, if not prohibitively costly, for firms, industries, and economies to switch quickly from an already established regime, with its associated trajectory of technical development, to exploit a quite distinct technological regime that had emerged elsewhere, under a different constellation of economic and social conditions.[13] The laggards, therefore, face varying degrees of difficulty in adopting and adapting the current practice of those who hold the productivity lead.

The second class of constraints on the potential productivity of coun-

---

12. See David (1975, chap. 1) for an introduction to the theory of "localized" technological progress and its relationship to the global bias of factor-augmenting technical change, and for a synthesis of some of the pertinent historical evidence. Related, more recent studies are noted below. Broadberry (1993) applies this general framework to interpret the historical evidence on manufacturing productivity leadership and technological leadership relationships between the United States and western Europe over the period from 1820 to 1987.

13. On hysteresis effects and path dependence in technological, organizational, and institutional evolution, see, for example, David (1975, 1985, 1988, 1993, 1994a, 1994b). The concept of technological regimes, or "paradigms" and "trajectories," is discussed by Dosi (1982, 1988), extending the work of Nelson and Winter (1977) and Sahal (1981).

tries concerns a more vaguely defined set of matters that has been labeled "social capability." This term was coined by Kazushi Ohkawa and Henry Rosovsky (1972). It covers countries' levels of general education and technical competence; the commercial, industrial, and financial institutions that bear on their abilities to finance and operate modern, large-scale business; and the political and social characteristics that influence the risks, the incentives, and the personal rewards of economic activity, including those rewards in social esteem that go beyond money and wealth.

An illustration may suggest the importance of the social and political constraints to which we refer. The 1989 level of value added per man-hour in Japanese manufacturing was 80 percent of the corresponding value in the United States, according to the careful comparison carried out by Van Ark and Pilat (1993). For the same year, Maddison's estimates (1993, Table 13) show that the overall level of productivity in Japan was only 65 percent of the American level. This difference may reflect many causes, but one important cause is surely the resistance of Japanese politics and society to the substitution of large-scale corporate farming and retailing and of foreign goods for the traditional very small-scale family farms and shops of that country. The productivity gap is especially pronounced in those industries where these influences have been especially strong: Wolff (1994) finds that in 1988, Japanese productivity in agriculture was just 18 percent of the U.S. level; the food, beverage, and tobacco industry's productivity was 35 percent of the American level, and for textiles the figure was 57 percent.

Over time there is a two-way interaction between the evolution of a nation's social capabilities and the articulation of societal conditions required for mastery of production technologies at or close to the prevailing "best practice" frontier. In the short run, a country's ability to exploit the opportunities afforded by currently prevailing best practice techniques will remain limited by its current social capabilities. Over the longer term, however, social capabilities tend to undergo transformations that render them more complementary to the more salient among the emerging technological trajectories. Levels of general and technical education are raised. Curricula and training facilities change. New concepts of business management, including methods of managing personnel and organizing work, supplant traditional approaches. Corporate and financial institutions are established, and people learn their modes of action. Legal codes and even the very concepts of property can be modified. Moreover, experience gained in the practical implementation of a production technique enhances the technical and managerial competencies that serve it, and thus supports further advances along the same path. Such mutually reinforcing interactions impart "positive feedback" to the dynamics of technological evolution. They may for a time solidify a leader's position or, in the case of followers, serve to counter the tendency for their relative growth rates to decline as catch-up proceeds.

On the other hand, the adjustments and adaptations of existing cultural attitudes, social norms, organizational forms, and institutional rules and procedures are not necessarily automatic or smooth. Lack of plasticity in such social structures may retard and even block an otherwise technologically progressive economy's passage to the full exploitation of a particular emergent technology (Freeman and Perez, 1988; Perez and Soete, 1988; David, 1991b). New technologies may give rise to novel forms of productive assets and business activities that find themselves trammeled by features of an inherited jurisprudential and regulatory system that had never contemplated even the possibility of their existence.[14] For laggards, the constraints imposed by entrenched social structures may long circumscribe the opportunities for any sustained catch-up movement.

To summarize our general proposition: countries' *effective* potentials for rapid productivity growth by catch-up are not determined solely by the gaps in levels of technology, capital intensity, and efficient allocation that separate them from the productivity leaders. They are restricted also by their access to primary materials and more generally because their market scales, relative factor supplies, and income-constrained patterns of demand make their technical capabilities and their product structures incongruent in some degree with those that characterize countries that operate at or near the technological frontiers. And they are limited, finally, by those institutional characteristics that restrict their abilities to finance, organize, and operate the kinds of enterprises that are required to exploit the technologies on the frontiers of science and engineering.

Taken together, the foregoing elements determine a country's effective potential for productivity growth. Yet another distinct group of factors governs the ability of countries to realize their respective potentials. One set of issues here involves the extent to which followers can gain access to complete and reliable information about more advanced methods, appraise it, and acquire the artifacts and rights needed to implement that knowledge for commercial purposes. A second set of issues arises because long-term,

---

14. On the problem of adapting intellectual property institutions to changes in the methods of acquiring knowledge of new technologies, and the problems of accommodating the needs of new technology innovations (in computer software and biotechnology, for example) within the existing legal framework of intellectual property, see David (1994a) and references therein.

aggregate productivity growth almost always entails changes in industrial and occupational structure. As a result, the determinants of resource mobility, particularly labor mobility, are also important. And finally, macroeconomic conditions govern the intensity of use of resources and the financing of investment and thereby affect the choices between present and future that control the R&D and investment horizons of businesses. By influencing the volume of gross investment expenditures, they also govern the pace and extent to which technological knowledge becomes embodied in tangible production facilities and the people who work with them.

We are now ready to put this analytical schema into use in a specific historical context: how the United States attained and sustained its productivity lead from 1870 to 1950, and then what changed during these years that released the catch-up and convergence boom of the postwar period.

Bases of the Postwar Potential for Catch-up and Convergence

The dramatic postwar record of western Europe and Japan creates a presumption that they began the period with a strong potential for rapid growth by exploiting American methods of production and organization. The productivity gaps separating the laggard countries from the United States were then larger than they had been in the record since 1870. However, the gains in prospect could only be realized if Europe and Japan could do what they had not been able to do before: take full advantage of America's relatively advanced methods. The insistent question, therefore, is why Europe, itself an old center of technological progress, had proved unable even to keep pace with the United States during the three-quarters of a century following 1870.[15] The answer we propose is that the difficulty lay in the failures of technological congruence and social capability, and that it was the gradual elimination or weakening of these obstacles that opened the way after the war to the strong catch-up and convergence of the postwar years.

---

15. Maddison (1991, Table 1.1) finds that the U.S. productivity advantage may have started well before 1870, perhaps as far back as 1820. But his estimates for these early years are exceedingly rough, and other estimates, at least for the United States, indicate that the American advantage increased little if at all between 1820 and 1870. In any event, industrialization in Canada, Australia, Japan, and several of the European countries had hardly begun before 1870. For that reason, it would be wrong to view all the countries that eventually came to be "industrially advanced" as having been similarly positioned throughout the pre-1870 era in regard to their respective effective potentials for catching up with the productivity leader.

Technological Congruence: Primary Materials

The American advantage stemmed first from America's more abundant and cheap supplies of primary materials.[16] Such supplies had a more important bearing on a country's growth potential in the nineteenth and early twentieth centuries than they have had since that time. This is true because food then constituted a larger share of consumer expenditure and GDP, and resources devoted to agriculture were a larger share of total factor input than they have been since that time. Moreover, America possessed abundant virgin forests and brushlands. In the Age of Wood that preceded the Age of Iron, this profusion of forest resources generated strong incentives to improve methods of production that facilitated their exploitation, to use them extravagantly in the manufacture of finished products (like sawn lumber and musket stocks), and to lower the costs of goods complementary to wood (such as iron nails, to take a humble example).[17]

Beyond that stage, the industrial technology that emerged during the nineteenth and early twentieth centuries, when America rose to productivity leadership and forged farther ahead, was based on minerals: on coal for steam power, on coal and iron ore for steel, and on copper and other non-ferrous metals for still other purposes. American enterprise, reprising its previous performance in rising to "industrial woodworking leadership" by combining technological borrowing from abroad with the induced contributions of indigenous inventors, now embarked upon the exploration of another technological trajectory—one that was premised upon, and in turn fostered, the rapid (and in some respects environmentally profligate) exploitation of the country's vast mineral deposits. In this technology, the costs of coal as a source of steam power, of coal and iron ore for steelmaking, and of copper and still other non-ferrous metals bulked larger in the total costs of finished goods than subsequently came to be true. Cheap supplies of these primary materials thus underlay America's growing comparative advantage as an exporter of natural resource–intensive manufactures during the period 1880–1929 (Wright, 1990, especially Table 6).

---

16. With some amendment, much of this section and the next follows the argument and evidence of several earlier papers: Rosenberg (1980), Wright (1990), Nelson (1991), David and Wright (1992), Nelson and Wright (1992), and previous work published individually and jointly by the present writers.

17. As Rosenberg (1976, chap. 2) has said, in describing America's rise to woodworking leadership during the period 1800–1850, "It would be difficult to exaggerate the extent of early American dependence upon this natural resource: it was the major source of fuel, it was the primary building material, it was a critical source of chemical inputs (potash and pearlash), and it was an industrial raw material par excellence."

By the eve of the First World War, America had attained world leadership in the production of nearly every major industrial mineral of that era. But this position had been attained only in part because of the nation's abundant natural endowment. Perhaps even more crucial were the nation's successes in rapidly uncovering the existence of its rich sub-surface mineral reserves, in devising new methods of refining and processing that were adapted to their sometimes peculiar chemical characteristics, and in building an efficient network of transportation by water and rail that reached throughout its very large territory.

Government policies and agencies played an active part in all those accomplishments, especially in subsidizing the extension of the railroad network into the American west, and by organizing and funding geological surveys and promoting the beginnings of systematic scientific research on subjects immediately relevant to the mineral industries. So did the newly formed faculties of engineering at the nation's institutions of higher education, both those at the older privately founded universities (like Columbia University's famous School of Mines) and those at the state colleges of more recent establishment under the terms of the 1862 Morrill Act (David and Wright, 1992). The peculiarities of the law of mining in the United States heightened the private, commercial incentives for investments in exploration and development. The federal government claimed no ultimate title to the nation's minerals, not even to those in the public domain. It offered free access to prospectors, and no fees or royalties were assessed against the minerals removed.

Finally, the incentives for minerals exploration and development stemmed even more largely from the demand that appeared as American manufacturing shifted towards the production of minerals-based capital and consumer goods. There was, therefore, a fruitful interaction between the development of primary materials supply, the advance of American technology, and the growth of manufacturing, construction, and transportation (Rosenberg, 1980; Wright, 1990; David and Wright, 1992).

The minerals-based, resource-intensive technology proved to be the dominant path of technical progress in all the presently advanced countries, but America gained substantial advantages in wholeheartedly embarking upon that path by undertaking infrastructural investments to explore, develop, and reduce the costs of access to her mineral resource deposits. Europe as a whole possessed known reserves of a number of the key minerals, such as iron ore, that in 1910 were as large as those identified in North America at the time, and the current rates of production of iron ore, coal, and bauxite in Europe as a whole exceeded those of the United States in 1913.[18] But when it came to petroleum, copper, phosphate, gold, and other minerals, America was out-producing the whole of Europe—even with Russia included. There was no nation in Europe, to say nothing of Japan, which approached the United States in the variety and richness of the mineral resources that actually had been developed, rather than remaining in "reserve" status. Out of fourteen important industrial minerals, America in 1913 accounted for the largest shares of world output of all but two—and for those two it was the runner-up. Given the still high transportation costs of the time and the relative importance of materials in the total costs of finished goods, this translated into a significant cost disadvantage for Europe and Japan vis-à-vis the United States in the production of finished manufactures.[19]

With the passing of time, however, the importance of these intercountry differences declined—for at least six reasons:[20]

First, technological progress reduced the unit labor input requirements in the mining, gas, and oil industries both absolutely and relatively. In the United States, for which the quantitative evidence is most readily available, unit factor costs of minerals production fell relative to unit factor costs in the rest of the economy. Table 3 illustrates these points, with the first panel focusing on absolute costs, and the second panel on relative costs. Compared to the non-extractive (or non-primary production) sector of the domestic economy, the unit costs of labor and capital in minerals decreased by 10 percent between the late nineteenth century and 1919, and then dropped by another 50 percent during the period from 1919 to 1957. Over the same long period, factor productivity in agriculture was merely keeping pace with that in the non-extractive activities as a whole, whereas in the forestry sector relative unit factor costs appear to have risen at an accelerated rate after 1919 (as shown in the second panel).

Second, mineral resources were discovered and developed in many parts of the world where their existence had remained unknown at the end of the nineteenth century, so costs of materials at points of origin and use outside the United States would have tended to fall. Furthermore, technological advance increased the commercial value of mineral resource depos-

---

18. See David and Wright (1992, Tables 1–2, and Figure 2). The following statements in the text are based on the same source, Figures 3–5, and Wright (1990, Chart 5).

19. For example, Wright (1990, p. 622) cites Foreman-Peck (1982, p. 874) to the effect that as late as the 1920s, "Ford UK faced steel input prices that were higher by 50 percent than those paid by the parent company."

20. These follow and elaborate on the lines of argument in Schultz (1951) and Nelson and Wright (1992).

TABLE 3

*Indicators of Productivity Growth in Production
and Use of Primary Products*

Relative output per worker in 1939 (1902 = 100)[a]	
Mining	280
Gas and oil	444[b]
Mining excluding gas and oil	178
Agriculture	164
Manufacturing	194

Unit costs (labor and capital) of gross product originating
in primary products sectors relative to unit costs of gross domestic
non-primary product[a] in United States

	Minerals	Agriculture	Forestry[d]
1870–1900 (average)	155	97	36
1900	155	94	47
1919	139	97	55
1937	78	91	100
1957	69	97	130

Energy and electricity consumption per dollar of GDP in 1920 prices
(1920 = 100)

	Energy consumption (Btu equivalents per dollar)		Electricity consumption (kwh's per dollar)
	Total[e]	In electricity generation	
1900[f]	86	77	20
1920	100	100	100
1950	64	97	268
1970	63	—	556

SOURCES: Panel A: Barger and Schurr (1944, Table 12). Panel B: Barnett and Morse (1963, Tables 6, 7, 8). Panel C: 1900–50 computed from data in Schurr and Netschert (1960, Tables 52, 58) and from Kendrick (1961, Table A-III) and estimated energy conversion estimates based on data in David (1991a) for 1902; extrapolations for 1950–70 based on Darmstadter (1972, Appendix, Table 1).

[a] Comparisons are for five-year averages centered on 1902 and 1939.
[b] Based on growth rate from 1902 to 1937.
[c] GDP less products of minerals industries, agriculture, forest products, and fishing.
[d] Estimates for sawn logs only; 1937 interpolated from 1930 and 1940 figures.
[e] Mineral fuels, hydropower, and wood for fuel.
[f] Electricity consumption estimates for 1902.

its that previously were neglected, and added new metals and synthetic materials to the available range of primary materials and agricultural products.

Third, petroleum came to be of increasing importance as a source of power for industry and transportation, and also as feedstock for the chemicals industry.

Fourth, transportation costs both by land and by sea declined markedly, which reduced the cost advantages enjoyed by exporters of primary products in the further processing of such materials.

Fifth, crude materials came to be processed more elaborately, and on this account, primary products became a smaller fraction of the final cost of finished goods. The consumption of primary materials declined per unit of final output, which had a similar effect. This is illustrated dramatically by a comparison of energy consumed in generating electric power with the electricity applied in industry and households. While electricity used per dollar of GDP more than quintupled between 1920 and 1970, energy consumed per dollar of GDP declined by a third (as shown in the third panel of Table 3).

Sixth, and finally, services in which the materials component is small became more important, compared with foods and manufactures, in which the materials component is larger.

For all of these reasons, differences in developed natural resource endowments have counted for less in recent decades than they had done earlier. One recent example of these changes deserves special notice. When the postwar period opened, it was widely expected that the well-worked, high-cost coal deposits of Europe and the more general lack of energy sources in Japan would pose serious obstacles to development for both. However, the rapid exploitation of cheap Middle Eastern petroleum and the development of low-cost transport by supertanker changed the picture. Energy problems became much less severe in Europe and Japan, which reduced what had been an important relative advantage of the United States.

Technological Congruence: Capital-Using and Scale-Intensive Technology

The technology that emerged in the nineteenth and persisted into the early twentieth century was not only resource-intensive, but also tangible capital–using and scale-dependent. Exploiting the technical advances of the time demanded heavier use of machinery per worker, especially power-driven machinery in ever more specialized forms. But it required operation on an ever-larger scale to make the use of such structures and equipment economical. Furthermore, it required steam-powered transport by rail and ship, itself a capital-intensive and scale-intensive activity, to assemble materials and to distribute the growing output to wider markets.[21] The im-

---

21. For a general discussion of the trend towards round-aboutness and increasing capital intensity in late-nineteenth-century industrial technology, the interested reader

portance of tangible capital supported by operation on a large scale was the message of all the early economists, beginning with Adam Smith and running through Bohm-Bawerk and Sidgwick to Taussig and Allyn Young. It is also a view supported by the economic history of technology and by statistical studies of American growth in the nineteenth and the early twentieth centuries.[22]

Tangible capital–using and scale-dependent methods again offered a technological path along which the American economy was drawn more strongly, and which the producers in the United States could follow more easily than their European counterparts during the late nineteenth and early twentieth centuries. We have seen how a rich natural endowment had supported American development of the minerals-based technology of the later nineteenth century. In a similar way, the early sparse settlement of America's virgin lands and its abundant forest resources made American wages relatively high and local labor supplies inelastic. And high wages in turn encouraged the development of the era's capital-intensive mechanical technologies. The heavy use of power-driven capital equipment was further supported by the relatively large, rich, and homogeneous domestic market open to American firms.

By 1870, the United States already had a larger aggregate domestic economy than any of its advanced competitors. Moreover, extensive investments in railroads and other transportation infrastructure were helping to realize its potential as an integrated transcontinental product market. Boosted by its comparatively rapid population growth (which was sus-

---

might begin with Abramovitz and David (1973a), Rosenberg (1976), and Hounshell (1984). With regard to the manufacturing industries in the United States and Britain, see the careful quantitative comparisons in James and Skinner (1985) and Broadberry (1993).

22. Growth accounting studies for the U.S. domestic economy in the nineteenth century show that tangible-capital accumulation was then the major source by far of the growth of output per man-hour and of its acceleration. See, for example, Abramovitz and David (1973a), David (1977), and Abramovitz (1993). But statistical analysis also indicates that the importance of capital accumulation in that era rested on a tangible capital–using bias of technological progress. Although a series of studies reports that the elasticity of substitution between tangible capital and labor is less than unity—which by itself would have reduced the income share of capital, which was the faster-growing factor—capital's share of GDP in fact rose markedly in the United States during the nineteenth century and remained stable into the early years of the twentieth century. There is, therefore, a strong presumption that technological progress was tangible capital-using not only at the aggregate level of the domestic economy, but within the industrial and agricultural sectors as well. For quantitative evidence on the elasticity of substitution and the bias of factor-augmenting technical change at the aggregate and industry levels in the United States, see David and van de Klundert (1965), Abramovitz and David (1973b), David (1975, chaps. 1, 4), David (1977), and Cain and Paterson (1981).

tained by a tide of international migration), the U.S. growth rate of real GDP between 1870 and 1913 outstripped those of all other industrializing countries. By 1913, therefore, the size of the American economy was over two and one-half times that of the United Kingdom or Germany, and over four times that of France (Maddison, 1993, Table 3). America's per capita GDP also topped those of the other industrial nations in 1913, exceeding that of the United Kingdom by 20 percent, France by 77 percent, and Germany by 86 percent (Maddison, 1993, Table 1.1). These differences indicate the advantage that the United States enjoyed in markets for automobiles and for the other new, relatively expensive durable goods, to which the techniques of a scale-dependent, capital-using technology (like mass production) especially applied.

The American domestic market was both large and well unified by an extensive transportation network. And it was unified in other ways that Europe at the time could not match. The rapid settlement of the country from a common cultural base in the northeastern and middle-Atlantic seaboards closely circumscribed any regional differences in language, legal systems, local legislation, and popular tastes. In fact, Americans sought consumer goods of unpretentious and functional design in preference to products that tried to emulate the more differentiated, elaborate, and custom-finished look of the old European luxury crafts. This taste structure, which was commented on repeatedly at international expositions where American manufactures were displayed alongside the top-quality wares of the Europeans, owed much to the spirit of democratic egalitarianism that prevailed over large sections of American society, and to the young nation's freedom from a heritage of feudal and aristocratic traditions and aesthetic values. It fostered the entrepreneurial strategy of catering to and actively creating large markets for the standardized products of large-scale production (Rosenberg, 1980; Hounshell, 1984).

The American development of mass-production methods was also encouraged by the country's higher and more widely diffused incomes, which supported an ample domestic market for the new metals-based durable goods. By contrast, Europe's lower and less equally distributed incomes initially restricted the market for such goods to its well-to-do classes, for whom standardized commodities had less appeal in any event, and thereby delayed the full application of American mass-production methods.

Finally, American land abundance and the level, unobstructed terrain of the Midwest and trans-Mississippi prairies were especially well suited to the extensive cultivation of grain and livestock under climatic and topo-

TABLE 4

Comparative Capital-Labor Ratios, 1870–1979

(*U.S. = 100*)

	Germany	Italy	United Kingdom	Average of three European countries	Japan
1870	73	—	117	—	—
1880	73	26	106	68	12
1913	60	24	59	48	10
1938	42	32	43	39	13
1950	46	31	46	41	13
1970	71	48	53	57	29
1979	105	66	64	78	52

SOURCE: Wolff (1991, pp. 565–79, Table 2).
NOTE: Labor input measured by hours worked, capital by gross fixed non-residential capital stock (Germany by net capital stock, so the German relatives are somewhat understated).

graphical conditions very favorable to the mechanization of field operations. None of these developments could be replicated on anything approaching the same comparative scale within European agriculture at the time. In this way, the "Westward Movement" helped perpetuate conditions of relative labor scarcity, which in turn favored the substitution of machinery (and horsepower) for human effort, and further stimulated technological innovations localized at the capital-intensive end of the spectrum of farming techniques (David, 1975, chaps. 4–5; Parker, 1972). And the recurring shifts of the farming frontier onto virgin soil contributed doubly to boosting nineteenth-century agricultural productivity growth in the still largely agrarian American economy.[23]

The effect of the American advantage in scale, buttressed by high wages relative to the cost of finance, is reflected in comparisons of U.S. capital-labor ratios with those in three large European countries and Japan. Table 4 offers some illustrative figures. In 1870, Britain may still have used more capital per worker than the United States. But by 1913, both the British and German ratios had sunk to about 60 percent of the U.S. fig-

23. Parker (1991, pp. 325–29) addresses the deeper issue of the endogeneity of technical and spatial innovation in the American agrarian context. There were, he suggests, two-way causal influences running between the westward movement and regional agricultural specialization, on the one hand, and technological progress in the development and improvement of farm machinery, on the other hand. This interaction was especially notable in the case of the mechanization of reaping and threshing small grains (which accounted for virtually all of the nineteenth-century American labor productivity growth in wheat and oats), and in the development of improved plows, seed drills, and row cultivators (which accounted for all the productivity growth in corn farming).

ure.[24] European (and Japanese) capital intensity, held back by wars and their aftermath, did not begin to catch up to the United States until after World War II, in conjunction with the postwar catch-up boom.

Again, however, these American advantages gradually waned in importance. As aggregate output expanded in Europe, the markets for more industries and products approached the scale required for most efficient production, with plants embodying technologies that had been developed to suit American conditions. Furthermore, the decline in transportation costs and the more liberal regime of international trade and finance that emerged between 1880 and 1913 encouraged producers to use international markets to achieve the scale required. From 1870 to 1913, the average growth rate of exports in continental Europe was 43 percent greater than GDP growth (Maddison, 1991, Tables 3.2, 3.15). Of course, there was a still greater expansion of trade during the 1950s and 1960s, when the growth of European exports exceeded the growth of their collective GDP (both in constant prices) by 89 percent. In this era, rising per capita incomes also helped assure that scale requirements in the newer mass-production industries producing consumer and producer durables would be satisfied for a widening range of commodities. As larger domestic and foreign markets appeared, laggard countries could begin to switch in a thoroughgoing way to exploit the capital-using and scale-dependent techniques already explored by the United States. This was a path toward catch-up that would prove to be especially important after World War II, even though it had begun to be followed by some large industrial enterprises in Europe and Japan during the interwar period (Denison, 1967, chap. 17; Denison and Chung, 1976, chap. 10).

---

24. Edward Wolff's figures in Table 4, which refer to gross reproducible, fixed, non-residential capital stock per person employed, go back to Maddison (1982). More recent estimates by Maddison, however, based on standardized assumptions regarding asset lives, revise his earlier estimates drastically. They put U.S. stock at a level over twice as high as the United Kingdom's as early as 1890 (Maddison, 1991, Table 3.9). And more recent, still unpublished figures suggest that the United States may already have enjoyed a substantial lead even in 1870.

In manufacturing, however, the capital-labor ratio in the United States was already 94 percent of the U.K. level in 1870, on the evidence of the official (Census) net stock figures. Stephen Broadberry's (1993) adjustments to standardize the service life assumptions underlying the American and British net capital stock figures—carried out by Broadberry for 1950 and later dates—would suggest that the corrected comparison for 1870 would show the capital-labor ratio in the United States to have already been at 150 percent of the U.K. level. One must bear in mind, however, that in 1870, at the end of the golden age of "High Farming" in Britain, heavy reproducible capital formation for drainage and other farm improvements had pushed Britain's agricultural capital-output ratio to a level well above that in the United States.

Still another significant cause of the decline in American advantage was a gradual alteration in the nature of technological progress itself. Towards the end of the nineteenth century, the former bias in the direction of reproducible tangible capital–using, scale-dependent innovations became less pronounced. New capital-augmenting techniques (like the assembly line and automatic railroad signaling, track-switching, and car-coupling devices) were found to increase the throughput rates achievable with fixed production facilities. Even more portentous for the coming century, the growth of the scientific knowledge base relevant to industry encouraged shifts in the direction of innovation that began to favor investment in *intangible* assets (both human and non-human) rather than the further accumulation of conventional, tangible capital goods such as structures and equipment. In other words, the effect of this alteration of the bias of scientific, technological, and organizational innovation, taken by itself, was that of raising the rate of return on intangible capital formation activities—most notably, education and organized R&D—in relation to the rate of return on investments in conventional tangible assets.

This view of the changing general thrust of technological progress at the beginning of the twentieth century finds strong support in the quantitative and qualitative evidence from the American experience (Abramovitz and David, 1973a, b; Kendrick, 1976; David, 1977; Abramovitz, 1993). We believe it applies equally to developments affecting Europe and Japan. One sees this shift reflected, first, in the trend of the share of tangible capital in the factor distribution of GDP. The latter had risen markedly in the middle of the nineteenth century, but then leveled off and declined just as markedly between the early 1900s and the mid-1950s. A second indication is found in the stability of rates of return to education in the face of huge increases during the present century in the proportions of the workforce who had comparatively extended periods of formal schooling. In the absence of some other influence (such as the hypothesized bias of technological change) acting upon the relative productivity and earnings of the more educated, the rising level of educational attainment among the labor force would have driven down the real rate of return on investment in education.

A third indication is to be seen in the rapid rise in organized research and development activities, whether measured as a fraction of corporate revenues or of aggregate output. Overall, according to estimates made by Kendrick (1994, Table 1B) "nonhuman tangible" capital formation—consisting of structures and equipment, utilized land, and civilian and military inventories—represented a secularly decreasing proportion of total real gross investment; the nonhuman tangibles' share declined from 64.9 percent in 1929 to 47.3 percent in 1990.[25] The share of investment devoted to intangible assets such as education, R&D, health, and others rose by a corresponding amount. Kendrick (1994, Table 2) also presents parallel figures showing the growing importance of intangible assets in the total real gross capital stock.

A final manifestation of the rising importance of intangible investment in education is the growth of the number of jobs requiring long years of schooling in relation to the jobs requiring less formal instruction—a trend that was firmly established in the United States during 1900–60, and that has continued unabated during the past three decades (Abramovitz, 1993; Katz and Murphy, 1992). The global dimensions of this trend bear on our contention that there has been an erosion of the part of the American growth advantage which depended upon close congruence between the scale requirements of a tangible capital–using technology and the size of the U.S. domestic market. While western Europe and Japan had lower levels of tangible capital throughout the first half of the twentieth century, they were able quite early to reach levels and trends of schooling more nearly approaching those in the United States, as shown in Table 5. Although the European levels fell back somewhat from their relative position as of 1913—largely because of the more widespread continuation into higher education in the United States—the significance of that limited reversal remains doubtful and uncertain in view of the roughness of the estimates and the differences in the "quality" and intensity of the school year among our small sample of countries. We conclude that the political and social conditions in most of western Europe and Japan were substantially congruent with the new human capital–using bias of technological progress, just as they were in America.[26] Consequently, as intangible capital became more important, America's special advantage waned.

---

25. The technologically driven shift in the structure of relative asset demands, therefore, should be seen to be a significant force that has operated to reduce the conventionally measured gross savings rate (in both real and nominal terms) in the American economy during the twentieth century. The fact that despite the recurrent urging by economists over a number of decades—for example, see Abramovitz and David (1973a), David and Scadding (1974), Eisner (1989), and Kendrick (1976, 1994)—the official national income accounts remain blind to the rising importance of intangible capital formation has been a factor contributing to the misplaced emphasis given forces impinging on the supply of savings in efforts to explain and find policy correctives for the U.S. economy's "declining savings rate" problem.

26. Inkeles (1981, pp. 20, 25) points out that while different countries followed distinctive historical paths towards the complete enrollment of all children in primary school, and eventually in secondary school, too, the industrialized nations arrived quite

TABLE 5

*Average Years of Formal Education of Population Aged 15–64
in Four European Countries and Japan Compared
with United States, 1913–89*

(U.S. = 100)

	1913	1950	1973	1989
France	89	86	85	87
Germany	100	90	82	72
Netherlands	87	78	79	78
United Kingdom	105	99	91	84
Average of four European countries	95	88	84	80
Japan	74	86	90	87

SOURCES: 1913, 1950, 1973 from Maddison (1987, Table A-12); 1989 from Maddison (1991, Table 3.8).

The United States led Europe—with Germany a possible exception—in the late-nineteenth-century development of organized industrial R&D (Mowery and Rosenberg, 1989). Its lead continued to widen until sometime in the 1950s, but thereafter the differential vis-à-vis the R&D efforts of other economically advanced nations began to disappear, and in recent decades the gap in the area of civilian and non–military-related R&D has been essentially closed. Nelson and Wright (1992) attribute the continuing American technological leadership through the period of the 1950s and 1960s to the country's heavy investments in higher education and R&D. There is a distinction, of course, between seizing leadership in technology and managing to catch up in the level of labor productivity. The laggard countries achieved their postwar labor productivity catch-up during 1950–73 mainly by exploiting the production techniques explored by American firms both in earlier times and contemporaneously. European and Japanese capabilities for assessing, acquiring, and adapting existing technology, moreover, were becoming stronger as their R&D investment accumulated. As they approached American levels of efficiency in some lines of production, however, the emphasis of their own innovative efforts gradually shifted towards the exploration of other technological trajecto-

---

rapidly at substantially the same destination in this regard; and ultimately the institutional and administrative structures of their educational systems resembled one another in many broad features. After World War II, all the leading nations of the West increased the proportion of GNP expended on public education, converging on the figure of 6 percent (direct costs) during the period 1955–75, but the national patterns of allocation of educational expenditures among the primary, secondary and tertiary levels remained quite variegated. See also Inkeles and Sirowym (1983).

ries. For example, Broadberry (1993) has suggested that western European industrial firms have been able to reassert a degree of localized technological leadership during the 1970s and 1980s—especially in the development of alternatives to Fordist, fixed-transfer-line, mass-production methods—because they had an advantage in marrying modern information technologies with the small-scale craft organization of production that was traditional in many of their branches of industry.

The Interdependence of Technological Congruence and Technological Progress

The preceding account has often referred to the technology with which American conditions were especially congruent as one that had "emerged" in the nineteenth century. This wording could suggest that we regard the path of nineteenth-century technological progress as exogenously determined. American superiority in making use of the opportunities presented by practical knowledge would then appear as just a happy accident, a fortunate concordance of American conditions with the character or biases of an autonomous path of progress. Was that really so?

It probably was, in some part. The inventions that opened the era of modern industrialization were mechanical inventions, and they drew upon the history of European experiments with labor-saving contrivances that stretched back to medieval times (White, 1968; Mokyr, 1990). That these inventions came first may have been accidental, but some opinion holds otherwise—supposing that the reason they appeared earlier was that they were more readily grasped by people whose everyday observations and experiences had implanted in them intuitions about the laws of mechanics (Parker, 1984, chap. 8). Systematic invention based on electricity, chemistry, solid-state physics, and molecular biology, which required more fundamental and obscure scientific knowledge, had to wait. Meanwhile, the progress of mechanical applications put pressure on the older sources of fuel and primary materials: timber, coal, iron ore, and the other metals. In an era of incomplete geographical exploration and high transport costs, America's natural resource endowment and its early development gave this country an advantage in exploiting the new opportunities.

At the same time, the water-powered and steam-powered mechanical inventions of the time were embodied in tangible and specialized capital equipment and driven by large, factory-sited, central sources of power, transmitted by elaborate and expensive systems of belts. All of this was economical only if operated on a sufficiently large scale. So America's superior market scale gave it another substantial advantage in exploiting the potential of the nineteenth century's path of mechanical progress.

But did the nineteenth-century path of technological progress that favored American productivity growth just "emerge"? Or alternatively, was it the product of a process of exploration, of learning and testing, that was itself shaped by the exceptional, American conditions of resource abundance, high wages, and large market size? After all, when businessmen, craftsmen, and engineers look to reduce costs, they do not search with equal vigor through every possible combination of materials, labor, capital, and scale. Rather, they concentrate on that segment of the spectrum of combinations which has already begun to reveal its economic opportunities and engineering challenges.[27]

In America in the nineteenth and the early twentieth centuries, conditions pointed this search process towards methods that spared the use of expensive labor by accepting intensive use of cheap materials or land, by equipping workers with better tools, and by organizing production on a large scale to spread the overhead of intensive capital use. Many familiar stories of American economic development are consistent with this hypothesis: the country's "wasteful" use of timber; its extensive land cultivation practices (including monoculture) which left soil exhaustion and erosion in the farmers' wake; and its innovative development of machine-made, "interchangeable" parts and later of mass production by assembly-line methods.

The logic of these endogenous mechanisms of technological change suggests that they may not only give direction to the search for progress, but also, in some circumstances, speed up the rate of advance. Insofar as the pace of learning depends on the cumulation of experience, it is influenced by the pace at which engineers and businessmen come into contact with new methods of production and with the capital goods in which they are embodied. Thus, the pace of technical advance may depend on the portion of production activities that involves constructing and installing new capital equipment and related structures, as well as on the growth rate of the cumulative gross stocks that constitute the setting for learning-by-

---

27. See David (1975, chap. 1) for the formulation and historical application of a model of "locally neutral stochastic learning" built on the Atkinson and Stiglitz (1969) concept of localized technical change, the literature of learning by doing following Arrow (1962), and Rosenberg's (1969) notion of "compulsive sequences" of innovation. Antonelli (1994) recently has expanded the concept of localized technological change and shown its applicability in numerous industrial contexts.

doing and learning-by-using capital-embodied technologies.[28] Therefore, if American scale induced larger demand for tangible capital, it would also have supported a rate of technological progress faster than that being endogenously generated in Europe.

Moreover, American scale would have worked to speed up the pace of progress in still another way. The very process of conceiving, designing, testing, and developing new methods and the equipment through which they work is itself an investment, the cost of which is less burdensome when spread over a larger output. It is ideas such as these that are embedded in the "new" growth theories that Paul Romer (1990) and others have put forward recently.

Manifestly, the two views we have sketched are not mutually exclusive. The path of advance that became dominant in the nineteenth century did not become established simply because Americans chose to use it. When Adam Smith wrote in 1776 that the division of labor opened the way to the substitution of tools for labor, and when he proposed his famous dictum that the division of labor is limited by the extent of the market, he did not have before him the American developments that would so thoroughly exploit these principles. The exceptional circumstances of the former colonists, whose Declaration of Independence had coincided with the publication of *The Wealth of Nations*, were propitious in that they so well satisfied the conditions for economic progress envisaged by its author. Thus, the technological investments undertaken by American inventors and entrepreneurs, and the direction in which American business firms pointed their efforts to raise efficiency, lay more directly on the dominant path of nineteenth-century technical progress than was true in the case of Europe; and the results of those investments were embodied in forms of machinery and in a scale of production operations that firms in Europe could not immediately imitate or readily adapt to their own circumstances.

Social Capability

Social capability has to do with those attributes, qualities, and characteristics of people and economic organization that originate in social and political institutions and that influence the responses of people to eco-

---

28. The dependence of the growth rate of efficiency on the growth of the gross stock of (cumulated) investment was hypothesized in Arrow's classic paper (1962) on learning by doing. See Rosenberg (1980) on learning by using in the case of complex production systems. The hypothesis that productivity growth is stimulated particularly by high investment rates in producers' equipment receives some empirical support from DeLong and Summers's study (1991) of international data for the post–World War II period.

nomic opportunity.[29] It includes a society's culture and the priority it assigns to economic attainment. It covers the economic constitutions under which people live, particularly the rights, limitations, and obligations involved with property, and all the incentives and inhibitions that these may create for effort, investment, enterprise, and innovation. It involves those long-term policies that govern particular forms of organization or activity, such as limited liability corporations and financial institutions, and the policies that may support or restrict such organizations. And it covers the policies that provide for the public provision of social services and those that support the accumulation of capital by investments in infrastructure and by public education or research. With all that in mind, we can do no more than suggest how the shifting state of social capability may have worked to inhibit and then release the forces of catch-up and convergence in the group of presently advanced countries.

One thing is clear enough at the outset. The differences in social capability within the group of presently advanced market economies are less important than those between this group and the less developed countries of the present time or those of a century ago. Even in the later nineteenth century, all of the presently advanced group had certain broadly similar features. All had substantially independent national governments at least as early as 1871.[30] Broadly speaking, all the countries except Japan share

---

29. "Social capability" is a subject that has drawn the attention of historians and economists for many years. De Tocqueville (1840) and Veblen (1915) are notable examples of older writings. There was a considerable addition to this literature in the years following World War II, and we depend on these writings in the pages that follow. We refer especially to the essays by Arthur H. Cole, Thomas C. Cochran, and others in the collective volume prepared by the Harvard Entrepreneurial Research Center (1949); to the series of biographies of businessmen edited by Miller (1952); to the essays on France by Sawyer (1951, 1954); to those on France and Germany by Landes (1949, 1951, 1954) and Gerschenkron (1953, 1954b, 1955); and to Wiener's controversial work (1981) on the role of culture and class in Britain's relative decline. In more recent decades the subject has been largely neglected and is only now being taken up again by economic historians, as in Parker (1984, 1991) and Lazonick (1994). An even fuller view of social capability would include the growing literature of public choice, economic organization, and institutions, not only in economics but also in political science and sociology.

30. Some qualifications are in order. Finland was acquired by Russia in 1809 but granted a constitution that gave the country a semi-independent status. Full independence was achieved only in 1917. Denmark has suffered several partitions of Schleswig-Holstein and their transfer between itself and Germany. The unifications of Germany and Italy were completed only in 1871. While Austria itself has survived to the present time, it lost its empire by the Treaty of St. Germain in 1919. Norway did not become fully independent until 1905, but gained substantial control of its internal affairs some decades earlier.

much of the older culture of western Europe. Most important, all the countries, again excepting Japan, have lived during the entire period under basically stable economic constitutions that provide for a system operated mainly by business enterprises coordinated by markets for goods, labor, capital, and land. In Japan, although a middle class of merchants had arisen even under the Shogunate, the country retained much of its older feudal character until the Meiji restoration of 1868. Thereafter, however, it was rapidly transformed and by the turn of the century had established its own form of private-enterprise, market economy (Rosovsky, 1961; Ohkawa and Rosovsky, 1972).

Beyond their economic constitutions, however, certain noteworthy differences worked to impair the ability of European countries to catch up to the United States during the late nineteenth and the early twentieth centuries. Nineteenth-century America presented a contrast with western Europe in its social structure, its people's outlook, and their standards of behavior. In America, plentiful land offered a widespread opportunity to achieve a satisfactory income by the standards of the time. It fostered a relatively equal distribution of income and wealth and an egalitarian spirit. America's Puritan strain in religion tolerated and even encouraged the pursuit of wealth. The older European class structure and feeling did not survive America's wider dispersion of property and opportunity. Americans judged each other more largely on merit, and with the lack of other signs of merit, wealth became the main badge of distinction. America's social and economic circumstances encouraged effort, saving, and enterprise, and gave trade and the commercial life in general a status as high as or higher than that of other occupations (de Tocqueville, 1840, bk. 1, chaps. 5, 8; bk. 2, chaps. 18, 19; Parker, 1991, pp. 24–25, 123, 242–49).

While the social backgrounds of economic life in the countries of nineteenth-century Europe were of course not uniform, there were certain commonalities in their divergence from American conditions of the time. In all the European countries, a traditional class structure—which separated a nobility and gentry from the peasantry, the tradesmen, and an expanding middle class—survived into the twentieth century. Social distinction rested more on birth and the class status it conveyed than on wealth. Insofar as social distinction did turn on wealth, inherited wealth and income counted for more than earned income or the wealth gained by commerce, and landed wealth stood higher than financial wealth and still higher than industrial or commercial wealth. The middle class who aspired to membership in the gentry or nobility bought rural seats and adopted upper-class standards of conspicuous consumption. Class lines were not impassable, but they were hard to cross. Wealth alone was not enough, whereas a step up in the status hierarchy could be gained through the adroit deployment of sufficient wealth in serving the crown or the nobility, or in contracting a socially advantageous marriage, or in purchasing a military or civil commission that entitled one to enter an occupation suitable to a gentleman. In short, the social order of western Europe diluted the characteristic American preoccupation with material success.[31]

These differences in the bases of social distinction—and therefore in the priority assigned to economic attainment—influenced many kinds of behavior that matter for productivity growth. They shaped the occupational choices of both the European gentry and the bourgeoisie. When family income was adequate, sons were pointed towards the occupations that the upper classes regarded as gentlemanly or honorific: the military, the civil service, the church, and, well behind, the professions. Even in the sphere of business, finance held pride of place, all to the detriment of commerce and industry (Landes, 1949, pp. 54–57; Wiener, 1981).

In Europe, a related tradition from pre-industrial times influenced education in a way that reinforced these pre-existing patterns of occupational choice. The curricula in the secondary schools continued to emphasize the time-honored subjects of the classics and mathematics; the faculties of Europe's ancient and most prestigious universities dwelt upon these and also theology, law, and medicine. Throughout Europe, university curricula emphasized what was regarded as proper for gentlemen destined for the clergy, the civil service, and the liberal professions (de Tocqueville, 1840, bk. 1, chap. 10; Wiener, 1981). Although training in engineering did win a place for itself in both France and Germany early in the nineteenth century, its character in both countries was theoretical, concerned with preparing an elite cadre of engineer-candidates to serve the state in administrative and regulatory capacities. In contrast, by the late nineteenth century, engineering schools in America clearly had evolved a more practical, commercial, and industrial bent.[32]

---

31. Note 29 offers citations to works that support what may seem to be a sweeping judgment.

32. See Emmerson (1973) on the intellectual foundations and the contrasting social realities that formed the context for engineering schools in Europe and North America. Especially notable was the contrast with the French *grandes ecoles*, which initially had a strong influence on American engineering education. Ferguson (1992, pp. 72, 208–9) notes that when the U.S. Military Academy was reorganized in 1817, the practical military and civilian engineering curriculum adopted was the one in use at the Ecole Polytechnique in Paris during 1795–1804; the heavily scientific curriculum that had been introduced at the Ecole Polytechnique after 1815 was essentially ignored, and never was widely adopted by American engineering schools. David and Wright (1992) discuss

In a notable series of articles, David Landes (1949, 1951, 1954) and John Sawyer (1951, 1954) argued that the French outlook and social structure, as these had survived from pre-industrial times and then developed after the Revolution, gave the French family a more important role in the new industrial era than was true in America. Together with other factors, mainly the smaller size of the French domestic market, this emphasis on family business restricted the size of French firms. Family-owned businesses assured their family's continuing control by pursuing financial self-sufficiency, which led to a notably cautious policy and resistance to profit seeking by expansion that might require external finance (Landes, 1949, p. 53). This delayed the adoption of the corporate form of organization. Where technology demanded a larger scale than family funds could satisfy, as in steel, the preferred business form for the maintenance of family control was, according to Landes (1951, p. 337, n. 10), the *commandite par actions*, "a form of sleeping partnership" in which ownership is represented by negotiable shares, but in which the "active partners are in sole charge of operations." The *Kommanditgesellschaft auf Aktien*, a similar arrangement, was popular in Germany. Alfred Chandler's great business history (1990, pt. 3) contends that the expansion of British firms and their development of managerial and merchandising capabilities were likewise limited by the desire of British entrepreneurs to keep control within their families.

Survivals of the pre-industrial social structure of France limited the scale of firms in other ways as well. One that we already have noted was an aristocratic taste for quality and individuality in consumer goods, a penchant that may also account for the excessive degree of "finish" and durability that some observers have seen in European tools and machinery. This pursuit of quality and distinction inhibited the development of mass production and supported the extreme fragmentation of retail trade in which tiny boutiques and specialty food stores offered limited lines of merchandise in an individual ambience. Similarly, a business ethos that can be traced back to the medieval guilds discouraged aggressive innovation and price competition, in favor of maintaining a high standard of quality in traditional product lines.

The French social structure and the outlook it inspired were doubtless different in elements and strength from those in other European countries. Yet something of the same character does seem to have been at work throughout western Europe. For example, in M. J. Wiener's picture of En-

---

differences between American and European educational institutions in the case of nineteenth-century mining engineering. In the twentieth century, the long delay in the appearance in Europe of schools of "business administration" and "management" conducted at the university and postgraduate levels is also worth notice in this connection.

glish society (1981), there is the same middle-class yearning to rise on the social ladder to the rungs occupied by the gentry and nobility. There is the same drain of talent from industry and trade into more honorific occupations in the civil service, the military, the clergy, and the law. There is the same pre-modern cast of secondary and higher education, an emphasis on the classical and theoretical as opposed to the practical. Britain was a laggard in the development of curricula in engineering and business, although this probably owes something to a peculiarly British distrust of the educated specialist and a preference in practical life for learning on the job. In addition, class feeling also delayed the spread of mass education at the primary level during the nineteenth century. As one of us (Abramovitz, 1989, p. 59) has written:

The upper class who controlled British politics in the nineteenth century were slow to be persuaded that mass education was needed and that state support was justified. The Church of England resisted the state schools that would be non-denominational. Moreover, when a State system was at last established, British working class feeling gave less than ardent support for its extension. Many workers resisted the view that schooling, at any rate schooling beyond the elementary grades, would be an advantage to their own class-bound children. The net result was that . . . the school system expanded more slowly than in the United States and more slowly also than in some continental countries (for example, Prussia).

Alexander Gerschenkron (1962, p. 64) drew a corresponding parallel between France and Germany:

Most of the factors mentioned by Landes [for France] find their counterpart in the German economy. The strength of preindustrial social values was, if anything, greater in Germany than in France. The family firm remained strong, and the lower entrepreneurial echelons, whose numbers bulked large, behaved in a way which was hardly different from that in France. The pronouncement made at the turn of the century, that modern economic development had transformed the top structure of the German economy while everything beneath it still remained medieval, was, of course, a deliberate exaggeration. But there was some meaning in that exaggeration. Such as it was, it applied to France as much as to Germany.

Evidently, the persistence of pre-industrial social values was widespread in Europe, and its connections with occupational choice, the character of education, the size of firms, the resistance to standardization, and the preference for quality over price suggest that these survivals had, indeed, inhibited European industrial development in the nineteenth century and for some time thereafter.

This conclusion has been disputed. Gerschenkron's main contention, for example (1954a, b; 1962, pp. 63–64), was that the influence of pre-industrial values on the economic development of France was overdrawn by Landes (1954) and Sawyer (1954). Instead, he argued for the importance of differences in natural resource endowment, income levels, and domestic market scale—in short, to differences we have referred to as "technological congruence." Landes and Sawyer, for their part, were careful not to make social structure and outlook the sole or even prime cause of the different pace of French and American development in the nineteenth century. In the face of Gerschenkron's criticism, however, they both strongly rejected his implied conclusion that these social factors were matters of negligible importance. And there the matter rests. Since it is extremely difficult to reduce the notion of "social capabilities" to a meaningful scalar magnitude, such considerations typically are omitted from formal economic models, and assertions as to their effects remain largely untested econometrically, despite the recent wave of interest in international comparative studies such as those surveyed by Fagerberg (1994). Unsatisfactory as this may be, we believe that such factors made some significant contribution to the U.S. pre-eminence in the late nineteenth and the early twentieth centuries. Thus, it would be still more unsatisfactory to leave them wholly out of consideration.

Neither social structure nor outlook, however, remained frozen in its nineteenth-century form. As economic development proceeded, the social status and political power of European business rose. The occupational targets of middle-class youth gradually shifted. Business and the pursuit of wealth as a road to social distinction (as well as material satisfaction) became more appealing. Entrepreneurs became more familiar with public corporations, more receptive to outside capital as a vehicle for expansion, and more experienced in the organization, finance, and administration of large-scale business. The small, specialized retail shop retained much of its old importance into the 1930s. But after World War II, the big, fixed-price chain stores expanded beyond the beachhead that companies like Woolworth and Marks and Spencer previously had established in Britain. The American-style supermarket, aided by the automobile and the home refrigerator, began to transform European retail food distribution.

The timing of this change around World War II is not accidental; the war itself had a profound impact on social structure and outlook. In the aftermath of the war, great steps were taken to democratize education. State-supported secondary schooling and universities were rapidly expanded, literally hundreds of new university campuses were constructed and staffed, and public support for the maintenance of university students was initiated. For virtually all the new students, the mecca became careers in industry, trade, and banking and finance, not the traditional honorific occupations.

In France, even the *polytechniciens* joined industrial firms. Curricula were modified to fit the more practical concerns of this much-expanded student population. Schools of engineering and business administration were founded or enlarged. Even Britain, the perennial laggard in educational reform, responded by opening its new system of comprehensive secondary schools and its new red brick universities and polytechnic colleges.

The most important change of outlook was in the public attitude towards economic growth itself. In the first half of the century, and particularly in the interwar years, the major concerns had been income distribution, trade protection, and unemployment. After World War II, it was growth that gripped people's imagination, and growth became the premier goal of public policy. Throughout Europe and in Japan, programs of public investment were undertaken to modernize and expand the infrastructure of roads, harbors, railroads, electric power, and communications. The demand for output and employment was supported by monetary and fiscal policy. The supply of labor was enlarged by opening borders to immigrants and guest workers. Productivity growth was pursued by expanding mass and technical education, by encouraging R&D, and by providing state support for large-scale firms in newer lines of industry. The expansion of international trade was promoted by successive GATT rounds and by the organization of the Common Market and the European Free Trade Area.

We hold, therefore, that many features of European (and Japanese) social structure and outlook had tended to delay catch-up in the nineteenth century. But these inhibitions weakened in the early twentieth century, and in the new social and political milieu of postwar reconstruction, they crumbled altogether. The traditional upper classes lost their hold on the outlook and aspirations of the growing middle class. The same forces tended to strengthen the political power of business corporations and trade unions, and to shift the directions of public policy accordingly toward institutional reforms and expansionary macroeconomic measures on which both interests could find agreement. In the aftermath of World War II, these developments joined to reinforce the vigorous catch-up process that had been released by the new concordance between the requirements of the forms of technology and organization that had appeared in America and the economic characteristics that now obtained in western Europe and Japan.

Conditions Promoting the Realization of Potential

The postwar period opened with a strong potential for European catch-up. But the actual realization of a strong potential depends on a variety of background conditions that, in the shorter term, govern the responses of businesses, labor, and governments to the opportunities before them. This background may be favorable or unfavorable, and it may persist for an extended span of years. Between 1914 and 1950—counting the difficult years of initial recovery from World War II—these short-term factors doomed the possibility of realizing what might by then have already been a strong potential for rapid growth by catch-up. During the quarter-century following the Second World War, however, the reverse was true. A full exposition of this subject would be a long story. Here, we can do no more than notice some of the important components.

New conditions favored the diffusion of technology. Transport, communications, and travel became faster and cheaper. Multinational corporate operations expanded, creating new channels for the international transfer of technology, management practices, and modes of conducting R&D. Further, heavier investment in R&D was encouraged by a closer connection between basic science and technological applications, while the open, international character of much of the basic science research community fostered the rapid dissemination of information about new and more powerful research techniques and instruments that were equally applicable for the purposes pursued in corporate R&D laboratories.

Industry was able to satisfy a growing demand for labor without creating the tight labor markets that might otherwise have driven wages up unduly and promoted price inflation. Some key factors here were that unions had been weakened by war, unprecedentedly rapid labor productivity growth in agriculture was freeing up workers from that sector, and Europe's borders were opened wider to immigrants and guest workers. U.S. immigration restrictions themselves helped to create more flexible labor-market conditions in Europe (Kindleberger, 1967; Abramovitz, 1979).

Governmental policies at both the national and international levels favored investment, trade, and the spread of technology. The dollar-exchange standard established at Bretton Woods, together with U.S. monetary and fiscal policy and U.S. capital exports, overcame the initial concentration of gold and other monetary reserves in the United States. They sustained a chronic American balance-of-payments deficit that redistributed reserves and ensured an adequate growth of money supply throughout the industrialized world.

These and other matters that bear on the factors supporting "realization" in the post–World War II era deserve more ample description and discussion, which one of us sought to provide on an earlier occasion (Abramovitz, 1979). We must confine this paper largely to the elements of a changing potential for rapid growth by productivity catch-up. Nonetheless, it is important to remember that the rapid and systematic productivity convergence of the postwar years rested on a fortunate historical conjuncture of strong potential for catch-up with the emergence of international and domestic economic conditions that supported its rapid realization.

Many of the elements forming that conjuncture have now weakened or disappeared; most plainly, the large productivity gaps that had separated laggards from the leader have now become very much smaller. The break-up of that favorable constellation of forces has slowed the rate of both catch-up and convergence within the group of advanced countries. The passing of the postwar conjuncture of potential and realization was in large measure the result of developments inherent in the catch-up process itself (Abramovitz, 1994).

Summing Up: Bases of Productivity Leadership and Limits of the Potential for Catch-up

America's position of productivity leadership was gained, and maintained for a remarkably long period, by a fortunate concordance between America's own exceptional economic and social characteristics and the nature of the path of technological progress that emerged and was developed in that region during the course of the nineteenth century. It was a concordance that other countries were not at first able to replicate or match by other means. So their potential ability to catch up or even to keep abreast of American productivity growth was limited.

The nineteenth- and early-twentieth-century path of technological progress was minerals-intensive, tangible capital–using and scale-dependent. America's superior concordance with the nature of this path rested on three elements. One was its superior endowment of natural resources and their early development. A second was its superior market scale. These were the elements of America's technological congruence and so the basis for a more far-reaching exploitation and development of the possibilities of tangible capital–using innovation, including mass production, than the natural resources and scale of European economies could afford in the same period. America's third advantage lay in the sphere of social capability. Its egalitarian and secular outlook made wealth and economic attainment the basis of social distinction, made business a respected occupation, and directed education and science to material ends. In Europe, by contrast, the social outlook was still colored by an aristocratic residue. Talent sought the older honorific occupations, schooling prepared gentlemen for them, and scientific effort was more largely bent towards learning for its own sake. A quest for family status and a reluctance to extend trust and financial control beyond the circle of kinship combined to restrict the size and scope of business enterprises. The persistence of a guild-like ethos, aristocratic standards of taste, and inequality of incomes were still further European obstacles to the standardization of products and the substitution of power and machinery for labor in American-style mass-production factories.

In time, however, the sources of America's exceptional productivity advantage eroded. The region's early superiority in providing cheap access to industrial raw materials and sources of power waned, and the importance of abundant natural resources for production decreased. America's advantage in exploiting the dominant tangible capital–using but scale-dependent character of nineteenth-century technological advance was also undercut. The domestic markets of the laggard countries grew larger. Cheaper transport and more liberal commercial policies opened wider markets, at least until 1913 and again, of course, in the post–World War II period itself. Per capita incomes rose in Europe and Japan and began to provide larger markets for automobiles and the other consumer durables that were especially suitable for mass production. Businessmen in Europe and Japan gradually gained experience with the organization, finance, and operation of large corporations. The bias of technological progress began to shift from its older scale-dependent, tangible capital–using bias to a newer intangible capital–using bias less dependent on scale. Capitalist development gradually weakened the hold of aristocratic values in Europe; the outlook and institutions of European society came to resemble America's more closely.

The post–World War II conjuncture of forces supporting catch-up has now largely done its work. It has brought the labor productivity levels of the advanced, capitalist countries within sight of substantial equality. The significant lags that remain among the advanced economies in the course of catching up are no longer to be found in a marked persistence of backward technology embodied in obsolescent equipment and organizations.[33] Rather, they lie in the remaining differences between American, European, and Japanese capital-labor ratios, and in the sphere of politics and social sentiments that protect unduly low-productivity agricultural sectors and traditional forms of organization in both farming and retail trade. The

---

33. A recent study by Dougherty (1991), applying the refined Tornqvist index procedures developed and implemented by Dale Jorgenson, reaches the following values for relative multifactor productivity (output per combined unit of labor and capital, relative to the United States = 100) in 1989: Canada, 101; Germany, 89; France, 112; United Kingdom, 102; Italy, 101.

great opportunities for rapid growth by modernization now belong to the nations of eastern Europe, South and Southeast Asia, and Latin America. Although it is correct to say that the argument presented here is immediately germane only to the experiences of the group of presently advanced countries during a particular historical epoch, the classes of conditions that figure importantly in the story told here, nevertheless, may have a considerably wider applicability. The work of Barro (1991), DeLong and Summers (1991), Mankiw, Romer, and Weil (1992), and still others, while confined to the post–World War II era, has considered a much wider cultural, political, and economic spectrum than the subset of industrially advanced market economies.[34] The findings of these studies seem to reflect the operation of mechanisms both of "local convergence" among the advanced economies and of "global divergence" between the advanced economies (joined by the few newly industrializing economies) and the remaining low-income countries.[35] Throughout the world, deep-rooted political obstacles and the constraints imposed by social capability, or, to use Veblen's (1915) words, by "the received scheme of use and wont," remain to be overcome.

Among the presently advanced capitalist nations, the question is whether substantial equality in productivity levels will long persist. Will a new bend in the path of technical advance again create a condition of superior technological congruence and social capability for one country? Or will conditions that support the diffusion and application of technical knowledge become even more favorable? Will technology continue to pose demands for "readjustment and rehabilitation" that many countries can meet? For the foreseeable future, convergent tendencies appear to be dominant. But the full potential of the still-emergent Age of Information and Communication is yet to be revealed. The industrialization of the huge populations of South and Southeast Asia may change the worlds of industry and commerce in ways that are now still hidden.

---

34. A considerable body of empirical work on convergence also has been produced using the international database, constructed by Kravis, Heston, and Summers (1982) and extended by Summers and Heston (1988), on GDP constant purchasing power equivalents for more than 100 countries in the period 1950–85. See Fagerberg (1994) for a recent survey. Although the time period covered is briefer, these data offer the advantage of being about a larger and more diverse sample of contemporary countries, within which differences in the degree of technological congruence and in social capabilities are likely to be more pronounced.

35. See Baumol (1986) for the initial suggestion that the international data showed the existence of "convergence clubs" rather than global convergence, and the econometrically rigorous tests for "local" as distinct from global convergence presented by Durlauf and Johnson (1992).

Our treatment of the problems of technological congruence and social capability has been highly general and suggestive. Although it may help us understand the path that we have already traveled, it is not yet able to reveal what lies along the road ahead. When examined more deeply and in greater detail, however, these concepts may yet supply insights into the likely shape of the future, and so a means of preparing for it more effectively.

References

Abramovitz, Moses, "Rapid Growth Potential and Its Realization: The Experience of the Capitalist Economies in the Postwar Period." In Edmond Malinvaud, ed., *Economic Growth and Resources*, vol. I. London: Macmillan, 1979.

———, "Catching-Up, Forging Ahead and Falling Behind." *Journal of Economic History*, 1986, 46(2), 385–406.

———, *Thinking About Growth*. Cambridge: Cambridge University Press, 1989.

———, "The Search for the Sources of Growth: Areas of Ignorance, Old and New." *Journal of Economic History*, 1993, 53(2), 217–43.

———, "Catch-Up and Convergence in the Postwar Growth Boom and After." In William Baumol, Richard Nelson, and Edward Wolff, eds., *The Convergence of Productivity: Cross-National Studies and Historical Evidence*. Oxford: Oxford University Press, 1994.

Abramovitz, Moses, and Paul A. David, "Reinterpreting Economic Growth: Parables and Realities." *American Economic Review*, 1973a, 63(2), 428–39.

———, "Economic Growth in America: Historical Parables and Realities." *De Economist*, May/June 1973b, 121(3), 251–72.

Amable, Bruno, "Endogenous Growth Theory, Convergence and Divergence." In G. Silverberg and L. Soete, eds., *The Economics of Growth and Technical Change: Technologies, Nations, Agents*, chap. 3. Aldershot, Hants.: Edward Elgar, 1994.

Antonelli, Cristiano, *The Economics of Localized Technological Change*. Norwell, Mass.: Kluwer Academic Publishers, 1994.

Arrow, Kenneth J., "The Economic Implications of Learning by Doing." *Review of Economic Studies*, June 1962, 29, 155–73.

Atkinson, Anthony B., and Joseph E. Stiglitz, "A New View of Technological Change." *Economic Journal*, Sept. 1969, 79, 573–78.

Barro, Robert J., "Economic Growth in a Cross-Section of Countries." *Quarterly Journal of Economics*, 1991, 106(2), 407–43.

Barro, Robert J., and Xavier Sala-i-Martin, "Convergence." *Journal of Political Economy*, 1992, 100(2), 223–51.

Baumol, William, "Productivity Growth, Convergence and Welfare: What the Long-Run Data Show." *American Economic Review*, 1986, 76(5), 1072–85.

Baumol, William, Sue Anne Batey Blackman, and Edward Wolff, *Productivity and American Leadership: The Long View*. Cambridge: MIT Press, 1989.

Broadberry, Stephen N., "Technological Leadership and Productivity Leadership in Manufacturing Since the Industrial Revolution: Implications for the Convergence Debate." Warwick Economic Research Paper, Department of Economics, University of Warwick, Feb. 1993.

Cain, Louis P., and Donald G. Paterson, "Factor Biases and Technical Change in Manufacturing: The American System, 1850–1919." *Journal of Economic History*, June 1981, 41 (2), 341–60.

Chandler, Alfred, *Scale and Scope*. Cambridge: Harvard University Press, 1990.

Darmstadter, Joel, "Energy Consumption: Trends and Patterns." In Sam Schurr, ed., *Energy, Economic Growth and the Environment*, Appendix. Published for Resources for the Future. Baltimore: Johns Hopkins University Press, 1972.

David, Paul A., *Technical Choice, Innovation and Economic Growth, New York: Essays on American and British Experience in the Nineteenth Century*. Cambridge: Cambridge University Press, 1975.

———, "Invention and Accumulation in America's Economic Growth." In K. Brunner and A. H. Meltzer, eds., *International Organization, National Policies and Economic Development*. Amsterdam: North Holland Publishing Company, 1977.

———, "Clio and the Economics of QWERTY." *American Economic Review*, 1985, 75 (2), 332–37.

———, "Path-Dependence: Putting the Past into the Future of Economics." Institute for Mathematical Studies in the Social Sciences Technical Report 533. Stanford University, Nov. 1988.

———, "Computer and Dynamo: The Productivity Paradox in a Not-Too-Distant Mirror." In *Technology and Productivity: The Challenge for Economic Policy*. Paris: Organization for Economic Cooperation and Development, 1991a.

———, "General Purpose Engines, Investment, and Productivity Growth: From the Dynamo Revolution to the Computer Revolution." In E. Deiaco, E. Hornel, and G. Vickery, eds., *Technology and Investment—Crucial Issues for the '90s*. London: Pinter Publishers, 1991b.

———, "Path-Dependence and Predictability in Dynamical Systems with Local Network Externalities: A Paradigm for Economic History." In D. Foray and C. Freeman, eds., *Technology and the Wealth of Nations*, Chap. 4. London: Pinter Publishers, 1993.

———, "The Evolution of Intellectual Property Institutions." In A. Aganbegyan, O. Bogomolov, and M. Kaser, eds., *System Transformation: Eastern and Western Assessments*. London: Macmillan for the International Economic Association, 1994a.

———, "Why Are Institutions the 'Carriers of History'? Notes on Path-Dependence in Conventions, Organizations and Institutions." *Structural Change and Economic Dynamics*, 1994b, 5 (2), 205–20.

David, Paul A., and John L. Scadding, "Private Savings: Ultra-Rationality, Aggregation and 'Denison's Law,'" *Journal of Political Economy*, Mar./Apr. 1974, 82 (2), pt. 1, 225–49.

David, Paul A., and Theo van de Klundert, "Biased Efficiency Growth and Capital-Labor Substitution in the U.S., 1899–1960." *American Economic Review*, June 1965, *55*, 357–94.

David, Paul A., and Gavin Wright, "Resource Abundance and American Economic Leadership." Center for Economic Policy Research Publication No. 267. Stanford University, Aug. 1992.

DeLong, J. Bradford, "Productivity Growth, Convergence and Welfare: Comment." *American Economic Review*, Dec. 1988, *78:5*, 1138–59.

DeLong, J. Bradford, and Lawrence Summers, "Equipment Investment and Economic Growth," *Quarterly Journal of Economics*, 1991, *106(2)*, 445–502.

Denison, Edward F., *Why Growth Rates Differ*. Washington, D.C.: Brookings Institution, 1967.

Denison, Edward F., and William Chung, *How Japan's Economy Grew So Fast*. Washington, D.C.: Brookings Institution, 1976.

De Tocqueville, Alexis, *Democracy in America*, vol. II. 1840. Reprint, New York: Vintage Books, 1945.

Dosi, Giovanni, "Technological Paradigms and Technological Trajectories: A Suggested Interpretation of the Determinants and Directions of Technical Change." *Research Policy*, 1982, *11(3)*, 147–62.

———, "Sources, Procedures, and Microeconomic Effects of Innovation." *Journal of Economic Literature*, 1988, *26(3)*, 1120–71.

Dosi, Giovanni, and Silvia Fabiani, "Convergence and Divergence in the Long-term Growth of Open Economies." In G. Silverberg and L. Soete, eds., *The Economics of Growth and Technical Change: Technologies, Nations, Agents*, chap. 6. Aldershot, Hants.: Edward Elgar, 1994.

Dougherty, John C., "A Comparison of Productivity and Economic Growth in the G-7 Countries." Ph.D. dissertation, Harvard University, 1991.

Dumke, Rolf H., "Reassessing the *Wirtschaftswunder*: Reconstruction and Postwar Growth in West Germany in an International Context." *Oxford Bulletin of Economics and Statistics*, Special Issue, Nov. 1990, *52(4)*, 451–91.

Durlauf, Steven, and Paul Johnson, "Local Versus Global Convergence Across National Economies." National Bureau of Economic Research Working Paper No. 3996. Cambridge, Mass., 1992.

Earle, Edward Meade, ed., *Modern France: Problems of the Third and Fourth Republics*. Princeton: Princeton University Press, 1951.

Eisner, Robert, *The Total Incomes System of Accounts*. Chicago: University of Chicago Press, 1989.

Emmerson, George S., *Engineering Education: A Social History*. New York: Abbot Newton, 1973.

Fagerberg, Jan, "Technology and International Differences in Growth Rates." *Journal of Economic Literature*, 1994, *32(3)*, 1147–75.

Ferguson, Eugene S., *Engineering and the Mind's Eye*. Cambridge: MIT Press, 1992.

Foreman-Peck, James, "The American Challenge of the Twenties: Multinationals and the European Motor Industry." *Journal of Economic History*, Dec. 1982, *42*.

Freeman, Christopher, and Carlotta Perez, "Structural Crises of Adjustment." In G. Dosi, C. Freeman, R. Nelson, G. Silverberg, and L. Soete, eds., *Technical Change and Economic Theory*. London: Pinter Publishers, 1988.

Friedman, Milton, "Do Old Fallacies Ever Die?" *Journal of Economic Literature*, Dec. 1992, *30(4)*, 2129–32.

Gerschenkron, Alexander, "Social Attitudes, Entrepreneurship and Economic Development." *Explorations in Entrepreneurial History*, Oct. 1953, 1–19.

———, "A Rejoinder." *Explorations in Entrepreneurial History*, May 1954a, 287–93.

———, "Some Further Notes on 'Social Attitudes, Entrepreneurship and Economic Development.'" *Explorations in Entrepreneurial History*, Dec. 1954b, 111–19.

———, "Social Attitudes, Entrepreneurship and Economic Development." In Leon H. Dupriez, with the assistance of Douglas C. Hague, eds., *Economic Progress: Papers and Proceedings of a Round Table Held by the International Economic Association*, pp. 307–29. Louvain: Institut de Recherches Economique et Sociales, 1955. Reprinted as chap. 3 in Gerschenkron (1962).

———, *Economic Backwardness in Historical Perspective*. Cambridge: Harvard University Press, 1962.

Harris, Donald J., "A Model of the Productivity Gap: Convergence or Divergence?" In Ross Thompson, ed., *Learning and Technological Change*, chap. 7. New York: St. Martin's Press, 1993.

Harvard Entrepreneurial Research Center, *Change and the Entrepreneur*. Cambridge, 1949.

Hounshell, David A., *From the American System to Mass Production, 1800–1932*. Baltimore: Johns Hopkins University Press, 1984.

Inkeles, Alex, "Convergence and Divergence in Industrial Societies." In M. O. Attir, B. Holzner, and Z. Suda, eds., *Directions of Change: Modernization Theory, Research and Realities*, chap. 1. Boulder, Colo: Westview Press, 1981.

Inkeles, Alex, and Larry Sirowym, "Convergent and Divergent Trends in National Educational Systems," *Social Forces*, Dec. 1983, *62(2)*.

James, John A., and Jonathan S. Skinner, "The Resolution of the Labor Scarcity Paradox." *Journal of Economic History*, 1985, *45(3)*, 513–40.

Katz, Lawrence F., and Kevin M. Murphy, "The Changes in Relative Wages, 1963–87: Supply and Demand Factors." *Quarterly Journal of Economics*, 1992, *107(1)*, 35–78.

Kendrick, John W., *Productivity Trends in the United States*. Princeton: Princeton University Press for the National Bureau of Economic Research, 1961.

———, *The Formation and Stocks of Total Capital*. New York: National Bureau of Economic Research, 1976.

———, "Total Capital and Economic Growth." *Atlantic Economic Journal*, Mar. 1994, *22(1)*, 1–18.

Kindleberger, Charles P., *Europe's Postwar Growth: The Role of Labor Supply*. Cambridge: Harvard University Press, 1967.

Kravis, Irving, Alan Heston, and Robert Summers, *World Product Income: International Comparisons of Real Gross Product, Phase III*. United Nations and World Bank. Baltimore: Johns Hopkins University Press, 1982. Also see earlier and later volumes in the same series.

Landes, David S., "French Entrepreneurship and Industrial Growth in the Nineteenth Century." *Journal of Economic History*, May 1949, 45–61.

———, "French Business and the Businessman: a Social and Cultural Analysis." In Edward M. Earle, ed., *Modern France, Problems of the Third and Fourth Republics*, pp. 334–53. Princeton: Princeton University Press, 1951.

———, "Social Attitudes, Entrepreneurship and Economic Development: A Comment." *Explorations in Entrepreneurial History*, May 1954, 245–72.

Lazonick, William, "Social Organization and Technological Leadership." In W. J. Baumol, Richard R. Nelson, and Edward N. Wolff, eds., *Convergence of Productivity*, chap. 6. New York: Oxford University Press, 1994.

Lucas, Robert, "On the Mechanics of Economic Development." *Journal of Monetary Economics*, 1988, 22, 2–42.

Maddison, Angus, *Phases of Capitalist Development*. Oxford: Oxford University Press, 1982.

———, "Growth and Slowdown in Advanced Capitalist Countries: Techniques of Quantitative Assessment." *Journal of Economic Literature*, June 1987, 25(2), 649–98.

———, *The World Economy in the 20th Century*. Paris: Development Centre of the Organization for Economic Cooperation and Development, 1989.

———, *Dynamic Forces in Capitalist Development*. Oxford: Oxford University Press, 1991.

———, "Explaining the Economic Performance of Nations, 1820–1989." In William Baumol, Richard Nelson, and Edward Wolff, eds., *The Convergence of Productivity: Cross-National Studies and Historical Evidence*. Oxford: Oxford University Press, 1993.

Mankiw, N. G., D. Romer, and D. N. Weil, "A Contribution to the Empirics of Economic Growth." *Quarterly Journal of Economics*, 1992, 108(2), 407–37.

Miller, W., ed., *Men in Business*. Cambridge: Harvard University Press, 1952.

Mitchell, B. R., and Phyllis Deane, *Abstract of British Historical Statistics*. Cambridge: Cambridge University Press, 1962.

Mokyr, Joel, *The Lever of Riches*. New York: Oxford University Press, 1990.

Mowery, David, and Nathan Rosenberg, *Technology and the Pursuit of Economic Growth*. Cambridge: Cambridge University Press, 1989.

Nelson, Richard R., "Diffusion of Development, Post–World War II Convergence Among Advanced Industrial Nations." *American Economic Review*, 1991, 81(2), 271–75.

Nelson, Richard R., and Sidney Winter, "In Search of a Useful Theory of Innovations," *Research Policy*, 1977, 6(1), 31–42.

Nelson, Richard R., and Gavin Wright, "The Rise and Fall of American Technological Leadership." *Journal of Economic Literature*, 1992, 30(4), 1931–64.

Ohkawa, Kazushi, and Henry Rosovsky, *Japanese Economic Growth*. Stanford, Calif.: Stanford University Press, 1972.

Parker, William N., "Productivity Growth in American Grain Farming: An Analysis of Its Nineteenth Century Sources." In R. W. Fogel and Stanley Engerman, eds., *The Reinterpretation of American Economic History*, pp. 175–86. New York: Harper and Row, 1972.

———, *Europe, America and the Wider World.* Vol. 1, *Europe and the World Economy.* New York: Cambridge University Press, 1984.

———, *Europe, America and the Wider World.* Vol. 2, *America and the Wider World.* New York : Cambridge University Press, 1991.

Perez, Carlotta, and Luc Soete, "Catching up in Technology: Entry Barriers and Windows of Opportunity." In G. Dosi, C. Freeman, R. Nelson, G. Silverberg, and L. Soete, eds., *Technical Change and Economic Theory.* London: Pinter Publishers, 1988.

Prados de la Escosura, Leandra, Teresa Dabán, and Jorge C. Sanz Oliva, "'De le Fabula narrative?' Growth, Structural Change and Convergence in Europe, 19th & 20th Centuries." Dirección General de Planificación, Ministerio de Economia y Hacienda (Spain), Documentos de Trabajo, Dec. 1993.

Romer, Paul, "Increasing Returns and Long-run Growth." *Journal of Political Economy*, 1986, 94, 1002–37.

———, "Endogenous Technological Change." *Journal of Political Economy*, 1990, 98(5), pt. 2, S71–S102.

Rosenberg, Nathan, "The Direction of Technological Change: Inducement Mechanisms and Focusing Devices." *Economic Development and Cultural Change*, 1969, 18(1), pt. 1. Reprinted in Rosenberg (1976).

———, *Perspectives on Technology.* New York: Cambridge University Press, 1976.

———, "Why in America?" In Otto Mayr and Robert Post, eds., *Yankee Enterprise: The Rise of the American System of Manufactures*, pp. 49–81. Washington, D.C.: Smithsonian Institution Press, 1980.

———, "Learning by Using." In *Inside the Black Box—Technology and Economics*, chap. 6. Cambridge: Cambridge University Press, 1982.

Rosovsky, Henry, *Capital Formation in Japan, 1868–1940.* New York: Free Press of Glencoe, 1961.

Sahal, D., *Patterns of Technological Innovation.* Reading, Mass.: Addison-Wesley, 1981.

Sawyer, John E., "Strains in the Social Structure of Modern France." In Edward Mead Earle, ed., *Modern France, Problems of the Third and Fourth Republics*, chap. 17. Princeton: Princeton University Press, 1951.

———, "The Entrepreneur and the Social Order, France and the United States." In Miller (1952, pp. 293–312).

———, "In Defense of an Approach: A Comment on Professor Gerschenkron's Social Attitudes, Entrepreneurship and Economic Development." *Explorations in Entrepreneurial History*, May 1954, 173–86.

Schultz, Theodore W., "The Declining Economic Importance of Agricultural Land." *Economic Journal*, Dec. 1951, 725–40.

Schurr, Sam H., Bruce C. Netschert, et al., *Energy in the American Economy, 1950–1975: Its History and Prospects.* Baltimore: Johns Hopkins University Press for Resources for the Future, 1960.

Solow, Robert M., "A Contribution to the Theory of Economic Growth." *Quarterly Journal of Economics*, Feb. 1956, 70(1), 65–94.

Summers, Robert, and Alan C. Heston, "A New Set of International Comparisons of Real Product and Price Levels." *Review of Income and Wealth*, 1988, 34, 1–25.

Taylor, Alan M., and Jeffrey G. Williamson, "Convergence in the Age of Mass Migration." National Bureau of Economic Research Working Paper No. 4711. Cambridge, Mass., 1994.

U.S. Bureau of the Census, *Historical Statistics of the United States, from Colonial Times*. Washington, D.C.: GPO, 1960.

Van Ark, Bart, and Dirk Pilat, "Productivity Levels in Germany, Japan and the United States: Differences and Causes." *Brookings Papers on Economic Activity: Microeconomics*, 1993, 2, 1–69.

Van de Klundert, Theo. C. M. J., and S. Smulders, "Reconstructing Growth Theory: A Survey." *De Economist*, 1992, 140(2), 177–203.

Veblen, Thorstein, *Imperial Germany and the Industrial Revolution*. New York: Augustus Kelly, 1915 [1964].

Verspargen, Bart, "A New Empirical Approach to Catching Up or Falling Behind." *Structural Change and Economic Dynamics*, 1991, 2(2), 359–80.

———, "Endogenous Innovation in Neoclassical Growth Models: A Survey." *Journal of Macroeconomics*, 1992, 14(4), 631–62.

White, Lynn, Jr., *Machina ex Deo: Essays in the Dynamism of Western Culture*. Cambridge: MIT Press, 1968.

Wiener, M. J., *English Culture and the Decline of the Industrial Spirit, 1850–1980*. Cambridge: Cambridge University Press, 1981.

Wolff, Edward N., "Capital Formation and Productivity: Convergence Over the Long Term." *American Economic Review*, 1991, 81(3), 565–79.

———, "Productivity Growth and Capital Intensity on the Sector and Industry Level: Specialization among OECD Countries, 1970–1988." In G. Silverberg and L. Soete, eds., *The Economics of Growth and Technical Change: Technologies, Nations, Agents*, chap. 8. Aldershot, Hants.: Edward Elgar. 1994.

Wright, Gavin, "The Origins of American Industrial Success." *American Economic Review*, 1990, 80(4), 651–68.

[4]

━━━

Chickens home to roost: from prosperity to stagnation in the postwar U.S. economy

DAVID M. GORDON

There can be little doubt that the twentieth century had become, by the 1950s, the American Century. In 1948 the United States economy accounted for roughly 45 percent of total global industrial production while real U.S. gross domestic product was nearly twice as large as the sum of real GDP in the U.K., Germany, France, and Japan combined.[1] Building on the Bretton Woods system, the power of U.S. corporations and the structure of postwar global finance assured that the dollar – backed by gold – was the pivotal international currency. U.S. military and nuclear power not only waged the Cold War against the Soviet bloc but was also deployed to keep the world safe for democracy and capitalism, mostly capitalism.

It seemed, indeed, that the sun might never set on the American Empire. "World opinion? I don't believe in world opinion," financial and presidential adviser John J. McCloy remarked scornfully in 1963. "The only thing that matters is power."[2]

This essay relies heavily on joint work with Samuel Bowles and Thomas E. Weisskopf, although they bear no responsibility for its presentation or conclusions. Significant passages in this essay have been reproduced, by permission, from *After the Waste Land*, by Samuel Bowles, David M. Gordon, and Thomas E. Weisskopf (Armonk, N.Y.: M. E. Sharpe, 1990).

1 Global industrial production data summarized in David M. Gordon, "The Global Economy: New Edifice or Crumbling Foundations," *New Left Review*, No. 168, March/April 1988, Table I. Comparison of real GNP based on data presented in Angus Maddison, *Phases of Capitalist Development* (Oxford: Oxford University Press, 1982), Tables A1, A6–A8.

2 Quoted in Alan Wolfe, *The Limits of Legitimacy: Political Contradictions of Contemporary Capitalism* (New York: The Free Press, 1977), p. 176.

Prosperity to stagnation in the postwar economy   35

Sic transit gloria imperiae. By the early 1980s the U.S. economy was no longer hegemonic, barely still dominant. The dollar had fallen from its pinnacle and U.S. trade deficits were beginning to soar nearly out of control. U.S. productivity growth lagged far behind its pace in other leading competing economies such as Japan and West Germany. The dreams and aspirations of U.S. workers and households were becoming clouded with hardship and uncertainty. Economic problems seemed pervasive. "It would be necessary to go back to the 1930s and the Great Depression," pollster Daniel Yankelovich concluded in 1979, "to find a peacetime issue that has had the country so concerned and so distraught."[3]

As background and foundation for many of the subsequent chapters in this book, this essay provides a brief overview of the rise and demise of postwar U.S. economic power. The essay begins with a summary of key indicators of U.S. economic performance in the postwar period, emphasizing the shifting tides from boom to stagnation. The second principal section then outlines the institutional foundations of the postwar U.S. economic system, sketching both the structural buttresses of prosperity and the sources of erosion of that institutional system. I conclude with an analysis of the burdens and inflexibilities imposed on the U.S. economy by the hierarchical structures upon which the U.S. corporate system was built. In the end, I argue, the U.S. economy was dragged into stagnation and crisis in large part by the costs of the very structures of power which had initially established its place in the sun. By the 1970s, it appears, the chickens had come home to roost.

THE TRAJECTORY OF THE POSTWAR U.S. ECONOMY

Things are going much better in the economy than most people realize. It's our attitude that is doing poorly.
— G. William Miller, Chair, Federal Reserve Board, 1978[4]

This section examines the performance of the U.S. economy in the postwar period, concentrating on its shift from boom to stagnation. I focus here on the years through the end of the 1970s. In our joint essay elsewhere in this volume, Samuel Bowles, Thomas E. Weisskopf, and I complete the story by examining the effects of right-wing economics on eco-

3 Quoted in William Bowen, "The Decade Ahead: Not So Bad If We Do Things Right," *Fortune*, October 8, 1979, p. 88.
4 Quoted in *Business Week*, January 15, 1978, p. 64.

36   *D. M. Gordon*

nomic performance during the 1980s, extending most of the indicators introduced here through 1989.

One of the problems in tracing the performance of any capitalist economy is separating trend from cycle. The economy continuously moves up and down its short-term roller coaster. In tracking its performance over the longer term, as a result, observations and measurements are crucially sensitive to the particular points in the cycle from which one begins calculations. Any economy can appear buoyant, for example, as it recovers from the pits of a deep recession or depression. Many of those enjoying momentary respite from economic hardship may feel, to borrow the title of a mid-1960s novel by Richard Farina, "been down so long it looks like up to me"[5] — even though, over the longer run, economic performance might not have improved at all.

In this essay, following relatively standard procedure, I control for the short-term effects of the business cycle by tracking the economy from one business-cycle peak to the next. And following the method deployed in joint work with Bowles and Weisskopf, I identify business-cycle peak years by looking at the ratio of actual gross national product (GNP) to "potential" GNP. The ratio of actual to potential GNP reaches a cyclical peak at the stage of an expansion when the economy's productive potential is most *fully* utilized.[6]

By this measure, there were seven business-cycle peaks in the period from the late 1940s through the late 1970s: 1948, 1951, 1955, 1959, 1966, 1973, and 1979. One can best study the economy's performance during the years of stable prosperity by examining data for the *entire* boom period from 1948 to 1966, ignoring the several short-term cycles in between. Then, in order to sharpen our focus on the contours of subsequent decline, I compare the boom period with two periods of economic

---

5 *Been Down So Long It Looks Like Up To Me* (New York: Random House, 1966).

6 The procedure for estimating potential output follows a method developed by the Council of Economic Advisors during the 1970s. For presentation and discussion of that method, see Peter K. Clark, "Potential GNP in the United States, 1948–80," *Review of Income and Wealth,* June 1979. For detail on our method of extending the CEA estimates of potential output, see Samuel Bowles, Thomas E. Weisskopf, and David M. Gordon, "Business Ascendancy and Economic Impasse: A Structural Retrospective on Conservative Economics, 1979–87," *Journal of Economic Perspectives,* Winter 1989, Data Appendix.

Prosperity to stagnation in the postwar economy   37

stagnation: the first phase from the cyclical peak of 1966 to that of 1973, and the second phase from the cyclical peak of 1973 to that of 1979.

Macroperformance

We can look first at some relatively standard measure of aggregate economic performance. Table 2.1 presents a set of data useful for this preliminary evaluation.

One common indicator focuses on output growth, normally measured as the rate of growth of real GNP. Beginning with this simple measure (row 1), we can see clearly the symptoms of stagnating economic performance after the mid-1960s. Real GNP growth averaged a healthy 3.8 percent a year from 1948 through 1966, then dropped to 3.1 percent in 1966–73 and subsequently dipped further to 2.5 percent in 1973–79.

Table 2.1. *From boom to stagnation: the deteriorating performance of the U.S. postwar macroeconomy*

| | Phase Averages | | |
	1948-66	1966-73	1973-79
[1] Real GNP growth rate (%)	3.8	3.1	2.5
[2] Real productivity growth rate (%)	2.6	1.8	0.6
[3] Rate of inflation (%)	2.2	5.0	7.7
[4] Index of monetary pressure (%)	-1.4	0.7	-0.8
[5] Rate of unemployment (%)	4.9	4.6	6.8

Sources: Growth rates are annual rates, calculated as logarithmic growth rates. Levels are calculated as average annual levels. *ERP* refers to *Economic Report of the President,* 1991.

[1] Rate of growth of real GNP ($1982): *ERP*, Table B-2.

[2] Rate of growth of output per hour of all persons, nonfarm business sector (1977 = 100): *ERP*, Table B-46.

[3] Rate of change of GNP price deflator: *ERP*, Table B-3.

[4] Rate of change of real money supply (M2) minus rate of change of real GNP: Real M2 from *Business Conditions Digest,* Series No. 106, adjusted for difference between rate of change of consumer prices, *ERP*, Table B-58, and rate of change of GNP deflator, *ERP*, Table B-3. Rate of change of real GNP same as in row [1].

[5] Rate of unemployment in civilian labor force: *ERP*, Table B-32.

38   *D. M. Gordon*

But is a decline in real GNP growth from 3.8 percent to 2.5 percent really so significant? How does one evaluate the impact of such a slow-down in economic growth?

The answer depends in part, of course, on how much benefit people derive from that economic growth. Do they have to work harder and harder to sustain it? Do its benefits flee the country or get plowed back into maintaining the existing capital stock?

Taking some of these complications into account, many economists prefer to focus on real GNP *per capita,* controlling for the size of the population which aggregate economic output is supposed to support. Bowles, Weisskopf, and I prefer an alternative measure of aggregate economic performance which we label "hourly income" – real net national income per hour of work. Hourly income differs from per capita GNP in three respects: (1) it deducts from gross national product the "capital consumption allowance" – that part of output needed simply to maintain the existing aggregate stock of structures and equipment; (2) it adjusts for inflation with a price index reflecting changes in the prices of *purchased* rather than produced commodities; and (3) it substitutes total *hours of work* for total population as the standard against which real income should be measured.[7]

None of these modifications is particularly controversial, but the third one – dividing by hours of work rather than population – is quite impor-tant. By focusing on hourly income, we can pay close attention to the standard of living we attain *in return for the amount of work we must perform in order to achieve that standard of living.* Increases in per capita GNP may not be desirable if we must work too many additional hours to achieve them.

Figure 2.1 presents data on average annual rates of growth of *hourly income.* These data underscore impressions of the turn from prosperity to stagnation. Hourly income grew rapidly from 1948 to 1966, slowed noticeably from 1966 to 1973, and declined even more dramatically from 1973 to 1979. By the evidence of this figure, the collapse of prosperity after the mid-1960s appears dramatic indeed.

There is one obvious source of these dramatic declines in hourly in-

---

7 For a detailed discussion of the concept of hourly income and its advantages over per capita GNP as a measure of the average level of well-being in a society, see Samuel Bowles, Thomas E. Weisskopf, and David M. Gordon, *Beyond the Waste Land: A Democratic Alternative to Economic Decline* (Garden City, N.Y.: Anchor Press/Doubleday, 1983), Appendix A.

Prosperity to stagnation in the postwar economy   39

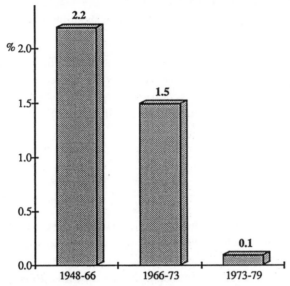

Figure 2.1. Growth of hourly income: average annual percent change in real net national income per hour.

come: the slowdown in the rate of growth of hourly output, or labor productivity. Hourly *income* did not grow as fast after the mid-1960s largely because hourly *output* did not rise as rapidly as during the postwar boom. Using the same benchmark years, we find (Table 2.2 row [2]) that the average annual rate of growth of U.S. hourly output – defined as real nonfarm business output per total employee hour – slowed from 2.6 percent in 1948–66 to 1.8 percent in 1966–73 and then again to 0.6 percent in 1973–79.[8]

8 Aggregate hourly income, defined as real net national income per hour of work, is conceptually very closely related to aggregate hourly output (productivity), defined as real net domestic output per hour of work. The only differences involve three technical distinctions: (1) real net national *income* is the nominal value of net national income/product divided by a *purchased*-output price index, while real *output* is the same nominal value of net national income/product divided by a *produced*-output price index; (2) *national income* includes income received by U.S. nationals from their activities abroad (e.g., foreign investment) and excludes income received by foreigners from their activities within the United States, while *domestic output* includes output produced by foreigners in the United States but excludes output produced by U.S. nationals abroad; and (3) the denominator in hourly income is hours of work by U.S. nationals anywhere, while the denominator in productivity is hours of work by all people within the United States.

40   *D. M. Gordon*

Judged by historical precedents in the United States earlier in the century, further, this decline in productivity growth rates seems relatively pronounced:[9]

• The economy's performance during the postwar boom compares favorably, for example, with the relatively prosperous years in the United States from the turn of the century through 1929, with productivity growth roughly 30 percent more rapid in the 1948–66 phase than during the 1901–29 period.
• By contrast, productivity growth during the stagnant 1966–79 cycle appears even more languid than during the Depression of the 1930s. Average annual productivity growth in the 1966–79 years was almost a fifth slower than from 1929 to the late-Depression peak of 1938.

These comparisons provide further indication that the erosion of macro-performance after the mid-1960s is notable and, by historical standards, relatively severe.

One additional correlate of stagnation after the mid-1960s was mounting inflationary pressure, giving birth to a new term – "stagflation" – for a new macroeconomic phenomenon – the unexpected combination of stagnating demand and accelerating price growth. Data for the rate of inflation are presented in row [3] of Table 2.1. They show a moderate and tolerable average annual rate of change of output prices of 2.2 percent a year in the 1948–66 boom. They then show an accelerating pace of inflation, rising to 5.0 percent in 1966–73 and 7.7 percent in 1973–79.

A traditional homily in economics suggests that inflation results when "too much money chases too few goods." We can assess the relative contribution of "too much money" and "too few goods" to accelerating inflation with a couple of simple calculations. "Too much money" would contribute to rising inflation if and when the rate of growth of the real

---

9   Data for 1947–79 from sources for row [2] in Table 2.1. Data for 1900–46 for nonfarm business sector real output from *Historical Statistics of the United States* (Washington, D.C.: U.S. Government Printing Office, 1976), Vol. I, Series D-684. (Business cycle peaks for pre-WWII cycles defined by peaks in series for capacity utilization, measured as the ratio of real GNP, from Nathan S. Balke and Robert J. Gordon, "The Estimation of Prewar Gross National Product: Methodology and New Evidence," *Journal of Political Economy* 97:1, February 1989, Table 10, to real potential GNP, from "natural real GNP" in Robert J. Gordon, *Macroeconomics* (Boston: Little, Brown, 1990), 5th ed., Table A-1.)

Prosperity to stagnation in the postwar economy   41

money stock exceeded the rate of growth of real output. Row [4] of Table 2.1 provides such an "index of monetary pressure," defined as the difference between the rates of change of the real money supply (M2) and of real GNP. If this measure is negative, it means that monetary factors were restrictive, with the money supply "leaning against" output pressure. If it is positive, it means that monetary influences were accommodating, amplifying inflationary pressure resulting from output growth. By this standard, as we can see from the table, "too much money" contributed to the acceleration of inflation in 1966–73, when the money supply grew relatively rapidly, but not at all in 1973–79, when money growth was restrictive.

A reasonable measure of "too few goods" is provided by the data for productivity growth. If productivity growth is buoyant, this means that the supply of goods is expanding rapidly relative to the resources available to produce them and inflationary pressure is unlikely to build. If productivity growth is tepid, by contrast, the supply of goods is expanding slowly relative to available resources, other things equal, and inflationary spurts may be likely because demand pressure bumps up against relatively limited supply. Looking back at row [2] in Table 2.1, we can see that "too few goods" made a marginal contribution to accelerating inflation in 1966–73, when the productivity slowdown was just beginning, but that it apparently made a major contribution in 1973–79, when productivity growth dropped abruptly. By the middle to late 1970s, it thus appears that the productivity slowdown – rather than demand-side pressure – played a crucial role in shaping the trajectory of deepening stagflation.

A final standard index of macroperformance focuses on unemployment. Conventional expectations through the late 1960s had anticipated a fairly sharp trade-off between inflation and unemployment. If the former went down in recessionary times, the latter would be expected to go up – and *vice versa*.

Beginning in the early 1970s, however, these expectations were confounded. Row [5] of Table 2.1 provides data on the rate of unemployment in the civilian labor force. Unemployment had remained above 5 percent during much of the 1950s but had begun to drop significantly by the mid-1960s. Thanks in part to the additional demand pressure generated by the Vietnam War, the unemployment rate fell below 4 percent in 1966–69, contributing to a somewhat lower average in 1966–73 than for the entire boom from 1948 to 1966. After the early 1970s, however, unemployment rose dramatically at the same time as the pace of inflation accelerated. Stagflation had taken firm roots. Many U.S. households were bound to be caught in a squeeze between slack labor markets and spiraling prices.

Further, the magnitude of the U.S. economic crisis was reflected in the international as well as the domestic arena. U.S. corporations lost much of the competitive advantage they had enjoyed in the early postwar period. In 1951, for example, the U.S. economy accounted for 30 percent of the world trade of the sixteen leading industrial nations; by 1971, the U.S. share had fallen to 18 percent.[10]

Even more dramatically, the U.S. economy took a running nose dive in the international rankings by per capita GDP. The United States ranked number one in 1950, in 1960, and again in 1970 – still more than 20 percent ahead of its nearest competitor. By 1980, however, the U.S. had dropped to number eleven (not counting the oil-rich Middle Eastern states), trailing Switzerland, Sweden, Norway, Germany, Denmark, Luxembourg, Iceland, Finland, the Netherlands, and Belgium in that order.

Despite these relative advances, however, other nations were suffering economically as well. All of the advanced capitalist economies experienced significant declines in the growth of output and productivity during the 1970s. Even in Japan, buoyantly successful in the postwar period, the rate of growth of GNP was less than half as rapid in the 1970s as it was in the 1960s.[11]

The worldwide character of the economic crisis thus emphasizes the extent to which the turn toward stagnation in the United States involved broader developments in the global economy, witnessing a generalized slowdown in the advanced economies, as well as specific tendencies within the domestic economy, underlying the slippage in the relative standing of the U.S. economy among the advanced countries.

Deteriorating well-being

However portentous the turn toward stagflation, stagnation in aggregate macroindicators does not by itself guarantee deteriorating working and

---

10 OECD, *National Accounts, 1950–1980*, Vol. I (Paris: OECD, 1982). Data for subsequent comparison of per capita GNP from ibid., p. 88 (with comparisons in current prices at current international exchange rates).

11 *Economic Report of the President*, 1991 (Washington, D.C.: U.S. Government Printing Office, 1991), Table B-110.

Prosperity to stagnation in the postwar economy   43

Table 2.2. *Impact of stagnation on people's well-being*

	Phase Averages		
	1948-66	1966-73	1973-79
[1] Rate change, real spend. hourly earnings (%)	2.1	1.1	-0.8
[2] Average hours worked per capita	659	691	707
[3] Rate change, real median family income (%)	3.1	2.2	-0.1

Sources: Growth rates are annual rates, calculated as logarithmic growth rates. Levels are calculated as average annual levels.

[1] Real after-tax hourly earnings of production workers ($1989): Thomas E. Weisskopf, "Use of hourly earnings proposed to revive spendable earnings series," *Monthly Labor Review*, November 1984, pp. 38–42, and annual updates by the present author.

[2] Hours worked divided by population: *National Income and Product Accounts*, Table 6.11:1; *Current Population Reports*, Series P-25.

[3] Real median family income ($1989): *Current Population Reports*, Series P-60, No. 160, Table 11.

living standards for the vast majority of households. It is plausible, though not particularly likely, that stagnation of aggregate output could squeeze net new investment or replacement investment or government services – but that wages, hours, and income might continue to improve substantially for most households.

Unfortunately for millions of Americans, however, the turn from prosperity to stagnation took its toll directly and fairly immediately. Table 2.2 reviews some of the most important indicators of this deteriorating well-being.

Roughly 90 percent of U.S. households depend on wage and salary income for their survival.[12] For this vast majority, two principal trends determine the level of income available to their households: take-home pay per hour of work and the total hours worked to support household members. Table 2.2 presents some basic data on both earnings and hours of the postwar period.

12   See Institute for Labor Education and Research, *What's Wrong with the U.S. Economy?* (Boston: South End Press, 1982), p. xi and notes, for analysis of the income sources of the bottom 90 percent of U.S. households in 1980. Underlying data are from Internal Revenue Service, *Statistics of Income, Individual Income Tax Returns.*

44   *D. M. Gordon*

Row [1] presents data on the rate of change of the average production worker's take-home pay – or *real spendable hourly earnings*.[13] Production workers comprised 81.3 percent of total employment in 1979[14] and represent that group in the labor force which is most clearly dependent on wage and salary income. Spendable hourly earnings measure the average worker's hourly wage and/or salary income plus other compensation – for example, medical benefits – minus personal income taxes and Social Security taxes. These earnings are expressed in constant dollars in order to adjust for the effects of inflation on the cost of living.

The data show a clear pattern. The average worker's real after-tax pay grew rapidly through the mid-1960s; its growth slowed in the first phase of stagnation, until the early 1970s, and then declined fairly sharply through the rest of the 1970s. By 1979, workers' take-home pay had fallen 6 percent *below* its postwar peak in 1972.

Row [2] presents data on average annual *hours worked per capita* by the U.S. population. This measure reflects the total amount of labor which U.S. households committed to the economy in order to support themselves and their dependents. The data on hours approximately mirror the data on real spendable hourly earnings. Not shown directly in the table, average hours per capita declined fairly steadily from the late 1940s until the early 1960s – as workers and households were able to take advantage of rising wage and salary income; hours fell from a peak during the Korean War of 704 hours per year to a postwar low of 627 hours in 1961. As row [2] indicates, this resulted in what turned out to be a relatively low average workload during the full 1948–66 period.

Average hours then rose in the mid-1960s when real earnings growth

13   For many years the Bureau of Labor Statistics provided a standard statistical series on "real spendable *weekly* earnings." This series was discontinued in December 1981 because it was judged that the average workweek had changed substantially over time (with shifts among part-time and full-time workers) and that the calculations made in the series for taxes were unrealistic. Although there is some validity to these claims, we believe that it is essential to be able to provide a continuous statistical series on the purchasing power of the take-home pay of production workers. We therefore developed an alternative series on real spendable hourly earnings, which is free of the two problems in the weekly earnings series. See Thomas E. Weisskopf, "Use of Hourly Earnings Proposed to Revive Spendable Earnings Series," *Monthly Labor Review,* November 1984.

14   Based on *Employment and Training Report* (Washington, D.C.: U.S. Government Printing Office, 1981), Table C-3.

Prosperity to stagnation in the postwar economy   45

began to slow. They continued to rise during the 1973–79 phase as households tried to stave off the squeeze of declining real hourly earnings (row [1]).

This increase in average annual hours per capita reflected an increase in the number of household members working outside the home, and not an increase in average hours per week. Faced with stagnating and then declining real spendable earnings, additional family members, particularly married women, sought work. The percentage of the adult population working or looking for work outside the home – a figure which had been roughly constant over the postwar period – began to rise in the mid-1960s, climbing from 59 percent in 1966 to 64 percent in 1979.[15] This extra labor helped sustain total household earnings, making possible continued increases in household consumption levels.[16] As the 1970s progressed, *Business Week* noted in 1980, it became more and more important to take into account "the sweat that goes into producing [household] income."[17]

This squeeze shows up quite clearly in data on real median family income (row [3]), a measure of the standard of living which the typical U.S. family could afford as the postwar period progressed. Families could sustain rapidly improving living standards during the decades of prosperity, with real median family income rising at an average annual rate of 3.1 percent in 1948–66. After the mid-1960s, however, the slowdown in hourly earnings began to take hold, with the rate of growth of real median family income in 1966–73 falling 30 percent below its pace during the boom years. After the early 1970s, finally, stagnation became fully manifest, with real median incomes actually declining slightly from 1973 to 1979. Despite the substantial increases in average hours worked (row [2]) in the second phase of stagnation, the decline in hourly take-home pay (row [1]) was so severe that family incomes could not keep pace with inflation.

By the second phase of stagnation, in short, the typical U.S. family was racing simply to stay in place. Prosperity had clearly given way to eroding well-being. The bloom was off the economic rose in the United States.

15 *Economic Report*, 1991, Table B-32, column for civilian labor force participation rate.
16 For a recent analysis of the increase in working hours since the 1960s, see Juliet B. Schor, *The Overworked American: The Unexpected Decline of Leisure* (New York: Basic Books, 1991).
17 *Business Week*, January 28, 1980, p. 73.

46   *D. M. Gordon*

INSTITUTIONAL FOUNDATIONS OF THE POSTWAR ECONOMY: CONSTRUCTION AND DECAY

> America has embarked on a career of imperialism, both in world affairs and in every other aspect of her life. . . . The path of empire takes its way, and in modern times . . . the scepter passes to the United States.
>
> — Management consultant, 1941[18]

> Between the fall of Vietnam and the fall of the Shah of Iran, the U.S. has been buffeted by an unnerving series of shocks that signal an accelerating erosion of power and influence. Although the shocks themselves have occurred primarily in the military and foreign policy arenas, they have deep-seated economic and monetary roots.
>
> — "The Decline of U.S. Power," *Business Week*, 1979[19]

Stagflationary pressures did not pass unheeded during the 1970s. Analyses of stagflation became a major growth industry in economics. Two standard kinds of explanations for the erosion of prosperity emerged within mainstream economics.

Those of relatively more conservative persuasion tended to regard the U.S. government as the principal culprit, ascribing deteriorating macroperformance to ill-advised and increasingly pervasive government interventions in the private economy.[20] In an introduction to a major collection of papers, *The American Economy in Transition*, published in 1980, for example, Martin Feldstein, Harvard economist soon to become chair of the Council of Economic Advisers under Ronald Reagan, concluded ominously:[21]

> The expanded role of government has undoubtedly been the most important change in the structure of the American economy in the postwar period. The extent to which this major change in structure has been the cause of the major decline in performance cannot be easily assessed. . . . Nevertheless, there can be no doubt that government policies do deserve substantial blame for the adverse experience of the past decade.

18   Quoted in William Appleman Williams, *Americans in a Changing World* (New York: Harper & Row, 1978), p. 314.
19   *Business Week*, March 12, 1979, p. 36.
20   For two rhetorical examples of this late-1970s conservative view, see Jude Wanniski, *The Way the World Works* (New York: Simon & Schuster, 1978); and William E. Simon, *A Time for Truth* (New York: McGraw-Hill, 1978).
21   "The American Economy in Transition: Introduction," in Feldstein, ed., *The American Economy in Transition* (Chicago: University of Chicago Press, 1980), p. 3.

Prosperity to stagnation in the postwar economy   47

By contrast, those of relatively more liberal inclination were inclined to blame the economy's deterioration on a variety of unanticipated "shocks" or "surprises" which distorted and disrupted an otherwise healthy economy.[22] For example, Robert J. Gordon, a leading liberal macroeconomist from Northwestern University, concluded at the end of the 1970s that "in the postwar period external events were the most important single destabilizing force, most obviously in the direct impact of Korean and Vietnam defense expenditures on real GNP and in the effect of the formation of the OPEC oil cartel in the 1970s on inflation and unemployment."[23] If only these shocks had been properly anticipated, according to this view, then stagflation might not have occurred.

Both of these orientations take the institutional structure of the private economy as given. Conservatives assume that the private sector in the postwar period was functioning according to the principles of perfect competition and that it would have continued to function effectively if the government had only minded its own business. Liberals assume that the prevailing mix of private and public sectors would have continued to enjoy smooth sailing if only turbulent weather hadn't intervened. In neither case is much attention paid to the actual structure and functions of private-sector institutions themselves. Nor do these mainstream economists imagine that the internal structure and contradictions of those institutions themselves might conceivably account for the turn from boom to bust.

Many economists outside the mainstream take the institutions of the private sector much more seriously. For some of us, indeed, these institutions hold the key to understanding the trajectories of capitalist economies in general and the fate of the postwar U.S. economy in particular. In our view, socioeconomic institutions shape relations among capitalists, workers, and other classes or groups of economic actors; they define the role of the state in the economy; and they determine the external relations of the capitalist sector with foreign capitalists and with other co-existing modes of production.

Following one line of approach, this perspective has been formalized in

22 Two useful examples of this inclination from the late 1970s are Otto Eckstein, *The Great Recession – With a Postscript on Stagflation* (Amsterdam: North-Holland Publishing, 1978); and Alan S. Blinder, *Economic Policy and the Great Stagflation* (New York: Academic Press, 1979).

23 "Postwar Macroeconomics: The Evolution of Events and Ideas," in Feldstein, ed., *The American Economy in Transition*, p. 156.

48   *D. M. Gordon*

recent years through analyses of prevailing "social structures of accumulation" (SSAs) – the constellations of institutions which condition growth and accumulation in a given capitalist economy.[24] If the constituent institutions of an SSA are operating smoothly and in a manner favorable to capital, capitalists will find their productive activities profitable and they will feel confident about the potential returns from investing in the expansion of productive capacity. But if the SSA begins to become shaky – for example, because some of its constituent institutions begin to lose their effectiveness and legitimacy, and/or because heightened class conflict or international rivalry begin to pose challenges to capitalist control – then capitalists will find production less profitable and will begin to cut back on domestic capital formation and instead devote their wealth to their own consumption, to financial investment, or to investment abroad. A slowdown of economic growth and a rise in unemployment will be likely to result. Under these circumstances costly social and economic conflicts often intensify, further eroding overall economic performance and reducing people's living standards.[25]

Viewed through the lenses of the SSA perspective, the postwar U.S. economy was based upon a new social structure of accumulation arising out of the ashes of the 1930s and the conflicts of World War II. In the account of the postwar U.S. SSA developed in my joint work with Bowles and Weisskopf, four main institutional dimensions provided the principal buttresses of U.S. corporate power in the postwar period and, building upon that power, the dynamics of rapid growth and accumulation.[26] We

24 The concept of a social structure of accumulation was introduced in David M. Gordon, "Up and Down the Long Roller Coaster," in Union for Radical Political Economics (ed.), *U.S. Capitalism in Crisis* (New York: Union for Radical Political Economics, 1978), and further developed and applied in David M. Gordon, Richard Edwards, and Michael Reich, *Segmented Work, Divided Workers: The Historical Transformation of Labor in the United States* (New York: Cambridge University Press, 1982). See also David M. Gordon, Thomas E. Weisskopf, and Samuel Bowles, "Power, Accumulation and Crisis: The Rise and Demise of the Postwar Social Structure of Accumulation," in R. Cherry et al., eds., *Macroeconomics from a Left Perspective*, Vol. I of *The Imperiled Economy* (New York: URPE, 1988).

25 A recent exploration of the foundations and implications of the SSA approach is available in David Kotz, Terence McDonough, and Michael Reich, eds., *Social Structures of Accumulation: The Political Economy of Growth and Crisis* (Cambridge: Cambridge University Press, 1994).

26 See Samuel Bowles, David M. Gordon, and Thomas E. Weisskopf, *After the Waste Land: A Democratic Economics for the Year 2000* (Armonk, N.Y.: M. E. Sharpe, 1990), Ch. 5.

refer to these four institutional dimensions as *Pax Americana*, the limited capital–labor accord, the capitalist–citizen accord, and the containment of intercapitalist rivalry. The subsequent turn of stagnation, we argue, was conditioned by the emergence of conflicts and contradictions along each of these four institutional axes.

In order to understand the deteriorating performance of the U.S. economy, by virtue of this argument, it becomes necessary to trace the construction, consolidation, and decay of each of these four institutional foundations. I provide here a brief review of each of those four dynamics of institutional development and crisis in turn.

Pax Americana

The United States emerged from World War II as the world's dominant economic and military power. In subsequent years, U.S. economic dominance assured a stable climate within which capitalist trade, investment, and output could grow rapidly throughout much of the world. Insistent U.S. leadership helped to lower tariffs and other barriers to trade. Marshall Plan aid to devastated European economies facilitated their economic recovery. U.S. direct private investment abroad contributed as well to the reconstruction and development of capitalist enterprise in many parts of the world.

For a time, at least, the system worked in the interests of both the U.S. and other active participants in the global economy. The dollars pumped into the world system by U.S. investment and foreign aid quickly returned through growing demand for U.S. exports. Booming foreign markets and stable world market conditions raised both corporate profits and private business expectations; this stimulated high rates of U.S. capital investment at home as well as abroad. Domestically, U.S. corporate leverage in international markets helped promote high rates of growth and capacity utilization.

None of these benefits emerged through private initiatives alone. The U.S. government adopted an increasingly interventionist international stance. U.S. corporations enjoyed huge productivity advantages at the beginning of the postwar period, to be sure, but aggressive political support of foreign investment and imposing military power joined to bolster this private-sector leverage. Drawing from a varied tool kit, the U.S. government built the military, economic, and political machinery to police much of the world.

Table 2.3 reviews some of the key indicators of the foundation which

50   *D. M. Gordon*

Table 2.3. *Institutional axis I: construction and erosion of*
Pax Americana

	Phase Averages		
	1948-66	1966-73	1973-79
[1] Rate change, real value of dollar (%)	0.0ª	-2.8	-2.9
[2] Rate change, real U.S. foreign dir. invest. (%)	7.2ª	4.0	1.4
[3] Defense outlays as percent of GNP (%)	9.0	7.7	5.0
[4] Rate change, rel. crude materials prices (%)	-2.0	1.1	-0.1
[5] Rate change, real cost of imports (%)	-0.6	1.6	3.8

ª Figure is for 1951–66. See also text note #27.

Sources: Growth rates are annual rates, calculated as logarithmic growth rates. Levels are calculated as average annual levels. *ERP* refers to *Economic Report of the President,* 1991.

[1] Rate of change, (real) multilateral trade-weighted value of the U.S. dollar: 1967–79, *ERP*, Table B-109, column for real series adjusted by changes in consumer prices; 1951–66, individual country exchange rates from U.S. Bureau of Labor Statistics, "Output Per Hour, Hourly Compensation, and Unit Labor Costs in Manufacturing, Twelve Countries, 1950–1982," unpublished tables, January 1984.

[2] Rate of change, real value of U.S. private direct investment abroad ($1982): U.S. Department of Commerce, *Selected Data on U.S. Direct Investment Abroad, 1950–76* (Washington, D.C.: U.S. Government Printing Office, 1982), and *Survey of Current Business*, updates various years. Deflated by price deflator for private nonresidential capital stock (1982 = 100), based on real and nominal series from U.S. Department of Commerce, *Fixed Reproducible Tangible Wealth in the United States, 1925–85* (Washington, D.C.: U.S. Government Printing Office, 1987).

[3] National defense outlays as percent of GNP: Defense outlays, 1948–61, *Historical Statistics of the United States* (Washington, D.C.: U.S. Government Printing Office, 1976), Series Y-473; 1962–79, *Statistical Abstract, 1989*, Table 526; GNP, *ERP*, Table B-1.

[4] Rate of change, ratio of nonagricultural crude materials price index to GDP price deflator: Crude materials prices from U.S. BLS disaggregated price data available from *Citibank Database*; GDP price deflator from *National Income and Product Accounts*, Table 7.4.

[5] Rate of change, ratio, imports price deflator to exports price deflator: *ERP*, Table B-3.

Pax Americana provided for U.S. economic prosperity – as well as its subsequent erosion:

• The Bretton Woods system featured fixed exchange rates, with each individual national currency pegged to the value of the dollar. This

Prosperity to stagnation in the postwar economy   51

exchange-rate stability fostered international trade and economic growth. Row [1] witnesses this fixed-exchange-rate regime, with the real value of the dollar remaining approximately constant throughout the boom period.[27]

- Reflecting the stability of the global economy and the favorable international access provided to U.S. corporations, U.S. foreign direct investment (row [2]) soared during the boom years. In the 1948–66 period, the real value of U.S. foreign investment increased by 7.2 percent — nearly twice the rate of growth of U.S. GDP.

- Driven by the political and military support which the U.S. government provided for *Pax Americana,* military expenditures also remained at very high levels after World War II and the Korean War. National defense outlays as a percent of GNP (row [3]) averaged 9.0 throughout the whole 1948–66 period, down somewhat from their post-WWII peak of 13 percent during the Korean War.

- U.S. capital gained access to foreign raw material and energy supplies on increasingly favorable terms. The relative price of nonfarm crude materials (row [4]), almost all of them imported, declined by an average 2.0 percent a year during the boom years, reflecting in particular the favorable access to imported oil which U.S. corporations and the government had been able to engineer during and after World War II.

- U.S. sellers sold in a seller's market and U.S. buyers bought in a buyer's market. One essential indicator of foreign market access is the real cost of imports, or the ratio of U.S. imports prices to U.S. exports prices. The lower the real cost of imports, the greater the quantity of goods and services that can be purchased abroad by a unit of real output produced in the U.S. economy. Between 1948 and 1966, the real cost of imports (row [5]) declined at an average annual rate of 0.6 percent a year, indicating that U.S. firms were able to purchase their input supplies on increasingly favorable terms. For U.S. corporations, the benefits of *Pax*

27 Official published data for the multilateral trade-weighted value of the dollar extend back only to 1967. From 1950 through 1966, the dollar values of almost all individual currencies remained approximately constant, with a few notable exceptions such as France's sharp devaluation in 1956–58. For the purposes of discussion, I have ignored these exceptions and treated the multilateral value of the dollar *as if* it remained exactly constant through 1966. For data on the dollar values of twelve leading individual currencies, see U.S. Bureau of Labor Statistics, "Output Per Hour, Hourly Compensation, and Unit Labor Costs in Manufacturing, Twelve Countries, 1950–1982," unpublished tables, January 1984.

52   *D. M. Gordon*

Americana showed up on the bottom line: as the imports grew relatively less expensive, everything else equal, domestic profitability could improve as well.[28]

None of these benefits occurred by accident. President Kennedy affirmed the principles of private–public partnership at the beginning of his administration, addressing a group of executives: "Our [national] success is dependent upon your profits and success. Far from being natural enemies, government and business are necessary allies. . . . We are anxious to do everything we can to make your way easier."[29]

Beginning in the early to middle 1960s, however, U.S. corporations faced growing challenges in both the First and the Third worlds. These challenges substantially weakened the international position of U.S. capital. By the mid-1960s, the structure of *Pax Americana* was tottering.[30]

The first challenge came from the recovery and increasing competitive vigor of corporations in Europe and Japan. By the mid-1960s, Japanese and European firms were enhancing their market shares at the expense of U.S. corporations not only overseas but also at home in the United States.[31]

This mounting international competition had many sources, but one of the sources of declining competitive advantage was undoubtedly the burden of U.S. military expenditures. The military role of the United States was indispensable in helping to police the postwar international system, but it also constituted an enormous drain on the productive capacity of the United States.[32]

---

28 For an analysis of the importance of the real cost of imports (the terms of trade) to domestic profitability, see Samuel Bowles, David M. Gordon, and Thomas E. Weisskopf, "Power and Profits: The Social Structure of Accumulation and the Profitability of the Postwar U.S. Economy," *Review of Radical Political Economics,* Spring–Summer 1986, 132–67.

29 Quoted in Wolfe, *The Limits of Legitimacy,* p. 214.

30 For detailed analyses of the demise of *Pax Americana* and the consequent changes in the structure of the global economy, see Joyce Kolko, *Restructuring the World Economy* (New York: Pantheon Books, 1988); and Mario Pianta, *New Technologies Across the Atlantic: U.S. Leadership or European Autonomy* (Brighton: Wheatsheaf Books, 1988).

31 Data on this mounting import competition is provided in the section below on intercapitalist rivalry. For a useful analysis of mounting competition among the advanced countries, see Philip Armstrong, Andrew Glyn, and John Harrison, *Capitalism Since 1945* (Oxford: Basil Blackwell, 1991), especially Ch. 10, "The Eclipse of U.S. Domination."

32 For an insightful analysis of the effect of the U.S. military on the U.S. econ-

Prosperity to stagnation in the postwar economy   53

Could this drain have been avoided? In retrospect we can see that the postwar international financial system required *both* a strong U.S. economy *and* a strong U.S. military – the former to reinforce the dollar's role as key currency, and the latter to stabilize the political relationships necessary to enforce U.S. access to foreign markets and secure the uninterrupted flow of dollars around the globe. But these requirements turned out to be as much competing as complementary, with military spending eventually sapping the economy's strength. When this contradiction became acute, by the mid-1960s, monetary stability began to unravel. There had been a growing glut of U.S. dollars on world money markets, partly as a result of defense expenditures abroad. Foreign countries became increasingly reluctant to hold dollars, sensing that the dollar's official exchange rate was overvalued, and demanded gold from Fort Knox instead. Eventually, by the early 1970s, the U.S. severed the relationship between gold and the dollar, effectively renouncing the dollar-based system of fixed exchange rates. With that declaration, the inevitable became actual and the foundations of international monetary stability were shattered.

Challenges from the Third World also began to undermine U.S. international domination in the 1960s. Foreign liberation movements came increasingly to focus their ire on the United States. The U.S. government initially rebuffed these challenges without much difficulty – as in Guatemala and Iran in 1954. But the failure of the Kennedy administration to overthrow Castro in the 1961 Bay of Pigs Invasion, and especially the long and humiliating failure to stem the revolutionary tide in South Vietnam marked a significant and escalating erosion of the U.S. government's capacity to "keep the world safe" for private enterprise.

A final challenge in the world economy came from exporters of raw materials, primarily in Third World nations. With U.S. political economic power teetering after the mid-1960s, the economic bargaining power of some of the Third World raw-material-exporting nations increased substantially. The OPEC cartel was the most visible and important example. In conjunction with multinational petroleum companies, it succeeded in shifting the terms of the oil trade sharply against the oil-importing nations, first in 1973 and then again in 1979.

The final two columns of Table 2.3 help us trace some of the consequences of this erosion in U.S. international political economic power:

omy, see Tom Riddell, "Military Power, Military Spending and the Profit Rate," *American Economic Review,* May 1988, 60–65.

54   *D. M. Gordon*

- Although the Bretton Woods system was not officially and finally dissolved until 1971–73, exchange rates began to fluctuate as early as 1967–68 when the drain on Fort Knox gold began in earnest. As a result, the real value of the dollar began to decline during the first phase of stagnation, falling at an accelerating rate from 1970 to 1973 and resulting in an average annual rate of change (row [1]) of −2.8 percent in 1966–73. When Bretton Woods was formally buried in 1973, the dollar was still apparently overvalued, resulting in a continuing decline of 2.9 percent per year in 1973–79. No longer officially the world's key currency, the dollar's sharp decline underscored how artificially inflated its value had become by the end of the boom years. The international hegemon had begun to seem more and more like a paper tiger.
- With mounting Third World hostility toward the U.S. as well as increasing global economic instability in the new flexible-exchange-rate regime after 1973, U.S. corporations became more and more reluctant to take the risks of direct investment abroad: the rate of growth of real U.S. foreign direct investment (row [2]) slowed considerably during the 1966–73 and 1973–79 phases, respectively, virtually ceasing its growth altogether in the middle to late 1970s.
- After increasingly successful challenges to U.S. political and military power, and with mounting demands on economic resources at home, the U.S. military machine became increasingly difficult to sustain. National defense outlays as a percent of GNP (row [3]) fell slightly during the 1966–73 phase, even with the Vietnam War effort at its peak. Then, with strong public reaction against the Vietnam War debacle, relative defense expenditures fell further in 1973–79 – to less than 60 percent their boom-phase levels.
- The rebellion of foreign raw materials exporters blew the cost of U.S. imported raw materials through the ceiling. Largely as a result of the OPEC oil price hike in 1973, the rate of change of relative nonfarm crude materials prices (row [4]) in 1966–73 reversed its earlier decline, now growing at a pace of 1.1 percent a year. And then, thanks in part to another oil price hike in 1979, relative crude materials prices maintained those higher levels during the 1973–79 phase, with an effectively zero rate of change from the previous cycle.
- As we saw above, the real cost of imports (row [5]) had improved during the boom period. After the mid-1960s, however, it began to rise, first increasing by 1.6 percent a year in 1966–73 and then even more substantially by 3.8 percent a year in 1973–79. This cost increase hit

Prosperity to stagnation in the postwar economy   55

U.S. corporations where they felt it most acutely, below the bottom line.

The limited capital–labor accord

The battle for postwar prosperity was also won on the home front. The limited truce between corporations and labor was a second essential element of the postwar SSA.

The limited capital–labor accord involved a restructuring of labor–management relations after the 1940s.[33] For those millions of U.S. workers to whom the accord was limited, it provided the carrot of real wage growth, improved job security, and better working conditions in return for acquiescence to complete corporate control of the production process and allocation of the profits from production. For those millions excluded from the accord, by contrast, corporations continued to wield a heavy stick of intensive supervision and the threat of job dismissal – with wages, job security, and working conditions continually falling behind those in the more advantaged sectors.

In many industries covered by the informal accord, corporations explicitly retained absolute control over the essential decisions governing enterprise operations – decisions involving production, technology, plant location, investment, and marketing. This set of corporate prerogatives was codified in the "management rights" clauses of most collective bargaining agreements. In return, unions were accepted as legitimate representatives of workers' interests. They were expected to bargain on behalf of labor's immediate economic interests, but not to challenge employer control of enterprises. Unions would help maintain an orderly and disciplined labor force while corporations would reward workers with a share of the income gains made possible by rising productivity, with greater employment security, and with improved working conditions.

There *were* productivity gains, as shown in Table 2.1, and there were real wage gains as well, as shown in Table 2.2. Job security also improved; the aggregate unemployment rate dropped to 3.8 percent by 1966, roughly one-quarter of its average level during the 1930s. But there was more to the limited capital–labor accord than simply its correlates in productivity growth, wage gains, and job security. Table 2.4 provides some of the key data for analyzing the contours of postwar capital–labor relations.

33   See Gordon, Edwards, and Reich, *Segmented Work, Divided Workers*, Ch. 5.

56   D. M. Gordon

Table 2.4. *Institutional axis II: construction and erosion of limited capital–labor accord*

	Phase Averages		
	1948-66	1966-73	1973-79
[1] Intensity of supervision (ratio)	0.18	0.21	0.22
[2] Union representation rate (%)	31.6	27.1	24.2
[3] Index of earnings inequality (ratio)	1.36	1.45	1.37
[4] Frequency of industrial accidents (rate)	3.5	4.1	5.1
[5] Cost of job loss (ratio)	0.31	0.21	0.22

Sources: Growth rates are annual rates, calculated as logarithmic growth rates. Levels are calculated as average annual levels.

[1] Ratio of nonproduction/supervisory employees to production/nonsupervisory employees: *Handbook of Labor Statistics* (Washington, D.C.: U.S. Government Printing Office, 1981), Table C-3.

[2] Union members as percentage of nonfarm employment. Union members: 1947–57, *Historical Statistics of the United States*, Series D591; 1958–77, U.S. Bureau of Labor Statistics, "Directory of National Unions and Employee Associations," Bulletin 2079, September 1980, Table 6; 1978–79, U.S. Bureau of Labor Statistics, "Corrected Data on Labor Organization Membership," USDL, 81-446, September 1981.   Nonfarm employment: *Economic Report of the President*, 1991, Table B-43.

[3] Weighted ratio of white male earnings to female and to black male earnings, for persons with income during year: Median income data from *Current Population Reports*, Series P-60, No. 162.

[4] Lost workday cases due to injury and illness, manufacturing, per hundred full-time employees: 1971–79, *Statistical Abstract*, various years; 1948–70, Peter Arno, "The Political Economy of Industrial Injuries," unpublished Ph.D. dissertation, New School for Social Research, 1984, Table 6.

[5] Portion of year's pay expected to be lost if dismissed from job: Samuel Bowles, David M. Gordon, and Thomas E. Weisskopf, "Business Ascendancy and Economic Impasse: A Structural Retrospective on Conservative Economics, 1979–87," *Journal of Economic Perspectives*, Winter 1989, Data Appendix.

In order to take full advantage of their renewed control, corporations dramatically expanded their supervisory apparatus. Overall, the resources devoted to managerial and supervisory personnel climbed significantly. Between 1948 and 1966, for example, the ratio of supervisory to nonsupervisory employees in the private business sector increased by nearly 75 percent – from roughly thirteen supervisory employees per

Prosperity to stagnation in the postwar economy   57

hundred nonsupervisory employees to more than twenty-two. For the period as a whole, this ratio, labeled in Table 2.4 as the "intensity of supervision" (row [1]), averaged 0.18.[34]

While the accord benefited some workers, it excluded others. The percent of nonfarm workers who were union members reached its peak at the time of the AFL–CIO merger in 1954 and then began to decline gradually through the mid-1960s as the limits on the accord held firm; the union representation rate (row [2]) averaged only about one-third for the full 1948–66 period. Meanwhile, unorganized workers, women, and minorities lost ground. The wages of workers in the "core" sector of industry outstripped those of workers on its periphery, increasing from 1.3 times noncore workers' earnings in 1948 to 1.5 times in 1966.[35] Income inequality by race and gender also increased through the 1960s. Row [3] presents a composite index of the degree of income advantages for white male over female and black male workers. This index of earnings inequality rose substantially from a ratio of 1.20 in 1948 to 1.45 in 1966, averaging 1.36 for the period as a whole.

Beginning in the early 1960s, two problems eventually emerged to shatter the limited capital–labor accord. The first involved those who had been excluded from its benefits, while the second involved the internal contradictions of the accord itself.

Corporations showed little interest in expanding the breadth of the accord, first of all, and unions grew comfortable with their privileges as

34 Not all the employees designated by official data as "nonproduction" or "supervisory" personnel are exclusively managers or supervisors, but by far the largest portion are. In 1980, for example, there were 13.9 million "supervisory" workers on private nonfarm payrolls. In the same year, according to detailed occupational data, there were approximately 11.5 million managers, clerical supervisors, and blue-collar worker-supervisors in the private sector. (This is an approximate estimate because detailed data on government supervisory personnel were not available from the census; the number reported here reflects an approximate deduction from the total number of managers and supervisors for those in government, assuming that equal proportions worked in those categories in both the public and private sectors.) All the rest of the 13.9 million certainly have supervisory responsibilities, since it appears that at least 8 million or so employees who are not managers or supervisors *also* supervise other employees. For data see *Employment and Training Report*, 1981, pp. 152–53; and Institute for Labor Education and Research, *What's Wrong with the U.S. Economy?* p. 220.

35 See Gordon, Edwards, and Reich, *Segmented Work, Divided Workers*, Figure 5.1A.

"insiders." As a result, the ranks of unions continued to drop as a percentage of nonfarm employment, with the union representation rate (row [2]) dropping to 27.1 percent in 1966–73 and further to 24.2 percent in 1973–79. The net effect for the labor movement was a significant narrowing of its reach.

As the ranks of those excluded from the benefits of the accord continued to swell, protest against the racism, sexism, and distributive injustice of the accord emerged through four different but effective movements: the civil rights movement, the welfare rights movement, the organization of the elderly, and the women's movement. These movements all led to government efforts at accommodation, including efforts at ensuring equal opportunity and affirmative action. Many of these programs cost money, and their growing costs reflected the mounting and increasingly expensive requirements of containing resistance to an unequal distribution of power and privilege. These movements helped eventually to provide real economic gains; as we can see in row [3], for example, earnings inequality by race and gender peaked in the 1966–73 phase and then began actually to decline as the government programs of the 1960s eventually took effect.

The accord began to encounter increasingly serious resistance from *inside* as well. Several factors contributed to this challenge. The first involves an apparent shift in attitudes and working conditions.

Rising real wages, heightened job security, and improved working conditions were increasingly taken for granted – as memories of the Depression receded and young workers replaced those who had struggled through the 1930s. This decline in *material* insecurity apparently led to greater concern about occupational health-and-safety issues, influence over workplace decisions, and opportunities for meaningful and creatively challenging work.[36] These spreading concerns could conceivably have been accommodated, but they tended to run up against the vast apparatus of bureaucratic control. The increasing intensity of supervision worked well for those workers who understood and still believed in the terms of the initial bargain, but it was less and less likely to remain effective when it confronted a labor force which – by age, education, and temperament – was increasingly resistant to arbitrary authority.

36 As the authors of the Report of a Special Task Force to the secretary of Health, Education, and Welfare, *Work in America* (Cambridge, Mass.: M.I.T. Press, 1972), concluded, "It may be argued that the very success of industry and organized labor in meeting the basic needs of workers has unintentionally spurred demands for esteemable and fulfilling jobs" (p. 12).

Prosperity to stagnation in the postwar economy   59

Compounding and partly precipitating these shifts in focus was a serious reversal of the improvement of working conditions during the postwar boom. Part of this reversal is captured by data on industrial accidents, presented in row [4] of Table 4. During the boom years, the industrial accident rate had declined fairly continuously, dropping by roughly 30 percent from 1948 to the early 1960s and resulting in a relatively low average rate of 3.5 in 1948–66. But mounting competition and declining profitability led to an intensification of the pace of production, with the accident rate climbing steadily through the two principal phases of stagnation. By 1979, the accident rate had reached a level roughly 80 percent higher than its levels of the early 1960s.

Rather than responding to frustration and friction in production by cutting back on the supervisory apparatus, however, corporations responded with further increases in the scale and scope of their institutions of production control. The intensity of supervision (row [1]) increased further to 0.21 in 1966–73 and then again to 0.22 in 1973–79. Nor were these continuing increases inevitable features of advanced technological societies. In deepening its top-heavy, hierarchical systems of management, U.S. corporations departed more and more noticeably from the more cooperative systems of labor relations practiced in leading competitors such as West Germany and Japan. By the late 1970s, for example, the ratio of administrative and managerial personnel to total nonfarm employment was almost three times as high in the United States as in West Germany and Japan.[37] Relying on top-down supervision was an expensive and apparently addictive habit. The bureaucratic burden was not easy to lift.

These contradictions of hierarchical organization were complemented by another and clearly critical problem for capital: the declining effectiveness of the traditional source of capitalist leverage over the workforce, the threat of unemployment. This threat is based on two simple facts of life in a capitalist economy: workers depend on getting jobs in order to live, and a significant number of workers at any time are stuck without a job.

Two developments in the postwar period reduced the effectiveness of this threat. First, the unemployment rate fell to unusually low levels in the mid-1960s. Second, the social programs won by social struggle in the

37 Based on commensurable tabulations of national occupational statistics, these comparative data are summarized and documented in David M. Gordon, "Who Bosses Whom? The Intensity of Supervision and the Discipline of Labor," *American Economic Review*, May 1990, 28–32.

1930s – social insurance, unemployment compensation, and others – were greatly expanded and augmented by new 1960s programs such as Medicaid, Medicare, food stamps, and Aid to Families with Dependent Children (AFDC). The combined effect of all these programs was to provide some cushion for those laid off from work.

To document this phenomenon and assess its relative impact, several of us have combined the two effects – lower unemployment and the cushion provided by social programs – into a single measure of the "cost of job loss."[38] This measure represents the portion of a year's expected overall income which is lost by a worker who is laid off. It varies with both the likelihood of remaining without a job for a long time – as when unemployment rises – and with the relative income lost when a worker is unemployed. The higher this measure, the greater the cost to the worker of job termination and the greater the potential corporate leverage over their workers through the threat of dismissal.

Row [5] of Table 2.4 traces the "cost of job loss." The cost of job loss was highest during the boom and significantly lower during the first phase of the crisis – boding poorly for the effectiveness of corporate threats of dismissal. It did rise marginally in the second phase, but remained on average well below its boom level. Moreover, the modest recovery from 1973 to 1979 was accomplished largely by rising relative unemployment (see row [5] of Table 2.1), not by further extensions of transfers and welfare benefits – underscoring the apparently enduring dependence of corporations on high unemployment for enhanced employee control.

Measured by the cost to workers of losing their job, employers' leverage over workers declined by roughly a third from the boom period to the first phase of crisis. This was bound to loosen their hold over labor and undermine their ability to maintain the profitability of production. There are several indications that workers began to take advantage of this reduced corporate leverage.[39]

---

38 The detailed sources and methods of estimating the cost of job loss are originally presented in Juliet B. Schor and Samuel Bowles, "Employment Rents and the Incidence of Strikes," *Review of Economics and Statistics,* November 1987. The data series is maintained and updated by the present author.

39 See Gordon, Edwards, and Reich, *Segmented Work, Divided Workers,* Ch. 5; and Bowles, Gordon, and Weisskopf, *After the Waste Land,* Chs. 5–6, for detailed discussion of these reactions.

Prosperity to stagnation in the postwar economy   61

I focus here on only one indicator, the frequency of strike activity. Because of the relatively cooperative contours of the postwar accord, strikes declined during the postwar boom itself; the number of workers involved in strikes as a percentage of all trade union members – the group of workers most likely to engage in strike activity – dropped substantially through the early 1960s.[40] But then, as workplace friction mounted after the mid-1960s and employer leverage eroded, strikes spread in the 1966–73 phase, increasing by 40 percent over their relatively low levels in the previous business cycle from 1959 through 1966. Only when unemployment rates climbed and corporations began to mount a sustained counteroffensive against labor did strike frequency subside again, declining by nearly 40 percent from 1966–73 to 1973–79.

It appears, on the basis of these several indicators, that the effectiveness of corporate control over labor was beginning to decline after the mid-1960s – as a result of both friction within the bureaucratic shell and the increasingly muted effect of the unemployment threat. This erosion of the limited capital–labor accord appears to have resulted in significantly reduced labor effort in production in the 1966–73 cycle, contributing to the first phase of slowdown in productivity growth.[41] With that productivity slowdown, profit margins also suffered mounting pressure, contributing to a decline in profitability after the mid-1960s (see data below). As the truce between capital and labor began to dissolve, so did one of the central foundations of U.S. corporate power and aggregate economic prosperity.[42]

40 Full documentation of this strike frequency variable is provided in Bowles, Gordon, and Weisskopf, "Business Ascendancy and Economic Impasse," Data Appendix.

41 See Thomas E. Weisskopf, Samuel Bowles, and David M. Gordon, "Hearts and Minds: A Social Model of U.S. Productivity Growth," *Brookings Papers on Economic Activity*, 2:1983, 381–441; and Bowles, Gordon, and Weisskopf, *After the Waste Land*, Ch. 7.

42 For reasons of space constraints, I concentrate here on developments during the 1966–73 phase. In 1973–79, corporations began to fight back, armed with the ammunition of rising unemployment, and a kind of political stand-off or stalemate between workers and corporations emerged – with the level of conflict much higher and the effectiveness of the accord substantially diminished compared to the boom years. For more on this part of the story, see Bowles, Gordon, and Weisskopf, *After the Waste Land*, Ch. 6.

62   *D. M. Gordon*

The capitalist–citizen accord

The Depression generated more than labor struggles. Millions also battled for tenants' rights and public housing, for social security and public assistance, for protection against the vagaries of life in capitalist economies. After World War II, these demands were at least partially accommodated. The state began trying to smooth the rough edges of the market economy without compromising the reign of profits as a guide to social priorities.

Three aspects of the expanded state role during the postwar boom years were crucial.

First, the government sought to reduce macroeconomic instability, hoping to avoid the kind of economic downturn which had threatened the survival of all the leading capitalist economies in the 1930s. Macropolicy sought quite modestly to moderate and guide the cycle, not to eliminate it, in the interests of political stability and profitability.

From the late 1940s to the mid-1960s, this effort succeeded. The results were felicitous: the first five postwar business-cycle recessions were more than two-thirds less severe – measured by the magnitude of their average-output slowdown – than business cycles during the comparable period of expansion after the turn of the century.[43]

Second, direct public support of business increased substantially at all levels of government – federal, state and local. This support became evident on both the tax and the expenditure sides of the ledger:

- On the expenditure side, government contracts provided guaranteed markets for many major corporations, especially in military production, while government subsidies favored many private businesses, particularly in nuclear power and agriculture. Even more important, government expenditures on transportation, communications, and other infrastructural facilities, as well as on education and research, lowered the costs of business for almost all private firms. Some of the resulting economic benefits were passed on to consumers through lower prices, but firms also profited from this public largesse.
- On the tax side, the government moved quickly and insistently to lower the tax burden on capital. This effect can be measured by an index constructed in joint work with Bowles and Weisskopf which we call

43 Based on data in Jeffrey Sachs, "The Changing Cyclical Behavior of Wages and Prices," *American Economic Review*, March 1980, Table 2.

Prosperity to stagnation in the postwar economy   63

Table 2.5. *Institutional axis III: construction and erosion of capital–
citizen accord*

	Phase Averages		
	1948-66	1966-73	1973-79
[1] Capital's share of tax burden (%)	37.5	28.5	26.4
[2] Personal transfer, share potential output (%)	5.9	8.6	10.7
[3] Rate change, index govt. bus. regulation (%)	3.8	16.1	10.3

Sources: Growth rates are annual rates, calculated as logarithmic growth rates. Levels are calculated as average annual levels.

[1] Share of total taxes falling on income from capital: Samuel Bowles, David M. Gordon, and Thomas E. Weisskopf, "Business Ascendancy and Economic Impasse: A Structural Retrospective on Conservative Economics, 1979–87," *Journal of Economic Perspectives*, Winter 1989, Data Appendix.

[2] Real personal transfer payments divided by potential output: Personal transfer payments, *National Income and Product Accounts*, Table 1.9:15, deflated by GNP price deflator, *Economic Report of the President*, 1991, Table B-3; potential output, from same source as in row [1].

[3] Rate of change, index of government expenditures on regulation of business: Same source as in row [1].

"capital's tax burden." It represents an estimate of the share of taxes at all levels of government which are borne by income from capital. Capital's tax burden had been heavy during World War II and continued to weigh mightily through the Korean War, reaching its post-WWII peak in 1951 of 45 percent of total taxes falling on capital income. It then fell continuously through the mid-1960s as government repeatedly sought to honor President Kennedy's prescription that "we are anxious to do everything we can to make your way easier" – dropping to only 33 percent in 1966. The average level during the boom years (row [1] of Table 2.5) was 37.5 percent.

Finally, the state committed itself to at least a margin of economic security for all Americans, whether aged, unemployed, or simply poor. Over most of the postwar period, up to 1966, unemployment insurance coverage grew, the size of the unemployment check relative to workers' take-home pay increased slightly, and the sum of social insurance, education, health, and general assistance programs inched upward as a fraction of GNP. These programs provided real benefits to many people but were nonetheless contained within the larger framework of capitalist priorities. For example, the distress of unemployment was reduced only by limited cash transfers to those who lost their jobs, not by structural changes guaranteeing everyone a job on a continuous basis.

The expanded state role thus provided benefits both to capital and to many citizens. Throughout the boom period, however, the central priority of profitability remained unchallenged. Charles Wilson, president of General Motors and President Eisenhower's designated secretary of defense, told his confirmation hearing in 1952 that "what was good for our country was good for General Motors, and vice versa."[44] Eric Goldman later reflected on the uproar which Wilson's comment provoked: "After all, was he not speaking precisely the feeling of generations of Americans who had labored . . . in the firm belief that what was good for their businesses was good for America, the land of business?"[45] As long as millions could benefit alongside business, the logic of profitability could continue to prevail.

But the bottom line was not to continue unchallenged for long.

As we saw in the previous section, several movements began during the 1960s to demand state cushions from the bumpy road of capitalist growth. As a result, fueled by expanding expenditures for Medicare, social security, and public assistance, transfer payments began to rise significantly in the mid-1960s. Row [2] in Table 2.5 charts this mounting burden of state expenditures, tracking the percentage of potential output committed to personal transfer payments at all levels of government. Averaging a modest and sustainable 5.9 percent during the boom years, the transfer share rose to 8.6 percent in 1966–73 and further to 10.7 percent in 1973–79 – nearly double its level in 1948–66. More and more citizens were insisting that their "entitlements" deserved at least as high a priority as government support for business.

A second challenge to the logic of profitability followed close behind. Beginning with occupational health-and-safety campaigns in the Oil, Chemical, and Atomic Workers Union and in the United Mine Workers, and equally with Ralph Nader's effective public mobilization around issues of consumer safety and product design, fueled by the notorious

---

44 Quoted in Eric F. Goldman, *The Crucial Decade and After: America, 1945–1960* (New York: Vintage, 1960), p. 239.
45 Ibid., p. 240.

Prosperity to stagnation in the postwar economy   65

Pinto exploding-gas-tank scandal, sustained by Love Canal and the periodic burning of the Cuyahoga River, a wide variety of movements emerged to challenge the hallowed identity of private greed and public virtue. The oldest of these movements – conservation – enjoyed a veritable rebirth and transformation in the late 1960s and early 1970s, sparking a series of popular and often militant campaigns demanding environmental protection, alternative energy sources, and a halt to nuclear power.

Although these movements were largely disconnected and focused on single issues, they had the combined effect of raising doubts about the primacy of private profitability in determining resource allocation and economic decision making. By the early 1970s, these several insurgencies had won a series of major legislative and legal victories, creating a sequence of agencies with major responsibility for corporate regulation – the National Highway Safety Commission (1970), the Occupational Safety and Health Administration (1970), the Environmental Protection Administration (1970), the Consumer Safety Administration (1972), the Mine Enforcement and Safety Administration (1973), and several others.

The increasing importance of such regulatory agencies is illustrated in row [3] of Table 2.5, which depicts the growth of an index of U.S. government regulatory expenses over the postwar period. After growing no more rapidly than real output during the boom years, government regulation took off in 1966–73 and continued its rapid growth in 1973–79.

The drive for government regulation pinched and business yelped. The government tried to ease the pain by continuing to lighten capital's tax burden; the share of taxes borne out of capital income (row [1]) fell further in 1966–73 and 1973–79. But this relief was not enough to salve the business community's discomfort. With mounting intensity beginning in the mid-1970s, corporations sought to roll back regulation and overcome citizen opposition. "We should cease to be patsies," one corporate executive urged at a series of management conferences in 1974–75, "and start to raise hell."[46]

The containment of intercapitalist rivalry

Large corporations in the United States emerged from World War II more powerful than ever. As the postwar period progressed, their power in-

46 Quoted in Leonard Silk and David Vogel, *Ethics and Profits: The Crisis of Confidence in American Business* (New York: Simon & Schuster, 1976), p. 67.

66   *D. M. Gordon*

Table 2.6. *Institutional axis IV: containment and intensification of
intercapitalist rivalry*

	Phase Averages		
	1948-66	**1966-73**	**1973-79**
[1] 200 largest firms' share industrial assets (%)	52.8	59.8	58.0
[2] Index of import competition (%)	5.6	8.6	10.3

Sources: Growth rates are annual rates, calculated as logarithmic growth rates. Levels
are calculated as average annual levels.

[1] Ratio of real imports to real GNP: *Economic Report of the President,* 1991, Table B-3.

[2] Share of industrial assets owned by largest 200 firms: *Statistical Abstract,* 1985,
Table 886, 1977, Table 923, and unpublished U.S. Bureau of the Census data.

creased – and their vulnerability to intercapitalist competition diminished. This protection against competition occurred both domestically
and internationally.

On the domestic front, large firms could use their monopoly or oligopoly positions to raise prices higher than would have prevailed in competitive markets. They could gain access to more favorable investment opportunities and use their funds to buy up more vulnerable competitors.

The indicator in row [1] of Table 2.6 illustrates one aspect of this
process. The largest 200 firms in the United States were able dramatically
to increase their ownership share of total industrial assets through the late
1960s, benefiting from both their general power and leverage throughout
the postwar years and an intense merger wave in the late 1960s: their
asset share increased from 47 percent in 1948 to 61 percent in 1971, with
the 1948–66 average of 52.8 percent increasing to 59.8 in 1966–73. The
largest corporations came more and more to dominate the economic
landscape, forming the core of what Harvard economist John Kenneth
Galbraith called the "new industrial state."[47]

For a time, at least, U.S. corporations were also able to enjoy considerable advantages over their foreign competitors. U.S. corporate size and
power enabled them to achieve economies of scale and to afford new
technology and product design while many foreign corporations lagged

47   *The New Industrial State* (Boston: Houghton-Mifflin, 1971), 2nd ed.

Prosperity to stagnation in the postwar economy   67

behind. The key role of the dollar and the flood of dollars circulating through the global economy provided ready markets for products made in the United States. And foreign competitors simply had difficulty penetrating U.S. domestic markets because of the scale and scope, as Harvard business historian Alfred D. Chandler, Jr., calls it, of U.S. corporations.[48] Through the boom period, as a result, imports averaged only 5.6 percent of GNP (row [2] of Table 2.6).

In the first decade and a half of the postwar period, in short, the great majority of large U.S. corporations did not have to worry much about price competition from rival suppliers of their product markets, and they could generally maintain a substantial margin of price over production cost. The containment of intercapitalist competition contributed to healthy balance sheets and high profits. By the early 1960s, however, new threats to the cozy position of the U.S. industrial giants began to loom on the horizon.

A first challenge came from the increasingly intense and effective competition waged by rival corporations in Europe and Japan. Having recovered from the devastation of World War II, and having built up their plant and equipment with the best of modern technology, these corporations were increasingly successful in competing with U.S. corporations – first in overseas markets and then also at home in the United States.

Imports had remained a low and constant or declining share of GDP over most of the postwar era. Around the mid-1960s, import penetration suddenly escalated. Between 1960 and 1970, imports rose from 4 to 17 percent of the U.S. market in autos, from 4 to 31 percent in consumer electronics, from 5 to 36 percent in calculating and adding machines, and from less than 1 to 5 percent in electrical components.[49] This import penetration showed up quickly in the aggregate data. As row [2] of Table 2.6 shows, the import share rose from 5.6 percent in 1948–66 to 8.6 percent in 1966–73 and then again to 10.3 percent in 1973–79.

But foreign competition was by no means the only challenge to the cozy oligopoly positions that had been enjoyed for so long by so many major U.S. corporations. A second challenge emerged from within the United States, in the form of growing domestic competition in many

---

48 *Scale and Scope: The Dynamics of Industrial Capitalism* (Cambridge, Mass.: Harvard University Press, 1990).

49 The industry data are from *Business Week,* June 30, 1980, p. 60, based on Commerce Department data.

industries. In part this growing competition could be attributed to the economic boom itself, which opened up new opportunities for "outsider" firms to break into markets previously controlled tightly by "insiders." And in part it was the result of increasingly effective antitrust activity on the part of a federal Justice Department pushed into action by a public growing more and more distrustful of big business.

In a major study of long-term trends in competition in the U.S. economy, economist William G. Shepherd concluded:

> The U.S. economy experienced a large and widely spread rise in competition during [the period from] 1958 [to] 1980. . . . Tight oligopoly still covers nearly one-fifth of the economy, but that share is down by half from 1958. Pure monopoly and dominant firms have shrunk to only about 5% of the economy, while the effectively competitive markets now account for over three-fourths of national income. Most of the shift appears to reflect three main causes: rising import competition, antitrust actions, and deregulation. Each has been important, but antitrust actions have had the largest influence.[50]

Row [1] of Table 2.6 shows the impact of this increased competition on the largest 200 firms' asset share: After a steady rise in their share of industrial assets through the early 1970s, the largest 200 firms' share actually declined some in the 1973–79 phase as new and rising giants began to challenge for market control.

U.S. corporations were thus pressured after the mid-1960s by increasingly intense product market competition and intercapitalist rivalry. Their ability to raise prices over costs to protect their profit margins, and their ability to close their own ranks against challenges from below, diminished apace.

The rise and decline of the SSA: profitability and accumulation

In a capitalist economy, two of the central barometers of the economy's vitality are provided by the level of profitability and the pace of accumulation. If the postwar economy had turned from prosperity to stagnation, this shifting dynamic should surely be evident in data on the rate of profit and the pace of accumulation.

50 William G. Shepherd, "Causes of Increased Competition in the U.S. Economy, 1939–80," *Review of Economics and Statistics,* November 1982, p. 624.

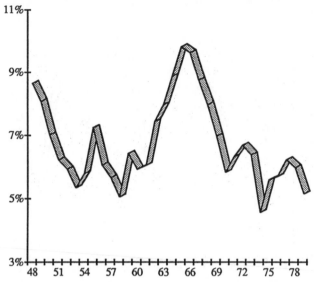

Figure 2.2. Declining profitability after the mid-1960s: net after-tax rate of profit, nonfinancial corporate business sector (NFCB).

The behavior of the (net) after-tax profit rate for U.S. corporate business is graphed in Figure 2.2. When the postwar U.S. social structure of accumulation was working well, profitability recovered from short-term recessions and achieved levels more or less comparable to its pre-recession peaks. Despite the depths of the 1957–58 and 1960–61 recessions, for example, the after-tax rate of corporate profits was far higher in 1965 than it had been in 1955, before these two recessions. After 1966, however, corporate profitability did not recover from the stresses of economic downturn. Following the recession of 1969–70, the after-tax profit-rate peak in 1972 was one-third lower than it had been in 1965. After the recession of 1974–75, once again, the after-tax profit-rate peak in 1977 had fallen below its 1972 peak. Operating through its normal cyclical mechanisms, *the U.S. economy was unable to reverse this process of decline by itself.*

The behavior of the (net) rate of capital accumulation by U.S. corporate business from 1951 to 1979 is graphed in Figure 2.3. This index measures the rate at which corporations are expanding their productive capital stock – one important determinant of the future productive potential of the U.S. economy. Like the rate of profit, the rate of capital

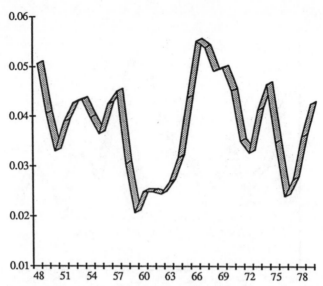

Figure 2.3. Stagnating accumulation after the mid-1960s: rate of growth of NFCB real net fixed nonresidential capital stock.

accumulation displays a pattern of significant cyclical fluctuations. The long-term trend in accumulation is not so clearly differentiated between the boom and the crisis periods as in the case of profitability. There is, however, an unmistakable downward trend in the accumulation rate after the mid-1960s; each cyclical peak and each cyclical trough after 1965 is lower than the previous one, just as in the case of profitability. As the pace of accumulation slowed, so did the productive potential of the economy.

Is there a link between the processes of institutional consolidation and decay outlined in the previous sections and the trends in profitability and accumulation sketched here? Bowles, Weisskopf, and I have been able to develop quantitative analyses which provide strong support for that connection.[51] The postwar SSA worked for U.S. capital as long as the several

51 Our most recent econometric analysis of U.S. corporate profitability is reported in Bowles, Gordon, and Weisskopf, "Business Ascendancy and Economic Impasse," Table 3. This model includes as explanatory variables seven quantitative indexes of capitalist power, which together reflect all four principal structures of the postwar SSA in the United States. Our regression (shown in row [3-1] of "Business Ascendancy") of the annual net after-tax rate of profit on variables accounts for 91 percent of the variance of U.S. profitability from 1955 to 1986. In a separate (unpublished) regression estimated for the period from 1955 to 1979, this same model accounts for 95

Prosperity to stagnation in the postwar economy   71

institutional foundations of its domination were effectively unchallenged. Once people began to challenge those power relations both at home and abroad, corporations could no longer enjoy the booming profits to which they had grown accustomed; stagnating investment was one of the perilous consequences.

THE COSTS OF KEEPING PEOPLE DOWN

> Even in the best state which society has yet reached, it is lamentable to think how great a proportion of all the efforts and talents in the world are employed in merely neutralizing one another. It is the proper end of government to reduce this wretched waste to the smallest possible amount, by taking such measures as shall cause the energies now spent by mankind in injuring one another or in protecting themselves against injury, to be turned to the legitimate employment of human faculties, that of compelling the powers of nature to be more and more subservient to physical and moral good.
>
> — John Stuart Mill[52]

percent of the variance of U.S. corporate profitability. Movements in the seven SSA variables account for 70 percent of the drop in the net after-tax rate of profit from the 1959–66 business cycle, when the profit rate reached its peak, to the 1973–79 cycle. (To determine the proportion of the decline in the net after-tax profit rate from 1959–66 to 1973–79 explained by different sets of independent variables, we used the same method described in our article "Hearts and Minds," Table 4.)

We have developed a parallel quantitative analysis of the slowdown in the pace of accumulation after the early 1970s in David M. Gordon, Thomas E. Weisskopf, and Samuel Bowles, "Power, Profits, and Investment: The Postwar Social Structure of Accumulation and the Stagnation of U.S. Net Investment since the Mid-1960s," New School for Social Research, Working Paper in Political Economy, No. 12, January 1993. Since profitability is a central determinant of investment, and since our SSA analysis helps illuminate the postwar trajectory of the rate of profit, we ought to be able to trace the influence of institutional consolidation and decline on investment *through* the mediating role of profitability. We find that an analysis of the investment slowdown which takes into account the erosion of the underlying institutional environment does a much better job of explaining annual movements in investment than one which ignores that environment. Through that analysis, for example, we find that the continuing erosion of capitalist power in the 1973–79 cycle accounts for fully three-fifths of the slowdown in investment from 1966–73 to 1973–79.

52 John Stuart Mill, *Principles of Political Economy* [1848] (London: Longmans, Green & Co., 1920), p. 979. I am grateful to Maurizio Franzini and Samuel Bowles for bringing this quote to my attention.

72   *D. M. Gordon*

If the stagnation of the U.S. economy after the mid-1960s had been purely the result of surprises or shocks, it might have been possible to adjust to the dislocations, fairly quickly steering the ship back on course within a relatively short period. But the institutional foundations of the SSA were enduring and relatively inflexible, making it difficult to shift course in midstream. Worse still, the postwar SSA built upon hierarchical relations of domination and subordination which could not so easily be abandoned.

Conflict and domination is generally more costly than cooperation and reciprocity. And once challenges to power begin to emerge, it is more likely than not that the powerful will respond – not by relinquishing it – but rather by extending and deepening their systems of control. If and when this course is chosen, it promotes tendencies toward the garrison state. An ever-increasing fraction of the nation's productive potential must be devoted simply to keeping the have-nots at bay.

These costs of keeping people down may be illustrated by a series of calculations of the scope and trends in what Bowles, Weisskopf, and I call "guard labor" and "threat labor."

In any society a significant number of people do not produce goods and services directly but rather enforce the rules – formal and informal, domestic and international – that govern economic life. The presence of some guard labor in an economy is hardly an indictment of an economic system: it is a fact of life that rules are necessary and that they do not enforce themselves. But some rules are harder to enforce than others, and some economic structures must rely more heavily on guard labor than others. In the workplace, for example, it takes large expenditures on surveillance and security personnel to enforce rules which workers often perceive as invasive, unfair, unnecessary, and oppressive.

It should come as no surprise, given the analysis of the preceding sections of this essay, that the amount of guard labor in the postwar U.S. economy was mammoth. We include the following enforcement activities in our estimates of guard labor – workplace supervisors, police, judicial, and corrections employees, private security personnel, the armed forces and civilian defense employees, and producers of military and domestic security equipment. By our estimates, for example, guard labor constituted fully 20 percent of nonfarm employment plus the armed forces in 1966.[53]

---

53   The full estimate of guard labor includes those in "supervisory occupations"; police, judicial, and corrections employees; private security guards; and military personnel on active duty, civilian employees of the Defense

Prosperity to stagnation in the postwar economy 73

Added to this burden is another category of unproductive labor in an inegalitarian society – the wasted activities of what we call "threat labor." As noted earlier, employers in conflictual workplaces rely on the threat of job dismissal to help intimidate their workers and extract greater labor intensity from them. The more hierarchical and conflictual the workplace, the more important the presence of this threat becomes. And the greater the reliance on this threat, the more important it becomes that unemployed workers clamor outside the workplace for jobs, making the threat of dismissal credible. We include three groups in our estimate of threat labor in the United States – the unemployed, "discouraged workers," and prisoners. Threat labor comprised another 6 percent of non-farm employment plus the armed forces in 1966.[54]

We can use these estimates of guard and threat labor to characterize the trajectories of institutional development in the postwar U.S. economy. To trace the evolution of the garrison state, I express these hierarchical

Department and those in defense-related employment. The data for those in supervisory occupations are based on the percentage of employees defined (in U.S. Department of Labor, *Dictionary of Occupational Titles* [Washington, D.C.: U.S. Government Printing Office, 1977], 4th ed.) as having "supervisory" or related "relations with people." Police, judicial, and corrections employees are drawn from U.S. Department of Justice, *Criminal Justice Statistics* (Washington, D.C.: U.S. Government Printing Office, various years); and *Historical Statistics,* numerous series. Data for private security guards are taken from *Statistical Abstract,* various years; and *Historical Statistics,* series D589, D591. Military personnel on active duty, civilian employees of the Defense Department, and those in defense-related employment are drawn from *Statistical Abstract,* 1989, p. 335. More detailed definitions, sources, and methods of our calculations, encompassing business cycle peaks from the late 1940s through the late 1980s, are available in a supplementary memorandum upon request from the present author.

54 The category of threat labor includes the unemployed; "discouraged workers" who would be unemployed if they had not dropped out of the labor force because they could not find work; and prisoners. The total number of unemployed are taken from *Economic Report,* 1990, Table C-33. The definition for the number of discouraged workers is drawn from *Statistical Abstract,* 1989, p. 395; data are based on U.S. Bureau of Labor Statistics, *Labor Force Statistics Derived from the Current Population Survey,* 1948–87, BLS Bulletin No. 2307, August 1988, Tables A-22, A-25. The number of prisoners is taken from U.S. Department of Justice, *Sourcebook of Criminal Justice Statistics, 1988* (Washington, D.C.: U.S. Government Printing Office, 1989), Table 6.31. As with the calculations on guard labor, more detailed definitions, sources, and methods for the estimates of threat labor are available in a supplementary memorandum upon request from the author.

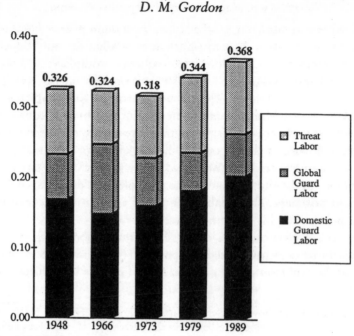

Figure 2.4. The costs of keeping people down: ratios of guard and threat labor to productive employment, 1948–89.

burdens as the ratio of guard and threat labor to all "productive" labor in the nonfarm economy – that is, all employment not devoted to guard activities. And I organize the data into three main categories: (1) "domestic guard labor," the sum of all "supervising" occupations as well as police, courts, corrections, and private guard employees; (2) "global guard labor," the sum of active-duty military personnel, civilian Pentagon employees, and defense-related employment; and (3) "threat labor," the sum of the unemployed, discouraged workers, and all federal and state prisoners.

Figure 2.4 plots these respective ratios for the postwar period at business-cycle peaks, extending the series through the end of the 1980s to anticipate a bit of the story outlined in the later essay by Bowles, Weisskopf, and myself. The graph traces the evolution of what could be fairly called a garrison state in the U.S. economy.

In 1948, for example, there were a total of nearly 33 people filling guard or threat roles for every 100 employed in "productive" slots – including 17 as domestic guard labor, 6.5 as global guard labor, and 9 as threat labor.

Prosperity to stagnation in the postwar economy 75

In the boom years from 1948 to 1966, the total burden of guard labor remained roughly constant, reflecting the consolidation of the postwar SSA. But some interesting changes in the composition of the garrison state took place. Because of the burdens and responsibilities of policing the world, on the one hand, the global guard labor ratio rose by 50 percent from 0.064 in 1948 to 0.10 in 1966. Because the carrot of the limited capital–labor accord rewarded some workers and allowed production relations to function effectively in some (limited) sectors without relying so heavily on either supervision or the threat of dismissal, on the other hand, the domestic guard labor ratio and threat labor ratio both diminished slightly, with the domestic guard labor ratio declining from 0.17 in 1948 to 0.15 in 1966 and the threat labor ratio falling from 0.09 to 0.08.

After the onset of stagnation in the mid-1960s, the total relative size of the garrison state again remained roughly constant – reflecting in part the inertial character of such hierarchical institutions. Again, however, some important changes in its internal composition occurred. Responding to friction at the workplace and the initial erosion of the limited capital–labor accord, corporations intensified their supervision of workers, with the domestic guard labor ratio increasing back to 0.16 in 1973. Corporations also became somewhat more dependent on the threat of dismissal, with the threat labor ratio increasing from 0.08 in 1966 to 0.09 in 1973.

Then, in the period of what we call mounting "political stalemate," the system came to rely more and more heavily on guard labor to try to beat back challenges to corporate power. The global guard burden continued to decline somewhat, in the period of the wind down from the Vietnam conflict, but domestic guard and threat activities more than compensated for that contraction. The domestic guard labor ratio increased once again, rising from 0.16 in 1973 to 0.18 in 1979. And the threat labor ratio grew as well, climbing from 0.09 in 1973 to 0.11 in 1979.

During the 1980s, as Bowles, Weisskopf, and I argue in our subsequent essay, right-wing economics relied even more heavily on direct assertion of hierarchical power in an effort to restore capitalist control. In the 1979–89 cycle, as a result, the garrison state increased its relative size even more. Remilitarization resulted in the global guard labor ratio rising back to 0.06. Increasing reliance on the stick in production generated a further increase in the domestic guard labor ratio from 0.18 in 1979 to 0.20 in 1989. And although the unemployment rate fell slightly (see row [5] of Table 2.1), the threat labor ratio remained roughly constant as the relative ranks of both discouraged workers and prisoners swelled.

76   *D. M. Gordon*

By 1989, after more than two decades of stagnation and crisis, the garrison state had swelled to gargantuan proportions. We estimate that roughly 34 million Americans were engaged in guard and threat labor in 1989 – over a third more people, for example, than all those employed in manufacturing industries at all occupational levels.

This is not an easy kind of economy to transform. Those who are used to exercising power over subordinates do not easily or willingly relinquish it. Or at least these are some of the lessons we might draw from the preceding analysis.

The American Century depended on the open and aggressive assertion of hierarchical power. The American Century began to ebb when workers, citizens, and foreign buyers and sellers began to challenge that power. U.S. corporations tried for a time to roll back those challenges. As we show in our later essay on the 1980s, however, the right-wing and business offensive ultimately failed either to restore underlying capitalist power or to revive the stagnant economy.

As the American Century continues to sputter to its ignominious conclusion, it is surely time for us to begin to organize our economy on more democratic foundations. Our joint analysis of the waste embedded in the postwar U.S. economy – the waste of misdirected and underutilized resources as well as of garrison employment – persuades us that a successful and effective program for economic recovery can advance rather than suppress the values of democracy, community, and fairness.[55] The American Century is not an experience which many of us should pine nostalgically to repeat.

55   See Bowles, Gordon, and Weisskopf, *After the Waste Land,* Chs. 11–14.

[5]

Sinking Ships?
Liberal Theorists on the American Economy

JULIE FROUD, COLIN HASLAM, SUKHDEV JOHAL,
JEAN SHAOUL and KAREL WILLIAMS

In the Asia-Pacific region, the conditions and consequences of East Asian success have understandably attracted more attention than the causes and implications of North American failure. In the American case, any failure must be relative when the US remains a bloc-sized market and the only surviving superpower. Thus, for Asians the US figures economically as an export opportunity and socially, for puritans like Lee Kuan Yew, as a warning about decadence. The discussion among Americans is altogether more interesting and this article focuses on the part of that discussion which takes the form of a debate about national competitiveness among American liberal democrats like Magaziner, Reich, Tyson and Krugman. This article analyses their debate and looks behind the differences of position which separate these protagonists to make two points about their shared *a priori*. First, it observes a problem shift within the American debate as the old 1980s problem of national uncompetitiveness is jettisoned in the 1990s; all the liberals now agree that Americans are no longer in the same boat and some of them are in sinking ships while others sail on serenely. Second, there is no policy solution corresponding to the new 1990s problem; the protagonists have moved from an industrial policy fix in the 1980s to an end of policy era in the 1990s where the question for American liberals is whether and how the political system can absorb the stresses created by increasing inequality.

OVERVIEW

The thoughtless who never doubt
Meet the thoughtful who never act.
They doubt, not in order to come to a decision but
To avoid a decision. Their heads
They use only for shaking. With anxious faces
They warn the crew of sinking ships that water
is dangerous.

Brecht, *In Praise of Doubt*

Julie Froud, Jean Shaoul and Karel Williams, University of Manchester; Colin Haslam and Sukhdev Johal, Royal Holloway, University of London

Asia Pacific Business Review, Vol.3, No.1, Autumn, 1996, pp.54–72
PUBLISHED BY FRANK CASS, LONDON

The American competitivity debate raises an Asian Pacific issue about whether and how the problems of the American economy relate to trade and intensifying regional and global competition. More broadly, the debate is a series of 'takes' on what is happening to the USA, why that country is in economic decline and what (if anything) can be done about it. Our article aims to observe and analyze this debate; quite deliberately, it is a commentary on, rather than an intervention in, the debate. The reading which we provide is more discourse analysis than academic review article; it focuses in depth on the *a priori* in a small number of representative texts rather than broadening the field of view by summarizing results and conclusions in a large number of texts.

Our analysis constructs the competitivity 'debate' around a set of authors united by a common social and political identity and a series of their texts which are separated by discursive differences. The authors are Robert Reich, Ira Magaziner, Laura d'Andrea Tyson and Paul Krugman. All are liberal Democrats with backgrounds in the same elite institutions of the East and West Coasts. Three of the four authors are academics who have variously held chairs at MIT, Harvard, Berkeley and Stanford; Magaziner is an ex-consultant who formerly worked for the Boston Group. Collectively, they have become President Clinton's policy intellectuals with three of the four occupying privileged official positions; Reich is Secretary of State for Labor, Magaziner is officially in charge of health reform and Tyson is effectively chief economic adviser. Krugman does not hold office but is hardly an outsider in these circles; his briefing book on the American economy was commissioned by the liberal *Washington Post*.

If the authors share an identity, their texts are interestingly different and, to demonstrate this point, our article concentrates on four book-length studies. Robert Reich's *The Work of Nations* (Reich, 1993: 329) and Laura d'Andrea Tyson's *Who's Bashing Whom* (Tyson, 1994: 296), written just before their authors went into government, represent mainstream attempts to reformulate the competitivity problem for the 1990s. Usefully, the two texts represent different genres: Reich is an easy reading, one big idea text for the airport bookstand, while Tyson is an academic monograph burdened with tables, statistics and references. As a first point of reference, we also include Magaziner and Reich's *Minding America's Business* (Magaziner and Reich, 1982); the difference of the texts of the 1990s can be measured against this classic statement of the competitivity problem from the early 1980s. Krugman's recent work provides a second obvious point of reference; his polemical articles in *Foreign Affairs* (Krugman, 1994a, 1994b) argue that the competitivity problem is meaningless and his book *The Age of Diminished Expectations* (Krugman, 1994c) attempts to provide an alternative more economically orthodox problem definition.

Our analysis and argument in this article raises questions about Krugman's thoughtlessness and makes an observation about Reich and Tyson's thoughtfulness. The competitivity debate was inaugurated by non economists; Magaziner and Reich used the discourse of business policy to argue the case for industrial policy. Krugman represents retaliation by orthodox economics; he attacks the competitivity problem as a way of diminishing the discourses which have appropriated issues which are properly the prerogative of economics. The result in Krugman's case is the intellectual equivalent of talk radio complete with the obligatory abusive references to those who 'don't know what they're talking about' (Krugman, 1994c: 252). But, paradoxically Krugman does not so much damage the competitivity problem, which he attacks, as raise questions about the economic discourse, which he champions; the questions arise because Krugman fails to read texts carefully, fails to engage the world with powerful empirics and fails to formulate an interesting alternative problem.

If Reich and Tyson are altogether more thoughtful and interesting to read, our aim is coolly to observe their (shifts of) position rather than defend their competitivity problem against Krugman. A comparison of these early 1990s texts with Magaziner and Reich shows a large and unnoticed slippage in the object of debate; the old problem of the 1980s about the national uncompetitiveness of the USA is resolved by the early 1990s into a new sectional problem about different social groups within the USA moving along different trajectories. This shift in problem definition undermines the distinctiveness of the liberal democrat position; as Reich and Tyson's problem definition changes, so the old 1980s fix of industrial policy for national regeneration becomes irrelevant. In terms of policy, Reich and Tyson have embraced a new quietism and passivity which is indistinguishable from Krugman's explicit policy of benign neglect. What the competitivity debate now signifies is an end of policy phase where the liberal democratic intelligentsia of America collectively abandons the idea of active intervention which would make some difference to the majority of the population.

The article which argues this reading is organized in a fairly straightforward way into two main sections; the first of these sections deals mainly with the competitivity problem definition while the second deals mainly with policy solutions and fixes. In each section we begin by considering Krugman's intervention as an index of the problems of orthodox economics before we move on to consider the mainstream competitivity literature. In considering the competitivity literature we emphasize slippage over time and difference between texts before demonstrating convergence and shared presuppositions.

THE END OF NATIONAL COMPETITIVENESS

The village of Hollywood was planned according to the notion
People in these parts have of heaven. In these parts
They have come to the conclusion that God,
Requiring a heaven and hell, didn't need to
Plan two establishments but
Just the one: heaven. It
Serves the unprosperous, unsuccessful as hell.

Brecht, *Hollywood Elegies*

SINKING SHIPS?   57

The Brechtian perception of America as the one place which could serve
as heaven for the rich and hell for the poor was denied in the classic 1980s
definition of competitiveness which put the emphasis on the prosperity that
all American citizens could share by virtue of their nationality. According
to the definition proposed by the Berkeley Round Table on the International
Economy in 1983, 'our economic competitiveness... (is) our ability to
produce goods and services that meet the test of international markets while
our citizens enjoy a standard of living that is both rising and sustainable' .
It is this 1980s national definition which Krugman engages without noticing
that Reich and Tyson have moved on to discuss sectional trajectories.

When Krugman presents himself as the defender of economic science, it
is worth remembering that the history of the sciences includes both the
triumphs of reason over ignorance and the crusades of the righteous against
alternative knowledges. In general, the righteous crusades are fiercest where
orthodox knowledge cannot deliver on its scientistic pretensions and their
outcome is inconclusive but revealing of orthodox habits of thought; it is the
orthopaedic surgeon who can neither understand nor cure low back pain
who righteously and ineffectually denounces the quackery and alternatives
of the osteopath and the chiropractor. Much inter-discursive dispute in the
human sciences takes the form of righteous crusades and so it is with
Krugman's crusade against competitivity which does not vindicate the
power of economics as raise doubts about the discourse's capacity to read
and to deliver empirical refutation.

Krugman's problems about reading are not an individual lapse. Donald
McCloskey may be an honourable exception, but most economists accept a
naive positivism which devalues text and reading as a problem because all
texts can be decomposed into hypothesis/elements. Thus, Krugman's
reading of competitiveness relies on the two devices of conflation and
translation which economists use to turn complex texts into simple refutable
hypotheses. The classic Berkeley economic definition is conflated with
President Clinton's political claim that each nation is 'like a big corporation
competing in the global market place' (Krugman, 1994a: 29). This
conflation allows Krugman to make some sharp points about the differences
between companies and countries without ever having to admit that the
identity of the two terms is not strictly implied by the classic definition. The
other device of translation allows Krugman to reinterpret the classic
definition as a series of refutable economic hypotheses which turn out to be
fallacious; thus competitivity means 'a country's economic fortunes are
largely determined by its success on world markets' (Krugman, 1994: 30)
although yet again this position is not strictly implied by the classic
definition. The refutation is then administered by a combination of first year
economic theory and basic arithmetic as when Krugman argues that foreign
trade can only reduce standards of living where the terms of trade
deteriorate substantially which they have not in the United States
(Krugman, 1994a, 32–3).

Just like Friedman in an earlier generation, Krugman aims to win every controversy by drawing his reader into the circle of orthodox economic assumptions. Unfortunately, in this case the empirical knockout depends on arithmetic whose proof or disproof value is limited. In communication with other economists, Krugman would usually use algebra; but this cannot be used to communicate with non-economists who either will not understand or will understand too clearly that modern economics is an exercise in rigorously developing the implications of highly contestable assumptions. When attempting to refute competitivity for a general audience, Krugman retreats onto arithmetic which allows him to make unkind points about other people's 'careless arithmetic' and so-called experts who do not 'know how to look up a standard industrial statistic' (Krugman, 1994b: 199). The sharp rejoinder must be that Krugman knows only how to look up the one ratio which always proves his point that the problem does not matter or matters less than his opponents make out. Thus the impact of international competitiveness is limited by the fact that exports account for only 10 percent of GNP and therefore 'national living standards are overwhelmingly determined by domestic factors' (Krugman, 1994a: 34).

The force of this arithmetical 'proof' is weakened by the observation that the same per cent of GNP device is used in Krugman's book to diminish other problems such as the US trade deficit, budget deficit and the hidden liability from the savings and loans crisis (Krugman, 1994c: 48–9). The choice of GNP as denominator in his preferred ratio does not tell us that the problem does not matter, it tells us what we already know: no event or process, up to and including the impact of railroads on the nineteenth century American economy, looks to be important if we evaluate it in this way and implicitly isolate it from the rest of the economy. Many of these diminished events will be of massive importance to relevant subsectors of the economy; in the US case, for example, imports account for 40 per cent of domestic production in durable tradeable goods. Furthermore, the national aggregate denominator of GNP is irrelevant in principle if, as Reich now argues, we are in a post national era where various sections and social groups within the one nation are moving along different trajectories determined by differences in their competitiveness.

It is hard to see how Krugman misses this basic shift in the problem definition of competitivity because the end of nationality is the one big idea in Reich's *The Work of Nations*. Reich's book begins in the first paragraph by announcing the end of 'national corporations' and 'national economies' and the introduction ends by burying 'the challenge of national competitiveness' (Reich, 1993: 8). This message is driven home with the watery image that 'Americans are no longer in the same economic boat' (Reich, 1993). Krugman's oversight about this shift is all the more difficult to understand because his book accepts and documents the facts which Reich in the 1990s is trying to explain. As Krugman demonstrates, while the real incomes of average Americans have stagnated, the American rich have got richer and the American poor have got poorer: the poorest fifth saw their incomes decline by ten per cent in the 1980s while the incomes of the top one per cent of families multiplied (Krugman, 1994c: 24–5). However, for Krugman, this is not a problem for economics because, after discounting the possibility that the rich, like the Sheriff of Nottingham, rob the poor, he confidently attributes the increasing poverty of the poor to a pathology which is 'in the domain of sociology'(Krugman, 1994c: 28).

Against this background, Reich deserves the intellectual credit for trying to relate the divergence of sectional experience and the growing contrast between rich and poor to one set of structural variables. He also deserves the credit for trying to integrate recent developments, such as the entrance of low wage Asian competitors, into his scenario of internationally relevant structural developments. In this respect, it is interesting to note that the more conservative Lester Thurow continues to represent the process of international competition as one of competition between different forms of advanced country, high wage capitalism. According to Thurow, the contest will be between Anglo-Saxon capitalism and the communitarian capitalism of Japan or Germany in a world effectively divided into triad blocs. Thurow predicts that in the next generation Europe will win a contest between established players, whereas Reich believes that the nature of the contest has already been changed by the entrance of new players, especially Asian players.

According to Reich, high value production is replacing high volume production which is being globally relocated in a world where 'almost anyone could undertake high volume standardized production' (Reich, 1993: 70). High wage countries, like the United States, can hold their own in high value product lines like speciality steels and chemicals and in services such as product design, marketing and consultancy which all meet unique customer needs. But 'high volume standardized production continues its ineluctable move to where labour is cheapest and most accessible around the world' (Reich, 1993: 70). Reich's scenario represents a recognisable variant on the end of mass production as announced by Piore and Sabel (Piore and Sabel, 1984). The difference is that our destination is not a local future in the form of industrial districts but a global future in the form of webs which often have their production facilities in Latin America or South East Asia (Reich, 1993: 171).

The result according to Reich is an institutional transformation of the US which in due course sends different social groups along different trajectories. The old order was dominated by 'core corporations'; these 'large hierarchical entities directed from the top down and acting en masse' were capable of generating long term employment at decent wages for white collar and blue collar America. The new order instead generates 'webs'; these centre on an elite of creative teams which identify and solve problems with everything else subcontracted in a way that threatens blue collar and junior white collar America because 'routine producers in the US ... are in direct competition with millions of routine producers elsewhere in other nations' who are prepared to work for much lower wages (Reich, 1993: 89,100,209). The institutional transformation thus creates winners and losers and sends different social groups along different trajectories of affluence and immiseration determined by 'the value that the world places on the work we do on ... our skills and insights' (Reich, 1991). The losers are the routine producers who account for around one quarter of the workforce and the winners are the creative 'symbolic analysts' in the 'fortunate fifth' who live by the skills of brokering, identifying and solving problems. The structural forces which represent disaster and a 'declining standard of living' for the routine producers represent opportunity for the symbolic analysts who are 'becoming ever more valuable in the world economy' as they 'are successfully selling their insights around the world' (Reich, 1993: 9).

Reich never provides the evidence which would sustain his vision of this new economic order. He presents almost no statistical evidence except on income distribution and, where Krugman chooses ratios that 'prove' his point, Reich prefers homiletic examples that illustrate his point; thus, we are told that the Pontiac Le Mans (nee Opel Kadett) was designed in Germany, assembled in Korea and sold in the United States without any information as to whether the case is representative of the auto business. More generally, Reich's book works by interpretative wrap and assertive identification so that a crucial category like 'symbolic analyst' is not a concept defined in a precise system of differences but a hold all crammed full of examples which include the denizens of Wall Street, Hollywood and Silicon Valley because they all live by 'manipulating symbols'. Against this background we would make two critical points: first, Reich's semiotics which present the symbolic analysts as the deserving rich are in themselves extraordinarily interesting; second, Reich's empirical claim that the symbolic analysts are doing well in the global economy is contradicted by the relevant evidence on high technology sector in Tyson's book.

Reich does not present the symbolic analysts as a meritocratic elite. As a class, their 'high incomes are more attributable to the good fortune of being reared in symbolic analysis households.... rather than ... unique talent or tolerance for hard work'; the symbolic analyst moves from comfortable suburb to affluent exurb in Reich's book, rather than *From Log Cabin To White House* as in Garfield's book. Nevertheless, social criticism is disarmed by Reich's insistence that this class of the increasingly affluent are the deserving rich because their reward depends on 'the value they add to the global economy through their skills and insights'. This impression of just reward is reinforced by the emphasis on symbolic analysis as 'creative problem solving' where 'the struggle over complex problems yields new insights and approaches relevant to ever more complex problems'. Reich does not give enough attention to the obvious anomalies where rich rewards reflect something other than insight; he does note the case of financiers who live by engineering the ownership changes of late capitalism; but he does not calculate how many of America's symbolic analysts operate in naturally sheltered sectors like law and accountancy or benefit from cost plus government contracts; nor does he count how many symbolic analysts operate in sectors like computer software and pharmaceuticals, where property rights inflate their incomes by allowing them to sell cheap product at fancy prices (Reich, 1993: 251, 255, 292).

Because Reichian semiotics presents the rich as deserving competitors rather than a structurally fortunate sheltered group, he predicts 'it is likely that Americans will continue to excel at symbolic analysis'. In his vision of the future a privileged high quality American supply intersects with an infinitely elastic global demand for symbolic analysts. The supply is guaranteed because America provides a high quality education for its fortunate children who can join existing agglomerations of symbolic analysts in Wall Street or Hollywood which provide the best opportunities for 'cumulative, shared learning'. At the same time, there is an infinite elasticity of demand for symbolic analysts because 'the global economy imposes no particular limits upon the number of Americans who can sell symbolic analytic services worldwide' so that even if all of the routine producers in America retrained as symbolic analysts 'real wages would still move steadily upwards' (Reich, 1993: 224–6, 247). These wild claims can hardly be substantiated and indicate an unconscious chauvinism which saturates much American discussion of Asian competition: we are asked to believe that Koreans or Chinese, who are already capable of assembling manufactures with cheap indigenous labour, will prefer in the long term to buy in expensive American labour as a way of obtaining design, marketing and financial services which they cannot replicate. Such hubris is not only unedifying but also implausible given the record of Japanese and European competition against the Americans in high technology.

Reich claims that America's symbolic analyst zones are 'wondrously resilient' because America's analysts 'are, by and large, succeeding in the world economy'; and, on Reich's classification, the class of symbolic analysts explicitly includes 'research scientists and engineers' (Reich, 1993: 177, 208, 240). Tyson's book about the trade performance of America's knowledge intensive high technology sector provides relevant evidence because this sector, as she defines it, employs one third of all US scientists and engineers in activities which are often exposed to international competition (Tyson, 1994: 35).

On the Guerriri and Miller classification, the high tech sector includes speciality chemicals and pharmaceuticals, power generating and electrical machinery, data processing and electronic office machinery, telecomms and electronic components as well as aircraft and scientific instruments. Tyson argues that the composition of economic activity and trade does matter. The high technology industries are inherently valuable because these are high value added activities which pay high wages; they are also R and D intensive in a way which generates externalities and spill over effects which cascade into the rest of the economy. Against this background, she describes how America is losing out in the triad competition between the established high wage players. USA, Europe and Japan together account for 75 per cent of global exports of high technology exports. But the American firms which once dominated high tech production and trade are now (like the Europeans) losing share: between 1980 and 1990, America's share of global high tech production declined by 11 per cent and Japan's increased by 59 per cent. Tyson, therefore concludes that 'Japan's growing ascendancy in technology intensive industries is a particular cause for concern' (Tyson, 1994: 10–11, 21, 53).

Tyson's book is dominated by a series of case studies of high technology trade which take up 200 pages in a 300 page book: in four substantial chapters the case studies cover cellular phones and super computers, semi conductors, commercial aircraft, video cassette recorders and High Definition TV. The remorselessly detailed narratives are a powerful device which build up the impression that foreign practices in the form of structural differences and trade barriers have inflicted 'substantial long term injury on American producers'. They also show by example how foreign governments and firms are willing to 'protect and promote' their strategic industries. The implication is that, as Tyson argues at the end of her semi conductor case study, 'if the United States fails to choose the semi conductor industry as a winner, American producers may well become long-run losers in the rigged game of international competition' (Tyson, 1994: 13, 194). And this kind of conclusion is supported by many well told stories about foreigners who did not play fair and blocked the products of the American good guys with established low cost positions. Thus, Motorola, the world's technical and cost leader in beeper pagers and mobile phones, was frustrated in the Japanese market by a variety of expedients including technical standards which prevented Motorola's cellular users from using their phones in the Tokyo-Nagoya area. Cray supercomputers were obstructed by the ability of Japanese manufacturers of large computers to sell their computers at a loss to public agencies which were willing to purchase technically inferior machines.

These are good stories but they raise almost as many questions as they answer. Tyson focuses on trade injury and largely ignores the decline of domestic military demand and effect of the end of the Cold War on American high tech production volumes and competitiveness. She also neglects the 'who is us' question which is more than relevant when the Motorola beepers which the Japanese blocked were designed and manufactured in Malaysia. But, most important of all, her economic explanation of why the high tech sector is valuable does not fit her own evidence which suggests a rather different social explanation.

Those interested in this issue should turn back from the case studies to the introductory chapters and specifically to the tables which show the economic characteristics of selected high technology industries in terms of value added per employee and their social characteristics in terms of employment of scientists and engineers (Tyson, 1994: 36–7). Examination of the value added table shows that the supposedly distinctive high value added characteristics of high technology industries are largely imaginary. The issue of value added productivity in high tech is raised by Krugman

(1994a: 37) in an attack on Magaziner and Reich; on this point we would agree with his arithmetic but dispute his economist's attribution of high productivity to capital intensity. In our view, the conditions of high value added productivity in high tech are heterogeneous; generally, value added productivity is mediocre in high tech except in those industries or businesses which have high flow techniques like chemicals, or legally protected property rights like pharmaceuticals. Because the high tech sector includes such activities, where productivity is typically twice as high as in the rest of manufacturing, value added per worker in all of high tech is 1/3rd higher than in manufacturing as a whole. But much of the rest of the high tech sector, like aircraft or scientific instruments, is strictly average or nothing special in terms of value added per employee. The high tech activities which differ in terms of value added productivity are however united by their social characteristics and a common composition of employment. Because the high tech activities are generally knowledge intensive, the high tech sector as a whole employs 85 scientists and engineers per 1,000 employees, which is twice as many as in manufacturing as a whole. The real difference is social not economic; the high tech sector as a whole has mediocre value added productivity but does employ more 'people like us', people whom Reich would call symbolic analysts.

There is an obvious difference of style and content between Reich who writes for the airport bookstand and Tyson who writes for the academic library. But, perhaps the difference is less than it seems, for, as we have observed, Reich and Tyson are talking about much the same thing. The difference is that Reich asserts that the symbolic analyst people are doing well whereas Tyson establishes that the high tech sectors are doing badly. In both cases the problem of national competitivity is displaced into sectional experience and signifies a social preference for people like us wrapped in a peculiar rhetoric about their justified rewards and high productivity. This hardly looks like a promising basis for policy formulation.

THE END OF POLICY?

> *The houses in Hell, too, are not all ugly.*
> *But the fear of being thrown onto the street*
> *Wears down the inhabitants of the villas no less than*
> *The inhabitants of the shanty towns*
> Brecht, *On Thinking about Hell*

The pessimistic Brechtian perception was that the insecurities attendant upon a divided society would undermine the democratic form of American politics. We will in due course consider the optimism of all our liberal democrat authors about the political implications of an increasingly divided society. But first we will consider the narrower and more technical question about the forms of economic policy which correspond to their current problem definitions. Here again, we will begin by considering Krugman and then briefly introduce Magaziner and Reich's work of the 1980s before establishing that all the texts of the 1990s by Krugman as well as Reich and Tyson converge on non-intervention and the end of economic policies which would make any difference to the majority of Americans.

In Krugman's reading, exaggeration of the policy threat posed by Clinton's house intellectuals is as fundamental to his intervention as the attempt to diminish their problem. On his account, the policy threat of the 1980s was 'a comprehensive industrial policy', as advocated by Magaziner and Reich; and the threat of the 1990s is 'strategic trade' policy which makes the unfair practices of the foreigners, as described by Tyson, into a model for American action. This tells us something about Krugman's motivations: in 'proving my point' (1994b), he protests against the justification of deviation from free trade by the illegitimate use of the so-called 'new theory of international trade' which he partly authored. But this tells us little about the world because Krugman is absurd when he claims that Clinton intellectuals like Reich and Tyson are as much of a threat in the 1990s as Laffer, Wanniski and the other supply-siders of the 1980s. The Clinton administration favours free trade not strategic trade or managed trade; this is an administration which has enlarged free trade by brokering a new GATT agreement, signing the NAFTA and bullying the Chinese into respecting intellectual property rights. Furthermore, as Krugman admits, industrial policy has simply not happened; Clinton's 1993 package of industrial subsidies and technological initiatives was tokenism. Krugman's explanation is that 'the political system has no appetite for a really major experiment' (1994c). He does not notice that industrial policy is more fundamentally intellectually obsolete because it is the form of intervention that corresponds to the old 1980s problem of uncompetitivity which is now superseded.

This point about the obsolescence of the old form of intervention can be demonstrated by turning to Magaziner and Reich's 1982 book where the policy prescription of industrial policy was derived from a characteristically 1980s style problem definition. Magaziner and Reich constructed their intellectual object through the categories of the discourse of business policy. 'Low wage businesses', such as shoes, clothing and electronics assembly were inexorably migrating to the developing countries and attempts to remain in these businesses were self-defeating because the USA's 'competitive position in low wage businesses will not improve'. But in 'complex factor cost businesses' the competition was 'primarily from developed countries' and here American firms could build competitive cost positions through investment in R and D, applications engineering and sophisticated marketing. According to Magaziner and Reich, these businesses in the aggregate accounted for 'more than half' of American manufacturing output and 'the majority' of American exports. More specifically, they listed industries such as commodity steel, motor bikes and autos and colour tv where they argued that 'certain businesses within these industries are salvageable and capable of being restored to competitive health' (Magaziner and Reich, 77, 87, 103, 106, 195).

Magaziner and Reich's solution of industrial policy was coherent with this problem definition. On the basis of case studies of steel, colour tv and an 'electro mechanical capital good', they argued that the primary, rectifiable cause of uncompetitiveness was defensive, reactive business strategy; thus, their chapter on colour tv detailed the past miscalculations of American management but concluded 'aggressive strategies are still possible for the three remaining US companies (in colour TV) if they have learned from past mistakes'. In this context, industrial policy was to play a secondary, reinforcing role: it would support aggressive management strategies in established and growing complex factor cost businesses by 'sharing risk, encouraging R and D and promoting rapid investment' (Magaziner and Reich, 167, 368). Where low wage business were inexorably declining, industrial policy would assist the 'reallocation' of capital and labour resources to the growing sectors which Magaziner and Reich assumed would be large enough to absorb the displaced resources. In the world of the 1990s, where Korea is the largest exporter of colour TVs and China has already overtaken Korea as the largest producer of colour TVs, Magaziner and Reich's 1982 vision of the future is passe. And industrial policy will not make a come back because nobody now believes it can be used to save and grow half or more of the American industrial base.

After industrial policy, the liberal Democratic economic policy interventions for the 1990s can be ranged across a fairly short continuum which ranges from explicit non-intervention, through whistling in the dark to intervention in special cases where it does not make much real difference. Krugman, Reich and Tyson neatly illustrate the three remaining possibilities: Krugman explicitly argues for doing nothing; Reich's policy of investment in training is whistling in the dark; and Tyson's 'cautious activist' trade policy represents casuistry about the special case. In all three texts it is important to emphasize that the end of policy recommendation is the corollary of a shift in the problem definition which in Krugman takes the form of a broadening into the problem of productivity just as in Reich and Tyson it takes the form of a narrowing onto sectional rather than national issues.

We have already argued that Krugman's refutation of competitivity fails because he does not represent the object of attack precisely and does not present decisive empirical counter evidence. In the next stage of our argument we will argue that he fails to displace competitivity with a different and more interesting problem. Krugman's preference for productivity slow-down as his new problem is fairly predictable. His preference is shaped by the orthodox economic concept of production as the combination of factor inputs to produce output and an earlier generation's empirical discovery that long-run economic growth depended on increases in 'efficiency' rather than the application of more inputs. Furthermore, the orthodox discourse provides Krugman with a ready made arithmetical ratio which measures efficiency as increases in output per unit of input; in the American case the arithmetic shows a productivity slow down from 2.5 per cent per annum rates of growth in the 1950s and 1960s to 1.26 per cent per annum rates in the 1970s and 1980s. If Krugman has an orthodox measure, it is not so clear that he has an alternative problem to competitivity because he and economics do not know what caused, or how to cure, productivity slow down: 'Why did it happen? And what can we do about it?' The answer to both is the same: 'We don't know'. Strictly, therefore, what Krugman has is a problem without any corresponding solution; productivity is the 'single most important factor affecting our economic well being' but 'it is not a policy issue because we are not going to do anything about it' (Krugman, 1994c: 18, 22).

Krugman does not establish the novelty of these positions in relation to earlier productivity discourse because, like many other economists, he is not interested in the history of discourse. If we reinstate this missing historical context, then we can see that Krugman's agnosticism represents a kind of dismal first. The problem of low productivity has a fifty year history and dates from the late 1940s when the Europeans first had to contemplate facing America under free trade rules. The 1950s reports of the Anglo American Council on Productivity on Britain's lag behind America are the discursive prototype for all those later reports by fearful and unsuccessful nations including the Americans who by the 1980s were comparing themselves unfavourably with Japan. For thirty years, successive reports followed the AACP model by fusing two discourses in a division of labour: economics would provide the measures of the productivity gap using the techniques pioneered by Rostas and others; while another discourse, classically a discourse of management, would identify the factor x whose presence in the more successful country caused high productivity and whose absence caused low productivity. Thus, the problem of low productivity was associated with a politics of emulating the more successful: in the 1950s the British firms were encouraged to adopt American management accounting and materials handling; just as, in the 1980s, the Americans were encouraged to adopt JIT, TQC, team working and MITI type industrial policy. It is easy to rubbish this approach: the efficiency measures were dubious, the identification of factor x was speculative and the politics of becoming somewhere else was always utopian. But, from our point of view, the more important point is that Krugman rejects the traditional division of labour between economics and another discourse so that he is left with the economic measure which was less than half of the original problem-solution couplet. Historically, this redefines the role and status of economics which no longer hopes to help fix the problem as a policy discourse but aims to observe the problem as a commentary discourse.

Commentary is not quite the end of policy because, like those other commentators who write newspaper editorials, Krugman knows what to do even without detailed analysis. The secret is a standard which can be applied to each new case or set of events; and in Krugman the standard is making the world more like economic theory. This point emerges most clearly in Krugman's various positions on the labour market. His attack on competitivity opens with a breathtakingly confident attribution of Europe's difficulties to a 'structural problem' of euro-sclerosis: economists believe that 'the taxes and regulations imposed by Europe's elaborate welfare states have made employers reluctant to create new jobs, while the relatively generous level of unemployment benefits has made workers unwilling to accept the kinds of low wage jobs that help keep unemployment low in the United States' (Krugman, 1994a: 28). The counterpoint is provided in Krugman's book where he discusses 'America's success in creating jobs' and presents the 1980s as 'a time of quite satisfactory job creation' without lingering over the question of low wages and the composition of employment. America's dynamism is attributed to 'America's highly competitive and flexible labour markets' in a way which must establish a generalized supposition in favour of untrammelled labour markets in America and labour market deregulation in Europe (Krugman, 1994c: 32, 36, 45).

Given the professional credo is hard quantification and rigorous algebra, it is contradictory and ironic when a positive economist like Krugman retreats into soft rhetoric and imagism where discourse works through language, assertive identification and appeals to authority. In practice, of course, the power of orthodox economics derives from the way in which it combines an institutional base, arcane techniques, simple epistemology and accessible rhetoric; those, like McCloskey, who analyze its discursive shifts and slides as rhetoric insist that these are the legitimate forms of argument within a community whose judgement and authority must be respected. And, in different ways, the work of both Reich and Tyson in the 1990s illustrates the extent of this authority outside the domain of orthodox economics: after resolving the national uncompetitivity problem into a sectional experience, Reich and Tyson both try to prescribe policy fixes which do not offend economic orthodoxy. Reich's fix could be represented in economic terms as investment in human capital which would allow Americans to compete more effectively on world markets. Tyson's fix could be represented as deviation from free trade in cases where the market does not operate; it is rather like the old 1980s arguments for industrial policy in cases of market failure.

Reich does raise the possibility of redistribution which is the most obvious technical fix for growing income inequality. But his discussion only brings out the implausibility of altruism by the symbolic analysts. The problem is that the basic arithmetic about the size of donor and recipient groups is profoundly discouraging: 'the fortunate fifth' who claim half of America's income must subvent a larger per cent of the population, maybe the majority. The redistributive problem posed by deindustrialization in late twentieth century America is arithmetically much more daunting than that posed by industrialization in early twentieth century Europe; in the case of Edwardian Britain, the work of Rowntree and others showed that the group which required income support accounted for only 10–30 per cent of the population. Politically, Galbraith's comfortable classes can't pay and won't pay for transfers to a much larger proportion of the American population; while some of them lobby for tax concessions for 'people like us'. In that case, by a process of elimination, Reich is left with just the one policy fix of training more symbolic analysts who could be recruited from the sections who are currently doing badly; the policy aim is 'to increase the potential value of what (American) ... citizens can contribute to global webs of enterprise' (Reich, 1993: 153). If this can be described as 'the real economic challenge' , it must be doubtful whether it is a credible solution. If individuals can compete more effectively, they will still depend on an uncertain global demand for highly paid symbolic analysts. And, as the processes of competition will continue unabated, the net outcome will depend on the balance between reskilling through training and deskilling through competition in tradeable goods. It is also worth remembering that in the Reichian scheme of things, some 30 per cent of the workforce is in personal services where training is presumably largely irrelevant.

Tyson's discussion of policy is even more depressing because she tries to solve the sectional problems of the high tech sector within even narrower parameters defined by economic orthodoxy; she is after all an economist who has always been inside the church whereas the lawyer Reich is a lapsed heretic who must now make concessions to the faith. Her proposals are economic casuistry in a precise technical sense: they involve the application of general rules to particular instances where circumstances alter cases. Tyson's economic casuistry on free trade parallels Catholic casuistry on marriage. Divorce cannot be countenanced but it is possible in special cases to sanction annulment of marriages which never really existed and annulment in such cases of course strengthens the institution. In the economic case the question is whether and when are deviations from free trade justified? Tyson's answer is that defensive deviations from free trade are justified in the special case of high tech where free trade never really existed.

Thus, her book rehearses a special case characterization of the high tech sector and emphasizes that her favoured policy instruments are defensive. High tech industries, like semi conductors or commercial aircraft, have oligopolistic or imperfectly competitive market forms with dynamic economies of scale and strategic interaction between firms. Their competitive fields are littered with structural impediments and institutional differences as nations struggle in a zero-sum game to capture 'a bigger share of the global rents from high technology production'. Inaction does not mean the market will determine the fate of America's high technology industries; 'instead they will be manipulated by the trade, regulatory and industrial policies of our trading partners'. But none of these special case characteristics justify large-scale offensive breaches with free trade. Tyson proposes defensive policies which 'deter or compensate for foreign practices that are not adequately regulated by existing multilateral rules'. Furthermore, Americans in their approach to active policy should reject those policy instruments, such as voluntary export restraints and price floors under imports, which 'impede competition and erect protectionist barriers' (Tyson, 1994: 13, 39, 254).

The immediate problem with this kind of casuistry is obviously the internal opposition from more conservative economists who require higher standards of proof. Within the discourse Tyson cannot clinch the argument for deviation because the fact that everybody else is interfering with high tech trade does not mean that it is economically rational or welfare improving for the US to do so. For the rest of us, the more important issue is the limited scope of the special case. By Tyson's own calculations, 76 per cent of American manufactured imports are low tech or medium tech and they should be left to free trade and competition; and, on the export side, Tyson explicitly rules out any attempt to generally open the Japanese market for American exports (Tyson, 1994: 22, 84). A few symbolic analysts in protected or promoted high tech businesses would appreciate that Tyson casuistry is different from Krugman 'do nothingism' or Reich-style 'whistling in the dark'. But from the American rust belt the difference might not be so obvious: all three authors share an economic vision of a future that does not work for the majority combined with the end of policy intervention that makes any difference.

This economic vision is combined with a corollary political assumption; Reich implicitly assumes and Krugman directly asserts that the economic outcome does not threaten the political status quo. In Reich, this outcome is implied by his watery imagery about Americans in different boats; some of those boats are sinking economically but his later discussion of the politics of redistribution implies that the political ship of state will sail on much as before. As for Krugman, his one endlessly repeated big idea is that Americans have over the past twenty years lived through a revolution of diminished (economic) expectations without 'drastic political reaction'; although GNP grew much more slowly than expected, 'things didn't fall apart and the centre held'. This political result is variously described as 'astonishing' or 'truly remarkable' but there is no intimation that the future will be very different because 'there is little political demand that we do better'. and 'that is probably the way it will be for the next decade'. These formulations irritatingly combine sense, imprecision and hyperbole. While it may be true that there has not been any 'drastic political reaction', the idea that 'the centre held' is highly contestable; as our discussion of the demise of industrial policy in the 1990s suggests, if the centre held, it did so by moving rapidly rightwards in a way which evacuated the traditional interventionist and solidaristic substance of centre left policy. The serious question about the future is how much further rightwards will the 'centre' move and under what conditions?

Krugman's implicit answer to this question is 'not very far, unless America has a major economic crisis'. The 'not very far' judgement is implicit in his assumption that populist politics is containable so that 'political experts' will retain control of what remains of economic policy.

The assumption about populist politics is contained in his two dismissive references to Ross Perot. In a brief reference to the 1992 presidential campaign, Perot is dismissed as another ignorant mechanic who promises to fix the economy. In a scenario of the 1996 campaign, Perot makes a more fanciful reappearance as an economic nationalist irritant in a chain of events which however only culminates in economic disaster when the Fed makes 'a crucial policy error'. For Krugman, this must be an uncharacteristic mistake because he is generally enthusiastic about the Fed's expertise in fine tuning the economy by varying interest rates and the money supply, even if he is forced to admit that in the 1980s the Fed induced the worst recession since the 1930s (Krugman, 1994c: xi, 3, 66, 216, 231). Maybe the record is irrelevant: what matters is that expert economists make policy at the Fed. They fought off one threat to their independence in from gold bugs and monetarists in the early 1980s and Krugman sees no reason why their independence should not continue through and beyond the 1990s.

Economic crisis is the only threat to this congenial prospect of policy making by the right set: as Krugman argues, 'attempts to change the economic system in a fundamental way, like President Roosevelt's (or Ronald Reagan's) occur only in the face of an economic crisis'. His idea of crisis is modelled on the events of 1929; a crisis originating in the financial sector blows hurricane-like through the real economy leaving a broad trail of disaster among rentiers and investors who are illiquid and managers and workers who suffer demand deficiency. Krugman claims reassuringly that this is now unlikely because 'stock market downturns need not cause severe downturns in the real economy' (Krugman, 1994c: 41, 215). This position is over sanguine because it almost certainly underestimates the potentially destructive impact of volatile international flows which are beyond national regulation and also underestimates the difficulties of propping up illiquid and embarrassed banks, a task which the Japanese are now contemplating with some trepidation. Even if Krugman's optimism about crisis is justified by events, we would be apprehensive about the political consequences of grumbling structural problems (inside and outside tradeable goods) which leave a narrower twister trail of disaster from which some Americans are sheltered and a few can make money.

Reich interestingly agrees with Krugman's political judgement that the political system can absorb the stresses of an increasingly divided society if the future turns out to be like the recent past. This emerges indirectly from Reich's analysis of how and why the democratic system has not generated an irresistible majority demand for redistribution at the expense of the fortunate fifth: tabloid trivialization in the media generates a basic lack of understanding; vestigial thinking about the national economy and myths about upward mobility limit mobilization; orthodox politics offers only a 'circle of political futility' which becomes a self fulfilling prophecy; and there is bargaining asymmetry when the fortunate fifth are globally mobile while many of the poor are dependent and immobile. The interesting thing about these arguments is that they apply most forcefully to the established forms of American party politics which have recently been rendered peculiarly unresponsive and immobile by the tendency of the system to give the Presidency to one party and Congress to another. But, even without this check, the system can undoubtedly contain and neutralize a good deal of pressure from below while Clinton, Gingrich and their successors wrangle over what a balanced budget means.

It would nevertheless be wrong to underestimate the destabilizing forces which already operate on the margins of the orthodox political system which increasingly looks like a leaky ship in heavy seas. The evacuation of the old centre ground by liberal democrats, and the perceived ineffectuality of the Clinton presidency, may signify the end of policy but it also creates a vacuum which waits to be filled by some kind of radicalism or populism. Furthermore, an increasingly divided society generates what Jesse Jackson has described as the politics of hurt and hate; much of this is now displaced onto social and cultural issues from guns and prayers to sexuality but these can always feedback unpredictably into the main political process. We have already seen Ross Perot's radical right trouble making about Nafta and the 'giant sucking sound' of jobs lost to low wage competitors; plus Pat Buchanan's campaigning which demonized the IBM chief executive responsible for downsizing. Against this background, it is reasonable to be apprehensive about the threat of an unstable post modern form of politics which would bypass the established institutions and processes; Perot and Berlusconi use TV to constitute the supporters club in a world where Italy and Canada show how long established parties of government can be wiped out.

The sunny political optimism of our liberal Democrat authors raises questions about whether they comprehend their own society. The middle America of junk food, Macjobs and conspiracy theories is remote from their experience. In his discussion of the symbolic analysts, Reich observes that 'never before has opulence on such a scale been gained by people who have earned it, and done so legally' (Reich, 1993: 219, 290–300). Some of this has trickled down into the liberal Democratic intelligentsia whose comfortable experience is nicely epitomized by the vignette which opens Krugman's chapter on the trade deficit (1994c: 43):

> One day recently I had a meeting in New York. Before leaving I set my Sharp VCR to record a tv programme I would miss while away. The I drove my Mazda to the airport, boarded an Airbus A 310, and while in transit finished some notes for the meeting on my Toshiba lap top computer. My suit was made in Hong Kong, my coffee cup in Portugal. It is quite possible that my breakfast cereal was the only American made product I encountered all morning.

This vignette, which reads like an 'idea' produced by the Alan Alda character in the film *Crimes and Misdemeanours*, reveals a life and a sensibility especially through the unconscious equation of manufactured 'products' with consumer goods. More broadly, it is not vulgar or reductionist to argue that class background and life experience shape and colour the values of intellectuals who share a common milieu. In his biography of Keynes, the greatest of all liberal democratic intellectuals, Roy Harrod argued that 'the assumptions of Harvey Road' influenced Keynes' approach to both policy and politics. What we have in Krugman, Reich and Tyson are the assumptions of that other Cambridge in Massachusetts, where Keynes' American counterparts of the 1990s believe their comfortable ship is unsinkable.

Time will tell whether they are right and, for the rest of us who spectate from outside America, the outcome is important in economic and social terms. The Asia Pacific region has narrow economic interests in free trade access to its major export market and broader social choices about whether it aspires to the American form of capitalism. The argument and evidence so far suggests caution about the stability of any form which combines high incomes for some and low wages for many.

REFERENCES

Krugman, P. (1994a), 'Competitiveness: A Dangerous Obsession', *Foreign Affairs*, March/ April, pp.28–44.
Krugman, P. (1994b), 'Proving My Point', *Foreign Affairs*, July/August, pp.198–203.
Krugman, P. (1994c), *The Age of Diminished Expectations: US Economic Policy in the 1990s*. Cambridge, MA.
Magaziner, I. and Reich, R. (1982), *Minding America's Business*. New York.
Piore. M. and Sabel, C. (1984), *The Second Industrial Divide: Possibilities for Prosperity*. New York.
Reich, R. (1991), 'Who is Them?', *Harvard Business Review*, March/April, pp.77–88.
Reich, R. (1993), *The Work of Nations: Preparing Ourselves for 21st Century Capitalism*. London.
Tyson, L. (1994), *Who's Bashing Whom?: Trade Conflict in High Technology Industries*. London.

[6]

The US Economic Model at Y2K: Lodestar for Advanced Capitalism?

RICHARD B. FREEMAN
Harvard and NBER
Cambridge, Massachusetts
Centre for Economic Performance
London School of Economics

La performance économique des années 90 suggère que les États-Unis pourraient avoir le bon niveau d'institutions et de politiques afin de devenir l'économie capitaliste de pointe dans la nouvelle économie de l'information. Cet article développe les critères servant à l'évaluation du niveau de pointe. Nous trouvons que les États-Unis sont un candidat légitime en terme d'emplois et de productivité lorsque la distribution n'est pas considérée. Le niveau de plein emploi des années 90 apporte encore plus de support à l'économie américaine en tant qu'économie de pointe même lorsque la distribution est considérée. Par contre, si le niveau de plein emploi n'est pas atteint, l'économie américaine va perdre de son éclat. De plus, l'effort américain dans l'augmentation des emplois chez les femmes et dans l'obtention du droit de propriété à plusieurs travailleurs méritent de l'attention.

The 1990s economic performance suggests that the US may have the right mix of institutions and policies to be the peak capitalist economy in the new information economy. This paper develops criteria for judging peak status. It finds that the US is a legitimate candidate for peak in terms of employment and productivity but not distribution. The 1990s full employment strengthens the case for the US as peak economy even on distributional grounds. But with anything less than full employment the US economy will lose its luster. Still, the US record in employing women and extending ownership to many workers deserves attention.

At the turn of the twenty-first century the US economy is the envy of the world, because throughout the 1990s it has generated higher employment and lower unemployment without inflation than most other advanced countries. In early 2000 the unemployment rate in the United States fell below 4 percent — lower than in Japan or Germany and other European Union (EU) countries, which have traditionally had lower unemployment than the US. The employment-population rate in the US was at an all-time peak, full employment was accompanied by a federal budget surplus, successful movement of welfare mothers to work, a booming stock market, and reduction in crime. From 1996 to 2000, moreover, real gross domestic product (GDP) rose by over 4 percent per year, while throughout the 1990s recovery, productivity in manufacturing grew more rapidly than in most other advanced countries.

Economists and policymakers did not anticipate the success of the US in these areas. In the mid-1990s the Federal Reserve thought that an unemployment rate below 6 percent would set off rising inflation. The government (Clinton and Gingrich)

S188   Richard B. Freeman

believed that the only way to reduce the federal budget deficit was to adjust downward the consumer price index to limit social security payments. Most experts feared that the welfare reforms of 1996 would create disaster for unskilled single mothers and their children and no one expected crime to fall. Long-term forecasts of US economic growth posited modest increases in productivity, in line with post-oil-shock patterns.

The US economy surpassed expectations by enough to suggest that the US might just have developed what afficionados of the new economy have claimed: the right mix of institutions and policies to assure full employment and sizeable productivity gains for the foreseeable future. If the US maintains these successes over the next 5 to 15 years and if persistent full employment reduces poverty and narrows the economic inequalities that have marred US economic performance, even the sharpest critics of the US model will have a hard time finding fault.

But perhaps the US economic performance at the outset of the twenty-first century is more a matter of luck than of the right economic institutions. Associated with the US boom is an unprecedented rise in consumer debt and balance of payments deficit and an extraordinary stock market bubble, none of which can continue ad infinitum. The US economy could just as readily come back to earth as the exemplar capitalist models of the 1970s and 1980s, Japan and Germany, and the 1960s-70s third-way ideal, Sweden, as continue along its new full employment prosperity.

The claim that the US (or any other economy) has found the best form of capitalism for the modern world rests on the notion that there is a single peak capitalist economic model. But does the economic world indeed have a single peak set of institutions or does it allow for diversity? The first section of the paper develops criteria for judging whether any economy is truly a peak and assesses which of these the US meets or does not meet. Section two argues that the key features of the US job

market that contribute to economic success are not, as many believe, deregulation and high rising inequality but rather expansion of opportunities for women and the growth of new "shared capitalist" institutions. The third section shows that US full employment is improving performance in the one area where the US economy has done poorest: distributing the gains of economic growth to all persons.

SINGLE-PEAKED VERSUS DIVERSE CAPITALISM

Behind the claim or belief that the US or any other country has developed *the* ideal form of capitalism for the twenty-first century is the notion that economic outcomes are related to institutions and policies according to a single-peaked social maximand. When institutions or policies produce a single peak in the space of social outcomes, one set of arrangements is indeed the global optimum. This is shown in the first landscape in Figure 1. The horizontal axis measures institutions along some general dimension (such as centralization of wage-setting or the role of unions or the state in economic decision-making) while the vertical axis represents aggregate output (GDP per capita or some variant thereof). In the first landscape the set of institutions N* (for nirvana) produces the highest output and every move in the direction of N* raises well-being. It behooves all economies to adopt the nirvana institutions as quickly as they can.

But there is nothing in economic logic that rules out very different institution-outcome landscapes. One alternative is a landscape with multiple peaks separated by valleys. Some of the multiple peaks may have similar heights, so that different institutional arrangements produce the same well-being, but most peaks are local optima, separated from higher optima by valleys that make it costly to change. The peak economy might have better outcomes than others, but it may not be worthwhile for countries with slightly lower outcomes to invest in change by going down from their peak.

FIGURE 1
Economic Institutions – Outcome Landscapes

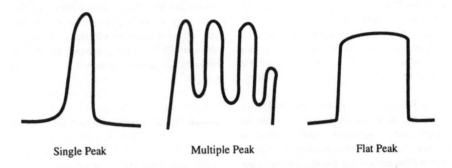

Single Peak   Multiple Peak   Flat Peak

It is also possible that different institutions produce similar levels of output, with little cost to changing them. This produces the flat peak in Figure 1. This is a Coasian world where institutions reflect different property arrangements and where side payments guarantee that whatever the arrangements, the economy reaches an efficient outcome. This diagram predicts similar GDP per capita (other social maximands) within a wide range of arrangements. Each country can do it "its own way" without suffering any economic penalty.

Belief in a single-peaked outcome function (whatever the outcome and its arguments) is deeply ingrained in economics. Models of optimizing behaviour assume convex functions so that first derivatives yield the maximizing conditions and second derivatives or matrices thereof have the appropriate sign. Even if individuals choose blindly, a single-peaked function will generate budget constraints so that those who pick institutions around the peak do better and eventually increase their share of markets. Marxian analysis also takes a single-peaked view of capitalism, predicting the growth of monopolies and proletariat in all countries.

In recent years globalization and the spread of information age technology have led observers on both the right and left toward a single-peaked view of the world. When the right argues for labour market flexibility or deregulation or privatization or contraction of the welfare state, it often claims that these are the only ways to attain efficiency in the modern world. When the left worries about social dumping, a race to the bottom, and trade-induced impoverishment of low-skilled workers, it does so from the same perspective: that there is only one efficient way to operate a capitalist economy.

But there is a case for diversified capitalism as well. Since the end of World War II living standards in advanced capitalist economies with differing institutions have converged. The coefficient of variation of GDP per capita, measured in purchasing power parity terms, among 18 major Organization for Economic Cooperation and Development (OECD) countries has declined over time as Japan and EU countries have closed much of the post-World War II gap with the United States. Comparative advantage argues for diversity. If Germany can operate a tripartite social partners model of

S190   Richard B. Freeman

capitalism better than the US while the US is more adept at a high mobility/decentralized wage-setting model, Germany will do better with its system than to mimic the US system and conversely. Game theory teaches us that interactive decision-making creates many potential outcomes, with institutional rules or norms determining equilibrium (Kreps 1990). This is more consistent with multiple or flat peaks — diversity — rather than single peak optima.

What factors might help us determine which landscape best describes the economics world, and whether the US or some other economy best represents the economic peak? Table 1 lists seven factors that differentiate peak landscapes from other landscapes and thus can guide an assessment of whether any economy has achieved peak status.

The first criterion for a single peak landscape is that the peak economy does better than other economies in various dimensions of aggregate economic performance. Over the long run, the natural measure of aggregate performance is GDP per capita or GDP per hour worked. But in any given period, the link between observed outcomes and long-term GDP

per capita or per hour is unclear. If there was general agreement on how to weigh the impact on long-term production of outcomes like inflation, balance of payments, unemployment, fiscal deficits, etc., we could form a single weighted average, as some analysts do with so-called misery indices of various forms. But there is no such general agreement. Some believe that inflation is the vampire's kiss and thus place great weight on inflation, while others weigh unemployment more heavily. Rather than argue over particular weights on aggregate performance, let us just stipulate that the peak economy must do better on various dimensions of aggregate performance.

The second criterion is distributional. The peak economy should produce higher incomes throughout much of the income distribution than competing economies. If one economy produces higher outcomes at *all* points in the income distribution, we would judge it as having a higher peak. Beyond that, there is no universally accepted weighting of distributions. Rawls values how the poorest fare; your local billionaire may value how the richest fare, while political economy considerations suggest that the middle of the distribution is important. My

TABLE 1

Evidence for Judging the Shape of the Institution-Outcome Landscape

	Single Peak	Multiple Peak	Flat Peak
Characteristics of N*			
1 N* dominates on several key aggregate outcomes	YES	NO	NO
2 N* has higher well-being in much of distribution	YES	NO	NO
3 N* dominates over extended period	YES	NO	NO
Landscape Near N*			
4 Near neighbours are also high	YES	NO	YES
5 Movements toward N raise well-being	YES	NO	NO
Landscape Away from N*			
6 Big jumps cost little	YES	NO	YES
7 Institutions converge (or outcomes diverge)	YES	NO	NO

Note: N* represents nirvana.

criterion for higher incomes throughout much of the distribution is a way of saying that distributional factors must enter any assessment.

The third criterion relates to the stability of the single peak over time. The economy with peak institutions must dominate other economies for at least a decade or so. Given that candidates for the peak, such as the United States, are likely to have high income per capita, and that other economies can take advantage of catch-up, I do not require that the peak economy grow more rapidly than other economies, only that it maintain an edge on outcomes over an extended period.

The fourth and fifth criterion relates to the convexity of the landscape space. As Figure 1 shows, N* lies at the top of a mountain, so that movements toward N* raise well-being. Neighbours with characteristics close to those of N* should also have good social outcomes; and copying this or that feature of the single peak economy ought to raise social outcomes.

The sixth criterion relates to large changes in institutions. Since there is only one peak, large-scale changes in policies or institutions toward peak institutions ought to be relatively costless. An economy that chooses radical reform ought to see economic improvements, not retrogression relative to others.

The seventh criterion refers to changes over time. If the single peak hypothesis is correct, and if countries seek to improve the economic well-being of their citizens with sensible policies, the peak should be an attractor in institution-outcome space. They should imitate the features of the peak economy. By contrast, economies that, for whatever reason, move away from peak institutions should suffer losses of economic well-being.

US Performance

How well does this decade's candidate for peak economy, the United States, fare by these criteria?

The US fulfills some of the criteria for peak economy, but fails others. It has produced sufficiently high employment-population rates and hours worked per employed adult and low unemployment rates for enough years to be the peak economy on this front (see Table 2, columns 1-3). The US has had lower unemployment than the EU for roughly a decade or so, though it had higher unemployment than Japan until 1998. Using employment to population rates, US success dates back to the 1980s or mid-1970s. In 1973 the US and OECD-Europe had the same employment-population rate. Since then the US rate has risen while the European rate has fallen to produce a 16-point differential in 1998!

But not until the late 1990s did the US outperform other economies in growth of GDP per capita

TABLE 2

Employment, Unemployment and Hours Worked, 1998

	Employment-Population	Unemployment Rate	Hours
	%	%	
US	73.8	4.5	1,957
UK	71.2	6.2	1,737
Canada	69.0	8.4	1,777
Australia	67.2	7.9	1,861
New Zealand	65.4	7.6	1,821
Eire	59.8	7.9	—
Japan	69.5	4.2	1,879
Germany	64.1	8.6	1,580
France	59.4	11.9	1,634
Italy	50.8	12.2	—
Belgium	57.3	9.4	—
Netherlands	69.8	4.3	1,365
Austria	67.4	5.5	—
Sweden	71.5	8.4	1,551
Finland	64.8	11.5	1,693
Norway	78.2	3.2	1,401
Denmark	75.3	5.1	—

Source: OECD (1999, Tables B and F).

or productivity and it trailed the others in growth of real compensation over the same period. Output per hour worked in the US was roughly on a par with output per hour worked in Germany, France, and some smaller EU countries in the 1990s (Freeman 1996; van Ark and McGuckin 1999; McKinsey Global Institute 1997) and has grown more slowly than in most other advanced countries since the 1970s. *The Economist* has argued that "if Germany and Japan can grow as fast (faster in the actual data) as America even when their incentives are blunted by an inflexible model, imagine what they might do were their economies to be set free"(10 April, p. 20). But it is the rapid growth of productivity in the US in the late 1990s, not a tortured interpretation of the US's slower productivity, that strengthens the case for the United States as peak economy.

Whether this growth performance is sustainable is, to be sure, highly debatable. The US has a low savings rate, but manages a reasonable investment to GDP ratio because it attracts considerable foreign capital and runs a large trade deficit. The US has an extremely productive research and development sector, and more venture capital than other countries, which should increase long-term economic performance. But it also has a huge consumer debt. The US has a highly educated workforce, but its lead has fallen relative to other advanced countries; and US workers have lower scores on adult literacy tests than workers in most advanced countries.

Even if rapid productivity growth can be maintained, the US has one major problem in meeting the criteria for peak economy status. This relates to the distributional criterion for judging a candidate peak economy. As Table 3 shows, while the US is number one in per capita income, it is number 13 in per capita income for those in the lower decile of earnings. It is not until the thirtieth to fortieth decile that the US surpasses most other advanced countries in per capita income. In addition, the fact that Americans work so much more than citizens of other countries implies that the US advantage in living

standards is less than indicated by GDP per capita. Greater hours worked per adult means less leisure, so that any social value function that weighted leisure would bring EU countries closer to the US in overall economic well-being. With hours per worker and per adult rising in the US relative to other countries, moreover, the US advantage in living standards actually eroded over the past 20 or so years.

In short, US performance has been clearly superior for an extended period on one outcome — full employment — and has been superior for a short period on one other outcome — productivity — but falls short of peak status on distributional grounds.

TABLE 3

Per Capita Income by Position in the Income Distribution, Relative to US Per Capita Income, 1996

	Per Capita	Lower Decile	Upper Decile
US	100	36	208
Switzerland	91	52	168
Norway	88	49	139
Japan	84	39	161
Denmark	81	44	126
Belgium	79	46	129
Canada	77	36	141
Austria	77	43	144
Germany	76	41	131
Netherlands	75	43	130
France	74	41	143
Australia	73	33	141
Italy	72	40	127
Sweden	69	39	110
Finland	68	39	107
UK	67	29	138
New Zealand	63	34	119

Source: Income per capita, *US Statistical Abstract, 1998*, Table 1355. Income Distribution estimates based on percentile figures relative to median for household income, Gottschalk and Smeeding (1997) usually 1991-92 figures.

Other Economies' Performance

According to the peak economy view of the economic landscape, the peak economy's closest economic neighbours should also do well while economies that adopt peak economy institutions should improve their relative economic position. The view of the United States as peak economy fails both of these criteria.

Close neighbours refers to neighbours in institution space, not in geography, but in fact the US's closest geographic neighbour, Canada, is also its closest institutional neighbour. The 1990s was a period of economic disaster for Canada. In 1990 Canada stood third in the GDP per capita league tables, below Switzerland and the US, but sufficiently above most EU countries to support the notion that North American institutions generated higher average living standards than those in other advanced countries. In 1997, following a decade of economic decline/stagnation Canada had fallen in the league tables to seventh position. One interpretation of the disparate performances of the United States and Canada is that the small differences between the two countries matter a lot, and that Canada has just not gone far enough toward the US model. Alternatively, some argue that Canada suffered from egregious macroeconomic policy. But the broader interpretation is that institutions-outcome landscape does not fit the single peak paradigm. Countries with similar institutions can do quite differently in any given time period.

In the European Union, the United Kingdom is generally viewed as the economy most similar to the US, and the reforms enacted by the Thatcher, Major, and Blair governments have brought the UK even closer to the American model. Has this improved the position of the UK in the league per capita income tables? No. In 1980 the UK was sixteenth in the league tables; in 1997 it was eighteenth (United States. Department of Commerce 1999). Perhaps the UK was not radical enough. Margaret Thatcher's reforms never touched the National Health Service, did not reduce the ratio of tax revenues to GDP to US levels, and left macroeconomic monetary policy in the hands of the government rather than the Bank of England. Perhaps without the reforms the UK would have fallen further in the league tables. But again, perhaps the correct interpretation is that the institutions-outcome space does not fit the single peak model.

Outside Europe, the economy that has undertaken the most radical reforms is New Zealand. New Zealand deregulated much of its labour market, freed its central bank from political control, and introduced a variety of free trade measures. It out-Thatchered Mrs T. With what result? In 1997 New Zealand ranked last in per capita income among advanced OECD countries with an income per capita 14 percent below that of its natural pair, Australia. In 1980 New Zealand was also last among the countries, with an income per capita 19 percent below that of Australia. Extenuating circumstances may explain the failure of radical reform to produce the expected outcomes. New Zealand had such serious problems prior to its reforms that absent the reforms it might have fallen even further. New Zealand may have screwed its monetary policy so badly that its labour and product market reforms had no chance to bring about recovery. Perhaps, but once more a simpler explanation is that the single peak landscape vision of capitalism is wrong.

What about the seventh criterion — the predicted movement of economies toward the peak institutional form? As there are many factors that differentiate the US model from others, it is difficult to determine whether economies are in fact becoming Americanized. In one readily measurable dimension, the extent of unionization and collective bargaining coverage, they are not becoming more like the US. Table 4 shows that union density and collective bargaining coverage rates diverged across OECD countries between 1980 and 1997. If the countries that moved further from the US on this dimension did especially poorly in GDP per capita, we might reconcile this pattern with a single peaked world (they screwed up), but the data do not show such a

TABLE 4
The Increasing Diversity of Labour Institutions, 1980-1994

	Density		Coverage	
	1980	1997	1980	1994-97
Declining density and coverage				
UK	50	30	70	44
US	22	16	26	18
Japan	31	21	28	18
New Zealand	56	30	67	31
Australia	48	35	88	80
Declining density and stable/rising coverage				
Austria	52	39	98	98
France	22	10	85	95
Germany	36	29	91	92
Italy	50	37	85	82
Netherlands	35	24	76	81
Portugal	52	30	70	71
Stable density/coverage				
Belgium	53	53	90	90
Canada	36	38	37	36
Denmark	79	76	69	69
Norway	55	55	75	74
Switzerland	31	23	53	50
Rising density and stable/rising coverage				
Finland	69	88	95	95
Spain	8	17	76	78
Sweden	78	86	86	89
No. 5 relative to no. 15	1.6	2.3	1.3	1.8

Source: OECD (1997, Table 3.3), with updates from Blanchflower (2000).

pattern. Sweden fell in per capita income, but so too did New Zealand.

Finally, it is important to recognize that few analysts regarded the US as the peak economy until the mid- or late 1990s. For much of the 1970s and 1980s, the 900-pound gorilla on the economic scene was Japan. American business was frightened by

Japanese economic performance — recall Ezra Vogel's *Japan as Number One*, or the best-selling business book *The Book of the Rings* by the fourteenth century Samurai warrior Musashi Musashi. The early Clinton administration looked jealously at some German institutions and sought to expand the US welfare state through mandated health insurance. Major business-school thinkers bemoaned Anglo-Saxon "short-termism" in capital markets and saw virtue in Japanese or German banking and ownership patterns (Porter 1990). Going back further, analysts in the 1970s thought that corporatist arrangements were a better way to fight inflation than the US-style decentralized wage and price-setting (Bruno and Sachs 1985).

In short, the safest reading of the empirical evidence is that the institutions-outcome space does not fit a single peak landscape but rather that the set of institutions that performs best varies with economic circumstances. The US may have found the right institutional mix for long-term economic success, but the case is far from proven, and the history of capitalist economies post-World War II should make even aficionados of capitalism, US-style, cautious in their reading of the late 1990s. In any case, whether the United States has found nirvana institutions on a single peak landscape or not, it is important to understand, as best we can at this time, what economic institutions have contributed to the 1990s' success of the American Model.

US INSTITUTIONS AND EMPLOYMENT CREATION

Many observers believe that the US employment success results from a non-regulated labour market and high and rising wage inequality. The absence of regulations allows firms to make more efficient use of its workforce, be it through downsizing or out-sourcing or otherwise changing work or pay arrangements. From this perspective, America has paid for its employment creation through falling real wages and conditions of work.

This view is erroneous. The US labour market is not an unregulated *laissez-faire* paradise (or hell, depending on your point of view). The US has not paid for its job creation with wage inequality. Rather, the US job market has contributed to the country's economic success by opening employment opportunities for female workers at an unprecedented rate and by developing new "shared capitalist" institutions that increase employee decision-making and financial stake in firms.

The US Job Market Is Not Unregulated

The view that the US job market is largely unregulated is fallacious. The United States has a considerable corpus of labour law covering everything from hours worked to occupational health and safety to protection of minorities and women. It has enough administrative and judicial rulings interpreting these laws to fill volumes and create employment for thousands of lawyers. For the most part, however, US laws protect workers as individuals rather than as members of a collective or group. Consider the following brief chronology of US job market regulations:

1960s-1970s legislation regulating treatment of discriminated groups. The *Equal Pay Act* of 1963, *Civil Rights Act* of 1964, amended in 1972; *Age Discrimination Act* of 1967; Executive Order 11246 requiring affirmative action, including numeric goals and timetables in increasing utilization of women and minorities;

1970s legislation regulating workplace health and safety and firm pensions. The *Occupational Health and Safety Act* of 1970 and federal *Mine Safety and Health Act* of 1977 regulating workplace conditions; the *Employee Retirement Income Security Act* of 1974 governing private pension plans; tax advantages granted to Employee Stock Ownership Plans.

1980s-1990s legislation enhancing individual employee rights. The *Americans with Disabilities Act* of 1990; *Civil Rights Act* of 1991; *Family and Medical Leave Act* of 1993; and *Employee Polygraph*

Protection Act of 1988. In addition, the *Worker Adjustment and Retraining Notification Act* of 1988 and *Immigration Reform and Control Act* of 1986 add further controls on employer behaviour in times of planned plant closures and employment of illegal immigrants. Most states adopted rules on wrongful dismissals that allow employees to sue for wrongful dismissal.

In the 1990s, moreover, Congress twice increased the minimum wage. It rejected business efforts to modify the *Fair Labor Standards Act* that requires time and a half overtime and failed to enact various Teamwork Bills to make it easier for employers to empower employee involvement committees. Regulations of hours worked and the ability of business to establish works-council-type arrangements are more stringent in the US than in the EU.

Because the federal government has few regulators to monitor these laws because the US has not developed a workplace-based system of monitoring and enforcement, the main mode of enforcement of labour laws has been through suits in court or worker complaints to agencies. Virtually every large firm in the US faces some legal suit about its employment practices every year. Firms have found the burden of employment law sufficiently large to lead many to seek private dispute-resolution alternatives in place of expensive legal suits. Hardly the sign of a *laissez-faire* labour market.

The US Did Not Buy Full Employment with McJobs and Wage Cuts

Observers critical of the US experience stress that much of US job growth consists of low paid, unskilled, fast-food-type jobs, of which *McDonald's* is the archetype. Looking at US job growth through an industry lens, American job creation has been concentrated in the service sector, particularly retail trade, which pays less than, say, manufacturing. But looked at through an occupation lens, US job growth has been in professional and managerial work. In 1999, 30 percent of the US workforce was in managerial and professional specialties compared to 23 percent in 1983. While the growth of employment was bifurcated with fast growth at both the top and bottom of the skill and wage distributions, on net US employment was more skilled in 1999 than it was in 1990 or 1980.

What about the claim that falling/stagnant real wages or poor productivity growth underlies the US jobs boom?

From the 1970s through the mid-1990s, there is some support for this proposition. Productivity growth was slower in the US than in EU countries or Japan. The real wages of American production workers fell while the real wages of workers in most OECD countries rose. But in the late 1990s, productivity growth is up, and real wages have increased commensurately. Even during the earlier period, moreover, the trade-off claim fails to explain the locus of employment growth. Given that the wages of low-skilled men fell sharply in the US, the trade-off argument suggests that their employment and hours worked should have grown. In fact, until the late 1990s, the American jobs miracle bypassed the low paid. From 1970 through 1990, annual hours worked for men in the bottom deciles of the earnings distribution fell while hours worked by those in the upper deciles were stable or rising (Juhn, Murphy and Topel 1991; Freeman 1997). Inequality in hours worked increased along with inequality in hourly pay, producing an even greater increase in annual earnings inequality. Employment of women, whose wages rose relative to that of men, increased most rapidly.

US experience with minimum wages also gainsays any wage-cut story of US job creation (Card and Krueger 1995). During the 1980s, the Reagan administration tried to create jobs for low-skilled Americans by maintaining the nominal value of the minimum wage while prices and other wages rose, without success. The modest increases in the minimum by the Bush and Clinton administrations and by various states in ensuing years had little discernible effect on employment. Comparisons of patterns of employment growth in Canada, France, and the

United States (Card, Kramarz and Lemieux 1996) or between Germany and the US tell a similar story (Freeman and Schettkat 1999). There is no clear relation across countries in the growth of employment among groups and in the pattern of wage changes.

US Jobs Growth is Growth of Jobs for Women

Perhaps the most important fact about US employment growth is that growth has been most pronounced among women. This is shown in Table 5, which records employment-population rates for the total population 16-64 years of age and for women and men, separately. Had the employment to population ratio of US women increased from 1973 to 1998 by the same percentage points as did the employment-population ratio of EU women, the aggregate US employment to population rate would have changed only marginally. All else being the same, the movement of women into (largely full-time) work added over nine percentage points to the total employment rate in 1998 and explained two-thirds of the 14 percentage-point difference between US and European employment rates.[1]

TABLE 5
Employment-Population Ratios in the United States, 1973-1998

	1973	1998	Change
All	65.1	73.8	8.7
Females	48.0	67.4	19.4
Males	82.8	80.5	-2.3

Note: Changes in OECD-Europe over the same period were:
     All, from 65.1 to 60.1;
     Females, from 43.2 to 49, a 5.8 percentage point increase; and
     Males, from 86.7 to 71.3, a 15.4 percentage point decrease.

Source: OECD (1996, Table A) and (1999, Table B).

The biggest increase in female employment was among married women with young children. Between 1960 and 1998 the proportion of married women, with children less than six years old, who were in the workforce increased from 18.6 percent to 63.7 percent. The proportion of married women; with children less than six years old in the workforce in 1997 exceeded the proportion of married women with children of school age (6 to 17) working in 1960 (39 percent), and was just 13 percentage points below the proportion with children of school age working in 1998 (76.8 percent) (US. Department of Commerce 1999, Table 659). The contrast with Western European women is striking. More American women with pre-school age children participated in the labour force in 1996 than did all European women, many of whom do not have children. This occurred without national daycare facilities or with the state hiring a majority of women, as in some Nordic countries, or with labour laws that give parents paid leave or other benefits to ease the burden of child care.

In addition, the position of women in the occupational hierarchy improved. In 1983 women were less likely to be in the high-wage executive and professional occupations than men (22 percent of women versus 25 percent of men). In 1998 they were more likely to be in those occupations (28 percent for women versus 25 percent for men) (ibid.).

In sum, *cherchez la femme* if you want the real lesson of US employment growth.

Shared Capitalist Institutions
A major component of the US economic model is the growth of shared capitalism, by which I mean a diverse set of mechanisms for worker participation in production decisions and in the financial stake of their firm and of capitalism more broadly.

On the decision-making side, America's best firms have delegated more decisions to workers through employee-involvement programs and team decision-making than ever before. In the mid-1990s over half of Americans reported that they worked in firms with employee-involvement committees; and one-third of workers said that they were members of employee-involvement committees of some form (Freeman and Rogers 1999).

On the financial sharing side, I have estimated that approximately 50 percent of the US workforce receives compensation related to company performance (Dube and Freeman 2000). Table 6 shows that approximately 25 percent of the workforce had a stake in their firm through some form of ownership. This includes working in a firm with an employee stock ownership plan (ESOP) (around 8 percent), or receiving a stock option through an employee stock option plan that covers the bulk of the workforce, or through the purchase

TABLE 6
Estimates of the Percentage of Employees with Pay Related to Company/Group Performance

	%
Based on worker representation and participation survey	54
Based on diverse surveys of programs*	45
Stock ownership programs	0.25
Profit/gain-sharing	0.25
Defined contribution pensions Invested heavily in company stock	0.11

Note: *If workers were covered by only one form of variable pay, our estimate would be the sum of the estimates for the bold categories in the table: 61 percent, of which 50 percentage points consist of ownership and incentive pay. But there is considerable overlap in coverage. On the basis of overlaps in the Worker Representation and Participation Survey, I estimate that the proportion of workers with any form of performance pay and ownership exceeds the sum of the proportions covered by each form separately by 33 percent = (41.9+29.6)/53.8. Thus, I reduce the 50 percent to 38 percent. I do not have data on the overlap with the estimated 11 percent of workers with 401k or other plans with sizable amounts of company shares, but anticipate that this will be modest, giving the 45 percent in the text.
Source: Dube and Freeman (2000).

of stocks in a firm offering discounts on purchases. A quarter of the workforce was covered by profit or gain-sharing. And approximately 10 percent of the workforce had a substantial proportion of their retire-ment funds invested in company stocks. Millions more had a stake in the performance of the economy through defined contribution pension fund ownership of other firms. In addition, in 1998 nearly 55 million workers were covered by a defined contribution private pen-sion plan (Profit-sharing/401(k) Council of America, www.psca.dcstats.hgtml,), which invested sizable sums in equities, giving them a stake in the performance of the economy outside their own firm. Unions had nearly twice as many private sector members in collectively bargained pension plans than they had members cov-ered by collective bargaining contracts.

These forms of shared capitalist arrangements have grown rapidly. All employee stock option plans barely existed in 1990 but have become the leading edge of US compensation policy by the year 2000. Electronics firms in particular could not attract the highly skilled workers they needed without offer-ing options. Firms like *Starbucks* give options not only to executives but also to their workers.

The view that the US economic model is one of the growth of labour with weak ties to the firm — the virtual employee working for the virtual com-pany as a contingent worker or consultant — misses the increased financial participation of employees in their firm and their increased role in workplace decision-making.

CAN FULL EMPLOYMENT RESOLVE DISTRIBUTIONAL PROBLEMS?

Until unemployment rates fell to 4-5 percent in the late 1990s, employment growth US-style, seemed incapable of raising the earnings of the bulk of the workforce, or of making much dent in poverty (Free-man 2000). Real earnings of production workers dropped by 14 percent in the private sector from 1973

to 1995. The pay of low-skilled workers in all sectors, particularly high school drop-out males, fell by over 20 percent. Median weekly earnings of all men fell while the median weekly earnings of women stagnated. The historic relationship between poverty and eco-nomic growth seemingly broke down in the 1980s (Blank and Card 1993; Cutler and Katz 1991), with more and more poor people residing in female-headed homes on welfare; and with the decline in real wages for the bulk of the male workforce.

But the experience of the late 1990s presents a different picture. The real hourly earnings of pro-duction workers in the private sector rose by over 5 percent from 1995 to 1999. The earnings of men with less than grade 9 education rose 7 percent from 1995 to 1998. The earnings of workers in the bot-tom decile of the earnings distribution increased by 8.7 percent from 1996 to 1998, and the wages of workers in the much maligned retail trade sector rose by 7 percent (Freeman 2000).

Over the same period, spurred in part by the booming economy and in part by changes in the welfare laws, the number of persons on welfare plummeted (Ellwood 2000). Many persons who had been on welfare, which invariably gave them pov-erty level incomes, moved into employment, where they received Earned Income Tax Credit monies which then raised their incomes. The rate of pov-erty began dropping after years of stagnation. While full employment did not reduce the level of inequal-ity or make a huge dent in poverty, the gains of eco-nomic growth finally "trickled down" the income distribution. *Conditional on full employment* the US economy began to reduce the principal flaw in eco-nomic performance and thus look more like a legitimate candidate for peak economy.

But can the United States maintain full employ-ment for long enough to lock in the gains in real wages, poverty reduction, and productivity growth to allow the country to pass the criteria for peak economy shown in Table 1?

Only a charlatan would claim to know the answer. Macroeconomists are divided over the potential for consistent rapid growth — believers in the new economy (US. Congressional Budget Office 1999) versus doubters (Godley 1999). Microeconomists do not understand why the economy managed to carry off the low unemployment with no inflation of the late 1990s (Katz and Krueger 1999). My intuition is that some of the 1990s changes in the US economy have made it easier to maintain full employment, but that eventually a negative shock coupled with the huge trade deficit, reliance on foreign capital, and substantial private debt and wealth dependent on the vagaries of the stock market will eventually produce a significant recession, whose costs will fall heavily on the lower half of the income distribution. In such a situation the US model will lose its lustre as a candidate for the single peak. But I could be as wrong as my macro colleagues were in foreseeing the late 1990s US economic boom. Maybe technological progress has raised productivity to new rates and the Internet will improve market efficiencies enough for the US to keep the late 1990s boom going and going and going like the *Energizer Rabbit.*

But if the US model falters in the next several years, who will replace it? Cool Britannia? A revived French economy? If Canada does well, some weirdos may even start touting the Maple Leaf Model /Modèle feuille d'érable. Sounds unlikely, but a decade ago no one would have predicted that Ireland or the Netherlands would be the great successes of the EU, or that the US would look like a winner and Japan a loser in the "War of the Models." There are a lot of alternative capitalist institutions out there, and every decade some economy leads the pack. In any case, I expect that whichever model emerges as the next candidate for peak will find a way to do what the US did so well in the 1990s — increase opportunities for women in the job market and expand shared capitalist institutions.

NOTE

[1]By contrast, the employment to population rate for men fell over the period, though much less sharply than in Europe. Part of the difference among men is due to large increases in enrolments in school in Europe, where students are less likely to work than in the United States. Part is due to more rapid movement of older men to early retirement in Europe. Among prime-age men, those between say 25 and 54, employment-population rates in the US and OECD-Europe are quite similar.

REFERENCES

Bernstein, J., L. Mishel and J. Schmitt. 1999. *The State of Working America: 1998-99.* Washington, DC: Economic Policy Institute.

Blank, R. and D. Card. 1993. "Poverty, Income Distribution and Growth: Are They Still Connected?" *Brookings Papers on Economic Activity* 2 (Fall): 285-325.

Blanchflower, D. 2000. "Globalization and Labor Market." Dartmouth College, unpublished paper

Bruno, M. and J. Sachs. 1985. *The Economics of Worldwide Stagflation.* Cambridge, MA: Harvard University Press.

Card D. and A. Krueger. 1995. *Myth and Measurement: The New Economics of the Minimum Wage.* Princeton, NJ: Princeton University Press.

Card, D., F. Kramarz and T. Lemieux. 1996. "Changes in the Relative Structure of Wages and Employment: A Comparison of the United States, Canada and France," NBER Working Paper No. 5487. Cambridge, MA: National Bureau of Economic Research.

Cutler, D.M. and L.F. Katz. 1991. "Macroeconomic Performance and the Disadvantaged," *Brookings Papers on Economic Activity* 2 (Spring):1-74.

Dube, A. and R.B. Freeman. 2000. "Shared Compensation Systems and Decision-Making in the US Job Market," paper presented at Commission for Labor Cooperation, North American Seminar on Incomes and Productivity, 24-25 February (www.naalc.org).

Ellwood, D. 2000. "Anti-Poverty Policy for Families in the Next Century: From Welfare to Work — and Worries," *Journal of Economic Perspectives* 14(1):187-98.

Freeman, R. 1997. *When Earnings Diverge: Causes, Consequences, and Cures for the New Inequality in the*

S200   Richard B. Freeman

U.S. NPA Report No. 284. Washington, DC: National Policy Association.

____ 2000. "The Rising Tide Lifts ...," paper presented at "Understanding Poverty in America" conference, Madison Wisconsin, 22 May.

Freeman, R. and J. Rogers. 1999. *What Workers Want*. New York: Cornell University Press.

Freeman, R. and R. Schettkat. 1999. "The Role of Wage and Skill Differences in US-German Employment Differences," in *Qualifikationsstruktur und Arbeitmarktflexibilitaet* special issue of the *Jahrbuecher fuer Nationaleckonomie und Statistik*. Cambridge, MA: National Bureau of Economic Research.

Godley, W. 1999. "Seven Unsustainable Processes." Special Report. Annandale-on-Hudson: Levy Institute.

Gottschalk, P. and T. Smeeding. 1997. "Cross-National Comparisons of Earnings and Income Inequality," *Journal of Economics Literature* 35(2):633-87.

Juhn, C., K. Murphy and R. Topel. 1991. "Why Has the Natural Rate of Unemployment Increased over Time?" *Brookings Papers on Economic Activity* 2:75-142.

Katz, L. and A. Krueger. 1999. "The High Pressure U.S. Labor Market of the 1990s," *Brookings Papers on Economic Activity* 1 (Spring):1-87.

Kreps, D. 1990. *Game Theory and Economic Modelling*. New York: Oxford University Press.

McKinsey Global Institute. 1997. *Removing Barriers to Growth and Employment in France and Germany*. Frakfurt, Paris, Washington, DC: McKinsey Global Institute.

Organization for Economic Development (OECD). 1999. *Employment Outlook*. Paris: OECD.

____ 1997. *Employment Outlook*. Paris: OECD.

____ 1999. *Employment Outlook*. Paris: OECD.

Porter, M. 1990. *The Competitive Advantage of Nations*. New York: The Free Press.

United States. Congressional Budget Office. 1999. "The Economic and Budget Outlook: Fiscal Years 2000-2009." Washington, DC: Government Printing Office.

____. Department of Commerce. 1999. *US Statistical Abstract*. Washington, DC: Government Printing Office.

van Ark, B. and R.H. McGuckin. 1999. "International Comparisons of Labour Productivity and Per Capita Income," *Monthly Labor Review* (July):33-41.

Vogel, E. 1985. *Japan as Number One: Lessons for America*. New York: Harper & Row.

[7]

ROBERT BRENNER

THE BOOM AND THE BUBBLE

TWO YEARS AGO, in autumn 1998, the international economy appeared to be in profound difficulty. The crisis that had broken out in East Asia in summer 1997 was in the process of engulfing the rest of the world. Stock markets and currencies had crashed outside the capitalist core. Russia had declared bankruptcy. Brazil was falling into depression. The Japanese economy had slipped back into recession. The American economy was not immune. In response to falling profits during the first half of 1998, especially in the still pivotal manufacturing sector, equity prices fell alarmingly from July through September. By October, a severe liquidity crunch threatened to plunge the US—and thereby world—economy into the danger zone. At that point, however, the Federal Reserve intervened. It bailed out the huge Long Term Capital Management hedge fund, on the grounds that, had it been allowed to fail, the international economy risked financial collapse; and lowered interest rates on three successive occasions, not only to counter the credit squeeze, but also to make crystal clear that it wanted equity prices to rise, to subsidize the consumption needed to keep the international economy turning over.

The upshot has been contradictory in the extreme. A US cyclical expansion that, up through 1995, had been even less vigorous than those of the 1970s and 1980s suddenly gathered steam. Since then it has delivered five years' rapid growth of GDP, labour productivity and even real wages, while reducing unemployment and inflation quite near to the levels of the long postwar expansion. Investment has boomed impressively. Although wildly over-hyped in the business press, US economic performance during the past half-decade has been superior to that of any comparable period since the early 1970s. On the other hand, the same period has witnessed the swelling of the greatest financial bubble in American history. Equity prices have taken leave of any connexion to underlying corporate profits. Household, corporate and financial debt have all reached record levels as a percentage of GDP, making possible an historic explosion of consumption growth. The resulting acceleration of imports has brought trade and current-account deficits to all-time highs. The result has been an unprecedented increase in the acquisition of US assets by the rest of the world, especially short-term holdings, which leaves the American economy theoretically vulnerable to the same sort of flight of capital, asset depreciation and downward pressure on the currency that wrecked East Asia.

The Boom opened the way to the Bubble, but the Bubble has blown up the Boom a good deal more. The problem, therefore, is to disentangle the one from the other. Only by determining the forces underlying each will it be possible to grasp the overall trajectory of the US economy, and gain some idea of where it is going. Have the tensions that nearly brought down the world economy just two short years ago been transcended? Will the current cyclical upturn broaden and deepen? Lurking behind these questions lies a bigger one. Is the American economy finally pulling out of the long downturn that overtook it around 1973, and on the verge of a new long upswing, like that of the 1950s and 1960s? Or, alternatively, does it face the sort of large-scale correction and reaction that ultimately overtook the Japanese bubble of the 1980s, in which the return to earth of over-priced equities and real estate set off a deep and extended recession?

I. PROFITABILITY REVIVAL: 1985–95

The roots of manufacturing revival in the US go back to the recession of 1979–82, when the record-high real interest rates which accompanied Volcker's turn to monetarism set off an extended process of industrial rationalization. Massive means of production and labour were eliminated in an explosion of bankruptcies not witnessed since the shedding of suddenly unprofitable plant and equipment during the Great Depression of the 1930s. The crisis of manufacturing was rendered deeper by the huge rise in the dollar which followed the major increase in real interest rates of these years. An acceleration of productivity growth in manufacturing was one palpable result. Another, however, was a series of record-breaking current-account deficits, as the runaway dollar sharply reduced US competitiveness. Between 1980 and

1985, manufacturing import penetration rose by one third. These trends could not be sustained, and soon issued in an abrupt and epoch-making reversal of policy.

Plaza Accord

The turning point—a watershed for the world economy as a whole—came with the Plaza Accord of September 1985, when the G5 powers agreed to take joint action to reduce the exchange rate of the dollar, to rescue a US manufacturing sector threatened with decimation. The Plaza Accord set off ten years of more or less continuous devaluation of the dollar against the yen and the Deutschmark, accompanied by a decade-long freeze on real-wage growth. It thereby opened the way for the competitive recovery of US manufactures, a secular crisis of German and Japanese industry, and an unprecedented explosion of export-based manufacturing development throughout East Asia, where currencies were for the most part tied to the declining dollar. Between 1985 and 1995, the dollar fell by about 40 per cent against the Deutschmark and 60 per cent versus the yen. In the same period, real wages in US manufacturing increased at an average annual rate of 0.5 per cent, compared to 3 per cent in Germany and 2.9 per cent in Japan. Meanwhile, the long-term shake-out of high-cost/low-profit means of production in the US economy was given a further major kick by the recession of 1990–91 and the subsequent extended 'jobless recovery'.

The combination of dollar devaluation, wage repression and industrial shake-out—and the increased investment that finally ensued after about 1993—detonated a fundamental shift in the modus operandi of US manufacturing towards overseas markets. From 1985 to 1997 exports increased at an average annual rate of 9.3 per cent, more than 40 per cent faster than between 1950 and 1970. Little by little, exports pushed the manufacturing sector forward, and thereby the whole economy. This restoration of international competitiveness made possible what turned out to be a major recovery of pre-tax profitability in manufacturing. As late as 1986, despite vigorous growth of productivity and stagnation of real wages, the rate of profit in manufacturing still remained more than 20 per cent below its level of 1978, and 50 per cent below its level of 1965. But from 1986 onwards manufacturing profitability increased rapidly. Its ascent was interrupted by the recession of 1990–91 and its aftermath but, by 1995, the pre-tax profitability of US manufacturing had risen by 65 per cent above its level of 1986 and was, for the first time in a quarter of a century, above that of 1973—although still a good third below its high tide in 1965.

It has become standard to downplay the importance of the manufacturing sector, by pointing to its shrinking share of total employment and GDP. But during the 1990s, the US corporate manufacturing sector still accounted for 46 per cent of total profits accruing to the non-financial corporate sector; in 1998 (the latest year for which there is data), it took 42.5 per cent of that total. It was the fall of profitability in the international manufacturing sector, beginning between 1965 and 1973, not only in the US but across the world economy, that was primarily responsible for the long downturn—the extended period from the early 1970s through the early 1990s marked by slow growth of output, investment and productivity, high unemployment and deeper and longer cyclical recessions.[1] By the same token, the recovery of pre-tax profitability in US manufacturing was the source of the rise in pre-tax profitability in the non-financial private economy, which climbed by 15.6 per cent between 1986 and 1995, approaching its levels at the end of the 1960s. This is clear from the fact that the pre-tax rate of profit in the non-financial economy outside of manufacturing remained roughly flat for this whole decade—even falling slightly.

The revival of profitability was further amplified by the tax breaks of the early 1980s, when Republicans and Democrats competed with one another to offer the greatest handouts to the corporations. By 1995, after-tax rates of profit in the non-financial corporate economy and in the corporate manufacturing sector had risen, respectively, to within 23 per cent and 24 per cent of their 1965 peaks, even though pre-tax rates were still 34 per cent and 35 per cent below their 1965 levels. The corporations further strengthened themselves, during the first half of the 1990s, by significantly reducing their dependence on borrowing—and so the proportion of their total profits owed to lenders. Between 1979

---

[1] Reduced manufacturing profitability was itself largely the result of the intensification of international competition, which led to the rise of over-capacity and over-production. The attempts made both by firms and states to reduce costs and improve competitiveness combined to produce the opposite effect, tending to exacerbate redundant production and to reduce the growth of aggregate demand. Profitability thus stayed down, and economic stagnation continued. See Robert Brenner, 'The Economics of Global Turbulence', NLR I/229, May–June 1998.

and 1991, net interest payments as a proportion of the total surplus (profits plus net interest) of non-financial corporations had averaged 31.8 per cent, and reached 37 per cent in 1991. By 1995, that figure had fallen to 20 per cent; it would average under 18 per cent for the remainder of the decade.

As the US economy slowly pulled out of the 1990–91 recession, this revival of profitability finally began to stir the real economy. For a long time manufacturing investment had languished. But between 1993 and 1998, it spurted forward at an average annual rate of 9.4 per cent, compared to 2.6 per cent between 1982 and 1990. In that same period, net capital stock in manufacturing grew at an average annual rate of 2.7 per cent, compared to just 1.3 per cent between 1982 and 1990. The investment recovery in the private economy outside manufacturing began at about the same time, and was ultimately stronger than within manufacturing. In turn, the acceleration of investment almost certainly helped to quicken productivity growth, already much improved by the long-term shake-out of obsolete means of production. The introduction of Japanese-style 'lean production' had intensified labour on the shop floor, while out-sourcing had reallocated many processes to non-unionized sectors in which workers lacked even minimal protection. In these years firms were also beginning to apply information technology to manufacturing production in significant ways (although its impact remained limited by low levels of investment). Between 1982 and 1990, despite the slowdown of investment growth, labour productivity in manufacturing thus increased at the average annual rate of some 3.3 per cent, about the same tempo as during the long postwar boom. But under the impetus of the accelerating increase of new plant and equipment from the early 1990s, it now jumped sharply to an annual average of some 4.74 per cent between 1993 and 1999. Nor was this faster rhythm simply the expression of a higher capital–labour ratio. For between 1993 and 1998 capital productivity itself continued to grow at the same 2.6 per cent pace it had reached in the 1980s expansion, making it clear that overall productiveness, taking into account both capital and labour, was rising impressively.

Services and finance

The picture was quite different in the non-manufacturing sector—services, construction, transport, utilities and mines. There improvement was sharply discontinuous and had to wait till 1996. Unlike the pattern in manufacturing, where solid productivity growth had been occurring long before the spurt of the 1990s, productivity in the non-manufacturing sector had recorded a truly dismal trajectory for almost two decades, growing at an average annual pace of 0.6 per cent between 1977 and 1995. Between 1995 and 1999, however, in the wake of the acceleration of non-manufacturing investment, and parallel to the leap upward of non-manufacturing profitability, it increased at an average annual pace of about 2.4 per cent, compared to around 2.7 per cent during the post-war boom between 1950 and 1973.

How, meanwhile, were financial institutions faring? The problems of trying to profit through lending in an era of international over-capacity and over-production in manufacturing had been brought home dramatically when the explosion of lending to Third World producers during the 1970s issued in the LDC debt crisis of the early 1980s, which shook the system to its foundations. The leading capitalist states naturally intervened to rescue the great international banks, using the IMF to insure their funds (as far as possible) by imposing the most crippling terms on the developing economies for their bridging loans. The 1980s foray by US savings and loan institutions and commercial banks into real estate followed a rather similar pattern, ending in the crash of the real-estate bubble and the collapse of many banks by the end of the decade. The resulting bail-out of the S&Ls cost American taxpayers the equivalent of three full years of US private investment. The leveraged mergers and acquisitions craze that so exemplified the financial attitudes of the era met the same sticky end. During the first half of the 1980s it did offer major gains, at a time when the profitability of new productive investment in manufacturing had reached its lowest point. But the field's potential for gain was soon constricted by over-entry, yielding steadily diminishing returns as the decade wore on and investors were obliged to pay ever more inflated prices for their takeovers. The shipwreck of the mergers and acquisitions movement contributed mightily to the declining condition of commercial banks, already suffering sharply reduced returns as a consequence of intensifying competition from a variety of non-bank lending institutions, such as insurance and finance companies, and of the trend to securitization.

The condition of the financial sector was further worsened by the onset of the recession of 1990–91. It was only another dramatic rescue operation by the government that averted a major crisis. This time, the Federal

Reserve brought down short-term real interest rates to zero to enable the banks to restore their balance sheets and resume profitable lending activity. As it turned out, financiers' problems would be dissolved with astonishing rapidity in the early 1990s. It has been the era of Clinton, Rubin and Greenspan, much more than that of Reagan and Volcker, that has witnessed the true ascendancy of finance in the American economy. When the Fed reduced short-term interest rates so sharply at the start of the decade, it enabled banks both to make windfall profits on the bonds they owned and to carry on their basic business—borrowing cheap, short-term, in order to lend dear, long-term—with unparalleled success. When Clinton promised to balance the budget by forswearing any new outlays not matched by spending cuts, he offered insurance to lenders that inflation would not eat into their profits. To allay any remaining doubts, in 1994 Greenspan raised interest rates sharply, by two and a half percentage points, to slow the expansion down.

Financial lift-off

Still, the ultimate foundation for the economic recovery of lenders and speculators was the return to health of the non-financial economy as the expansion of the 1990s progressed. The banks in particular achieved a stunning turnaround. Loan demand grew rapidly, and loan losses plummeted. Whereas in 1990 just 30 per cent of all bank assets were officially classified as 'well capitalized', the figure had risen to 97 per cent by 1996. As the economy began to prosper, moreover, banks were finally able to take maximum advantage of the process of deregulation under way since the end of the 1970s, expanding revenues from off-balance-sheet activities, such as fees from the sale of mutual funds. Meanwhile, the movement toward bank concentration begun in the 1980s accelerated, as the share of bank assets held by the top 50 bank holding companies reached 64 per cent in 1996, up from 57 per cent in 1986, while the number of commercial banking organizations fell to 7,500 from 11,000 a decade earlier. Perhaps most important, the Fed insured that the gap between what the banks paid for their short-term borrowing and what they received for their long-term lending remained 'unusually wide'.[2] The outcome was truly epoch-making. During the 1990s, US financial institutions in general, and commercial banks in particular,

---

[2] OECD, *Economic Survey. The United States 1997*, Washington, D.C. 1997, pp. 71, 176, n. 26.

achieved their highest rates of return on equity in the postwar era, and did so by a goodly margin. Indicative of the new state of affairs, financial-sector profits came to constitute a greater percentage of total corporate profits than at any time in postwar history. To put the icing on the cake, equity prices went through the roof.

By the middle of the 1990s the US corporate sector as a whole had significantly improved its condition compared to a decade earlier, largely by means of extended and brutal processes of rationalization and re-distribution. Manufacturers had engaged in wave after wave of shake-out, casting off vast quantities of outdated and redundant plant and equipment and 'downsizing' tens of thousands of employees to achieve substantial improvements in productivity. They had hugely increased their profits at the expense of workers, by means of a decade-long freeze on the growth of real wages, and at the expense of their overseas rivals, via a decade-long devaluation of the dollar. Only near the end of this recovery process did they begin to substantially step up investment and thereby productivity growth. As we have seen, it was the revival of profitability in the manufacturing sector, amplified by a major reduction in corporate taxes, that accounted virtually in toto for the recovery in the rate of profit of the non-financial sector as a whole through 1995. After 1995, this increased substantially in the non-manufacturing, mainly service sector as well, bringing profitability in the business economy as a whole still closer to the high plateau of the long postwar boom. With the real economy on a firmer foundation, the financial sector could exploit deregulation, as well unstinting government subsidy and support, to achieve an unexpected turnaround. If this symbiosis between manufacturing, service and financial sectors could be maintained, would not the US economy have finally left the long downturn behind?

II. WATERSHED: 1995–98

In the world economy, however, the recovery of American manufacturing between 1985 and 1995 had put enormous pressure on the export-oriented economies of Japan and Germany, not to speak of Western Europe as a whole. The deep recessions and large-scale industrial shake-outs experienced by Japan and Western Europe during the first half of the 1990s, under the pressure of fast-rising currencies, may fruitfully be considered the analogue of the crisis in US manufacturing

in the first half of the 1980s, following the Volcker shock, the take-off
of the dollar, and the Reagan-Regan lurch toward finance. Indeed,
Japanese and West European difficulties may have been aggravated by
the American head-start in the elimination of high-cost, low-profit firms
in similar circumstances. US revival took place at the expense of its leading rivals. But there was a price for this. In the first half of the 1990s
the underlying stagnation of the world economy as a whole, plagued by
manufacturing over-capacity and further slowed by wage repression and
tightening of credit, had not been overcome. The US recovery itself was
still constricted by the ever slower growth of world demand, and related
intensification of international competition in manufacturing. It cannot
be over-stressed that, even by the mid 1990s, the world economy showed
little sign of breaking out of its long stagnation. In fact, growth was significantly slower in this half-decade throughout the advanced capitalist
economies than in any comparable period back to 1960. This was true
not only of the Japanese and European economies, mired in deep recessions, but even of the US economy itself, which grew even more slowly
between 1990 and 1995 than it had during the 1970s and 1980s.

Such slow growth, it must be said, was anything but distressing for
the Clinton administration, which virtually from its inception combined
monetary hawkishness and fiscal stringency of a sort not seen since the
days of Eisenhower—pending a full recovery of business profitability.
Not only did Clinton reject the kind of deficit spending that had pulled
the US and international economy out of every recession since the
start of the 1970s, he embarked on a budget-balancing crusade which
reduced the Federal deficit as a percentage of GDP from 4.7 per cent
in 1992 to virtually zero in 1997. Moreover, when the economy began
to show signs of life, the Federal Reserve, as we have seen, raised interest rates by a full three percentage points between February 1994 and
February 1995. Indeed, according to public opinion polls, 'many people
thought the country was still in recession right up to 1995'.[3] It was hardly
surprising that between 1990 and 1995, American GDP, labour productivity and real wages grew even more slowly than they had during the
1970s and 1980s.

---

[3] *Economic Report of the President 1996*, Washington, DC, 1996, p. 46; Rich Miller et
al, 'How Prosperity is Shaping the American Economy', *Business Week*, 14 February
2000.

Starting in 1996, however, there was a break in the pattern. In that year, and the one that followed, the growth of every major economic variable palpably accelerated, even including (with a lag) real wages. Clearly, the recovery of profitability in the manufacturing sector, based heavily on dollar devaluation, wage restraint and corporate tax relief—and only very recently amplified by the boom in investment—was beginning to pay off. In 1997, as real exports grew by 14 per cent, the economy flourished as it had not done for several decades, and it began to appear that the US might finally lead the world economy out of the doldrums. The expansion of the US domestic market which was making possible export-led growth internationally was no longer being driven, as it had been for decades, primarily by US government deficits, but, to an important degree, by rising exports and capital investment, founded upon increasing competitiveness and rising profit-rates. Yet just at the moment when faster growth began to take hold in the US economy, from the end of 1995, its foundations started to be transformed by two closely interrelated developments. On the one hand, a sudden rise in the dollar began to undermine US manufacturing exports, by driving up the relative cost of American goods and indirectly precipitating the end of the East Asian boom. On the other hand, an exploding stock-market bubble, financing a feverish growth of indebtedness, began to shift the driving force of expansion towards domestic consumption, and in so doing to speed up substantially the growth of the US economy.

Reverse Plaza

The turning point in the germination of both of these developments, and indeed the evolution of the world economy during the second half of the 1990s, was the agreement forged by the US, Japan and the other G7 powers that would come to be called the 'Reverse Plaza Accord'. During the first part of 1995, in the wake of the collapse of the peso and the subsequent US bail-out of the Mexican economy, there was a new run on the dollar, sharply accentuating its secular fall over the previous decade. A cheap currency had, of course, been an indispensable precondition for the revival of profitability in the US manufacturing and non-financial economy as a whole, and Washington had more than welcomed it, returning between 1985 and 1995 to the policy of 'benign neglect' towards the dollar that had prevailed during most of the 1970s. So when the dollar plummeted during the early months of 1995, the Clinton administration not only did nothing to stand in its way, but even turned up the pressure on Japan, threatening to close off the US market for Japanese cars if Japan did not agree to open up its market to US auto-parts.

By April 1995, however, the same low dollar that had been helping to drive the US manufacturing economy for a decade had brought the Japanese to the edge of collapse. The yen had risen by 60 per cent over its level at the start of 1991, and by 30 per cent over its level at the beginning of 1994, to a record-high exchange rate of 79 against the dollar. At this astronomic height, Japanese producers could not even cover their variable costs, and the Japanese growth machine appeared to be grinding to a halt. Despite what had been, right up to this juncture, their almost obsessive concern with manufacturing competitiveness, US authorities were in no position to regard this development with equanimity. They had just been shocked by the Mexican crisis, which, arising 'from nowhere', had shaken the international financial system. A Japanese version would obviously be very much more dangerous. And even if a Japanese crisis could be contained, it might easily precipitate a large-scale liquidation of Japan's enormous holdings of US assets, especially Treasury Bonds. Such a development would drive up interest rates, frighten money markets, and possibly catalyse a recession at the very moment when the US economy finally appeared to right itself. The next presidential election was, moreover, beginning to loom. Led by Treasury Secretary Robert Rubin, the US not only summarily dropped its campaign to force open the Japanese auto-parts market, but entered into an arrangement with the Japanese and Germans to take joint action to drive down the yen (and Deutschmark) and push up the dollar. This was to be accomplished in part by lowering Japanese interest rates vis-à-vis American, but also by stepping up Japanese and German purchase of dollars, as well as intervention by the Treasury itself to support the US currency.[4]

This was a momentous agreement, representing a total about-face in the policies both of the US and its main allies and rivals, in much the same way as had the original Plaza Accord of 1985. The US relinquished the advantage the cheap currency had given its manufacturing sector for almost a decade. But it secured in exchange the prospect of a huge inflow of funds that could be expected to help cover its rising current-account deficit and push up equity prices, as well as a flood of cheap imports

---

[4] For this and the previous paragraph, see R. Taggart Murphy, *The Weight of the Yen*, New York 1996; J. B. Judis, 'Dollar Foolish', *New Republic*, 9 December 1996.

which could be counted on to exert strong downward pressure on prices, relieving the Fed of much of the job of containing inflation. In a sense, the Clinton administration was favouring lenders and stock-market speculators at the expense of manufacturers, in much the same way as the Reagan administration had done during the first half of the 1980s. It may have believed that a slimmed-down US manufacturing sector could now successfully withstand a rise of the dollar. It may also have felt that increasing profitability in services and growing domestic consumption could make up for any decline in manufacturing profitability and export growth. In any event, powerful reverberations from this deal were felt immediately throughout the world system, in just the opposite way that the dramatic effects of the original Plaza Accord had been registered from 1985. A rising currency now began to squeeze American (rather than Japanese and German) manufacturing; Japanese and German industries (rather than US) initiated (short-lived) recoveries; and East Asia slid from record boom in the wake of the Plaza Accord to regional depression in the wake of Reverse Plaza. At the same time, a huge financial bubble now blew up in the US, enabling the American economic expansion to accelerate on the basis of rising shares, increasing debt and runaway consumption—much as the bubble in Japan had done, after 1985.

Equity surge

From the time of the Volcker recession at the start of the 1980s, the US stock market had been enjoying an historic ascent. This had been interrupted by the stock-market crash of 1987; but when not only the US Fed but also the Japanese financial authorities took decisive action to cut short the collapse in equity prices, many investors began to believe that the stock market would never be allowed to drop too severely, and the bull run continued. Between 1990 and 1993, the rising market was driven further up when Greenspan reduced short-term real interest rates to zero, in order to rescue debt-burdened corporations and failing banks—opening the way for a massive expansion of liquidity. Since opportunities to profit were still relatively limited in a US real economy only slowly recovering from recession, the resulting flood of extra-cheap money poured into the stock market, catalysing a major new escalation of equity prices in these years. Still, by the end of 1995 share prices, even after a rapid increase over the better part of a dozen years, had failed to outdistance the growth of corporate profits. It could indeed be said without too much exaggeration that the dramatic rise in equity prices up to that point basically reflected the recovery of profitability in the US economy from its depressed state in the recession of the early 1980s. Between 1980 and 1995 the index of equity prices on the New York Stock Exchange climbed by a factor of 4.28, while after-tax profits increased by a factor of 4.68. But from this point onwards, share prices quickly lost contact with underlying corporate profits, as the stock-market bubble blew up.

Clearly, the recovery of profitability that had begun a decade previously, and the high levels of investor confidence this had created, were necessary conditions for the surge of equity prices that took place from 1995–96. The forces that actually powered it are less easy to specify. But it is hard to avoid the conclusion that the dramatic transformations in international financial conditions and flows set off in the course of 1995 were largely responsible. In March 1995, in the wake of the Mexican bailout, the Fed ended the credit-tightening campaign it had begun about a year earlier and, starting in July 1995, lowered rates by about three-quarters of a point during the subsequent half year. Perhaps even more significant, the measures taken to implement the Reverse Plaza Accord not only began to drive up the dollar, thereby amplifying increases in the value of US assets (including equities) for internationally oriented investors, but also unleashed a torrent of cash from Japan, East Asia and the world at large into US financial markets, sharply easing the cost of borrowing for share-purchases.

In April 1995, the Bank of Japan cut the official discount rate, already a very low 1.75 per cent, to 1 per cent and, the following September, reduced it further to 0.5 per cent. This did help to bring about the desired effect of reducing the yen's value. But rather than strongly stimulating a domestic economy in which profit rates were still too low to justify much long-term investment in new plant and equipment, Japan's ultra-low interest rates had the effect of pumping up the global supply of credit, as a major portion of increased Japanese liquidity leaked out of the country. US investors, in particular, fabricated a very profitable 'carry trade', borrowing yen in Japan at a low rate of interest, converting them into dollars, and using the latter to invest around the world. Much of the proceeds found their way back into the US stock market.[5]

---

[5] *Weight of the Yen*; Ron Bevacqua, 'Whither the Japanese Model?', *Review of International Political Economy*, vol. 5, no. 3, September 1998, pp. 410–23.

Meanwhile, Japanese authorities were pouring money into US government securities and US currency, and encouraging Japanese insurance companies to follow suit by relaxing regulations on overseas investment. Governments from East Asia, aiming to hold down the value of local currencies so as to sustain export growth, did the same and were followed by private investors, especially from hedge funds, from all over the world. In 1995 the rest of the world thus bought US government securities worth $197.2 billion, two and a half times the average for the previous four years, following up with purchases of $312 billion in 1996 and $189.6 billion in 1997. Of these purchases, by far the greater part were Treasury instruments—$168.5 billion in 1995, $270.7 billion in 1996, and $139.7 billion in 1997. The grand total of more than half a trillion dollars of US Treasury instruments purchased by foreigners in these three years covered not only the total new debt issued by the US Treasury in this period, but a further $266.2 billion of US government debt previously held by, and now bought from, US citizens.[6]

Such enormous purchases could not but dramatically ease conditions on US money markets, driving down interest rates and freeing a flood of liquidity to purchase US equities. Between January 1995, when they hit their peak in the wake of the bond-market crunch of 1994, and January 1996, interest rates on thirty-year Treasury bonds fell sharply from 7.85 per cent to 6.05 per cent. This near 25 per cent reduction in the cost of long-term borrowing over the course of 1995 was a major factor in catalysing the stock-market bubble. So, too, was the new take-off of the dollar, triggered by dramatic purchases of the currency by US authorities, in coordination with their Japanese and German counterparts, in May and August of 1995; and subsequently propelled by the tidal wave of foreign purchases of US government securities. The dollar's exchange rate against the yen shot up by 50 per cent in the short period between April 1995 and the end of 1996.

---

[6] Board of Governors of the Federal Reserve System, *Flow of Funds Accounts of the United States. Flows and Outstandings* [henceforth FRB, *Flow of Funds*], Table F.107 Rest of World (flows) and Table F.209 Treasury Securities (flows); OECD, *Economic Survey. United States 1995*, Paris 1995, pp. 55–8; OECD, *Economic Survey. United States 1996*, Paris 1996, pp. 49–51; OECD, *Economic Survey. United States 1997*, Paris 1997, pp. 73–5. The difference between total government securities and total Treasury instruments purchased by the rest of the world in these years was made up of government agency securities, bonds issued by entities like FNMA or FIX.

With interest rates falling so sharply and the dollar rising so rapidly, the stock market could not but take off. After having risen respectively by just 2 and 1.8 per cent in 1994, the S&P 500 and the NYSE jumped up by 17.6 and 14.6 per cent in 1995, by far the biggest increases since 1989. Both indexes rose by a further 23 per cent during 1996, and by December of that year Greenspan was already issuing his famous warning against 'irrational exuberance'. Investors ignored his admonition. In 1997, the S&P 500 increased by another 30 per cent, the NYSE an additional 27 per cent. The expansion of the US equity price bubble beginning in 1995 was soon amplifying the accelerating growth in the economy at large. Major sales of shares, especially to corporations that financed their buybacks through debt, added substantially to households' buying power. At the same time, the inflation of asset values resulting from the rise in stock prices appeared to justify a historic running down of household savings, as well as a big increase in household borrowing. Acceleration of consumption in turn gave a major fillip to what appeared to be an increasingly powerful boom, while the rise in US imports and current-account deficit helped pull the world economy out of the recessions of the first half of the decade. The non-manufacturing sector was the principal beneficiary at home. With consumption growth accelerating, demand for its products expanded accordingly. Since its output was composed mainly of non-tradeables, far from being hurt by the flood of imports cheapened by the high dollar, it enjoyed lower-cost imports. Non-manufacturing investment rose very rapidly and, as already noted, brought about a real leap in the growth of productivity. Between 1995 and 1997, long-flat (though never extremely reduced) profitability in the service sector rose by 22 per cent, taking the rate of profit in the non-financial private economy as a whole to within 19 per cent of its 1965 peak.[7] It appeared that the economy was finally operating on all cylinders.

Debacle of 1998

By the autumn of 1997, the East Asian crisis had only just begun to unfold, and the US economy was at the zenith of its manufacturing-led revival. In 1996 and 1997, manufacturing output and exports continued to grow rapidly. Costs of production, moreover, were still falling sharply, as the annual growth of labour productivity averaged 3.2 per cent, the

---

[7] In 1997, *after-tax* non-financial corporate and corporate profit rates came within 15 and 9 per cent, respectively, of their 1965 high-points.

output-capital ratio 6 per cent, and nominal compensation a mere 2.2 per cent in these years. Nevertheless, over the same two-year period, the real effective exchange rate of the dollar rose by 20 per cent, and its value versus the yen by 50 per cent, placing powerful downward pressure on the prices of tradeable goods. Manufacturing product prices were thus forced down at an average annual rate of 3.5 per cent in 1996 and 1997, with the result that the rise of the manufacturing rate of profit—and that of the private economy as a whole—originating in the mid 1980s and only briefly interrupted in the recession of the early 1990s, finally came to an end during the second half of 1997.[8]

When the Asian crisis hit, US producers had to face not only stepped-up competition from their rivals in Japan, Germany and elsewhere in Western Europe who were benefiting from falling currencies. They also had to confront the collapse of hitherto dynamic East Asian export markets and the flooding of US domestic markets by East Asian imports, made extraordinarily cheap by the depreciation of East Asian currencies. The growth of US exports, an essential motor of the boom, plummeted in real terms from 14 per cent in 1997 to 2 per cent in 1998, from an average annual rate of 17.4 per cent in the third quarter of 1997 to minus 0.5 per cent in the second and third quarters of 1998. US real imports, meanwhile, continued to expand at an 11.8 per cent clip in 1998, compared to 14.2 per cent in 1997. With export and import prices tumbling by 3.1 per cent and 5.9 per cent respectively in 1998, the US manufacturing sector was set for a fall; the corporate manufacturing profit rate fell by about 12 per cent, vis-à-vis 1997.[9] Declining corporate profits in turn exerted downward pressure on equity markets. Share prices of the smaller companies represented on the Russell 2000 were most vulnerable, falling by 20 per cent between April and the first week in August. By that point, the elite S&P 500 had itself begun to drop, losing 10 per cent from its mid-July peak; in the wake of the Russian default, it fell a further 10 per cent. The stock-market decline threatened to put a quick end to the US expansion by destroying business confidence and sending

---

[8] Cf. OECD, *Economic Survey. United States 1999*, Paris 1999, p. 32, esp. Figure 7. 'After a rapid rise from 1992 to the middle of 1997, corporate profits have weakened recently, and their share of the national income has begun to drop.'
[9] Bureau of Economic Analysis, 'National Income and Product Accounts: Second Quarter 2000 GDP and Revised Estimates: 1997 Through First Quarter 2000', 28 July 2000.

into reverse the rising tide of domestic consumption. With much of the rest of the international economy in crisis, a recession in the US now threatened to plunge the world into depression.

III. THE BUBBLE SUSTAINS THE BOOM

By late September 1998, a major crisis was unfolding in the US. The Russian default triggered a flight to quality in the bond markets, manifested in the emergence of huge differentials between the interest rates paid on relatively safe US Treasuries and those on less secure corporate bonds, LDC sovereign debt, and even certain European government issues. The shares of commercial banks dropped precipitously, on fears of big losses on loans to emerging nations. But the greatest losses were sustained by the hedge funds and proprietary trading desks of commercial and investment banks, collectively known as Highly Leveraged Financial Institutions (HLFI), which lost untold billions of dollars after accumulating huge long positions in high-risk, poorer-quality, higher-yielding debt instruments, offset by short positions in developed nations' government bonds.

The watershed came on 20 September, when the huge Long Term Capital Management hedge fund (LTCM) admitted to the US government that it was facing insolvency. It was at this juncture that the US Fed intervened. It brought together a consortium of fourteen Wall Street banks and brokerage houses to organize a $3.6 billion bail-out of LTCM. Greenspan justified this rescue operation of a non-bank on the grounds that, had the Fed failed to act, the international financial system would have been put in jeopardy.[10] The Fed then made its famous three successive interest-rate cuts, including one dramatic reduction between its regular meetings. If its immediate aim was to counteract the danger of financial markets seizing up, a broader goal was from the start to revive equity prices, and keep the long-running bull market going. The Fed's interest-rate reductions thus marked a turning point, not so much because the resulting fall in the cost of borrowing was all that great, but because it gave such a strong positive signal to investors that it wanted

---

[10] On the unfolding financial crisis of autumn 1998, see Peter Warburton, *Debt and Delusion. Central Bank Follies that Threaten Economic Disaster*, London 2000, pp. 263–6.

stocks to rise, in order to stabilize a domestic and international economy that was careening toward crisis. Greenspan vigorously denied, of course, that his interest rate reductions were at all designed to affect share prices. But investors did not have to be reminded that his intervention at this juncture was hardly the first of his bail-outs of financiers and corporations. In October 1987, he had intervened to counter the stock-market crash, and between 1990 and 1992 he had reduced real short-term interest rates to zero to rescue failing banks and deeply indebted corporations, in the wake of the S&L and commercial banks crises, and the leveraged mergers and acquisitions debacle. Nor had it escaped their notice that the US Treasury and Federal Reserve had gone out of their way to rescue the leading international banks at the time of the Latin American debt crisis of 1982; the American investors who stood to suffer huge losses as a result of the Mexican collapse of 1994–95; and the international banks, once again, at the time of the crisis in East Asia of 1997–98.

Investors were thus confirmed in their view that Greenspan simply would not allow stock prices to fall too far, all the more so because they realized how dependent the current economic expansion had become on consumption and thus the bull market. In truth, Greenspan probably had little choice. The main foundation of the US expansion, the recovery of manufacturing profitability, had given way under the impact of the rising dollar and the worsening of world over-production that had resulted from the crisis in East Asia. Between 1987 and 1997 export growth had been responsible for almost one-third of total growth of GDP—in 1998 and 1999 taken together, for only 7 per cent. To avert a downturn on an international scale, the Fed was in effect substituting a new form of demand stimulus—increased private debt, both corporate and consumer—for the old Keynesian kind, based on public deficits. The American stimulus would function much as it had in the mid 1970s and early 1980s to pull the world away from recession.

The Fed's decisive intervention in the equity and credit markets in autumn–winter 1998 not only put a stop to the frightening fall of the stock market of the previous summer but enabled it to skyrocket further, without the benefit of any rise in profits at all. Thus, during 1998 and 1999, the NYSE Index increased by 20.5 per cent and 12.5 per cent, respectively, even though after-tax corporate profits net of interest grew by minus 3.9 per cent and 4.6 per cent. In the same two years, the

S&P 500 Index increased by 27 per cent and 19 per cent, respectively, despite earnings for S&P 500 firms of 0 per cent in 1998 and 17 per cent in 1999. The Fed jumped in to re-assure the credit markets yet again at the end of 1999, ostensibly in response to possible Y2K disruption. By pumping sufficient liquidity into the banking system to bring the Federal Funds Rate suddenly down from 5.5 to below 4 per cent—the widest deviation from its target rate in nine years—Greenspan paved the way for a final frantic, upward leap in the equity markets during the first quarter of 2000. By March 2000, the S&P 500 had risen 20 per cent above its level at the end of October 1999. It now stood at 3.3 times its level at the end of 1994. The technology and internet-dominated NASDAQ had exploded in much more extreme fashion, up from 2736 in early October 1999 to 5000 in March 2000.

Corporate buy-backs

If the conditions making for the continual expansion of the bubble were nurtured by the Fed, equity prices were themselves directly, and consciously, pushed up by the corporations. In the course of the leveraged mergers and acquisitions craze of the 1980s, firms had initiated the practice of buying up their own stock through ever increasing assumption of debt. The remarkable outcome was that corporations made the overwhelming majority of net purchases of equities during this era: no less than 72.5 per cent between 1983 and 1990. Although their capital expenditures were quite limited in this period, corporate cash flow covered only about 87.5 per cent of such outlays, leaving 12.5 per cent to be financed by borrowing. It follows that fully 100 per cent of corporate stock purchases in those years were financed by further borrowing. Corporate stock purchases absorbed 50 per cent of corporate borrowing and amounted to 125 per cent of retained earnings (after-tax profits of enterprise minus dividends) and 25 per cent of corporate cash flow (retained earnings plus depreciation).[11]

During the first three years of the 1990s, in the wake of the corporate debt crisis, firms pretty much ceased both to buy back stocks or to borrow. But, beginning in 1994, taking up where they had left off during the leveraged mergers and acquisitions movement of the 1980s,

---

[11] FRB, *Flow of Funds*, Table F.102 Non-farm Non-financial Corporate Business (flows); Table F.213 Corporate Equities (flows).

they went ever more deeply into debt. As in that earlier era, moreover, they did so hardly at all for the purpose of funding investment in new plant and equipment, which continued to be covered mainly out of internal funds, but instead mainly for the purpose of buying back stocks. The resumption of the mergers and acquisitions movement, which has accelerated in recent years, accounted for some of these operations. Somewhat lower real interest rates, which made the cost of borrowing cheaper, together with a tax system that is lighter on capital gains than dividends and allows corporations to write off interest payments entirely, were also important factors. But it is clear that, as the 1990s progressed, mounting stock buy-backs were increasingly driven by the desire of corporate executives, taking an increasing part of their salaries in the form of stock options, to drive up company stock values simply to line their own pockets. They have had no hesitation in resorting to ever more debt to accomplish this. By 1999, the corporate debt-to-equity ratio of S&P 500 companies had shot up to 116 per cent, compared to 84 per cent at the end of the 1980s, when the corporate debt crisis had paralysed both banks and corporations.[12] In the years 1994–99 inclusive, borrowing by non-financial corporations amounted to $1.22 trillion. Of that total, corporations used just 15.3 per cent to fund capital expenditures, financing the rest of such purchases out of retained earnings plus depreciation, while they devoted no less than 57 per cent or $697.4 billion, to buying back stocks—an amount equal to about 75 per cent of their retained earnings and 18 per cent of their cash flow.

Bubblemania

By the first quarter of 2000, the value of corporate equities, their market capitalization, had soared to $19.6 trillion, up from $6.3 trillion in 1994. The incongruity of this figure, and this ascent, was evident from many angles. Most definitive, of course, was the lack of connexion between the rise of share prices and the growth of output—and particularly of profitability—of the underlying economy. Market capitalization as a percentage of GDP had needed just five years between 1995 and early 2000 to *triple* from 50 per cent to 150 per cent of GDP—despite the fact that after-tax corporate profits had risen by only 41.2 per cent in the interim. By contrast, it had taken a full thirteen years between 1982 and 1995 just

---

[12] Daniel Bogler and Gary Silverman, 'US Risky Debt Threat to Banks', *Financial Times*, 22 February 2000.

to double from 25 per cent to 50 per cent of GDP—even though corporate profits had risen by 160 per cent in the intervening period.[13] Equally
telling was the unprecedented divergence between companies' valuations on the stock market in terms of the price of their equities and the
value of the financial and physical capital that they possessed. In the first
quarter of 2000, the ratio of the stock-market value of US non-financial
corporations to their net worth—known as Tobin's Q—reached 1.92, up
from 0.94 in 1994 and 1.14 in 1995, and from an average of 0.65 for
the twentieth century as a whole. This was some *50 per cent* higher than
this ratio's previous peaks during the twentieth century, which came,
not surprisingly, in 1929 (at 1.3) and 1969 (at 1.2), at the very conclusions of the stock market booms of those decades.

With corporations' shares costing so much more than the means of
production and financial assets that they owned, it would seem to have
been only common sense for investors to buy new plant and equipment and the like, rather than purchase equities, in order to secure
any given amount of capital. That they so often did the opposite was a
clear indication that a bubble was in progress.[14] Finally, in March 2000,
the price-to-earnings ratio for the corporations represented on the S&P
500 index—the ratio of what it costs, on average, to buy a share with
respect to the annual earnings (profits) that share represents—reached
about 32. In view of the extent to which the rise of share prices had
diverged from the increase of profits, it is not surprising that this was
again a record—at least one third higher than this ratio's previous peaks
during the twentieth century, and about two and a half times its historical average of 13.2. The annual rate of return on equities—the so-called
earnings yield, which is simply the price–earnings ratio inverted—was
thus extremely low in historical terms—around 3 per cent, compared to
the historical average of 7.7 per cent. One might therefore have expected
that stocks would have been regarded as an increasingly bad investment.

---

[13] Martin Wolf, 'Walking on Troubled Waters,' *Financial Times*, 12 January 2000.
Wolf's figures do not jibe perfectly with those in the most recent FRB, *Flow of
Funds*, but they are close enough.

[14] FRB, *Flow of Funds*, B.102. Balance Sheet of Nonfinancial Corporations, line 37;
Andrew Smithers and Stephen Wright, *Valuing Wall Street: Protecting Wealth in
Turbulent Times*, New York 2000, p. 10, Chart 2.1, and pp.146–54, 257. Net worth
is defined as financial assets plus their tangible assets in real estate, equipment and
software, and inventories at what it would currently cost to replace them, minus
their liabilities.

That the opposite was the case was indicative of the fact that equities were being purchased, for the most part, simply on the expectation that their prices would go up further, irrespective of corporations' rates of return, and one more sign of the bubble dynamic.[15]

Household debt

Meanwhile, private citizens were launched on their own spree. Between 1994 and the first quarter of 2000, the value of equities held by households rose from $4.5 trillion to $11.5 trillion.[16] Buoyed by this enormous asset appreciation, households felt they had the wherewithal to decrease savings and step up borrowing to an historically unprecedented degree. Between 1950 and 1992, the personal savings rate had never gone above 10.9 per cent and never fallen below 7.5 per cent, except in three isolated years. Between 1992 and the first half of 2000, it plummeted from 8.7 per cent to 0.3 per cent. Conversely, household borrowing soared— although as a percentage of GDP it did not quite reach the record levels of the 1980s, probably because borrowing by working-class families to compensate for declining incomes was not as widespread as in the earlier period. Still, by 1999 household debt as a proportion of personal disposable income reached the all-time high of 97 per cent, up from an average of 80 per cent during the second half of the 1980s. Throughout this same period, 1994–99 inclusive, households were in every single year net sellers of equities, for a total of $218 billion. Put crudely, corporations, with some significant help from state and local government retirement funds and life insurance companies, made the net purchases that drove up the stock market, largely by means of stepping up their borrowing. Households took advantage of the resulting inflation of asset values not just to increase their borrowing and decrease their savings, but to realize significant capital gains.[17]

In order to respond to the skyrocketing demand for loans from households and corporations, to cover increased consumption as well as the purchase of equities, financial institutions had vastly to expand their

---

[15] *Valuing Wall Street*, pp. 226 and 227, esp. Chart 22.1.

[16] FRB, *Flow of Funds*, Table L.213 Corporate Equities (levels).

[17] FRB, *Flow of Funds*, Table F.213 Corporate Equities (flows). The figure given here for net sales by households is derived by subtracting net equity purchases by mutual funds of $882 billion in these years from net household equity sales of $1.1 trillion.

own borrowing. Between 1995 and 1999, financial-sector borrowing increased by two and a half times and averaged just about 10 per cent of GDP, more than double the average of the previous decade. This was manifest in the rapid growth of the money supply. Between 1995 and 1999, M3 grew at an average annual rate of just under 8.3 per cent, compared to 1 per cent a year between 1990 and 1995. Such a burst of borrowing by the financial sector could not have occurred without the blessing of the Federal Reserve, which might, for example, have increased interest rates or reserve requirements had it wished to keep down the growth of debt to fund stock purchases and consumption. But containing the bubble could not have been farther from Alan Greenspan's mind. Indeed, during the years 1998–99, financial-sector borrowing averaged 12 per cent of GDP, which was 75 per cent higher than in any previous year on record. In the same two years, just to be sure that available liquidity was great enough to support the enormous binge taking place, the government itself, through such entities as the Federal National Mortgage Association and the Federal Home Loan Mortgage Association, lent a cool $0.6 trillion to consumers for house purchases and the like. Its own borrowing to do so amounted to almost 30 per cent of total financial-sector debt in these years. By the end of 1999, household, corporate and financial debt were all at their highest levels as percentages of GDP in postwar US history.

Runaway consumption

As savings collapsed, debt mounted and big capital gains were realized, personal consumption sped up, playing an ever greater role in driving economic growth. After increasing at an average annual rate of 2.9 per cent and accounting for about two-thirds of the growth of GDP between 1985 and 1995, household expenditures grew at an average annual pace of 4.2 per cent between 1995 and 1999, when they were responsible for 73 per cent of GDP increase. As the Fed and the Treasury must have hoped, moreover, this more than made up for the collapse of exports from the end of 1997, increasing at the torrid average annual rate of 5 per cent and accounting for four-fifths of a GDP growth of 4.3 per cent a year in 1998–99. All told, after having increased at a rate of 2.4 per cent between 1989 and 1995, GDP grew at a rate of 4.15 per cent between 1995 and 1999. Of this, according to the Federal Reserve, about a quarter could be attributed to the 'wealth effect' of the skyrocketing stock market. Put another way, stock-market-driven consumption boosted the growth of GDP in this period by about one-third. Real wages, too, finally began to increase substantially in 1998 and 1999, averaging 3.3 per cent in the non-farm sector, after having averaged 0.3 per cent between 1986 and 1996, giving a further major lift to consumption in these years.

US supply could not keep up with this level of demand. By 1998–99 the increase in gross domestic purchases was outrunning that of gross domestic product by 25 per cent. Goods produced abroad had to fill the gap, and real imports of goods and services rose at the very rapid pace of 11.2 per cent per annum between 1995 and 1999, compared to 6.1 per cent per annum between 1985 and 1995. Such ballooning US imports were critical in reviving the world economy from 1995, and indispensable in preventing it from falling into depression in the wake of the East Asian crisis of 1997–98. During the early years of the 1990s, the US current account deficit had come back somewhat from its record highs of the mid to late 1980s. But, from 1994–95, as the economy began to expand, the external balance started to slide again. Once export growth collapsed and consumption accelerated in 1998, trade and current-account deficits exploded. In 1999 and 2000, both set new records.

To finance these, the US had no choice but to incur growing liabilities to overseas purchasers. Foreign investors, however, hardly needed coaxing to purchase American assets, and their rush to get hold of them helped considerably to swell the bubble. The process got under way in 1995, when Japanese and other East Asian governments sought to keep down their exchange rates by purchasing US government securities, and private buyers followed suit to take advantage of the rising dollar. But in 1997, the composition of overseas purchases shifted significantly. Various East Asian governments were obliged to liquidate dollar assets in an effort to support their plummeting currencies. On the other hand, private investors abroad increasingly saw the US as a safe haven in a world under threat of recession and stepped up foreign direct investments, becoming even more central players in US equity and corporate bond markets. In the first quarter of 2000 they were responsible for 30 per cent of total purchases of shares—up from 15 per cent in 1999 and 7 per cent in 1998—and 40 per cent of total bond purchases—up from 33 per cent in 1999 and 20 per cent in 1998.

The growth of foreign entry into these markets amplified the US asset boom, as overseas lenders directly and indirectly subsidized debt-driven consumption, so that US demand could subsidize their own exports. The fact remains that the bulk of the assets they bought could be liquidated with relative ease—their private purchases of US Treasuries, corporate bonds and equities between 1995 and the first half of 2000 amounting to around $1.6 trillion, compared to around 900 billion in direct investments. By the first half of 2000, gross US assets held by the rest of the world reached $6.7 trillion, or 67 per cent of US GDP, compared to just $3.4 trillion, or 46 per cent of GDP, in 1995. Of these, $3.49 trillion were composed of privately held US treasury certificates, corporate bonds and equities, compared to $1.2 trillion in direct investments.[18] The dependence of American prosperity—and the prospects for global expansion—on unprecedented foreign purchases of US assets, is stark. So, too, is the vulnerability of the US boom to any withdrawal of overseas confidence.

IV. THE CONTOURS AND CHARACTER OF THE BOOM

Given the extraordinary hype surrounding it, the contours of the expansion of the 1990s and the boom to which it has given rise should be kept in perspective. In 1999 Alan Greenspan gushed: 'We are witnessing, this decade in the US, history's most compelling demonstration of the productive capacity of free peoples operating in free markets.' He had clearly been seduced by his own creation. Taking the data at face value, there are no grounds yet for thinking that we have entered a 'new economy'—if by 'new economy' is meant one of unique (or even unusual) productivity and vitality, in historical terms, and not just greater dynamism than during the long downturn of the two decades after 1973.

The performance of the US economy in the decade of the 1990s as a whole did not remotely compare to that of the first three decades of the post-war era. The decade's business cycle has been stronger, but not dramatically so, than those of the 1980s (1979–90) or the 1970s (1973–79). Moreover, to the degree it did improve upon its predecessors, this was

---

[18] FRB, *Flow of Funds*, Table L.107 Rest of the World (levels). Between 1995 and 2000, *net* US assets held by the rest of the world doubled, reaching $1.4 trillion, or 14.2 per cent of GDP, compared to just $0.7 trillion, or 9.4 per cent of GDP a brief five years before. 'Net assets' here simply means gross assets held by the rest of the world, minus liabilities of the rest of the world to US entities (which here includes the market value of foreign equities held by US residents).

entirely due to the growth acceleration after 1995.[19] Till then, American economic performance in the 1990s failed to better that of the 1970s and 1980s, let alone that of the 1950s and 1960s. In terms of the growth of GDP, it was actually worse. Since 1995, the expansion has become considerably more powerful. But even the boom of the four and a half years between 1995 and the middle of 2000 has, at best, barely been able to match the twenty-three-year economic expansion between 1950 and 1973, in terms of the average annual growth of GDP—4.15 per cent versus 4.2 per cent; of labour productivity—2.7 per cent versus 2.7 per cent; of real wages—1.8 per cent versus 2.7 per cent; or of the rate of unemployment—4.7 per cent versus 4.2 per cent (and that long period, unlike the present short one, included several recessions). Of course, the magnitude of the expansion of the US economy during the long post-war upturn did not remotely compare to that of Japan, or of most of Western Europe.

It should also be pointed out that the pace of US job creation during the 1990s has been less than that during the upswings of the 1970s and 1980s, and has delivered such low rates of unemployment mainly because the expansion started with little labour-market slack, compared to those predecessors. Moreover, the growth of real wages has been reasonably rapid only since 1998. In fact, as late as 1997 the real hourly-wage level in the non-farm economy was no higher than it had been in 1992. For production and non-supervisory workers, the situation was very much worse: by 1999, their average hourly real wage had failed to surpass its level of 1970, and was still more than 5 per cent below its 1979 peak. Meanwhile, notoriously, the distribution of wealth over the course of the 1990s got much worse: between 1989 and 1997, the top 1 per cent increased its net worth by 11.3 per cent, the top 5 per cent by 10 per cent, the top 10 per cent by 4.1 per cent, and the bottom 90 per cent by minus 4.4 per cent.[20]

---

[19] Indeed, if one were to consider only the *expansion* of the 1990s, i.e. the period in the business cycle from the point it hits bottom and turns up (the trough), 'it has not been the expansion with the highest rate of growth, [and] even during the last four years, average growth only just reached that of the expansion of the 1980s and remained well short of that of the 1960s.' Bank for International Settlements, *70th Annual Report 1999–2000*, Basel, 5 June 2000, p. 13. The reason that the business cycle of the 1990s as a whole looks slightly better than its predecessors of the 1980s and 1970s is that the recession of 1990–91 with which it began was much shallower than those of 1974–75 and 1979–82.

Perhaps most telling of all, the rate of growth of labour productivity achieved in the US manufacturing sector since 1993, the evidence most commonly cited for the emergence of a 'new economy', is not clearly better than that of its leading rivals. Whereas US manufacturing productivity increased at an annual rate of 4.7 per cent between 1993 and 1999, German and French manufacturing productivity grew at the average rates of 5 per cent (through 1998) and 4.25 per cent, respectively. During the same period, Japanese manufacturing productivity lagged somewhat, averaging 3.7 per cent, but was clearly held down by recession (yielding less than zero productivity growth for a couple of these years). In fact, between 1990 and 1998, non-farm labour productivity growth in the Euro area as a whole was roughly equal to that of the US, averaging about 2 per cent a year, and the increase in total factor productivity was somewhat higher.[21]

A new vitality

Bearing all this in mind, it remains true that, when the burst of growth beginning in 1996 is taken into account, the business cycle of the 1990s did mark a modest improvement over that of the 1970s and 1980s, and the recent four-to-five year US boom does represent a clear discontinuity in the context of the past quarter-century's long stagnation. How should the numbers be interpreted? It is clear that during the course of the 1990s the American economy displayed a major increase in vitality, expressed in interrelated accelerations in investment and productivity growth in the non-farm economy, after very extended periods of investment stagnation and slow productivity gains.[22] Between 1995 and the middle of 2000, real business plant and equipment averaged respec-

---

[20] Bank for International Settlements, *70th Annual Report 1999–2000*, p. 14; Lawrence Mishel et al, *The State of Working America 2000–2001* (preliminary edition), Ithaca 2000, p. 121, Figure 2A; Lawrence Mishel et al, *The State of Working America 1998–1999*, Ithaca 1999, p. 264, Table 5.6.

[21] US Bureau of Labor Statistics, 'International Comparisons of Manufacturing Productivity and Unit Labor Cost Trends, Revised Data for 1998', News Release, p. 7, Table B and p. 17, Table 1; 'Europe's Economies: Stumbling Yet Again?', *Economist*, 16 September 2000, p. 78, chart 2.

[22] In what follows, I tend to accept, especially for the sake of argument, the government's revised economic statistics, and try to present a coherent picture based on them. But it must be emphasized that changes in methods of measurement have been very great, and the resulting numbers may decisively over-state the growth of the key variables.

tively 17 and 9.7 per cent as a percentage of GDP, compared to 14.6 and 6 per cent during the eight-year expansion of the 1980s, and 13.4 and 3.4 per cent during the nine-year expansion of the 1960s. During the same four-and-a-half-year period, non-farm labour productivity growth averaged 2.7 per cent, compared to 1.6 per cent between 1990 and 1995 and 1.4 per cent between 1973 and 1990.[23]

In light of this increase in the rate of capital accumulation, the figures indicating a parallel upsurge in the growth of labour productivity, even if overstated, would appear mostly to carry conviction, despite the technical controversy surrounding them. The case is fairly clear-cut for manufacturing, simply because the acceleration of both productivity and investment has been so pronounced, and has occurred where one would expect it. In the period between 1993 and 1999, the rate of growth of manufacturing labour productivity was more than one-third greater than that during the business expansion between 1982 and 1990. It seems only reasonable to view this impressive improvement as stemming from the 100 per cent increase in the rate of growth of the capital stock in the same period, compared to 1982–90. This is especially so since, for the first time since the long downturn began around 1973, the capital–labour ratio was able to grow consistently during an expansion, increasing at an average annual rate of 1.8 per cent between 1993 and 1998, compared to 0 per cent between 1975 and 1979, and 1982 and 1990.[24] It is significant that in the durable goods sector, labour productivity growth jumped to approximately 7 per cent for 1993–99, compared to 3.9 per cent between 1982 and 1990. This is where one would have anticipated productivity gains to be disproportionately located, since it

---

[23] Bank for International Settlements, *70th Annual Report 1999-2000*, p.13 Figures on the growth of real investment in this period have been called into question, because they appear, in part, to be based on the attribution of unrealistically huge declines in prices to components of investment growth. However, the fact that the growth of non-farm business investment *in nominal terms* was also so rapid— averaging 9 per cent per annum during the business expansion of the 1990s (1991–2000), compared to 4.9 per cent for the business expansion of the 1980s (1982–90), when inflation was significantly higher—gives some credence to the evidence that capital accumulation was indeed quite rapid. *Economic Report of the President 2000*, p. 326, Table B-16.

[24] In the business cycles of the 1970s and 1980s, gains in the capital–labour ratio were made only during the recessions, as a consequence of sharp absolute falls in the size of the labour force, rather than of the growth of the capital stock compared to the growth of the labour force.

was here that the acceleration of investment was mainly concentrated—with an increase of durable goods investment averaging 12.3 per cent between 1993 and 1998, against 6.3 per cent for non-durable goods. It is here, too, that the leading growth industries are to be found: industrial and commercial machinery, including computers, and electrical machinery, including semi-conductors.

Productivity gains in the remainder of the economy are more difficult to evaluate, because of their extreme discontinuity. Labour productivity in non-manufacturing increased at an average annual rate of about 2.4 per cent between 1995 and 1999, after having barely grown at all during the previous eighteen years. Even by 1995, the level of labour productivity in this sector was a scant 4 per cent higher than it had been in 1977. The fact that non-manufacturing productivity did not begin to increase until the growth of output accelerated, beginning in 1996, has led a number of analysts to discount it as a by-product of this more rapid, perhaps unsustainable output growth. By this reasoning, the uptick in recorded labour-productivity growth outside of manufacturing is largely a result of increased pressures on workers in response to fast-rising demand, an expression of the speed-up common to the later phases of the business cycle, when investment growth typically subsides. What calls this account into question, however, is that the growth of investment during the 1990s has, very atypically, actually accelerated as the business cycle has matured, creating the strong possibility that the rise in registered output per hour is an expression of increased plant and equipment at workers' disposal, not just their increased effort. Average annual investment growth in the non-manufacturing sector in nominal terms has thus been well over 10 per cent during the business expansion that began in 1991—more than twice as high as in the comparable expansion of the much more inflationary 1980s—and reached its highest point during the first half of 2000. Over that same period, moreover, nominal investment in information processing and software increased as a proportion of the total from about 30 to 35 percent. It is hard to believe that employers made such large expenditures over such an extended period, if these were not contributing a good deal to their profitability by substantially increasing their productivity growth.

The containment of inflation during the 1990s is in line with the preceding analysis. Accounting for stable prices during the first half of the decade is hardly a problem. In those years, real wage growth was effectively zero, so upward pressure from costs on prices was minimal. With GDP increase in these years also very limited, the growth of demand was even lower than in the 1970s and 1980s. Just to make sure, as noted, the Fed raised interest rates very sharply in 1994. What requires more explanation is the low rate of inflation over the next half-decade, in the face of a rapid growth of GDP, a major fall in unemployment and acceleration of real wages. No doubt the weakened position of workers continued to be a critical factor in keeping down price increases. Private-sector union density averaged below 10 per cent of the labour force during the second half of the 1990s, notwithstanding the efforts of the AFL–CIO under a new leadership. Despite low unemployment, moreover, workers' insecurity remained great, as layoffs and job turnover continued to run very high and the huge proportion of the labour force in low-wage slots continued to undercut the bargaining position of those with better pay. While ever tighter labour markets have naturally forced up wage growth to a significant degree, they have not so far squeezed profits or lifted prices significantly, and are unlikely to do so, simply because corporations at present have the power to force real wage increases into line with productivity growth.[25]

The main active force in keeping down inflation during the second half of the decade has probably been the very slow growth in the prices of world manufactures and US imports—results of the high dollar and crisis conditions abroad. Especially with the East Asian economies in the doldrums, import prices of industrial inputs have been very stable. Moreover, with world demand sluggish from 1997 through 1999, raw material—and, especially, oil—prices have been kept down until very recently. Finally, since the dollar has risen so much in value, goods from overseas are that much cheaper in the US. Under these circumstances, it has been extremely difficult for American sellers of tradeable goods to push up prices. Even so, it is difficult to discount the anti-inflationary impact of the rapid growth of productivity in US manufacturing, which limited the average annual growth of its unit labour costs between 1995 and 1999 to minus 1.2 per cent. Increased productivity growth has clearly been important outside of manufacturing as well, as price increases have also been kept down in the non-farm economy as a whole—i.e., beyond the tradeable goods sector.

---

[25] This is not, of course, to doubt that should demand side problems manifest themselves in the form of slower growth of output or prices, sticky wages would either squeeze profits or lead to greater inflation.

Finally, and crucially, the rapid increase of the capital stock, by preventing capacity utilization from increasing much over the length of the expansion, despite the accelerating growth of GDP, will also have been critical in containing costs and prices. Even despite the record-breaking length of the 1990s expansion, the factory operating rate at the beginning of 1999 was more than a percentage point below its average over the past 30 years. To make the same point another way, capacity utilization was a bit lower in 1999 than in 1993. During the last two and a half years, from 1997 through the first half of 2000, real wage growth in the non-farm economy has averaged 2.9 per cent per year—yet the increase in unit labour costs over the same period has averaged just 1.6 per cent, only a little higher than that of product prices, at 1.4 per cent.

In sum, an explosive growth of household consumption, based on a record run-down of savings and unprecedented growth of private indebtedness, began to amplify the US expansion in 1996, and secured its continuation in 1998. What also distinguished the economy's trajectory in these years was that rapidly expanding demand was met by fast growing supply and little inflation, i.e. by rising output rather than rising prices. Ultimately responsible for this improvement in performance was the major increase in pre-tax and after-tax profit rates, originating in the manufacturing sector between 1985 and 1995, but spreading beyond it between 1995 and 1997 and bringing about a very significant revival, if not total recovery, of overall non-farm profitability by comparison with the postwar boom. During the 1970s, due to the growth of Federal deficits, public and private borrowing combined as a percentage of GDP was 50 per cent higher than in the later 1990s. But because profit rates were significantly lower, corporations had relatively smaller surpluses available for investment, while many were on the edge of bankruptcy. The result was 'less bang for the buck'—relatively bigger price increases and relatively smaller investment, productivity and output increases, in response to any given increase in aggregate demand. During the 1980s, public and private deficits combined were higher as a percentage of GDP than in the 1970s. But still-low profit rates and record-high real interest rates kept investment and productivity growth to a minimum. In this context, as the increase of debt drove the expansion, inflation was held down by very slow nominal (as well as real) wage growth, as well as a very high dollar during the first half of the decade.

By contrast, during the early to mid-1990s, as pre- and (even more) after-tax profitability approached the peaks of the mid 1960s—unleashing increased investment, industrial capacity and productivity growth through the second half of the decade—domestic supply could keep up with debt-driven demand in a way that it could not through most of the long period that preceded it. Not only were price increases held down, but rising wages were accommodated without much pressure on the rate of profit, at least outside the manufacturing sector (which was indeed squeezed by falling world prices from 1998). If an 'artificial' debt-based increase in demand, founded ultimately in rising equity prices, drove the boom after 1995, the economy was able to respond with considerably more vigour than it had for a long time.

V. CAN THE BOOM BE SUSTAINED?

The question, of course, is whether the boom can be sustained. Will the excesses of the bubble that have driven the boom so far upward find their nemesis in a down-side over-correction, as they did in Japan at the start of the 1990s? Well aware of this danger, the US authorities are counting on the hectic expansion of US household consumption—before it subsides—to place the economy on a sounder footing, catalysing a smooth transition from the international crisis of 1997–98 to a sustained world upturn. By animating export-led expansions throughout the global economy, and so setting off a reciprocal acceleration of overseas demand for American goods, US consumption growth will—in the favoured scenario—enable American manufacturers to recover the levels of export growth they enjoyed up to 1997, and thereby regain their former rates of profit. At the same time, it is hoped, investment outside of manufacturing will keep growing sufficiently fast to sustain productivity gains at least at the level of the past four to five years, thereby raising the rate of profit in services yet higher. The economy could then break its current addiction to debt-driven consumption, shifting the basis of the boom to exports and investments—and therewith a sounder foundation for elevated equity prices (which could, in the meantime, have seen a 'correction', but would have been prevented from crashing).

As of the middle of 2000, the US economy seemed to be developing in much the manner hoped for by US authorities. It was booming in an extraordinary fashion, actually accelerating its pace in a way rarely seen so late in a business expansion. Over the previous twelve months, GDP had grown by 6.1 per cent. In the same period, non-farm labour productivity had increased at the astounding pace of 7 per cent—far beyond the quite respectable 4.1 per cent achieved the year before. This result is almost certainly attributable to still accelerating investment, which increased 14.2 per cent for the year, growing at an annual rate of 18 per cent during the first half of 2000. On the other hand, despite the big jump in GDP and productivity growth, real wages rose just 1.4 per cent during the year ending in the middle of 2000, half the 2.7 per cent increase of the twelve months before that, and crept up a mere 0.8 per cent on an annual basis during the first half of 2000. Firms, meanwhile, were able to raise prices significantly faster than in the previous year, especially during the first half of 2000, when they increased at an annualized pace of 2.7 per cent. Things could hardly have been going much better for capital. It is no wonder that, during the first half of 2000, corporate profits (ex-interest) rose at a 14 per cent annual pace.

Meanwhile, the expanding US economy did indeed stimulate faster growth throughout much of the world, especially parts of East Asia and Western Europe, and was benefiting in turn from increased overseas sales. Korea, for example, had seemingly emerged from its crisis. Its exports to the US shot up by 20–25 per cent in 1999 and the first half of 2000, while Korean GDP grew 11 per cent in 1999 and was projected to expand almost as fast in 2000. Taiwan, Hong Kong and Singapore were doing about as well. The Euro economies, whose exports to the US market increased at an annualized rate of 11 per cent for 1999–2000, were expanding as rapidly as they had ever done since the end of the 1980s, at an average annual rate of better than 3.5 per cent, with unemployment declining. In this dynamic context of cyclical international upturn, US export growth also picked up speed— real goods exports increasing by 13.3 per cent for the year ending in the middle of 2000, compared to 2.2 per cent in 1998 and 4 per cent in 1999. The policy scenario of Greenspan–Summers–Clinton seemed to be in the process of realization, and the vista of a new long upturn seemed anything but a fantasy.

To help ensure the desired outcome, from June 1999 to 2000, Greenspan reversed his 1998 policy of reducing interest rates to push up equity prices, raising short-term interest rates to date by a total of

1.75 per cent. The tightening was quite mild, to say the least. By summer 2000, rising prices meant that real interest rates had still failed to rise above their level when the tightening began. The Fed Chair apparently hopes that, in the same way that his patent desire for a rise in equity prices drove up the stock market in autumn 1998, without the need for dramatically reduced borrowing costs, his unconcealed wish for them now to slow their ascent—or even sustain a modest 'correction'—will bring the required outcome without his having to take stronger steps. The aim is explicitly to slow down household consumption—and therewith imports—by cooling off equity markets.[26] It remains, however, an open question whether the US can pull this off without jeopardizing its own expansion, and exposing the rest of the world to the risk of stagnation, or worse. The course that the US economy must negotiate is one that would largely return it to the more export-oriented path that it had been pursuing up through 1997—ideally, this time, complemented by accelerated export growth among the US's trading partners and rivals, too. A mutually expanding world division of labour would, as in the textbooks, confer sufficient gains on all parties to sustain a coordinated international expansion. To further underwrite the whole process, the US non-tradeables non-manufacturing sector would have to sustain a virtuous upward spiral of high rates of profit, leading to higher investment and productivity growth, unleashing in turn faster wage growth and a dynamically expanding domestic market.

International over-production?

But neither the return to a path of complementary rather than competitive international expansion, nor the continuation of an investment boom in the non-tradeables sector can be taken for granted. It must be remembered, to begin with, that right up through 1998, the world's leading manufacturing economies—in the US and East Asia, in Western Europe and Japan—had continued to find it difficult, if not impossible, to expand and prosper together, in the face of international over-capacity and over-production in manufacturing. From 1995, as we have seen, the rising dollar and stepped-up growth of the US economy spurred fast-rising US imports, which in turn detonated a new cyclical upturn across

---

[26] By autumn 2000, Greenspan's wish was coming true, as the S & P 500 index had essentially stagnated for months, and the technology and internet dominated NASDAQ index, central site of the bubble, had fallen by 40 per cent.

much of the world, pulling Western Europe and Japan out of the doldrums, just as they had done in the wake of the cyclical downturns of the mid 1970s and early 1980s (but had notably failed to do during the first half of the 1990s, when slowed US growth and a low dollar had ratified West European and Japanese recessions). Indeed, in 1997 the growth of GDP for the G7 and OECD economies taken together hit a peak for the decade. But the high exchange rates in the US, and the East Asian economies tracking the dollar, so essential to export revival in Japan and Western Europe, led in short order to declining competitive performance, falling profitability and economic slowdown for US manufacturing, and an all-out crisis in East Asia—which threatened, by autumn–winter 1998, to pull the world economy, including the US, back into recession or worse. International over-capacity and over-production, manifested in ongoing downward pressure on the rate of profit in international manufacturing, had once again reared its ugly head.

According to a survey by the *Economist* taken early in 1999, 'Thanks to enormous over-investment, especially in Asia, the world is awash with excess capacity in computer chips, steel, cars, textiles, and chemicals . . . The car industry, for instance, is already reckoned to have at least 30 per cent unused capacity worldwide—yet new factories in Asia are still coming on stream.' The *Economist* went on to assert that: 'None of this excess capacity is likely to be shut down quickly, because cash-strapped firms have an incentive to keep factories running, even at a loss, to generate income. The global glut is pushing prices relentlessly lower. Devaluation cannot make excess capacity disappear; it simply shifts the problem to somebody else'. The upshot, it concluded, was that the world output gap—between industrial capacity and its use—was approaching its highest levels since the 1930s.[27]

From 1998 onwards, as we have seen, the growth of debt-driven consumption came to substitute for increasing manufacturing com-

---

[27] 'Could It Happen Again?' *Economist*, 22 February 1999. As the Bank for International Settlements put it several months later: 'The overhang of excess industrial capacity in many countries and sectors continues to be a serious threat to financial stability. Without an orderly reduction or take up of this excess capacity rates of return on capital will continue to disappoint, with potentially debilitating and long-lasting effects on confidence and investment spending. Moreover, the solvency of the institutions that financed this capital expansion becomes increasingly questionable.' *69th Annual Report 1998–1999*, Basel, 7 June 1999.

petitiveness and rising exports in pushing the US economy forward, enabling it to finesse for the time being these system-wide problems. But the question that imposes itself is whether the US can now reverse the process, at the same time as its rivals sustain their own export-driven expansions. The international recovery that has gathered force since 1999 has provided little clear evidence that the world's leading manufacturing economies can finally expand together, at least without the benefit of a US current-account deficit that is setting new records every year—i.e., without the continuation of the US consumption boom. US export growth has indeed responded crisply to an emerging international economic expansion, which has been made possible largely by the rise of US imports. But it has hardly done so unproblematically, since the level of American imports as of the middle of the year 2000 is a full 30 per cent above that of American exports. What this means is that exports would henceforth have to grow about a third faster than imports just to prevent the trade deficit from widening further. In the year ending at mid-2000, US exports grew by about 13 per cent, but imports increased by about 22 per cent. Were that pace of import growth to continue for the rest of this year, exports would have to grow at an impossible 28.5 per cent annual rate just to hold the trade gap to its present $30 billion per month. It is therefore very hard to see how the current-account deficit can avoid hitting 4.5 or 5 per cent of GDP in 2000, setting a new record.

In the current international expansion, just as in that of 1996–97 (and, indeed, the previous cyclical recoveries of the first part of the 1980s and the middle of the 1970s), the US's main rivals and partners in Western Europe and East Asia have depended upon a combination of sharply reduced exchange rates (notably the very low Euro) and a sizzling US import market to accelerate growth. Were the growth of American GDP and the American market to slow down significantly, it is hard to believe that the overseas stimulus to US exports would increase. On the contrary, for the world market to expand sufficiently to absorb US export growth at its current rapid rate, it would seem that US imports and the US current-account deficit must increase disproportionately. The implication is that for the American and world economy to continue to grow vigorously, the reigning pattern of expansion must continue to prevail—though this would obviously do nothing to reduce the current account deficit, indeed would be likely to make it worse.

By the same token, it is far from clear that US manufacturers can, at the current level of the dollar, easily escape the kind of downward pressure on their profits and their pace of capital accumulation that they experienced in 1998 and 1999, under the impact of the international economic slowdown. During the first half of 2000, profits (not including interest) in the corporate manufacturing sector had still failed to rise above their level of 1997, even though real goods exports grew by 13 per cent. This was despite the fact that personal consumption expenditures continued to explode upwards, as they had in 1999, at the astonishing—and probably unsustainable—annual rate of 5.35 per cent. It did not help, of course, that the Euro plummeted in this period. But then again, a low Euro has been pivotal for the European recovery that has helped drive US exports.

In the final analysis, the fundamental source of strength for the US non-financial economy since 1995, and especially since 1997, has been its capacity to maintain, and even increase, its aggregate profitability, despite the powerful downward pressure in the interim on the manufacturing profit rate. This strength has derived, in the first instance, from the remarkable performance of its non-manufacturing sector. There the profit rate rose sharply between 1995 and 1997 and continued to increase sufficiently to compensate for the decline in the manufacturing profit rate in 1998 and 1999. In fact, during the first half of 2000, total profits (not including interest) in the non-financial corporate economy were $93 billion dollars higher than they had been in 1997, and the non-manufacturing economy accounted for all but $3 billion of that increase. As a consequence, the profit rate in the non-financial corporate economy—including manufacturing—remained in 1999 as high as it had been in 1997, and will probably increase in 2000. On the basis of these rising returns, investment in the non-manufacturing sector rose even faster than in the non-farm economy as a whole from 1995 through the present, and very markedly so from 1998, as manufacturing investment growth appears to have fallen significantly from that point.[28] In turn, with non-manufacturing investment accelerating, non-manufacturing productivity growth, almost non-existent over the previous two decades, broke from its torpor and also sped up remark-

---

[28] In 1998, the last year for which there is relevant data, manufacturing investment (in nominal terms) fell to 2.6 per cent, compared to 10.8 per cent for the previous four years, while non-manufacturing investment rose to 13.2 per cent, compared to 9.1 per cent.

ably, clearly accelerating in the last two years. With real wage growth lagging, higher investment, leading to higher productivity growth, has brought still higher profitability.

The spectre of Japan?

The question is whether this can be sustained. For not only did the fevered growth of personal consumption provide an enormous incentive for new investment in plant and equipment in this sector, but it was indispensable to its realization—just as it also enabled the manufacturing sector to limit its losses in 1997 and 1998. Despite the collapse of export growth, from around 10 per cent per year in nominal terms between 1985 and 1997, to 0 per cent a year in 1998 and 1999, and the parallel fall in manufacturing competitiveness, the decline in the rate of manufacturing profit was held down to 10–12 per cent or so—in large part because durable goods consumption suddenly grew at the phenomenal pace of 11 per cent a year between 1997 and the middle of 2000, having increased at a 6.5 per cent pace between 1991 and 1997. The problem is, of course, that the fast-rising consumption that paved the way for accelerating investment, and cushioned the slowdown in manufacturing during the second half of the 1990s, was itself dependent upon the running down of household savings and the enormous increase in household debt. Yet, given the unprecedented ratio of household debt to household income and the fall of the savings rate below zero, it is not easy to see how borrowing can continue to rise sufficiently to sustain consumption growth—and, therefore, how consumption growth can continue to drive the economy.

This is especially so, given the likely diminution, if not disappearance, of the wealth effect derived from soaring equity prices. Indeed, were equity prices to cease to rise for any length of time, it is difficult to see how they could be prevented from falling rather sharply (since the 1990s, equities have largely been purchased on the expectation that they would go further up in value, rather than for their rate of return). The US economy would then find itself in a position not unlike that of Japan at the end of its bubble era. Prevented by its high-priced currency from returning to an export-oriented path of growth, its manufacturing sector would be unable to dynamize the economy. With equity prices—and thus borrowing and consumption growth—returning to earth, its non-manufacturing, non-tradeables sector would find itself without the fast-expanding home market that could valorize its huge expansion of plant and equipment. With dollar-denominated costs too high to exploit the growth of international demand, and with domestic demand falling off, a return to stagnation would be on the agenda. Corporations, now without the net worth that hitherto constituted their collateral, due to the declining prices of their shares, would now not only find borrowing much more difficult but would find the interest rates on their existing obligations starting to rise.

But were the US economy obliged to accept a significant slowdown to accommodate the end of the bubble, it is by no means clear that this could be accomplished without disruption. For if US growth were to cool off sufficiently to curb import growth, it is difficult to see how the rest of the world economy could fail to decelerate too—with unpredictable consequences, especially in East Asia, which has depended so overwhelmingly on a fast-growing US market. This would undercut the US's own export expansion. But it is doubtful if the difficulties would end there. For if American GDP growth were to slow, and equity prices to drop at all significantly, US assets in general would lose some of their attraction to foreign purchasers. Speculative foreign purchases of US shares and corporate bonds have recently been muliplying at an unsustainable rate. Any serious attempt to flee these assets would put enormous downward pressure on the dollar. In this case, the Fed would be caught in a double bind. It would need to reduce interest rates to provide the liquidity to keep the economy turning over and defend US assets, but it would, even more, need to raise interest rates to attract an inflow of funds from overseas, to maintain the dollar for the US to fund its record-breaking current-account deficit. Yet how high would interest rates have to go to counteract the enormous downward pressure on the dollar, if overseas holders sought to liquidate their portfolios? Such a scenario would risk setting off interacting declines in asset markets and the currency, driven by a panicky flight of capital, with devastating consequences for the real economy. This, as we know, is what happened in East Asia in 1997–98. But, of course, it could not happen here.

Part II
Liberal Capitalism: The UK

[8]

The Decline of the British Economy: An Institutional Perspective

BERNARD ELBAUM AND WILLIAM LAZONICK

This paper attributes the relative decline of the British economy in the twentieth century to rigidities in its economic and social institutions that had developed during the nineteenth-century era of relatively atomistic competition. Inherited and persistent constraints impeded British firms from acquiring the market control, authority in labor relations, or managerial hierarchy necessary to avail themselves fully of modern mass production methods. At the societal level there was an interrelated failure to transform the character of British educational and financial institutions, labor-management relations, and state policy in order to promote economic development. By performing better in these respects late-industrializing countries were able to surpass Britain in economic growth.

THE British economy, once the workshop of the world, seems to have fallen victim to some century-long affliction. For lack of an adequate generic diagnosis, many observers have termed this affliction the "British disease."[1] There are signs, however, that the disease may be spreading, and the recent competitive reverses of American industry in the face of Japanese and European challenges have sparked renewed interest in explanations of economic growth and decline. The Japanese success in particular has recently received most of the attention from economists and policy makers, but there is yet, we would argue, much to be learned from Britain's economic failure.

In Britain itself, the ideology directing current government policy assumes that the nation's decline has been due to the obstruction of the self-regulating market economy by trade union power and state intervention. This ideological perspective finds intellectual reinforcement in orthodox economic theory that, in both its liberal and conservative variants, views the capitalist economy as fundamentally an atomistic market economy. According to economic orthodoxy, the perfection of market competition and economic prosperity go hand in hand.

Although this proposition goes back to the time of Adam Smith, it has

Journal of Economic History, Vol. XLIV, No. 2 (June 1984). © The Economic History Association. All rights reserved. ISSN 0022-0507.

Bernard Elbaum is Assistant Professor of Economics, Boston University, Boston, Massachusetts 02215, and William Lazonick is Associate Professor of Economics, Harvard University, Cambridge, Massachusetts 02138. This paper synthesizes new research on British industrial decline, much of which will appear in a forthcoming Oxford University Press volume edited by Elbaum and Lazonick. They wish to thank the participants at the Anglo-American Conference on the Decline of the British Economy (held at Boston University on September 30-October 1, 1983) for their help in shaping the perspective presented here, and to Lance Davis and Michael Edelstein for their comments at the 1983 Economic History Association meetings.

[1] See, for example, G. C. Allen, *The British Disease* (London, 1976).

Elbaum and Lazonick

never been adequately supported by comparative examination of the historical experiences of capitalist economies. In particular, the issue of Britain's decline has largely been avoided by neoclassical economic historians who have been preoccupied with demonstrating that turn-of-the-century British managers "did the best they could" by optimizing subject to given constraints.[2] Neoclassical economists who have confronted the problem of explaining national decline simply assume that the mainspring of the wealth of nations is free market competition and proceed as a matter of course to blame Britain's economic misfortunes on either market imperfections or "noneconomic" factors such as the cultural peculiarities of businessmen or workers.[3]

By contrast, the historical perspective presented below attributes the decline of the British economy to the rigid persistence of economic and social institutions from the nineteenth-century era of relatively atomistic competition. In such countries as the United States, Germany, and Japan, successful twentieth-century economic development has been based on mass production methods and corporate forms of managerial coordination. But in Britain adoption of these modern technological and organizational innovations was impeded by inherited socioeconomic constraints at the levels of the enterprise, industry, and society. Entrenched institutional structures—including the structures of industrial relations, industrial organization, educational systems, financial intermediation, international trade, and state-enterprise relations—constrained the ability of individuals, groups, or corporate entities to transform the productive system.

Britain's problem was that economic decision makers, lacking the individual or collective means to alter prevailing institutional constraints, in effect took them as "given." In failing to confront institutional constraints, British businessmen can justifiably be accused of "entrepreneurial failure."[4] But the cause of the failure was not simply cultural conservatism, as some historians have implied. If British society was pervaded by conservative mores, it was in this respect certainly no worse off than Japan or continental European countries that were precapitalist, tradition-bound societies when Britain was the workshop of the world. The thesis of entrepreneurial failure casts no light on why Britain, the first industrial nation, should have been less

---

[2] Donald N. McCloskey, ed., *Essays on a Mature Economy: Britain After 1840* (London, 1971); Donald N. McCloskey and Lars Sandberg, "From Damnation to Redemption: Judgments on the Late Victorian Entrepreneur," *Explorations in Economic History*, 9 (Fall 1971), 89–108; R. C. Floud, "Britain 1860–1914: A Survey," and L. G. Sandberg, "The Entrepreneur and Technological Change," both in *The Economic History of Britain since 1700*, ed. Roderick Floud and Donald McCloskey, vol. 2 (Cambridge, 1981).

[3] See, for example, Richard E. Caves, "Productivity Differences among Industries," in *Britain's Economic Performance*, ed. Richard E. Caves and Lawrence B. Krause (Washington, D.C., 1980).

[4] David Landes, *The Unbound Prometheus* (Cambridge, 1969), chap. 5; Martin Wiener, *English Culture and The Decline of the Industrial Spirit, 1850–1980* (Cambridge, 1981).

Decline of the British Economy   569

successful than later industrializers in shedding customary attitudes that encumbered economic performance.

Britain's distinctiveness derived less from the conservatism of its cultural values per se than from a matrix of rigid institutional structures that reinforced these values and obstructed individualistic as well as concerted efforts at economic renovation. In our view, the causes and consequences of such institutional rigidities remain central to understanding the long-term dynamics of economic development as well as the current crisis of the British economy.

THE CONSEQUENCES OF COMPETITIVE CAPITALISM

In the third quarter of the nineteenth century, the British economy experienced a "long boom" that represented the culmination of the world's first industrial revolution. After three centuries of international conflict for the control of world markets and after seven decades of intense capital investment in productive capacity, Britain emerged unchallenged in the world economy. On the basis of national domination of world markets, there was much in the way of opportunity for aspiring merchants and manufacturers. As they entered into commerce and industry, the structure of British industry became extremely competitive. By today's standards, Britain's major nineteenth-century staple industries—textiles, iron and steel, coal mining, shipbuilding, and engineering—were all composed of numerous firms with small market shares. Their industrial structures were also characterized by a high degree of vertical specialization: distribution of intermediate and final products relied upon well-developed market mechanisms, often involving specialized merchant firms.

The managerial organization and technology employed by nineteenth-century British firms were comparatively simple. Characteristically, firms were run by owner-proprietors or close family associates. Managerial staffs were small, and methods of cost accounting and production control were crude or nonexistent. The development of industrial techniques typically relied upon trial and error rather than systematic in-house research. Most enterprises were single-plant firms that specialized in particular lines of manufacture of intermediate or final products. Industries exhibited a high degree of regional concentration based upon geographical advantages as well as external economies provided by local access to skilled labor supplies, transport facilities and distribution networks, capital, and product markets.

Up to the 1870s the long-term financing for these business ventures came from country banks, personal family fortunes, and retained earnings. After the collapse of the country banks in the Great Depression of the 1870s, financial institutions had little involvement in the long-term finance of British industry. The purchasers of share capital tended instead to be individuals—among them many shopkeepers and skilled workers—who invested their savings locally. With British firms able to tap local as well as internal sources of long-term financing, there is no evidence that they were short of capital in the decades prior to World War I. The last decades of the nineteenth century also saw the extension of national banks and the development of a highly liquid national capital market. But industrial firms were reluctant to risk loss of control by issuing equity on the national market or incurring long-term debt. Financial institutions provided only short-term working capital to British industry (mainly through overdraft accounts), and as a result never developed the institutional expertise to serve the demand for long-term capital that did arise. Instead they exported most of their capital, usually in exchange for fixed-interest bonds, to finance large-scale (typically government-backed) foreign projects such as railroads. A consequence of these arrangements was the separation of provincial industrial enterprise from national financial institutions based in the City of London, a characteristic feature of the British economy well into the twentieth century.[5]

Another outcome of British capitalism as it developed in the last half of the nineteenth century was the consolidation of job control on the part of many groups of workers in industry. During the "long boom," individual capitalists, divided by competition, opted for collective accommodation with unions of skilled and strategically positioned workers rather than jeopardize the fortunes of their individual firms through industrial conflict while there were profits to be made. The labor movement also made important legislative gains that enhanced the ability of workers to organize unions, build up union treasuries, and stage successful strikes.

A distinguishing feature of the British labor movement was its two tiers of bargaining strength. Workplace organizations enjoyed substantial local autonomy in bargaining, backed by the leverage that national unions could exert on employers during disputes. From the fourth quarter of the nineteenth century, as intermittent but often prolonged recessions occurred and as foreign competition began to be felt by many industries, capitalists were unable to replace the job control of shop-floor union organizations by managerial control. Despite the introduction of many skill-displacing changes in technology, the power of the union organizations that had developed earlier had simply become too great. Attempts by Parliament and the judiciary to undermine the trade union movement—most notably by means of the Taff Vale decision—resulted in the emergence of a distinct political party representing the interests of labor.

---

[5] Michael Best and Jane Humphries, "The City and the Decline of British Industry," in *The Decline of the British Economy*, ed. Bernard Elbaum and William Lazonick (Oxford, forthcoming).

Decline of the British Economy   571

THE CHALLENGE OF CORPORATE CAPITALISM

Elsewhere, from the late nineteenth century (notably in Japan, Germany, and the United States) corporate capitalism was emerging to become the dominant mode of economic organization. Corporate capitalism was characterized by industrial oligopoly, hierarchical managerial bureaucracy, vertical integration of production and distribution, managerial control over the labor process, the integration of financial and industrial capital, and systematic research and development.[6]

Oligopoly, by helping to stabilize prices and market shares, facilitated long-run planning, particularly where large-scale capital investments were involved. Managerial coordination of product flows within the vertically integrated enterprise permitted the achievement of high-speed throughputs that reduced unit costs. Vertical integration of production and distribution provided the direct access to market outlets that was a precondition for the effective utilization of mass production methods. Managerial control over the labor process in turn facilitated the introduction of new, high-throughput technologies. Integration of financial and industrial capital, along with managerial bureaucracy, made possible the geographic mobility of capital and the rapid expansion of capacity to produce for new or growing markets. Systematic research and development, particularly in such science-based industries as electrical and chemical manufacturing, provided the mainspring of technological innovation. Across countries, the degree of coordination of economic activity by the state and large financial institutions varied, with significant implications for economic performance. But the experience of successful capitalist economies in the twentieth century demonstrates the ubiquitous importance of the visible hand of corporate bureaucratic management.

In order to compete against the corporate mass production methods being developed in Germany, Japan, and the United States, British industries required transformation of their structures of industrial relations, industrial organization, and enterprise management. Vested interests in the old structures, however, proved to be formidable (if not insurmountable) obstacles to the transition from competitive to corporate modes of organization. Lacking corporate management skills and opportunities, British industrialists clung to family control of their firms. Even where horizontal amalgamations did take place, the directors of the participating firms insisted on retaining operational autonomy.[7] In any case, very few of these managers had the broader

---

[6] Alfred D. Chandler, Jr., *The Visible Hand* (Cambridge, Massachusetts, 1977); Alfred D. Chandler, Jr., and Herman Daems, eds., *Managerial Hierarchies* (Cambridge, Massachusetts, 1980).

[7] Leslie Hannah, *The Rise of the Corporate Economy: The British Experience* (Baltimore, 1976); Alfred D. Chandler, Jr., "The Growth of the Transnational Industrial Firm in the United States and the United Kingdom: A Comparative Analysis," *Economic History Review*, 2nd ser., 33 (Aug. 1980).

entrepreneurial perspectives or skills needed to develop modern corporate structures.[8]

The British educational system hampered industry by failing to provide appropriately trained managerial and technical personnel. On the supply side, the existing system of higher education was designed almost explicitly to remove its "aristocratic" students as far as possible from the worldly pursuit of business and applied science.[9] On the demand side, there was comparatively little pressure to transform this system as highly competitive businesses could not afford to hire specialized technical personnel and were further reluctant to support industry-wide research institutes that would benefit competitors as much as themselves.[10] Given the lack of interest of business and the educational establishment in fostering managerial and technical training, it is not surprising that the British state, rather passive towards industrial development in any case, took little initiative to make education more relevant to economic development.

Nor was leadership for industrial transformation forthcoming from other sectors of the British economy. The financial sector kept its distance from direct involvement in industry, preferring instead to maintain its highly liquid position by means of portfolio investment, mostly abroad. The orientation of Britain's bankers towards liquidity and protection of the value of the pound sterling was reinforced by the undisputed position of the City of London as the financial center of the world. The concentration of banking in the City also gave rise to a relatively cohesive class of finance capitalists with much more concerted and coherent power over national policy than industrial capitalists, who were divided along enterprise, industry, and regional lines.

In the absence of a shift to corporate enterprise structure, British industrialists also had little incentive or ability to challenge the shop-floor control of trade union organizations. In the United States and Germany a critical factor in the development of high-throughput production was the ability of management to gain and maintain the right to manage the utilization of technology. In most of Britain's staple industries, by contrast, managers had lost much of this "right to manage," reducing their incentive to invest in costly mass production technologies on which they might not be able to achieve high enough throughputs to justify the capital outlays. During the first half of the twentieth century, British unionism was able to consolidate its positions of control at both the national and workplace levels, aided by the

---

[8] William Lazonick, "Industrial Organization and Technological Change: The Decline of the British Cotton Industry," *Business History Review*, 57 (Summer 1983), 195–236.

[9] Julia Wrigley, "Seeds of Decline: Technical Education and Industry in Britain," in *The Decline of the British Economy*.

[10] David Mowery, "British and American Industrial Research: A Comparison, 1900–1950," in *The Decline of the British Economy*.

Decline of the British Economy   573

growing strength of the Labour Party and the emergency conditions of two world wars.

Lacking the requisite degree of control over product and input markets, British managers confronted severe obstacles in adapting their enterprise structures to take advantage of new market opportunities. As a result, in the late nineteenth and early twentieth centuries firms continued for the most part to manufacture traditional products using traditional technologies.

How these firms structured production depended very much on the prospects for selling their output. Contrary to typical textbook theory, Britain's competitive firms did not as a rule assume that the market could absorb all the output they might produce at a given price. Indeed they produced few manufactures in anticipation of demand. Almost all production was to order, much of it for sale to merchants for distribution to far-flung international markets.

In the heyday of British worldwide economic dominance, these arrangements proved advantageous to British firms. Unlike many of their international competitors, who had access only to much more confining markets, Britain's international marketing structure meant that British firms could get enough orders of similar specifications to reap economies of long production runs, and had a large enough share in expanding markets to justify investment in (what were then) up-to-date and increasingly capital-intensive plant and equipment. But the tables were turned by the spread abroad of tariff barriers and indigenous industrialization. Because Britain had already industrialized, its domestic market for such staple commodities as textiles or steel rails had reached a point of at best moderate growth potential. Under these circumstances, British firms could not find at home a market that could match the dramatic rates of expansion of the foreign markets foreclosed to them. Indeed, given its dependence on international markets, British industry was severely constrained to keep its own domestic markets open to the products of foreign firms.

Taking advantage of their more secure and expansive domestic markets, foreign rivals, with more modern, capital-intensive technology, attained longer production runs and higher speeds of throughput than the British. By virtue of their reliance on the corporate form of organization—in particular on vertical integration of production with distribution and more concentrated market power—Britain's rivals were better able to rationalize the structure of orders and ensure themselves the market outlets required for mass production. From secure home bases these rivals also invaded market areas and product lines where the British should have been at no comparative disadvantage.

Forced to retreat from competition with mass production methods, British firms sought refuge in higher quality and more specialized product lines where traditional craftsmanship and organization could still command a competitive edge—in spinning higher counts of yarn and weaving finer cloth, making sheets and plates of open hearth steel, and building unique one-off ships. Unfortunately for the British, in a world of expanding markets, the specialized product of the day all too often turned out to be the mass production item of tomorrow. The arrival of mass production methods and the pace and timing of decline varied among the major staple industries, with British shipbuilding, for example, still holding a commanding competitive position as late as World War II. But all eventually met a similar fate.[11]

INSTITUTIONAL RIGIDITY

From the standpoint of the neoclassical model of competition, these developments would lead one to expect a British response to competitive pressures that would imitate the organizational and technological innovations introduced abroad. In fact, the British only adapted patch-work improvements to their existing organizational and productive structure. Facing increasingly insecure markets and lacking the market control requisite for modern mass production, the British failed to make the organizational renovations that could have allowed them to escape competitive decline.

With the massive contractions of British market shares that occurred in the 1920s and early 1930s, firms in the troubled staple industries alternated between scrambling for any markets they could get and proposals for elimination of excess capacity and concentration of productive structure. In a period of contraction the market mechanism was anything but an efficient allocation mechanism, in part because existing firms remained in operation as long as they could hope for some positive return over variable costs, their proprietors living, so to speak, off their capital. Coordinated attempts to eliminate excess capacity were confounded by numerous conflicts of interest between owner-proprietors, outside stockholders, management groups, customers, banks and other creditors, and local union organizations. In particular the involvement of the national banks in the attempts to rationalize industry was aimed more at salvaging their individual financial positions than at developing a coherent plan for industry revitalization. In light of the failure to achieve coordination the rationalization programs that were implemented in the interwar period were half-hearted and of limited effectiveness.

During the interwar period and beyond, the rigid work rules of British

[11] Edward Lorenz and Frank Wilkinson, "Shipbuilding and British Economic Decline, 1880–1965"; Bernard Elbaum, "British Steel Industry Structure and Performance before World War I"; William Lazonick, "The Decline of the British Cotton Industry"; Stephen Tolliday, "Industry, Finance, and the State: Steel and Rationalization Policy"; all in *The Decline of the British Economy*.

Decline of the British Economy   575

unions remained an impediment to structural reorganization. Entrenched systems of piece-rate payment often led to higher wage earnings in more productive establishments, deterring firms from scrapping old capacity and investing in new. Union rules also limited management's freedom to alter manning levels and workloads, which in mechanical, labor-intensive industries such as textiles had particularly adverse effects on the prospective benefits of new technology.[12] In general, management could be sure that the unions would attempt to exact a high price for cooperation with any plans for reorganization that would upset established work and pay arrangements. On the other hand, amidst industrial decline the strong union preference for saving jobs even at low wage levels was an additional conservative influence on a generally unenterprising managerial class.

Given this institutional structure, Britain's staple industries were unable to rationalize on the basis of the profit motive. They relied too much—not too little—on the market mechanism. To be sure, there were some highly successful enterprises such as Imperial Chemical Industries and Unilever that emerged in new industries during the interwar period.[13] But in terms of our perspective on capitalist development, these firms are the exceptions that prove the rule: success was ultimately based on control over product and input markets and the ability to transform internal managerial and production structures to maintain control. Furthermore, even the new industries were not immune to the wider institutional environment. The slow growth of demand in new product market areas hampered the emergence of large firms and created a need for consolidation of industrial structure. In chemicals, fabricated metals, and electrical machinery, newly amalgamated firms suffered from a dearth of appropriately trained managerial personnel and, initially, experienced serious difficulties in overcoming vested interests and in establishing effective coordination of their enterprises. In automobile manufacturing, competitive performance was undermined after World War II by a long-established management strategy of using labor-intensive techniques that helped breed control of shop-floor activities by highly sectionalized union organizations.[14]

THE IMPACT ON GROWTH

If difficult to quantify precisely, the overall impact of these institutional rigidities on British economic performance was undoubtedly

[12] Lorenz and Wilkinson, "Shipbuilding and British Economic Decline," and Lazonick, "The Decline of the British Cotton Industry."

[13] William Reader, *Imperial Chemical Industries: A History*, 2 vols. (Oxford, 1972); Charles Wilson, *The History of Unilever: A Study of Economic Growth and Social Change*, 2 vols. (London, 1954), and *Unilever 1945–1965: Challenge and Response in the Post-War Industrial Revolution* (London, 1965).

[14] Wayne Lewchuk, "The British Motor Vehicle Industry: The Roots of Decline," in *The Decline of the British Economy*.

considerable. Throughout the pre-World War I years, the staple industries remained economically preponderant. According to the 1907 Census of Production, the largest of these industries—coal, iron and steel (including non-electrical machinery and railway equipment), textiles, and shipbuilding—alone made up roughly 50 percent of total net domestic industrial production and 70 percent of British exports. During the long boom of the third quarter of the nineteenth century there was a rapid increase in British output per head that drew important impetus from growth and technological advance in the staple industries.[15] Subsequently, from 1873 to 1913 a marked slowdown in aggregate productivity growth occurred, with some evidence that growth was particularly sluggish from the late 1890s to World War I.

Detailed industry-level evidence is useful for assessing the accuracy of the aggregate data and the reasons for the prewar productivity slowdown. British cotton enterprises, for example, did not reorganize the vertical structure of production in order to adopt more advanced technologies. Instead they chose to compete on the basis of traditional organization and techniques by cutting raw material costs and intensifying workloads.[16] The resultant cost-savings, augmented by the benefits of well-developed external economies, enabled the cotton industry to expand its output and exports despite stagnating labor productivity in the 15 years or so before World War I. In the British steel industry there was significant ongoing productivity advance in the newer sectors of open hearth steelmaking. Bessemer practice, however, was comparatively stagnant after 1890 as firms were deterred from investing in new, large-scale facilities by a sluggish domestic market, overseas protection, an increasing threat from foreign imports, and fragmented industrial structure.[17]

British growth in output per head not only slowed in the last quarter of the nineteenth century, but also began to lag relative to latter-day industrializing economies that were developing the institutional bases for corporate capitalism. British growth rates first fell behind those of other countries in the 1870s and 1880s. Serious losses in international competition were first sustained between 1899 and 1913 and were interlinked with the failure of British industry to match the productivity advances achieved abroad by fully availing itself of the benefits of mass production methods. With the exception of wartime intervals, the gap in relative productivity growth performance between Britain and most of its competitors has remained substantial ever since.

During the interwar period the competitive weaknesses of the staple

---

[15] R. C. O. Matthews, C. H. Feinstein, and J. C. Odling-Smee, *British Economic Growth, 1856–1973* (Stanford, 1982), p. 26.

[16] William Lazonick and William Mass, "The Performance of the British Cotton Industry, 1870–1913," *Research in Economic History*, 9 (Spring 1984).

[17] Elbaum, "British Steel Industry Structure and Performance."

Decline of the ·British Economy   577

industries became evident, while the productivity performance of the British economy as a whole remained poor by international standards. There remains, however, considerable controversy over the connection between the performance of the staple industries and that of the aggregate economy. According to one influential perspective, the weak performance of the interwar economy was largely due to the relative lack of mobility of resources from the "old" to the "new" industries.[18] This argument, however, is open to criticism on several grounds. It assumes that the old industries imposed effective supply constraints on the growth of the new—a rather dubious proposition given the high unemployment levels, ongoing capital export, and the housing boom that characterized the interwar period. If there were supply constraints on the growth of the new industries it was because of the failure of financial and educational institutions to infuse industry with sufficient long-term venture capital and the types of personnel required.

This argument also implies that the basic problem of the British economy was one of structural adjustment out of industries in which comparative advantage had been lost and possibilities for technical advance had for the most part been exhausted. Yet there is little evidence that shifts in comparative advantage were the root of the competitive problems of Britain's staple industries. Some international competitors in these industries, facing prices for labor and resources greater than or equal to the British, were nonetheless more successful because they adopted major technical advances. Recent evidence also indicates that interwar productivity gains in Britain's staple industries were comparable to those in the new industries (although much of the measured gains in productivity reflect the closure of obsolescent capacity).

The staple industries contributed significantly to Britain's relatively poor interwar growth performance mainly because they still bulked large in the economy and lagged behind seriously in international standards of technological and managerial practice. In 1924 staple manufacturing industries still accounted for 45 percent of all manufacturing net output. By 1935 this figure had fallen to 35 percent but remained at roughly that proportion into the late 1940s.[19] With persistent excess capacity in the staple industries, firms that had long ago written off their plant and equipment always stood ready to "ruin the market" for firms that might otherwise have invested in the modernization of plant and equipment and enterprise structure. Divided by competition, the firms of Britain's staple industries were unable on their own to rationalize capacity.

[18] Derek H. Aldcroft and H. W. Richardson, *The British Economy, 1870–1939* (London, 1969).
[19] G. N. von Tunzelmann, "Structural Change and Leading Sectors in British Manufacturing, 1907–1968," in *Economics in the Long View*, ed. Charles P. Kindleberger and Guido di Tella (New York, 1982), vol. 3, pp. 28–30.

578   *Elbaum and Lazonick*

THE BARELY VISIBLE HAND

What British industry in general required was the visible hand of coordinated control, not the invisible hand of the self-regulating market. Given the absence of leadership from within private industry, increasing pressure fell upon the state to try to fill the gap. Even before World War I, calls were made for greater state intervention. By the interwar period the British state had assumed a distinctly more prominent role in industrial affairs, macroeconomic regulation, and provision of social and welfare services.[20]

With further growth of state intervention after World War II—extending to nationalization of industry and aggregate demand management—critics have pointed accusing fingers at the government for failing to reverse, and even for causing, relative economic decline. At various times and from various quarters the state has been blamed for undermining private-sector incentives and the natural regenerative processes of the free market economy, for absorbing resources that would have been employed more productively in manufacturing, or for failing to provide British industry with a needed environment of macroeconomic stability and a competitively valued exchange rate.

In historical perspective, however, state activism must be absolved from bearing primary responsibility for Britain's relatively poor economic performance. In the late nineteenth century, at the outset of relative decline, the most singular features of the British state were its small size and laissez-faire policies. Even in the post-World War II period, British levels of government taxes, expenditures, and employment were not particularly high by European standards. Indeed, a distinctive feature of British state policy throughout recent history has been its reluctance to break from laissez-faire traditions. It is only in the second instance that state policy is implicated in British decline, by virtue of its failure to intervene in the economy more decisively in order to take corrective measures. The consequences of this failure of state policy first became evident in the interwar period.[21]

THE LIMITS OF INTERWAR INTERVENTION

The Irrationalities of Rationalization Policy

State intervention between the wars included programs aimed at rationalizing the depressed staple industries in order to rid them of excess capacity and facilitate modernization. The problem of excess capacity had been exacerbated by the vast and imprudent expansion of

[20] Charles Feinstein, ed., *The Managed Economy* (Oxford, 1983).
[21] Peter Hall, "The State and Economic Decline in Britain," in *The Decline of the British Economy*.

Decline of the British Economy   579

investment and overdraft borrowing during the short but frenetic boom of 1920/21. The prolonged state of depressed trade that followed in the 1920s placed the banks' loans in serious jeopardy. At that time the Labour government was also considering direct intervention as a means of reorganizing the failing industries and alleviating industrial depression. This combination of circumstances prompted the Bank of England to step in.

For the Bank, rationalization was an economically viable and politically desirable alternative to more far-reaching forms of government intervention that threatened to go as far as nationalization and "encroaching socialism." Bank of England Governor Montagu Norman conceived of intervention as limited, temporary, and exceptional. The Bank's approach was highly consensual and "quasi-corporatist." Firms were encouraged to form trade associations and develop their own plans for industry rationalization. Within the trade associations, firms were authorized to negotiate common pricing policies, mergers, and production quotas. Even then individual firms were reluctant to have the Bank of England intervene, and it was only the stick of bankruptcy and the carrot of support for tariff protection that enabled it to do so.[22]

When the Bank intervened more directly, it was as a merger promoter rather than as an investment bank. Where the market did not respond, the Bank was unwilling to put up its own funds. With the Bank and Treasury allied in keeping a tight hold on the public purse strings, the public funds devoted to backing rationalization schemes were negligible. Yet the Bank found that its efforts at voluntary persuasion had little influence over the allocation of market sources of finance.[23]

As for the government, its interwar industrial policies were confined largely to monitoring industrial affairs through the Import Duties Advisory Committee, established under the 1932 tariff legislation, and to legislative schemes aimed at reducing excess capacity in industries such as textiles. Like the Bank of England, the Advisory Committee pursued influence through conciliation and suasion, seeking no powers of centralized control over industry. Lacking the requisite authority to shape industrial development, the committee found itself overseeing a process of industrial quasi-cartellization that ensured profits for weak and strong firms alike. Government legislation generally responded to the wishes of industry trade associations with similar results.

Public attempts at rationalization left British industry with the worst aspects of both competitive and monopolistic worlds. Productive structure remained highly fragmented and inefficient, while quasi-cartellization and tariff barriers (or imperial preference) protected existing producers from competitive pressure. Rather than achieving its objec-

---

[22] Best and Humphries, "The City and the Decline of British Industry"; Lazonick, "The Decline of the British Cotton Industry"; Tolliday, "Industry, Finance, and the State."

[23] Tolliday, "Industry, Finance, and the State."

tive of promoting industry rationalization, interwar policy inadvertently reinforced preexisting institutional rigidities.

The Underdevelopment of Industrial Research

State policy initiatives in the area of research and development originated at the onset of World War I with concern over the inability of British industry to supply technologically sophisticated materials of strategic military importance. Major policy initiatives included the establishment of a state-owned corporation (British Dyestuffs) and state-subsidized industrial research associations for the promotion of cooperative research and development by firms in the private sector. British Dyestuffs, however, was handicapped by a lack of trained chemists in top management positions and a reliance on chairs in universities for research efforts.

Government promotion of industrial research associations reflected a concern that few firms in Britain were large enough to undertake their own in-house research and development programs. As many as 24 Research Associations were established in industries ranging from woolen textiles to laundering. But firms often lacked the in-house technical expertise required to evaluate and employ the results of extramural research. As a result, Research Associations failed to gather the anticipated financial support from the private sector, and their impact on innovative performance was modest. Government-sponsored cooperative research proved to be an inadequate replacement for the in-house research capabilities of modern corporations.[24]

The Ruin of the Regions

Industrial decline in the interwar period created severe problems of regional unemployment and decaying infrastructure because of the high degree of local concentration of the staple industries. Interwar regional policies were, however, a limited and ad hoc response to diverse political pressures for regional aid, rather than a coherent attempt to deal with the social costs and benefits of relocation of economic activity. The most consistent element in regional policy was the reluctance of the government to become directly involved in industrial development. Instead, the state sought to alleviate regional disparities by policies directed towards improving the operation of labor and capital markets.

The effectiveness of these policies was constrained by macroeconomic conditions, the limited size of the programs, and the underlying assumption that facilitating the operation of market mechanisms would suffice to combat regional problems. Initially, the government promoted labor transference by providing assistance for individual workers or

---

[24] Mowery, "British and American Industrial Research."

Decline of the British Economy   581

households to move to more prosperous regions. But the unemployed workers in the depressed regions were mainly adult males, who were heavily unionized, whereas many of the expanding industries sought primarily new entrants to the labor force, particularly women and juveniles.

By 1937 the emphasis had shifted to moving jobs to unemployed workers by providing businesses with special sources of finance and subsidized factory rentals. Provision of capital to firms in the depressed areas, however, could not overcome the limits on investment demand posed by depressed regional markets. Nor could it overcome the inability of the single-industry family firms that predominated in interwar Britain to manage diversified industrial and regional operations. Expanding industries, which had already begun to develop in the South prior to the stagnation of the 1920s, continued to grow in these more prosperous areas during the interwar period.[25]

The Protection of the Pound

Following the lead of Keynes, a long line of economists have argued that interwar macroeconomic policies had seriously adverse effects on the British economy. A contrast is often drawn between the industrial depression of the 1920s, when restrictive policies preceded the 1925 resumption of the gold standard at the prewar parity, and the relatively strong performance of the economy in the 1930s, when devaluation and protectionism were forced upon the government. Yet if the deflationary impact of the macroeconomic policies of the 1920s seems beyond dispute, there has been a lively debate about its significance for the trend in growth of output per head. Detailed examination of the staple industries, which were the most seriously affected by the 1920s depression, indicates that slack domestic demand, intensified international competitive pressure, and high interest rates *exacerbated* rather than caused problems of excess capacity, shrinking profit margins, and a heavy debt burden. The problems of the staple industries were structural and long-term in character, and if dramatized during the low waters of recession, were also an increasingly evident undertow during the high tides of prosperity before and after the interwar period.

THE LEGACY OF HISTORY

The British economy of the post-World War II period inherited a legacy of major industries too troubled to survive the renewed onslaught of international competition that began in the 1950s. As competitive pressure mounted, the state began to nationalize industries such as coal,

[25] Carol Heim, "Regional Development and National Decline: The Evolution of Regional Policy in Interwar Britain," in *The Decline of the British Economy*.

steel, and automobiles that were deemed of strategic importance to the nation, and (with the exception of steel in 1951) that were in imminent danger of collapse. But nationalization, however necessary, was by no means a sufficient response to Britain's long-run economic decline. Public ownership overcame the problem of horizontally fragmented private ownership, but not inherited problems of enterprise productive structure, managerial organization, and union job control. Nationalized enterprises still had to confront these problems while attempting to overcome the technological leads already established by competitors.

Although the British government was called upon willy-nilly to play an increased role in industrial affairs, the basic theoretical and ideological framework guiding public policy has remained that of the self-regulating market economy. The rise of Keynesianism has led to widespread acceptance of interventionist fiscal and monetary policies, but for the most part has left unchallenged the neoclassical belief in the inherent dynamism of unfettered market competition.

The monetarist policies of the Thatcher government have taken the neoclassical perspective to its extreme. Invoking laissez faire ideology, Thatcher has attacked the power of the unions and sought revival through the severity of market discipline. But the supposition that there are forces latent in Britain's "free market" economy that will return the nation to prosperity finds little confirmation in historical experience. The only foundation for the free-market perspective appears to be the tradition of orthodox economic theory itself.

There is considerable irony in the neoclassical focus on free market competition as the engine of economic dynamism. The focus derives from the fundamental assumption of neoclassical theory that firms are subordinate to markets. History suggests, however, that successful development in the twentieth century has been achieved by markets being made subordinate to firms. The main thrust of the perspective presented here is that the British economy failed to make a successful transition to corporate capitalism in the twentieth century precisely because of the very highly developed market organization of the economy that had evolved when it was the first and foremost industrial nation.

By now, Britain's relative economic decline has persisted through enough ups and downs in the business cycle to indicate that its roots lie deeper than inappropriate macroeconomic policies. If contemporary economic discussion nonetheless is usually preoccupied with obtaining the right monetary and fiscal policies, it is because there has been comparatively little criticism of the microfoundations of neoclassical theory and related versions of laissez faire ideology. Despite the prominence of mass production methods in corporate economies, conventional economic theory has failed to analyze the associated

Decline of the British Economy   583

developmental process of productivity growth and technological change.

If existing institutional arrangements seriously constrained the actions of individual British industrialists and rendered impotent intervention by the state, the example of late-developing nations suggests that a purposive national program can enjoy considerable success in adapting institutions to meet growth objectives. The task for political economy is to identify those elements of the prevailing institutional structure that will promote and those that will hinder alternative strategies of socio-economic development. The argument presented here contends that planning at the levels of the 'enterprise, financial institutions, and the state has become increasingly important for international competitiveness and economic growth, even within the so-called market economies. To elaborate and modify this perspective will require historical studies of the interaction of planning and market forces in economic activity and the resultant impact on performance. Thus far we have only begun to research this perspective, and to test the various hypotheses generated by it. But we view the synthesis presented here, as well as the research upon which it is based, as important foundations for understanding modern economic development.

[9]

OXFORD REVIEW OF ECONOMIC POLICY, VOL. 4, NO. 3

THE FAILURE OF TRAINING IN BRITAIN: ANALYSIS AND PRESCRIPTION

DAVID FINEGOLD
Pembroke College, Oxford

DAVID SOSKICE[1]
University College, Oxford

I. INTRODUCTION

In the last decade, education and training (ET) reform has become a major issue in many of the world's industrial powers. One theme which runs throughout these reform initiatives is the need to adapt ET systems to the changing economic environment. These changes include: the increasing integration of world markets, the shift in mass manufacturing towards newly developed nations and the rapid development of new technologies, most notably information technologies. Education and training are seen to play a crucial role in restoring or maintaining international competitiveness, both on the macro-level by easing the transition of the work force into new industries, and at the micro-level, where firms producing high quality, specialized goods and services require a well-qualified workforce capable of rapid adjustment in the work process and continual product innovation (see Fonda and Hayes in this issue).

This paper will highlight the need for policy-makers and academics to take account of the two-way nature of the relationship between ET and the economy. We will argue that Britain's failure to educate and train its workforce to the same levels as its international competitors has been both a product and a cause of the

[1] The authors would like to thank Kay Andrews, Geoffrey Garrett, Ken Mayhew, Derek Morris, John Muellbauer and Len Schoppa for helpful comments; and to acknowledge intellectual indebtedness to Chris Hayes and Prof. S. Prais. Research on comparative aspects of training was financed in part by a grant to D. Soskice from the ESRC Corporatist and Accountability Research Programme.

0266-903X/88$3.00 © 1988 OXFORD UNIVERSITY PRESS AND THE OXFORD REVIEW OF ECONOMIC POLICY LIMITED

OXFORD REVIEW OF ECONOMIC POLICY, VOL. 4, NO. 3

nation's poor relative economic performance: a product, because the ET system evolved to meet the needs of the world's first industrialized economy, whose large, mass-production manufacturing sector required only a small number of skilled workers and university graduates; and a cause, because the absence of a well educated and trained workforce has made it difficult for industry to respond to new economic conditions.

The best way to visualize this argument is to see Britain as trapped in a low-skills equilibrium, in which the majority of enterprises staffed by poorly trained managers and workers produce low-quality goods and services.[2] The term 'equilibrium' is used to connote a self-reinforcing network of societal and state institutions which interact to stifle the demand for improvements in skill levels. This set of political-economic institutions will be shown to include: the organization of industry, firms and the work process, the industrial relations system, financial markets, the state and political structure, as well as the operation of the ET system. A change in any one of these factors without corresponding shifts in the other institutional variables may result in only small long-term shifts in the equilibrium position. For example, a company which decides to recruit better-educated workers and then invest more funds in training them will not realize the full potential of that investment if it does not make parallel changes in style and quality of management, work design, promotion structures and the way it implements new technologies.[3] The same logic applies on a national scale to a state which invests in improving its ET system, while ignoring the surrounding industrial structure.

The argument is organized as follows: section two uses international statistical comparisons to show that Britain's ET system turns out less-qualified individuals than its major competitors and that this relative ET failure has contributed to Britain's poor economic record. Section three explores the historical reasons for Britain's ET problem and analyses the institutional constraints which have prevented the state from reforming ET. Section four argues that the economic crisis of the 1970s and early-1980s and the centralization of ET power undertaken by the Thatcher Administration have increased the possibility of restructuring ET, but that the Conservative Government's ET reforms, both the major changes already implemented and the Bill which has just passed through Parliament, will not significantly improve Britain's relative ET and economic performance. The fifth section proposes an alternative set of ET and related policies which could help Britain to break out of the low-skill equilibrium.

II. INTERNATIONAL COMPARISONS

i) Britain's Failure to Train

Comparative education and training statistics are even less reliable than cross-national studies in economics; there are few generally agreed statistical categories, wide variations in the quality of ET provision and qualifications and a notable lack of data on training within companies. Despite these caveats, there is a consensus in the growing body of comparative ET research that Britain provides significantly poorer ET for its workforce than its major international competitors. Our focus will be on differences in ET provision for the majority of the population, concentrating in particular on the normal ET routes for skilled and semi-skilled workers. This need not be technical courses, but may - as in Japan or the US - constitute a long course of general education followed by company-based training.

---

[2] 'Equilibrium' is not meant to imply that all British firms produce low-quality products or services, or that all individuals are poorly educated and trained. A number of companies (often foreign-owned MNCs) have succeeded in recruiting the educational élite and offering good training programmes.

[3] An excellent discussion of the differences in each of these dimensions between British and German companies is contained in Lane (1988).

D. Finegold and D. Soskice

The baseline comparison for ET effectiveness begins with how students in different countries perform during compulsory schooling. Prais and Wagner (1983) compared mathematics test results of West German and English secondary schools and found that the level of attainment of the lower half of German pupils was higher than the average level of attainment in England, while Lynn (1988, p. 6) reviewed thirteen- year-olds' scores on international mathematics achievement tests from the early 1980s and found that 'approximately 79 per cent of Japanese children obtained a higher score than the average English child'. The results are equally disturbing in the sciences, where English fourteen year-olds scored lower than their peers in all seventeen countries in a recent study (Postlethwaite, 1988).

This education shortfall is compounded by the fact that England is the only one of the world's major industrial nations in which a majority of students leave full-time education or training at the age of sixteen. The contrast is particularly striking with the US, Canada, Sweden and Japan, where more than 85 per cent of sixteen year-olds remain are in full-time education. In Germany, Austria and Switzerland, similar proportions are either in full-time education or in highly structured three or four-year apprenticeships. Britain has done little to improve its relative postion. It was, for example, the only member of the OECD to experience a decline in the participation rate of the sixteen-nineteen age group in the latter half of the 1970s. (OECD, 1985, p. 17) Although staying-on rates have improved in the 1980s - due to falling rolls and falling job prospects - Britain's relative position in the OECD rankings has not.

The combination of poor performance during the compulsory schooling years and a high percentage of students leaving school at sixteen has meant that the average English worker enters employment with a relatively low level of qualifications.

Workers' lack of initial qualifications is not compensated for by increased employer-based training; on the contrary, British firms offer a lower quality and quantity of training than their counterparts on the Continent. A joint MSC/NEDO study (1984, p. 90) found that employers in Germany were spending approximately three times more on training than their British rivals, while Steedman's analysis (1986) of comparable construction firms in France and Britain revealed that French workers' training was more extensive and less firm-specific. Overall, British firms have been estimated to be devoting 0.15 per cent of turnover to training compared with 1-2 per cent in Japan, France and West Germany (Anderson, 1987, p. 69). And, as we will show in Section four, neither individuals nor the Government have compensated for employers lack of investment in adult training.

ii) Why Train? The link between ET and Economic Performance

Britain's relative failure to educate and train its workforce has contributed to its poor economic growth record in the postwar period. While it is difficult to demonstrate this relationship empirically, given the numerous other factors which effect labour productivity, no one is likely to dispute the claim that ET provision can improve economic performance in extreme cases, i.e. a certified engineer will be more productive working with a complex piece of industrial machinery than an unskilled employee. Our concern, however, is whether marginal differences in the quality and quantity of ET are related to performance. We will divide the evidence on this relationship in two parts: first, that the short-term expansion of British industry has been hindered by the failure of the ET system to produce sufficient quantities of skilled labour; and second, that the ability of the British economy and individual firms to adapt to the longer-term shifts in international competition has been impeded by the dearth of qualified manpower.

A survey of the literature reveals that skill shortages in key sectors such as engineering and information technology have been a recurring problem for UK industry, even during times of high unemployment. The Donovan Commission (1968, p. 92) maintained that 'lack of skilled labour has constantly applied a brake to our economic expansion since the war', a decade later, a NEDO study (1978, p. 2) found that 68 per cent

OXFORD REVIEW OF ECONOMIC POLICY, VOL. 4, NO. 3

of mechanical engineering companies reported that output was restricted by an absence of qualified workers. The problem remains acute, as the MSC's first *Skills Monitoring Report* (May, 1986, p. 1) stated: 'Shortages of professional engineers have continued to grow and there are indications that such shortages will remain for some time, particulary of engineers with electronics and other IT skills.'

The shortages are not confined to manufacturing. Public sector professions, i.e. teaching, nursing and social work, which rely heavily on recruiting from the limited group of young people with at least five O-levels, are facing a skilled (wo)manpower crisis as the number of school-leavers declines by 25 per cent between 1985 and 1995. In the case of maths and science teachers, the shortages tend to be self-perpetuating, as the absence of qualified specialists makes it harder to attract the next generation of students into these fields (Gow, 1988, p. 4; Keep, 1987, p. 12).

The main argument of this paper, however, is that the evidence of skill shortages both understates and oversimplifies the consequences Britain's ET failure has on its economic performance. Skill shortages reflect the unsatisfied demand for trained individuals within the limits of existing industrial organization, but they say nothing about the negative effect poor ET may have on how efficiently enterprises organize work or their ability to restructure. Indeed, there is a growing recognition among industry leaders and the major accounting firms that their traditional method of calculating firms' costs, particularly labour costs, fails to quantify the less tangible benefits of training, such as better product quality and increased customer satisfaction (*Business Week*, 1988, p. 49).

There are, however, a number of recent studies which show the strong positive correlation between industry productivity and skill levels. Daly (1984, pp. 41-2) compared several US and UK manufacturing industries and found that a shift of 1 per cent of the labour force from the unskilled to the skilled category raised productivity by about 2 per cent, concluding that British firms suffered because 'they lacked a large intermediate group with either educational or vocational qualifications'. The specific ways in which training can harm firm performance were spelled out in a comparison of West German and British manufacturing plants (Worswick, 1985, p. 91): 'Because of their relative deficiency in shop-floor skills, equivalent British plants had to carry more overhead labour in the form of quality controllers, production planners . . . the comparative shortage of maintenance skills in British plants might be associated with longer equipment downtime and hence lower capital productivity.'

Likewise, employee productivity levels in the French construction industry were found to be one-third higher than in Britain and the main explanation was the greater breadth and quality of French training provision (Steedman, 1986).

While these studies have all centred on relatively comparable companies producing similar goods and services, a high level of ET is also a crucial element in enabling firms to reorganize the work process in pursuit of new product markets, what Reich has called 'flexible-system' production strategies (Reich, 1983, pp. 135-6). 'Flexible-system' companies are geared to respond rapidly to change, with non-hierarchical management structures, few job demarcations and an emphasis on teamwork and maintaining product quality. They can be located in new industries, i.e. biotechnology, fibre optics, or market niches within old industries, such as speciality steels and custom machine tools.

A number of recent studies have highlighted the role of training in 'flexible-system' production: in Japanese firms, Shirai (1983, p. 46) found that employees in 'small, relatively independent work groups . . . grasped the total production process, thus making them more adaptable when jobs have to be redesigned'. Streeck (1985) took the analysis one step further in his study of the European car industry, arguing that the high-quality training programmes of German automakers have acted as a driving force behind product innovation, as firms have developed more sophisticated models to better utilize the talents of their employees. Even in relatively low-tech industries, such as kitchen manufacturing, German

D. Finegold and D. Soskice

companies are, according to Steedman and Wagner (1987), able to offer their customers more customized, better-quality units than their British competitors because of the greater flexibility of their production process--a flexibility that is contingent on workers with a broad skill base.

III. WHY HAS BRITAIN FAILED TO TRAIN?

Economists normal diagnosis of the undersupply of training is that it is a public good or free ride problem: firms do not invest in sufficient training because it is cheaper for them to hire already skilled workers than to train their own and risk them being poached by other companies. While the public good explanation may account for the general tendency to underinvest in training, it does not explain the significant variations between countries' levels of training nor does it address the key public policy question: Given the market's inability to provide enough skilled workers, why hasn't the British Government take corrective action? To answer this question we will look first at why political parties were long reluctant to intervene in the ET field, and then, at the two major obstacles which policy-makers faced when they did push for ET change: a state apparatus ill-equipped for centrally-led reform and a complex web of institutional constraints which kept Britain in a low-skills equilibrium.

i) Political Parties

Through most of the postwar period, the use of ET to improve economic performance failed to emerge on the political agenda, as a consensus formed among the two major parties on the merits of gradually expanding educational provision and leaving training to industry. Underlying this consensus was an economy producing full employment and sustained growth, which covered any deficiencies in the ET system. The broad consensus, however, masked significant differences in the reasons for the parties' positions: For Labour, vocational and technical education were seen as incompatible with the drive for comprehensive schooling, while the Party's heavy dependence on trade unions for financial and electoral support prevented any attempts to infringe on union's control over training within industry (Hall, 1986, p. 85). In the case of the Conservatives, preserving the grammar school track was the main educational priority, while intervening in the training sphere would have violated their belief in the free market (Wiener, 1981, p. 110). An exception to the principle of non-intervention came during the war, when the Coalition Government responded to the manpower crisis by erecting makeshift centres that trained more than 500,000 people. When the war ended, however, these training centres were dismantled.

ii) The State Structure

One of the main factors which hindered politicians from taking a more active ET role was the weakness of the central bureaucracy in both the education and training fields. On the training side, it was not until the creation of the Manpower Services Commission (MSC) in 1973 (discussed in section four) that the state developed the capacity for implementing an active labour market policy. The staff of the primary economic policy-making body, the Treasury, 'had virtually no familiarity with, or direct concern for, the progress of British industry' (Hall, 1986, p. 62) and none of the other departments (Environment, Trade and Industry, Employment or Education and Science) assumed clear responsibility for overseeing training. There was, for example, a dearth of accurate labour market statistics, which made projections of future skill requirements a virtual impossibility (Reid, 1980, p. 30). Even if the state had come up with the bureaucratic capability to develop a coherent training policy, it lacked the capacity to implement it. Wilensky and Turner (1987, pp. 62-3) compared the state structure and corporatist bargaining arrangements of eight major industrialized nations and ranked the UK last in its ability to execute manpower policy.

OXFORD REVIEW OF ECONOMIC POLICY, VOL. 4, NO. 3

While responsiblity over education policy in the central state was more clearly defined, resting with the Department of Education and Science (DES), the historical decentralization of power within the educational world made it impossible for the DES to exercise effective control (Howell, 1980; OECD, 1975). Those groups responsible for delivering education, local authorities (Jennings, 1974) and teachers (Dale, 1983), were able to block reforms they opposed, such as vocationalism. The lack of central control was particularly apparent in the further education sector, an area accorded low priority by the DES until the 1970s (Salter and Tapper, 1981).

The main obstacle to ET reform, however, was not the weakness of the central state, which could be remedied given the right external circumstances and sufficient political will, but the interlocking network of societal institutions which will be explored in the following sections, beginning with the structure, or lack of it, for technical and vocational education and entry-level training.

iii) The ET System

Technical and work-related subjects have long suffered from a second-class status in relation to academic courses in the British education system (Wiener, 1981). The Norwood Report of 1943 recommended a tripartite system of secondary education, with technical schools to channel the second-quarter of the ability range into skilled jobs; but while the grammar schools and secondary moderns flourished, the technical track never accommodated more than 4 per cent of the student population. In the mid-1960s two programmes, the Schools Council's 'Project Technology' and the Association for Science Education's 'Applied Science and the Schools', attempted to build an 'alternative road' of engineering and practical courses to rival pure sciences in the secondary curriculum (McCulloch et al. 1985, pp. 139-55). These pilot experiments were short-lived due to: 1) conflicts between and within the relevant interest groups, 2) minimal co-ordination of the initiatives and 3) the absence of clearly defined objectives and strategies for implementing them (ibid., pp. 209-12).

The efforts to boost technical education were marginal to the main educational tranformations of the postwar period: the gradual shift from division at eleven-plus to comprehensives and the raising of the school-leaving age to fifteen, and eventually sixteen in 1972. The education establishment, however, was slow to come up with a relevant curriculum for the more than 85 per cent of each age cohort who were now staying longer in school, but could not qualify for a place in higher education. Success for the new comprehensives continued to be defined by students' performance in academic examinations (O- and A-levels), which were designed for only the top 20 per cent of the ability range (Fenwick, 1976) and allowed many students to drop subjects, such as mathematics and science, at the age of fourteen. The academic/university bias of the secondary system was reinforced by the powerful influence of the public schools, which while catering for less than 6 per cent of students produced 73 per cent of the directors of industrial corporations (Giddens, 1979), as well as a majority of Oxbridge graduates, MPs and top education officials; thus, a large percentage of those charged with formulating ET policy, both for government and firms, had no personal experience of state education, much less technical or vocational courses.

The responsibility for vocational education and training (VET) fell by default to the further education (FE) sector. The 1944 Education Act attempted to provide a statutory basis for this provision, declaring that county colleges should be set up in each LEA to offer compulsory day-release schemes for fifteen-eighteen year-olds in employment. The money was never provided to build these colleges, however, with the result that 'a jungle' of different FE institutions, courses and qualifications developed (Locke and Bloomfield, 1982). There were three main paths through this 'jungle': the academic sixth form, the technical courses certified by independent bodies, such as City & Guilds, BTEC or the RSA, and 'the new sixth form' or 'young stayers on', who remain in full-time education without committing to an A-level or specific training course (MacFarlane Report, 1980). A host of factors curtailed the numbers pursuing the intermediate route: the relatively few careers requiring these qualifications, the lack of maintenance support for FE

D. Finegold and D. Soskice

students and the high status of the academic sixth, which was reinforced by the almost total exclusion of technical students from higher education.

The majority of individuals left education for jobs which offered no formal training. Those who did receive training were almost exclusively in apprenticeships. The shortcomings of many of these old-style training programmes, which trained 240,000 school-leavers in 1964, were well known: age and gender barriers to entry, qualifications based on time-served (up to seven years) rather than a national standard of proficiency and no guarantee of off-the-job training (Page, 1967). The equation of apprenticeships with training also had the effect of stifling training for positions below skilled level and for older employees whose skills had become redundant or needed updating.

In the early 1960s the combination of declining industrial competitiveness, a dramatic expansion in the number of school-leavers and growing evidence of skill shortages and 'poaching' prompted the Government to attempt to reform apprenticeships and other forms of training (Perry, 1976). The route the state chose was one of corporatist compromise and minimal intervention, erecting a network of training boards (ITBs) in the major industries staffed by union, employer and government representatives (Industrial Training Act, 1964). The ITBs' main means of overcoming the free-rider problem was the levy/grant system, which placed a training tax on all the companies within an industry and then distributed the funds to those firms that were training to an acceptable standard, defined by each board (Page, 1970).

The boards created a fairer apportionment of training costs and raised awareness of skill shortages, but they failed to raise substantially the overall training level because they did not challenge the short-term perspective of most companies. The state contributed no new funds to training and each board assessed only its industry's training needs, taking as given the existing firm organization, industrial relations system and management practices and thus perpetuating the low-skill equilibrium. Despite the Engineering ITB's pioneering work in developing new, more flexible training courses, craft apprenticeships remained the main supply of skilled labour until Mrs Thatcher came to power in 1979.

iv) Industrial/Firm Structure

Industry Type. One of the main reasons that British industry has failed to update its training programmes is the concentration of the country's firms in those product markets which have the lowest skill requirements, goods manufactured with continuous, rather than batch or unit production processes (Reich, 1983). An analysis of international trade in the 1970s by NEDO found that the UK performed better than average in 'standardized, price-sensitive products' and below average in 'the skill and innovation-intensive products' (Greenhalgh, 1988, p. 15). New and Myers' 1986 study of two hundred and forty large export-oriented plants confirmed that only a minority of these firms had experimented with the most advanced technologies and that management's future plans were focused on traditional, mass-production market segments.

Training has also been adversely effected by the long-term shift in British employment from manufacturing to low-skill, low-quality services. Manufacturing now accounts for less than one-third of British employment and its share of the labour market has been declining. The largest growth in employment is in the part-time service sector where jobs typically require and offer little or no training. The concentration of British service providers on the low-skill end of the labour market was highlighted in a recent study of the tourist industry (Gapper, 1988).

While the type of goods or services which a company produces sets limits on the skills required, it does not determine the necessary level of training. Recent international comparisons of firms in similar product markets (i.e. Maurice et al., 1986; Streeck, 1985) have revealed significant variations in training provision depending on how a company is organized and the way in which this organizational structure shapes the

OXFORD REVIEW OF ECONOMIC POLICY, VOL. 4, NO. 3

implementation of new technologies. In the retail trade, for instance, 75 per cent of German employees have at least an apprenticeship qualification compared with just two percent in the UK. The brief sections which follow will outline how, in the British case, the many, integrally-related components of firms' organizational structures and practices have combined to discourage training.

Recruitment. British firms have traditionally provided two routes of entry for young workers: the majority are hired at the end of compulsory schooling, either to begin an apprenticeship or to start a semi- or unskilled job, while a select few are recruited from higher education (HE) for management posts (Crowther Report, 1959). (Nursing is one of the rare careers which has sought students leaving further education (FE) at the age of 18.) As a result, there is little incentive for those unlikely to gain admittance to HE to stay on in school or FE. Indeed, Raffe (1984, Ch. 9) found that Scottish males who opted for post-compulsory education actually had a harder time finding work than their peers who left school at sixteen. Vocational education is perceived as a low status route because it provides little opportunity for career advancement and because managers, who themselves typically enter employment without practical experience or technical training, focus on academic examinations as the best means of assessing the potential of trainees.

Job design and scope. After joining a company, employees' training will depend upon the array of tasks they are asked to perform. Tipton's study (1985, p. 33) of the British labour market found that 'the bulk of existing jobs are of a routine, undemanding variety' requiring little or no training. The failure to broaden individuals' jobs and skill base, i.e. through job rotation and work teams, has historically been linked to craft unions' insistence on rigid demarcations between jobs, but there is some evidence that these restrictive practices have diminished in the last decade. The decline in union resistance, however, has been counterbalanced by two negative trends for training: subcontracting out skilled maintenance work (Brady, 1984) and using new technologies to deskill work (Streeck, 1985). The latter practice is particularly well documented in the automobile industry, where British firms, unlike their Swedish, Japanese and German rivals, have structured new automated factories to minimize the skill content of production jobs, instead of utilizing the new technology to increase flexibility and expand job definitions (Scarbrough, 1986). Tipton concludes (p. 27): 'the key to improving the quality of training is the design of work and a much needed spur to the movement for the redesign of work . . . may lie in training policies and practice'.

Authority Structure. In the previous section we used job design to refer to the range of tasks within one level of a firm's job hierarchy (horizontal scope); how that hierarchy is structured - number of levels, location of decision-making power, forms of control - will also effect training provision (vertical scope). *A Challenge to Complacency* (Coopers and Lybrand, 1985, pp. 4-5) discovered that in a majority of the firms surveyed, line managers, rather than top executives, are generally responsible for training decisions, thereby hindering long-term manpower planning. British firms also lack structures, like German work councils, which enable employees to exercise control over their own training.

Career/Wage Structure. A company's reward system, how wages and promotion are determined, shapes employees' incentives to pursue training. While education levels are crucial in deciding where an employee enters a firm's job structure, these incentives are low after workers have taken a job because pay and career advancement are determined by seniority not skill levels (George and Shorey, 1985). This disincentive is particularly strong for the growing number of workers trapped in the periphery sector of the labour market (Mayhew, 1986), which features part-time or temporary work, low wages and little or no chance for promotion.

Management. Linking all of the preceding elements of firm organization is the role of management in determining training levels. The poor preparation of British managers, resulting from a dearth of technical HE or management schools and a focus on accounting rather than production, is often cited as a reason for the lack of priority attached to training in Britain (i.e. Davies and Caves, 1987). A recent survey of over 2,500 British firms found that less than half made any provision at all for management training

D. Finegold and D. Soskice

(Anderson, 1987, p. 68). In those firms which do train, managers tend to treat training as an operating expense to be pared during economic downturns and fail to incorporate manpower planning into the firm's overall competitive strategy. For managers interested in career advancement, the training department is generally seen as a low-status option (Coopers and Lybrand, 1985, pp. 4-5). And for poorly qualified line managers, training may be perceived as a threat to their authority rather than a means of improving productivity. It is important, however, to distinguish between bad managers, and able ones who are forced into decisions by the institutional structure in which they are operating. We will explore two of the major forces impacting on their decisions, industrial relations and financial markets, in the following sections.

v) Financial Markets

The short-term perspective of most British managers is reinforced by the pressure to maximize immediate profits and shareholder value. The historical separation of financial and industrial capital (Hall, 1986, p. 59) has made it harder for British firms to invest in training, with its deferred benefits, than their West German or Japanese competitors, particularly since the City has neglected training in its analysis of companies' performance (Coopers and Lybrand, 1985). Without access to large industry-oriented investment banks, British firms have been forced to finance more investment from retained profits than companies in the other G5 nations (Mayer, 1987).

vi) Industrial Relations

Just as the operation of financial markets has discouraged training efforts, so too the structure, traditions, and common practices of British industrial relations have undermined attempts to improve the skills of the work force. The problem must be analysed at two levels: a) the inability of the central union and employer organisations to combine with government to form a co-ordinated national training policy; and b) the historical neglect of training in the collective bargaining process.

Employer Organizations. The strength of the CBI derives from its virtual monopoly status - its members employ a majority of Britain's workers and there is no competing national federation. But while this membership base has given the CBI a role in national training policy formulation, the CBI lacks the sanctions necessary to ensure that employers implement the agreements which it negotiates with the Government. The power lies not in the central federation, nor in industry-wide employers' associations, but in individual firms. The CBI's views on training reflect its lack of control, as Keep (1986, p. 8), a former member of the CBI's Education, Training and Technology Directorate, observes: 'The CBI's stance on training policy . . . was strongly anti-interventionist and centred on a voluntary, market-based approach. Legislation to compel changes in training policy . . . was perceived as constituting an intolerable financial burden on industry.'

This free-market approach, combined with the absence of strong local employer groups, like the West German Chambers of Commerce, has left British industry without an effective mechanism for overcoming the 'poaching' problem. Among the worst offenders are the small and medium-sized firms, poorly represented in the CBI, which lack the resources to provide broad-based training.

Trade Unions. There are four key, closely connected variables which determine the effectiveness of a central union federation in the training field (Woodall, 1985, p. 26). They are: degree of centralisation, financial membership and organisation resources, degree of youth organisation and structure and practice of collective bargaining. Woodall compared the TUC with European central union federations and found it weak along all of these axes. Like the CBI, it could exert a limited influence on government policy, but it lacked the means to enforce centrally negotiated initiatives on its members.

The TUC has had to deal with 'the most complex trade union structure in the world', (Clegg, 1972, p. 57)

OXFORD REVIEW OF ECONOMIC POLICY, VOL. 4, NO. 3

while having little control over its affiliated unions. And whereas the German central union federation, the DGB, claims 12 per cent of its member unions' total receipts, the TUC has received less than 2 per cent and devotes only a small fraction of these resources to training. This inattention to education and training is reflected in unions lack of involvement in the transition from school to work. Britain's major youth organisations, the National Union of Students and Youthaid, grew outside the formal union structure and have often criticized the labour movement for failing to address the needs of the nation's school-leavers, particularly the unemployed. The unco-ordinated nature of British collective bargaining, with agreements varying from coverage of whole industries to small portions of a particular factory, and the lack of central input in the negotiations further hinder TUC efforts to improve training provision. The combination of these factors prompted Taylor (1980, p. 91) to observe that 'by the standards of other Western industrialised nations, Britain provides the worst education services of any trade union movement.'

Although we have broken down this analysis into separate sections for conceptual clarity, it is essential to view each element as part of a historically evolved institutional structure which has limited British ET. In the next part we will examine how the economic crisis of the 1970s destabilized this structure, creating the opportunity for the Thatcher Government's ET reforms.

IV. MRS THATCHER'S EDUCATION AND TRAINING POLICIES

During the 1970s a confluence of events brought an end to the reluctance of central government to take the lead in ET policy-making. The prolonged recession which followed the 1973 oil shock forced the Labour Government to cut public expenditure, necessitating a re-examination of educational priorities. This reassessment came at a time when the education system was drawing mounting criticism in the popular press and the far Right's 'Black Papers' for allegedly falling standards and unchecked teacher progressivism (CCCS, 1981). The response of the then Prime Minister, Callaghan, was to launch the 'Great Debate' on education in a now famous speech at Ruskin College, Oxford in October 1976, where he called on the ET sector to make a greater contribution towards the nation's economic performance (*TES* 22/10/76, p. 72).

The increase in bipartisan political support for vocational and technical education was matched by a strengthening of the central state's capacity to formulate ET policy. The Manpower Services Commission (MSC), a tripartite quango funded by the Department of Employment, was established in 1973 to provide the strong central organization needed to co-ordinate training across industrial sectors which was missing from the industrial training board structure. In practice, however, the ITBs were left to themselves, while the MSC concentrated on the immediate problem of growing youth unemployment. The Commission supervised the first substantial injection of government funds into training, beginning with TOPS (Training Opportunities Scheme) and later through YOP (Youth Opportunities Programme). The rapid increase in government spending, the MSC budget rose from £125 million in 1974-5 to £641 million in 1978-9, did little to improve skills, however, since the funds were concentrated on temporary employment, work experience and short-course training measures and the demands for quick action precluded any long-term manpower planning.

Spurred on by its new rival, the MSC, the DES set up the Further Education Unit (FEU) in 1978, which produced a steady stream of reports that helped shift educational opinion in favour of the 'new vocationalism', (i.e. *A Basis for Choice*, 1979). The Department teamed up with the MSC for the first time in 1976 to launch the Unified Vocational Preparation (UVP) scheme for school-leavers entering jobs which previously offered no training. Although this initiative never advanced beyond the early pilot phase, it set a precedent for subsequent reform efforts.

D. Finegold and D. Soskice

The state structure was in place for the new Thatcher Government to transform the ET system. The first half of this section will outline three distinct phases in the Conservatives' ET reform efforts (see Table

Table 1: Mrs Thatcher's Education and Training Policies

Phase/Date	Characteristics	Programmes		
		Education	Youth Training	Adult Training
I. Preparation 1979-81	Market orientation Weaken resistance Lack overall strategy	Budget cuts	Apprenticeship collapse	Dismantle ITBs
II. NTI 1982-86	Focus on 14-18s Concern with youth unemployment Enterprise economy Increase central control	TVEI Pilot-National Programme in 4 yrs	YTS/ITeCs NCVQ YOP;1 yr YTS; 2 yr YTS YTS apprentice route	TOPS/JTS/CP TOPS-new JTS Focus on adult unemployment
III. Expansion 1987-	Education-new priorities Adults - first attempt at coherence.	GERBIL/CTCs TVEI extension or extinction?	Weaken MSC Compulsory YTS NCVQ finish in 1991.	Weaken MSC Training for employment 600,000 places; no new money.

1), examining how the Government has avoided many of the pitfalls which plagued past efforts at change, while the latter portion will argue that these reforms, while leading to significant shifts in control over ET, will not raise Britain's relative ET performance.

i) Phase 1: Preparation

It is only in retrospect, that the first few years of the Thatcher Administration can be seen as an effective continuation of the movement towards greater centralization of ET power. At the time, Government economic policy was dominated by the belief that controlling the money supply and public expenditure were the keys to reducing inflation and restoring competitiveness. Education and training accounted for approximately 15 per cent of the budget and thus needed to be cut if spending was to be curtailed. The cuts included: across the board reductions in education funding, a drop in state subsidies for apprenticeships and the abolition of seventeen of the twenty-four training boards (one new one was created), despite the opposition of the MSC. The financial rationale for the cuts was underpinned by the then strongly held view of the Government that training decisions were better left to market forces.

The net effect of these cuts, coming at the start of a severe recession in which industry was already cutting back on training, was the collapse of the apprenticeship system. The number of engineering craft and technician trainees, for example, declined from 21,000 to 12,000 between 1979 and 1981, while construction apprentice recruitment fell by 53 per cent during the same period (from EITB and CITB in TUC Annual Report, 1981, pp. 434-5). The destruction of old-style apprenticeships, combined with the Government's attacks on trade unions' restrictive practices through industrial relations legislation, meant that when the state eventually chose to reform initial training within companies, there was only minimal resistance from organized labour and employers.

OXFORD REVIEW OF ECONOMIC POLICY, VOL. 4, NO. 3

ii) Phase II: 'The New Training Initiative'

By 1981 the deepening recession and the dramatic rise in youth unemployment which it caused compelled the Government to reassess its non-interventionist training stance. While the Conservative's neo-liberal economic philosophy offered no immediate cure for mass unemployment, it was politically essential to make some effort to combat a problem which the polls consistently showed to be the voters' primary concern (Moon and Richardson, 1985, p. 61). This electoral need was highlighted in a Downing Street Policy Unit paper from early 1981:

'We all know that there is no prospect of getting unemployment down to acceptable levels within the next few years.(Consequently) we must show that we have some political imagination, that we are willing to salvage something - albeit second-best - from the sheer waste involved.' (Riddell, 1985, p. 50.)

What this 'political imagination' produced was the New Training Initiative (NTI) (1981), whose centerpiece, the Youth Training Scheme (YTS), was the first permanent national training programme for Britain's school-leavers. YTS replaced YOP, which had begun as a temporary scheme in 1978 to offer a year's work experience and training to the young unemployed. In just four years, however, YOP had swelled to more than 550,000 places, and as the numbers grew so did the criticism of the programme for its falling job-placement rates and poor quality training. YTS attempted to improve YOP's image by upgrading the training content, 'guaranteeing' a year's placement with at least thirteen weeks off-the-job training to every minimum age school-leaver and most unemployed seventeen year-olds and more than doubling the programme's annual budget, from £400 to £1,000 million.

Despite these improvements, the scheme got off to a difficult start, with a national surplus of close to 100,000 places, as school-leavers proved reluctant to enter the new programme. In response, the MSC implemented a constant stream of YTS reforms: the scheme was lengthened from one to two years, with off-the-job training extended to twenty weeks, all sixteen and seventeen year-olds, not just the unemployed, were made eligible, some form of qualification was to be made available to each trainee, and monitoring and evaluation were increased by requiring all training providors to attain Approved Training Organisation (ATO) status. While the majority of YTS places continue to offer trainees a broad sampling of basic skills ('foundation training') and socialization into a work environment, some industries, such as construction, engineering and hairdressing, have used the scheme to finance the first two years of modernized apprenticeships.

The other major ET reform originating in this period was the Technical and Vocational Education Initiative (TVEI), launched by the Prime Minister in November 1982. TVEI marked the Thatcher Administration's first attempt to increase the industrial relevance of what is taught in secondary schools, through the development of new forms of teacher training, curriculum organisation and assessment for the fourteen-eighteen age group. Under the direction of MSC Chairman David (now Lord) Young, the Initiative grew extremely rapidly, from fourteen local authority pilot projects in 1983 to the start of a nationwide, £1 billion extension just four years later. Lord Young conceived TVEI as a means of fostering Britain's 'enterprise economy', by motivating the vast majority of students who were not progressing to higher education: 'The curriculum in English schools is too academic and leads towards the universities. What I am trying to show is that there is another line of development that is equally respectable and desirable which leads to vocational qualifications . . .' (*Education*, 19 Nov. 1982, p. 386).

This line of development was extended into the FE sector in 1985 with the introduction of the Certificate of Pre-Vocational Education (CPVE), a one-year programme of broad, work-related subjects for students who wished to stay on in full-time education, but were not prepared for A-levels or a specific career path.

D. Finegold and D. Soskice

In 1985 the Government set up a working group to review Britain's increasingly diverse array of vocational qualifications. The De Ville Committee's Report (1986) led to the establishment of the National Council for Vocational Qualifications (NCVQ) which has the task of rationalizing all of the country's training qualifications into five levels, ranging from YTS to engineering professionals, with clear paths of progression between stages and national standards of proficiency. The Council, which is scheduled to complete its review in 1991, will be defining broad guidelines for training qualifications into which the courses of the independent certification bodies (i.e. RSA, BTEC, City and Guilds) can be slotted.

Taken together these initiatives represent a dramatic reversal in the Government's approach to ET. The scope and pace of reform was made possible by the centralization of power in the hands of the MSC, an institution which has proved adept at securing the co-operation required to implement these controversial changes. In the case of YTS, the MSC has thus far retained trade union support, despite protests from over one-third of the TUC's membership that the schemes lead to job substitution and poor-quality training (*TUC Annual Reports*, 1983-86), because the TUC leadership has refused to give up one of its last remaining channels for input into national policy-making.

The MSC has also become a major power in the educational world because it offered the Conservatives a means of bypassing the cumbersome DES bureaucracy (Dale, 1985, p. 50). The Commission was able to convince teachers and local authorities, who had in the past resisted central government's efforts to reform the curriculum, to go along with TVEI through the enticement of generous funding during a period of fiscal austerity and the use of techniques normally associated with the private sector, such as competitive bidding and contractual relationships (Harland, 1987). Its influence over education increased still further in 1985, when it was given control over 25 per cent of non-advanced further education (NAFE) funding, previously controlled by the LEAs. This change has, in effect, meant that the MSC has the power to review all NAFE provision.

iii) Phase III: Expanding the Focus

The constantly changing nature of ET policy under Mrs Thatcher makes it hazardous to predict future developments, but early indications are that education and training reform will continue to accelerate in her third term. The combination of a successful economy (low inflation, high growth and falling unemployment) and a solid electoral majority has enabled the Conservatives to turn their focus toward fundamental social reform. As a result, the narrow concentration of ET policy on the fourteen-eighteen age group appears to be broadening to include both general education (The Great Education Reform Bill (GERBIL), 1987) and adult training (Training for Employment, 1988).

The 1987 Conservative Election Manifesto signalled the emergence of education reform as a major political issue. While GERBIL is primarily an attempt to raise standards by increasing competition and the accountability of the educational establishment, a number of its provisions will impact on the vocational education and training (VET) area: the National Curriculum, which will ensure that all students take mathematics and science until they reach sixteen; City Technical Colleges, which may signal the beginning of an alternative secondary school track, funded directly by the DES with substantial contributions from industry; the removal of the larger Colleges of Further Education (CFEs) and Polytechnics from LEA control, freeing them to compete for students and strengthening their ties with employers; and increased industry representation on the new governing body for universities, the UFC (University Funding Council).

At the same time, the Government has begun restructuring adult training provision. Over the previous eight years, the MSC concentrated on reducing youth unemployment, while financing a succession of short-duration training and work experience programmes for the long-term unemployed: TOPS (Training Opportunities Scheme - short courses normally based in CFEs), JTS, and new-JTS (Job Training

OXFORD REVIEW OF ECONOMIC POLICY, VOL. 4, NO. 3

Scheme - work placement with minimal off-the-job training for eighteen-to-twenty-fours), and the CP (Community Programme - state-funded public work projects). In February 1988 the Government's White Paper, *Training for Employment*, introduced a plan to combine all of these adult initatives into a new £1.5 billion programme that will provide 600,000 training places, with initial preference given to the eighteen-to-twenty-four age group. To attract the long-run unemployed into the scheme the Government is using both carrot and stick: a training allowance at least £10 above the benefit level, along with increases in claimant advisors and fraud investigators to ensure that all those receiving benefit are actively pursuing work.

The new scheme will be administered by the Training Commission, the heir to the MSC. The Employment Secretary surprised both critics and supporters when he announced that the Government's most effective quango would come to an end in 1988. The new Training Commission lacks the MSC's employment functions, which have been transfered to the DoE, and its governing board structure has been altered to give industry representatives, some now appointed directly rather than by the CBI, effective control. The changes seem to indicate that the Thatcher Government no longer feels the need to consult trade unions and wants to play down the role of the CBI in order to push forward its training reforms.

The Government has also started to devote a limited amount of resources to broadening access to ET for those already in employment. The DES is expanding its PICKUP (Professional, Industrial and Commercial Updating) Programme, which is now spending £12.5 million a year to help colleges, polytechnics and universities tailor their courses more closely to employers' needs. And in 1987, the MSC provided start-up money for the Open College, which along with Open Tech uses open-learning techniques to offer individuals and employers the chance to acquire new skills or update old ones.

iv) Problems with Mrs Thatcher's ET Policies

While Mrs. Thatcher has brought about more radical and rapid changes in the ET system than any British leader in the postwar period, there are a number reasons to doubt whether her reforms will succeed in closing the skills gap which has grown between Britain and its major competitors. Rather than detail the shortcomings of specific programmes, we will focus on two major flaws in this Government's ET policy: the lack of coherence and weakness in the many initiatives designed to change the transition from school to FE or employment (reforms for the fourteen-eighteen age group) and the absence of an adult training strategy and sufficient funding to facilitate industrial restructuring.

The Transition from School to Work. Oxford's local education authority has coined a new term, 'GONOT'. GONOT is the name of a committee set up to coordinate GCSE, OES, NLI, OCEA and TVEI,[4] just some of the reforms introduced by the Government since 1981 for the fourteen-eighteen age group. The need to create abbreviations for abbreviations is symptomatic of the strains which the Conservatives' scatter-shot approach to ET policy has placed on those charged with implementing the reforms. The case of TVEI provides a clear illustration of the difficulties created by this incoherence.

When TVEI was first announced one of its primary objectives was to improve staying-on rates. This goal has since been de-emphasized, however, because TVEI's sixteen-eighteen phase comes into direct conflict with YTS. Students have a dual incentive to opt for the narrower training option: first, because YTS offers an allowance, while TVEI does not, and second, because access to skilled jobs is increasingly

---

[4] These initials stand for: General Certificate of Secondary Education (GCSE), Oxford Examination Syndicate (OES), the New Learning Initiative (NLI) -- part of the Low-Attaining Pupils Programme (LAP), Oxford Certificate of Educational Achievement (OCEA) -- part of the Record of Achievement Initiative and, of course, TVEI.

D. Finegold and D. Soskice

limited to YTS apprenticeships. The failure of the MSC to co-ordinate these programmes is evident at all organizational levels, from the national, where the headquarters are based in different cities, to the local, where the co-ordinators of the two initiatives rarely, if ever, come into contact.

The success of individual TVEI pilot schemes is also threatened by recent national developments. Local TVEI consortia, for example, have built closer ties between schools and the FE sector to rationalize provision at sixteen-plus, a crucial need during a period of falling student numbers. But these consortia are in jeopardy due to GERBIL's proposals for opting out, open enrollment and the removal of the larger Colleges of Further Education (CFEs) from LEA control, which would foster competition rather than co-operation among institutions. Likewise, TVEI's efforts to bridge traditional subject boundaries and the divide between academic and vocational subjects are in danger of being undermined by the proposed national curriculum with its individual subject testing and the failure to include academic examinations (GCSE and A-level) in the National Review of Vocational Qualifications (DeVille Report, 1986, p. 4).

These contradictions stem from divisions within the Conservative Party itself. Dale (1983) identifies five separate factions, industrial trainers, populists, privatizers, old-style Tories and moral educationalists, all exercising an influence on Thatcher's ET policies. Do the Conservatives, for instance, want to spread technical and vocational subjects across the comprehensive curriculum (the TVEI strategy) or ressurrect the old tripartite system's technical school track (the City Technical College route)? Another conflict has emerged in the examination sphere, where modular forms of assessment pioneered under TVEI and GCSE, which are already improving student motivation and practical skills (HMI, 1988), have been stifled by Conservative traditionalists, such as the Minister of State at the DES Angela Rumbold, insisting on preserving the narrow, exclusively academic focus of A-levels and university admissions (Gow, 1988, p. 1). The splits within the Party were highlighted in a leaked letter from the Prime Minister's secretary to Kenneth Baker's secretary, indicating Mrs Thatcher's reservations concerning the forms of assessment proposed by the Black Committee to accompany the National Curriculum (Travis, 1988, p. 1).

Emerging from this unco-ordinated series of reforms appears to be a three-tiered, post-compulsory ET system (Ranson, 1985, p. 63) which will not significantly raise the qualifications of those entering the work force: At the top, higher education will continue to be confined to an academic élite, as the White Paper 'Higher Education - Meeting the Challenge' (1987) projects no additional funds for HE in the next decade, despite growing evidence of graduate shortages; the middle rung of technical and vocational courses in full-time FE seems equally unlikely to expand, given that the Government refuses to consider educational maintenance allowances (EMAs) and that the extension funding for TVEI appears inadequate to sustain its early successes (Dale, 1986); the basic training route, then, will remain YTS, a low-cost option which has not succeeded in solving the skills problem (Deakin and Pratten, 1987; Jones, this issue). As of May 1987, more than half of all YTS providers had failed to meet the quality standards laid down by the MSC (Leadbeater, 1987). And though the quality of training may since have improved, organizations are finding it increasingly difficult to attract school-leavers on to the scheme, as falling rolls lead to increased competition among employers for sixteen year-olds to fill low-skill jobs (Jackson, 1988).

Restructuring/Adult Training. As we have shown (section 2.2), the capacity for continuously updating the skills of the work force is a key factor in the process of industrial restructuring, either at firm or national level. But in the rush to develop new ET initiatives for the fourteen-eighteen sector, the Conservatives have neglected the largest potential pool of trainees: adults in employment. The Government has not secured sufficient extra resources from any of the three basic sources of funding for post-compulsory ET, the state, individuals or companies, to finance a major improvement in British ET performance.

The largest increase in expenditure has come in the state sector, but it is crucial to examine where the money was spent. Although the MSC's budget tripled (to £2.3 billion) during the Conservatives' first two terms, only just over 10 percent of these funds were spent on adult training, the vast majority on the

OXFORD REVIEW OF ECONOMIC POLICY, VOL. 4, NO. 3

long-term unemployed. Those courses, like TOPS, which did offer high-quality training geared to the local labour market, have been phased out in favour of the much-criticized JTS and new-JTS, which offer less costly, lower-skill training (Payne, 1988). This emphasis on quantity over quality was continued in the new 'Training for Employment' package, which proposes to expand the number of training places still further without allocating any new resources. Mrs Thatcher's efforts to improve training within companies have been largely confined to a public relations exercise designed to increase 'national awareness' of training needs (*Training for Jobs*, 1984). Former MSC Chairman Bryan Nicholson made the Government's position clear: 'The state is responsible for education until an individual reaches sixteen. From sixteen to eighteen, education and training are the joint responsibility of industry and government. But from eighteen on, training should be up to the individual and his employer.' (Press Conference at People and Technology Conference, London, November, 1986.)

The Conservatives, however, have had little success in convincing the private sector to assume its share of responsibility for training. While the MSC has been gradually placing a greater portion of YTS funding on employers, the bulk of the cost is still met by the state. In fact, an NAHE study (1987) revealed that private training organizations were making a profit off the MSC's training grants. The Government may be regretting its decision to do away with the one legislative means of increasing employers' funding for training, as this remark made last year by Nicholson indicates: 'Those industries who have made little effort to keep the grand promises they made when the majority of ITBS were abolished should not be allowed to shirk forever.' (Clement, 1986, p. 3)

Mrs Thatcher has made somewhat more progress in her attempts to shift the ET burden on to individuals, who can fund their own ET either through direct payments (course fees, living expenses) or by accepting a lower wage in exchange for training. The state has compelled more school-leavers to pay for training by removing sixteen and seventeen year-olds from eligibility for benefits and then setting the trainee allowance at a level well below the old apprenticeship wage. It has also forced individuals staying on in full-time education to make a greater financial contribution to their own maintenance costs through the reduction of student grants, a policy which seems certain to accelerate with the introduction of student loans.

These measures, however, are not matched by policies to encourage adults to invest their time and money towards intermediate or higher-level qualifications. This failure can be traced to three sources: lack of opportunity, capital and motivation. The state's assumption of the full costs of higher education (HE), among the most expensive per pupil in the world, has resulted in a strictly limited supply of places. Those individuals who wish to finance courses below HE level suffer both from limited access to capital and a tax system which, unlike most European countries, offers employees no deductions for training costs (DES, 1988). But the main reason for workers' reluctance to invest in their own training is that the Government has done nothing to alter the basic operation of British firms which, as we saw in section three, are not structured to reward improvements in skill levels.

This underinvestment in ET raises the question: If it is true that training is critical to economic restructuring and that Mrs Thatcher has failed to improve Britain's poor ET record, why has the UK grown faster than all the major industrial nations, except Japan, over the last eight years? Part of the answer lies in the Conservatives' success in creating more efficient low-cost production and services economy. A series of supply-side measures, weakening Wage Councils and employment security legislation, subsidizing the creation of low-wage jobs (the Young Workers Scheme) and attacking trade unions, have improved labour mobility and company profitability. Training programmes, like YTS, have played a pivotal role in this process, providing employers with a cheap means of screening large numbers of low-skilled, but well-socialized young workers (Chapman and Tooze, 1986). The liberalization of financial markets, with the resultant pressure on firms to maximize short-term profits, and the explosion of accountancy-based management consultancy (*Business Week*, June 1988) have further reinforced industry's cost-cutting approach. The irony is that while Britain is striving to compete more effectively with low-cost producers

D. Finegold and D. Soskice

such as South Korea and Singapore, these nations are investing heavily in general education and training to enable their industries to move into flexible, high technology production.

V. POLICIES FOR THE FUTURE.

This section suggests in broad terms what policies could remedy the insufficiencies of our system of education and training. It covers both those in the sixteen to twenty age group and the (far larger) adult labour force. We take the quantitative goal to be the broad level which the Japanese, German and Swedes have achieved, namely where about 90 per cent of young people are in full-time highly-structured education and training until nineteen or twenty. And, less precisely, that major improvements take place in the training of those already in the workforce, both by the employer and externally.   Training of managers, in particular of supervisers, is treated in relation to these goals.

What type of education and training? There is broad agreement about the need to raise ET standards and levels, but less about its content. This reflects the failure of the (opposed) ET methodologies of the post-war decades: manpower planning, on the one hand, and human capital theory, on the other. Manpower planning has proved too inflexible in a world in which long-run predictions about occupational needs can seldom be made. And the rate of return calculations underlying human capital approaches to optimal training provision have foundered on the difference between social and market valuations. While both approaches have a role to play when used sensibly, few practitioners would see either as sufficient to determine the content of ET.

Reform of education and training is seen in this section as part of the process of 'managing change'. This context argues for three general criteria as determining the content of education and training.

First, the uncertainty of occupational needs in the future requires *adaptability*. Many people in the labour force will have to make significant career changes in their working lives, which will require retraining. There is some agreement that successful retraining depends on a high level of general education and also on previous vocational training. Moreover, as much training for new occupations covers skills already acquired in previous ET (e.g. computing skills), a modular approach to training is efficient.

Second, ET needs to equip workers with the skills required for *innovation in products and processes* and the *production of high quality goods and services*.   One implication is that participation in higher education will have to steadily increase. And there is a more radical implication, as Hayes and others have stressed: effective innovation and quality production requires participation; that means that workers and managers should acquire not just technical competence, but also the social and managerial skills involved in working together. We may need increasingly to blur the distinction between management ET and worker ET. The implications are various: a high level of general education, sufficiently broad that young people are both technically competent and educated in the humanities and arts; strong emphasis on projects, working together and interdisciplinary work; vocational education and training which provides management skills as well as technical understanding. More generally, ET should be designed to reduce class barriers (not only as a good in itself, but also) because of the requirements of innovation and high-quality production.

Third, ET must be *recognisable* and *useful*, so that employers want to employ the graduates of the ET system and young people and adults want to undertake ET. There is a potential tension here with the previous paragraph. For the abilities stressed there are at present only demanded by a minority of companies. Vocational education is thus a compromise between the characteristics needed in the longer term and the skills and knowledge which companies can see as immediately useful to them. A second

OXFORD REVIEW OF ECONOMIC POLICY, VOL. 4, NO. 3

implication of the need for recognition and usefulness is that there be a widely agreed and understood system of certification, based on acceptable assessment.

Much policy discussion, sensibly, concerns potential improvements within the broad context of the existing framework of ET provision within the UK. As a result less thought has been given to the wider transformations which we believe the management of change and the move to a high skills equilibrium imply. The discussion of this section thus takes a longer-term perspective.

There are five interdependent parts to these recommendations for reform: reforming ET provision for the sixteen to twenty age group; training by companies; individual access to training; the external infrastructure of ET; and the macro-economic implications of a major ET expansion.

i) The Education and Training of Sixteen to Twenty Year-Olds

The focus of this section is on how incentives, attitudes, institutions and options can be changed so that young people will choose to remain in full-time education and training until the age of nineteen or twenty, rather than entering the labour market or YTS at age sixteen.

For two reasons the next decade offers a window for reform which was not previously open. First, the demographic decline in the sixteen-plus age cohort will mean a drop of nearly a third over the next ten years in the numbers of young people aged between sixteen and nineteen. It will therefore be an ideal period for bringing our system into line with that of other advanced countries. For the resource cost, although considerable, of a substantial increase in the ET participation ratio of sixteen to nineteen year-olds will be significantly less than in the past decade.

The second reason was spelt out in section four. The institutional constraints against change are in two ways significantly weaker now than a decade or two decades ago. Unions at national level, far from seeking to frustrate change, would support it in this area; they would see it as a means of regaining membership, rather than a threat to the bargaining position of existing skilled workers. The education system (teachers, LEAs, educationalists, teachers unions) no longer sees itself as having the right to determine education policy alone; central government has far stronger control over it than in the past, and this will increase over the next decade as opting out develops; the larger CFEs will no longer be run by LEAs; teachers unions are moving away from the belief that they can successfully oppose government to the view that they need to cultivate wider alliances, including industry; and educationalists today are far more aware of the role which schools can play in helping children to get employment. In addition political parties are no longer constrained as they were (say) two decades ago in formulating policy in these areas.

What basic requirements are implied for a sixteen to twenty ET system by the discussion in the introduction above? Five should be stressed:

— Good general education, covering both technical subjects and the humanities.

— This should be designed to encourage interaction (project etc.) and reduce social class differences.

— Rising percentage over time going into HE, and ease of switching between more vocational and more academic routes.

— Structured vocational training for those not going on to HE, with acquisition of broad skills, including communications and decision-making competences.

— Modularisation and certification.

D. Finegold and D. Soskice

Despite the 'window of opportunity'" how feasible is the sort of major change envisaged? Aside from the question of financing, formidable problems will need to be resolved:

(a) Young people have the option at sixteen to remain in full-time education. About 65 per cent choose not to. Raising the legal minimum school leaving age to eighteen is politically not a possibility, and in any case it is desirable that young people should choose to stay on. How are incentives to be structured and attitudes changed to raise the staying-on rate to above 80 per cent?

(b) Relatively few businesses are currently capable of providing high-quality training. And, while employer organisations are becoming more committed to involvement in ET, effective action on their part will require a co-ordinating capacity which is beyond their present power or resources.

(c) In comparison to other countries with well-developed vocational training systems the UK lacks an effective administrative structure and a major research and development capacity.

Of these constraints the first must be overcome. It will be argued in this section that the involvement of employers and their organisations and a proper state infrastructure will be needed to achieve both this and the ET desiderata set out above. To see why this is the case, we look first at why sixteen year-olds choose to leave education and training, and with this in mind, examine the experience of sixteen-twenty ET in other countries.

Why do such a large proportion of young people choose to join the labour market or YTS at sixteen? There are two main reasons. The first is financial. On YTS or social security young people get a small income. If they remain in full-time education they receive nothing (their parents receiving child benefit). There are therefore strong inducements to leave full-time education at sixteen. The demographic shrinking of the sixteen-plus age group (while it will make reform easier) will, in the absence of reform, strengthen the incentive to leave; this is because employers are accustomed to recruiting from this age group, directly or nowadays through YTS, since it provides relatively cheap and pliable labour, so that relative earnings at sixteen-plus may be expected to rise.

In the second place, staying on in full-time ET has not been seen as a bridge to stable employment. The best route to employment for most sixteen year-olds today is via YTS, which is used by many employers as a screening device for the choice of permanent employees. YTS trainees who show themselves to be co-operative have a high probability of securing permanent employment; and that probability will rise as the demographic decline in the sixteen-plus age cohort sets in.

Foreign experience can give an idea of different possible systems of sixteen-twenty ET, as well as alerting to some of the problems.

— One country often cited as an exemplar is the US. About 75 per cent of the relevant age group graduates from high school by age eighteen after a broadly based course, more academically geared for those going on to HE, more vocational for those going directly into the labour market. Over 40 per cent go on to two year junior colleges or university, producing a remarkably educated population. But there are problems with the education and training of those who do not go on to HE. In many areas, lack of co-ordinated employer involvement has meant there is no clear bridge between education and employment. The 'Boston compact', under which a group of companies guaranteed training and employment against for good high school performance, acknowledged this need. And lack of involvement by companies in sixteen to twenty ET has limited firms' provision of training for manual workers and low-level white collar workers.

— France has a more highly structured system of initial vocational training. Less able children can go to vocational schools from fourteen to eighteen, and end with craft-level qualifications. More emphasis in the future is being placed on the various higher-level vocational *baccalaureat* courses, from

OXFORD REVIEW OF ECONOMIC POLICY, VOL. 4, NO. 3

sixteen to nineteen, which turns out technician engineers with managerial skills. Compared with the UK, both routes are impressive, especially the second. But, as in the US, there is limited employer involvement. One consequence is staying-on rates at sixteen-plus well below the Northern European and Japanese, and a higher rate of youth unemployment. A second is limited training for manual workers in companies.

— In the Germanic (Germany, Austria, Switzerland) system, those going on to higher education spend two years from sixteen to eighteen in a high school before taking the *abitur*. Those working for vocational qualifications become apprenticed at sixteen for three or four years and follow a highly structured, carefully monitored system of on-the-job and off-the-job training and education, with external exams on both practical and theoretical subjects.

— In the Scandanavian (Norway, Sweden) system, young people remain in the same college between sixteen and eighteen, specialising in vocational or academic areas; vocational education is then completed in vocational centres post-eighteen.

— Denmark has been actively experimenting with post-sixteen ET in the last two decades. The Danes have been moving towards a system in which all young people remain within the same educational institution between sixteen and eighteen, more or less a tertiary college. If they choose the vocational route, they move into a two year apprenticeship at eighteen, for which much work will have already been covered in the college.

Both the Germanic and Scandinavian systems succeed in attaining very high participation rates for thw sixteen-eighteen age groups, and in delivering high-quality vocational training as well as good general education. There are, however, arguments against both Germanic and Scandinavian systems as the optimal model for the UK, despite the fact that both systems are greatly superior to our own. The main argument against applying the Scandinavian system to the British context is that Britain lacks the infrastructure to make it work: the close involvement of employer organisations with the public system of vocational education. Moreover, there is powerful union and state pressure on companies to maintain training standards.

The Germanic system also has disadvantages, in part because it would be based too strongly on employers if transplanted to the UK. There are four reasons why we should be wary of advocating a German-type division at sixteen between academic education and an employer-based three or four-year apprenticeship:

— The greater the employer involvement (unless restrained by powerful employer organisations and unions as in Germany), the more the apprenticeship will reflect the short term needs of the employer. This is illustrated by the otherwise excellent EITB engineering apprenticeship scheme in the UK: broken into modules, employers select those modules most relevant to their own needs, rather than to the longer-term needs of the trainee.

— Few UK employers are in a position to run quality three or four year apprenticeships; but these would be needed across the board in public and private sectors, and in industry and services.

— If young people were to move into employer-based apprenticeships at sixteen, it would *de facto* close them off from higher education.

— Equally, by dividing the population at sixteen, the opportunity to reduce class distinctions would not be taken.

How, then, should sixteen-twenty ET evolve in the future? We believe a system very roughly along Danish lines is the most feasible model to aim for, given the current UK position.

40

D. Finegold and D. Soskice

(1) *A common educational institution from sixteen to eighteen.* Apart from the Germanic countries, the US and Scandanavia, as well as Japan (more or less), have a common institution from sixteen to eighteen. France and Denmark have both been moving towards it as a matter of conscious choice. It is an obvious vehicle for encouraging a rising percentage of young people to go on to higher education at eighteen. Equally it has a necessary part to play in reducing class differences.

(2) *Accelerated apprenticeships post-eighteen: the bridge to employment.* The Germanic and Scandinavian systems, and Japan and South Korea, provide at least four years of ET post-sixteen. This could be done in the UK by short, highly structured apprenticeships, which would at the same time build clear bridges to employment. If further training was carried out mainly in vocational schools post-eighteen, this bridging perception would be less clear; of course, vocational schools would be important post-eighteen, since UK companies would require considerable help if they were to provide high-quality training. The next section 5.2 discusses how companies could develop high-quality training capacities: it is evident that if they can the benefits would go beyond sixteen-twenty ET; the need for companies in both public and private sectors to develop effective training capacities is central to the management of change.

(3) *Linking post-eighteen apprenticeships with pre-eighteen ET.* In order for two-year apprenticeships to be of high quality, considerable preparatory work towards them will need to have been completed pre-eighteen. It is also important to make clear to students the link between what is expected from them in the sixteen-eighteen period and their subsequent training opportunities. Preparatory work covers both general and vocational education. The role of a good general education, covering technical subjects and the humanities, has already been stressed, as has the parallel need for vocational education to include the acquisition of broad skills including communications and decision-making competences, with emphasis on developing individual initiative and team-work through projects. Vocational education will also be focused in part on the chosen apprenticeship area. Thus, for those who choose it at sixteen, there will be a 'vocational' route, with specific and general requirements for particular apprenticeship areas.

(4) *Modules and certification.* Vocational qualifications would be awarded and HE entrance requirements satisfied by successfully completed modules. In the case of HE the modules would all be taken in the common institution; it would be natural to think of AS levels as module-based (the original intention), and that the major part of the most common route to satisfying HE entrance requirements would consist in completing the modules needed to gain so many AS levels. To gain a vocational qualification, and to fulfil the condition for entry to an apprenticeship, a substantial proportion of the necessary modules could and should be completed pre-eighteen. A modular system in a single institution provides considerable flexibility. Most students would choose early on a vocational or an HE route; but if some proportion of AS modules were allowed for vocational qualification purposes and some proportion of vocational modules for entry into HE, those students who wished to do so could keep their options open for longer. Modules could also be used to broaden HE entry requirements, and to increase the general education component in vocational qualification. There might in addition be a case for a college graduation diploma, as in many countries, based on successful completion of modules.

(5) *Employer co-ordination and involvement.* A high degree of employer co-ordination and involvement will be needed to make this system work. That is the positive lesson of Northern Europe. Local co-ordination is necessary to link 'training' employers with educational institutions and with students. At a regional and national level, employer involvement is needed to help develop curricula, monitoring of 'trainers', assessment procedures, and so on. This will require more powerful employer organisations, nationally, sectorally and locally than the UK has now. How this might be achieved is further discussed below.

(6) *Role of unions.* Many 'training' employers, especially in the public sector, are unionised, so that union co-operation will be needed. Union involvement in curriculum development and the like will also be

OXFORD REVIEW OF ECONOMIC POLICY, VOL. 4, NO. 3

important in balancing the power of employer organisations. This again is a lesson from the experience of Sweden and Germany.

(7) *Local and national government.* Government has played a key role in providing a coherent framework for the sixteen-twenty ET system at local, regional and national level in each of the countries discussed, with the exception of the US. The UK lacks institutional coherence in this area, and has only a limited research and policy-making capacity.

(8) *Education maintenance allowance and financial incentives.* A central purpose of the reform strategy suggested above has been to construct a clear bridge from education to employment so that young people stay within a well-structured ET system from the age of sixteen to nineteen or twenty. This is in line with the instrumental view of education taken by most young people who leave at sixteen (Brown, 1987). But to be successful in raising the sixteen-plus participation rate, it is also necessary to ensure that leaving at sixteen is less attractive than staying on. This will require, first, an educational maintenance allowance for those who stay on, at least equal to state payments for those who leave. More fundamentally, it raises the question of reducing employer incentives to hire sixteen year olds, and convincing them to stop seeing the sixteen-plus age group as its main recruiting ground for unskilled and semi-skilled labour (Ashton & Maguire, 1988). This is discussed in the next section.

ii) Developing the Training Capacity of Employers

International comparisons suggest that UK employers devote a smaller share of value added to training expenditures than any other major advanced country. For radical reform to be successful, the attitude of employers will have to change, as has been seen in the discussion in the last section of post-sixteen ET and restructuring: specifically, the development by employers of a training capacity is necessary for a system of accelerated apprenticeships. In addition to sixteen-twenty ET, a training capacity is needed for restructuring within organisations for training and retraining existing employees.

In looking at restructuring, it is useful to distinguish between retraining by the existing employer, which will be referred to as internal retraining, and retraining elsewhere, primarily in state/union/employer-organisation or private vocational training centres. This will be referred to as external retraining and will be discussed below. Roughly the internal/external retraining distinction corresponds to that between internal (e.g. changing product composition within a company) and external (e.g. closures/running down an industry) restructuring.

With internal restructuring companies meet declining demand by product innovation. In countries where product innovation strategies are emphasised they are associated with reliable sources of long-term finance, and long-term relations with suppliers which the company does not wish to disrupt. More important, they are associated with internal training capacities in companies, a retrainable workforce with on-the-job flexibility and a high perceived cost to making workers redundant (Streeck et al., 1985; Sorge and Streeck, 1988; Hotz-Hart, 1988). The high perceived cost may arise from legal requirements, as in Germany, or collective bargaining power, as in Sweden, or from a basic communitarian view of the enterprise, as in Japan (Dore, 1987). Cost reduction strategies under these circumstances will tend to focus on reducing capital or material or financing costs, rather than labour saving changes. Again, retraining capacities are critical.

In the UK much more use has been made of external restructuring. This reflects the lack of the characteristics described in the last paragraph as associated with internal restructuring in countries such as Germany, Japan and Sweden. Instead the UK is characterised by:

D. Finegold and D. Soskice

(i) The organisation of production around relatively standardised goods and services, with low skill requirements and cost-cutting rather than technically competent management; aggravated by:

— the public goods problem; and

— the pressure of financial institutions and, in the public sector, cash limits against long-term investment activity.

(ii) The lack of pressure from employees to maintain training; and the ease with which companies can make workers redundant without being required to consider product innovation and retraining as alternative ways of maintaining employment.

(iii) The lack of an effective infrastucture. Few sectors of the economy have well developed training structures, with worked out systems of certification, training schools, and information and counselling for companies. Employers organisations are weak, and unions are seldom equipped to provide good training services to their members.

The difficulties involved in increasing company expenditure on training and ensuring it is of the right quality are thus substantial. In a longish-term perspective two general points may be made:

— The increase in the educational level of young people entering the labour force and a different attitude to adult education and training will make it easier for companies to move to a higher skills equilibrium.

— Policies to change company behaviour on training should be one part of a co-ordinated strategy to help companies focus on marketing, product innovation, new technology, high-quality production, and provision of long-term finance. Education and training policies should be closely linked to industrial and regional policies; but to trace out these links would be beyond the scope of this paper. Four main policy directions are set out here: how they might be financed, where not implicit, is discussed below.

(1) *Financial incentives*. There is little question that companies in both public and private sectors need financial incentives (positive or negative) if they are significantly to increase their training activities. This is because, for the foreseeable future, there will be a divergence between private and public returns because of the public good problem and the low-skills equilibrium. (The general strategy advocated in this paper is designed to reduce the divergence over time, but specific incentives will be necessary until then.)

The form of the incentives is critical. A minimum legal requirement is unlikely to be productive, at least by itself. It might take one of two forms: a requirement to spend a certain minimum percentage of value added or payroll on training; and/or a requirement to carry out certain types of training, e.g. to take so many apprentices, with a significant enough penalty to gain compliance. One problem with both approaches is that some companies may be better placed to carry out effective training than others. In addition, the minimum percentage approach (by itself) says nothing about who gets trained: in France this approach led to senior managers being sent to expensive hotels in the French Pacific to learn English. And the 'minimum number of apprentices' approach poses formidable quality problems.

A sensible approach, at least to start with, is to give financial incentives to companies (private and public) who are prepared to train and undergo the monitoring and other conditions necessary to ensure both quality and coverage (i.e. that training covers apprenticeships and semi-skilled workers as well as managers, etc.). The further conditions are discussed in the next paragraph. These incentives would not need to be uniform across industries, regions or types of training.

(2) *Meisters and certification.* How are we to ensure that companies train to the right quality and over the desired coverage? In Japan, Germany and similar countries, the role of the supervisor in both industry and services is different to the UK superviser, (see e.g. Prais and Wagner, 1988). In those countries supervisors (in German *'meister'*) are technically skilled as well as playing a management role; moreover they have major responsibility for training. In the German system, they have themselves to pass a rigorous training after having gained a technician or craft-level qualification. The above suggests ideas along the following lines:

(a) A distinction should be drawn between certified skills and non-certified skills. This would be similar to the distinction between marketable and firm-specific skills. In practical terms it would reflect those that the NCVQ included as certifiable.

(b) Companies wishing to participate in the training of employees for certified skills would be required to employ certified 'training supervisers', i.e. similar to German *meisters*.

(c) The Government could then negotiate with employer organisations tariffs for different certified skills, and use this as one means of influencing the size and distribution of training. Those companies would then get automatic payments for certified training, subject to periodic inspections and subject to satisfactory results of trainees in external assessment.

In summary, financial incentives should be used, not just to produce a desired amount of training, but also to ensure that companies acquire a training capacity and supervisory staff with a professional commitment to training.

(3) *Changing the age structure of hiring.* Specific disincentives will be needed to dissuade businesses from hiring sixteen-eighteen year olds over the next decade.

(4) *Employee representation.* Again, as in Northern Europe, it is sensible to give employees a role in decision-making on training within companies. They have an interest in the acquisition of certified skills. For this role to be effective, decisions on training would need to be codetermined between management and employees. In addition, continental experience suggests that employee representatives need union expertise if they are to challenge low-spending management with any chance of success.

In particular, it is important to enable employees to challenge management decisions on redundancies. In the German model, management is required to reach an agreement with the works council on how redundancies are to be dealt with. The cost to management of not reaching an agreement means that managers emphasise innovation and retraining in their long-term planning.

(5) *External infrastructure.* Both (2) and (3) impose strong demands on an external infrastructure. Companies will in practice rely heavily on the advice of employer organisations, whom they can trust at least to give advice in the interest of the sector they represent, if not in the interest of the individual company. Employees need the advice of unions if they are to challenge company decisions on training and redundancies. Public or tripartite bodies will be required to provide R & D on training technology and labour market developments (e.g. skill shortages); to run a system of certification; and to provide training where it is needed to complement company training. How this can be done is discussed in 5.4.

iii) A Culture of Lifetime Education and Training.

There is an apparent lack of interest by adults in the UK in continuing education and training. In countries with good training systems, a strong belief by individuals in the benefits of ET reinforces the system: parents can see the value of education and training for their children; employees put pressure on laggardly employers to provide training; the public good problem which companies face is reduced by individuals

D. Finegold and D. Soskice

paying for the acquisition of marketable skills. Yet in the UK little adult training takes place which is not paid for by the employer; this is in particular the case for unskilled and semi-skilled employees and for the unemployed. Why is human capital theory wrong in asserting that individuals will be prepared to pay for the acquisition of marketable skills? Why especially is this the case when vacancies for skilled jobs coexist with high unemployment and insecure semi-skilled employment?

In the first place, individuals seldom have access to financial resources sufficient to finance any extended period of vocational training:

(a) Borrowing. Financial institutions are reticent about lending without security for training, except for a few cases where returns from the training are high. This is not particular to UK financial institutions. Banks in most countries will not lend for ET purposes to individuals, unless the loans are guaranteed or subsidised or unless the bank has close connections and knowledge of a community. This likely reflects both moral hazard and adverse selection problems.

(b) There is limited access to state subsidy for most adult vocational training, particularly for maintenance, but also for tuition. Individual expenditure on training is in general not tax deductible. The unemployed likewise have limited access to funds: their retraining possibilities seldom relate to those areas in which there are vacancies.

(c) Major reductions in income are seldom feasible for those who are employed; *a fortiori* for those who are unemployed.

Secondly, the individual return from much vocational training is not high. There are several reasons for this:

(a) The low-skills equilibrium organisation of work means that the marginal productivity of skills for individual workers is below what it would be in an economy where a large enough proportion of the workforce was skilled to permit a high-skills pattern of work organisation.

(b) For a large proportion of the workforce (manual and low-level white-collar) there reflects the organisation of work discussed. Second, differentials for skilled workers were heavily compressed in the 1970s, and though they have widened since, they are still not high in comparison to high-skill countries. (Prais and Wagner, 1988.)

(c) A large proportion of the workforce does not have the basic education required to proceed to craft-level vocational training; so a major prior investment is necessary.

(d) The existing system of certification is unhelpful, as the NCVQ has emphasised. Aside from being confusing, it fails to give employers real guarantees in many areas as to the competences of the certified employee, because of the lack of proper assessment procedures. In addition, and more important, portability is limited. In the modern economy skills obsolesce. The acquisition of new skills should not involve returning to square one, as it frequently does today.

(e) Finally, for those who are currently employed, and wish independently to take leave to pursue education or training, there is seldom a guarantee that they will be able to keep their job.

This means that major self-financed training or retraining is not seen as a realistic possibility, if it is considered at all, by most unskilled or semi-skilled workers or those who are unemployed. Moreover, with the exceptions of a few unions who provide good counselling services, little advice is available.

(1) *A comprehensive external training system.* Those who seek, or might be persuaded to seek, external training fall into two categories with some overlapping: people with clear goals and courses in mind, adequate previous education and training, but held back by unavailability of finance or employment insecurity; and the unskilled, semi-skilled and unemployed with little belief in the possibility of effective retraining. For both groups adequate financing is necessary. There is a strong case for formalising a system

OXFORD REVIEW OF ECONOMIC POLICY, VOL. 4, NO. 3

of education credits for adults. These credits would be intended for training not covered by companies. The general question of financing is considered below, but it should be noted here that if individuals had their own 'training accounts', into which education credits were put, these credits could be added to by saving, perhaps topped-up by public funding. For most people in the second group, additional financing will be necessary, since it will not be reasonable to expect them to save enough. It is of great importance that those threatened by redundancy or made redundant are given sufficient resources for long periods of ET. Along Swedish lines, a reasonable income might be conditioned on in effect a contract to train for a given range of skills in which there are vacancies or in which employment is likely.

For this group, much more is required than financing. Also needed are counselling, an information system covering vacancies and future areas of demand, structured basic education if necessary, training and retraining facilities (though they might be in the private sector and hired by the state), and a support system to facilitate mobility if needed. How an external retraining system might be set up is discussed in the next section.

(2) *Returns to skills.* This is an important problem to which there are few easy solutions. We argued above for policies to encourage the development of a supervisory grade with technical qualifications: if successful, that would help the concept of a career ladder based on skills. It is harder for the government to intervene in the process of wage determination, and widen skill differentials even if there is case for doing so. In our view, the more sensible approach is to give incentives to employers to increase training, on the one hand, and to develop an external training policy to help redundant and potentially redundant workers, who have less need of incentives to acquire skills, on the other.

iv) Institutional Infrastructure

Radical reform of ET requires a more effective institutional infrastructure than presently exists. Our view is that radical reform is not a simple political option, but one requiring major institutional changes which will be difficult to bring about in the UK, at least if reform is to realise its full potential. This returns the argument to those economic historians that our basic economic problems lie in our institutions.

It was argued in section four that the old constraining infrastructure has broken down; and that the Government has substituted increased centralised control via the MSC (as was) and the DES, combined with the use of contracts with training agencies. The centralisation of policy-making has not been accompanied by a significant expansion of the very limited research and information-gathering capacities of the MSC and the DES. A parallel can be drawn between this system and large conglomerates controlled by a small financially-oriented headquarters. The new system will become more pronounced as: (a) local education authorities have a diminished role in post-sixteen ET, with the removal of polytechnics and the larger CFEs from their control, with the decline in importance of TVEI, and with the possible opting out of secondary schools; (b) the wide variety of course-development, assessment and accreditation bodies are encouraged to behave more competitively; and (c) the NCVQ becomes more a body carrying out government instructions, especially in relation to certification of YTS trainees, than a forum in which different points of view, of the business community, of unions and of educationalists and trainers can be expressed.

The new system is hardly adequate for dealing with YTS and ATS; it has major drawbacks if it is to carry through radical reform. We will argue that a different system needs to be developed in which employers organisations, unions, educationalists and the regions should all ideally play a more important part; and in which the role of government should be more concerned with the provision of information, research and development, and coordination, than with unilateral policy-making.

D. Finegold and D. Soskice

(1) *The need for better information, R & D, and co-ordination.* The reforms discussed in the preceding sub-sections involve major course developments: for sixteen-eighteen year olds; for accelerated appren-ticeships; for those at work; for *meisters*; for those undertaking external retraining; together with development of assessment procedures, certification and accreditation of examining bodies. It will be necessary to co-ordinate academic examining boards with vocational training institutions such as BTEC; and to co-ordinate the activities of the vocational institutions themselves. Also, it is important to allow experimentation and thus course development by individual teachers or trainers, and a mechanism is needed to permit the diffusion of best-practice innovations. All this demands a much greater role of government in the R & D and co-ordination process. This might perhaps be on the lines of regional labour market and regional education boards in Sweden.

For two broad reasons, a more effective ET system also requires involvement by the social partners (employers' organisations and unions) as well as educational institutions and the Government. The first is to ensure that policy-making is conducted in a balanced way, (2) below. The second is to bring about the participation of companies (3), and employees (4).

(2) *Multilateral participation in ET governance.* Running a complex ET system is a principal-agent problem. However clear the ideas of the Government (the principal) and however effective its own research and development activities, the co-operation of teachers and trainers as agents is essential to efficient course development, assessment, etc. But educators will have their own interests. (Japan is a case in point, where educationalists dominate the development of sixteen-eighteen education, business has no influence, and where rote learning still plays a major role.) A tempting solution is for governments to use expert civil servants as additional agents; of course it is important that government experts should be involved, but there is a danger: if detailed polcy-making is left to government experts and educationalists, the former may assimilate over time the goals of the latter, particularly if governments change.

A more effective solution is to balance the interests of educators against the interests of employers and those of employees. Hence the case for involving their representatives as additional agents, to bring about more balanced objectives. If this is to be successful, both employers' organisations and unions need expertise; here again Northern European experience, where the social partners have their own research institutions, in some cases financed by the state, is suggestive. Moreover, as employers' organisations and unions acquire expertise, so a common culture of understanding and agreement on a range of training issues gets built up by professionals on all sides. Thus the agents, with their different interests but shared culture, become players in a co-operative game over time in which compromise and flexibility are available to meet changing conditions. (For a broader use of this type of approach, see the insightful Lange, 1987.)

A similar case can be made for involving representatives of regions in addition to central government. For individual regions will have their own economic goals, and more political stability than central government. Again, effective involvement requires expertise. This reinforces the argument for regional labour market and regional education boards.

(3) *Employers' organisations and the participation of companies.* Most companies see no gain in participating in training in marketable skills and associated activities to a socially optimal degree. This is both because of the standard prisoner's dilemma problem and the low skills equilibrium. As a partial solution to both problems we suggested the use of financial incentives to encourage the building up of a training capacity within companies. Important though that is by itself, its effectiveness can be greatly enhanced through employers' organisations. First, getting companies to train in the right way is difficult for government, because of an assymetry of information: the company knows much more about how good its training is than the Government. Companies are often loathe to be monitored by, or give detailed information to, government, because they distrust the use to which the information will be put. Employers'

OXFORD REVIEW OF ECONOMIC POLICY, VOL. 4, NO. 3

organisations are in a better position to engage the co-operation of companies, because they are seen to be on the side of companies as a whole. Secondly, powerful employers' organisations, as in Germany, can sanction free-riders more cheaply than the Government. This is the case where employers' organisations distribute a range of valued services to companies, not necessarily just in the training area; and have a degree of discretion over their distribution. One of these services may be training advice; others might be in, say, export marketing. This gives the organisation potential sanctions, which might enable it, for instance, to organise local co-ordination of companies with respect to the bridge between education and employment; or to prod companies into increasing training activities.

(4) *Employees and unions.* Unions have several important roles to play in an effective ET system, as mentioned above. Here we want to stress the role of unions in promoting employee involvement in training decision-making. Such involvement is a critical component of high-skill economies. If it is to be effective, employees must be properly backed up by union advice and expertise.

Much of the argument of this sub-section is influenced by the study of why the Scandinavian and Germanic ET systems have been successful. There is an important research agenda here for the UK. We do not want to suggest the type of powerful employers organisations or union confederations in those countries, or regional government as in Germany is transplantable, it is not. But there is a strong case for giving muscle to employers' organisations and unions, and to regions and perhaps metropolitan areas, in the training field. Unions are moving in the UK (some much faster than others) to consider training as a core area of their interests. Business organisations are moving less fast, but in the right direction. Radical reform of ET will need a push by government. One possibility, for a radical reforming government, is to give the social partners the resources to develop major expertise in training. A second is to consider whether chambers of commerce can play a more significant role at local level, so as to enable them to develop local employer networks. Third, to consider the possibilities of regional labour market and regional education boards as quadripartite institutions, with educationalists and regional representatives as well as the social partners.

5. Macroeconomic and Financing Implications

The preceding four sub-sections have looked at the micro aspects of policies needed for transforming the post-sixteen education and training system. They have suggested how to change incentives facing individuals and organisations; how co-ordinating and providing institutions could be built up; and how training policies should be seen as part of a broader micro-economic strategy directed at changing ways in which companies operate. If successful these changes carry great benefits in terms of macro-economic performance. But to be successful they require a major injection of resources.

In a steady-state, the benefits can be assumed to outweigh the resource cost. But in the process of the transforming the system, resource costs would be likely to precede the benefits of additional resources. There is not the space in this article to discuss in detail the financing of this gap. But we want to make some brief points to indicate why we believe that increased expenditures in this area can be more easily managed than in many others.

The increased resources devoted to ET can be met in one or more of three ways:

— an increase in GDP;

— a reduction in other expenditures;

— an increase in imports.

There are two reasons why some part of the resource cost can be met by reduction in other expenditures. First, specific forms of taxation or quasi-taxation can be exploited with minimal economic damage.

D. Finegold and D. Soskice

— A training levy on companies who do not undertake certified training. It will be difficult for these companies to pass on the levy in the form of higher prices if some competitors are undertaking certified training and hence not paying the levy. And since most of the non-training companies are likely to be in the sheltered sector of the economy, any reduction in their activity levels as a result of the levy will have the beneficial effect of transferring business to training competitors.

— Individual training accounts. If individuals choose to contribute to an individual training account, it will come from a voluntary reduction in consumers expenditure.

Second, other government expenditures will be reduced:

— Reduction in government expenditures on YTS and other MSC related activities which would be phased out as a new system of sixteen-twenty ET developed.

— Reduction in government expenditures on education and training post sixteen as a result of demographic decline.

Thus some part of the necessary resources can be met from reduced expenditure elsewhere but without relying on an increase in general taxation. The damage caused by the latter is not only political, but also, via its inflationary potential, economic. But there are limits beyond which it may be unwise or impossible to push these reductions.

This means that the resources to finance a training programme will have to come in part from increased GDP and increased imports. The point to be made here is that the standard problems associated with an expansionary policy can be more easily handled within the context of a training programme than in other cases.

The first problem is that of inflation caused by the increased bargaining power of employees as employment rises. Appropriate increases in the skilled workforce can reduce inflationary pressures in two ways. Directly, it reduces skilled labour bottlenecks and the power of 'insiders' relative to outsiders. Indirectly, it facilitates wage restraint especially if unions are involved in the training institutions.

The second problem is financing the external deficit and the public sector deficit, at least without a fall in the exchange rate or a rise in the interest rate. Avoiding these consequences requires: that inflation does not increase; and that the increase in the PSBR and the external deficit are seen as eventually self-correcting. The last paragraph was concerned with inflation. A training programme can, more easily than most programmes involving increased government expenditure, be credibly seen as self-correcting in its effect on the PSBR and the external deficit.

VI. CONCLUDING REMARKS

The UK has long suffered from a low-skills equilibrium in which the ET system has delivered badly educated and minimally trained sixteen year-old school-leavers to an economy which has been geared to operate - albeit today more efficiently - with a relatively unskilled labour force. Some companies have broken out of this equilibrium with the aid of strategic managers, to see training and innovation as core activities. Most have not.

Despite the much-vaunted reforms of the ET system of the last few years, major improvements are unlikely to be brought about:

— The majority of children will still leave school at sixteen, and will gain a low-level training in YTS; referring to the certification of YTS by the NCVQ, Jarvis and Prais argued that it would lead to 'a

OXFORD REVIEW OF ECONOMIC POLICY, VOL. 4, NO. 3

certificated semi-literate under-class - a section of the workforce inhibited in job-flexibility, and inhibited in the possibility of progression'. (*Financial Times* , 1/7/88, quoting Jarvis and Prais, 1988.)

— There are no substantive policies to remedy the vacuum in training in most companies.

— There are no measures to undertake the depth education and training frequently needed in a rapidly restructuring world economy to enable those made redundant acquire relevant skills.

We have argued the case in section 5 for: full-time education to eighteen, with 'accelerated' apprenticeships thereafter, for those not going on to higher education; building up training capacities within companies; and an external retraining system to deal with restructuring between companies and industries.

Instead of summarising these proposals, we want to underline certain points which have not always been adequately brought out in discussions of reform:

— It is important to think in terms of the incentives which face individuals, rather than make the mistake of some educators of just talking about institutions or educational innovations. But equally the economist's mistake, of treating of incentives as only financial, must be avoided. We lay stress on the idea of enabling individuals to see career progressions: thus importance is attached to the bridge from education to employment for sixteen to twenty year-olds.

— Companies should be seen not as profit-maximising black boxes, but as coalitions of interests, particularly among managers. We argue that, rather than incentives being used to increase the amount of training as such, they can more effectively be used if they increase a company's training capacity, by giving companies an incentive to train or hire meisters, or training supervisors. This produces a stake in training as a company activity.

— Along similar lines, employees should be given a role in training decision-making within the company. Here, there are lessons to be learned from industrial democracy procedures in Germany and Sweden. This reinforces the idea of groups within the company with a stake in training.

— More generally, the problem of moving companies from a low-skill to a high-skill equilibrium involves much more than training and education. It requires changes in management style, R & D, financing, marketing, etc. so training policy should be seen as part of a wider industrial strategy.

— Countries with successful ET systems devote substantial resources to research on education and training and labour market developments. In the UK today policy-making has become highly centralised but based on limited information and research.

— Successful countries also place great reliance on employers' organisations and unions. In the UK their role in the governance of training has been progressively reduced. If radical reform is to be successful, it will be important to build up the expertise and involvement of the social partners.

To conclude, the UK is becoming isolated among advanced industrialised countries. They have either attained or are targeting a far higher level of generalised education and training than is being considered here. This should be worrying enough in itself. What makes it more so, is the progress made by other countries with substantially lower labour costs: South Korea has currently 85 per cent in full-time education to the age of seventeen or eighteen, and over 30 per cent in higher education. (*Financial Times* ,30/6/88.)

REFERENCES

Anderson, A. (1987), 'Adult Training: Private Industry and the Nicholson Letter, in Education &
        Training UK 1987, Harrison, A. and Gretton, J.(eds.), *Policy Journals*, pp. 67-73.
Brady, T. (1984), *New Technology and Skills in British Industry*, Science Policy Research Unit.
Business Week (1988), 'How the New Math of Productivity Adds Up', pp. 49-55, June 6.

Callaghan, J. (1976), Ruskin College Speech, *Times Educational Supplement*, 22 October, p. 72.

Centre for Contemporary Cultural Studies (1981), *Unpopular Education*, London, Hutchinson.

Chapman, P. and Tooze, M. (1987), *The Youth Training Scheme in the UK*, Aldershot, Avebury.

Clegg, H. (1972), *The System of Industrial Relations in Great Britain*, Oxford, Basil Blackwell.

Clement, B. (1986), 'Industry Threatened over Training Lapses', *Independent*, p. 3, 29 November.

Coopers and Lybrand Associates (1985), *A Challenge to Complacency: Changing Attitudes to Training*, MSC/NEDO, Moorfoot, Sheffield.

Crowther Commission (1959), *15 to 18*, Report to the DES, HMSO.

Dale, R. (1983), 'The Politics of Education in England 1970-1983: State, Capital and Civil Society', Open University, unpublished.

— (1983), Thatcherism and Education, In Ahier, J. and Flude, M. (eds.), *Comtemporary Education Policy*, London, Croom Helm.

— (1985), The Background and Inception of TVEI, in Dale (ed.), *Education, Training and Employment*, Milton Keynes, Open University.

— (forthcoming), TVEI: From National Guidelines to Local Practice.

Daly, A. (1984), 'Education, Training and Productivity in the U.S. and Great Britain', NIESR no. 63, London.

Deakin, B. M. and Pratten, C. F. (1987), Economic Effects of YTS, *Department of Employment Gazette*, 95, 491-7.

Department of Education and Science (1987), Education Reform Bill, 20 November.

— (1988), *Tax Concessions for Training*, HMSO, May.

Department of Employment (1988), *Training for Employment*, HMSO no. 316, February.

Department of Education and Department of Education and Science, *Training for Jobs*, HMSO, Jan.

De Ville, H. G. et al. (1986), *Review of Vocational Qualifications in England and Wales*, Report to MSC and DES, April.

Donovan, Lord (1968), *Royal Commission on Trade Unions and Employers' Associations 1965-1968* Report, HMSO, London.

Dore, R. (1987), *Taking Japan Seriously*, Athlone Press, London.

Fenwick, I. G. K. (1976), *The Comprehensive School 1944-1970*, London, Methuen.

Gapper, J. (1987), '£500,000 scheme to boost training in tourist sector', *Financial Times*, 17 March.

George, K. D. and Shorey, J. (1985), 'Manual Workers, Good Jobs and Structured Internal Labour Markets', *British Journal of Industrial Relations*, 23:3, pp. 425-47, November.

Giddens, A. (1979), 'An Anatomy of the British Ruling Class', *New Society*, 4 October, pp. 8-10.

Gow, D. (1988), 'Fury at A-Level Rejection', *Guardian*, p. 1, 8 June.

Gow, D. (1988), 'Teaching Shortage Catastrophe Feared', *Guardian*, p. 4, 16 June.

— and Travis, A. (1988), 'Leak Exposes Thatcher Rift with Baker', *Guardian*, p. 1, 10 March.

Greenhalgh, C. (1988), *Employment and Structural Change: Trends and Policy Options*, mimeo, Oxford.

Hall, P. (1986), *Governing the Economy*, Oxford, Polity Press.

Harland, J. (1987), 'The TVEI Experience', in Gleeson, D. (ed.)*TVEI and Secondary Education*, Milton Keynes, Open University.

Hotz-Hart, B.. (1988), 'Comparative Research and New Technology: Modernisation in Three Industrial Relations Systems', in Hyman, R. and Streeck, W. (eds.) *New Technology and Industrial Relations*,

Howell, D.A. (1980), 'The Department of Education and Science: its critics and defenders', *Educational Administration*, 9, pp. 108-33.

Hyman, R. and Streeck, W. (eds.) (1988), *New Technology and Industrial Relations*, Oxford, Blackwells.

Independent (1986), 'Managers "a Decade Out of Date"', 11 December.

Jackson, M. (1988), 'More leavers shun youth training scheme', *Times Educational Supplement*, 19 February, p. 13.

OXFORD REVIEW OF ECONOMIC POLICY, VOL. 4, NO. 3

Jennings, R. E. (1977), *Education and Politics: Policy-Making in Local Education Authorities*, London, Batsford.
Keep, E. (1986), *Designing the Stable Door: A Study of how the Youth Training Scheme was Planned*, Warwick Papers in Industrial Relations No. 8, May.
—— (1987), *Britain's Attempts to Create a National Vocational Educational and Training System: A Review of Progress*, Warwick Papers in Industrial Relations no.16, Coventry.
Lane, C. (1988), 'Industrial Change in Europe: the Pursuit of Flexible Specialisation', in *Work, Employment and Society*, forthcoming.
Lange, P. (1987). *The Institutionalisation of Concertation*. *International Political Economy*, WP no. 26, Duke University.
Leadbeater, C. (1987), 'MSC criticises standard of youth training', *Financial Times*, 13 May, p. 1.
Lynn, R. (1988), *Educational Achievement in Japan*, Basingstoke, MacMillan.
MSC (1981), *A New Training Initiative, a Consultative Document*, HMSO, May.
—— (1986) *Skills Monitoring Report*, MSC Evaluation and Research Unit, Sheffield.
Maurice, M., Sellier, F. and Silvestre, J. J. (1986), *The Social Foundations of Industrial Power: A Comparison of France and West Germany*, Cambridge, MIT Press.
Mayer, C. (1987), 'The Assessment: Financial Systems and Corporate Investment', *Oxford Review of Economic Policy*, Winter.
Mayhew, K. (1986), 'Reforming the Labour Market', *Oxford Review of Economic Policy*, Summer.
McArthur, A. and McGregor, A. (1986), 'Training and Economic Development: National versus Local Perspectives', *Political Quarterly*, 57, 3, July-September, pp. 246-55.
McCulloch, G. et al. (1985), *Technological Revolution? The Politics of School Science and Technology in England and Wales since 1945*, London, Falmer.
Macfarlane, N. (1980), Education for 16-19 Year Olds, report to the DES and Local Authority Associations, HMSO, December.
Moon, J. and Richardson, J. (1985), *Unemployment in the UK*, Aldershot, Gower.
Morton, K. (1980), *The Education Services of the TGWU*, Oxford University, Ruskin College Project Report.
National Economic Development Council (1984), *Competence and Competition: Training in the Federal Republic of Germany, the United States and Japan*, London, NEDO/MSC.
—— (1978), *Engineering Craftsmen: Shortages and Related Problems*, London, NEDO.
New, C. and Myers, A. (1986), *Managing Manufacturing Operations in the UK, 1975-85*. Institute of Manpower Studies.
Nicholson, B. (1986), Press Conference at People and Technology Conference, London, November.
OECD (1975), *Educational Development Strategy in England and Wales*, Paris.
—— (1985), *Education and Training After Basic Schooling*, Paris.
Page, G. (1967), *The Industrial Training Act and After*, London, Andre Deutsch.
Perry, P. J. C. (1976), *The Evolution of British Manpower Policy*, London, BACIE.
Postlethwaite, N. (1988), 'English Last in Science', *Guardian*, 1 March.
Prais, S. J. and Wagner, K. (1983), Schooling Standards in Britain and Germany, London, NIESR Discussion Paper no. 60.
Raffe, D. (1984), *Fourteen to Eighteen*, Aberdeen University Press.
Rajan, A. and Pearson, R. (eds.) (1986), *UK Occupational and Employment Trends*, IMS, London, Butterworths.
Ranson, S (1985), 'Contradictions in the Government of Educational Change', *Political Studies*, 33, 1, pp. 56-72.
Reich, R (1983), *The Next American Frontier*, Middlesex, Penguin.
Reid, G. L. (1980), 'The Research Needs of British Policy-Makers', in McIntosh, A. *Employment Policy in the UK and the US*, London, John Martin.
Riddell, P. (1983), *The Thatcher Government*, Oxford, Martin Robertson.
Salter, B. and Tapper, T. (1981), *Education, Politics and the State*, London, Grant McIntyre.

D. Finegold and D. Soskice

Scarbrough, H. (1986). 'The Politics of Technological Change at BL.', in Jacobi, O. et al. (eds.) *Technological Change, Rationalisation and Industrial Relations.* **city, pub?

Sorge, A. and Streeck, W. (1988). 'Industrial Relations and Technological Change', in Hyman and Streeck (1988).

Steedman, H. (1986), 'Vocational Training in France and Britain: the Construction Industry', *NI Economic Review*, May.

Steedman, H. and Wagner, K. (1987), 'A Second Look at Productivity, Machinery and Skills in Britain and Germany', *NI Economic Review*, November.

Streeck, W. (1985), 'Industrial Change and Industrial Relations in the Motor Industry: An International Overview', Lecture at University of Warwick, 23/10/85.

Streeck et al. (1985). 'Industrial Relations and Technical Change in the British, Italian and German Automobile Industry'. IIM discussion paper 85-5, Berlin.

Taylor, R. (1980), *The Fifth Estate*, London, Pan.

Tipton, B. (1982), 'The Quality of Training and the Design of Work', *Industrial Relations Journal*, pp. 27-42, Spring.

TUC Annual Reports, 1980-1986.

Wiener, M. (1981), *English Culture and the Decline of the Industrial Spirit*, Cambridge, Cambridge University Press.

Wilensky, H. and Turner, L. (1987), *Democratic Corporatism and Policy Linkages*, Berkeley, Instititute of International Studies.

Woodall, J. (1985), 'European Trade Unions and Youth Unemployment', unpublished Kingston Polytechnic Mimeograph, London.

Worswick, G. D. (1985), *Education and Economic Performance*, Gower, Aldershot.

[10]

The British production regime: a societal-specific system?

Jill Rubery

Abstract

The 'Hoover' affair has reawakened interest in Europe in the British production regime as the closest to a free market regime in Europe. This paper argues that in fact the British production regime is another example of a societal-specific system in which institutions and social arrangements are central to the specific characteristics of the British system. The low-skilled, low-wage employment system, with high shares of long and part-time employment emerges out of the interaction of institutional and social arrangements, including family and distribution systems as well as the institutions of labour market and industrial organization. This interaction creates both internal coherence and internal conflicts, but adjustment to internal conflicts does not necessarily result in escape from the vicious circle. Similarly the impact of international integration is not necessarily convergence of national models, for, as in the British case, 'internationalization' takes effect through institutions, sometimes resulting in increasing divergence.

The so-called 'Hoover' affair has reawakened interest within Europe in the British production regime. Britain is becoming notorious within the European Union as the one country not to endorse the high-skill, high-value-added model for the future of an integrated Europe. The notion of competitive advantage based on productivity and skill may be an ideal-type model to which no individual country conforms, let alone the European Union as a whole. Nevertheless, most European governments at least aspire to these goals, accepting that Europe can compete effectively in world markets only if it eschews the temptation of trying to undercut other European countries and Third World countries on the basis of low wages.

In contrast, the UK government has distanced itself from other European countries by disowning this objective. The UK is content to compete for jobs and for trade on the basis of low wage levels, even at the expense of productivity. In the early 1980s it directly endorsed the view that future jobs in

Economy and Society Volume 23 Number 3 August 1994
© Routledge 1994

336   *Jill Rubery*

the UK would not even be 'low tech' but in fact 'no tech' (Lawson 1984). These differences in approach came to a head over Maastricht when the UK government demanded an opt-out clause on the grounds that Britain would lose out in world competition if it was not able to offer inward investors the lowest pay and working conditions among advanced European countries. The potential significance of this policy became more evident recently in the controversial decisions of Hoover to transfer a plant from France to Britain in order to take advantage both of weak regulations on employment and a newly negotiated deal offering flexible employment contracts and low overhead costs. John Major, in keeping with the earlier position of Nigel Lawson, announced that Europe could have the charter but Britain would have the jobs.

One aspect of the 'Hoover affair' which should not be overlooked is that the decision to switch locations was associated with the negotiation of new employment conditions, leading to deteriorating standards in the British Hoover plant. This has put the debate over Maastricht and the social dimension to Europe into a more dynamic perspective. Britain is not only concerned to hold on to its current advantage in wage levels but also to enhance it by placing further pressure on wages and conditions in many parts of the employment system.

This distinctive British approach to competition within Europe provokes mixed reactions within the rest of the European Union. While at one level the UK can be, and often is, regarded as a maverick, pursuing its own very particular, but also self-defeating and destructive, model of economic development, there remains an underlying interest within all European states in the functioning of the UK production system. This arises out of the presumption, propagated by the UK government, that the UK production regime is the closest to a pure market regime. The experiment in so-called free market economics underpins the interest in what might otherwise be considered a marginal and not very successful model of economic and social organization, measured by indicators such as trade performance or productivity levels. Nevertheless, according to advocates of the free market approach, the UK may provide a pointer to the future organization of Europe, once the historical baggage of a commitment to a welfare state and to national industrial policy is dispensed with. Even those who reject this model still feel obliged to pay attention to developments within the UK in order to better understand the enemy 'within' (not only 'within' the European Union, but also a potential model which may emerge within any of the individual nation states).

Societal systems: the case of Britain

The purpose of this paper is to contribute to the continuing debate over the existence and persistence of different production regimes in Europe through the study of the specificities of the UK production and labour market system.

The approach adopted is related to the societal system model, whereby the characteristics of a nation's production system are seen as interrelated with a whole set of social and economic conditions and institutions (Maurice *et al.* 1986). This societal system approach has developed in opposition to the notion of a universalist process of convergence between nation states as a consequence of international integration based on free trade.[1] From this perspective there is no one 'best way' of organizing production, and economic organization must be regarded as socially embedded, and not as 'distorted' by social factors and institutions. Each societal system is seen to have a certain internal coherence, which generates both the society's specific 'comparative advantage' within the international economy but also at the same time forecloses other options or paths of development and inhibits individual organizations from breaking free and developing alternative modes of operation. This societal systems approach, developed initially through comparisons between France and Germany but also applied to a limited extent to Britain (see, for example, Lane 1992; Sorge 1991), has the merits of the holistic approach to analysis. Factors and characteristics of an economic system are treated in context and the complex correlations between the economy and the society are fully understood. For example, a system of training is related not only to firms' production needs but also to the career paths and expectations of workers and indeed to the system of reproduction of skills that operates within the society.

However, a societal systems approach also has its dangers. Two in particular need to be highlighted here (Rubery 1992). First, there is a danger, as in any comparative analysis, of stressing the internal coherence and functioning of the productive system, and of thus paying less attention to the internal contradictions and tensions and the pressures for change inside and outside the system. An important source of these pressures and tensions will be the extent to which the system delivers an efficient and productive system of organization as tested by world trade (Wilkinson 1983). The societal effect school in LEST has in fact paid relatively little attention to the issue of competitive success and to the tensions that arise under economic failure. Such tensions are now, for example, evident in Germany where a previously successful and coherent societal system may be unable to continue to deliver the economic prosperity on which the system is based. The responses to such pressures do not necessarily move a productive system in a direction in which the underlying problems may be solved. For example, short-term fiscal problems may push an economy to cut back on the social and economic infrastructure which may be a necessary precondition for the economic development necessary to resolve the long-term contradictions between aspirations and current output levels (Wilkinson 1983).

Comparative analysis also tends to over-stress the functionalism of the aspects of societies that it identifies (as has constantly been identified as a problem within for example social anthropology). In developing society models to explore inter-country differences, the diversity within societies

338   *Jill Rubery*

tends to be reduced to averages and norms which again may disguise as much as they reveal.

The second and related danger is a tendency to analyse societal systems as static and to pay insufficient attention to the ways in which systems evolve over time. The dynamic element in analysis is critical to the debate over European convergence and integration. What we need to distinguish between are differences in countries' production systems that exist at present but which may be expected to disappear over time (for example, differences attributable to stages of economic development or to the still incomplete integration into the wider European market), and differences that relate to inherently different ways of operation and organization and which may be expected to increase as much as decrease over time.

The societal effect approach tends to emphasize the second over the first set of differences; if differences were primarily related to stages of development, then convergence may need to be orchestrated over a long time period (a two-tier Europe is often advocated, for example, to allow some countries longer to converge), but no long-term obstacles to convergence are held to exist. However, even if this convergence hypothesis is rejected, the question of change in societal systems over time must still be addressed. One important set of influences on this process of change will in fact be the process of international integration itself. These influences, as we discuss below, may create tensions and contradictions, leading to transformations of societal systems. Yet such transformations will not necessarily bring about convergence – each particular societal system will respond in a different way to common forces[2] – but direct attention needs to be paid to the impact of internationalization, not only of trade but also of technology, consumption patterns, intellectual and political ideas and ideologies. Societal systems that have previously been more isolated from the influences of the international community may experience relatively rapid and pervasive change as a consequence of these multi-dimensional influences.

This analysis of the advantages, disadvantages and shortcomings of the societal effect approach provides the basis for the following schematic analysis of the British productive system. Though this model has already been subject to much debate and analysis, we aim to contribute further to the discussion in two particular ways. First, we highlight some aspects of the interrelationships within the societal system which have been relatively neglected, at least in terms of the discussion of differences in labour market structures. Second, at the same time as highlighting these interrelationships and internal coherence, we will also focus on the tensions and forces for change, thus introducing a more dynamic element into the analysis of production regimes. We start the analysis by focusing on the internal coherence of the system, and in particular the interrelations between production, consumption and social reproduction in the British context. In the second section we identify both the sources of tensions and conflicts within the UK system and consider the role of international influences on developments within the British system of production. We conclude by examining first of all the long-term prospects for Britain and, second, the impact on the European integration policy of Britain pursuing its policy of remaining outside the social dimension to Europe.

The British production system: the interrelations between production, consumption and social reproduction

The British production system is often characterized as a low-skill, low-value-added system of production, which competes in world trade and for foreign investment on the basis of low wages and lack of restrictions on the employment of labour (Finegold and Soskice 1988; Ashton *et al.* 1989; Keep 1989; Lane 1992). This production system has been described as a low-skill 'equilibrium'. The lack of a skilled labour force is argued not to be a problem from the perspective of individual British employers as they have in fact adjusted their systems of work organization and production to make minimum demands on the work-force, other than acceptance of low wages and working-time patterns determined by management (short part-time work where necessary; long and flexible working hours where necessary (Marsh 1991)).

The literature on training and skills, which has grown extensively in Britain over recent years, has gone quite a long way towards explaining the basis of this low-skill equilibrium position. These analyses have argued that the low-skill labour force is a consequence of the long-term policy adopted towards training and education in the UK, reinforced by cultural attitudes and practices. Some analysts have also extended the debate to include the industrial relations system and particularly the absence of high trust relations. These analyses have already identified the many faceted obstacles which confront individual firms or organizations which wish to break out of this mould and develop a more skill-intensive production system. However, the set of factors that interact to create a low-skill equilibrium production system can be identified as even wider than the labour market and industrial relations systems (Best 1990). Other aspects of the UK production regime identified as contributing to relative failure include a lack of managerial expertise inhibiting moves towards a higher value added or higher skilled and more flexible production system, the historical limited role of the state and, of course, the influence of the finance system (Lane 1988, 1992; Williams *et al.* 1990).

All aspects of a country's production, consumption and social reproduction systems are necessarily interrelated. At one level this statement may be considered a truism, similar for example to the interdependencies of the circular flow of income. However, at another level these interdependencies are critical for understanding the ways in which different modes of operation are embedded in a societal system. It is not possible, for example, to look at the high share of women who work part-time in the UK without analysing the full set of reinforcing factors that have led to this outcome: favourable social security systems, the dominance of large firms in the service sector which have developed sophisticated working-time planning systems, the lack of child-care facilities and the establishment of standards of living based on a norm of a male bread-winner on long hours and a female part-time worker (Gregory 1991; O'Reilly 1992; Marsh 1991; Rubery 1989).

To understand how societies may move into self-reinforcing vicious or virtuous circles it is necessary to examine these interactions and interrelation-ships between elements of the societal system, instead of the alternative cross-sectional and ahistorical approach to data analysis. Yet it is also necessary, for purposes of analysis, to be selective about the components of the system which should be highlighted and at which interactions or links take on critical importance. This selection is necessarily subjective, varying according to the analyst's interests and competences as well as between countries. For example, the dominance accorded to the educational system by the LEST would not necessarily be found in other societal systems where educational divisions may be less related to the structuring of employment than in France. The selection of areas for analysis also reflects the issue or question to be addressed. Our interest here is in the type of labour market organization that the UK production regime generates, and this leads to a somewhat different list of criteria than in analyses focused on, for example, differences in business systems (Lane 1992), although of course the two impact upon each other.

The interrelationships that we have chosen to highlight in the case of Britain are: first, the relationship between consumption, distribution and production systems; second, the relationship between the systems of education and training, career paths in the labour market and the production system; third, the relationship between the labour market system and the organization of families and social reproduction (see figure 1). The elements included here that are often neglected in discussions of, for example, UK training and skills policy or UK working-time patterns, are on the one hand the influence of the consumption and distribution systems and on the other the social reproduction system. Nevertheless other relevant elements, such as the industrial relations regime, the fiscal regime and the financial regime, which have been more fully discussed elsewhere, are either omitted from the discussion or alluded to only in passing.

Consumption, distribution and the production system

Much of the debate around changing competitive requirements in the 1980s and 1990s has centred on the increased need for higher quality output, more customized to meet consumer tastes and with the emphasis on non-price competition. Part of the economic convergence argument depended on the notion that increased penetration of markets had resulted in firms having to

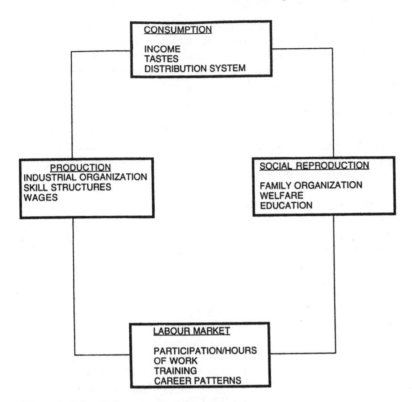

Figure 1 Selected elements of a societal system

compete on variety and style and not simply on producing standard commodities at the lowest possible price (Piore and Sabel 1984; Best 1990). This argument assumed that the penetration of international markets would have similar impacts on consumption patterns in all countries. One of the main arguments that has been made explaining Britain's poor economic performance has been the absence of a suitably trained managerial and non-managerial labour force to meet these new production requirements. However, this argument presupposes that the main constraint on the UK production regime moving up-market was to be found in the labour market, and associated government policies towards labour.

Indeed, the emphasis on increasing quality in product markets has tended to confuse similarities in trends with similarities in outcomes and indeed levels. Search for higher quality in some markets certainly implied the development of designer-based luxury products, but in countries such as the UK the trend to higher quality was still compatible with mass marketing of relatively cheap commodities. Studies of consumer goods industries in the UK have found that these changes in consumer tastes, far from providing manufacturing firms with the basis for moving towards a higher-value-added production system and creating scope for the development of new products, have instead acted as an additional constraint imposed upon organizations geared up to produce standard low-quality commodities (Rubery and Wilkinson 1989). Instead of being able to produce in large batch against stable demands, firms have had to provide goods against short-run and variable orders but priced on the basis of large batch standard commodities. Flexibility in the production systems in many consumer industries has thus been used to provide flexibility to the large and dominant retail chains and not to enhance the market position of the producer.

The British low-wage economy has been reflected in the maintenance of low-price and low-quality distribution outlets. The dominance of large retailers, and indeed large companies in other service areas such as catering, has restricted the development of manufacturers and service producers designed to serve the higher end of the market; where demands for higher quality products develop these are often in practice served by imports as the scale of the domestic market is too small or too fragmented for British producers accustomed to dealing with large retail chains. Thus, in the case of the footwear industry, we found the paradoxical position of the small flexible Italian firms receiving the large batch advance orders from British retailers, with the larger and more Tayloristic UK firms expected to pick up the small repeat and flexible orders as the season progressed (Courault 1992; Rubery and Wilkinson 1989). Similar findings in clothing, hosiery and furniture (Rubery *et al.* 1987; Rubery *et al.* 1992; Best 1990) all suggest that in large areas of consumer production British manufacturers have the 'worst of all worlds', lacking the independence and power to move into high-value-added, small batch production but denied the stability and size of orders necessary to reap traditional benefits of economies of scale. However, as the experiments of industrial policy in the early 1980s revealed, there is no easy solution for the independent producer; the domestic market infrastructure appropriate for a higher-value-added production system may not be in place and a producer may well be adopting an entirely rational strategy in remaining within the network of the dominant retailers. These arguments provide important caveats to the debate about training; many studies have bemoaned the short termism of UK producers and their unwillingness to invest in developing high skills and training. Such strategies may be a necessary condition for developing a more effective industrial strategy but they are by no means sufficient, and training staff in the absence of an effective industrial strategy is likely to lead both to a waste of resources and to frustration on all sides at the under-utilization of skills.[3]

The vicious circle in which producers are trapped is only one part of the problems restricting the adjustment of the UK economy to modern trading conditions. Another problem is that profitability of capital does not necessarily depend on the development of a strong manufacturing and servicing base. A particular feature of the UK government policy since 1979 has been the support of a profit-based strategy for firms at the expense of any consideration of the development of the real economy which may be necessary to sustain the profitability of the UK production system. Most British firms do not see themselves as producers but as asset managers; issues such as developing new products and technologies to enhance Britain's long-term competitiveness are treated very much as of second- or third-order importance to ensuring a decent return on capital even if this means divesting all direct manufacturing activities. This 'hollowing out' of the British economy is a further, and arguably equally important reason why individual organizations will not necessarily take the steps needed to develop a high-value-added skilled production system (Williams *et al.* 1990; Cutler 1992). It is also a demonstration of one further feature of the UK production system often referred to in the literature: that is, the dominance of accountants over engineers in steering organizational strategy, a dominance that in turn can be related to historical trends in the education system and to the specific relationships between the city and industry in Britain.

The current discussion of the UK production system cannot take on board the analysis of the specific development of the UK, let alone an historical analysis of how and why the development took a particular form. Our main focus here is on the various elements that contribute to the maintenance of a 'low-skill' production system, although some may argue the more interesting question is why there is so little concern with the real economy in all its aspects in the management of the British economy.

Skills, training and the labour market

Numerous comparisons of the UK and German and French firms in different industries have revealed not only a skill deficiency in the UK labour force but also a system of low skill embedded in industrial and work organization (see, for example, Steedman and Wagner 1987, 1989; Lane 1988, 1990). Firms minimize their requirements for skilled staff by using a detailed division of labour and by compensating for lack of skill on the production side by the use of supervisors and quality control inspectors. This alternative may be argued to be potentially just as cost effective as a high-skill, mass-training system, particularly given the risk of poaching. However, studies also make clear that the skill deficiencies are not fully compensated for: productivity is markedly lower per person employed, such that differences in pay between skilled and unskilled are unlikely to offset these productivity differences; UK firms are geared to the production of low-quality products; and UK firms are more likely to make more limited use of capital equipment, both by investing less and by making less effective use of such equipment as is installed. Managers and employees lack the basic educational knowledge necessary to programme

344   *Jill Rubery*

and implement the equipment effectively and the interactive capacities of office equipment and the like are under-utilized because of a lack of both trained staff and managerial expertise to implement such systems.

The reasons for this low-skill equilibrium have been variously attributed first to the voluntarist approach to training in the UK, which apart from a brief interlude from 1964 to 1981 has historically almost always been left to the market and to training within firms independently of the education system. The other major factor has been argued to be the negative attitude towards vocational education or training within the UK cultural system. The new vocational qualifications, NVQs, could be interpreted as an attempt to overcome this long-term historical disregard for vocational skills and training; the NVQs assess skills on the basis of actual competences at work and are thus an alternative to academic study and abstract training on the route to qualification. This new approach to training could equally well be regarded as a method of consolidating the low-skill base of the British economy; the levels set by NVQs compare unfavourably to, for example, the standards expected in the German system and the emphasis on competences alone means that there is no attempt to combine basic education in core subjects with vocational training, but instead an emphasis on narrow job-related competence testing unconnected to abstract knowledge and understanding (for a critique of firm-specific and narrow job training, see Streeck 1989).

The low-skill system in Britain can be argued to arise out of a number of strongly reinforcing factors. These include:

i)   the maintenance of a large batch, low-value-added production system as described above;

ii) the influence of the élitist educational traditions in the UK which tend to divide children at an early age into those that are expected to achieve within academic subjects and those that are not, with the majority falling into the latter category;

iii) the lack of government intervention in the training system, such that firms are not compelled to train and often are not able to make use of readily available training systems;

iv) the prevalence of a low-wage system which reduces employers' incentives to train as more skilled workers may demand higher wage levels;

v)   the relationship between vocational training and union craft organization, such that training outside these areas has been neglected, and within them training has been regarded as akin to supporting trade union restrictive practices;

vi) the low-trust industrial relations systems that exist in at least parts of the British production system and which therefore inhibit the development of a highly skilled flexible production system;

vii) and, last but by no means least, the absence of a strong relationship between training and career prospects in Britain.

In many of the comparative case studies British workers have been implicitly criticized for their lack of interest in training and their desire to move out of trainee positions into a 'proper job'. Such attitudes may however be entirely rational and indeed forward thinking within a UK context. It is certainly clear that completion of a YT training course does not provide a passport to stable employment or to jobs with chances of advancement (Bynner and Roberts 1990). These problems also apply to those who stay on within the education system to undertake education or training past the age of 18 but not related to higher education. Evidence suggests that members of the same cohort who succeed in obtaining a job at 16 fare better than those who seek to advance their education or training (Clarke 1991). One of the major problems for the new system of NVQs in gaining widespread acceptance by workers and employers is the question as to what benefit they will be in enhancing careers. If employers choose to ignore such qualifications, as they appear to do for a wide range of vocational qualifications at present, then the system itself will prove to be unworkable as there will be no incentive on the part of employees to obtain NVQ qualifications. Thus in Britain, outside the apprenticeship system which affected primarily craft male manual workers, the relationship between training and career opportunities has been at best indeterminate and at worst negative. In Germany we perhaps find the opposite system, which in some respects is no more rational than that found in the UK. Here because of the widespread use of the apprenticeship system as a credential for entry into intermediate and higher-level jobs, young people are willing to take on and complete a lengthy training in an occupation where the prospects for employment are extremely limited (Bynner and Roberts 1990; Maier and Quack 1992). They use this training then as a passport to another occupation where they may have actually very limited opportunity to use the skills they have learnt, although the general education that goes with the apprenticeship may be more transferable and useful in all occupations.

The labour market and social reproduction

The features that distinguish the UK labour market from that of its European competitors are linked not only to the specific industrial organization in Britain but to the specific form of social organization.

Three schematic examples can be given.

First, the high levels of low-skill part-time work among women are related to:

i)   the continuing tendency for women in Britain to quit the labour market at childbirth, which results in a large supply of female returners who are often unable to re-enter at a level equivalent to their qualifications;
ii) the absence of child-care support, either from the state or from extended family arrangements;
iii) the prevalence of a social norm that it is appropriate for women with children to work part-time but not full-time. This social norm may have

even greater influence than the presence or absence of child care (see, for example, the comparison with the United States where women do work full-time in the absence of any state-provided child care). Alwin *et al.* (1992) provide evidence on differences in social attitudes towards mothers in full-time and part-time work in the UK, Germany and the US, which endorse the actual practices in those countries.

Second, the tendency for men to work long hours in Britain (Marsh 1991) is not only a consequence of employer policy in the absence of regulation. All evidence suggests that British men are willing to work long hours and often deliberately seek jobs with overtime opportunities. This preference may at least in part be related to family organization and family budgets. First, the expectation that male full-timers will work long hours in the UK may restrict the opportunities for women to consider taking on full-time work. The norm of the woman in the partnership working part-time may then increase the willingness of men to seek overtime work as a means of supplementing family income. Thus, the model of men working long full-time hours and women working part-time may be reinforced by the actions of individuals to increase family income. It is notable that this model of the nuclear family is taken to be the common-sense model within British society but bears little resemblance to the models adopted in other European states. For example, in the Scandinavian countries the model is more one of short full-time work for both partners (Jonung and Persson 1993) or in France of medium full-time work for both, with even part-timers effectively working a short full week.

Third, the organization of the UK labour market can be seen to be strongly related to the system of education and training and of income support for the young. The low participation in higher education in Britain has meant that the youth labour market is both large and consists of workers who are seeking entry into long-term employment on a full-time basis. In contrast, in other countries much of the youth labour market consists of people who are still partially in education or training and who may be seeking, for example, temporary or part-time work to provide income support for their education. One factor which has perhaps decreased the number of young people willing to train in Britain is that the family system is geared to young people making independent contributions to their upkeep at an earlier age than in many countries. There is considerable pressure on young people to find a 'proper job' when leaving school, and even within the higher education system support for young adults has up until recently been provided primarily by the state and not by the family system. The lack of a tradition of family-based support for education and training thus places an additional obstacle in the way of policies designed to increase the scale of further and higher education and training in Britain.

The British productive system: coherence or conflict?

The model we have presented so far has been of a coherent and interlocking system of consumption, production and social reproduction, all tending towards the establishment and reinforcement of a low-skill, low-value-added economy. In many aspects there is considerably validity in a vicious circle approach to the UK economy, but it would be wrong to present the system as an harmoniously and smoothly adjusting model, albeit in a downward direction away from a prosperous, skill-based system. Conflicts and tensions, whether suppressed or overt, are inherent in the UK system as indeed in any 'societal model'. In considering these conflicts, tensions and indeed pressures for change, it is useful to discuss first those that relate to what could be called the real economy – to disharmonies in the various balance sheets of the economy. In the second section we look at the British model and how it has survived, adapted and changed in response to more external influences, in particular to the spread of ideas and ideologies across nation-state boundaries, including the increasing influence of or knowledge of other modes of operation.

Tensions, conflicts and imbalances in the British productive system

The British productive system could be, and is often described as, providing an alternative mode of competition to that of the highly regulated and high-wage economy. The advantages of the British system are identified in its supposed flexibility and in its ability to compete on the basis of labour costs. However, identification of a different mode of competition does not guarantee that this mode is capable of delivering competitive success when measured in terms, for example, of the balance of trade. It is in the relative failure of the British productive system to deliver competitive success on world markets that the strongest tensions and conflicts in the UK model arise. The imbalance in trade arises from both consumption and production patterns. British labour costs are not sufficiently low to allow successful competition in standard low-wage-cost commodities; British consumers have developed tastes for commodities that can often best be met from imports. This is either because they are high quality and high tech goods which British firms do not produce or because Britain, as a low-wage economy but with well-developed and internationalized consumption patterns, consumes high-fashion products produced at low cost, often imported from the Third World. These imbalances on the foreign exchange markets are kept in check by monetary and fiscal policy which restricts the level of employment, thereby causing tensions between the employed and the unemployed. Unlike the textbook model of competition between firms, competition between nation states will not necessarily result in the elimination of unproductive regimes. Nation states do not disappear under competitive pressure and will usually continue to survive even under conditions of great indebtedness. Thus long-term relative failure is still a possible outcome, even if this failure leads to internal tensions and conflicts.

In addition to these macro-economic imbalances there are conflicts and tensions at a micro level. British firms have adjusted to a long-term low-skill equilibrium, but this does not prevent the emergence of skill shortages whenever the economy speeds up a little or even whenever a firm wishes to expand over and above its planned level.

Deregulation of the labour market has encouraged the growth of low-wage employment. It has also provided the opportunity for substantial increases in pay for those at the top end of the pay hierarchy, in both public and private sectors. These developments are likely to cause major problems in the future particularly in the public sector. The system of national industry-level bargaining and national pay and grading scales was argued by Conservative governments to have led to the over-payment of wages for the less skilled relative to so-called market rates. However, perhaps the more important effect was to keep the lid on salaries of managerial and professional staff within the public sector. Deregulation and individualization of pay has provided the opportunity for some cutbacks in wages for the low paid but the rapid rises in managerial salaries and in performance-related pay may be a long-term problem for public sector expenditure, and for the wage bill of private sector organizations. Of course, the most likely way within the current political context that these problems will be addressed is to exert further pressure on the middle and low paid in order to provide the funds for the increases for the higher paid. But there may be a limit to the costs savings that can be achieved through such strategies.

The UK has long been a low-wage, low-productivity economy with balance of payments problems. The long-term persistence of these characteristics does not mean that they do not generate tensions and conflicts. Indeed, it is arguable that the industrial relations reforms of the 1980s were designed to suppress the conflict that constantly evolved over the level of wages within the UK economy. The combination of high unemployment, industrial relations legislation and a weakened trade union movement and Labour party may have acted to reduce the level of overt conflict. This does not mean, however, that there is not underlying tension and conflict over the distribution of both income and employment and that the British labour force has finally and forever accepted its role as the social dumping ground of Europe.

Nor is it the case that the 'model' of the nuclear family on which both labour market and social policy is based, that is of a male bread-winner and a female second income or part-time worker, is either fully accepted or adopted by the majority of the population. True, most women who return to work within the context of a nuclear family do so on a part-time basis and rarely move back into full-time work. However, there are many households that do not conform to this model; there are more single parents, divorced and separated couples and more women staying on at work or returning to work very quickly after having children (McRae 1991). The current cohort of female returners may be keener to return to full-time work than the older cohorts, so it may be dangerous to predict future behaviour on the basis of past patterns. The result of these changes is increasing problems of poverty for women not embedded in the standard nuclear family, as women's wage and employment opportunities are still geared to second-income-earner status. There are other tensions over the long hours of work and lack of child care in the increasing number of families with two full-time workers. However, if women resist their use as a low-paid part-time labour force, as is indicated by the higher share of women using maternity leave provisions rather than quit the labour force, changes in the educational system may be generated through an alternative labour supply for low-paid part-time jobs. The switch from student grants to loans is increasing the number of students seeking to supplement their income while studying through work, and in the future Britain could follow the US route towards the use of youth rather than female labour in many catering and retail-type activities. Thus, adjustments can take place in the sources of labour supply for particular types of jobs, but the analysis of this adjustment process requires an understanding of institutional and non-market arrangements, such as the education and training system and the family system. The British production regime is as much conditioned by and related to forms of social organization as other European regimes, even if these institutions increasingly lack coherence and stability.

Towards convergence or divergence: the impact of international ideas, ideologies and modes of operation

The British productive system has so far been analysed as if it has developed in isolation from the world economy and the international transmission of ideas, ideologies and modes of operation: in short, as if Britain was an isolated island whose only point of contact with the rest of the world was through trade. Instead, Britain has been the recipient of large amounts of inward foreign investment, which has brought with it not only capital but different managerial ideas and ideologies; it is integrated into the ideological and political debates of the international community; and it has itself sought to use the experience of other nations in designing and developing its own productive system. With these different but reinforcing channels of influence from the external community, it might be expected that the possibility of divergence in productive systems is being steadily eroded. If not forced to conform by the pressures of world trade, the international integration of firms and the spread of ideas freely across national boundaries might be expected to do the trick.

What is interesting, however, is the way in which these international influences can reinforce and increase as well as reduce differences. Contact with the rest of the world helps to highlight differences and indicate problems in the British productive system. For example, it is arguable that the current low level of interest in training in Britain would be even less if it were not for the role of foreign multinationals in stimulating interest in techniques of human resource management. Perhaps more significant is the adoption of the term human resource management in Britain to signify moves to minimize the role of unions in the work-force, but without the commitments to the investment in human resources and the associated employment guarantees that such a term implies.

A similar use can be seen to have been made of the concept 'Japanization'. Firms legitimate the changes they make to working conditions and modes of operation by reference both to the economic threat from Japan and to the established practices of Japanese firms (Marchington and Parker 1990: 100; Ackroyd *et al.* 1988). However, many of these changes are not towards a more skill-intensive production system but towards increased flexibility over working time and a reduced role for trade unions. No mention is made by employers of increased job security, and performance-related pay and internal competition between individuals is substituted for the Japanese model of team working achieved through job security and seniority-related pay.

There are many examples of how practice or policies pursued in other countries have been used in the UK context either to reinforce existing practice or to legitimate change. Even the neo-liberal experiment in the UK has been justified by reference to the fact that all European states have been concerned about the degree of labour market regulation and are seeking to deregulate their own systems; but this debate has ignored the differences in the starting points between Britain and other member states. Deregulation of the British labour market in the 1980s, when it started with a much lower degree of regulation than other European states, has acted to increase the degree of divergence between the economies even if their regulatory trends appear to be in the same direction. Even the European ideal of a social dimension to the labour market has been used internally within Britain for ends that are not directly related to the European issue itself. The British Labour Party espoused the social charter idea and the notion of individual employment rights in part to enable it to refuse to promise to re-establish the pre-Thatcher status quo in industrial relations legislation. This move was arguably as much connected with an attempt to distance itself from the trade unions in order to increase its chances of being elected as with any specific commitment to or interest in Europe.

In the area of training and education the use and misuse of international comparisons has been rife. The employer-led Training and Enterprise Councils were apparently modelled on a successful American system, but in reality these systems in the US were both less successful and less important than the UK government would have us believe (Bailey 1990; Peck 1992). The establishment of NVQs has been justified as a move towards raising the status of vocational skills, following practice in Germany and elsewhere, but little attention has been paid to the setting of lower attainment levels in Britain or to the exclusive focus on competences without the simultaneous continuing extension of general education that is the hallmark of the German system.

From even these examples it is clear that the spread of international ideas and the process of 'learning' from other countries does not necessarily lead to convergence, as it is the interpretation and implementation of the ideas within a specific community which matters. In fact, the whole internationalization and integration trend depends not on automatic and inevitable market forces, but on how these influences are taken up and used within specific consumption, production and social reproduction systems.

To take the spread of international consumption patterns, it is arguable that in the UK there has been a rapid internationalization of tastes, especially in the area of food, partly because of the tendency of the British to seek the sun abroad during their annual holidays. Yet this internationalization is firmly within the control of the large retailer, who determines which particular brand of Italian bread or French cheese will be the next to be introduced on a mass scale into British households. The more fragmented distribution systems in other European countries, and indeed perhaps a better cuisine, has reduced the spread of 'international' consumption patterns.

In production, as we have already argued, the international move towards more flexible production systems has also taken a specific form in the UK; just in time and small batch production systems are being introduced, but to meet the demands of the retailer and not to enhance the producer's position within the consumer market. Flexible employment systems are being used not to enhance the skill level of the labour force but to increase work intensification (Brunhes *et al.* 1989).

Social reproduction systems are also open to 'internationalization'. In Britain, the spread of feminist ideas has, as elsewhere, been associated with the increased integration of women into the economy. But in a deregulated labour market women are facing decreasing wages in part-time jobs, and where employed in higher-level jobs, for example in the public sector, they are in practice providing a relatively cheap alternative to men who are leaving the public sector as pay and prospects decline.

Conclusion

The British productive system has not evolved in isolation from the international community. The need to trade and compete within the international community helps to expose the deficiencies of the system as a long-term answer to economic growth and prosperity. However, the adaptations to the system that are called forth by these failures are not necessarily those that will enhance the long-term success of the British economy or bring it into convergence with other European states. Some of the remedies that are called for to solve British economic ills, including increased flexibility of the

352   *Jill Rubery*

labour force, less government expenditure and intervention, are often justified in the name of practices and policies found in other states. The different starting points and cultural and economic conditions in these states are glossed over. Moreover, these adaptations may postpone the fundamental adjustments required by the system to move onto a virtuous path of upskilling and growth. The problem of European convergence is thus not a static one; it is not simply a question of how to eliminate current differences but also of how to stop countries moving onto different tracks, and competing against each other not only on the basis of current differences in labour costs but on their ability to drive costs even lower (as in the case of Hoover). The British productive system is not static but is constantly evolving, under the influence of international integration and international practice. Yet the specific form that the evolution takes is determined by the ways in which these international influences are taken up and embedded into British-specific institutions and practices. The responses made by British firms to changes in product market conditions are constrained by the presence or absence of other institutions and institutional arrangements – by the power of the dominant retailers on the one hand and the absence of institutional arrangements to generate a supply of skilled labour on the other. Thus, the British productive system demonstrates the danger of assuming that deregulation will lead to efficient and productive adaptions to changing market conditions. Yet demonstration of the unsuitability of the British productive system as a model of feasible future development for Europe is not sufficient. The European integration process does not have to result in long-term relative success but can equally well result in long-term relative failure and decline. In this context European states and European citizens may well be right to worry about the potential destabilizing effect of the British productive system uncontrolled by even the minimum regulatory regime that may emerge out of the Maastricht treaty.

Manchester School of Management
UMIST

Notes

1   This societal effect school is perhaps the best known but by no means the only approach to stress the social embeddedness of economic organization. Other examples include the associated work by Lutz, who undertook the German part of the original French/German comparisons, the work by Sorge and Warner (1986) on Germany and Britain, the business systems approach developed by Whitley (1992), the productive systems approach of Wilkinson (1983) and the work of the International Working Party on Labour Market Segmentation (Castro *et al.* 1992; Tarling 1987; Wilkinson 1981).
2   The approach adopted here is similar to that advocated with respect to the analysis of the articulation between the spheres of production and social reproduction. Instead of seeing social reproduction systems as either determined by the economic production systems or, as in more culturalist arguments, entirely independently determined, the

argument has been made that each sphere should be considered 'relatively autonomous'. For example, developments in the production sphere influence the path of development of social reproduction, but the adaptations these bring about are not determined by the economic system but arise out of the dynamic of development within the social reproduction sphere (Humphries and Rubery 1984).

3   In the study of skills and training in the clothing industry young people in Britain were implicitly criticized for their lack of interest in training (Steedman and Wagner 1989). Yet this could be regarded as an entirely rational approach, given the concentration of the industry on low-value-added products and the poor job prospects in the industry.

References

Ackroyd, S. *et al.* (1988) 'The Japanisation of British Industry?', *Industrial Relations Journal* 19(1): 11–23.

Alwin, D., Braun, M. and Scott, J. (1992) 'The separation of work and the family: attitudes towards women's labour-force participation in Germany, Great Britain and the United States', *European Sociological Review* 8(1): 13–37.

Ashton, D. *et al.* (1989) 'The training system of British capitalism: changes and prospects', in F. Green (ed.) *The Restructuring of the UK Economy*, Brighton: Harvester-Wheatsheaf.

Bailey, T. (1990) 'The mission of the TECS and private sector involvement: lessons from the PICs', Conference on US and UK Education and Training Policy in Comparative Perspective, University of Warwick, June.

Best, M. (1990) *The New Competition*, Oxford: Polity Press.

Brunhes, B., Rogot, J. and Wasserman, W. (1989) *Labour Market Flexibility: Trends in Enterprise*, Paris: OECD.

Bynner, J. and Roberts, K. (eds) (1990) *Youth and Work: Transition to Employment in England and Germany*, London: Anglo-German Foundation.

Castro, A., Méhaut, P. and Rubery, J. (eds) (1992) *International Integration and Labour Market Organisation*, London: Academic.

Clarke, K. (1991) *Women and Training: A Review*, Manchester: EOC Discussion Series.

Courault, B. (1992) 'Footwear manufacturers and the restructuring of distribution in the shoe industry: a challenge to the flexible specialisation analysis', in A. Castro *et al.* (eds) (1992).

Cutler, T. (1992) 'Vocational training and Britain's economic performance', *Work, Employment and Society* June.

Finegold, D. and Soskice, D. (1988) 'The failure of training in Britain: analysis and prescription', *Oxford Review of Economic Policy* 4(3).

Gregory, A. (1991) 'Patterns of working hours in large-scale grocery retailing in Britain and France: convergence after 1992?', *Work, Employment and Society* December.

Humphries, J. and Rubery, J. (1984) 'The reconstitution of the supply-side of the labour market: the relative autonomy of social reproduction', *Cambridge Journal of Economics* December.

Jonung, C. and Persson, I. (1993) 'Women and market work: the misleading tale of participation rates in international comparisons', *Work, Employment and Society* 7(2): 259–74.

Keep, E. (1989) 'A training scandal?', in K. Sisson (ed.) *Personnel Management in Britain*, Oxford: Blackwell.

Lane, C. (1988) 'Industrial change in Europe: the pursuit of flexible specialisation in Britain and West Germany', *Work, Employment and Society*, June.

—— (1990) 'Vocational training, employment relations and new production concepts in Germany: some lessons for Britain', *Industrial Relations Journal* Winter.

—— (1992) 'European business systems: Britain and German compared', in R. Whitley (ed.) (1992).

354   *Jill Rubery*

Lawson, N. (1984) 'Mais lecture', reprinted as 'The British experiment', *Public Money* September.

McRae, S. (1991) *Maternity Rights in Britain*, London: Policy Studies Institute.

Maier, F. and Quack, S. (1992) *Occupational Segregation of Women and Men in Germany*, Report for the EC Network on the Situation of Women in the Labour Market.

Marsh, C. (1991) *Hours of Work of Women and Men in Britain*, EOC Research Series, London: HMSO.

Maurice, M., Sellier, F. and Silvestre, J-J. (1986) *The Social Foundations of Industrial Power*, Cambridge, Mass.: MIT Press.

Marchington, M. and Parker, P. (1990) *Changing Employees Relations*, Basingstoke: Macmillan.

O'Reilly, J. (1992) 'Banking on flexibility', *International Journal of Human Resource Management* March.

Peck, J. (1992) 'TECs and the local politics of training', *Political Geography* July.

Persky, J. (1992) 'Regional competition, convergence and social welfare – the US case', in A. Castro *et al.* (eds) (1992).

Piore, M. and Sabel, C. (1984) *The Second Industrial Divide*, New York: Basic Books.

Rubery, J. (1989) 'Precarious forms of works in the UK', in G. Rodgers and J. Rodgers (eds) *Precarious Jobs in Labour Market Regulation: The Growth of Atypical Employment in Western Europe*, Geneva.

—— (1992) 'Productive systems and international integration', in A. Castro *et al.* (eds).

Rubery, J. and Wilkinson, F. (1989) 'Distribution, flexibility of production and the British footwear industry', *Labour and Society* 14(2): 121–40.

Rubery, J. *et al.* (1987) 'Flexibility, marketing and the organisation of production', *Labour and Society* March.

Rubery, J., Humphries, J. and Horrell, S. (1992) 'Women's employment in textiles and clothing', in R. Lindley (ed.) *Women's Employment: Britain in the Single European Market*, Equal Opportunities Commission, London: HMSO.

Sengenberger, W. (1992) 'Future prospects for the European Labour market: visions and nightmares', in A. Castro *et al.* (eds) (1992).

Sorge, A. (1991) 'Strategic fit and the societal effect: interpreting cross-national comparisons of technology, organisation and human resources', *Organization Studies* 12(2): 161–90.

Sorge, A. and Warner, M. (1986) *Comparative Factory Organisation: An Anglo German Comparison of Management and Manpower in Manufacturing*, Aldershot: Gower.

Steedman, H. and Wagner, K. (1987) 'A second look at productivity, machinery and skills in Britain and Germany', *National Institute Economic Review* 122.

—— and —— (1989) 'Productivity, machinery and skills: clothing manufacture in Britain and Germany', *National Institute Economic Review* May.

Streeck, W. (1989) 'Skills and the limits of neo-liberalism: the enterprise of the future of as place of learning', *Work, Employment and Society* March.

Tarling, R. (ed.) (1987) *Flexibility of the Labour Market*, London: Academic.

Whitley, R. (ed.) (1992) *European Business Systems*, London: Sage.

Wilkinson, F. (ed.) (1981) *The Dynamics of Labour Market Segmentation*, London: Academic.

—— (1983) 'Productive systems', *Cambridge Journal of Economics* 7(3/4): 413–30.

Williams, K. *et al.* 'The hollowing out of British manufacturing', *Economy and Society*, December.

[11]

European Business Systems:
Britain and Germany Compared

Christel Lane

Business systems (Whitley, 1991) are understood as the sum of general practices and value orientations which characterise both the internal organisation of business units and their relations with their external environment. They are regarded as constituted by the social-institutional environment in which they are embedded. It is now widely accepted that the impact of such social-institutional factors is so significant that they can almost be regarded as additional factors of production which become the basis of competitive advantage or disadvantage (Elbaum and Lazonick, 1987; Maurice et al., 1980; Sorge and Warner, 1986; Streeck, 1990). Such business systems should neither be viewed as 'iron cages', which prevent managerial strategic choice and policy innovation from below (from the labour movement) or above (government reform), nor as generalisable 'business recipe', freely transferable from one national context to another. Business systems do not prevent change at the level of the individual business unit. Incremental adaptation in response to challenges from the global economic system can occur within the parameters of the business system and be absorbed in nationally specific ways. But radical change against the grain of the wider institutional fabric will be difficult to sustain in the long run. Institutional transformation at sectoral or societal level can be successfully achieved, provided that the inter-relatedness of given institutional complexes is taken into consideration.

The adoption of the term 'system' does not imply a functionalist equation of system durability with effectiveness or success, as will become evident from the evaluation of the British system. Lastly, it should be noted that influence does not flow unidirectionally from social institutions to business systems, but that there occurs reciprocal conditioning of business organisations and institutional complexes.

Business systems receive their distinctive character at a very early stage of the industrialisation process, but develop and adapt over time in response to broader economic and technological challenges as well as social and political pressures. Britain and Germany have undergone the industrialisation process at very different times and under highly divergent circumstances, as well as experiencing the discrepant political and economic consequences of being winners and losers respectively in two world wars. Britain's early start on the road to industrialism and its experience of incremental social change since that time have made for an exceptional degree of continuity in deeply implanted social-institutional patterns. Germany's experience of political and social upheaval has brought some ruptures in these patterns. But even in Germany there has been striking institutional inertia within radical political change (in the financial and training systems), and the post-war period has demonstrated the exceptional stability of the new structures, such as the system of industrial relations.

The business systems of these two societies have, therefore, developed along fundamentally different lines and, given their common European heritage and similar size and industrial structure, provide the material for a very instructive comparison. In both cases it is possible to identify nationally bounded, homogenous systems which override regional/industrial differences and to delimit them, in the case of Germany, from those of neighbouring countries or, in the case of Britain, from countries shaped by the Anglo-Saxon tradition (the USA and Australia). These countries share some of the crucial institutional factors, though not the whole bundle of interacting institutional complexes. These contrasting systems will be analysed only in relation to manufacturing industry.

This chapter is structured in the following way. The first section contains brief descriptions and comparisons of institutional complexes in the two societies, commonly seen as having an impact on business systems either singly or in combination. The state, the financial system and the system of education and training are accorded the strongest and most pervasive impact. A lesser, though by no means insignificant, influence is attributed to the network of business associations and to the system of industrial relations. The second section discusses the impact of the above complexes on the following four aspects of British and German business systems: the nature of firms and their patterns of growth; market organisation; coordination and control systems; and employment and personnel practices. An attempt is made to systematise these institutional influences in tabular form and to record their differential strength. Such representation inevitably oversimplifies relations and ignores both interrelations *between* institutions and the way business practices strengthen and sustain institutional arrangements. The

66 European business systems

conclusion summarises the argument and relates the evolving business systems to a brief outline of current and projected national business performance.

The Social-Institutional Environment of Business Systems

The State

The institution of the state is seen to be particularly influential in moulding business systems as it exerts both a direct influence and an indirect one through its shaping of the other institutional complexes under discussion. In Germany, there has occurred a significant disjuncture between pre- and post-war forms of state. Although there was significant variation in this respect during the period 1871–1945, one can nevertheless talk of a centralised and interventionist state throughout this time, and the legacy of this period has left a considerable impact on the business system. Since the Second World War, a democratic political system has become firmly implanted. The state has assumed a federal structure which grants local states (*Länder*) significant economic resources and competences and thus makes it more likely that state-sponsored support for industry is attuned to local needs, particularly those of the small firm (Allen, 1987: 88 ff.). The Länder governments develop regional growth plans, promote exports and innovation and plan and finance vocational education, corresponding to local need.

The system of proportional representation for political parties has resulted in frequent coalition governments. It has ensured that governments enjoy majority support and political legitimacy and that policy initiatives have not usually been overturned after government changes. The resultant high degree of political stability has strongly contributed to a stable framework for industrial decision-making. Legitimacy and stability have also been boosted by the well-established procedures for consultation and cooperation with the representatives of both capital and labour.

The political philosophy of the social Market Economy, dominant since the Second World War, emphasises competition in the free market and eschews detailed intervention in industry but compensates labour for the social costs which the working of the market inevitably imposes. This philosophy respects and perpetuates the long-established German tradition of industrial self-regulation and self-help, based both on the banking system and on the dense network of trade associations and Chambers of Industry and Commerce. Individual businesses cannot rely on the state to share business risks nor expect to be bailed out in times of trouble. The non-interventionist stance of the state, however, does not mean that the state remains aloof from industrial concerns. Together with the federal bank, it provides a stable economic environment as well as uniform regulatory frameworks, resulting in considerable national homogeneity of structural arrangements. In recent decades, the state has adopted a more proactive role, particularly in the area of technological innovation, where financial support for specific innovation projects has been aimed at the establishment of inter-industrial cooperative networks and at the intensification of existing ties between firms and research institutions (Sorge and Maurice, 1990: 162 on the engineering industry). Local states have been more interventionist than the central state, but such intervention is rarely direct and is exercised through the medium of, and in consultation with, regional trade associations.

In Britain, the structure of the state and the philosophy of state–industry relations have provided a very different institutional/ideological framework. The state has long been very centralised and during the 1980s has striven to undermine remaining structures of local power. The structure of the British state, particularly the dominance of the independent Bank of England over fiscal/financial policy and the preeminence of the Treasury, have had a very negative impact on industrial policy (Hall, 1987: 282). The absence of constitutionally regulated representation of regional economic interests has made elected representatives very vulnerable to local pressures and has resulted in an unstable and haphazard representation of regional and other specialist economic interests. Regional policy has concentrated on transferring funds to depressed areas but has neglected to tie them to restructuring (ibid.: 274). The electoral system, which has recently given rise to an executive, based on the support of only a minority of voters, undermines the legitimacy of government policy and makes it vulnerable to reversal by a change in the party of government (Gamble, 1985: 209). The systematic exclusion of the unions from consultative forums during the Thatcher years has further diminished the legitimacy of many policies. Together, these factors have resulted in an unstable economic framework and, in some areas, perpetually changing institutional structures and procedures, as, for example, in the case of the training system and the agency dealing with technology policy.

Local political bodies did adopt a more interventionist stance during the 1980s in an effort to revive the economic strength of their locality. But their limited budgets and the absence of intermediate institutions, facilitating liaison with most of the firms in

68   *European business systems*

the area or industry, have endowed their efforts with only limited success.

In the area of industrial policy, the philosophy of *laissez-faire* has been dominant during most of the post-war period (with the exception of the late 1960s/early 1970s) and reached its apex during the 1980s in the idea of the minimalist state. Frequent economic crises have, however, forced governments to abandon this non-interventionist stance. Consequently, industrial policy – if, indeed, it deserves this title – has been haphazard and ineffective in instituting any long-term and sustained industrial change, and in several instances (Concorde, shipbuilding, the nuclear reactor programme) badly misdirected. Although the financial resources made available during recent decades have been roughly comparable to those in other advanced European societies they have mainly been used 'as inducements and not for sanctioning purposes' (Hall, 1987: 275) and thus rarely effected restructuring. State reluctance to intervene has been mirrored by industry's insistence on a hands-off policy. Comprehensive regulatory frameworks on aspects of industrial organisation were never developed although, paradoxically, beginnings were made during the 1980s in the areas of industrial relations and vocational training. But the principle of voluntarism is still being upheld and makes for considerable diversity and complexity in the institutional structures bearing on business systems.

The Financial System

Large British firms have traditionally raised their capital mainly by issuing shares on the stock market, and the financial institutions have never tied the provision of capital to demands for, and involvement in, the restructuring of individual firms or whole sectors. At the present time, the bulk of new investment, as in the case of Germany, comes from internally generated funds (Edwards and Fischer, 1991: 17). Among outside sources of finance, institutional investors predominate, and the banks are only one group of players among several. The banking system is highly centralised, and bank lending tends to be short-term and has not entailed the establishment of close industry–bank relations. The British financial system has imposed constraints on industrial managements of high, short-term returns on capital, without offering any support or monitoring functions. The ease of takeover has lent additional urgency to the achievement of short-term returns on capital and high dividend payouts (*Bank of England Quarterly Bulletin*, August 1991: 364). In addition, it has encouraged the search for economic gain from purely financial transactions to the detriment of concentration on manufacturing concerns (Williams et al., 1990).

The legitimacy of the takeover option has also militated against enterprise growth from small to medium size (Hughes, 1990) and has thus contributed to the creation of a polarized industrial structure. Thus, to sum up, the essence of the British relation between the financial and the industrial sector lies not so much in a shortage of investment capital but more in the conditions under which it is made available (Best and Humphries, 1987).

The German financial system is mainly based on bank credit, and the stock market remains underdeveloped. The large universal banks form the centre of the financial system, and they maintain very close links with industry. Banks own substantial amounts of industrial equity, as well as acting as proxies for small investors. Long-term relationships are built up between given banks and firms, and this relationship is not only expressed in mutual board membership but is also accompanied by consultancy and supervision, though not usually by interference in management (Edwards and Fischer, 1991). The high degree of concentration of corporate control (in terms of bank ownership and/or voting rights), together with legal safeguards, written into company statutes, make hostile takeover rare. Groups of banks have acted as 'crisis cartels' to assist in the restructuring of traditional industries or to rescue ailing giants.

The high degree of bank concentration at national level (the Big Three) is counterbalanced by decentralisation at the level of local states. Smaller firms tend to obtain credit from the many regional cooperative and municipal banks. The close relation of the former with local industry is evidenced by the fact that their boards are typically composed of local industrialists (Sabel et al., 1987: 36). This provides not only a close connection between industry and banking but also forges horizontal links between SMEs in a region. This more assured financial support enables SMEs to grow more easily into medium-sized firms than is the case for their British counterparts.

The System of Education and Training

Industry depends not only on money capital but also on human capital, in the form of skills, professional expertise and scientific/ technological knowledge. This section will focus on the system of vocational education and training (VET); on management education; and on the generation and transfer of scientific knowledge.

Germany is known for its highly developed system of VET, sustained by the long survival of the craft sector, but now diffused

70   *European business systems*

throughout industry. It is a dual system, i.e. both college- and industry-based, and provides nationally standardised courses for both manual and lower non-manual occupations from the apprenticeship level upwards to that of the master craftsman and/or engineer. It thus offers career ladders and ensures homogeneity of competence and orientation at various hierarchical levels. Examination and certification by Chambers of Craft and Industry safeguard standards and ensure vocational education a relatively high prestige, as well as tying promotion to increase in qualification. Financing is a joint effort by employers and the state (two-thirds and one-third respectively), and the coverage of both theoretical and practical aspects of VET results in broadly based skills and competences. Unions are involved in course design in a consultative manner but have never had the strong influence of their British counterparts. During the 1970s and 1980s, partly as a result of union and more general public pressure, training was significantly stepped up, increasing the proportion of apprentices in the labour force from 4.5 per cent in 1964 to 6 per cent in 1986 (Marsden and Ryan, 1991: 259, table 11.2). The increase in provision, together with the high market value of vocational qualifications, has resulted in a high participation rate – 65 per cent of the eligible group in the 1980s – and in a broadening of appeal also to those already in possession of academic qualifications. The 1980s also witnessed a substantial increase in advanced (certified) and further training (internal) (Janoski, 1990).

In Britain VET has always been of secondary importance and has never attained the same social prestige as German VET nor the same wide social diffusion. The weaknesses of the British system are now widely recognised, and a fundamental overhaul of the whole system is in train, but current business recipes have been only marginally affected by new practices. The two main components of British VET are the traditional apprenticeship system and the Youth Training Schemes (YTS). The former trains mainly craftsmen to high standards of practical competence and traditionally provided a springboard to the higher levels of technician and engineer. The shortcomings of the traditional apprenticeship have come to be seen as insufficient external monitoring of standards, the union-determined rigidity of acquired skills and the low and declining level of its take-up/provision from 3 per cent of the industrial labour force in 1964 to a mere 1.2 per cent in 1986 (Marsden and Ryan, 1991: 259, table 11.2).

The YTS schemes have overcome the problems of demarcation and low diffusion, but are fundamentally flawed by their low standards of attainment and their lack of legitimacy among both trainees and employers (ibid.). The greater formalisation and professionalisation of technician and engineering training in recent years have destroyed the former ease of progression to higher levels of the career ladder. The biggest discrepancy with the German system exists at the supervisory level, where a total absence of training schemes has resulted in foremen of low technical competence, unsuited to execute a training function (Prais and Wagner, 1988).

Management education is an important focus of study not only for its obvious impact on levels and nature of technical competence but also for its influence on managerial identity and value orientations. The latter become reinforced by the connection between social origin and educational route adopted. Management education has become increasingly 'professionalised' in both Britain and Germany, but professionalisation has proceeded to different degrees and in different directions. Comparative data from the 1970s and 1980s, collected by NEDO (1987: 2, table 1), show the German proportion of graduate managers to be significantly higher at 62 per cent, as compared with the British 24 per cent. When we examine the content of management education, we find the following contrast: among German managers those with an engineering education dominate (although business economics is becoming more prevalent among younger managers), whereas a more general educational preparation in arts, social sciences and management studies is acceptable in Britain. But high flyers frequently possess a more specialised accountancy qualification, and engineers are sought after in certain industries and staff functions. The second important difference between the countries is the British emphasis, from the 1960s onwards, on a postgraduate general management education on the American model. In Germany, in contrast, this generalist approach has received no institutionalised recognition, and additional qualifications highly rewarded are either a doctorate in science or engineering or, alternatively, an apprenticeship (NEDO, 1987: 2; *Manager Magazin*, 1986: 11, 343).

The third kind of expertise needed by manufacturing firms in many sectors lies in the area of Research and Development (R & D). The problem is not merely one of producing the scientific/technological knowledge but also one of transfer between knowledge producers and users. The relation between industry and research departments in institutes of higher eduction is said to be closer in Germany than in Britain (van Tulder and Junne, 1988; Mowery, 1987). In Germany, this close tie between scientists and industry was forged at the beginning of the industrialisation process (Trebilcock, 1981: 63) and is ascribed to two developments

72   *European business systems*

in higher and further education. The first is the founding of technical universities and their early (1899) attainment of equality of status with traditional universities, which created and legitimated a more applied tradition (Sorge and Maurice, 1990: 147). The second is the founding of the vocationally oriented *Fachhochschulen* (polytechnics) at the end of the nineteenth century, which are both very practice- and locality-orientated and a valuable resource particularly for SMEs (Sabel et al., 1987; van Tulder and Junne, 1988: 171). Lastly, research institutes are also based in industry and are organised on a sectoral or transsectoral basis. They were first founded in 1911 and receive support both from central and state governments, as well as from trade associations and individual firms (Best, 1990: 99). They constitute a valuable collective resource, close to industry's needs, which is particularly beneficial to SMEs.

In Britain, the importance of R & D was recognised much later than in Germany. Up to the First World War, there was still 'a wide-spread abjuration of science in industry' (Levine, 1967: 70), and even in later periods it never acquired the centrality it had in German industry, despite an excellent science base in universities (Mowery, 1987). The broad development of a vocational tradition in higher education occurred only in the 1960s with the introduction of polytechnics and technological universities. The latter have not attained the same status as their more traditional counterparts, nor have they managed to sustain an undiluted vocational/applied focus. Also industry has been less forthcoming in sponsoring university research and, with the exception of the government-funded research associations between the world wars (Mowery, 1987: 205 ff.), has not benefited from the provision of research-based knowledge on a collective basis. Although government funding and direction of R & D has increased in more recent decades, it is generally considered remarkably unsuccessful (Mowery, 1987).

Trade Associations and Chambers

Although the collective organisation of firms on an industry and geographical basis is common in both societies, there are important differences between them in the support given to such associations and in the breadth of functions and services provided by them. In Germany, the surviving craft tradition is still embodied and defended by the Chambers of Industry, Commerce and Craft which are prominently involved in training. As statutory bodies, the Chambers can impose a compulsory levy on firms. They are thus well endowed and provide a variety of producer services, particularly for the SMEs (Streeck, 1986). The trade associations, formed on the nationally uniform principles of both industry and territory, enjoy high levels of membership participation and exercise a wide range of functions, ranging from the provision of services such as research facilities, via tasks of self-administration of the industrial community (industrial restructuring or arbitration between buyer and supplier firms), to political presentation and negotiation with state agencies – as, for example, participation in the formulation of technology policy. Separate regional and national associations represent employer interests vis-à-vis the unions. (For details see Simon, 1976; Streeck, 1986.) Lastly, employer associations act jointly with unions in self-administration bodies in such areas as labour market policy and social insurance provision (Janoski, 1990).

In Britain, Chambers of Commerce do not enjoy statutory status and are thus much more marginal to industry. Trade associations are not subject to uniform regulation and have grown historically in a more haphazard manner, often leading to wasteful overlap and competition for membership. The resulting lower membership, less secure financial basis and voluntarist constitution curtail the width and depth of functions they are able to perform and leave British firms more institutionally isolated. The latter affects SMEs more severely than large firms, which are more able to buy in consultancy services or keep up political pressures. (For a British–German comparison, see Grant, 1986). Many of the self-administration functions, noted in the German context, do not exist at all in British associations but are handled by the state. This lack of cohesion and consequent inaction is particularly damaging in the area of sectoral restructuring, given that neither banks nor the state have taken an active role. Thus, the contrast between British and German associations can be summed up in the following way: British associations act defensively to protect members against public policies or global competition; German associations, in contrast, also take a proactive and strategic role in shaping their sector (Allen, 1987: 96).

The System of Industrial Relations
The system of industrial relations (IR) influences business organisation both through its structural features and through the tenor of its underlying class relations. In both respects the British and German systems are polar opposites. The German system is highly juridified and nationally homogenous. The representation and defence of the interests of labour are served by a dual structure: industry-based trade unions, authorised to engage in collective

74   *European business systems*

bargaining and to call strikes in defence of their claims; and enterprise-based organs of codetermination and consultation, functioning firstly through elected employee representation at board level and secondly, and more importantly, through works councils. This orderly structure, with clear lines of differentiation according to area of competence and lines of support and enforcement, has made for effective conflict resolution and methods of interest representation. The underlying ideological goals of social partnership and industrial harmony have, during the post-war period, achieved a large measure of acceptance and have become expressed in what has been called a cooperative style of IR. Union organisation on an industry basis, together with a strong central organisation, results in solidaristic rather than sectional demands and facilitates the formulation of social demands, going beyond shop-floor concerns. The degree of unionisation is moderately high – 40 per cent – and unions are well organised to pursue their claims. Employer organisations also have a high degree of cohesiveness and strength, but on the whole share the unions' commitment to the current structure and style of IR.

The British system of industrial relations has grown incrementally over a long historical period, and until the 1980s was regulated only by tradition and custom. Multi-unionism has entailed different modes of bargaining, but during the post-war period decentralised plant bargaining has become very common. Unions have been relatively strong, particularly in large firms, and have resisted the introduction of parallel bodies of representation. Bargaining has usually been about issues close to the shop floor, and work stoppages and other forms of conflictual behaviour have been readily practised to lend force to claims. Widely adopted practices of job demarcation have introduced a high level of rigidity into work organisation which was, in any case, strongly influenced by unions. An adversarial style of industrial relations and a high level, by European standards, of conflict were tolerated by relatively weakly organised employers. The 1980s saw extensive change in many of these aspects, but it is too early to judge how permanent they are. Although union membership dropped considerably during the 1980s, the degree of organisation – at 50 per cent – is still considerable, and shop-floor organisation has remained intact. At the national level, however, union influence is now weak.

To conclude this section on the institutional environment of business organisations in the two societies, a systematic overview of the effects of institutional differences is given in Table 3.1. These contrasting effects can be further summarised by pointing to

Table 3.1   *Effects of institutional differences in Britain and Germany*

	Britain	Germany
The state		
Decentralization of economic policy-making	Low	High
Reliance on intermediate organisations and self-regulation of industry	Low	High
Stability of economic framework	Low	High
Legitimacy of policy-making	Medium	High
Degree of state involvement:		
risk sharing	Low	Low
regulatory	Low	Medium
The financial system		
Degree of pressure for high short-term return on capital	High	Low
Participation in rationalisation of firms/industries	Low	High
Ease of takeover	High	Low
Impact on industrial concentration	High	High
Attention to 'small firm' needs	Low	Medium
The system of education and training		
(a) *Vocational education and training*		
Prestige of VET	Low	High
Availability of highly skilled, flexibly deployable human resources	Low	High
Homogeneity of competences/orientations within firm	Low	High
(b) *Management education*		
Availability of managers with high level of technical competence	Low	High
Availability of managers with high level of 'generalist' training	Medium	Low
(c) *Scientific research*		
Degree of industry–university cooperation	Low	High
Degree of industrial self-organisation of R & D	Low	High
Trade associations and chambers		
Degree of industrial self-administration	Low	High
Degree of formalisation of inter-firm relations	Low	High
The system of industrial relations		
Effectiveness of conflict resolution	Low	High
Degree of flexibility in labour deployment	Low	High
Union recognition of 'the right to manage'	Medium	High
National homogeneity of negotiated bargains	Low	High

76   *European business systems*

the resulting degree of either isolation or social embeddedness in which business organisations find themselves. Whereas German business organisations are connected by a multiplicity of ties both to a very dense socio-institutional framework and to each other, their British counterparts tend to be more institutionally isolated. These structural features are reflected in, and reinforced by, different business philosophies. Whereas British firms jealously guard their independence and espouse voluntarism and arm's-length relationships, German firms lean more towards a limited communitarianism and a willing acceptance of some regulatory frameworks.

The Impact on Business Organisation

The Structure and Development of Firms

In both Britain and Germany the large managerial enterprise is now the dominant type of firm. But this superficial similarity hides important differences in the timing of the transition from the personal to the managerial enterprise and in both developmental paths and current organisational structures.

In Germany, extensive state involvement and long-term bank lending at the beginning of industrialisation led to the early establishment of large firms in key industries of the time, such as coal, steel and electrical (Kocka, 1975a: 89). Vertical integration and diversification (in related products/processes) emerged relatively early, due to a number of reasons: the underdevelopment and lack of transparency of markets and the absence of merchant middlemen; the availability of organisational models and management techniques for large complex units provided by the highly developed and positively perceived public bureaucracies which pre-dated industrialisation; the early dominance of joint stock companies – in both 1887 and 1907 four-fifths of the 100 largest manufacturing firms were joint stock companies (Kocka and Siegrist, 1979: 82); and from the dominance of investment banks, sufficiently strong to finance such growth patterns and to insist on rationalisation of merged units (Best, 1990: 102; Kocka, 1975b; Kocka and Siegrist, 1979: 82).

Early diversification was not only associated with under-developed and uncertain markets but also with the intention to utilise capital-intensive plant and know-how more effectively (Siegrist, 1980: 81). Thus, of the 100 largest manufacturing firms in 1907, two-thirds had integrated both backward and forward, as well as being diversified, and by 1927 this trend had proceeded even further (Kocka and Siegrist, 1979; Siegrist, 1980). (This pattern was very close to that established in the USA at this time and much more advanced than that found in Britain (ibid.: 82, 87).) But in contrast to both the US and the British pattern of diversification, German efforts rarely resulted in conglomerates: firms stayed in commercially or, more frequently, technically related areas (Dyas and Thanheiser, 1976: 89, 96; Kocka and Siegrist, 1979; Siegrist, 1980). Management educational background in engineering is bound to have influenced this diversification strategy.

Although the early reasons for vertical integration, connected with economic backwardness, lost their force as economic development proceeded, these growth patterns survived their origins. Consequently, persistent structures and habits were available when new impetuses for integration arose at later times. The cartel movement, particularly its development of sales syndicates (see below, on market organisation), which achieved a peak during the 1920s, provided one such impetus (Dascher, 1974; Dyas and Thanheiser, 1976: 52), and various tax measures during the post-Second World War period provided another (Dyas and Thanheiser, 1976: 54).

Family ownership of substantial share holdings and/or control of large companies was common in the decades around the turn of the century (Kocka and Siegrist, 1979) and has remained relatively significant even in later decades. But it has proved much less of an obstacle to the development of modern organisational and management forms than in Britain. Thus concentration increased steadily, joint stock companies proliferated and diversification was vigorously promoted. By 1907, personal enterprises (both top and middle management functions are executed by owners) had been replaced by entrepreneurial ones (only top management functions remain in the hands of owners), and by 1927 increasingly by managerial enterprises (managers have replaced owners at both levels) (Siegrist, 1980). Two likely reasons for this reconciliation of family control and modern business organisation come to mind: expansion financed by bank credit was less likely to lead to loss of family influence; and the bureaucratic management tradition, associated with a high level of education, integrity and a sense of duty and accountability, checked fraudulent activity and thus lessened the fear of passing control to non-family middle managers, as well as requiring family managers to acquire an adequate level of education.

Expansion of firms occurred both by internal and external growth. Merger movements occurred around the turn of the century, in the mid-1920s – the creation of the two giants IG Farben and Vereinigte Stahlwerke – and again in the late

78 *European business systems*

1960s/early 1970s, but they were less common than in Britain. Merger waves were also clearly distinguished from their British equivalents by two facts: first, they were followed by thorough rationalisation of capacity and organisation, and, indeed, were often undertaken with the explicit goal of rationalisation in mind (Best, 1990; Dascher, 1974: 130). This crucial difference was undoubtedly due to the fact that German banks undertook the rationalisation of sectors, rather than just of firms. Secondly, mergers were predominantly horizontal and aimed to eliminate competition rather than create conglomerates (Dyas and Thanheiser, 1976: 50 ff.).

By 1927, large German companies were mostly associations of legally independent companies, organised under a mother company, and they assumed the forms of a holding company or of a trust (*Konzern*) (Siegrist, 1980: 86). Some of the giants, like IG Farben and Siemens, deliberately accompanied growing size by decentralisation measures (Dascher, 1974: 131), but generally centralisation was more pronounced than in comparable British firms. Centralisation received a further impulse during the Nazi period, particularly during the war years, when political direction became very strong. Divisionalisation came only from the 1960s onwards. It made less progress than in the UK and has experienced a partial reversal during the 1980s (Cable and Dirrheimer, 1983: 46). This difference is said to be due to two facts: first, incompatibility with pre-existing structures, such as functional specialisation and collegiate management (Dyas and Thanheiser, 1976); and second, better pre-existing owner control by banks and families, obviating the necessity for improved control through divisionalisation (Cable and Dirrheimer, 1983: 49).

The close relation between industry and banking received its organisational expression in the two-tier board structure (a supervisory and a management board) in 1870 (Dyson, 1986), affording banks a supervisory and advisory role. The latter has endured even after the decline of bank lending as an important source of new capital and an attendant reduction in bank influence over individual firms. (In the 1971–85 period, internally generated funds formed by far the largest part of investment capital for joint stock companies (AG) in manufacturing, although bank loans were of greater importance for other manufacturing firms (Edwards and Fischer, 1991: 19–22).) Although the supervisory board is potentially influential – it can reject management strategic decisions and block reappointment of incompetent managers – it does not have the legal power to force the adoption of alternative strategies. In general, management does not feel unduly constrained by the board (see Lane, 1989: ch. 2).

Most of the features of large German firms, crystallised during the first 50-odd years of industrial development, have endured up to the present time. The American intervention during the early post-war years brought some partial, though temporary, reversal of concentration and a more effective curtailment of cartellisation (Berghahn, 1986). Thus, at the present time, large German firms remain highly concentrated, diversified (but not conglomerates), centralised (Child and Kieser, 1979) and vertically integrated. The fragmentation strategies of the 1980s, discussed for Anglo-Saxon countries, such as splitting-off or spinning-off divisions or departments into independent units, are said to have found no parallel among large German companies, with the exception of Siemens and Loewe Opta (Weimer, 1990: 129). Greater rationalisation of acquired firms is still indicated by the much lower number of establishments per company than in Britain (Prais, 1981). Family ownership and control has, of course, greatly receded, and the managerial firm has long since been the norm, but family control of large firms has nevertheless remained more significant than in Britain (Scott, 1985: 128).

State protection of the artisan sector in engineering and more traditional industries ensured the survival of SMEs and the early establishment of business ties and attitudinal cross-fertilisation with the large-firm sector. The greater survival in Germany of small and medium-sized family-owned and -managed enterprises presents one of the most striking differences from the British pattern (Doran, 1984). Historically, the family has been regarded as a business resource – in terms of capital, labour and patterns of organisation – which is combined with a more calculative orientation towards its external environment (Kocka, 1975a: 93). But a third important reason for its superior survival capacity is no doubt the German financial system and the greater protection from hostile takeover afforded by it.

Due to the absence of either state or bank involvement, British firms grew only slowly up to 1880. The first merger wave during the 1880–1918 period affected mainly firms in traditional industries such as textiles and brewing, and due to the adoption of a loosely federated holding company structure did not lead to actual capital concentration, permitting economies of scale (Hannah, 1976a; Levine, 1967: 43 ff.). In 1919, according to Chandler (Chandler and Daems, 1980: 28), 'there were few middle and almost no top salaried, non-owning career managers working in British enterprises'.

The creation of large publicly-quoted multiple-site companies in a cross-section of industries came only at the end of the 1920s

80 *European business systems*

(Hannah, 1976a). The new ease of raising capital on the stock market at that time led to a rapid expansion of the corporate sector and to the development of the then modern industries. Hannah (1980) dates the emergence of the modern company to the early 1930s whereas Chandler (Chandler and Daems, 1980) is inclined to postpone it to the post-war period, pointing to the underdevelopment of many features commonly associated with modern status.

The lack of involvement of financial institutions in industry meant that both individual firms and industries were seldom forced to restructure and modernise. Not only did the family-dominated large enterprise persist much longer than in Germany but it also proved less able to reconcile family control with modernisation of organisation structures and modes of management (Pollard, 1965: 23). Among the 200 largest firms, family directors were a clear majority of board members well into the post-war period (Hannah, 1980: 53), and family vested interest often inhibited desirable change (Hannah, 1976b: 12).

Although British historical data on business structure for the early (pre-Second World War) period are patchy (Hannah, 1980: 82) some generalisations can nevertheless be made. Large companies, in the majority of cases, remained very loose federations of family firms under a holding company structure. Vertical integration and diversification remained relatively low, and the absence of a management hierarchy, together with low levels of managerial competence, prevented organisational and technological innovation on the scale experienced in Germany. Although individual companies, such as ICI, began to develop a sizeable R & D facility during the 1920s, most companies lagged behind their continental competitors in this respect too.

The main structural and managerial transformations in British large companies came about in the 1960s. A further important merger wave led to a level of capital concentration which gave Britain the most highly concentrated large-firm sector in the world. Mergers were now more frequently followed by structural modernisation, but even in the 1960s the loose holding-company structure persisted in many of the large companies (Hannah, 1976b: 199). The remnants of family capitalism were finally superseded by managerial capitalism. This period also saw the widespread adoption of divisionalisation, adapted from the American pattern to British organisational forms. Diverging evaluations of the effects of this implantation make an unambiguous comparative assessment impossible. (See, for example, Hannah, 1980; Cable and Dirrheimer, 1983; Best, 1990: 102.) Although traditional, technologically sluggish firms still have an undue weight in the British economy, there are now a significant number of technologically advanced and innovative firms. One final feature of British large firms is that they have always been, and still are, much more international in character than their German counterparts, with both outward and inward direct investment on a significantly higher level.

The large modern British corporation thus developed significantly later than its German counterpart, and development involved more drastic change, stimulated particularly by the American example. Growth by merger and acquisition, without the intervention of either banks or the state, was more predominant than in Germany. The resultant current organisational pattern still preserves some distinctively British features. The level of concentration is higher and that of family influence lower than in German firms. Vertical integration, internal rationalisation and centralisation are still less pronounced, and diversification is more often of the conglomerate type. Despite a high incidence of share ownership by financial institutions, there has occurred no institutionalisation of this tie at board level, and their active participation in, and control over, strategic decision-making remains rare.

Due to lack of state involvement in this industrial transformation, the British small-firm sector was left exposed to market forces. The consolidation of large corporations in a cross-section of industries led to the rapid decline, from the late 1930s onwards, of small manufacturing firms which was only halted in the early 1970s and reversed in the 1980s. (The decline in both numbers and employment share of small – < 200 employees – and very small – < 50 employees – establishments began in the 1935–48 period and continued until 1973, when it reached its lowest point (Hughes, 1990: 10, table 8). This exceptionally rapid decline, due to both competitive pressure from large firms and the higher incidence of acquisition and takeover, has given Britain a somewhat unbalanced industrial structure and composition. Particularly notable in comparison with Germany is the low incidence of family-managed craft enterprises (Doran, 1984) and of medium-sized companies (Hughes, 1990). These features have crucial effects on market organisation.

Market Organisation
The current dominance, in both societies, of large, impersonally owned corporations has led to the prevalence of a relatively low degree of market organisation in each, but there are nevertheless some important differences between them. These relate chiefly to the manner in which market relationships are organised. These

82   *European business systems*

different patterns have been significantly shaped by the timing and especially the speed of the industrialisation process in the two countries.

In Germany one needs to distinguish between a large-firm and a small-firm pattern of market organisation. The large German corporation is said to have a significantly higher degree of vertical integration than its British counterpart, retaining both up-stream supply functions and down-stream distribution functions under its own control. Kocka (1975a: 82) traces the origins of this back to Germany's very rapid industrialisation process which gave no scope for the development of a market tradition and resulted in mistrust of merchants and suppliers. Other external influences, detailed in the second half of this chapter, have perpetuated this feature since that formative period. Recent comparative data on manufacturing depth (calculated in terms of the relation between number of employees and turnover in *Wirtschaftswoche*, 1989, 38: 146 ff.) show that this remains much greater in all of Germany's major industries than in its competitor countries. The more recent claim (Altmann and Sauer 1989; Sabel et al., 1987) that substantial vertical disintegration has occurred in both large and smaller firms, evidenced in the contracting out of more manufacturing and design tasks has, as yet, not received substantiation by large-scale cross-sectoral surveys (Weimer, 1990: 127–8).

The relatively high degree of vertical integration has led one commentator (Herrigel, 1989) to speak of the 'autarkous' large German firm. But such a characterisation neglects the many ways in which even large German firms have always maintained links with other firms and the many institutional supports for such links. The prime historical example of extensive market organisation is given by the far-reaching cartelisation of German industry which started in the 1890s and reached a peak in 1929–30 (Best, 1990: 96 ff.; Dyas and Thanheiser, 1976: 52). Cartels and syndicates (cartels with joint marketing arrangements), although particularly strong in the heavy industry sector, affected the majority of large firms in all sectors and, by 1938, provided 50 per cent of industrial output (Kocka, 1980). They regulated competition not primarily by price control but by sectoral rationalisation. The latter aimed, firstly, at the universal application of scientific methods and techniques, and secondly, at cooperative effort in all phases of the industrial process (ibid.). Cartelisation was made illegal, through American intervention, in the aftermath of the Second World War (Berghahn, 1986), and today it is of limited importance.

Historical dominance of horizontal combination has exerted a strong formative influence on large German firms, and many forms of cooperation have remained prevalent up to the present day. The pattern of financial interlocks, expressed in interlocking directorships, has remained very prevalent and dense (Scott, 1985: 130). Close links with customers and suppliers are maintained in the same way. Connections with firms in the same industry are cultivated through the strong and active trade and employers' associations (Grant, 1986; Wilks and Wright, 1987), which have a well-known record for organising collective activities in such diverse areas as R & D, export diplomacy and wage setting respectively.

Such horizontal links between both competitors and suppliers are much more pronounced among SMEs and have recently been commented upon in the discussion of German industrial districts, such as those of Baden-Württemberg (Sabel et al., 1987; Herrigel, 1989). Cooperative ties are said to be particularly developed among craft enterprises, and Weimer (1990: 103) claims that 'the economic success of the craft sector could even be attributed to the fact that firms in the sector succeeded at an early stage in setting up powerful self-help and interest groups', albeit with considerable state support. It is, however, notable that, in contrast to other industrial societies (e.g. Italy or the Southeast Asian countries), inter-firm networks do not rest on direct, personal and familial ties but on an institutionalised form of market organisation through Chambers and business associations. This renders market organisation very stable and effective but may lack the flexibility of networks built on personal contacts.

The existence of such mediated horizontal cooperation is well documented for the state of Baden-Württemberg by the work of Sabel et al. (1987) and is shown to pre-date the more recent emergence of industrial districts in countries like Italy. This capacity to cooperate, they point out, is premised on a market strategy of specialisation in complementary products which in turn depends on the regulation of competition by intermediate bodies, such as sectoral trade associations. Cooperation has been practised in such activities as advertising and selling in foreign markets, research and training (ibid.: 22 ff.). There is, as yet, little systematic research on such horizontal links between SMEs in other German regions. But it should be noted that the preconditions for such cooperation – sectoral agglomerations of small and medium-sized craft enterprises, active trade associations and an abundance of skilled labour – can also be found in other German states. In the craft sector more generally, the following collective practices are common: collective purchasing in the food sector; the provision of joint pension funds to improve the attractiveness of small firms

84   *European business systems*

to scarce skilled labour; and the formation of cooperatives of small building firms in order to gain and carry out larger contracts (Weimer, 1990: 106). One striking instance of cooperation of SMEs, reported in the *Economist* (4 November 1989: 112), speaks of the formation of a consortium with a predominance of '*Mittelstand*' firms to get the licence to build and run Germany's first mobile telephone service.

Britain, in contrast, has traditionally accorded the market more emphasis in the coordination of economic activities. But it has been associated with a pattern of market organisation where inter-firm relations are purely contractual, restricted in scope, short-term and conducted at arm's length or even in an adversarial style (Hirst and Zeitlin, 1989). The historically high geographic concentration of industry and the more drawn-out British process of industrialisation meant that, in the past, large firms could rely on a 'highly developed and efficient system of markets' with a developed network of marketing middlemen (Hannah, 1980: 63, 64). While these could be regarded as equalling hierarchies in efficiency up to a certain stage of industrial development, market relationships proved inadequate to the tasks of industrial restructuring and technological modernisation.

A more recent emphasis on the importance of market organisation to competitive strategy has focused on the peculiar quality of British market organisation, which is seen to militate against the evolution of trust relationships. Relations between firms are no longer mediated by family networks, and their regulation through trade associations is fragmented and underdeveloped. Although there exists a large variety of such industry-based associations, they are much less effective than their German counterparts and tend to provide more individual than collective goods. Their relatively weak influence over firms in a given sector precludes them from adopting regulatory functions, such as in the area of competition, and thus leaves smaller firms unprotected (see, for example, the account of Whitson (1989) on the foundry industry). Large firms are also said to be very insular and to disdain contact with small, innovative firms, except as acquisitions (Saxenian, 1989: 464). Hence it is significant that the recent small-firm revival has not led to any horizontal cooperation in the face of ever-increasing demands on small-firm capability by large buyers. Industrial districts, although a feature of British industrial life in the past (Sabel and Zeitlin, 1985), are notably absent at the present time.

Coordination and Control Systems

Turning to the organisational structure within establishments, the studies of the French Aix Group and of their British and German associates have revealed that British and German patterns are also divergent at this level. This work, together with the many excellent studies by the National Institute of Economic and Social Research, have now convincingly related these organisational divergencies to the differing approaches to both vocational training and management education. Whereas British production units tend to be highly compartmentalised both vertically and horizontally, German ones are characterised by more permeable boundaries in both respects. Thus in Britain task differentiation is strong between production and maintenance workers, between technical and supervisory workers and between management and technical staff. This is said to create operational rigidity, as well as problems of communication and of dual authority. In Germany, in contrast, due to the higher level of technical expertise at all levels, roles are defined in a more fluid manner and facilitate not only task integration and a high degree of flexibility but also a lower level of overall staffing (see, for example, the findings of Finlay, 1981).

A much greater German emphasis on the utilisation of shop-floor expertise makes production and associated functions the organisational hub of establishments, whereas the British preoccupation with financial matters gives much greater emphasis to relevant managerial positions. A particularly pronounced difference between the two national organisational configurations exists at the supervisory level, where the German *Meister*'s technical, managerial and pedagogical expertise makes him/her a pivotal figure at various organisational interfaces in a way which has no parallel in the role of the largely untrained British foreman (Prais and Wagner, 1988).

The lesser emphasis on production tasks and the disassociation of technical and supervisory authority in British manufacturing firms also result in a different conception of managerial identity and claim to authority, which are shaped by both social origin and education. British managers are much more likely to see themselves as generalists than technical specialists and, due to their frequently very low level of formal education, claim positional rather than expert authority (Lawrence, 1980), particularly at lower levels. At top level, authority is also often derived from the social capital of upper-class background, giving rise to claims of natural leadership skills. Positional or class-based authority is, of course, more fragile and open to challenge as credentialism is becoming ever more

86   *European business systems*

widely accepted. Where authority is knowledge-based, it is usually financially oriented.

In Germany, in contrast, legitimacy of managerial authority is almost invariably based on certified skill, and the latter ranges from the craft-based type – witness the many managers with a completed apprenticeship – to the research-based variety, as evidenced in the significant proportion of managers with doctorates in science subjects (Lane, 1989: 92–3). These organisational differences have become expressed in, and reinforced by, profoundly different business orientations. Whereas the productivist ethos of the German firm suffuses all hierarchical layers and acts as an integrating mechanism, the British predominantly financial orientation fails to provide such a common focus.

These different bases of authority in the two societies have some influence on the way authority is exercised, although other factors also affect managerial style. Such influences are patterns of primary socialisation in the family, types of ownership and enterprise size, the political culture of the wider society, the industrial relations system and the social/educational distance between managers and managed. As argued elsewhere (Lane, 1989: ch. 4), the common stereotypes of authoritarian German versus democratic British managerial style no longer capture the complex reality, particularly where German managers are concerned. During the post-war period, far-reaching democratisation of political and industrial relations, as well as of parent–child and teacher–pupil interaction, has notably undermined the authoritarian tendency so evident in Germany's earlier history. Autocratic management style is also curbed by the collegiate form of top management. The trend towards a more democratic management has, however, been more pronounced in the large corporations than in the small and medium-sized family-managed firms where paternalistic and authoritarian styles have remained more prevalent (Kotthoff 1981). In both large and smaller firms the craft ethos, with its emphasis on worker autonomy, imposes democratic norms on shop-floor management–employee relations (Lawrence, 1980; Maurice et al., 1980). In the administrative sphere, in contrast, management control in most aspects remains much more centralised than in British firms (Child and Kieser, 1979; Horovitz, 1980; Weimer, 1990: 130). Power distance, defined as the difference between the extent to which managers can influence the behaviour of employees and vice-versa, was found to be of the same magnitude in both societies (Hofstede, 1980).

In British society, there has been relatively little change in the institutional structures impinging on management style until the

1980s. The democratic or constitutional management style is said to have predominated in most operational spheres (Gallie, 1978; Maitland, 1983), although it is by no means certain to what extent loose control had a normative basis and to what extent it resulted from management weakness and/or incompetence (Maitland 1983). Management style can also be seen as shaped by enterprise growth through undigested acquisitions, which made a decentralised form of management 'more natural' (Hannah, 1976a: 97). During the 1980s, high unemployment, the weakening of the unions and government moral support for management led to a widespread reassertion of the right to manage, but not to a fundamental change in management style (Edwards, 1987). Although paternalism is also more common in British smaller firms, the difference between large firms and SMEs is not as marked as in Germany, due to the much looser connection in contemporary Britain between family and business.

Employment System and Personnel Procedures

In both countries the employment system is heavily influenced by the system of VET and, to a lesser degree, by industrial relations practices. In both societies the apprenticeship system, providing workers with certified skills which possess validity on a national labour market, has historically accorded occupational labour markets an important place in employment systems (Marsden and Ryan, 1991: 256 ff.). Standardised payment norms for standardised skills have been enforced by union influence. But in recent decades, internal labour markets have gained more importance in both Britain and Germany, albeit for different reasons and with different structural outcomes, and the employment system of both countries is now characterised by a mixture of partially overlapping principles. This blending of internal and occupational structures is said to have been accomplished more successfully in Germany (ibid.).

In Germany's large corporations internal labour markets have become very developed, and employment security has been high by European standards. Such firms train large numbers of apprentices and retain most of them after the completion of their training course (Casey, 1986). Although such training is not firm-specific, its broad and flexible nature nevertheless makes it a valuable resource which large firms are anxious to retain. Further flexibility is acquired by more informal and firm-specific upgrading of training (*Weiterbildung*), which greatly increased in volume during the 1980s, and by works councils' support for the flexible utilisation of core labour (Bosch, 1988: 180). Employment stability as a

88　*European business systems*

function of employer investment in training is reinforced by
employee pressure through codetermination structures (works
councils and representation on supervisory boards) (Streeck, 1984).
The attraction of external labour markets is reduced by the following circumstances: first, wage determination at regional/industry
level entails relatively low wage differentials between large firms;
and second, promotion into technical, supervisory and often
managerial positions, although dependent on further formally
certified training, is rendered more likely by loyalty to a given firm
and thus best pursued in internal labour markets. The much-
discussed drive towards numerical flexibility during the 1980s
appears to have had only a minimal impact on large manufacturing
firms (Lane, 1989).

Although initial recruitment of managers now occurs predominantly on external labour markets, promotion is still dependent on
long, loyal service and thus mainly internal. Thus top management
teams have considerable depth of expertise and knowledge about
one industry which is consistent with their predominantly 'productivist' orientation but may impede the development of broader
strategic visions. In smaller firms management is usually not
divorced from ownership and tends to come from a craft background. Such firms also train a large number of apprentices, but,
in contrast, are unable to retain more than a few on completion of
training.

The newly trained surplus workers have to move via external
labour markets to larger firms; but, given that their training is
frequently in outmoded or irrelevant trades, are forced to enter
large firms initially as semi-skilled workers. Their background is,
however, not totally irrelevant. Managerial practices of work
organisation have to take some cognisance of their skills, attitudes
and expectations, and have increasingly been influenced to extend
the 'responsible autonomy' approach downwards in the manual
hierarchy (Kern and Schumann, 1984; Schumann et al., 1990). In
several industries formerly dominated by semi-skilled workers, such
as the chemical and steel industries, a policy of formal upgrading
to skilled status was adopted in the 1980s (ibid.).

Employment/personnel policy in Germany is thus internally very
consistent. Training, employment, promotion, pay and work
organisation practices are logically connected and reinforce each
other. They are designed to stimulate the acquisition of formal
qualifications and to create and retain the long-term commitment
of workers. Although the latter are equipped to obtain employment
on external labour markets, both push (recession) and pull (reward
of qualification plus loyalty by promotion) factors have inclined

large-firm workers increasingly towards internal markets. The ideology of the works community has been an additional contributory factor. The latter originated in the 1889 writings of the influential reformist economist Gustav Schmoller (Homburg, 1991), and has frequently been reinterpreted since then in line with the dominant political ideology (Plumpe, 1991). During the postwar period it has again become an accepted integrating mechanism. The active involvement in, and assumption of co-responsibility for, business administration by the works council (Lane, 1989: 232 ff.) and the predominantly cooperative style of industrial relations are related factors which increase worker commitment to the firm.

In Britain the development of internal labour markets is combined with different employment and personnel practices, and consistency between the various elements is much lower. The increasing importance of internal labour markets from the late 1950s onwards can be attributed to several factors: the shift in the locus of pay bargaining from the industry level to that of the firm (Sisson, 1987: 90 ff.); the decline of industries with a high concentration of skilled workers, such as shipbuilding and engineering; and the steep overall decline over the last 25 years of apprenticeship training and skilled workers (Marsden and Ryan, 1991: 257 ff.). Large employers have not only moved to company- or plant-level pay bargaining but have also favoured internal promotion, company training schemes and flexibility agreements (ibid.). But the establishment of internal markets has affected different types of worker unevenly, and employment security was significantly reduced during the 1980s – although this affected industry much less than the service sector (Lane, 1989: 282 ff.). Furthermore, security of employment has never figured as prominently on union agendas as it has in Germany. A comparison of employment stability in the mid-1980s shows this to be significantly lower in Britain than in Germany – 30 per cent of British, as compared with 46 per cent of German, workers had been with the same employer for more than ten years (*Arbeitsmarktchronik*, 1986, 24: 1, Wissenschaftszentrum Berlin).

Hence the development of internal structures in British firms has remained uneven and incomplete (Marsden and Ryan, 1991: 257), and management attachment to an ideology of worker involvement and commitment is very recent and still fragile. The long tradition of a 'minimum involvement' philosophy and of a purely contractual approach, espoused by both sides of industry, cannot be easily superseded. Thus work organisation strategies have only very partially moved towards the 'high skill–high autonomy' principles of flexible specialisation (Hirst and Zeitlin, 1990; Wood, 1989),

90   *European business systems*

and training and skill upgrading have been uneven and patchy. Marsden and Ryan (1991: 257) point out that internal upgrading is mainly confined to new and foreign-owned plants and that flexibility agreements have almost totally bypassed the semi-skilled. This is partly attributable to existing union structures and practices. The continued segregation of semi-skilled workers from skilled craftsmen in separate unions makes it difficult to overcome demarcation practices. The numerical dominance of the unions of the semi- and unskilled has led to very low wage differentials compared with skilled workers, and the union-controlled apprenticeship system prevents adult workers from gaining access to traditional craft training. Informal upgrading from craft worker to technician, engineer or managerial status, while relatively common in some industries up to the early 1980s, has been made more difficult by the greater formalisation of technical training on the one side and the trend towards management recruitment from graduates on the other. But even in the early 1980s, Sorge et al. (1983) found the continuity from worker to technician jobs to be significantly greater in Germany than in Britain.

Management promotion in Britain is more often gained by movement between firms. The generalist education and/or predominantly financial orientation among top managers and the more diversified nature of British firms makes movement between firms and even industries relatively easy, and more frequent movement between firms gives British managers a wider industrial perspective. At the same time, however, it is bound to lower identification with, and commitment to, the employing firms. The lack of provision of structural supports for worker loyalty and commitment by the employing firm, the greater managerial turnover and the traditional union rejection of responsibility for enterprise competitiveness make it unlikely that the hoped for increases in employee involvement will materialise in the near future.

Table 3.2 provides a summary, in systematic form, of the impact of the institutional environment on the development and current structure of British and German business organisations.

Conclusions

The above analyses have shown that the British and German business systems possess sufficient stability and distinctiveness to merit the application of this concept. But there is a much greater looseness of fit between the elements of the British system which, as Knights et al. (Chapter 9 in this volume) point out, leaves it much more vulnerable to 'becoming unlocked'. The tight integration of

Table 3.2 *Impact on business organisation*

	Britain	Germany
Development and structure of firms		
Transition to managerial enterprise	Late	Early
Development of modern industries	Late	Early
Degree of vertical integration	Medium	High
Degree of structural rationalisation	Low to medium	High
Degree of centralisation	Low	High
Owner control	Low	LEs: low
		SMEs: High
Emphasis on technological innovation	Low to medium	High
Incidence of conglomerates	High	Low
Market organisation		
Degree of polarisation between large and SMEs	High	Low
Degree of horizontal inter-firm cooperation	Low	LEs: medium
		SMEs: High
Reliance on personal networks	Low	Low
Reliance on institutionalised networks	Low	High
Coordination and control systems		
Compartmentalisation of business units	High	Low
Delegation to middle management	High	Low
Granting of shop-floor work autonomy	Medium	High
Managerial style:		
large firms	Facilitative	Facilitative
SMEs	–	paternalist/ autocratic
Employment system and personnel procedures		
Development of internal labour markets	Medium	Medium
Development of employee competences	Low	High
Degree of employment stability	Medium	High
Degree of employee commitment/ involvement:		
workers	Low	High
managers	Medium	High

elements in the German case, conversely, make the system much more stable and able to withstand the potential dislocating effects of changes in markets and technology, as demonstrated by Sorge (1991: 181) for the mechanical engineering industry.

The identification of such national business systems has been undertaken by focusing on constituent structures at a high level of

92 *European business systems*

generality and does, therefore, not preclude the existence of diversity within these systems. In the German case, the dual structure of large vertically integrated corporations on the one side and owner-managed SMEs on the other was seen as characterised by more common than divergent features and thus deemed to be part of the same system. In both Germany and Britain there exists also considerable diversity along sectoral and regional lines. This is more pronounced in the British case, due to the absence of homogenising national regulatory frameworks. The national business system should be seen as a dominant pattern (Sorge, 1991: 183) which accommodates a measure of sectoral/regional variety. It is impossible to understand the success/failure of a region (see Saxenian's (1989) analysis of the Cambridge high-tech industry) or sector (Sorge and Maurice, 1990) without consideration of the overarching national business system.

The two business systems have been portrayed as polar opposites in all their fundamental components. German firms have been described as being embedded in an institutional framework, which provides them with multiple support structures and gives them access to capital, human resources and technical know-how on very favourable terms, as well as encouraging them to combine these resources in a highly productive way. British firms, in contrast, have been described as institutionally isolated and hence more reliant on internal resources which are often lacking in both quantitative and qualitative terms. Structural isolation of British firms has long been recognised as a resource-depleting influence on the business system. A long history of reform projects to remedy this situation exists, but only very partial institutional change has been achieved to date.

It will be obvious from this evaluation that the sometimes asserted functional equivalence of different business systems (Maurice et al., 1980), i.e. the claim that these systems merely constitute different ways of reaching the same final goals, is rejected by this analysis. The analysis offered by Porter (1990) and Whitley (1991), that institutional environments, shaping business systems, give different nations a competitive advantage in different industries, is more persuasive. Thus the combination and flexible utilisation of highly skilled workers/advanced technology and engineering skill/high R & D intensity is said to give German firms an edge in the machine tool and car industries, whereas British firms, according to Porter (1990), fare better where mass production of standardised products, supported by marketing skill, is required, such as in food and drinks or, less spectacularly, in industrial segments such as electronics and data processing, where the continuity from craft worker to engineer is less compelling (Sorge, 1991: 176).

But this argument is no longer as persuasive as it was in the recent past. The changes in the international division of labour, the greatly intensified competition and market volatility and the radical advances in several core technologies in recent decades have all acted to erode the boundaries between industries and undermine the plausibility of the mass/customised production distinction. Diversified quality production (Sorge and Streeck, 1988) and associated human resources and technology management requirements are gradually confronting all industrial sectors and call for more homogeneous management adjustment strategies across sectoral boundaries. The implications of this for British policymakers have now been widely recognised. But unless there is more widespread recognition of the social embeddedness of business systems, and reform becomes less piecemeal, success will continue to elude them.

References

Allen, C.S. (1987) 'Germany. Competing Communitarianisms', in G. Lodge and E. Vogel (eds), *Ideology and National Competitiveness: an Analysis of Nine Countries.* Boston: Harvard Business School Press.

Altmann, N. and Sauer, D. (eds) (1989) *Systemishe Rationalisierung und Zulieferindustrie.* Frankfurt: Campus.

Berghahn, V.R. (1986) *The Americanisation of West German Industry 1945–1973.* Leamington Spa/New York: Berg.

Best, M.H. (1990) *The New Competition. Institutions of Industrial Restructuring.* Cambridge: Polity Press.

Best, M.H. and Humphries, J. (1987) 'The City and Industrial Decline', in B. Elbaum and W. Lazonick (eds), *The Decline of the British Economy.* Oxford: Clarendon Press. pp. 223–39.

Bosch, G. (1988) 'Der bundesdeutsche Arbeitsmarkt im internationalem Vergleich: Eurosklerose oder "Modell Deutschland"', *WSI-Mitteilungen,* 3: 176–85.

Cable, J. and Dirrheimer, M.J. (1983) 'Hierarchies and Markets. An Empirical Test of the Multidivisional Hypothesis in West Germany', *International Journal of Industrial Organization,* 1: 43–62.

Campbell, A., Sorge, A. and Warner, M. (1989) *Microelectronic Product Applications in Great Britain and West Germany. Strategies, Competence and Training.* Aldershot: Gower.

Casey, B. (1986) 'The Dual Apprenticeship System and the Recruitment and Retention of Young Persons in West Germany', *British Journal of Industrial Relations,* 24 (1): 63–82.

Chandler, A.D. and Daems, H. (1980) 'Introduction', in A.D. Chandler and H. Daems (eds), *Managerial Hierarchies.* Cambridge, MA: Harvard University Press.

Child, J. and Kieser, A. (1979) 'Organization and Managerial Roles in British and

94   *European business systems*

West German Companies: an Examination of the Culture-free Thesis', in C.J. Lammers and D.J. Hickson (eds), *Organizations Alike and Unlike*. London: Routledge and Kegan Paul.

Dascher, O. (1974) 'Probleme der Konzernverwaltung', in H. Mommsen, D. Petzina and B. Weisbrod (eds), *Industrielles System und Politische Entwicklung in der Weimarer Republik*. Düsseldorf: Droste Verlag. pp. 127–35.

Doran, A. (1984) *Craft Enterprises in Britain and Germany*. London: Anglo-German Foundation.

Dyas, G. and Thanheiser, H.T. (1976) *The Emerging European Enterprise*. London: Macmillan.

Dyson, K. (1986) 'The State, Banks and Industry: the West German Case', in A. Cox (ed.), *The State, Finance and Industry*. Brighton: Wheatsheaf.

Edwards, J.S.S. and Fischer, K. (1991) *Banks, Finance and Investment in West Germany since 1970*. Discussion Paper No. 497, Centre for Economic Policy Research, London, January 1991.

Edwards, P.K. (1987) *Managing the Factory*. Oxford: Basil Blackwell.

Elbaum, B. and Lazonick, W. (eds) (1987) *The Decline of the British Economy*. Oxford: Clarendon Press.

Finlay, P. (1981) 'Overmanning: Germany vs. Britain', *Management Today*, August: 43–7.

Gallie, D. (1978) *In Search of the New Working Class: Automation and Social Integration within the Capitalist Enterprise*. Cambridge: CUP.

Gamble, A. (1985) *Britain in Decline*. 2nd edn, Macmillan.

Grant, W. (1986) *Why Employer Organization Matters*. Working Paper No. 46, University of Warwick.

Hall, P.A. (1987) 'The State and Economic Decline', in Elbaum and Lazonick (1987). pp. 266–302.

Hannah, L. (1976a) *The Rise of the Corporate Economy*. London: Methuen.

Hannah, L. (1976b) *Management Strategy and Business Development*. London: Macmillan.

Hannah, L. (1980) 'Visible and Invisible Hands in Great Britain', in Chandler and Daems.

Herrigel, G. (1989) 'Industrial Order and the Politics of Industrial Change: Mechanical Engineering', in P.J. Katzenstein (ed.), *Industry and Politics in West Germany*. Ithaca, NY: Cornell University Press.

Hirst, P. and Zeitlin, J. (eds) (1989) *Reversing Industrial Decline*. Oxford/New York: Berg.

Hirst, P. and Zeitlin, J. (1990) *Flexible Specialization versus Post-Fordism: Theory, Evidence and Policy Implications*. Working Paper, Birkbeck Centre for Public Policy, London.

Hofstede, G. (1980) *Culture's Consequences*. London: Sage.

Homburg, H. (1991) 'The "Human Factor" and the Limits of Rationalization: Personnel Management Strategies and the Rationalization Movement in German Industry between the Wars', in S. Tolliday and J. Zeitlin (eds), *The Power to Manage? Employers and Industrial Relations in Comparative Historical Perspective*. London/New York: Routledge.

Horovitz, J. (1980) *Top Management Control in Europe*. New York: St Martin's Press.

Hughes, A. (1990) *Industrial Concentration and the Small Business Sector in the UK: the 1980s in Historical Perspective*. Working Paper No. 5, Small Business

Research Centre, University of Cambridge, August 1990.

Janoski, T. (1990) *The Political Economy of Unemployment. Active Labour Market Policy in West Germany and the United States*. Berkeley, CA: University of California Press.

Kern, H. and Schumann, M. (1984) *Das Ende de Arbeitsteilung?* Munich: C.H. Beck.

Kocka, J. (1971) 'Family and Bureaucracy in German Industrial Management, 1850–1914', *Business History Review*, 45: 133–56.

Kocka, J. (1975a) *Unternehmer in der Deutschen Industrialisierung*. Göttingen: Vandenhoek und Ruprecht.

Kocka, J. (1975b) 'Expansion – Integration – Diversifikation. Wachstumsstrategien industrieller Grossunternehmen in Deutschland vor 1914', in H. Winkel (ed.), *Vom Kleingewerbe zum Grossbetrieb*. Berlin: Dunker und Humblot. pp. 203–26.

Kocka, J. (1980) 'The Rise of the Modern Industrial Enterprise in Germany', in Chandler and Daems.

Kocka, J. and Siegrist, H. (1979) 'Die hundert groessten deutschen Industrie-unternehmen im spaeten 19. und fruehen 20. Jahrhundert', in N. Horn and J. Kocka (eds), *Law and the Formation of the Big Enterprise in the 19th and Early 20th Century*. Göttingen: Vandenhoek und Ruprecht.

Kotthoff, H. (1981) *Betriebsraete und Betriebliche Herrschaft*. Frankfurt: Campus.

Landes, D. (1969) *The Unbound Prometheus. Technological Change and Industrial Development*. Cambridge: Cambridge University Press.

Lane, C. (1989) *Management and Labour in Europe. The Industrial Enterprise in Germany, Britain and France*. Aldershot: Edward Elgar.

Lawrence, P. (1980) *Managers and Management in West Germany*. London: Croom Helm.

Levine, A.L. (1967) *Industrial Retardation in Britain, 1880–1914*. London: Weidenfeld & Nicolson.

Maitland, I. (1983) *The Causes of Industrial Disorder: a Comparison of a British and a German Factory*. London: Routledge and Kegan Paul.

Marsden, D.W. and Ryan, P. (1991) 'Initial Training, Labour Market Structures and Public Policy: Intermediate Skills in British and German Industry', in P. Ryan (ed.), *International Comparisons of Vocational Education and Training for Intermediate Skills*. London: The Falmer Press. pp. 251–85.

Maurice, M., Sorge, A. and Warner, M. (1980) 'Societal Differences in Organising Manufacturing Units', *Organization Studies* 1. 63–91.

Mowery, D. (1987) 'Industrial Research, 1900–1950', in Elbaum and Lazonick (1987). pp. 189–222.

NEDO (National Economic Development Office) (1987) *The Making of Managers*. Report on behalf of the MSC, NEDC and BIM. London: NEDO.

Plumpe, W. (1991) 'Employers' Associations and Industrial Relations in Postwar Germany: the Case of Ruhr Heavy Industry', in S. Tolliday and J. Zeitlin (eds) (1991) *The Power to Manage? Employers and Industrial Relations in Comparative Historical Perspective*. London: Routledge. pp. 176–203.

Pollard, S. (1965) *The Genesis of Modern Management*. London: Edward Arnold.

Porter, M.E. (1990) *The Competative Advantage of Nations*. London: Macmillan.

Prais, S. (1981) *Productivity and Industrial Structure: a Statistical Study of Manufacturing Industry in Britain, Germany and the US*. Cambridge: Cambridge University Press.

Prais, S. and Wagner, K. (1988) 'Productivity and Management: the Training of

96   *European business systems*

Foremen in Britain and Germany', *National Institute Economic Review* (February): pp. 34–47.

Sabel, C., Herrigel, G., Deeg, R. and Kazis, R. (1987) *Regional Prosperities Compared: Massachusetts and Baden-Württemberg in the 1980s.* Discussion Paper of the Research Unit Labour Market and Employment, Wissenschaftszentrum Berlin.

Sabel, C. and Zeitlin, J. (1985) 'Historical Alternatives to Mass Production: Politics, Markets and Technology in Nineteenth Century Industrialization', *Past and Present*, 108: 133–76.

Saxenian, A.L. (1989) 'The Cheshire Cat's Grin: Innovation, Regional Development and the Cambridge Case', *Economy and Society*, 18 (4): 448–77.

Schumann, M., Bäthge-Kinsky, V., Neumann, U. and Springer, R. (1990) *Breite Diffusion der Neuen Produktionskonzepte – Zoegerlicher Wandel der Neuen Arbeitsstrukturen.* Zwischenbericht, Soziologisches Forschungsinstitut Göttingen.

Scott, J. (1985) *Corporations, Classes and Capitalism.* London: Hutchinson.

Siegrist, H. (1980) 'Deutsche Grossunternehmen vom späten 19. Jahrhundert bis zur Weimarer Republik', *Geschichte und Gesellschaft*, 6 (1): 60–102.

Simon, W. (1976) *Macht und Herrschaft der Unternehmerverbaende.* Opladen.

Sisson, K. (1987) *The Management of Collective Bargaining.* Oxford: Blackwell.

Sorge, A. (1991) 'Strategic Fit and the Societal Effect: Interpreting Cross-National Comparisons of Technology, Organization and Human Resources', *Organization Studies*, 12 (2): 161–90.

Sorge, A. and Warner, M. (1986) *Comparative Factory Organisation, An Anglo-German Comparison of Management and Manpower in Manufacturing.* Aldershot: Gower.

Sorge, A., Hartmann, G., Warner, M. and Nicholas, I. (1983) *Microelectronics and Manpower in Manufacturing. Applications of Computer Numerical Control in Britain and West Germany.* Aldershot: Gower.

Sorge, A. and Maurice, M. (1990) 'The Societal Effect in Strategies and Competitiveness of Machine-tool Manufacturers in France and West Germany', *International Journal of Human Resources Management*, 1 (2): 141–72.

Sorge, A. and Streeck, W (1988) 'Industrial Relations and Technical Change: the case for an extended perspective', in R. Hyman and W. Streeck (eds) *New Technology and Industrial Relations.* Oxford: Basil Blackwell. pp. 19–47.

Streeck, W. (1984) 'Co-determination: the Fourth Decade', in B. Wilpert and A. Sorge (eds), *International Perspectives on Organizational Democracy.* Chichester: John Wiley.

Streeck, W. (1986) *The Territorial Organization of Interests and the Logics of Associative Action. The Case of Artisanal Interest Organization in West Germany.* Discussion Paper, Research Unit Labour Market and Employment, Wissenschaftszentrum Berlin.

Streeck, W. (1990) 'On the Institutional Conditions of Diversified Quality Production'. Unpublished Research Paper, University of Wisconsin, Madison, July 1990.

Trebilcock, C. (1981) *The Industrialization of the Continental Powers 1780–1914.* London: Longman.

van Tulder, R. and Junne, G. (1988) *European Multinationals in Core Technologies.* Chichester: John Wiley.

Weimer, S. (1990) 'Federal Republic of Germany', in W. Sengenberger, G.W. Loveman and M.J. Piore (eds), *The Re-emergence of Small Enterprises.*

Industrial Restructuring in Industrialised Countries. Geneva: International Institute of Labour Studies.

Whitley, R. (1991) *Societies, Firms and Markets: the Social Structuring of Market Economies*. Paper prepared for the 10th EGOS Colloquium, Vienna, 15–18 July 1991.

Whitson, C. (1989) 'Rationalizing Foundries', in S. Tailby and C. Whitson (eds), *Manufacturing Change: Industrial Relations and Restructuring*. Oxford: Basil Blackwell.

Wilks, S. and Wright, M. (eds) (1987) *Comparative Government and Industry Relations*. Oxford: Clarendon Press.

Williams, K., Williams, J. and Haslam, C. (1990) 'The Hollowing Out of British Manufacturing and its Implications for Policy', *Economy and Society*, 19 (4): 456–90.

Wood, S. (ed.) (1989) *The Transformation of Work?* London: Unwin Hyman.

[12]

OVERVIEW:
CAPITAL AND CONTROL
City–industry relations

Martha Prevezer

Better and more widely diffused knowledge is a remedy for that excessive confidence which causes a violent expansion of credit and rise of prices; and it is also a remedy for that excessive distrust that follows. One of the chief sources of disturbance is the action of the general public in providing funds for joint-stock companies. Having insufficient technical knowledge, many of them trust just where they should not: they swell the demand for building materials and machinery and other things, just at the time at which far-sighted people with special knowledge detect coming danger...

(Alfred Marshall, *Money, Credit and Commerce* (1923))

INTRODUCTION

In assessing the relationship between the financial sector and industrial sector within a country, looking exclusively at the structure of financing and its cost omits much that is significant. In particular the financial sector plays an important role in the control of companies, as an intermediary for other share-holders, and as a collector and storehouse of information about companies. This intermediary role occurs through the connection between the willingness to lend or take equity stakes in a company and the control that such creditors or owners subsequently have over what happens within the company. In the context of equity-holding, the debate has been over the different connections between ownership and control, their separation to varying extents depending on the strength of the stock market, and on the effect such separation has on different types of investment. In Chapter 12, Derek Morris contrasts 'inside control', where concentrated ownership confers control, with 'outside control' where there is dispersed ownership and no overlap of owners and managers, and control comes through a more open stock market and tradeability of the companies.

193

CITY AND INDUSTRY

We develop the idea that the type of contractual relationship that is developed between the shareholder or the bank and the company is significant in shaping observed patterns of shareholding or bank lending to the corporate sector. It is the nature of the contractual relationship which is built into the institution, and how this evolves, which has contributed to the perceived characteristics of dependence or otherwise of companies on either markets or banks. Such an approach provides an overview for the more detailed discussion of different ownership and control structures, and their influence on the stock market, which is developed in the chapter by Derek Morris.

This chapter also provides a brief overview of some of the main trends in the financing of companies that underlie the debates that are examined in more detail elsewhere in the book. We look at various aspects of the capital structure of non-financial companies in the UK and US, Germany and Japan. It has been popular practice to distinguish between the UK and US whose companies' financing structures are thought to be more 'market oriented' than Japan's and Germany's, where it is thought that company financing is more dependent on the banks deriving from closer ties between the banking and company sectors. We examine the validity of this dichotomy and look at changes in company capital structures over the 1980s through a variety of measures. It brings out how far differences between countries in their corporate control structures are reflected in debt and equity structures and levels of dividend pay-out. If providers of finance have better information channels, they may be prepared to advance funds more cheaply and for longer periods, thereby permitting higher debt–equity ratios. If firms have long-term relationships with others in a supply chain, as happens frequently in Japan, this may result in larger outstanding claims on one another in the form of trade credits extended and received and this will again increase some measures of the ratio of debt to equity. The funding of employees' separation payments in Japan and pension entitlements in Germany also influences debt–equity ratios depending on whether such implicit or explicit claims on the firm are regarded as debt or equity. So financial ratios, as well as telling us something about the relative cost of finance, are also influenced by the corporate control structures that are looked at in detail in the next chapter.

Finally, we look at the performance and competitiveness of the UK's financial sector, in terms of its growth and productivity in comparison with UK manufacturing, and where its strengths lie in competing with other financial centres. The question is then addressed of whether the particular strengths and expertise developed by this sector, and for which London is famous as a financial centre, have proved beneficial to those parts of the domestic economy most reliant on local sources of finance. The argument here is that, whereas London has excelled above most financial centres in its innovativeness and introduction of new products and services, these have for the most part been geared towards the international global economy, and similar sorts of expertise

OVERVIEW

and local information networks have not existed for smaller companies without access to the international capital markets. It is in these areas that the financial sector has been failing with regard to its support for domestic and smaller-scale industry.

INFORMATION AND CONTROL IN FINANCING COMPANIES

We can think of contractual relationships along a spectrum from specific 'classical' contracts which are legalistic with clauses intended to cover most fore-seeable contingencies, to longer-term more 'obligational' or 'implicit' contracts which do not stipulate exactly what their terms are, where the relationship is assumed to continue over a longer period of time, and where the contract itself is a sign of commitment with the precise terms of the relationship negotiable. Broadly speaking, the Anglo-Saxon world has developed a system making greater use of classical contracts in many areas of business, whereas Japan has developed more obligational relations in many spheres of transactions. In order to have relational or obligational contracts, information flows have to be effective and management time must be invested in their establishment.

It was Coase (1937) who first thought of the firm as a system of contracts which, by reducing transactions costs, improved on pure market transactions between individual agents. Transactions costs are important in the relationship between the provider of finance and the firm for two main reasons – infor-mation asymmetries and agency problems leading to moral hazard. Asymmetry of information arises whenever the firm has better information of the details of investment projects and their likely success than an outsider. For an introductory discussion of asymmetric information and the problems arising from it, see Estrin and Laidler (1994). This is coupled with the agency problem arising from the split between owners and managers. The monitoring by owners and the different paths of expansion that managers will take under different ownership structures have been analysed by Jensen and Meckling (1976). It will be hard for an owner who is an outsider to monitor what uses are made of the finance provided; and because decisions about investment inherently involve uncertainty and long payback periods, so the outsider to the firm will find it hard to ascertain whether or not the outcome of the investment has been due to good management.

How do these general observations fit in with the actual institutions that provide finance in the different countries? Different types of contract underlie the relationships between market and company and between bank and company. We look first at the nature of shareholding and the different obligations and rights that it confers in the different systems.

195

CITY AND INDUSTRY

THE NATURE OF SHAREHOLDING IN THE UK, JAPAN AND GERMANY

To a greater extent than with Japanese and German shareholding, the UK shareholder is the owner with ultimate responsibility and rights. In principle it is to the shareholder that managers are accountable and shareholders are entitled to the residual earnings in return for which they are the ultimate risk-bearers (Dimsdale 1994). The system has evolved to cope with this by individual shareholders holding a wide portfolio of shares and consequently reducing risk. In addition, the shares are freely tradeable on the stock market. The consequence is very low concentrations of holdings of shares in any one company by any particular shareholder, even the large institutional shareholders. Shareholders have the right to appoint managers by voting at the annual general meeting. The chairman of the board and non-executive directors on the board are meant to represent and safeguard shareholders' interests in the running of the company. In practice this is not very tightly controlled. The recent recommendations of the Cadbury Committee on corporate governance were intended to strengthen these positions and thereby increase the effectiveness of shareholder representation and lessen managerial autonomy. Another feature of UK shareholding in particular is the equality of shareholder status; thus the small shareholder has equivalent rights as the large, and access to the same information. It is expressly forbidden that groups of shareholders should have privileged access to 'insider' information. Shareholders are all equally outsiders. One of the drawbacks of this is the comparative insulation of shareholders from the type of information they would need to be able to monitor managerial performance more directly. This accentuates the asymmetry of information referred to above, where in effect managers have access to much more detailed and pertinent strategic information of which shareholders are by definition deprived. Accompanying the exclusion from information is the moral hazard problem of not being able to judge whether the agent, in this case the manager, is acting in the shareholders' interests. A further feature in the UK system is that three-quarters of holding of equity is done by institutional shareholders – pension funds, insurance companies and the like. These have their own constitutions which demand that they serve their pension-holders' or trustees' interests above all. They can best do this by diversifying their portfolios and spreading the risk from any one particular shareholding. It is not in any individual pension fund's interest that the managers of the fund become too involved in either accumulating information about any one company or intervening with the management of the company on the basis of acquired information. In terms of Hirschmann's choice between exit or voice,[1] it is more sensible to exit by selling the shareholding than to voice misgivings and try to change management or management strategy directly.

OVERVIEW

The countervailing force in the UK system is the strength of the stock market and the development, through the market's openness and liquidity, of what has come to be called the market for corporate control. This means that not only are particular shares freely tradeable but whole companies may be bought and sold. This makes companies more sensitive to their own share prices than they otherwise would be, and in effect the institutions or shareholders can express approval or disapproval for any particular management strategy by buying or selling shares and its consequent effect on the share price, to which management are attuned. This mechanism provides a means whereby share-holders indirectly monitor the activities of managers. Share prices therefore respond quickly to news or information, and when the market reflects all avail-able information in the prices, it is said to be informationally efficient. In terms of our original distinction in the kind of contract that is established, these contracts are classical with the rights to sell shares at any time and no constraints or obligations posed on that right to sell.

Many of these features of UK shareholding stand in contrast to Japanese shareholding practices. Whereas the structure of equity-holding in terms of its split between institutions and household shareholdings is roughly equivalent in the ratio of 3/4 to 1/4 in both countries, the nature of institutional share-holding has some significant differences in Japan from practices in the UK. Such shareholders are more likely to be insiders with some kind of contact with the company whose shares they own. These contacts include being a bank, a supplier, another company where there are cross-shareholdings by each company of the others' shares, or they may belong to the *keiretsu* group which is influential in financing the company. These contacts may provide infor-mation. The counterpart to this is that trading is much more constrained. It has been estimated that during the 1980s something like two-thirds of equity was in the form of stable shareholding – *antei kabunishi* – which is distinct from interlocking shareholding – *kabushiki mochiai*. These stable share-holdings amount to an implicit agreement not to sell the shares to third parties or at least to consult the management when wishing to do so. It does not prevent the trading of shares, but certainly mutes it (Masuyama 1994). Accordingly, the most actively traded shares in Japan have been those of the household sector, the opposite of the UK case. Takeover activity has been much less than in the UK and there have been no hostile takeovers. The cost of such stability in shareholding has been the lower rate of return on equity that Japanese shares have given to investors. Management has been freer to pursue higher growth and market-share strategies at the expense of the rate of profit on investment. However, there will be increasing pressure for the market to become more open, for shares to become more tradeable and hence for the return on equity to rise to levels equivalent to those in the West. Precise comparisons between such measures as the rate of return on equity in Japan and the UK or US are fraught by differences in accounting conventions which affect price–earnings ratios and such measures (Corbett 1994). However, it is

CITY AND INDUSTRY

the balance between the competing interests of shareholder and manager that are likely to change. Another feature of Japanese balance of interests is the greater obligations that are built into company structure towards their employees. This again attenuates shareholder rights in considering the growth path that a company should adopt. Lifetime employment, substantial in-house training, lower mobility of employees and management between companies (but not within companies) than is found in the UK and US, all are part of the system of obligations within companies towards employees. These sorts of contract that exist between company and employees are of the relational, implicit type referred to above (for discussion see Odagiri 1992).

German shareholding does not have as many explicit constraints on it as does its Japanese counterpart. There is no equivalent to stable shareholding agreements, and ownership rights can be sold in a fairly liquid market. However, there are greater barriers than exist in the UK to the transfer of control over a company (Franks and Mayer 1990). These are partly enshrined in the ability to issue non-voting shares so that capital can be raised without ceding control. The banks often have the proxy voting rights for shares held with them. They have to state how they are going to vote and shareholders are informed of their intentions and they must fulfil those intentions. Such proxy voting rights mean that a greater concentration of voting power can be built up through the banks. They may find themselves in a position of being able to block certain decisions and the thwarting of some takeovers has followed from the build-up of that sort of power. Another feature built into the German system that curtails shareholders' rights in comparison with those in the UK is the co-determination system whereby employees' rights are enshrined in company statutes. This affects the structure of boards which we discuss below; it also widens the formal accountability of managers to include employees as well as shareholders. This may in practice not amount to substantial curtailment of managerial prerogative; however, it marks more than a symbolic difference in terms of attitude towards the sovereignty of the shareholder.

THE ROLE OF THE BANKS AND THE MONITORING FUNCTION

The counterpart to having a weaker market mechanism for transferring control rights over a company, as is the case in Germany and Japan, is a more informal but nevertheless substantive network of information gathering and more direct monitoring and intervention in the managers' sphere of influence. The banks perform a central role in this. The main bank in Japan or the Hausbank in Germany, although not having an exclusive banking relationship with its client company, will have built up knowledge about the working and competencies of a company and there is again more of an implicit longer-term relational agreement emphasizing the continuous nature of the relationship (Schneider-Lenne 1994). Banks hold equity stakes in companies, although these are limited to 5 per cent of equity in any one company in Japan and in Germany

OVERVIEW

came to 12 per cent of equity in 1988. They also have a role as lender. As the following section indicates, this in fact in terms of lending as a source of finance for new investment has been more substantial in Japan than elsewhere. Banks also have seats on company boards, in particular on supervisory boards in Germany and they form part of the *keiretsu* in Japan. In addition to the proxy voting rights mentioned above, these features create a concentration of information about companies within the banking sector allied with substantial influence through various channels. This does not mean that the banks dictate activity in the industrial sector in those countries. It does mean that companies may find themselves subject to greater pressure from that quarter instead of from the stock market and via the share price, as happens in the UK. This divergence in the systems of governance partly reflects the structure of ownership, especially when it comes to the smaller and medium-sized companies. Far fewer of the German *Mittelstand*, that body of medium-sized companies on which the strength of the German economy has depended, are publicly quoted companies than their UK equivalent-sized counterparts. It is not surprising therefore that the influence of the stock market should be replaced by other mechanisms, in particular for these medium-sized companies which fits their ownership structure. Aoki (1989) has written of the delegation to the main bank in Japan of the monitoring function by the shareholders and sees the phenomenon of overborrowing in the interests of the bank as a type of agency fee for the bank for doing so.

CHANGES IN THE UK BANK–INDUSTRY RELATIONS OVER THE 1980s

There have been major changes in the UK financial sector, mainly through deregulation, that have affected the way that the UK banks have done business with various parts of the corporate sector (McWilliams and Sentance 1994). The major changes in the financial system included:

- the abolition of foreign-exchange controls in 1979 widening opportunities for lending;
- the removal of the corset in 1980 which had restricted the interest-bearing eligible liabilities of banks;
- the abolition of hire purchase controls on consumer credit;
- the ability of the building societies from 1983 to raise funds through certificates of deposit and further deregulation in 1986 in the Building Societies Act;
- the entry of the clearing banks into the mortgage market;
- the breakdown of informal rules preventing equity withdrawal.

In addition, 'Big Bang' brought major changes from 1986 in the structure of the provision of financial services and the margins on those services. The changes affecting business most acutely have been the globalization and liberalization

CITY AND INDUSTRY

of financial markets whereby a wide range of new financial instruments became available (such as swaps, options, convertibles). These instruments plus much easier direct access for large companies to the developing Eurobond markets and commercial paper markets, coupled with the internal development of the Treasury functions inside large companies, have meant that the relationship banking which did exist between large UK companies and their banks became less necessary from the companies' point of view. For the banks, their business shifted in composition as a consequence of the financial deregulatory measures listed above, and their proportion of lending to the personal sector increased (from 14 per cent of total bank lending in 1980 to 28 per cent in 1991) and the share of lending to business fell from 70 per cent of total lending in 1980 to under 50 per cent by 1991.[2] To offset this decline in the share of lending going to business there was an increase in leasing and in lending to security dealers, which reflect the changes in method of companies obtaining finance rather than in the amount of finance available. Bank lending to business as a proportion of GDP continued to rise throughout the 1980s from 23 per cent in 1980 to 49 per cent in 1990. However, this has to be seen in the light of bank lending forming a shrinking proportion of large companies' liabilities in the second half of the 1980s, replaced by their issuing commercial paper and other methods of raising finance. It became the case in the late 1980s that large companies could raise finance more cheaply through direct access to capital markets than the cost of borrowing from banks. Below we analyse companies' balance sheets and chart their main sources of finance.

One of the consequences of these changes in the structure of bank lending was increased pressure on banks' profitability. Partly due to the liberalization measures listed above, greater competition in the 1980s squeezed net interest margins, in particular on domestic lending. Margins (interest income as a proportion of interest-earning assets) and spreads (the difference between the rate paid on interest-bearing assets and on deposits) on domestic lending declined. Margins fell from 7 per cent in 1980 to 4 per cent in 1990. This occurred mainly in two periods: between 1980 and 1983 as interest rates fell, margins declined although spreads increased; between 1987 and 1990 there were lower spreads due to greater competition for loans, in turn owing to lower margins on mortgage lending and on lending to large companies and due to changes in the deposit mix on the liabilities side (*Bank of England Quarterly Bulletin*, November 1991). In addition costs did not decline, as retail branch networks have been maintained and there was a greater reliance on labour-intensive fee-generating activities. The broad strategy of the banks was to focus on personal sector customers as large companies looked directly to the markets to satisfy their financial needs. This was despite the fact that banks' most stable sources of non-interest fee income continued to be fees and commissions from the corporate sector.

Whilst bank business with large companies became less of a priority, the number of small businesses registered for VAT rose dramatically during the

OVERVIEW

1980s. The banks responded to this by expanding its services to small and growing companies. By 1991, 95 per cent of NatWest's commercial customers were small businesses (having a turnover of less than £1 million per annum). Barclays quoted a figure of 80 per cent for the proportion of business customers in 1992 with a turnover of less than £100,000 (McWilliams and Sentance 1994). Small businesses are higher risk and need more servicing, both factors contributing to increasing costs to the banks. In effect, banks provided loan capital to small businesses at rates which, whilst higher than those charged to larger customers, were below those charged by venture capital companies for similar sorts of risk. The Treasury and Civil Service Select Committee of 1991–2 on Banking Codes[3] criticized the banks for insufficient monitoring of companies' performance, making little use of local information which might have been gathered. The committee pointed to the centralization of decision-making in banks with the erosion of authority at the local branch level. It also pointed to the heavy weighting of short-term loan finance and very little use of longer-term loan or equity finance, which was not desired by either companies or banks. Banks have come in for criticism for inadequate assessment of the risk involved in their lending and for adopting too short-term a view of companies' prospects. More information on business prospects and managerial ability coupled with more imagination concerning the forms of finance used may be needed. However, small businesses have to be willing to disclose information and cede some control in exchange for longer-term and more stable financing.

The net effect has been a greater reliance by the banks on higher-risk lending to smaller businesses, which themselves are more exposed to cyclical pressures. This was coupled with the expansion of bank lending to the personal sector and the erosion of longer-term relationships with their more traditional larger corporate customers due to competitive pressures and liberalization of capital markets.

The question of finance for small business has been a recurring theme in the question of Britain's economic performance since at least the time of the Macmillan Committee in 1931 which had identified a considerable finance gap. Many of the features of the financial structure of small businesses are well known – high levels of trade credit, low proportions of equity in total debt and heavy dependence upon short-term borrowing from the banks. With these arrangements the problems of small business are inevitably compounded in times of recession – in 1993 as in 1931. Hughes (1994) has suggested that the situation has probably improved for small businesses in the 1980s as some of the recommendations of the Wilson Committee in 1979 have been implemented – including the Loan Guarantee Scheme (1981) and the Business Expansion Scheme (1983). In addition, new equity markets have been established and the venture capital industry has expanded rapidly. New business start-ups have proliferated during the 1980s, but the death rate is considerable. Hughes, however, points to problem areas remaining in high technology or

CITY AND INDUSTRY

otherwise innovative manufacturing where finance gaps may still exist. His own suggestion is for clubs of small firms to form Mutual Guarantee Schemes which are quite widespread in mainland Europe. These can be used to reduce problems of informational asymmetry in arranging loans as well as encouraging industrial coordination.

CAPITAL STRUCTURE: A COMPARISON OF GERMANY, JAPAN AND THE UK

Are these differences described above in the relative importance given to shareholders, banks and other stakeholders (such as employees and suppliers) in the different systems reflected in either companies' capital structure or in the pay-out ratios that we observe? There are a number of differences in dividend pay-out ratios, debt–equity ratios and the structure of liabilities and assets on companies' balance sheets that suggest that these differences in the balance of power between different institutions or in conventions are reflected in the way companies organize their financing. Higher dividend pay-outs, more contested takeover activity and higher rates of return on equity may be evidence of greater accountability to the stock market.

Dividend pay-out ratios have been lower in Japan, Germany and the US than in the UK (see Table 1). There are several possible explanations. One is that fear of takeover induces higher distributions. More specifically, pay-outs may be a signal of commitment to some minimum standard of performance, and

Table 1 Ratio of dividends to gross income of non-financial corporations (percentage)

Year	UK	US	Japan
1974	–	24	17
1975	–	20	18
1976	–	20	17
1977	36	19	16
1978	37	20	15
1979	41	20	13
1980	45	23	14
1981	45	22	14
1982	49	25	15
1983	48	23	13
1984	45	21	12
1985	46	20	10
1986	34	22	12
1987	39	22	10
1988	42	21	10
1989	41	28	–

Source: OECD Financial Statistics

OVERVIEW

failure to achieve that standard sends a bad signal to the market. Below, Derek Morris discusses the possibility that these signals 'jam' and the consequences of that happening. Higher pay-out ratios may also be a mechanism whereby better monitoring by investors of managers can occur. If managers are made to distribute earnings rather than retain them, it diminishes their autonomy and forces them back to the market for more funds than they otherwise would have needed. It provides an avenue whereby, indirectly, shareholders can obtain more information on investment plans and direction that a company is taking than they would otherwise have if distributions were lower.

This is not to suggest, however, that retained earnings are unimportant as a source of finance for new investment; they are particularly important in the UK, US and Germany (see Figure 1). The arguments made as to why retained earnings have assumed such a predominant position in financing for invest-ment in some ways diminish the force of the monitoring argument about high pay-out ratios. It is precisely because of the asymmetry of information about investment prospects for a particular firm where insiders understand the risks better than outsiders, that insiders (managers) prefer to rely on internal finance for riskier projects such as research and development which are particularly hard for outsiders to understand and assess. External financing is deemed unsuitable through posing too many constraints on the use to which the money is put, and managers prefer if possible to exercise their autonomy in areas where they feel the risk aversion and lack of information of investors will make the terms of

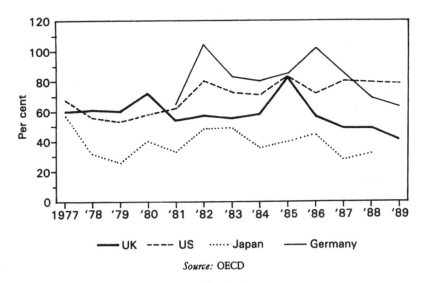

Source: OECD

Figure 11.1 Self-financing ratio.
Note: Germany: Issues of shares included in non-financial sources; break in German series in 1986

203

CITY AND INDUSTRY

external financing more onerous than the opportunity cost of using internal finance.

Lower self-financing and greater use of debt for financing new investment in Japan might also be consistent with this story, if banks are relatively better informed and are effectively insiders to managerial strategy (see Figure 2). Debt financing has been consistently higher in Japan than in the other countries. It has been argued that this use of bank borrowing may be an implicit form of monitoring that reduces the agency costs referred to above. Another distinction between Japanese financing ratios and those in the UK, US and Germany is the greater stability of financing proportions in Japan. There has been a more constant share of debt financing in particular (see Table 2). By contrast, in the other countries external finance has been used as a residual measure as needed, with considerable volatility in debt financing as a consequence. This difference may also be attributable to the banks having more of an insider role in Japan than elsewhere. In this respect at least, German use of bank financing resembles that of the UK more than that of Japan.

These features of corporate control are also reflected in companies' balance sheets. On the liabilities side, in the UK and US there seems to be a higher proportion of equity than in Germany and Japan (Figure 3). In comparisons with Germany this depends on how pension provisions are classified. Table 3 shows debt–equity ratios for Germany defining pension provisions as both debt and equity. They are debt-like having a fixed obligation for repayment at a

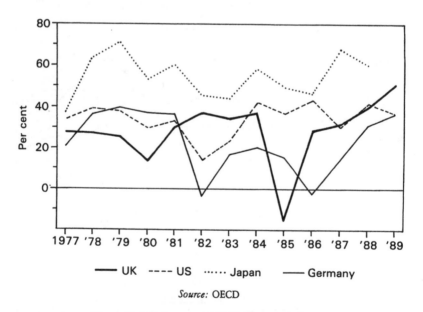

Source: OECD

Figure 11.2 Debt as a proportion of total sources.

Table 2 Sources of finance as a proportion of total sources

	UK		Germany		US		Japan	
	1977–80	*1981–9*	*1977–80*	*1981–9*	*1977–80*	*1981–9*	*1977–80*	*1981–9*
Debt	23.4	30.4	33.2	18.4	35.1	33.7	56.3	54.2
Of which short-term debt	22.9	21.3	–	–	22.0	10.8	42.2	32.4
Of which long-term debt	0.5	9.2	–	–	13.1	22.9	14.1	21.7
Share issues	9.1	13.2			3.6	–5.3	5.1	6.4
Internal sources	67.5	56.4	66.8	81.6	61.3	71.6	38.6	39.5

Source: OECD Financial Statistics

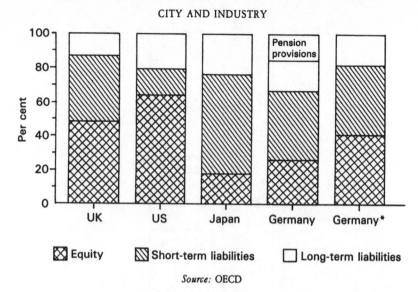

CITY AND INDUSTRY

☒ Equity   ☒ Short-term liabilities   ☐ Long-term liabilities

Source: OECD

Figure 11.3 Liabilities of non-financial companies as a proportion of total liabilities, 1977–89.
* Provisions are included as equity
NB: Japanese time period covered is 1977–88

Table 3 Debt–equity ratio of non-financial enterprises*

Year	Japan	US	UK	Germany Provisions classified as debt	Germany Provisions classified as equity
1974	–	0.56	–	–	–
1975	5.60	0.52	–	2.56	1.84
1976	5.72	0.50	–	2.62	1.85
1977	5.49	0.51	1.06	2.60	1.82
1978	5.49	0.50	1.08	2.68	1.84
1979	5.49	0.49	1.06	2.77	1.88
1980	5.16	0.48	1.06	3.02	1.92
1981	5.04	0.47	1.10	3.09	1.96
1982	5.02	0.47	1.13	3.06	1.89
1983	4.84	0.50	1.10	3.05	1.83
1984	4.77	0.56	1.09	3.00	1.76
1985	4.40	0.61	1.04	2.99	1.72
1986	4.22	0.67	1.04	2.90	1.63
1987	4.36	0.71	1.03	4.19	1.51
1988	4.19	0.76	1.03	4.25	1.52
1989	–	0.82	1.14	4.33	1.53

* Gross liabilities less equity as a proportion of equity
Source: OECD Financial Statement

OVERVIEW

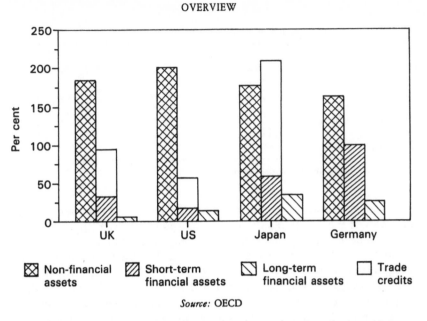

Source: OECD

Figure 11.4 Assets of non-financial companies as a proportion of value-added.

certain date. On the other hand they have been represented as social capital and in effect are part of equity over which managers have a relatively free rein. If they are counted as equity, then debt–equity ratios are comparable between Germany and the UK. Treating pension provisions as equity better reflects the type of relational contract that exists between the employee and employer in a German company. Short-term trade credits and short-term borrowing are very important on both the assets and liabilities side of Japanese balance sheets. They are significantly higher than credits extended in other countries. In Figure 3 such borrowing is marked as short-term liabilities; in Figure 4 trade credits are marked separately. Such borrowing and lending between companies reflects the inter-company network of financing and again is an example of the less explicit more relational contracting that occurs between Japanese companies.

THE PERFORMANCE AND COMPETITIVENESS OF THE FINANCIAL SECTOR

The growth of the financial sector of Britain's economy was quite remarkable during the 1980s. On a broad definition of the sector (including business services, such as computing, estate agency and accounting), output growth comfortably outstripped that of the economy as a whole, as shown in Table 4.

CITY AND INDUSTRY

Table 4 Output and employment in the financial sector

| | Employees (GB) thousands | | Growth rates 1979–90 (% p.a.) | |
	1979	1990	Output (UK)	Employment
Finance and banking	443	621	6.5	3.3
Insurance	214	261	7.7	1.8
Business services	798	1548	7.7	6.4

Source: CSO Service Trade Statistics (various issues)

Recession notwithstanding, the sector actually grew somewhat faster in the early part of the decade than in the second, post-'Big-Bang', period.

The same is true in an international comparison, and we can see from Figure 5 that the UK stands out when compared to the G6 economies. The disaggregated picture of the growth of the sector in Table 4 shows that, although output growth was rather similar between the different industries, employment growth differed considerably, reflecting differences in productivity performance. The really big generator of jobs was in business services rather than in banking and insurance. As shown elsewhere in this volume, this

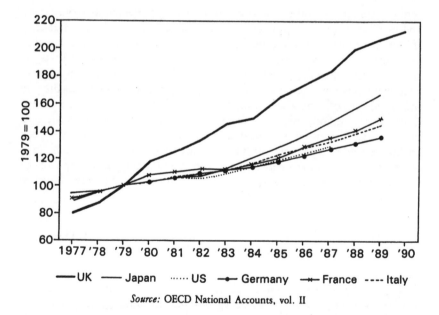

Source: OECD National Accounts, vol. II

Figure 11.5 Growth in the output of financial, insurance, real estate and business services (G6).

OVERVIEW

reflects a huge structural change in terms of the inputs of business services –
which comprises all manner of technical, legal, accounting and advertising
services – that are required by other sectors of the economy, including business
services themselves (Barker and Forsell 1992). Some have interpreted this as a
fundamental shift towards an 'information-intensive economy', a structural
shift observed in other advanced economies. In both banking and finance and
insurance, similar output gains have been translated into fewer jobs and hence
a superior productivity performance. In part this reflects the rapidity of
technical change – many of the underlying transactions are on a large scale and
relatively homogeneous, so the scope for advance is correspondingly enormous.
It should be borne in mind, however, that output measures can be unreliable
in this sector, and some have argued that there may be systematic under-
recording of output in some of the industries (Smith 1989). An interesting
feature of productivity growth in the entire sector, as indicated in Figure 6, is
that after the rapid growth in the period 1977–83 it stagnates thereafter, and
over the whole period 1979–90 it is little faster than that of the economy as
a whole.

The question of the competitiveness of the sector has been heightened by
the creation of the European Single Market and the possibility that the
dismantling of barriers in financial services might allow rapid penetration of

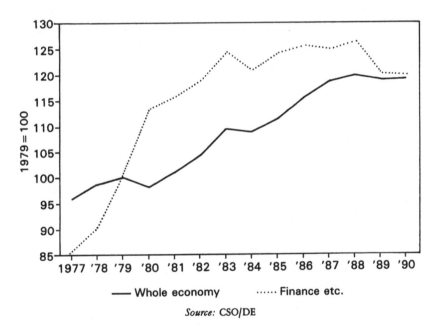

Source: CSO/DE

Figure 11.6 Labour productivity in the UK financial sector against the whole economy.

CITY AND INDUSTRY

markets by the most competitive financial institutions in the Community. The Cecchini (1988) report suggested that the UK was a relatively low-cost supplier of a variety of financial services but it is not clear how far higher costs in other markets, especially in Germany, reflect implicit services of the kind discussed above – e.g. the long-term commitments that are attached to bank lending. These 'club effects' amount to significant attributes of non-price competitiveness. It is certainly the case that many commentators are not expecting an easy entry for UK institutions into domestic markets. Smith (1992) cites evidence from the Swiss market, where the relative ease with which it is now possible to obtain banking licences and the abandonment of the banking cartel has made little difference to foreign banks' access to it. In general, entry into the smaller markets in the EC may be easier than into the larger markets of Germany and Italy (Bank of England 1989).

Although it may not be true across the entire range of financial services, the role of non-price competitiveness may be just as great if not greater in this area than in manufacturing. Sources of trading advantage are likely to arise from the specialized expertise and innovativeness of institutions rather than technology (which is relatively accessible to all the major players) and productivity advantages, and so the traditional role of comparative costs may be slight. The sources of competitive advantage for the institutions of a particular country such as the UK stem in part from the peculiarities of its national economy which may give it an edge in some areas. However, as Smith (1992) points out, the weakness of the UK domestic economy is unlikely to stand it in good stead in this regard.

Table 5 International banking analysed by centre (gross lending – percentage share of total world market)

	1990 (Q3)
Belgium	3.3
Luxembourg	4.8
France	6.8
Germany (Federal Republic)	5.0
Italy	2.1
Netherlands	2.9
Switzerland	2.4
Swiss Trustee Account	4.1
UK	19.1
Canada	1.1
Japan	20.4
US	8.1
'Offshore' banking centres	18.7

Source: Bank for International Settlements

OVERVIEW

The City's strengths have lain in international finance rather than in the provision of finance for the domestic industrial sector. London has been the centre for almost 20 per cent of gross lending in international banking, on a par with Japan (Table 5). London has become the centre of international bond dealing, looking at the number of firms by centre (Table 6). London also has a large number of companies quoted on its stock exchange, both domestic and foreign companies, although many of these are not large companies. Thus London as a financial centre is providing a valuable service to international

Table 6 Association of international bond dealers (number of firms by centre)

	All firms[a]	Reporting dealers[b]
UK	205	73
Switzerland	151	1
Luxembourg	76	5
Germany	68	–
Hong Kong	48	1
Netherlands	58	–
US	29	–
France	49	5
Belgium	39	2
Other	211	10

[a] End September 1990
[b] Those firms which report prices on a daily basis (end September 1990)

Table 7 International stock exchanges (primary market statistics for equities, end-1990)

Exchange	Market value of domestic equity (£bn) end-1990	Number of listed companies, end-1990	
		Domestic	Foreign
Tokyo	1,482.8	1627	125
Osaka	1,221.0	1138	0
New York	1,389.1	1678	96
London	445.0	2006	553
NASDAQ*	736.9	3875	256
Frankfurt	176.5	389	354
Paris	159.3	443	226
Zurich	85.7	182	240
Amsterdam	77.2	260	238
American	35.1	789	70

*National Association of Securities Dealers (USA) Automated Quotations
Source: Bank of England Quarterly Bulletin

CITY AND INDUSTRY

companies, and has been more successful than other financial centres by such measures (Table 7).

Therefore in assessing the performance of this sector, we need to consider it in its various parts and for the different functions and services that it needs to perform. There have been many institutional changes centred on the financial sector in the 1980s. These have had mixed effects on the competitiveness both of the sector in itself and in terms of the knock-on effects of what the sector can provide to UK industry.

CONCLUSION

Control mechanisms and relations between the financial and industrial sectors are important for information collection and monitoring by the financial sector of the industrial sector. The relevant financial intermediary may be institutions connected with the stock market or with the banks. In which system do these features work best? We have described here the 'inside' system where financial intermediaries are in the position of accumulating inside information about companies and exercising some measure of control or monitoring as a consequence; the Japanese and German institutions resemble this to some extent. We contrast this with the 'outside' system where information gathering and monitoring occur through institutions that are kept at arm's length from companies and work through markets. Longer-term investment and higher risk investment by companies may be made easier by the types of inside relations that are more prevalent in Japan and Germany than in the UK and US.

The inside–outside dichotomy fits to some extent with some of the features we observe in the capital structures in the different countries, in particular their split between debt and equity. German pension provisions and Japanese trade credits are examples of longer-term obligations and relationships between those stakeholders that constitute the wider nexus of 'inside' financing relationships than occur in the 'outside' UK and US. In the UK and US, on the other hand, the importance of the market is manifest in higher dividend pay-outs and the greater sensitivity that companies display towards their share price.

How well does the UK financial sector perform? In comparison with UK manufacturing, the financial sector broadly defined has grown rapidly over the 1980s and has achieved substantial productivity growth. Its expertise and competitiveness benefits the international community and larger companies with access to global capital markets more than domestic companies confined to local financing mechanisms. The UK financial sector is stronger in areas where outsider control which does not require local and personal knowledge is appropriate and where markets predominate. Thus it has been extremely innovative and competitive in producing new financial instruments, in developing Eurobond markets and in hosting stock markets for international companies. The sector fails in relation to the provision of local domestic finance

OVERVIEW

where detailed knowledge, risk assessment at the local level, and regional commitment and imagination are necessary.

NOTES

1 Hirschmann, A. (1970) *Exit, Voice and Loyalty*, Cambridge, MA: Harvard University Press.
2 *Source: Bank of England Quarterly Bulletin*, various issues, from McWilliams and Sentance (1994).
3 *Source:* House of Commons Treasury and Civil Service Committee Third Report 1991–92 Session, 'Banking codes of practice and related matters'.

REFERENCES

Aoki, M. (1989) *Information, Incentives and Bargaining in the Japanese Economy*, Cambridge: Cambridge University Press.
Bank of England (1989) 'London as an international financial centre', *Bank of England Quarterly Bulletin*, November, pp. 516–29.
Barker, T. S. and Forsell, O. (1992) 'Manufacturing, services and structural change 1979–1984', in C. Driver and P. Dunne (eds), *Structural Change in the UK Economy*, Cambridge: Cambridge University Press.
Cadbury, A. (1992) *Committee on the Financial Aspects of Corporate Governance*, London: HMSO.
Cecchini, P. (1988) *1992: The European Challenge*, London: Gower.
Coase, R. (1937) 'The nature of the firm', *Economica*, vol. 4, pp. 386–405.
Corbett, J. (1994) 'An overview of the Japanese system', in N. Dimsdale and M. Prevezer (eds), *Capital Markets and Corporate Governance*, Oxford: Oxford University Press.
Dimsdale, N. (1994) 'The need to restore corporate accountability', in N. Dimsdale and M. Prevezer (eds), *Capital Markets and Corporate Governance*, Oxford: Oxford University Press.
Estrin, S. and Laidler, D. (1994) *Introduction to Microeconomics*, second edition, Oxford: Philip Allan.
Franks, J. and Mayer, C. (1990) 'Corporate ownership and corporate control: a study of France, Germany and the UK', *Economic Policy*, April, pp. 191–231.
Hirschmann, A. (1970) *Exit, Voice and Loyalty*, Cambridge, MA: Harvard University Press.
House of Commons Treasury and Civil Service Committee on Banking Codes and Related Matters (1992) Third Report 1991–1992 Session.
Hughes, A. (1994) 'The problems of finance for smaller businesses', in N. Dimsdale and M. Prevezer (eds), *Capital Markets and Corporate Governance*, Oxford: Oxford University Press.
Jensen, C. M. and Meckling, W. H. (1976) 'Theory of the firm: managerial behaviour, agency costs and ownership structure', *Journal of Financial Economics*, vol. 3, pp. 305–60.
McWilliams, D. and Sentance, A. (1994) 'The changing relationship between the banks and business in the UK', in N. Dimsdale and M. Prevezer (eds), *Capital Markets and Corporate Governance*, Oxford: Oxford University Press.

CITY AND INDUSTRY

Masuyama, S. (1994) 'The role of the Japanese capital markets and the effect of cross-shareholdings on corporate accountability', in N. Dimsdale and M. Prevezer (eds), *Capital Markets and Corporate Governance*, Oxford: Oxford University Press.

Odagiri, H. (1992) *Growth Through Competition and Competition Through Growth*, Oxford: Oxford University Press.

Prevezer, M. and Ricketts, M. (1994) 'Corporate governance: the UK compared with Germany and Japan', in N. Dimsdale and M. Prevezer (eds), *Capital Markets and Corporate Governance*, Oxford: Oxford University Press.

Schneider-Lenne, E. (1994) 'The role of the German capital markets and universal banks, supervisory boards and inter-locking directorships', in N. Dimsdale and M. Prevezer (eds), *Capital Markets and Corporate Governance*, Oxford: Oxford University Press.

Smith, A. D. (1989) 'New measures of service sector output', *National Institute Economic Review*, no. 128, May, pp. 75–88.

Smith, A. D. (1992) *International Financial Markets: The Performance of Britain and its Rivals*, Cambridge: Cambridge University Press.

ACKNOWLEDGEMENT

Figures 11.1, 11.2, 11.3, 11.4 and Tables 1, 2, 3 have been reproduced from Prevezer, M. and Ricketts, M. (1994) 'Corporate Governance: the UK compared with Germany and Japan', in N. Dimsdale and M. Prevezer (eds), *Capital Markets and Corporate Governance*, Oxford: Oxford University Press, with permission of Oxford University Press.

[13]

The hollowing out of British manufacturing and its implications for policy

Karel Williams, John Williams and Colin Haslam

Abstract

This article presents new evidence on the 'hollowing out' of British manufacturing. It shows that large British firms are building up their overseas activities while the manufacturing operations which remain in Britain are increasingly sheltered and low tech. The authors argue that these developments set limits on the effectiveness of national industrial policy. Britain's peculiar national problems must in any case be seen as part of a larger European problem about German manufacturing predominance

This paper charts and analyses the continued erosion of Britain's real, productive manufacturing base. We argue that a process of 'hollowing out' is under way as giant British firms are shifting out of manufacturing and into dealing and service activities. At the same time these large British firms are building up their overseas manufacturing whilst the manufacturing operations which remain in Britain are increasingly sheltered and low-tech. These complex, interrelated developments are important because they have major economic, social and political consequences. In earlier work (e.g. Cutler *et al.* 1986) we argued that the decline of manufacturing was undermining the male blue collar employment base and would generate a structural trade constraint. We now argue that the process of erosion has gone so far that it sets limits on the effectiveness of a national industrial policy. If British manufacturing decline is to be halted, Britain's problem must be seen as part of a larger European problem in which nearly 40 per cent of EC manufacturing production is now centred in Germany. That problem can only be solved through EC-wide policy initiatives. From this wider perspective, national policy can play its role as an adjunct to European industrial policy.

Basic distinctions

In this section we provide some basic information about the relation between

Economy and Society Volume 19 Number 4 November 1990
© Routledge 1990 0308-5147/90/1904-0456 $3.00/1

the British financial sector and the real economy, before drawing the distinction between production, services and dealing as distinct kinds of real economic activity with very different consequences. Here, it is a question of recovering some elementary distinctions which are not made in the economics textbooks and which are suppressed by the particular concept of enterprise stressed by Thatcherism. This bogus concept, which is now officially taught in Britain's universities, tends to establish the equivalence of all market based economic activities. In this and the next section, our task is to distinguish between different economic activities and their consequences.

The first issue concerns the relation between the financial sector and what economists call the real economy. It is often supposed that, in capitalist economies, the function of the financial sector is to serve the real economy by mobilising household savings and transferring them to industrial and commercial companies which use them for new productive investment. In some advanced economies, such as Japan, the pattern of flows does fit this model. But, as Mayer (1987) has recently demonstrated, industrial and commercial companies in the British real economy have long been self-financing and the financial sector makes little or no net contribution to the finance of physical investment. Mayer observes that, in the period 1970–85, 'the non-financial corporate sector could have been floated off separately from the financial sector with no net consequence for corporate investment' (Mayer, 1987: 9). This pattern arises partly because the inflow of funds from the financial sector into the real economy is usually balanced by a reverse flow of funds into the financial sector as industrial and commercial companies buy financial assets: Mayer shows that, between 1970 and 1984, 30 per cent of the total finance of the non-financial corporate sector went into acquiring financial assets. The industrial and commercial company sector does occasionally go into deficit, as in 1974 or 1988–9. But these occasional deficits do not arise because the industrial and commercial company sector is investing in new productive assets. The emergence of a £23.4 billion deficit in 1989 appears to have been mainly the result of mergers and acquisitions which have latterly been 80 per cent paid for in cash (*Financial Times*, 6 April 1990). The deficit was incurred to finance changes in the ownership of assets.

The implication of all this is that the financial and the real economies are not discrete entities coupled in one invariant, productive relation; the sectoral boundaries are blurred and the relation is variable. Further complications arise because the 'real economy' includes all industrial and commercial companies which engage in a variety of heterogeneous activities such as the production of manufactures, the sale of services and dealing in assets. Official statistics do not exactly measure the extent of any of these activities because it is impossible to classify them precisely. To take one example of this difficulty; trucking or cleaning activities undertaken 'on own account' by a manufacturing firm will usually be regarded as manufacturing activity; but, when these same activities are undertaken by specialist sub-contractors, they

458   *Karel Williams, John Williams and Colin Haslam*

will always be classified as services. It is therefore difficult to judge the changing balance of different activities within the national economy.

The demand for the service function is high and rising in all the advanced economies. But the share of services in GDP is not rising rapidly because there is competition between services and goods which discharge a service function; cinema seat sales, for example, have shown a secular decline with the development of TV and VCRs. Nevertheless, services, have the greatest weight in output and employment; over the past forty years in Britain, services have accounted for around half of GDP. It is impossible to provide a similar measure of dealing. All we can say is that dealing is not confined to a specialist asset trading sector of property companies and investment trusts; historically, dealing is an adjunct of manufacturing and its importance is now increasing. In Britain and America, giant manufacturing firms have often bought other firms; Prais (1976) and Hannah (1977) long ago showed that increasing concentration in Britain since 1914 is primarily caused by acquisition. More generally, the competitive international exchange of manufactures and the breakdown of the Bretton Woods system of fixed exchange rates has encouraged a vast expansion in financial dealing; in all the advanced countries, large manufacturing companies are adept at foreign exchange dealing, interest rate swaps, offshore bond issues and such like.

Very little of this complexity is registered in orthodox micro economic theory. The micro textbooks are based on simplifying productivist assumptions. They identify real economic activity with manufacturing undertaken by a management dedicated to the operation of one going concern: bought in physical inputs of resources, labour and capital are combined so that the firm realises profit through the manufacture of a product which has use value for the consumer. This is unsatisfactory when much productive manufacturing activity is concerned with the problems and opportunities which arise in the co-ordination and integration of multi-process, multi-product operations (Williams *et al.*, 1989a). It is even more relevant for the immediate argument that the textbooks ignore the possibility that the firm may pursue profit in a variety of ways as well as, or instead of, manufacturing. In particular there has emerged a widespread opportunistic culture of the deal.

When we discuss the hollowing out of British manufacturing, we should not assume there was an earlier age of innocence when giant manufacturing firms concentrated exclusively on making things. Manufacturing, services and dealing have always been inextricably intertwined inside and around the firm. But there are serious questions about the relative importance of manufacturing production in a hierarchy of real economic activities. It is equally important to investigate the character and quality of manufacturing and to inquire whether such operations are located inside the national economy. We can suppose that production, services and dealing are differently weighted in various national economies at different times and that domestic production is variably articulated into an international division of labour. In the next section, we explain why the relative weight of the different activities, inside the national economy, does matter.

Why production matters

There is no simple answer to the question of whether and why manufacturing production matters: it all depends on national circumstances and the criteria adopted. In considering the British case it is useful to distinguish between the narrow private interest of shareholders, the social interest of labour, and the broader national interest. From the shareholder's point of view, manufacturing, services and dealing are all the same insofar as their sales turnover generates profit which can be distributed as dividend. Regardless of source, profit is profit; a pound of profit made through foreign exchange dealing, property trading or renting video recorders is just as good as a pound of profit earned through making widgets. But from labour's point of view or the national interest, sales turnover in the various activities is very different because these pounds will have very different labour contents and the tradeability of different kinds of output varies considerably.

The contrast in labour content is clearest between dealing and manufacturing. Dealing rests on differences in exchange value which create the possibility of instant realisation without physical transformation; the office block which was bought last month for £5 million can be immediately revalued and, with luck, sold this month for £8 million. Subject to tax regulations, almost all this profit is available to capital because labour claims a very modest share of the increase in value. A small number of executives can run many large deals; thus, property companies with a large asset base and substantial dealing profits typically generate very little employment. The position in manufacturing is completely different because this activity adds value through the relatively slow physical transformation of bought-in materials and components. It is often supposed that modern manufacturing has carried the substitution of capital for labour to the point where labour is a trivial part of total costs of production. As we have argued elsewhere (Williams *et al.*, 1989b) this is simply not so; in British manufacturing now, labour accounts for 25–30 per cent of total costs (including bought-in components) and labour accounts for 70 per cent of net output or value added (excluding bought-in components). For this reason, it is practically impossible to realise manufacturing profit from sales turnover or value added without generating a substantial quantum of employment. The amount of employment generated is substantial, even in the most capital intensive and automated manufacturing activities: chemicals and electronics still generate substantial employment because their production and development processes eliminate direct labour but create new requirements for indirect maintenance workers and design and development staff.

460   *Karel Williams, John Williams and Colin Haslam*

It could be argued that the balance between production and dealing does not matter provided service employment expands. Many service activities are much more labour intensive than manufacturing because activities as diverse as tourism and medicine require personal service. We know that service activities are the major source of employment in all the advanced economies; according to British official statistics, more than 15 million work in the service sector, while less than 5 million work in manufacturing. During the Thatcher years, the service sector has been the source of new job creation. Tory ministers boast of 3.5 million new jobs created since 1981; these are *all* service jobs created in a decade when manufacturing employment has continuously declined. But the new service jobs are poor compensation for lost manufacturing jobs; the new service jobs are predominantly poorly paid, part time jobs which in Britain are taken by female, second-wage earners. In Britain, the expansion of service employment at the expense of manufacturing is creating problems about the composition of employment because it undermines the traditional assumption that blue collar employment offers a wage which is adequate for the maintenance of a nuclear family.

Service output (like dealing) is, in any case, not a good substitute for manufacturing output because it generates much less tradeable output; cookers and fridges, for example, are internationally traded but restaurant meals are not. This point is of considerable importance in the relatively small open economies of northern Europe which all have a comparatively high propensity to import manufactures; in Britain (as in France, Italy and West Germany) imports now capture more than 25 per cent of the domestic market for manufactures. It is hard to see how this propensity to import manufactures can be covered without a domestic manufacturing sector that generates compensating export sales of domestic products. This general need becomes an imperative for any economy, like that of Britain, facing a severe balance of payments constraint. In the mid-1980s, Britain was shielded from the consequences of manufacturing decline by the windfall gain of North Sea oil. But the balance of payments surplus in North Sea oil has rapidly declined because oil prices are lower and production has fallen away; these factors, plus interruption of supply, reduced the 1989 surplus on oil to just £1.4 billion. Financial services are internationally traded and, in the mid-1980s, Tory ministers like Nigel Lawson were optimistic about an expansion in the surplus on invisibles. These hopes have been disappointed; while the British manufacturing trade deficit burgeoned in the late 1980s, Britain's surplus on financial services declined. In 1986 the surplus on all invisibles (including financial services) peaked at £9.3 billion and by 1989 had fallen to £4.1 billion. City spokesmen now figure prominently in the media as interpreters of the national economy; for understandable reasons, they never make the point that their own sector contributes little to that economy by way of job creation, and that its traditional positive contribution to the trade balance is rapidly eroding.

Having established that from a broad social and national point of view, (domestic) manufacturing does matter, we can now turn to examine the pattern of hollowing out in British manufacturing. But, before we do so, we will make one final point about the mechanics of dis-employment in an unsuccessful manufacturing sector or national economy. Because manufacturing output has a relatively high labour content, any stagnation or decline in real manufacturing output has predictable consequences for manufacturing employment. If manufacturing employment is to be maintained or increased then manufacturing output must grow more rapidly than the rate of increase of labour productivity (or the rate of real wage increase, if that outstrips the rate of growth of labour productivity). The reason for this is straightforward: in normal circumstances labour claims a high (near 70 per cent) share of net output and any increase of labour's share quickly threatens to wipe out the relatively small residual claimed by capital in the form of profit. In these circumstances, management typically responds by sacking workers which renormalises labour's share. Tory propaganda about irresponsible wage claims 'pricing workers out of jobs' does have some basis in economic fact. But it is also an exercise in scapegoating and half truth because it ignores the issue of the trend of manufacturing output which is the other element in the equation. If there is one law of the manufacturing labour market it is that real net output falls in recession, followed by *pari passu* reductions in manufacturing employment: this was the general pattern in the advanced economies in the downturns after 1973 and 1979 (Williams *et al.*, 1989b). Tory ministers are silent about the linkage between output and employment for good reasons; through fiscal and monetary policy, the government is partly responsible for the level and trend of output.

The record of 'British manufacturing'

It is not easy to follow the progress of manufacturing from official statistics or company reports and accounts. In the census of production and elsewhere, companies are assigned to official categories on the basis of a judgement about their dominant activities. Even publicly quoted companies are not obliged to provide any comprehensive breakdown of profits by type of business or geographic source. From the available sources, it is difficult to judge whether, in the aggregate, there has been a tilt away from the real, productive activity of manufacturing; and, in specific cases, it is not easy to determine what kind of manufacturing is being undertaken or where. But all the sources show that the British activities officially and unofficially classified as manufacturing have not been doing well over the past twenty years. And a sample of reports from giant companies suggests that there has been a substantial shift to overseas manufacturing over the past decade.

   In social and national terms, what matters is the aggregate of output and employment generated inside the national economy by all manufacturing firms. If we define British manufacturing in this way and compare it with other national manufacturing sectors, Britain has two melancholy distinguishing

462   *Karel Williams, John Williams and Colin Haslam*

Table 1 Real output, employment, productivity and profit in British manufacturing, 1973–89

| Year | Real Output[a] | | Employment[a] | | Labour productivity[b] | | Profit[c] |
	£ billion (1980 prices)	Index 1973 = 100	Total Thou.	Index 1973 = 100	Annual percent increase	Index 1977 = 100	%
1973	66773	100.0	7859	100.0	6.9	95.4	7.4
1974	65934	98.8	7906	100.6	0.8	96.2	5.6
1975	61394	91.9	7506	95.5	1.9	98.0	5.5
1976	62504	93.6	7262	92.4	1.1	99.1	5.9
1977	63732	95.4	7317	93.1	0.9	100.0	7.8
1978	64142	96.1	7272	92.5	1.4	101.4	7.8
1979	64025	97.4	7171	91.2	0.5	101.9	6.7
1980	58470	87.7	6985	88.9	5.1	107.1	5.6
1981	54962	82.4	6294	80.1	6.0	113.5	4.8
1982	55079	82.6	5919	75.3	8.5	123.1	5.9
1983	56657	85.0	5540	70.5	5.5	129.9	6.7
1984	58938	88.5	5397	68.7	3.2	134.1	7.5
1985	60692	90.7	5395	68.6	3.3	138.6	8.7
1986	61218	91.6	5338	67.9	4.9	147.6	9.2
1987	64569	96.7	5049	66.0	6.5	154.9	10.4
1988	69043	103.4	5110	67.3		145.2	
1989	72449	108.5		67.3		152.4	

Sources:
(a) Eurostat National Accounts, Economy and Finance Series
(b) Bureau of Labor Statistics, Washington, DC, Monthly Labor Review
(c) OECD Paris, contact

Notes:
1   Labour productivity is defined as output per person employed
2   Profit is defined as gross operating surplus as per cent of gross capital stock

characteristics. Firstly, Britain is the only advanced country where real manufacturing output shows no sustained growth over the past twenty years. In 1989, UK real manufacturing output was less than 10 per cent up on the level of the cyclical peak year of 1973; other European national manufacturing sectors show growth rates of 17–75 per cent over the same period. Secondly, the British record is dominated by unusually sharp cyclical fluctuations and severe downturns after 1973 and 1979. In the post-1979 downturn, British real net manufacturing output fell by nearly 15 per cent, a fall which was twice as large as in any other OECD country. The British pattern is that recovery on the upswing restores output loss, but the manufacturing sector then turns down when the level of the previous cyclical peak has been regained. The pattern seems likely to be repeated in the early 1990s; manufacturing output has already (mid-1990) been flat for nearly a year.

The downturns are usually damaging because they destroy jobs for the reasons explained in the previous section. If employment declined gently after

1973, it did not after 1979; 1.8 million manufacturing jobs, one quarter of the 1979 total, were wiped out in just five years at the beginning of the 1980s. Dis-employment, on this scale was associated with another dramatic change; Robinson (1985) calculates that more than 20 per cent of manufacturing capital was scrapped in this downturn and thus domestic manufacturing capacity was dramatically reduced. This miserable and wasting downturn did peculiarly have a political dividend for the Tories who had aggravated the downturn with their monetarist policies. When the economy turned round after 1983, the Tories were able to represent the cyclical upswing as a 'supply side miracle'; it was the dynamics and extent of the previous output, employment and capacity fall which made the post-1982 record look impressive.

The two indicators which looked good on the upswing were profit and labour productivity. The recovery of profit was a modest one which, on the CSO measure, did not bring the return on assets into double figures. This was the predictable result of cyclical recovery after wholesale sacking had taken labour costs out. Much the same point could be made about labour productivity. Manufacturing labour productivity growth rates of 5 per cent plus were not unprecedented; they had been achieved in earlier periods when output was growing rapidly. Equally, in previous cycles the trend of employment had lagged behind the trend of output; there was nothing new about sackings continuing into the output upswing, as they did after 1983. Before the 1980s, high rates of labour productivity had never been sustained when output growth stopped; and that is what is happening again in the early 1990s. Manufacturing output has been flat since September 1989 and, by January 1990, the rate of growth of manufacturing labour productivity had fallen to an annual rate of 0.6 per cent (*Financial Times*, 17 March 1990). Over the whole output cycle, from peak to peak, between 1980 and 1989 manufacturing output per man increased at a rate of about 4.25 per cent per annum; this is only fractionally better than the secular rate achieved in the late 1960s and early 1970s (*Bank of England Quarterly Bulletin*, August 1989: 376).

As the manufacturing sector moves into another downturn, we can look back to the 1980s and balance the temporary revival of profit and spurt in productivity against flat output and declining employment. The 1980s profile is of a hollowed out manufacturing sector which is in progress to decline. British manufacturing may be viable in a narrow, private sense but it has failed in a broader social sense because its achievements are won by sacking workers in line with reduced output. Our manufacturing sector is also a failure, from a national point of view, in generating a surplus of tradeable goods. Significantly, the deficit on manufactured trade first emerged in 1983 after the wave of scrapping and capacity reduction; the deficit reached crisis point when the economy ran out of capacity after recovery was stoked for political reasons in the run up to the 1987 election. By 1989, the manufacturing sector reached a record 102.3 per cent level of capacity utilisation (*NIER*, Februrary 1990), the deficit on manufactured trade burgeoned to £24.4 billion and that created an

464   *Karel Williams, John Williams and Colin Haslam*

Table 2 Stock levels at Lucas, GKN and Ford

	Lucas		GKN		Ford	
	Stock/ turnover ratio	*Number of weeks stock*	*Stock/ turnover ratio*	*Number of weeks stock*	*Stock/ turnover ratio*	*Number of weeks stock*
1981	3.8	13.7	4.1	12.7	3.3	15.8
1982	4.0	13.0	4.0	13.0	3.4	15.3
1983	4.1	12.7	4.5	11.6	3.6	14.4
1984	4.7	11.1	4.6	11.3	3.4	15.3
1985	5.2	10.0	4.6	11.3	3.7	14.1
1986	5.6	9.3	4.6	11.3	3.5	14.9
1987	5.6	9.3	4.7	11.1	3.9	13.3
1988	5.2	10.0	5.5	9.5	4.0	13.0
1989	5.4	9.6	5.8	9.0	4.2	10.2

Source: Lucas, GKN and Ford (UK) *Report and Accounts,* various years

overall payments deficit of £19.1 billion which amounts to approximately 4 per cent of GDP. This deficit can only be managed by adopting high interest rates which bridge the trade gap by attracting short term, hot money to London and reduce the gap by depressing domestic activity and the demand for imports. The government present high interest rates as a measured   response to (monetary) inflation; it would be more honest to admit that high interest rates are necessary because manufacturing failure can only be managed by (real) deflation.

If we turn to look at different sectors of manufacturing or individual companies, the striking fact is that few sectors or individual companies buck the trend; it is, for example, extraordinarily difficult to find manufacturing sectors or companies with strong organic growth of sales or value added. The chemicals and pharmaceuticals sector is an honourable exception. Elsewhere, healthy rises in sales at a company level are usually the result of acquisition rather than organic growth. Even more worrying, at the company level, there is very little evidence of progress with fundamentals in the management of manufacturing, new product development and marketing.

In production management, the evidence of stock levels is particularly significant. Stock levels are an index of integration in multi-process manufacturing operations; stock/turnover ratios or number of weeks sales cover, as disclosed in company accounts, provide a kind of window onto manufacturing operations. The Japanese manufacturing sector as a whole runs on less than 6 weeks sales cover, while best practice firms like Toyota run on 2 weeks stocks. In Britain there is considerable room for improvement because the manufacturing sector as a whole runs on 12–13 weeks stocks (Williams *et al.*, 1989a). Several major British companies have made attempts at 'Japanisation', with stock reduction a major objective. It is now clear that programmes, such as Ford's 'After Japan' programme, usually have limited success. As Table 2 below shows, Lucas and GKN have achieved something but are nowhere near Japanese standards, and their improvement may not be sustained as the economy turns down cyclically in the early 1990s; it is usual for stock cover to decline at cyclical peaks like 1988–9 and then to increase on the downswing.

In product development and marketing the only broad based successes are in chemicals and pharmaceuticals. Some companies have achieved a narrower success by retreating into specialist niche markets; TI, for example, sold its machine tools, white goods and bicycle interests to concentrate on industrial seals and fasteners. For the rest, the verdict of a recent FT survey of engineering will do,

> After the changes of the past decade it is now more difficult than ever to find large British industrial companies which have generated strong organic growth by developing their own products and using them to take market share away from foreign competitors ... For all the talk of improved efficiency ... virtually no sector of British manufacturing has been able to plunder global markes with new world beating products of their own design. (*Financial Times*, 1990, February 21)

It is, of course, naive to expect the development and export of 'world beating' exports from the British factories of British firms. Many giant British manufacturing firms have long met part, or all, of the demands of foreign customers by overseas production rather than export from Britain. This is part of a larger pattern of internationalisation of production. Foreign owned firms have long accounted for a small but significant share of the manufacturing output produced in Britain; American multinationals make up the largest group of foreign owned firms producing in Britain and, in recent years, they have accounted for 12–15 per cent of the manufacturing output produced in Britain. While the decisions of these American firms have justifiably been a focus of public concern, it is the decisions of British owned firms which are more important. In the aggregate, according to the 1986 Census of Production, British owned firms account for four-fifths of the gross (or net) manufacturing output produced in Britain (Dillow, 1990). The decisions of larger British firms about manufacturing location have major repercussions for the level of domestic manufacturing output and employment.

We investigated the role of overseas production by taking a sample of 25 giant British manufacturing firms from the 1989 *Financial Times* Top 500 list. For these companies, we obtained data on domestic and overseas employment totals since 1979. All the firms in the sample are British owned giants with current sales turnover of more than £2 billion. In every case, we checked that these were predominantly manufacturing firms by obtaining information on their turnover by activity for the current year; two-thirds of the combined turnover of the 25 firms is in manufacturing SIC 2–3 (excluding food, drink and tobacco) and nearly 80 per cent is in SIC 2–4 (including food, drink and tobacco). One of the complications is that there are large differences between

466   *Karel Williams, John Williams and Colin Haslam*

Table 3 Domestic and overseas employment in 25 giant British manufacturing firms, 1979–89

	Total employ-ment thou.	Domestic em-ployment thou.	Domestic as percent of total	Overseas em-ployment thou.	Overseas as percent of total
sub-period (a)					
1979	1839.8	1139.9	62.0	699.9	38.0
1983	1488.6	802.0	53.9	685.6	46.1
sub-period (b)					
1985	1480.8	805.8	54.4	675.0	45.6
1989	1705.2	807.2	47.3	898.1	52.7

Sources: Datastream plus company communications

Notes: The firms are: BAT; ICI; Hanson; Unilever; GEC; BAe; B. Steel; BICC; Pilkington; BTR; BOC; BET; Glaxo; GKN; Hawker Sid; Lucas; Reed Int.; Bowater; T and N; Ferranti; Bunzl; DRG; Delta; BBA; Simon Eng.

giant firms which individually have considerable weight in the sample. A couple of real giants, ICI and Unilever, have a large commitment to, and weight in, overseas employment; while a handful of defence and aerospace firms, like British Aerospace, are still largely British based. The composition of the sample influences conclusions about the level of domestic and overseas employment but, we would argue, it does not undermine conclusions about the trend of domestic and overseas employment. Our conclusions about the trend of employment broadly corroborate those of an earlier Labour Research Department (1987) study of forty UK manufacturing companies. In these companies, domestic employment decreased by 415,000 between 1979 and 1986, at the same time as overseas employment increased by 125,000.

The results of our survey are summarised in Table 3. Overseas employ-ment has always been important in British owned giant firms; in our sample, it accounted for 38 per cent of total employment in 1979. But the relative importance of overseas employment increased markedly over the decade of the 1980s; by 1989, overseas employment accounted for 53 per cent of total employment. The shift in proportion was accounted for by a decline in the absolute numbers employed in domestic manufacturing and an increase in the numbers employed overseas. Between 1979 and 1989, overseas employment increased by some 200,000, or 28.3 per cent while domestic employment declined by 330,000 or 29.1 per cent. Further analysis of sub-periods (1979–83 versus 1985–9) shows that the decline in domestic employment and the increase in overseas employment were not synchronised and simultaneous developments. In the downswing of the recession, from 1979 to 1983, domestic manufacturing employment declined by just over 330,000 with overseas employment more or less completely flat. The lost domestic manufacturing jobs were never found again; in the later 1980s, on the upswing, the growth was almost entirely in overseas employment. The cut backs in domestic employment may have been an inevitable defensive response to the limits of the domestic market in recession; subsequent growth in overseas employment suggests that many giant British firms have now deliberately chosen strategies which limit their exposure to the domestic market.

This development might be excused if giant British firms were building up manufacturing operations in continental European countries where it would strengthen the competitive position of British companies in the run up to the single market. It is possible to find individual companies which are implementing such strategies; in auto components. GKN, for example, has built up German manufacturing to supply the car assemblers who lead the European industry. More typically, however, the build up of overseas employment is concentrated in the United States. This issue cannot be explored systematically because there is no publicly available information which breaks down overseas employment by region or country. But it is significant that the largest absolute and relative increases in overseas employment after 1979 occur in companies with active strategies of American acquisition; in our 25 company sample, no less than 33 per cent of the total increase in overseas employment since 1979 is accounted for by just two companies, Hanson and BTR, which have made substantial American acquisitions. This indication is corroborated if we turn to examine the pattern of outward direct investment flows from the UK; in 1987, for example, 71 per cent of outward direct investment went to North America and 16 per cent to Europe.

Those who write stockbrokers' circulars are concerned only with the private shareholder interest and, from this point of view, they celebrate the shift offshore. When listing 'the strengths of British mechanical engineering', a recent Wood Mac circular emphasised the point that only 40 per cent of the turnover of the 20 largest British engineering companies is now generated in the UK (County Nat West, 1989). From a broader point of view, offshore production aggravates our social and national problems by stripping out British employment and exports in a way which leaves behind only a rump of manufacturing activity which is not well placed to withstand European competition. Worse still, in the next section, our case studies of giant firms suggest that part of the rump is not manufacturing at all, while the manufacturing that does remain is increasingly sheltered and/or low tech.

Giant British firms: some pathological cases

We turn now to case studies which provide us with a different perspective on hollowing out. Case studies are a guide to commitment to manufacturing; in individual cases it is possible to judge the balance between manufacturing and other activities, as well as the kind of manufacturing undertaken. We recognise that it is difficult to generalise from particular cases; in the nature of

468   *Karel Williams, John Williams and Colin Haslam*

things, the results of case studies are suggestive not conclusive. But the cases of giant firms – such as GEC, British Aerospace and Hanson – are significant. In themselves, such giant firms have considerable weight; for example, taken together, these three giant firms employ more than 175,000 workers in the UK. And through their demand for components and services, they create the environment in which many small and medium firms operate. Our concern is that these giant firms are leading the retreat from manufacturing and adapting to hollowing out in a way which deprives us of 'national champions'.

When we started to work on British manufacturing, we produced a revisionist case study of GEC (Williams, 1983) which was then widely regarded as a successful company. Against this, we then argued GEC was a company in retreat from manufacturing and especially manufacturing for contested markets. GEC had built up a £1 billion cash mountain which it was unable or unwilling to use for productive investment; while GEC was quitting or not trying in difficult contested markets (like microchips or consumer electronics) and retreating into the cosy cost plus world of defence contracting where it had a sheltered role as a national supplier. Since 1981, GEC has made a bewildering variety of defensive and offensive strategic moves. Many of these moves were difficult to interpret and some of them came to nothing; AEG, for example, went to Daimler Benz not GEC. But the strategic results by 1990 are completely consistent with our earlier analysis. And, because profits have been flat since 1982, even the financial press now agrees with us; Lord Weinstock's considerable intelligence is not harnessed to any constructive productive outcome.

With the purchase of Plessey, GEC has completed its retreat into defence contracting. The purchase of Plessey by Siemens and GEC was originally dressed up as a joint venture whose constructive purpose was to deal with the problems of GPT, the British telecoms manufacturer that lacks the resources to develop a new generation of public switching equipment. This purchase now turns out to be a break up operation from which Siemens and GEC get the bits they want while, for the time being, they leave GPT to wither on the vine (*Financial Times*, 4 April 1990). GEC has picked up Plessey's aerospace, avionics and naval systems divisions, the MOD having retracted its traditional objection to monopoly in domestic defence contracting which had frustrated earlier attempts to buy Plessey. The other, more dramatic, development is GEC's metamorphosis into a kind of investment holding company with a curious portfolio of gilts and electrical shares. The cash mountain has grown so that by 1987 cash and short term investments stood at £1,730 million, a sum equal to 33 per cent of 1987 sales. Money market investment is now GEC's largest wholly owned activity and probably the company's largest single source of profit. This situation arises because, under threat of takeover and break up, in late 1988 and early 1989 GEC entered into a series of joint ventures; by spring 1989 it looked as though around half of GEC's assets and workers were being backed into joint ventures. In all these deals, strategic control and day by day management was shared with, or ceded to, the foreign partner. Thus, in the largest of these joint ventures, GEC's power generating equipment business, which accounted for 25 per cent of GEC sales, was backed into a new Anglo-French joint venture with the Alsthom division of CGE; the new company will be French managed and its corporate headquarters will be in France.

In many ways this abdication through joint venture represents the logical culmination of Weinstock's longstanding preoccupation with financial control and rate of return. GEC is becoming a rentier capitalist firm whose profits increasingly come from short term investment and shareholdings in electrical businesses which somebody else manages. GEC's remaining direct responsibility for manufacturing is increasingly confined to defence contracting where the profitability of development and production is guaranteed even if, like Marconi AWACs, the equipment does not work. Of course, GEC is only one company, but it is not alone in its retreat from manufacturing. It is interesting, for example, to make the comparison with British Aerospace which provides significant further evidence. BAe and GEC are the largest of our diversified engineering companies; each company has sales of £3 billion plus and a market capitalisation of near £6 billion. And BAe has latterly been moving in the opposite direction from GEC. Ten years ago, BAe was almost 100 per cent oriented to defence, but now it has diversified, through building up a civil aircraft business and acquiring Rover cars, so that 54 per cent of the company's turnover is currently in non-defence activities (Datastream).

Although BAe is diversifying into new areas of manufacturing, its commitment to these activities is limited. Rover Cars is, and will remain, a minor producer making less than 500,000 vehicles a year. When Rover was bought from the state, BAe insisted it would not be bound to fulfil any corporate investment plan and it should be free to sell the business on after five years. Meanwhile, BAe's downside risk is minimised by a joint venture deal with Honda which supplies new models like the 200/400 which Rover assembles. In civil aviation, there is the same preoccupation with minimising downside risk; BAe has a politically privileged position as the British participant in the Air Bus consortium whose planes are the natural first choice of Europe's national carriers. BAe's problem is that its risk avoiding diversification has not been profitable; in 1989, £310 million out of a total trading profit of £360 million will be earned by military aircraft, weapons and electronics systems. This problem is being dealt with by building up non-manufacturing activities. Defence service contracts for the Saudis and others will be a lucrative source of income in the 1990s. The sale of surplus land from Royal Ordnance and Rover has been a major source of windfall profits which is now being developed as a mainstream business. BAe's most recent strategic move was the purchase of Arlington, a property company, and 'property development' should account for 13–14 per cent of trading profit in 1989 and 1990. According to recent reports (*Financial Times*, 29 January 1990) BAe's chairman, Professor Smith, 'is toying with the idea of moving the company into the financial services business'.

470   *Karel Williams, John Williams and Colin Haslam*

Professor Smith has recently protested that BAe is a manufacturing company. His company's actions speak louder than the chairman's words: BAe is another company in retreat from manufacturing. The line of retreat may be different at GEC but it is essentially the same story; both BAe and GEC limit their commitment to risky manufacturing for contested markets and abdicate responsibility for developing manufacturing businesses and managing manufacturing operations. BAe and GEC are not alone and they do not represent the limit point of low commitment to manufacturing. In collapsed sectors like electronics, all the smaller British household names have quit the field of contested high tech manufacturing; thus Thorn-EMI has sold its Ferguson TV and Inmos chip business as well as the Thorn lighting business and now prefers to earn profit through TV rental and music publishing. Meanwhile, in the 1980s we have seen the rapid development of giant companies which have a completely instrumental approach to manufacturing which is used as a cover for dealing in assets; the two classic examples here are Hanson and BTR which, in terms of market capitalisation, are now our two largest diversified manufacturing companies.

By any standards, Hanson is now a very large company: it employs 90,000 in Britain and the United States and it has a market capitalisation of nearly £13 billion, more than twice as large as BAe or GEC. Hanson grew very rapidly during the 1980s; on our calculations, Hanson's real sales turnover increased more than five times between 1979 and 1989. This was achieved in Britain and the United States mainly through acquisition rather than organic growth. Major purchases of the 1980s include Imperial Tobacco, SCM and, most recently, Cons Gold. A substantial proportion of what is acquired is subsequently divested and the company's success in 'increasing shareholder value' rests on a formula of buying companies cheap and selling dear. After analysing 100 Hanson deals, Dickers concludes that the typical deal involves selling companies for one third more than was paid for them (Credit Suisse, 1990). The takeover and break up of SCM in the USA shows how lucrative this dealing can be. In January 1986, SCM cost Hanson £930 million and disposals have since recovered 166 per cent of the purchase price; the remaining businesses, including SCM chemicals and a 48 per cent share in Smith Corona Typewriters, are currently generating annual profits equal to 30 per cent of the original purchase price. Everything is for sale if the price is right. When Cons Gold was taken over in 1989, it was generally assumed that Hanson would sell the South African mines but retain the aggregates business which fitted in with existing Hanson interests in construction materials; the latest annual report discloses that all of Cons Gold is being sold.

More typically, however, Hanson does retain and operate part of what it buys and, to that extent, Hanson is a manufacturing company. The pattern of retention is explained by Hanson's preference for sheltered, low tech businesses which are slow-changing and do not require major investment. On this point, Lord Hanson is quite explicit: 'we avoid areas of very high technology. We do not want to be involved in businesses which are highly capital intensive' (Goold and Campbell, 1987). In Britain, Hanson subsidiaries with the right characteristics for retention have a major presence in tobacco, batteries and bricks; the classic example is bricks where the 1990 acquisition of Armitage brings Hanson's share of the British brick market to nearly 45 per cent. In the United States, Hanson's product lines include Jacuzzi hot tubs, cement, the whitening pigment titanium oxide and lighting equipment; one of Hanson's American subsidiaries is the world's largest producer of wheelbarrows and shovels (*Independent*, 4 June, 1990).

Subsidiaries which begin to display the wrong characteristics are likely to be divested. Thus Hanson sold a turbocharger business whose managers wanted to invest strategically in new technology; their investment plan projected several years of negative cash flow and, as Hanson managers explained, 'This worried us a lot. We sold the business shortly afterwards' (Goold and Campbell, 1987). Newly acquired subsidiaries have their characteristics ruthlessly adjusted by teams of accountants who identify saleable assets and strip out unnecessary operating expenditure. A senior manager at Imperial's brewing division has explained what happened after that takeover, when Hanson sent in a team of accountants:

> They didn't ask any questions at all about products or distribution and weren't interested in our plans for the business . . . All they were interested in was the bottom line. They went through every document we had about property valuation, leases, freeholds, pension plans and salary structures but about the business itself they just didn't want to know . . . What they wanted to do was to cut the cash, cut the overheads and make the assets sweat. (*Marketing*, 30 July, 1987)

We have no doubt that Hanson is a deal-driven company. This point is proved by the way in which all the company's financial resources are now being mobilised in preparation for further acquisition. The 1989 Report discloses that the company has £5.25 billion in cash, a sum equal to 75 per cent of the value of annual sales turnover. Hanson has also recently converted loan stock into ordinary shares with the aim of raising its borrowing limit which now stands between £15 and £18 billion (*Financial Times*, 2 March, 1990). If we add together cash and borrowing power, Lord Hanson has the resources to go into the stock market tomorrow and buy 10 per cent of British manufacturing. Because any such move would make big waves in a small pool, it is almost certain that future major acquisitions will be made in the United States. The retention of low tech manufacturing subsidiaries from previous deals is both a support and cover for the next round of even larger deals. Mature manufacturing businesses act as cash cows whose earnings fill in the gaps between deals, while these manufacturing operations usefully distract attention from asset trading. Britain's largest diversified manufacturer is essentially a company whose earnings growth depends on Lord Hanson's ability to put deals together and take companies apart.

Hanson is not alone in its preoccupation with dealing and manufacturing.

472   *Karel Williams, John Williams and Colin Haslam*

The modus operandi at BTR is very similar. BTR's management has the same explicit preference for undemanding low tech manufacturing and the same capacity for dealing in assets; the most recent move was an unsuccessful $1.6 billion bid for Norton, the American abrasives manufacturer. And the smaller success stories of British engineering in the 1980s have been acquisitive mini conglomerates like Williams Holdings, Evered, Tomkins and Suter. In the aftermath of the recession, they usually played a variant on Hanson's game: the trick was to buy bombed out companies with undervalued assets and considerable scope for rationalisation through sacking workers, selling surplus land and passing on unwanted businesses. A possible defence would be that these large firms acquire small firms as a way of buying in innovation and dynamism: but none of these cases fit such a pattern. The spread of the new style of asset sweating has exactly the same consequences as more traditional forms of retreat; manufacturing activities are always demoted in the hierarchy of corporate activities while dealing and services are promoted.

Finally, we would note that case study of giant firms gives us a new insight into hollowing out. GEC, BAe and Hanson are all hollowed out to the extent that they are not like Siemens, Fiat or Thomson-Brandt; the British giants are distinguished by lack of commitment to manufacturing, absence of world class productive capability and indifference to market presence. This conclusion has a double significance. First, it raises doubts about the assumption of productive essentialism which underpins much current discussion of British industrial policy. For example, in *Beyond the Policy Review* (1989) it is assumed that the problem is external financial institutions which encourage 'short-termism' in firms that would otherwise be productively virtuous. Our evidence on hollowing out suggests this counter-factual assumption is very dubious. Second, our conclusion indicates that with the exception of a handful of chemical and pharmaceutical companies, like Glaxo and ICI, Britain no longer has any 'national champions'. There are still signboards with familiar corporate names outside the factories on the by-passes and dual carriageways, but these boards no longer signify what they did twenty years ago. Old style British industrial policy which seeks positive results through promoting national champions has been rendered obsolete by manufacturing retreat.

Conditions of hollowing out

In most of the advanced countries, manufacturing firms are trading companies, shifting into services and building up financial activities and in some advanced countries offshore production is being developed. But these activities are usually undertaken to defend the firm's manufacturing base and generally do not reflect a lack of commitment to manufacturing. Defence and strengthening of the manufacturing base is the aim of a diversifying firm like Daimler Benz which has bought into white goods, electronics and aerospace through the purchase of AEG and MBB. The aim is the same in a firm like

Thomson-Brandt which strategically is moving in the opposite direction through divestment and purchase which focuses the firm on two core manufacturing businesses of TV and micro chips. A similar defensive logic underlies some well-publicised manufacturing moves into services; Sony has bought into Columbia so that it can create a vertically integrated company which produces programme material as well as the hardware for home entertainment. In other cases, activities like financial services are being built up as complements or supplements to manufacturing. This development is particularly pronounced in Japan where successful manufacturing firms are accumulating funds faster than they can deploy them in their manufacturing businesses (Ballon and Tomita, 1989); 20 per cent of Toyota's profits this year should come from financial operations. But that development is not at the expense of Toyota's obsessional commitment to the production and marketing of motor cars; the cars business is one of the main beneficiaries of the glut of funds because investment in new capital equipment is no longer rationed in Toyota car factories (Company visit, March 1990). Commitment to manufacturing is equally manifest in the development of offshore production by Japanese electronics and car companies. The aim has been to become more competitive through exploiting low wages and to increase market share despite trade friction. This does not involve the stripping out of domestic value added and employment; Japanese car export volume to the United States has not fallen as transplant production has come on stream and the value of such exports is likely to increase as the Japanese factories concentrate on luxury and sporting models.

If the behaviour of manufacturing firms elsewhere is superficially similar but really different, the questions about giant British manufacturing firms are fairly specific. Why, in Britain, are trading services and finance being developed as part of a retreat from manufacturing which is not taking place elsewhere? Why do giant British firms have such a strong bias against manufacturing of all kinds except for the simpler or more sheltered varieties, where returns are guaranteed? Why, when giant British firms move offshore, do they so often move to the United States rather than adjacent West Europe? These questions can, of course, be answered in a variety of ways within different intellectual frameworks. Our own approach (see Williams, 1983) has always been to emphasise the force of institutional and organisational conditions which operate differently in various advanced economies. It is an approach which does not commend itself to orthodox social scientists who are preoccupied with similarities and universal frameworks. But, if we are interested in differences, the obvious starting point is the behavioural difference of British manufacturing in terms of profit performance and distribution of earnings.

In any survey of British manufacturing over the last twenty years, two points immediately stand out: first, the British manufacturing sector is relatively unprofitable compared with other national manufacturing sectors; and, second, the British manufacturing sector has a high propensity to distribute earnings to shareholders.

474   *Karel Williams, John Williams and Colin Haslam*

Table 4 Profitability of various national manufacturing sectors

	1973	1981	1988
USA	20.7	10.8	18.5
UK	7.4	5.9	11.4
Germany	13.6	11.6	17.3
Italy	9.0	14.9	16.4
Japan	22.4	19.6	20.6

Source: OECD (communication)

Note: Profit equals gross operating surplus as per cent of gross capital stock

Table 4 illustrates long run profitability. Whatever the measure of profit and whatever the sub-period, up to the late 1980s, British manufacturing is less profitable than other national manufacturing sectors. British manufacturing in the late 1980s did attain average levels of profitability. But, as Nigel Lawson would say, that is a 'blip'; current British levels of profit can hardly be sustained in the recession which will be produced by the deflationary cure for trade deficit. Even more interesting are the differences in patterns of distribution. Table 5 provides a long run comparison of distribution patterns in Britain and Germany.

On distribution, the picture is broadly the same right back to the early 1970s; the proportion of GOS paid out as dividend to keep the shareholders happy in British manufacturing is typically 3–4 times as high as in German manufacturing (Meyer and Alexander, 1990). The contrast with patterns of distribution in other advanced countries, especially Japan, is equally marked.

What do these behavioural differences signify? The absence of profit in British manufacturing is an index of the pervasive disorganisation of production and marketing inside firms. Case studies by the National Institute (e.g. Daly *et al.*, 1985) and general surveys (e.g. New and Myers, 1986) identify productive disorganisation as a constraint on the firms manufacturing in Britain. New and Myers show that, despite a massive shakeout in the recession, the lamentably poor delivery performance of British manufacturing did not improve at all between 1975 and 1985. There was also no improvement in the proportion of lead time used productively and no overall reduction in stock levels. The NIESR case studies of metal working and kitchen cabinet manufacture document these problems at a micro level and show that management and supervisors lack training and technical knowledge; so perhaps the failure to improve performance is not surprising. On the marketing side, the Doyle, Saunders and Wong (1987) survey shows that the marketing function is grossly underdeveloped and ineffective in British owned firms which often fail to make a basic analysis of market segments or customer needs and set very modest marketing targets. This kind of disorganisation makes manufacturing a peculiarly unrewarding activity and retreat from manufacturing must often be the line of least resistance.

Table 5 Dividends and interest payments as a share of gross operating surplus in British and West German manufacturing, 1970–84

	West Germany			United Kingdom		
	Dividends as percent of GOS	*Interest as percent of GOS*	*D + I as percent of GOS*	*Dividends as percent of GOS*	*Interest as percent of GOS*	*D + I as percent of GOS*
1970	4.7	15.3	20.0	22.6	26.6	49.2
1975	3.4	20.3	23.7	13.1	41.8	54.9
1976	3.0	18.2	21.2	13.3	38.8	52.1
1977	3.9	17.8	21.7	10.4	26.9	37.3
1978	3.4	16.7	20.1	11.0	23.8	34.8
1979	4.4	17.2	21.6	16.4	28.2	44.6
1980	3.5	20.9	24.4	14.4	33.9	48.3
1981	3.3	24.9	28.2	15.3	30.7	46.0
1982	3.6	25.8	29.4	15.0	29.1	44.1
1983	3.3	22.2	25.5	15.4	23.5	38.9
1984	3.7	22.0	25.7	14.8	23.0	37.8

Source: Eurostat National Accounts, *ESA – Detailed Tables by Sector*, table S10.

Note: GOS includes dividends and income payments received.

Retreat is also encouraged by an overdevelopment of financial control together with the acceptance of financial rules and representations as a self-contained guide to action. Most giant British firms are organised on a divisional basis, with considerable emphasis on financial control through capital budgeting and product costing. Our own case study work on Japan (Williams and Haslam, 1991) shows that the Japanese organise the relation between the financial and the productive in a completely different way. Their workshops are run on tight physical standards, with the emphasis on 'Kaizen' or constant, positive improvement. This contrasts sharply with the Anglo-American way of cost accounting which polices the negative financial variances. Senior Japanese managers use financial measures as guides to the extent and kind of productive improvement which is necessary if the firm's market objectives are to be met; for example, a particular project should go ahead but development costs will have to be reduced or machine utilisation must be improved. This is quite different from the Anglo-American way of capital budgeting where the financial rule is everything; for example, a particular project will not go ahead if it does not meet a target rate of return (at given levels of productive efficiency). The Anglo-American way is ineffectual and it may well be counter-productive in disorganised firms; where competition is intense, financially controlled British and American firms respond negatively to the internal limits set by their own disorganisation rather than respond positively to the external requirements of the market. Insofar as the dominant British forms of organisation and calculation mediate an external environment, their main function is to reinforce external pressure from the stock market.

476   *Karel Williams, John Williams and Colin Haslam*

The high levels of distribution to shareholders reflect external stock market pressure for earnings. It is very difficult for major British manufacturing firms to resist these pressures. In Britain large manufacturing companies are almost always publicly quoted and their shareholders have no loyalty or commitment to existing management. Nearly 60 per cent of ordinary shares are owned by institutions (Stock Exchange, 1990) whose managers deal actively in the (vain) hope of bettering the performance of the FT index; the velocity of dealing has increased to the point where the average share is held for 4 to 6 years (Bain, 1987). Fund managers will always sell if they are offered a small premium over yesterday's close. In this environment, take-over is an ever present threat for firms whose profit performance is mediocre. As for firms with decent earnings, they are likely to be tempted into external growth through acquisition as a substitute for organic growth: profits push up the p/e ratio and/or generate cash resources which both make take-over easier.

The pursuit of profit is part of any capitalist system; the British have constructed a peculiar national system for swapping ownership in pursuit of profit. The scale of these ownership transfers is truly staggering. In the merger boom of the 1960s, nearly half of all British quoted companies were acquired. The late 1980s saw another merger boom; in the peak years of 1988 and 1989, 2,263 manufacturing and non-manufacturing companies were acquired at a cost of £48 billion (CSO, 1990). Apologists for the stock market would argue that all will benefit if assets are transferred to new owners who can increase shareholder value by securing a higher rate of return. But, on the evidence of the 1960s merger boom, this is not exactly what happens in Britain. The shareholders of the taken-over company do benefit if there is a cash offer and they take the money. But Meeks's (1977) classic study shows that, after the acquired and acquiring companies are put together, the profits of the combined companies, in the seven years after take-over, are typically lower than those of the separate companies before take-over. The results of the current merger boom may be different and high profits would benefit shareholders. But, from the point of view of labour and the national interest, there would be little gain unless the profits come from domestic manufacturing. As long as production is disorganised and marketing is ineffectual, retreat from manufacturing is the surest way of increasing profits. In this context, the stock exchange, which wants profits, and does not care where or how they are made, is a malign and destructive influence on manufacturing.

Institutional conditions can again be invoked to explain why the United States of America is the main centre of attraction for the manufacturing companies who are slipping away from Britain. Acquisition and merger in the United States is subject to anti-trust regulation, but otherwise free. Crucially, in America there are no institutional obstacles to hostile takeover; such obstacles are commonplace in continental Europe where many companies are bid-proof. Three quarters of the multi-billion value of UK international purchases of manufacturing and non-manufacturing companies is in the United States; whereas, until 1987, UK companies typically bought just

10–25 EC companies at a cost which was usually below £50 million (Cutler *et al.*, 1989). The primary influence of institutional conditions is reinforced by similarities in the culture of management in Britain and the United States. In both countries there is the same emphasis on achieving profit through financial control. In shifting to the United States, British companies are following institutional fault lines rather than realising new productive opportunities.

In this international context, a hollowed out British manufacturing sector is the logical result of internal disorganisation and external stock market pressure. If this conclusion is accepted, it can only deepen our pessimism because hollowing out is determined by national and international conditions which are long standing and difficult to reform; abolition of the British stock exchange is hardly within the realms of the possible for Mr Kinnock, reform of the American stock exchange is not within the realm of the thinkable. Insofar as internal disorganisation is a major factor, we must also have doubts about the efficacy of any industrial policy which concentrates on changing strategy; operational incapacity is likely to set limits on the benefits from strategic intervention. In this sober frame of mind, we turn to consider the policy options in the next two sections of this paper.

The implications for policy

Industrial policy is a prominent theme in centrist and left discussion of Britain's industrial decline; if we exclude the radical right, all men of goodwill agree that some form of active industrial policy might help to reverse our decline. The shape of politics in the 1990s is unclear, but the claims of industrial policy are pressed in the Labour Party's *Policy Review* (1989) and in Heseltine's *Challenge of Europe* (1989). The irony is that industrial policy is arriving politically just when traditional national industrial policy is increasingly constrained economically by external developments. After all, the premise of traditional policy is that the object of intervention is inside the national economy; policy aims to act on the population of firms inside the national manufacturing sector which is to be revived or redirected. But, in Britain now, this is a very shaky premise. The hollowing out of manufacturing has gone so far that we have lost national champions which could be easily regulated or usefully taken into public ownership; the resurrection of British manufacturing is an altogether more formidable task than the redirection of British manufacturing.

Some part of this is recognised in current discussions of British industrial policy. There is an increasing recognition that the existing model of industrial organisation has failed to solve the problems of British manufacturing; other approaches are being presented as constructive ways forward. The two main contenders have been Japanisation (Oliver and Wilkinson, 1988) and flexible specialisation (Hirst and Zeitlin 1989; also Thompson (ed.) 1989). These

478   *Karel Williams, John Williams and Colin Haslam*

Table 6 Share of textiles, clothing and furniture in British manufacturing value added and employment, 1987

	Textiles	Footwear/ clothing	Furniture/ timber
Sectoral value added as percent of manufacturing value added (SIC 2–4)	3.2	3.5	3.2
Sectoral employment as percent of manufacturing employment (SIC 2–4)	4.7	7.0	4.1

Source: P.A. 1002, Census of Production, 1987

interventions have usefully transformed the industrial policy debate, but there are strong reasons for doubting whether Japanisation and flexible specialisation have enough weight and leverage to transform the prospects and performance of British manufacturing.

In particular both flexible specialisation and (thus far) Japanisation are in Britain associated with small and medium sized enterprises (which in the Japanese case are branches of giant parents). This prompts several comments. In the first place one of the distinguishing peculiarities of British manufacturing is the size of the small and medium enterprises sector which accounts for a smaller share of output than in most other advanced countries. In Britain, 23 per cent of employment in manufacturing in the late 1970s was in enterprises with less than 200 employees; whereas, at the other extreme, in Italy, one third of manufacturing employment may be in small businesses with less than 20 employees (Bannock, 1985). Networks of small firms may have something to offer a country like Britain. Equally, inward investment by productively capable firms from Japan might be one of the ways of reviving a hollowed out manufacturing sector whose domestic firms have a limited capacity to 'Japanise' and are, in any case, quitting the domestic market. The problem is the scale of likely and actual developments on both these fronts.

Up to the present time, in Britain at least, small and medium networks are most relevant to a limited number of sectors especially textiles, clothing and furniture which have traditionally been the preserve of small firms. The immediate problem is that these three sectors have a modest weight in British output and employment.

As Table 6 shows, even if these sectors are broadly defined to include footwear and timber, they account for only 9.9 per cent of manufacturing value added; their share of manufacturing employment is higher at 15.8 per cent because these are relatively low wage sectors. The three core sectors of British manufacturing capability in 1987 were mechanical engineering, electrical engineering and motor vehicles, none of which as yet show signs of significantly shifting to a small firm base. These sectors, in contrast to those displayed in Table 6, accounted for 28.9 per cent of British manufacturing value added and 29.4 per cent of manufacturing employment. But even for a sector like clothing and even on the most optimistic assumptions, it would not be possible to develop small firm networks to the point where they accounted for all (or most?) of the production. For the immediate future the conclusion must be that the policy of encouraging small firm networks offers very little leverage on overall manufacturing performance.

As for Japanese inward investment, that has attracted media attention which is out of all proportion to its real importance. For a start, despite a sharp recent spurt induced by their fears of having their exports shut out of 'fortress Europe', the Japanese are not the only or the most important direct investors in the UK. In 1987 Japan ranked eighth (below e.g. Canada, France and the Netherlands) in a table of foreign-owned UK manufacturing production (Lloyds Bank, 1990). The flow of Japanese direct investment into the UK is still dwarfed by American direct investment; US firms directly invested 31.7 $ billion in Britain the year to end-December 1989, whereas the Japanese invested only 4.2 $ billion (Nomura Research, Communication). Japanese direct investment in manufacturing is smaller still and is conspicuous mainly because it has gone into the much publicised construction of new factories on green field sites. But the number of these factories and the total amount of employment generated is trivial. By early 1990 there were only 125 Japanese factories in Britain which employed a total of 25,000 employees of whom 1,000 were Japanese; by way of contrast, more than 500,000 workers are employed in American owned British factories (Economic Development Briefing, 1990; *Independent*, 30 May 1990). If the scale of Japanese manufacturing in Britain has been greatly exaggerated, it is also doubtful whether this development brings significant economic benefits to our national economy.

Japanese manufacturing firms have been welcomed because they bring superior manufacturing techniques to Britain. That may be so, but, from a social point of view, the crucial economic issues is whether new Japanese factories bring extra value added and employment to the failing British manufacturing sector. A strategic panic about 1992 and fortress Europe has recently brought three Japanese car manufacturers to Britain. But the net medium term benefits can only be limited when Nissan, Toyota and Honda are each developing small, 200,000 cars a year, plants which will succeed mainly by displacing domestically produced Ford and Rover output. Unless these new factories export a high proportion of their output, the national benefit (in terms of value added and employment) could be negligible or negative because the British content level of Japanese transplant production will be lower than that of the indigenous car production which is displaced. On this point, the results of an earlier wave of Japanese investment in British electronics factories are hardly reassuring. Table 7 summarises data from the 1986 census of production on variations in plant level labour productivity between British and foreign owned plants; this source is unique because it allows us to relate labour input to gross output (including bought in parts and components) as well as to net output (or gross value added, excluding bought in parts and components).

480   *Karel Williams, John Williams and Colin Haslam*

Table 7 British labour productivity in manufacturing by plant ownership

	Gross output		Net output (Gross Value Added)	
	Per operative	Per employee	Per operative	Per employee
UK owned plants	100	100	100	100
EC owned plants	150	136	140	128
German owned plants	157	138	153	134
Japanese owned plants	167	182	75	81
US owned plants	188	171	161	146
Total Foreign owned	174	160	152	140

Source: 1986 Census of Production, re-calculated in Dillow (1990)

As enthusiasts for Japanese manufacturing techniques would expect, gross output per operative or employee is higher in Britain's Japanese owned factories than in British factories. On this basis, the performance of Japanese factories is also better than that of German owned factories in Britain and, per employee but not per operative, is better than US owned factories. But, if we measure the performance of Japanese owned factories on a net output basis, Japanese superiority collapses; the net output per operative in the Japanese owned factories of 1986 was only 75 per cent of the net output per operative in British owned factories and fared even less well in comparison with German and US owned factories. Presumably, the discrepancy between gross and net productivity in the Japanese case arises because a substantial part of the value of the final product is accounted for by components which arrive in styrene trays from Japan.

The benefits of Japanisation may not, therefore, be either as overwhelming or as axiomatic as is commonly assumed. Insofar as an inflow of Japanese investment in manufacturing, or an extension of flexible specialisation, contribute to the improvement of British manufacturing performance they are to be welcomed. The problem is that for the forseeable future each of these developments necessarily has a limited leverage. Because of this their beneficial results are likely to be negated by forces which operate in the opposite direction.

The most important of these opposing forces is the giant British firm which operates its own anti-industrial policy. There is little doubt that, in a deflationary environment, Lords Weinstock and Hanson or Professor Smith can destroy jobs and reduce exports faster than they can be created by local networks or Japanese newcomers. This point is proved by the record of the 1980s; as we have seen, over the last decade, the top 25 British owned firms destroyed 200,000 British manufacturing jobs and acquired or created a similar number overseas, while all the Japanese newcomers created just 25,000 manufacturing jobs. The anti-industrial policy of giant British firms is an acute problem which will not go away because the highly concentrated structure of British manufacturing puts so much economic power into the hands of a small number of giant firms. If we consider the 100 British owned manufacturing companies with the largest stock market capitalisation, our rough calculations suggest that the home and overseas sales turnover of these companies adds up to a sum equal to 45 per cent of the total output of manufacturing industry in Britain. In other national economies, industrial policy can concentrate on positive tasks; in Britain it is equally important to address the issue of damage limitation by neutralising the anti-industrial policies of our giant firms. From this perspective, the most obvious traditional instruments of industrial policy are some form of selective public ownership and/or a regulatory regime that includes a variety of sticks and carrots.

The Alternative Economic Strategy is dead and nationalisation is desperately unfashionable, but it is still worth considering public ownership of some firms, like GEC, if only because it would break the connection with the stock exchange. The immediate practical problem is that any nationalising government must suffer the consequences of the stock exchange when it takes companies into public ownership. The social objective of public ownership is to obtain economic leverage by capturing sales turnover, which represents productive or market presence, and also to capture value added or net output which determines the amount of employment that can be sustained inside the firm. But, under any system of nationalisation with compensation, the purchase price which the government pays for the manufacturing firm has to be based on the stock market valuation of that firm's (distributed) earnings. We have already observed the high propensity of British firms to distribute profit in the form of dividend to shareholders; we can now add the point that the price/earnings ratio for British manufacturing companies, currently around 11 : 1, is much the same in Britain as elsewhere in Europe. These two facts increase the cost of any nationalisation programme and reduce the economic leverage obtained for a given expenditure of public money. Because British distribution ratios are high and the p/e ratio is the same as elsewhere in Europe, the capitalised stock market valuation of each ECU of turnover is much higher in Britain than, for example, in Germany. In Britain £1 spent on nationalising a manufacturing firm buys only 30p of sales and 10p of value added; in Germany, DM 1 spent on the same object buys DM 1 of sales and 30pf of value added.

It could be argued that this is only a tactical difficulty; if the benefits of nationalisation are considerable, it may be worth paying the price. But these benefits are doubtful because nationalisation offers ownership without control. State control of nationalised enterprises is elusive because the formulation and execution of strategy must be delegated to enterprise managers. The strategists who export jobs and the dealers and traders who neglect manufacturing would become the high priests of the newly nationalised temple of manufacturing. Non-productive habits and productive incapacity together ensure that the relation between putting capital in and getting saleable manufacturing output is by no means certain and direct. This point is

482   *Karel Williams, John Williams and Colin Haslam*

proved by the history of nationalised coal, steel and cars in Britain in the decade after the mid-1970s; on our calculations £9.5 billion of state funds were wasted on supporting ill-conceived and poorly-executed management strategies in these three industries (Williams *et al.*, 1986). Our case history of the Edwardes recovery strategy at BL (Williams, 1987), like our work on coal (Cutler *et al.*, 1985) and on steel (Haslam, 1989) shows that successive Labour and Tory politicians and civil servants failed to question, leave alone control, management strategies which involved large scale investment on the basis of very dubious assumptions about the market and productive possibilities.

This point is pertinent because filling out hollowed shells is likely to be an expensive business, however it is attempted. The starting point is that, under current conditions of intense national competition, many giant British manufacturing firms are not going concerns. Under state or private ownership, they can only quickly become internationally competitive, going concerns if they are given large sums of state money to invest. If the economic results of state subvention are uncertain, it is also true that there are now external political constraints on pumping state money into industrial regeneration. The EC would insist on inspecting the terms and conditions on which funds were being supplied to nationalised or private firms: interest free equity capital or soft loans would be challenged in the European courts. The EC has vigorously pursued nationalised manufacturing firms, like Renault in France whose debt write offs were sanctioned on condition of capacity reduction, and has been prepared to impose hefty fines. The Commission would be more fiercely opposed to nationalised or private manufacturing firms who tried to increase capacity with soft state loans. Equally, the Commission would make it difficult to operate the kind of planning agreements which the left advocated in the 1970s. Under the 1992 regulations, it is doubtful whether the Commission can adequately police and prohibit existing purchasing policies which covertly favour national producers; but new purchasing policies of an overtly discriminatory kind would be an easy target. Financial incentives for compliance with planning agreements would be equally unacceptable.

As British manufacturing continued to decline economically through the 1980s, so Europe moved on politically. Most British economists and politicians have been slow to notice that the rules of the whole industrial policy game have been changed by the renaissance of the EC through the 1992 programme. Under current EC law and practice, active national industrial policies are now rather like trade unions in nineteenth-century Britain; their existence is tolerated, but any form of activity will be legally harassed. In making this point, our aim is not to sanction a futile Thatcherite anti-Europeanism which scapegoats Brussels restrictions and regulations. As we argue in the next section, it is essential to take a broader view of the European problem; Europe is both, in terms of manufacturing trade, the economic source of our real problems and the political sphere in which these problems have to be addressed.

The European dimension

By insisting on the European dimension our recent work breaks with the national preoccupations of our earlier work on British decline; the first major result of this problem shift is a new book *1992 – The Struggle for Europe* (Cutler *et al.*, 1989). The logic of this shift is inescapable. By concentrating on the national condition of hollowing out, we were only analysing half a problem. The other half is what fills the space left by hollowing out and under what economic and political conditions does this infilling take place. The short answer to both these questions is European manufactured imports, especially German imports, which enter freely because Britain is a member of the European Community. This point is perfectly illustrated by the composition of the British trade deficit. Britain's trade deficit arises entirely from manufactured trade with Europe; Britain's manufactured trade with the rest of the world is still in surplus. And, above all, the European deficit arises from manufactured trade with Germany; two-thirds of Britain's total deficit with Europe is caused by trade with Germany (Cutler *et al.*, 1989). This pattern of trade is the result of German manufacturing strength which creates problems for all of Germany's trading partners within the EC. If this point is still controversial, this is because British political and economic discourse about Europe is founded on a series of misconceptions about the economic status of different European countries, about the uniqueness of Britain's problems and about the benefits of trade.

The memory of great power status and Thatcher's theatrical foreign policy still colour British popular perception of Britain's national power and relative status within Europe. It needs to be emphasised that the four major European national economies (West Germany, France, Italy and Britain) are not of roughly equal weight in productive terms. Their national populations of 55–60 millions are roughly equal so that each of the four countries has around 18 per cent of total EC population. But West Germany has much the greater economic weight: in 1985, West Germany had a 38.0 per cent share of EC 12 manufacturing output compared with 23.0 per cent for France, 16 per cent for Italy and just 12.8 per cent for the UK (Cutler *et al.*, 1989). West Germany is already Europe's regional economic superpower and we expect Germany's predominance will be reinforced by German reunification and the general collapse of the East European police welfare states. Whatever the difficulties and dislocations of German reunification a second economic miracle should raise East Germany to the productive level of the West before the year 2000. And that implies Germany's national share of EC 12 manufacturing output will rise to 50 per cent. The share of a more broadly defined 'centre' is even larger if the centre is defined to include Germany plus contiguous areas of North France, Belgium, Holland and Denmark. The reality of Europe is centralisation of production and the prospect is for more of the same.

From this point of view, the British trade deficit, which is usually discussed as a national problem, should be seen as part of a larger European problem.

484   *Karel Williams, John Williams and Colin Haslam*

The centralisation of production is associated with general trade imbalance which creates structural problems at the periphery. The strength of West German manufacturing is such that West Germany runs large trade surpluses with Europe and the rest of the world: West Germany's 1989 trade surplus was in total larger than that of Japan whose population is twice as large. Around half the German surplus is earned in Europe and the general pattern is that *all* the EC countries (with the trivial exception of Ireland) run deficits on manufactured trade with Germany which amounted to some 32 million Ecu in 1987. Export success creates manufacturing jobs in Germany, and the trade deficits elsewhere create constraints which prevent North European countries from adopting expansionary policies to reduce unemployment. Trade constraint is a reality not only in Britain but also in France where the Mitterand reflationary experiment of 1980–1 was frustrated by a rising deficit on manufactured trade with Germany. The reality is that intra-European trade is a mechanism for passing the parcel of unemployment to weaker countries. Even the European countries with a strong manufacturing trade performance struggle to escape these constraints; in 1987 Italy, for example, managed a manufacturing surplus of 1.3 billion Ecu with the other EC countries but her manufactured trade with Germany was 2.8 billion Ecu in deficit.

All this is invisible in liberal market economics which maintains that free trade benefits all and, if the market generates increased inequality, automatic equilibriating mechanisms should solve the problem. Against this, we would support the historical school who argued that the rules of free trade usually benefit stronger and more advanced countries. For Germany now, European free trade is a crucial support of German economic predominance (just as world free trade was for the British in the nineteenth century). Free trade allows the Germans to manufacture in Germany and then distribute via wholly owned subsidiaries throughout Europe; as Edzard Reuter, the chairman of Daimler-Benz, observed in a recent interview, 'Europe is our future home market' (*Financial Times*, 23 April, 1990). The German national economy is managed so that German manufacturers are encouraged to seek their own salvation through trade; under a system of export-Keynesianism, the domestic monetary and fiscal policy regime is usually fairly restrictive so that German manufacturers have to find sales and value added from export markets. West Germany's manufacturing sector has responded magnificently and, as a result, Germany has a higher propensity to export manufactures than any comparable advanced country; fully half of West Germany's manufacturing output is exported, compared with around one third in France, Britain and Italy (Cutler *et al.*, 1989). This division of responsibility between the state and the private manufacturing sector is completely misunderstood by the many non-German politicians and economists who believe that other European countries could be like Germany if they adopted responsible monetary and fiscal policies.

It is equally important to resist the misconception that market mechanisms will somehow or other correct the centralisation of production. West German wages are the highest in Europe but German manufacturing is not migrating to the lower wage declining industrial regions of North Europe or the underdeveloped Southern agricultural countries. This point is proved by the disparity between Germany's investment in domestic manufacturing and her direct investment in foreign manufacturing; in 1988, the German investment in domestic capacity was nine times higher and most of the direct investment went to North America (not other European countries). West Germany's output, especially in mechanical engineering, consists of high value added products which incorporate much 'technik'; unlike, say, electronics assembly work, this kind of production does not migrate naturally to low wage areas. It is not surprising, therefore, that, in Europe over the 1980s, regional and national disparities of income increased. The EC regional and social funds are an inadequate and inappropriate response to this problem. After the CAP has claimed the lion's share of the EC's limited budget, only 0.3 per cent of the Community's GDP is available to these funds. Furthermore, three-quarters or more of their expenditure is concentrated on infrastructural improvement and youth training. In liberal market terms these are desirable objects because this kind of intervention aims to make the market work better. In practice, the effects on trade generated inequality are double edged; infrastructural improvement, for example, helps peripheral countries to export, but it also makes it easier for the Germans to export from the centre.

What we are proposing is that Britain's industrial problems should be reconceptualised as part of a larger European problem about centralised production and unbalanced trade. The nature of the problem shift is summed up by the exchange between Holmes and Watson in *Silver Blaze* about the 'curious incident of the dog in the night-time':

'The dog did nothing in the night-time'
'That was the curious incident' remarked Holmes.

For Watson, what happens is the centre of attention; while, for Holmes, what does not happen may be equally, or more, important. So it is with the hollowing out of British manufacturing. Like Watson, we have been preoccupied with the way in which British firms (or irresponsible American multinationals) are leaving Britain; while those who want an unlikely happy ending to the story put the emphasis on the coming of the Japanese. As Holmes would see, the more important point is that the Germans are not coming, on any significant scale, to manufacture in Britain, or anywhere else on the periphery of Europe. Instead, the Germans are sending us their finished exports to fill the hollowed out space and that must set an absolute limit on the possibility of national industrial policy. The German firms who do not manufacture in Britain are simply beyond the reach of our national government. There is no point in having planning agreements with the distributors of AEG or BMW in their smart post-modernist warehouses in

486   *Karel Williams, John Williams and Colin Haslam*

Milton Keynes or Swindon. These problems can only be tackled by a European industrial policy.

The task of a European industrial policy is formidable and the constraints on such a policy are considerable. Britain is the worst case north European country but there are declining industrial regions in other northern countries, like Belgium and France. Furthermore, income levels are much lower and unemployment levels are much higher in the underdeveloped southern countries. Income levels in Portugal are not much higher than in Poland or Bulgaria, while the Spanish rate of unemployment is near 20 per cent. With the exception of Spain, none of the Southern agricultural countries are increasing their share of European manufacturing production and exports. The problem of centralised production and unbalanced trade could easily be solved through some form of protection. But that option has been partially blocked with the renaisssance of the EC through the 1992 programme. The members of the EC all accept trade without tariffs, they are now committed to partial removal of non-tariff barriers and beyond that to monetary union. Free trade is the ark of the European covenant. In the 1970s or early 1980s, the British left proposed protection as part of the AES and we ourselves endorsed selective protection in our work of the mid-1980s (e.g. Williams *et al.*, 1987a). These proposals are now incredible and obsolete; protectionism in one country would attract massive retaliation.

Nevertheless, it is necessary to address the problem of centralised production and unbalanced trade. Even within a framework of free trade in manufactures, it should be possible to devise policy measures which encourage decentralisation of production and allow weaker countries to live with payments problems. There is much to be said for Germanisation, not least because the German model gives a role to strong unions as well as to competent managers. But, if the German model is economically relevant and socially desirable, we must be cautious about whether and how it can be realised on the periphery. An imitative Germanisation on the periphery is unlikely to succeed because indigenous firms in countries like Britain are unlikely to cure the long standing performance gap with West German firms; as Table 8 showed, German-owned plants in Britain have levels of labour productivity which are 33 to 50 per cent higher than British-owned competitors and there is no evidence that this gap is being closed. The new-found enthusiasm for work force trainng in Britain may be welcome, but it is surely unrealistic to suppose that an improved supply of technically trained workers will in itself transform performance if the national demand is for low skilled workers and their financial controllers. In that case, it is necessary to contemplate measures which direct or encourage German firms to locate outside Germany.

This kind of decentralisation of production should be the first objective of policy. The limited budget of the EC rules out many of the more traditional kinds of policy instruments which have been used at a national level to promote regional balance; the EC, for example, does not have the resources to bribe German firms into relocation. And that may be no great loss because unfocused policies of bribery are ineffectual. One main remaining possibility is variation of national fiscal regime as a way of encouraging decentralisation; this does not put any demand on the EC budget and could be effective if it was tightly focused on the residual of profit. The EC's 1992 programme for fiscal harmonisation has run into the sand and that failure leaves open the possibility of creating fiscal differences for industrial policy purposes. The 'unlevel field' could be promoted in a variety of ways, there is for example considerable scope for varying the incidence of corporation tax which, as a recent study showed (IFS, 1989), takes a substantial proportion of manufacturing profit in all the EC countries. At the simplest, there could be general rebates of corporation tax on profits which arise from manufacturing in Britain and in the southern agricultural countries; this difference would provide an incentive for German firms to relocate. A more elaborate scheme could provide incentives for indigenous firms to expand output in the peripheral countries. One such proposal would involve a scheme of 'value added promotion' where extra corporation tax rebates would be offered to British based firms which improved on their past record of output growth; the aim here would be to redress the anti-industrial policy of giant British firms in a way which would be compatible with a broader European initiative that aimed to influence German firms.

The second major objective of policy should be to make it easier for weaker countries to live with structural problems about trade deficit. For the foreseeable future, weaker countries like Britain will have to live with trade constraints which prevent the adoption of expansionary policies and force the adoption of deflationary policies. From the point of view of damage limitation in Britain this is crucial; the devastating, irreparable damage to labour and the national interest is concentrated in periods of recession when output drops. The current proposals for moving towards EMU will exacerbate the situation because, as exchange rates become increasingly fixed, the whole burden of (deflationary) adjustment will fall on the weaker countries; the Italian option of crawling peg devaluation will be increasingly closed off. If EC plans go ahead, there is, however, one policy option which would help Britain and that option is control of portfolio capital exports. Within the EC, free trade in goods is twenty years old but free trade in money is still not complete and several European countries may yet have to reintroduce controls as a way of controlling pressure on weak currencies. Our proposal here is simply that countries with problems about visible trade balance should be free to restrict capital movements. For Britain a bar on portfolio investment would be easiest to administer and would probably be sufficient because Britain exports about £10 billion of portfolio capital each year. If these exports were blocked, Britain's trade deficit, even at its 1989 level of around £20 billion, would, at a stroke, be halved.

These proposals are probably not adequate to the double economic task of decentralising production and palliating the consequences of centralisation.

488   *Karel Williams, John Williams and Colin Haslam*

They are also politically problematic. If the German national interest is narrrowly defined, most of what we propose could be represented as anti-German. We would argue that a stable Europe with constraints on levels of economic inequality is in the long-term interests of Germany along with the rest of Europe. None the less, the Germans would probably initially have to be pressured into concession by an EC coalition of disadvantaged governments. If such a coalition now seems impossibly remote, in three or four years time things may be very different; present political alignments and identifications will change with the passing of Thatcher and the pressing of European economic integration (especially monetary union) on terms which disadvantage all the weaker countries. Amidst much which is uncertain one trend which is reasonably predictable is that the EC must address the so called 'deficit of democracy' and give more power to the European parliament. As that happens, one person one vote becomes a radical principle; there may be 77 million citizens in re-united Germany but there are 260 million in the other 11 EC countries. Fortunately, none of this is our immediate concern. The articulation and implementation of the policies we recommend is a matter for Europe's politicians. As intellectuals, we are mainly responsible for defining problems and suggesting lines of attack which are practical and appropriate to the problem diagnosed. Like all the rest, our own approach to policy can be criticised because its solutions are underdeveloped, inadequate or difficult to implement. But, we do believe that the various approaches promote and incorporate different kinds of problem definitions, some of which are more realistic and relevant than others. And it is never possible to solve imaginary problems. In writing this paper, our main aim has been to challenge the irrelevant problem definitions which underpin the current British debate on manufacturing decline. The process of hollowing out has gone much further than most are prepared to admit. That creates peculiar national problems because the giant firms which have such a large weight in output and employment are both productively feeble and pathologically anti-industrial. And these national peculiarities need to be set in a European context where the problems created by German manufacturing predominance, inside a regional free trade area, have to be recognised.

K. and J. Williams
University College of Wales, Aberystwyth
C. Haslam
East London Polytechnic

References

Bain, A. (1987) 'Economic Commentary', *Midland Bank Review*, Summer.
Ballon, R. and Tomita, I. (1989) *The Financial Behaviour of Japanese*
Corporations, USA: Kodansha International.
Bank of England Quarterly (1989) August: 376.

Bannock, G. (1985) Going Public, London: Economist Publications.

County Nat West Woodmac (1989) *Focus on Engineering.*

Credit Suisse – First Boston (1990) *Hanson*; London.

CSO (1990) *Acquisitions and Mergers, MA4*, London: HMSO.

Cutler, T., Haslam, C., Williams, J. and Williams, K. (1985) *The Aberystwyth Report on Coal*, Aberystwyth: UCW.

Cutler, T., Williams, K. and Williams, J. (1986) *Keynes, Beveridge and Beyond*, London: Routledge & Kegan Paul.

Cutler, T., Haslam, C., Williams, J. and Williams, K. (1989) *1992 – The Struggle for Europe*, Oxford: Berg.

Daly, A., Hitchens, D. and Wagner, K. (1985) 'Productivity, machinery and skills in a sample of British and German manufacturing plants', *National Institute Economic review*, February.

Dillow, C. (1990) *A Return to a Trade Surplus? The Impact of Japanese Investment on the UK*, Nomura Research Institute.

Doyle, A., Saunders and Wong (1987) 'A comparative study of US and Japanese marketing strategies in the British Market', University of Warwick, mimeo.

Economic Development Briefing (1990) *Japanese Business Investment*, London.

Financial Times (1990) 29 January.
—— (1990) 21 February.
—— (1990) 2 March.
—— (1990) 17 March.
—— (1990) 4 April.
—— (1990) 6 April.
—— (1990) 23 April.

Goold, M. and Campbell, A. (1987) *Strategies and Style: The role of the centre in managing diversified corporations*, Oxford: Blackwell.

Hannah, L. (1977) *Concentration in Modern Industry.*

Haslam, C. (1989) 'The British Steel Corporation: a case study on the rationality of strategy enterprise calculation', unpublished University of Wales Ph.D. thesis.

Heseltine, M. (1989) *The Challenge of Europe, Can Britain Win?*, London:

Weidenfeld & Nicolson.

Hirst, P. Q. and Zeitlin, J. (eds) (1989) *Reversing Industrial Decline*, Leamington Spa: Berg.

IFS (1989) *Corporate Tax Harmonisation and Economic Efficiency*, Report No. 35: London.

Independent, The (1990) 30 May.
—— (1990) 4 June.

Labour Party (1989) *Policy Review.*

Labour Research (1987) 'UK firms seek rosier clime', May.

Lloyds Bank (1990) *Economic Bulletin*, June.

Marketing

Mayer, C. (1987) *New Issues in Corporate Finance*, London: CEPR Discussion Papers, 181.

Mayer, C. and Alexander, I. (1990) *Banks and Securities Markets: corporate financing in Germany and the UK*, London: CEPR Discussion Paper 443.

Meeks, G. (1977) *Disappointing Marriage: a case study of the gains from merger*, Cambridge: Cambridge University Press.

National Institute Economic Review (1990) February.

New, C. and Myers, A. (1986) *Managing Manufacturing Operations in the UK, 1975–85*, London: British Institute of Management.

Oliver, N. and Wilkinson, G. (1988) *The Japanization of British Industry*, Oxford: Blackwell.

Prais, S. J. (1976) *The Evolution of Giant Firms in Britain, 1909–70*, Cambridge: Cambridge University Press.

Robinson, P. (1985) 'Capacity constraints, real wages and the role of the public sector in creating jobs', *Fiscal Studies*, 6 (2).

Stock Exchange (1990) *Quality of Markets Bulletin*, March.

Thompson, G. (ed.) (1989) *Industrial Policy: USA and UK Debates*, London: Routledge.

Williams, K., Williams, J. and Thomas, D. (1985) *Why Are the British Bad at Manufacturing?*, London: Routledge.

Williams, K., Haslam, C., Williams, J. and Wardlow, A. (1986), 'Accounting

490   *Karel Williams, John Williams and Colin Haslam*

for failure in nationalized enterprises',
Economy and Society, 15 (2).
Williams, K., Williams, J. and
Haslam, C. (1987a) *The Breakdown of
Austin Rover:* a case study in the failure of
business strategy and industrial policy,
Leamington Spa: Berg.
Williams, K., Cutler, T., Williams, J.
and Haslam, C. (1987b) 'The end of
mass production?', *Economy and Society*,
16 (3).
Williams, K., Williams, J. and

Haslam, C. (1989a), 'Why take the
stocks out? Britain vs Japan', *Inter-
national Journal of Operations and
Production Management*, 9 (8).
Williams, K., Williams, J. and
Haslam, C. (1989b), 'Do labour costs
really matter?', *Work, Employment and
Society*, 3 (3) Sept.
Williams, K. and Haslam, C. (1991)
'How far from Japan?', *Critical
Perspectives in Accounting*, (forthcoming).

4. Britain under 'New Labour': a model for European restructuring?[1]

Hugo Radice

INTRODUCTION

The sweeping victory of 'New Labour' in the May 1997 elections was not marked by expectations of dramatic change in the political–economic institutions, practices and policies inherited from 'Thatcherism': the Labour leadership had carefully avoided, over several years, making the sort of promises that helped to return a Socialist government in France shortly after. Nevertheless, it is fair to say that many on the left and centre-left expected that *some* central aspects of the Thatcher model would go. There would clearly be no return to Keynesian fiscal activism or public ownership, but Labour had flirted with institutionalist critiques of Thatcherism, particularly with regard to the labour market (skills and training, minimum wage) and the capital market (corporate governance, financial short-termism) and this suggested a possible shift towards a 'social market', 'trust-based' or 'organized' variety of capitalism. Even some of the big business allies of the Labour leadership seemed to be sympathetic to this (for example, David Sainsbury and Chris Haskins).

Some 10 months later, however, there had been continuity more than change. The more visible changes – towards central bank independence, away from 'Euro-scepticism' – have been not only modest, but also not inconsistent with the inherited neoliberalism. Meanwhile, the government has renewed the privatization programme, has still not decided on its minimum wage policy, is stalling on the restoration of trade union rights, is pursuing US-style 'welfare-to-work' policies, maintaining the British nuclear 'deterrent', and so on. More generally, the government has trumpeted its belief that the 'flexibility' of modernized, globalized British capitalism makes it an appropriate model for continental European economies mired in high unemployment and slow growth.

The major exception to this has been the new government's acceptance of the Social Chapter, and its stated commitment to participate in future EU developments of labour and welfare measures. This has in principle met one of the main objectives of the British labour movement, which during the 1980s dropped its opposition to European integration, seeing Brussels instead (especially during the Delors presidency) as a potential source of support against the ravages of Thatcherism. However, the positive assessment by the unions of New Labour's engagement with its EU partner states has to be tempered by an understanding of the radical changes wrought in the past 20 years in the economic and managerial environment facing labour *throughout Europe*, not just in Britain.

This chapter explores the nature of the 'British model' and examines some of its causes and consequences. The general context of this appraisal is the continuing and connected debates on, first, the myths and realities of globalization and regionalization, and, second, the restructuring of work organization and the markets for labour and capital: that is, the direction of change, and possible convergence, of distinct national 'industrial orders' or 'business systems' (see, for example, Berger and Dore, 1996; Boyer and Drache, 1996; Hirst and Thompson, 1996; Lane, 1995; Radice, 1998; Smith and Elger, 1997). The next section summarizes some of the historically rooted features of the British model; the third section considers how far this model matches the current transnational ambitions of capital in general (that is, is globalization inherently 'Anglo-Saxon'?); the fourth section examines some aspects of the Anglo-Saxon model by comparison with alternative 'organized' models; and the chapter concludes with a summary prognosis for European labour.

THE BRITISH MODEL

A large literature developed from the 1960s on the historical 'peculiarities' (Fine and Harris, 1985) of British capitalism, mainly trying to explain the inexorable relative decline of Britain's economic performance in general, and its manufacturing sector in particular (the literature as a whole is summarized well in Coates and Hillard, 1995). On the right, the blame for decline was placed on the trade unions, the welfare state, or the 'anti-business' attitudes of the intelligentsia and the media; on the left, it was placed instead on the historical dominance of trade and finance over industry, the legacy of empire and post-imperial pretensions, or the amateurism of managerial elites both private and public.

In the 1980s, Thatcherism strove to break the syndrome of decline on the basis of a distinctive neoliberal critique, which placed the blame firmly on the strength of organized labour, and the excessive size and interventionism of the state. Extensive privatization, welfare cuts and anti-union laws were followed by a feverish boom in the late 1980s, centred on financial services and property development, and bringing with it a substantial redistribution of income and wealth from poor to rich (for details, see the essays in Michie, 1992). Those who rejected the neoliberal diagnosis and policies were not surprised when nemesis arrived, most notably in Britain's departure from the European Exchange Rate Mechanism (ERM) in 1992. Nevertheless, the relative rate of decline in several indicators of economic importance had halted or at least slowed by the mid-1990s.

In the meantime, a rather different critical literature arose which looked more deeply at the institutional foundations of the British political economy. Most notably, *The State We're In*, by *Guardian* journalist Will Hutton, became an unexpected best-seller in 1995: Hutton offered a powerful critique of Britain's institutions, centred on finance and industry but extending into many other areas also. But behind this lay a large and still growing body of academic work, on a range of topics:

1. A major programme of research at the National Institute of Economic and Social Research examined the differences in *productivity* between Britain and other European countries on a sectoral basis, and linked these differences to *training systems and the deployment of skills* (Prais, 1995).
2. On *innovation performance*, important weaknesses were revealed, such as the preponderance of defence-related work in industrial R&D and in the public finance of innovation, and the apparent inability to carry a strong research base forward into commercial development (for example, Walker, 1993).
3. Students of *labour markets and industrial relations* argued that the shift towards more decentralized, company- or plant-level bargaining, and 'numerical flexibility' through reliance on external labour markets, were perpetuating shopfloor antagonisms and a mutual lack of commitment between management and labour. Hence the apparent victory over labour in the Thatcher period could not shift British industry on to the higher productivity growth path expected from new technologies and new forms of work organization (for example, Visser and van Ruysseveldt, 1996).
4. The longstanding criticisms of the dominance of the City (the London-based centre of the financial services sector) over industry re-emerged in the more precise form of the *'short-termism' thesis*: this argues that the stock-market-based system of industrial finance, coupled with the dominance of private institutional investment funds (life assurance, pensions), compels businesses in general to pay attention to dividend payments and share price rises, rather than to long-term investments in innovation or training (for example, Dimsdale and Prevezer, 1994).
5. The overcentralized nature of the British state and the absence of strong regional institutions have been blamed for the persistence of *large re-*

gions of industrial decay and high unemployment, which have either
missed out on the Thatcherite booms or experienced only the growth of
low-skill, low-wage assembly work (for example, Hudson et al., 1997).

Important though these arguments are, the focus on *national* institutions
and practices has tended to draw attention away from one of the most important features of the British political economy, namely the extremely high
internationalization of capital: although this is taken into account in many of
the contributions to these debates (for example, on regional development or
on innovation), it has received rather little attention in its own right (but see
Fine and Harris, 1985; Radice, 1995). Levels of foreign investment, both
inward and outward, are far higher in relation to the size of the economy
when compared to the other three large European economies (see Barrell and
Pain, 1997). As well as high levels of foreign *direct* investment, *portfolio*
investment – again, both inward and outward – is also very much higher,
while London dwarfs other European financial centres in the issuing and
trading of global financial instruments of all kinds. Discussion of the consequences of this internationalization has focused on four issues in particular.

First, the general role of London as a financial centre is widely seen as
having encouraged, for many decades, government policies aimed at supporting a high value of the pound, high interest rates and an advanced liberalization
of capital markets in general and foreign capital movements in particular.
These policies in turn have supposedly damaged the growth of both exports
and investment, and hence the growth of output, productivity, employment
and real wages.

Second, the importance of overseas assets and employment to British-
based firms, and of foreign-owned assets and employment in the UK economy,
has made successive British governments firmly committed to a liberal policy
regime on foreign direct investments, both in the UK itself and in intergov-
ernmental policy forums such as the OECD and the ILO. This has subjected
British workforces and communities to forms of blackmail by mobile capital;
reduced levels of corporation tax to among the lowest in Europe; and led to
government expenditure on industrial support being devoted mainly to giving
incentives to foreign investors.

Third, British businesses, especially in manufacturing, were seen as substituting investment abroad for investment at home. Before Thatcherism took
hold, the argument was that British capital was escaping low profit and
growth rates at home (or poor industrial relations in the anti-union version)
by investing in more dynamic regions such as continental Europe or North
America. More recently, such investment is seen as motivated by the search
for cheaper labour, or for a superior technology or production environment,
depending on the sector. However, the view that production abroad substi-

tutes directly for exports, thus hitting output and jobs at home, is too simplistic, because it ignores the need in many sectors for firms to get behind tariff or non-tariff barriers, or to be 'embedded' in local networks, if they are to supply local markets at all (for example, witness the rapid growth in FDI in the USA by first Japan and then Germany).

Lastly, inward direct investors, whether from the USA (before 1970 and since 1990), continental Europe (since 1970) or Japan (since 1980), are widely criticized for creating mostly low-wage, low-skill employment, especially in so-called 'screwdriver' assembly plants.[2] The recent scale of these investments further reflects the desire of non-European investors in particular to use Britain as a low-cost platform for supplying Europe as a whole. While this view accords with the evidence in consumer electronics and many areas of engineering, other sectors such as pharmaceuticals and finance are, it has been argued, attracting 'high-quality' investments from abroad (though doubt has been cast on the UK success in pharmaceuticals by Froud *et al.*, 1997). Even in the automotive industry, the demise of the last British-owned mass assembler belies continuing strength in important component and sub-assembly areas (such as diesel engines), as well as automotive design. Nevertheless, what is undeniable is the transfer of *strategic control* of large parts of the British economy to foreign ownership.

This deep internationalization of the British economy was a major reason why capital so readily accepted the Thatcherite programme (Radice, 1986). Deregulation went furthest and fastest in financial services, but other sectors also welcomed their increased freedom to invest abroad (the last remaining controls on capital export were abolished in 1979), which enabled them to compete globally despite the apparently weak national economic performance. After 1979, North Sea oil revenues, a savage industrial recession and the accompanying high value of sterling encouraged a vast outflow of both portfolio and direct investments. But long after the disappearance of these short-term conditions, the financial sector has continued willingly to supply funds to successful British-based transnational corporations (TNCs) to finance takeovers and other investments abroad. On top of this, British disclosure rules and the general aura of the UK's financial success have also enabled them to tap foreign sources of finance. In a broader historical perspective, from around 1960, the *reinternationalization* (following a period of relative closure since 1931) of British capital steadily undermined the *economic* viability of the corporatist alternative presented by Labour and the centrist wing of the Tory party. After 20 years of this, British *politics* then quickly succumbed to the traditional, dominant, nineteenth-century ideologies of free markets (neoliberalism) and free trade (globalization).

At the same time, this deep internationalization is closely linked to the traditional dominance, economic and political, of the financial sector. Financial capital comes into its own in periods of economic crisis: it provides the means by which capitals can withdraw from unprofitable production, regroup and then transform themselves again into productive form. It also provides a haven in which capital can obtain its highest form, the nirvana of M–M', the circuit of money capital: making money out of money without having to extract surplus-value directly from production. Although Britain is no longer the 'rentier state' of the pre-1914 period when measured by the net income from foreign investments as a proportion of national income, the return on its net assets abroad, plus the transaction income from trading in financial instruments of all kinds, contributes a far more important share of total profits than in any other major European economy.

GLOBALIZATION, NEOLIBERALISM AND THE 'ANGLO-SAXON' MODEL

The conclusion from the analysis so far is that the 'British model' is now not simply one of flexible markets in the abstract (which means of course nothing more than the freedom of capital to accumulate by whatever means), but concretely one of untrammelled international mobility for capital, and of the dominance of financial interests and motives. This suggests that the British model may be, not only the ideal exemplar of financial orthodoxy and neoliberalism, but also a particularly suitable vehicle for the project of globalization.

The problem here lies first in disentangling the myths and ideologies of globalization from the realities. In centre and left-wing circles, both in Europe and elsewhere, there is a great deal of scepticism about globalization. This scepticism is associated in particular with institutionalism, regulation theory and various other schools of critical political economy (post-Fordist, post-Keynesian, neo-Schumpeterian and so on) (for example, Hirst and Thompson, 1996; Boyer and Drache, 1996; Ruigrok and van Tulder, 1995; Wade, 1996; Weiss, 1997). The common sceptical viewpoint is that globalization is most important as an *ideology* of big business: first, the extent and/ or depth of globalization has been exaggerated in order to present it as an inevitable and irreversible trend; and second, the reduction in the ability of nation-states to defend the interests of their citizens, when threatened by this trend, has also been exaggerated, in order to disarm potential opposition. These two propositions are accepted as regards the exaggeration for ideological and political effect; however, the sceptics tend to make the opposite mistake of underplaying the realities of globalization, and likewise of overstating the capacity of individual nation-states (or, sometimes, regional blocs) to impose priorities other than those of 'global' capital.

At the heart of this misunderstanding is the tendency of the sceptics to accept at face value an a priori and indeed *essential* opposition between capital and the nation-state. Ironically, the general form of this supposed opposition (market versus state) is at the heart of the neoliberal theory they claim to oppose. If the existing form of state is seen as intrinsically *capitalist*, representing the interests of capital in general, and the *nation*-state is seen as intrinsically part of a worldwide inter-state system (rather than an autonomous political agent) then it is precisely this opposition between 'capital' and the 'nation-state' which is revealed as an ideological veil. It is true that for a particular historical period – generally between about 1870 and 1970 – the working classes were able to make important gains within the political framework of the nation-state, but that was in the context of imperial rivalries exploding in world wars; the creation of mass trade unions, socialist parties and later the Soviet challenge; and, from 1929, cataclysmic economic depression which shook capitalism to its foundations. In the last 25 years or so, capitalist classes have quite unexpectedly recovered their confidence by reversing many of the post-war gains of labour. Not only have they 'restructured' workplaces, labour markets and so on, they have also re-established a global private financial system and restructured the nation-state system itself. The Keynesian ideal of a global regulatory system governing international trade, investment and finance has been reconstituted as a normative agency for enforcing the will of global capital markets – and this transformation has been, remember, *willingly accepted* by the vast majority of governments (any that disagreed are, almost without exception, no longer in power). They have, furthermore, turned the ancient humanist ideal of political internationalism into the exclusivist form of the regional trade bloc.

The sceptics argue that this is too pessimistic a conclusion; they feel that a renewed programme of 'reregulation' and reform is still feasible. This is entirely possible, but the sceptics do not offer any realistic road to change. In the light of the history of our nearly finished century, it is surely realistic to be pessimistic about the willingness of *capitalism* to reform *itself* beyond the most minimal measures. But by confining themselves to the political terrain of the nation-state, or at best the regional bloc, the sceptics are themselves being pessimistic *about labour*, and about labour movements in particular. The alternative to capitalist 'globalization' surely starts from the internationalization of labour, not the defence of the capitalist nation-state.

From this perspective, it is realistic to see the British, or more generally 'Anglo-Saxon', model as a serious economic and political threat to labour throughout Europe, and indeed throughout the world. The British state pioneered the liberalization of capital controls, the acceptance of IMF conditionality (in 1976), the mass privatization of public utilities and the dismantling of laws and regulations offsetting the inbuilt disadvantages of

66   *Global money, capital restructuring and labour*

labour in labour markets and in the workplace. Thatcherism found its strongest ally in Reaganomics, and fostered the resurgence of free-market economics
everywhere. The 'daughter' states of the 'white dominions', Australia and,
still more, New Zealand, have in some respects taken Thatcherism further.
Meanwhile, the Third World debt crisis which exploded in 1982 led in due
course to the forced acceptance of neoliberalism throughout the underdeveloped world. The Anglo-Saxon model has dominated *politically* the restoration
of capitalism in the Soviet bloc, even though compromises have been necessarily in practice. And now the latest 'regional crisis', in East and South-East
Asia, is openly being exploited in an effort to force open the last bastions of
state-led 'developmentalism'.

It should be stressed that none of this means that Anglo-Saxon capitalism
is inevitable and irreversible. On the contrary, it is subject to very widespread
resistance. The point to emphasize is that, 20 years ago, the Anglo-Saxon
model seemed to be on the ropes, with the USA following Britain into
stagflation and relative industrial and economic decline. Now, New Labour's
version of the British model fully adopts the ideology of globalization, adding to it the even more vacuous ideology of 'modernization', which, despite
the lip-service paid to training, seems to mean nothing more than achieving
world market competitiveness by squeezing wage costs. The British model
looks strong and self-confident, while the proponents of 'organized' or 'trust-
based' industrial success are on the defensive (Streeck, 1997).

THE ANGLO-SAXON MODEL VERSUS AN 'ORGANIZED' ALTERNATIVE

It might well be objected that the Anglo-Saxon model's current success is
merely conjunctural: that Britain's present relative boom arose only because
her departure from the ERM triggered a premature end to the recession which
persists elsewhere in Europe. Certainly, there is no shortage of commentators
who continue to argue that important core features of the German or Japanese
industrial orders (these are the two customary comparators in British debates)
still represent fundamentally superior *principles* for capitalism (for example,
Albert and Gonenc, 1996; Perkin, 1996). Before considering this point concretely in relation to European restructuring, we need to go a bit further into
these principles.

In a classic contribution on work organization under capitalism, Friedman
(1977) argued that two basic ways of establishing the control of capital over
labour could be identified: *direct control*, typified by Taylorism, and *responsible autonomy*, typified by the then fashionable alternative of 'job
enlargement', or earlier by the Hawthorn experiments. In Friedman's view,

these could be seen as sequential alternatives, or subject to variation across sectors, or across levels within the hierarchy of skill and pay. In addition, he saw the form of control as closely related to the nature of labour markets and the evolution of labour's own organizations; and both the forms of labour control *and* their effectiveness as conditioned especially by the fundamental antagonism between labour and capital and the outcome of class struggles. This sort of approach was reflected in other writings in the new 'labour process' tradition, and in the various strands of the regulation school. The roots of this analysis lie in Marx's identification of the basic contradiction in the capitalist labour process: while the capitalist who buys labour power owns the potential for value creation, that potential still has to be extracted. Neither the length of the working day, nor the intensity of work, can be determined by appeal to any economic law; nor can the effective and timely conversion of raw materials and equipment into products saleable at a profit. Friedman's two types of control represent abstract strategies, while the capitalist must find concrete institutions and practices that can give an acceptable degree of control in the particular circumstances.

In the more recent debates, however, this point of origin has been lost, and instead we are asked to 'see' these abstract strategies as forming (obviously in connexion with other phenomena) the basis for different 'industrial orders'. In an extreme case, Lipietz (1997) sets out a chain of variant combinations of the two strategies, which are identified as distinct possible *national models*, ranging from the 'neo-Taylorism' of the USA (maximal direct control) to the 'Kalmarism' of Sweden (maximal responsible autonomy, or 'negotiated involvement'). The significance of this is the hypothesis that the latter is, first, preferable and, second, open to political choice.

But does capitalism offer such a straightforward choice; and if so, does it do so on a *national* basis? If the answer to these questions is a simple 'yes', then throughout Europe labour can indicate its clear preference for the model of negotiated involvement, especially if it continues to be associated with higher wages, better work conditions, more jobs, a superior welfare system and so on. But what if the answer is more complicated? Suppose that *some* workers are offered negotiated involvement, while others are subject to direct control? What if the dividing line between them runs, not neatly along national boundaries, but rather across and between regions, sectors, firms, individual plants, 'segmented' labour markets and, finally, workgroups? What if the price for Kalmarism in Sweden is neo-Taylorism in Portugal? And what if employers *in reality* offer subtle mixes of the two, as in the supermarket checkout, where workers benefit from the bar-code reader, but are thereby subject to stringent invisible policing of their pace of work? Realistic answers to these questions lead to the conclusion that labour movements need, now as ever, to question the *basic right to control*, not just its modalities, and to

68   *Global money, capital restructuring and labour*

develop complex and multifaceted strategies which challenge division and exclusion.

Matters turn out to be just as complicated when we consider the question of corporate ownership, finance and control. Models of corporate governance exist primarily to regulate relations between individual owners of capital. For all the talk about 'stakeholder' models which 'incorporate' the interests of labour or the public at large, their basic aim is to secure a legal structure within which the capitalist labour process can take place, under conditions where the scale of production requires a collective or corporate form of capital. The vaunted German model of two-tier board with worker representation still leaves the final say in the hands of the owners: in the end, it is the traditional organizational strength of labour that matters, not having seats on the board.

It is true that the very existence of a legal framework at all gives the lie to the ideology of the free market, since only the state has historically been able to provide 'rules of the game' for the conduct of business. In certain respects and under certain historical conditions, the dominant owners of capital have had to make deals with the state, as in the case of patent systems or the principle of limited liability, which restrict the exercise of ownership rights. The embedding of employee rights, as in Germany, Austria and Sweden, occurred in specific historical circumstances when the political power of capitalists was at its weakest, through defeat in armed conflict or class struggle. Naturally, those who support employee rights argue that such 'stakeholder' forms of governance generate intrinsically superior economic performance, in the sense of long-term growth in productivity and living standards. In addition, it can be argued that a more 'stakeholder'-type system is likely to persist as a *consequence* of superior performance (in capitalist terms): so long as there are enough profits in aggregate to keep all capitalists content, they will cooperate and even extend the benefits of accumulation to employees. However, when this condition no longer holds, they seek to assert their individual ownership rights and to focus on improving performance through cutting wage costs.

The Anglo-Saxon model of corporate governance, on the other hand, evolved historically as a means of drawing into capitalist accumulation the monetary hoards of a large and varied middle class, either through direct share ownership (the USA) or via investment intermediaries (the UK), thereby allowing the banking system to concentrate on financing transactions rather than on accumulation. It substitutes stock market liquidity for the negotiated relations required between the much smaller number of owners typical of continental Europe; and it resolves the problematic relationship between industrial and banking capital also found in the latter. Despite being apparently prone to speculative disasters, the Anglo-Saxon system provides flexibility for capital, and a wider base of economic and political support for the capitalist class. The critique of 'short-termism' may appeal to the left, but it has yet to make serious political headway.

The clear conclusion from this is that corporate governance is, as much as work organization, a 'contested terrain'. From a capitalist standpoint, a market-based system of finance and control is both economically and politically preferable, although concessions may have to be made at times of acute political weakness.

EUROPE AT A CROSSROADS?

The argument above suggests that the two broad models of industrial order can only be judged from a class standpoint. What, then, can we say about the concrete prognosis for Europe? In order to simplify matters, let us take for granted that we are talking about two or more industrial orders in the broad sense, in which 'sub-systems' of industrial relations, labour markets, training systems, finance, state industrial policies and so on are all quite closely interlocked. Let us also assume that, broadly speaking, Europe remains capitalist, in the sense that it remains divided between a capitalist class and a working class, with interests that are fundamentally irreconcilable, but which nevertheless are in practice accommodated through the outcome of industrial and political struggles. In that case, there seem to be two general propositions which follow from the analysis so far: first, that in the present circumstances of deeper internationalization and, especially, transnational restructuring, there is a process of permeation or mutual erosion of national orders; and second, that in these same present circumstances, capitalists are seeking to shift Europe as a whole towards a more Anglo-Saxon model.

The cross-penetration of capital in Europe, especially since the Single Market, is an undeniable fact. While restructuring in some sectors might take place primarily on a national basis, accompanied by competition through exports, cross-border mergers and takeovers have grown enormously, and have added to the Europe-wide restructuring of production in existing transnational groups (including those based outside Europe). The present preoccupation with monetary union seems to have suspended further EU legislation in areas like company law and industrial relations for the time being. But even in the absence of such changes, cross-border capital flows and production integration entails the mutual accommodation of hitherto separate markets, institutions and practices. A *European* capitalism is emerging.

At the same time, in so far as there is a fusion between different industrial orders, it seems that New Labour's claim to offer a superior model of capital-

70   *Global money, capital restructuring and labour*

ism is credible from a capitalist standpoint. The privatization movement has spread from Britain right across Europe. Employers everywhere, backed by bodies like the IMF and the OECD, call for more flexible labour markets.[3] Independent shareholders are challenging cosy networks that maintain corporate control through cross-shareholdings and interlocking directorships.[4] Some academics, at least, suggest systematic shifts towards a more liberal model, for example in France (Schmidt, 1996) or Germany (Streeck, 1997), even if these claims are disputed by others (for example, on Germany, by Carlin and Soskice, 1997). Above all, however, the internationalization of capital – *not* just 'Europeanization', but including investments to and from other regions of the world economy – is deepening in the other larger European economies (and has long been apparent in smaller ones like the Netherlands and Sweden).

So 'which labour next?' In terms of a response to these trends, only three conclusions will be suggested. First, it is clearly *European* labour. Of course, it is in principle open to the left in any country to pursue a national road, to seek to block the processes of European integration in order to preserve past gains, or even to advance further the interests of labour; but the existing reality of integration makes this option highly doubtful except in very distasteful political company. Secondly, programmatically, we have nothing to lose by advocating reforms towards a more humane capitalism, but we have to recognize that they will not be readily conceded, without a struggle, to more than a thin layer and/ or in favoured core locations in Europe. If such reforms are to be permanent, and to provide a springboard for more radical change, they must be universal across Europe, and based upon the *highest* levels of employee and union rights, the *highest* levels of welfare, not the lowest. Thirdly, we have to integrate our own organizations and our own politics at the European level, if we are to have any chance of succeeding in this.

NOTES

1. For advice on the revision of this chapter, I am grateful to participants at the Bergamo conference, and to my colleagues Rumy Husan and Paul Marginson.
2. Although critics of poor UK productivity say much the same about UK-owned companies: see, for example, Prais (1995, ch. 3).
3. For example, BDI president Hans-Olaf Henkel, on a recent visit to England (as reported in *The Guardian*, 28 November 1997, p. 22).
4. See Jack (1997) for a detailed account of recent shake-ups in the French alliance system.

REFERENCES

Albert, M. and R. Gonenc (1996), 'The future of Rhenish capitalism', *The Political Quarterly*, **67**(2), 184–93.

Barrell, R. and N. Pain (1997), 'The growth of foreign direct investment in Europe', *National Institute Economic Review*, **160**, 63–75.

Berger, S. and R. Dore (eds) (1996), *National Diversity and Global Capitalism*, Ithaca, NY: Cornell University Press.

Boyer, R. and D. Drache (eds) (1996), *States against Markets: The Limits of Globalization*, London: Routledge.

Carlin, W. and D. Soskice (1997), 'Shocks to the system: the German political economy under stress', *National Institute Economic Review*, **159**, 57–96.

Coates, D. and J.V. Hillard (eds) (1995), *UK Economic Decline: The Key Texts*, London: Harvester Wheatsheaf.

Dimsdale, N. and M. Prevezer (eds) (1994), *Capital Markets and Corporate Governance*, Oxford: Oxford University Press.

Fine, B. and L. Harris (1985), *The Peculiarities of the British Economy*, London: Lawrence & Wishart.

Friedman, A. (1977), *Industry and Labour: Class Struggle at Work and Monopoly Capitalism*, London: Macmillan.

Froud, J., C. Haslam, S. Johal, K. Williams and R. Willis (1998), 'British pharmaceuticals: a cautionary tale?', *Economy and Society*, **27**(4), 554–84.

Hirst, P. and G. Thompson (1996), *Globalization in Question*, London: Polity Press.

Hudson, R., M. Dunford, D. Hamilton and R. Kotter (1997), 'Developing regional strategies for economic success', *European Urban and Regional Studies*, **4**(4), 365–73.

Hutton, W. (1995), *The State We're In*, London: Jonathan Cape.

Jack, A. (1997), 'New tricks for old dog', *Financial Times*, 26 June, p. 29.

Lane, C. (1995), *Industry and Society in Europe: Stability and Change in Britain, Germany and France*, Aldershot: Edward Elgar.

Lipietz, A. (1997), 'The post-Fordist world: labour relations, international hierarchy and global ecology', *Review of International Political Economy*, **4**(1), 1–41.

Michie, J. (ed.) (1992), *The Economic Legacy 1979–92*, London: Polity Press.

Perkin, H. (1996), 'The third revolution and stakeholder capitalism: convergence or collapse?', *The Political Quarterly*, **67**(2), 198–208.

Prais, S.J. (1995), *Productivity, Education and Training: An International Perspective*, Cambridge: Cambridge University Press.

Radice, H. (1986), 'Le thatcherisme et ses alternatives: quel est l'avenir du capitalisme britannique?', in L. Jalbert and L. Lepage (eds), *Néoconservatisme et restructuration de l'état*, Montréal: Presses Universitaires de Québéc.

Radice, H. (1995), 'Britain in the world economy: national decline, capitalist success?', in D. Coates and J.V. Hillard (eds), *UK Economic Decline: The Key Texts*, London: Harvester Wheatsheaf.

Radice, H. (1998), '"Globalization" and national differences', *Competition and Change*, **3**, 263–91.

Ruigrok, W. and R. van Tulder (1995), *The Logic of International Restructuring*, London: Routledge.

Schmidt, V.A. (1996), *From State to Market: The Transformation of French Business and Government*, Cambridge: Cambridge University Press.

Smith, C. and T. Elger (1997), 'International competition, inward investment and the restructuring of European work and industrial relations', *European Journal of Industrial Relations*, **3**(3), 279–304.

Streeck, W. (1997), 'German capitalism: does it exist? Can it survive?', *New Political Economy*, **2**(2), 237–56.

Visser, J. and J. van Ruysseveldt (1996), 'From pluralism to ... where? industrial relations in Great Britain', in J. van Ruysseveldt and J. Visser (eds), *Industrial Relations in Europe*, London: Sage.

Wade, R. (1996), 'Globalization and its limits: reports of the death of the national economy are greatly exaggerated', in S. Berger and R. Dore (eds), *National Diversity and Global Capitalism*, Ithaca, NY: Cornell University Press.

Walker, W. (1993), 'National innovation systems: Britain', in R.R. Nelson (ed.), *National Innovation Systems: A Comparative Analysis*, Oxford: Oxford University Press.

Weiss, L. (1997), 'Globalization and the myth of the powerless state', *New Left Review*, **225**, 3–27.

[15]

Political Studies (1999), XLVII, 643–660

Models of Capitalism in the New World Order: the UK Case

DAVID COATES

University of Manchester

In the debate over economic performance which has preoccupied UK policy makers for the last four decades, foreign 'models' of more successful capitalisms elsewhere have been an important point of reference. Those models have been variously market-led (USA), state-led (Japan) or negotiated/consensual (Germany/Sweden). Of late the UK's own internal economic and social settlement has itself been offered as a viable model for once successful foreign economies now in competitive difficulties. The key features of these various models are analysed, and the UK's changing post-war position on the map of models is traced. The changing fortunes of these models are then related to developments in the global economy; and an assessment made of the adequacy (and desirability) of the kind of economic order now being canvassed in the UK by the present Labour Government.

Questions of economic performance have been central to political debate in the UK for over four decades now. From the moment at which it became obvious that the post-war UK economy was insufficiently productive and competitive to sustain a world role for the UK state, the political class has been engaged in a perpetual search for a new economic settlement. From the late 1950s at least, that search for a settlement has turned the attention of UK policy makers outwards. It has obliged them to measure UK economic performance against the performance of other leading capitalist economies, and it has predisposed them to see foreign models of capitalist success as sources for their own policy design. The foreign model in vogue has shifted over time, and varied with the political persuasion of the policy makers involved. The USA has always had an enormous appeal for policy makers of the centre-right. Sweden and Germany have been equally attractive poles of thinking for policy makers of the centre-left (as indeed, briefly, was France in the early 1960s): and Japan has been variously interpreted by right and left as simultaneously an exemplar of free-market economics, statist industrial development, and trust-based capitalism. The model in question has therefore varied; but what has not varied has been the openness of the UK policy debate to the notion that capitalism comes in a range of forms, and that the policy trick is to lock the UK into the best form available.

Of late, of course, this deference to foreign modelling has gone into reverse; and has done so for at least two broad sets of reasons.

1. One is that the foreign models hitherto canvassed as superior have themselves run into difficulties. The first model to lose its street credibility (a loss it was later to recoup) was the American model post-Vietnam,

644   *Models of Capitalism*

when the fall of the dollar, the rise of European and Japanese competition, and the low rate of productivity growth in US manufacturing
combined briefly to erode American economic dominance. The second
casualty was European: as first the Swedish economy, and more recently
German social-market capitalism, fell victim to slow rates of growth, the
export of capital, and the rise of unemployment. And then, in 1997, the
Asian model fell too: as first South Korea and then Japan ran into that
financial storm (and linked industrial recession) in which Brittan at least
found the 'modest consolation ... that we should now hear rather less
about the much canvassed virtues of Asian capitalism'.[1] By 1998 that is,
'trust-based' capitalism in both its Asian statist and European welfare
versions had become insufficiently resilient to act as any kind of model
for either Conservative or New Labour policy makers.

2.   By then, in any case, those policy makers were not looking for foreign
models any more. As the 1980s progressed, the Conservatives increasingly offered the Thatcherite resetting of UK capital–state–labour
relations as a general model for capitalist reconstruction; and New
Labour has more recently decided that its 'third way' between Thatcherism and old-style social democracy is *the* answer both to the diminished
competitiveness of Western European welfare capitalism and to the
unexpected emergence of Japanese financial instability.[2] As the century
closes, the policy debate in all the leading chancelleries of the capitalist
world still turns on the design of successful economic and social models:
but leadership in that policy debate has shifted back to the very 'Anglo-
Saxon' way of running capitalism which hitherto has been so subject to
critique and ridicule.

This rise and fall of models has been accompanied by the associated rise and
fall of the academic literatures most closely associated with them. Initially those
literatures were largely constructed around individual models, as predominantly
nationally/regionally focused explanations of economic performance. There
was a literature on US economic performance and decline;[3] and a parallel
literature on the earlier UK experience of similar post-imperial under-
performance.[4] There was a literature on Scandinavian corporatism;[5] and
another on the sources of the post-war Japanese economic miracle.[6] Those
literatures, of course, remain: though many elements within them now need
considerable resetting in the light of recent events (events which have served to
highlight the very *thin* empirical base on which many of the claims about
'foreign strengths' in those individual national studies often rested). Then from
the mid-1980s, and under the impact of intensified global (and academic?)

---

[1] S. Brittan, 'Asian model, R.I.P.', *Financial Times*, 4 December 1997, p. 24.

[2] Tony Blair, speech to the European Socialists' Malmo Congress, 6 June 1997.

[3] Surveyed in S. D. Cohen, 'Does the United States have an International Competitiveness
Problem', in D. P. Rapkin and W. P. Avery (eds), *National Competitiveness in a Global Economy*
(Boulder CO, Lynne Reiner, 1995), pp. 21–40.

[4] Surveyed in D. Coates, *The Question of UK Decline* (London, Harvester Wheatsheaf, 1994).

[5] Surveyed in D. Coates, 'Labour Power and International Competitiveness: a Critique of
Dominant Orthodoxies', in L. Panitch and C. Leys (eds), *The Socialist Register 1999* (London,
Merlin, 1998), pp. 1–31.

[6] Surveyed in S. Wilks, *The Promotion and Regulation of Industry in Japan* (London, Macmillan,
1991).

competition, individual national studies were progressively supplemented by new comparative analyses of relative economic performance, comparative analyses which – in the Anglo-Saxon world at least – often took the form of a critique of dominant US and UK institutions and practices. Of course, mainstream economics in the 1980s blithely went on its predominantly neo-liberal way, in apparently total ignorance of these predominantly sociological and institutional forms of analysis; but the very enthusiasm of mainstream economics for self-referential market-based theorizing simply fuelled the production of literatures (not least by a new generation of economic historians and comparative political scientists) which insisted on the social embeddedness of economic institutions and on the resulting 'path dependent' nature of national capitalist development.[7] In the journals of academia, neo-liberal economists crossed swords with the new institutionalists, and witnessed the emergence of 'new growth theorists' willing to advocate a role for state action that was, at one and the same time, both post neo-classical and post-Keynesian. In the world beyond, advocates of market capitalism clashed with advocates of statist and corporatist forms of capitalist regulation; and in the UK at least, the centre of policy making shifted in line with these academic fashions: moving from Keynesian corporatism in the 1970s into neo-liberal market forms of capitalist regulation in the 1980s, and by the late 1990s, into a messianic enthusiasm for flexible labour markets and investments in human capital that derived from a particular reading of the new growth theory.

The paper that follows attempts to do two things. It attempts to clarify the polar positions in the now well-established debate on capitalist models, and to chart the changing position of the UK economy on that map of models. It also seeks to use the notion of capitalist models to anticipate the difficulties which are likely to be met by current UK policy makers if they continue to rely on the policy prescriptions of new growth theory in their pursuit of a high growth trajectory for the UK economy. The paper will argue that the New Labour remodelling of that economy represents only a minor shift from the model pursued by its Conservative predecessor; and falls far short of the remodelling characteristic of mainstream European social democracy. It will also suggest that such a minor restructuring is unlikely to eradicate the deep-seated sources of UK economic weakness to which the earlier policy initiatives of both Old Labour and Thatcherism were also – in model terms – a response. The underlying thesis of this paper is that the space for the establishment of a range of economically successful capitalist models is now diminishing; and that ironically the UK, having missed the opportunity to exploit that range when it existed, is now aligning itself with a model which will perpetuate, rather than resolve, UK competitive weaknesses.

The Nature of Capitalist Models

Of course, there is nothing particularly unusual about academics and political commentators differentiating types of capitalism. On the contrary, there is a

---

[7] See in particular D. C. North, *Institutions, Institutional Change and Economic Performance* (Cambridge, Cambridge University Press, 1990); and J. Rogers Hollingsworth and R. Boyer (eds), *Contemporary Capitalism: the Embeddedness of Institutions* (Cambridge, Cambridge University Press, 1997).

646   *Models of Capitalism*

long academic tradition of splitting capitalism into different stages. Marxists have been doing it for years: differentiating between 'early capitalism' and 'late',[8] between 'liberal capitalism', 'monopoly capitalism' and 'state monopoly capitalism',[9] and between 'organized' and 'disorganized' capitalism.[10] Liberal and Schumpeterian scholarship has been equally active, differentiating 'stages of economic growth',[11] splitting early capitalism from the later 'mixed economy',[12] and even locating stages of competitive development (labelled, by Porter for instance, as respectively 'factor-driven', 'investment driven', 'innovation driven' and 'wealth driven').[13] In both marxist and non-marxist hands, the argument has been much the same: that capitalism as an economic form can be distinguished in different time periods by the qualitatively distinct mixes of technologies, forms of business organization, characters of labour forces and state functions that come to predominate within it. In arguments of this kind, it is not so much that different models of capitalisms co-exist. They may, but that is not the main point. The main point is that over the life-cycle of capitalism as a whole, different forms of social organization and political structuring emerge as dominant for a period; and capitalism as a whole has, in consequence, to be understood as moving inexorably from one model to another over time.

These traditions of periodizing capitalism are not absent from the current debate on contemporary capitalist models. On the contrary, there is a strong marxist presence in that debate, and an equally potent Schumpeterian one. The marxist voice in the models debate has been largely French – in part a regulationist presence concerned with the fate of Fordist and post-Fordist social structures of accumulation.[14] The Schumpeterian influence has largely been American; particularly evident in Lazonick's use of Alfred Chandler's work to sustain a periodization of capitalism into first proprietary, then managerial and finally collective capitalisms,[15] but present too in the explanations offered by Reich, and by Dertouzas *et al.*, on the recent decline of the US economy.[16] Both regulationist and Chandleresque periodizations easily lend themselves to the competitiveness agenda of the capitalist models debate, and slide effortlessly from a diachronic to a synchronic form. Stages of capitalism slide into models of capitalism, where a stage dominant in the past becomes outmoded by a stage dominant in the present and by one embryonically signalled for future dominance. The future is post-Fordist or collective (and really Japanese!). Competitiveness lies with the 'new competition' rather than with 'the old'.[17] It

[8] See E. Mandel, *Late Capitalism* (London, Verso, 1973).

[9] See B. Jessop, *The Capitalist State* (Oxford, Martin Robertson, 1982).

[10] See S. Lash and J. Urry, *The End of Organized Capitalism* (Cambridge, Polity, 1987).

[11] See W. Rostow, *The Stages of Economic Growth: a non-communist Manifesto* (Cambridge, Cambridge University Press, 1960).

[12] See A. Crosland, *The Future of Socialism* (London, Cape, 1956).

[13] M. Porter, *The Competitive Advantage of Nations* (London, Macmillan, 1990), pp. 545–60.

[14] See A. Lipietz, *Towards a New Economic Order* (Cambridge, Polity, 1992); and R. Boyer, 'French Statism at the Crossroads', in C. Crouch and W. Streeck (eds) *The Political Economy of Modern Capitalism* (London, Sage, 1997), pp. 71–101.

[15] See W. Lazonick, *Business Organization and the Myth of the Market Economy* (Cambridge, Cambridge University Press, 1991).

[16] See R. Reich, *The Next American Frontier* (Harmondsworth, Penguin, 1984); and M. Dertouzos, R. K. Lester and R. M. Solow, *Made in America: Regaining the Productive Edge* (New York, Harper Perennial, 1990).

[17] See M. Best, *The New Competition: Institutions of Industrial Restructuring* (Cambridge, Polity, 1993).

lies with systems of 'reflexive accumulation' of either a 'collective' (Japanese), 'practical' (German) or discursive (Anglo-American) form.[18] It does not lie with Fordist forms of accumulation of the kind that enabled the USA to replace the UK in world economic domination; and economies that have not caught up, or which find the move out of Fordism difficult, are likely to experience economic decline.

However the periodizers are not the key players in the debates on capitalist models. The key players are the 'new institutionalists': particularly (in what is actually a very rich and heterogeneous grouping) those economists, political scientists and comparative sociologists who are committed to the notion of the necessary social embeddedness of all economic institutions, and to the resulting path-dependent and socially-specific nature of resulting economic trajectories.[19] Such new institutionalists have been very productive of late,[20] generating a literature bedecked with an initially bewildering variety of different typologies, labels and number of cases. The incentive to create these overlapping typologies has come from a number of sources. A sensitivity in the work of many scholars to the *peculiarities* of each national social formation has triggered a listing of models by nation/region, with as many labels as there are social units in the research frame; while the parallel *fracturing of academic disciplines* has triggered a listing of models by single distinguishing feature. So we have 'the Scandinavian model', 'Asian capitalism', German 'social market' capitalism, 'American liberal capitalism', even Russian 'mafia capitalism'; and we have typologies of welfare systems, of cultural networks, of forms of corporate organization, of systems of investment provision, of modes of labour market regulation, and of state-economy relations. We have 'liberal', 'corporatist' and 'social democratic' welfare regimes;[21] 'individualistic' or 'communitarian' value systems;[22] 'J', 'G', or 'A' forms of corporate organization;[23] 'bank-based' or 'stock-market' based forms of credit provision;[24] 'co-ordinated' and 'non-co-ordinated' forms of labour market regulation;[25] and 'market-led', 'negotiated/consensual' and 'state-led' forms of economic management.[26] Hardly surprising then, that the literature on models gives us not one, but several, listings of capitalist types,

---

[18] See S. Lash and J. Urry, *Economies of Signs and Space* (London, Sage, 1994).

[19] See in particular Hollingsworth and Boyer, *Contemporary Capitalism*; and Crouch and Streeck, *The Political Economy of Modern Capitalism*.

[20] 'in the 1980s a welter of studies showed advanced capitalist societies to vary profoundly in the way they dealt with the … core institutions of capitalism' (Crouch and Streeck, *The Political Economy of Modern Capitalism*, p. 2).

[21] See G. Esping-Andersen, *The Three Worlds of Welfare Capitalism* (Princeton, Princeton University Press, 1990).

[22] See L. Thurow, *Head to Head: the Coming Economic Battle among Japan, Europe and America* (New York, William Morrow, 1992); or, for an even more differentiated typology, C. Hampden Turner and F. Trompenaars, *The Seven Cultures of Capitalism* (London, Piatkus, 1993).

[23] Lash and Urry, *Economies of Signs and Space*.

[24] J. Zysman, *Governments, Markets and Growth: Financial Systems and the Politics of Industrial Change* (Ithaca, Cornell University Press, 1983).

[25] See D. Soskice, 'Reinterpreting Corporatism and Explaining Unemployment', in R. Brunetta and C. Dell'Arringa (eds), *Labour Relations and Economic Performance* (London, Macmillan, 1990), pp. 170–214.

[26] D. Marquand, *The Unprincipled Society* (London, Cape, 1988). For other state typologies, see F. Block, 'The Roles of the State in the Economy', in N. Smelser and R. Swedberg (eds), *The Handbook of Economic Sociology* (Princeton, Princeton University Press, 1994), pp. 691–710; and R. Wade, *Governing the Market: Economic Theory and the Role of Government in East Asian Industrialization* (Princeton, Princeton University Press, 1990).

with a seemingly endless number of categories inside the various typologies. Capitalism comes in two forms for some writers,[27] in three for some,[28] in four for others,[29] or in an infinite variety of internally-differentiated national types for the really committed new institutionalists.[30] But what it does not do is come in one form alone. On that much the new institutionalist scholarship is quite clear.

Putting order on all that complexity is difficult; but it is worth noting how – beneath all the nuanced differentiation – clear polar types of capitalist model regularly re-appear. For this is a literature concerned with competitiveness; and competition is uniquely a practice generative of winners and losers. So literatures concerned with competitiveness tend ultimately to bifurcate, or at least to map out only limited numbers of likely scenarios. The classic formulations certainly did. Albert, for example, argued himself, with due recognition of complexities, down to a distinction between two models: one 'American' (and not Anglo-American, since UK welfare provision was far too European), the other 'core European' (really a mixture of Rhine capitalism and Alpine). For Albert, 'the neo-American model was based on individual success and short-term financial gains; the Rhine model, of German pedigree but with strong Japanese connections, emphasizes collective success, consensus and long-term concerns'.[31] Similarly, Thurow played with a single distinction between Anglo-American and Japanese-German capitalisms, before eventually setting up his head-to-head as a three way fight between the USA, Japan and Europe. Intriguingly too Albert had the USA winning, and Thurow had Europe!

In fact, there are real dangers in setting up any simple two-case model of capitalist types. Certainly the great weakness of any modelling that collapses Japan and Germany into a similarly 'communitarian' or 'trust' based model (to be set against an Anglo-American individualistic one) is its failure to spot the very different role of labour movements in the Japanese and German cases, and therefore to see the very different sources of what, through liberal individualistic eyes, may initially seem to be a similar set of communitarian cultures. In Japan, the labour movement has historically been weak, and the main sources of cultural specificity have been broadly right-wing (conservative, religious and nationalist). In the European welfare capitalisms (especially post-war Sweden, but also to a lesser degree Germany) labour movements have been historically strong, and the sources of market-regulating cultures have been predominantly centre-left, social democratic ones. The result has been that Japanese capital has had to deal with a very different set of welfare, worker and trade union rights than has Western European capital; and has consolidated a very different set of institutional props for what are – on the surface – quite similar patterns of wage differentials, job security, labour turnover and training in the two systems.

---

[27] See M. Albert, *Capitalism against Capitalism* (London, Whurr, 1993).

[28] See L. Thurow, *Head to Head*; D. Marquand, *The Unprincipled Society*; and H. Perkin, 'The Third Revolution', in G. Kelly *et al.* (eds), *Stakeholder Capitalism* (London, Macmillan, 1997), pp. 35–48.

[29] See R. Boyer, 'French Statism at the Crossroads'; and R. Dore, 'The Distinctiveness of Japan', in Crouch and Streeck, *The Political Economy of Modern Capitalism*, pp. 19–32.

[30] See Hollingsworth and Boyer, *Contemporary Capitalism*. For a defence of national differences in the face of globalization, see J. Zysman, 'The myth of the global economy: enduring national foundations and emerging regional realities', *New Political Economy*, 1, 2 (July 1996), 157–184.

[31] M. Albert, *Capitalism against Capitalism*, p. 19.

Those props in Europe have been largely public (state) props. In Japan, of course, they have been largely private (and corporate).

Moreover, any simple 'US versus the rest' tendency in the models literature can only obscure a much more variegated range of differences in who really are the key players (or stakeholders) in each particular capitalist model. Again, the Anglo-Saxon version of stakeholding is reasonably straightforward. The shareholders are the key stakeholders in those capitalisms in which large corporations raise the bulk of their external capital in open financial markets, and where the level of short-term profit yield, executive salaries and dividend distribution drive the whole system. And such a narrow base of stakeholding clearly differs from more bank-based systems of industrial finance, and from systems where interlocking sets of corporations sustain each other in long-term strategies of market capture and profit consolidation. Industrial companies, financial institutions and public agencies, that is, interact differently in a variety of national contexts; and any modelling of capitalist types has to make space for that national differentiation.

This is why Thurow's specification of three geographical areas of future capitalist competition is probably a better guide to the basic choices here than a simple polarity of the Albert kind. For the choices do seem to triangulate around a capital–labour–state set of overlapping polarities, a set which then allows a range of positioning within the parameters of the triangle as a whole. The three-way nature of the basic choices before us here can be isolated schematically in a variety of diagrammatic forms. Boyer has recently produced one;[32] Hart has produced another;[33] Hutton has a third.[34] Figure 1 here is a fourth. All of them constitute a diagrammatic response to the recognition that the core institutional settlement that capitalism has taken (both temporarily and spatially) varies around the central question of who/what decides how capital accumulation will be organized; and that that response can best be measured around two intersecting axes: one charting the degree of state regulation over private capital; the other recording the strength of labour rights in the face of the private ownership of the means of production. Is capital accumulation the private concern of individual entrepreneurs and firms – which it is in forms of capitalism that are predominantly market-led? Or is that accumulation a matter settled in some relationship between private firms and the state; or is it negotiated within industrial and political systems in which organized labour also has a voice?

The answers to these questions are invariably matters of degree: which is why a triangular representation of ideal types (allowing for a scaling of position along each dimension of the triangle) seems to work better than a simple set of boxes. Alongside dimension 'A' in Figure 1, for example, particular models can be distinguished by the set of labour rights within which private capital is obliged to operate: very few such rights at point 'a', very many at point 'aa'. Along dimension 'B' in Figure 1, models can be differentiated by the political strength of labour movements (and by the associated provision of welfare rights and government policy on full employment): with labour movements strong at

[32] R. Boyer, 'French Statism at the Crossroads', p. 92.

[33] J. A. Hart, *Rival Capitalists: International Competition in the United States, Japan and Western Europe* (Ithaca, Cornell University Press, 1992), p. 281.

[34] W. Hutton, *The State We're In* (London, Cape, 1994), p. 282.

650   *Models of Capitalism*

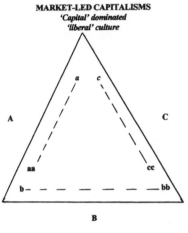

Figure 1. *Models of Capitalism*

point 'b', weak at point 'bb'. Along dimension 'C' in Figure 1, models can be differentiated by the degree of autonomy of private firms from state regulation, direction and control: with high levels of autonomy at point 'c', and with high levels of state regulation at point 'cc'. Moreover, each of the defining points of the triangle tends to be associated with a particular cultural mix, and each face of the triangle tends to be associated with a particular distribution of power and rewards. So, as we rotate the triangle, different political ideologies and associated value systems come into view: liberal political ideologies and values when we get to market-led capitalism, social democratic ideologies and values when we get to negotiated/consensual forms of capitalism, and conservative or nationalist ideologies and values when we reach state-led capitalisms. As we drop down the triangle from top to bottom, the number of stakeholders tends to widen and income inequalities tend to diminish; and as we move across the triangle from right to left, the distribution of social power tends to even out. And so on.

What the diagram suggests is that, in ideal-typical:

- *market-led* capitalisms, accumulation decisions lie overwhelmingly with private companies, who are left free to pursue their own short-term profit motives and to raise their capital in open financial markets. In such capitalisms, workers enjoy only limited statutory industrial and social rights, and earn only what they can extract from their employers in largely unregulated labour markets. State involvement in economic management is limited largely to market-creating and protecting measures; and the dominant understandings of politics and morality in the society as a whole are individualistic and liberal in form.

- In *state-led* capitalisms by contrast, accumulation decisions are again primarily seen as the right and responsibility of private companies, but those decisions are invariably taken only after close liaison with public agencies, and are often indirectly determined through administrative guidance and bank leadership. In such capitalisms, labour movements tend still to lack strong political and social rights; but there is space for forms of labour relation which tie some workers to private corporations through company-based welfare provision. The dominant cultural forms in such capitalisms are likely to be conservative-nationalist in content.

- In *negotiated* or *consensual social* capitalisms the degree of direct state regulation of capital accumulation may still be small; but the political system entrenches a set of strong worker rights and welfare provision which gives organized labour a powerful market presence and the ability to participate directly in industrial decision making. The dominant cultural networks in these capitalisms are invariably social democratic ones.

It is possible to use this triangle for a number of purposes. As we will see later, it is certainly possible to superimpose upon it a mapping of the changing centres of gravity of state policy towards competitiveness. But the main initial value of the triangle is as a guide to the positioning of whole national economies. It does not seem unreasonable, as a first approximation, to position the USA towards the market-led end of the triangle, Japan nearer the state-led end, and Sweden and Germany along the axis linking market and social capitalism together (see Figure 2). Certainly a number of comparative studies do precisely that.[35] The question before us here is where to position the UK.

There seems little doubt that, prior to 1979, the UK economy had settled nearer the German than the US model as far as labour rights and welfare provision were concerned. The labour codes surrounding trade unionism in the mid-1970s gave workers the right to join a union of their choice, gave those unions immunity from civil damages across a wide range of trade disputes, and afforded their members (and non-unionized workers as well) extensive welfare rights and access to industry-wide (and industry-provided) retraining. National trade union officials participated directly in an expanding set of tripartite consultative and executive agencies; and a system of wages councils guaranteed minimum earnings in a series of industries in which trade unionism was weak. The labour codes surrounding workers and their unions in the UK in the 1970s did not, however, give workers or their representatives membership of supervisory boards on German lines (the attempt to introduce a limited degree of industrial democracy was blocked).[36] Nor did the state pursue the full range of active labour market policies characteristic of the Swedish model during the same decade.

The UK economy prior to 1979 also possessed a large public sector, and was characterized by active and extensive state involvement in the provision of private industrial investment funds. At its peak, the National Enterprise Board

---

[35] Hart and Thurow for two.

[36] See D. Coates, *Labour in Power? A Study of the Labour Government 1974–79* (London, Longman, 1980), pp. 131–42.

652   *Models of Capitalism*

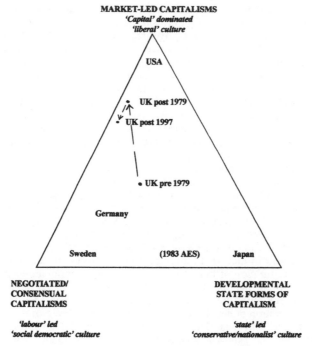

Figure 2. National Models of Capitalism

held a controlling interest in a considerable number of major UK-based manufacturing companies (including British Leyland, Rolls Royce 1971, Alfred Herbert and Ferranti); and the Government made extensive use of regional aid to shape the geographical dispersal of private investment. The Government (both Labour after 1974 and Conservative before 1974) ran a series of incomes policies which periodically involved price controls and/or voluntary price restraints; and by 1979 had taken to itself powers to blacklist firms which were in breach of nationally-specified wage norms. The UK state never developed a local equivalent of the Japanese Ministry of International Trade and Industry (though at least one major scholar in the field has argued that Labour's Ministry of Technology in the late 1960s was potentially a super-MITI in the making):[37] but in spite of the failure of the UK to develop a full-blown developmental state in the 1970s, it is nonetheless clear that prior to the arrival of the Conservatives in power in 1979 the UK economy stood nearer to the state-led than to the market-led end of side 'C' of the triangle in Figure 1.[38] Figure 2 suggests a possible location for the UK 'model' prior to the Thatcher era.

[37] See D. Edgerton, *England and the Aeroplane, an Essay on a Militant and Technological Nation* (London, Macmillan, 1991), p. 105.
[38] For a discussion of why that failure occurred, see D. Coates, *The Question of UK Decline*, pp. 204–9.

DAVID COATES   653

Post-1979, of course, the UK economy was significantly repositioned. Trade union rights were substantially eroded, though basic welfare provision remained. Industrial training was privatized and recast in TEC form. Large swathes of the public sector were privatized, regional industrial aid was cut, the whole edifice of tripartite decision making structures was dismantled, and state involvement in industrial investment was heavily curtailed. Even the close working relationship between the UK state and the defence industries was subject to new market forms of regulation. By 1997, that is, the UK had long been repositioned far closer to the ideal typical 'market-led' model than had hitherto been the case; and was indeed by then – as was earlier noted – being heavily 'marketed' as *the* successful growth model to be adopted by more statist or corporatist forms of capitalist economy.

Under New Labour very little of that repositioning has yet been abandoned. New Labour has defined itself sharply both against Old Labour in its pre-1979 governmental form, and against Old Labour in its 1983 Bennite 'alternative economic strategy' form (a form which, if implemented, would have moved the UK down towards the corporatist and statist side of the triangle). A certain degree of repositioning has been signalled that, if implemented, will move the UK back slightly towards the German model: most notably a commitment to state involvement in industrial retraining and the raising of skill levels, plus a very modest restoration of basic trade union rights, a minimum wage and the formal adoption of the Social Chapter. But New Labour is not about to shift UK plc towards any kind of 'developmental state' model; and has actively eschewed any notion of detailed state regulation of industry. Nor is it willing to re-establish any fully negotiated/consensual structure of industrial decision making that would extensively empower trade unions again. New Labour's 'third way' – its way of 'combining economic dynamism with social justice in the modern world', as Tony Blair said in The Hague in 1988 – privileges 'macro-economic stability ... competition, liberalization and open markets', and addresses 'supply side weakness, not' by 'over-regulation and burden on business' but by targeting 'education, skills, technology, better infrastructure and transport systems'.[39] And significantly for our purposes here, New Labour's adoption of the Social Chapter, and introduction of a national minimum wage, will – according to Tony Blair – still leave the UK with 'the most lightly regulated labour market of any leading economy in the world'.[40] The UK economy under New Labour, that is, will still be a market-led form of capitalism, but one in which – in line with new growth theory – the state plays an active role in enhancing investment in human capital.

The Viability of Capitalist Models

The modest nature of these proposed re-alignments by a self-proclaimed government of the centre-left stands in sharp contrast with the depth of critique of market-led capitalism associated with recent centre-left intellectual

[39] Tony Blair, speech at the Annual Friends of Nieuwspoort dinner, The Ridderzaal, The Hague, 20 January 1998.
[40] Tony Blair, foreword to the DTI White Paper *Fairness at Work*, 1998: (http://www.dti.gov.uk/ir/fairness/foreword/html).

commentaries on capitalist models. That critique has been built around a number of linked themes.

1. One is that economies pursuing more negotiated/consensual forms of capitalist management achieve growth rates and levels of international competitiveness that are at least as good as those achieved by more market-led forms of capitalism; while at the same time attaining social targets (on welfare rights, job security and income equality) that are distinctly superior.[41] In their defence of organized labour as a key 'social partner' in the regulation of economies dominated by privately-owned companies, the advocates of Swedish corporatism and German social-market capitalism regularly cite the 'beneficial constraints'[42] imposed on capital accumulation by strong worker and trade union rights. By blocking off low wage sweat-shop routes to short-term profitability, such constraints are said to oblige local capitalists to prosper by investment and innovation (to move into what Streeck called 'diversified quality production');[43] and by generating a strong sense of job security and corporate identification in the workforce, they are also said to enable organized labour to co-operate fully in the job changes and reskilling processes necessarily associated with such high value-added production processes.

2. A parallel, though normally differently-focused, argument from centre-left intellectuals emphasizes the superiority of the 'developmental state' model over the Anglo-Saxon one; and stresses in particular the superiority of the modes of industrial, social and political organization underpinning Japanese post-war economic success.[44] In much of the centre-left's comparative writings on Japan, particularly those produced in the 1980s, emphasis is placed on the long-term nature of Japanese industrial planning (at both corporate and state levels), a long-termism that is supposedly rooted in the close (non-market-mediated) relationships that exist in Japan between financial and industrial capital, and between private firms and the state. This apparent Japanese propensity for 'voice' rather than 'exit' strategies in the management of economic life is also often related to the job security afforded to core workers by Japanese life-time employment policies; and to the non-confrontational industrial relations that Confucian value-systems are said to consolidate. Against market-led forms of capitalism, centre-left enthusiasts for Asian models emphasize the competitive advantages of 'trust-based' systems of

---

[41] For typical examples of this form of argument, see L. Kenworthy, *In Search of National Economic Success: Balancing Competition and Co-operation* (London, Sage, 1995); A. Henley and E. Tsakalotos, *Corporatism and Economic Performance* (Aldershot, Edward Elgar, 1993); or J. Pekkarinen et al. (eds), *Social Corporatism: a Superior Economic System?* (Oxford, Oxford University Press, 1992).

[42] See W. Streeck, 'Beneficial Constraints: on the Economic Limits of Rational Voluntarism', in Hollingsworth and Boyer, *Contemporary Capitalism*, pp. 197–219.

[43] W. Streeck, *Social Institutions and Economic Performance: Studies of Industrial Relations in Advanced Capitalist Economies* (Aldershot, Edward Elgar, 1992), p. 5.

[44] For representative formulations of this argument at each end of the 1980s, see C. Johnston, *MITI and the Japanese Miracle* (Stanford, Stanford University Press, 1982); and L. D'Andrea Tyson and J. Zysman (eds), *Politics and Productivity: how Japan's Development Strategy Works* (New York, Harper Business, 1989).

DAVID COATES   655

economic regulation; and use the argument that 'trust' is the missing ingredient in market-led capitalisms to link their enthusiasm for Japanese capitalism to that for the very different systems of European welfare-capitalism.[45]

Both sets of arguments about the superiority of non-market-led models of capitalism share a common critique of neo-liberal economics, and a common reading of the economic weakness of the UK under Thatcher and Major and of the USA under Reagan and Bush. According to Hutton, for example, liberal economics is flawed in three ways: by its narrow view of economic rationality (and associated faith in the capacity of the price mechanism to trigger self-correcting market responses), its commitment to the law of diminishing returns and its belief in unregulated markets mechanisms as self-regulating optimizers.[46] Like the conservative Fukuyama, centre-left intellectuals tend to 'think of neo-classical economics as being, say 80% correct ... there is a missing 20% of human behaviour of which neo-classical economics can give only a poor account'.[47] In consequence they are able to treat Anglo-Saxon ways of running capitalism as inherently outmoded and inappropriate to a modern world in which 'the nature of work is fundamentally different from the way it is conceived in the free market tradition and embodied in the techniques of Fordist production' and in which 'successful capitalism [now] demands a fusion of co-operation and competition'.[48] So Marquand is able to explain twentieth century UK economic under-performance as a consequence of the dominance of outmoded liberal ideas (what he terms 'the mental furniture of the age of steam');[49] and Lazonick is able to treat Anglo-Saxon economies of the US and UK kind as trapped in a nineteenth century time-warp, blocked in an age of 'collective capitalism' by the inability of their policy-makers to 'confront the myth of the market economy and the meagre analytical tools that the proponents of this myth have labelled *science*'.[50] The cumulative impact of this embedded liberalism within Anglo-Saxon economies is – on this argument – a long-term loss of international competitiveness: a loss variously related by centre-left intellectuals to the short-termism (and high dividend requirements) of stock market-led capital provision, and to the adversarial nature of industrial relations triggered by market-led personnel strategies. According to centre-left critics of market-led capitalisms, the absence of trust relationships along dimension 'C' of Figure 1 leaves US- and UK-based private firms vulnerable to competition from East Asian and German multinationals who enjoy long-term relationships with their local banking systems and (in the Japanese case) with the planning agencies of the state; a weakness then compounded by the associated absence of trust relationships along dimension A of Figure 1, by what Lazonick at least called 'the Achilles heel of US manufacturing ... [its] organization of work on the shop-floor ... and [its] dramatic weakening of the labour movement at precisely the time when unions needed to be brought into

[45] The classic example of this 'fusion of enthusiasms' is the widely-cited ch. 10 in Hutton, *The State We're In.*

[46] Hutton, *The State We're In*, p. 236.

[47] F. Fukuyama, *Trust: the Social Virtues and the Creation of Prosperity* (New York, Free, 1995), p. 13.

[48] Hutton, *The State We're In*, pp. 254–5.

[49] D. Marquand, *The Unprincipled Society*, p. 8.

[50] W. Lazonick, *Business Organization and the Myth of the Market Economy*, p. 349.

656   *Models of Capitalism*

the investment decision-making process in both the private and the public sectors'.[51]

Of late, such advocates of non-market-led capitalisms have been put on the defensive by the difficulties of first the European and then the East Asian economies.[52] What looked in happier times like long-term relationships of trust between the suppliers and deployers of capital now stand condemned as inadequate financial regulation and systematically-induced corruption; and Streeck's 'beneficial constraints' are widely condemned as machines for the destruction of employment. In truth, centre-left defences of humane capitalism were always heavily challenged from both their left and their right. They were (and continue to be) challenged by a tradition of marxist scholarship unimpressed by capitalist models of any kind: one concerned in particular with the degree of labour exploitation hidden behind the facade of capitalist trust relationships, and with the fragility of class compacts and national corporatism in an age of expanding proletarianization and intensified global competition.[53] And they were (and continue to be) challenged by a tradition of liberal scholarship committed to the very market forces that the centre-left historically sought to control.

In fact the underperformance of certain capitalist models (the UK before 1979, European welfare capitalism since) has long been explained by liberal economists in exactly the reverse terms to those deployed by intellectuals of the centre-left: as underperformance triggered by the *blunting* of market forces by political interference and labour-market regulation. Liberal scholarship on specific economies has long argued that innovation and change are made more difficult by strong trade unions, high welfare and tax regimes, and over-active governments; and that flexibility (particularly in labour markets) alone holds the key to competitiveness.[54] Such arguments, as we know, held centre-stage in the UK for two decades after 1979, where they shaped economic policy under the Conservatives and inspired the Labour Party to abandon its original commitments to public ownership, Keynesianism and full employment. They also were the standard intellectual tools of a whole series of international regulatory agencies throughout the same twenty year period; and are now enshrined in the convergence criteria of the Maastricht treaty on European monetary union. And, of course, current understandings (in both policy making and academic circles) of the economic imperatives associated with intensified global competition are predominantly liberal in kind. Statism is out. Keynesianism is out. Welfare provision and trade union rights are heavily under siege. In terms of the triangular relationships laid out in Figures 1 and 2, the current policy consensus in the corridors of power in advanced capitalism is steadily shifting back towards market-led solutions to rising unemployment and slow rates of economic growth. As New Labour formulates its 'third way', its

---

[51] W. Lazonick, *Business Organization and the Myth of the Market Economy*, pp. 188–9.

[52] See W. Streeck, 'German capitalism: does it exist? Can it survive?', *New Political Economy*, 2, 2 (July 1997), p. 247.

[53] See P. Burkett and M. Hart-Landsberg, 'The Use and Abuse of Japan as a Progressive Model', in L. Panitch (ed.), *The Socialist Register 1996* (London, Merlin, 1996); and D. Coates, 'Labour Power and International Competitiveness: a Critique of Dominant Orthodoxies'.

[54] See R. Bacon and W. Eltis, *Too Few Producers* (London, Macmillan, 1976); A. Lindbeck, 'What is wrong with the West European economies?', *The World Economy*, 8, 2 (1985), 153–76; and M. Olson, *The Rise and Decline of Nations* (New Haven, Yale University Press, 1982).

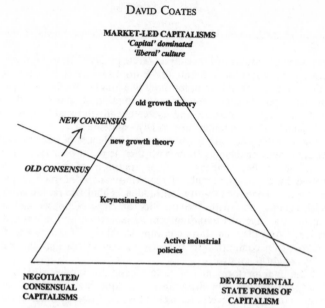

Figure 3. The Changing Policy Consensus

rejection of old-style social democracy is suddenly the only story in town (see Figure 3).

Where the marxist and liberal critics of the new institutionalism converge is in their common recognition that this policy shift is not accidental. Where they differ is in their assessment of the likely viability of the convergence now under way. For certainly on a marxist reading of the logics of contemporary capitalism, changes in the global economy are now squeezing the space for certain kinds of capitalist model. It is not just, as Zysman has it, that 'national models of growth in the advanced countries are not collapsing, but are rather undergoing a common transition along distinct trajectories'.[55] It is rather that the extensive industrialization of East Asia (and the associated proletarianization of the Asian rural poor) is qualitatively altering the balance of class forces on a world scale; and if that is not requiring a straightforward convergence in the relationships within capitalist classes (and between capital and the state), it *is* squeezing the space within which different relationships between capital and labour can be easily sustained. Globalization, understood in this sense of renewed industrialization on a global scale, has qualitatively altered the class parameters from those within which negotiated/consensual models of capitalism were initially created and sustained in Western Europe in what – for the western European labour movements – now does look as though it was capitalism's 'golden age'. There may still be a space for the protection of existing (and construction of new) developmental state forms of capitalism; but those

[55] J. Zysman, 'The myth of the global economy', p. 159.

were never in the past (and will not be in the future) necessarily superior to Anglo-Saxon forms of capitalism as far as labour was concerned. But what is now becoming clear is that an increasingly integrated global economy will allow fewer and fewer spaces for social democratic models of capitalism. Odd ones may find a 'niche' for themselves for a brief moment of time (as Pontussen hopes Swedish social democracy may yet do in the new international division of labour: what he calls finding 'a swimmable eddy of the Rhine rather than drown in mid-Atlantic'):[56] but the rest will no doubt go in pursuit of their own versions of New Labour's 'third way': and that will take them back towards market-led forms of capitalist regulation behind a rhetoric of policy modernization and welfare reform.

For the moment, in the UK at least, New Labour is full of modernizing self-confidence: with leading government figures apparently convinced that they have found *the* way to protect employment and living standards for the bulk of their electorate.[57] But they would do well to be cautious for at least two sets of reasons: one specific to the UK, one more general to the Anglo-Saxon model.

1. The structural weaknesses of the UK economy to which the centre-left new institutionalists drew attention, and which the rise of Western European and Asian capitalism highlighted so starkly through the 1970s and 1980s, have not gone away, and will not go away simply by the introduction of welfare-to-work schemes and/or life-long learning. For quite contrary to the Thatcherite and neo-liberal claims which New Labour now seems so content to follow, those institutional weaknesses lay predominantly on the side of capital, not of labour: and the new government's enthusiasm for capital de-regulation therefore robs it (and the labour movement) of any levers by which to tackle deep-seated inadequacies in investment, innovation and change. If the whole world *is* going in an Anglo-Saxon direction, Labour ministers would do well to remember that the UK (as a leading Anglo-Saxon economy) has already spent half a century slipping down every league table that they would now recognize as important, as well as a few others (on income equality, social justice and the like) which most of them would probably now discount. The arrival of previously corporatist/state developmentalist economies in the Anglo-Saxon 'camp' will not of itself automatically reverse the historical vulnerability of UK-based producers to their competitive superiority; and may actually amplify/intensify UK competitive weakness by creating a 'level playing field' between UK-based producers short of adequate investment and generously-invested foreign-based producers suddenly enjoying falling private and social wage bills. Tony Blair may feel personally superior as he flies around the world extolling the virtues of the UK's 'third way'; but the personal feelings of even key members of the political class are no guide to the actual strengths of the economies over which they formally preside. The UK is able to present itself as a role model for others now primarily because its dominant classes have for so long been at the forefront of the export of

---

[56] J. Pontussen, 'Between Neo-liberalism and the German Model: Swedish Capitalism in Transition', in Crouch and Streeck, *The Political Economy of Modern Capitalism*, p. 70.

[57] There are many examples of this optimism and self belief. See in particular Gordon Brown's 'Personal view: no quick fix on jobs', *Financial Times*, 17 November 1997, p. 16.

capital which has become again a defining feature of global capitalism, after the brief 'national capitalist' interregnum of the long post-war boom.[58] What the UK experienced since the 1960s – footloose capital in pursuit of short-term profit – is very much more the global norm than it was in the 1960s: and is everywhere weakening established industrial classes (both national bourgeoisies and their associated labour forces) as it did so spectacularly in the UK after 1960. But this belated convergence in the habits of capitalist classes, and especially in the habits of their financial sections, is small comfort to a UK industrial base which has been eroded by more than three decades of what Rowthorn and Wells properly term 'negative de-industrialization';[59] and ought equally to be small comfort to New Labour ministers now charged with the protection of UK-based employment and living standards. Far from extolling the virtues of globalization, New Labour ministers would do well to ask themselves if the internationalization of UK capital which so undermined investment in UK-based jobs and services will be turned around by merely the provision of macro-economic stability, industrial retraining and a low minimum wage; and to consider, if it will not, what kind of European-wide social democratic political initiatives are required to pull multinational corporate power back under labour control.

2.   And even if the future is Anglo-Saxon, what comfort are we to take from the progressive collapse of western European welfare capitalism as a viable capitalist model? Right-wing political forces might enjoy that victory, but left-wing ones should not. For if market-led capitalism is all that is left in its place, then the weaknesses of that model – as both a developmental engine and as a guarantor of minimum standards of welfare provision and worker rights, of the kind laid out by its critics in easier times – will simply become generalized through the world economy, and intensified there by the spread of world competition. Unregulated markets in an environment of extensive proletarianization and global capital mobility will generate an upward and permanent momentum in economic activity only if the central contradictions of a capitalist mode of production are suddenly and miraculously a thing of the past. But if they are not, we all face a long period of 'ratcheting down' (of wages, job rights, employment and welfare) and of 'ratcheting up' (of longer hours, intensified work routines, greater income inequality, and generalized economic insecurity). For, as Marx put it long before it became fashionable to talk of globalization and the convergence of capitalist models, we seem now at last to be approaching that point at which 'the bourgeoisie ... through its exploitation of the world market ... compels all nations, on pain of extinction, to adopt the bourgeois mode of production. In one word, it creates a world after its own image': that point, moreover, where perhaps 'man is at last compelled to face with sober senses his real conditions of life, and his relations with his

---

[58] For this and much else, see H. Radice, 'Britain under New Labour: a model for European restructuring?' (unpublished paper, available from the author at the Leeds University Business School).

[59] B. Rowthorn and J. Wells, *Deindustrialization and Foreign Trade* (Cambridge, Cambridge University Press, 1987), p. 228.

660   *Models of Capitalism*

kind'.[60] It is 150 years since Marx wrote *The Communist Manifesto*. Contemporary developments suggest that, though its production was maybe a little premature, its central message has now at last found its time.

(*Accepted*: 22 July 1998)

[60] K. Marx, 'The Communist Manifesto', reprinted in *Marx-Engels: Selected Works* (London, Lawrence and Wishart, 1968), pp. 38–9.

Part III
The Models Compared

[16]

CONTINUITIES AND CHANGES IN SOCIAL SYSTEMS OF PRODUCTION: THE CASES OF JAPAN, GERMANY, AND THE UNITED STATES

J. Rogers Hollingsworth

In twentieth-century capitalism, there have been several changes in perceptions about the relative effectiveness of specific management styles and work organizations (Boyer, 1991; Chandler, 1962, 1977, 1990; Piore and Sabel, 1984; Sabel, 1982). Changes in technology, relative prices, and consumer preferences have been instrumental in altering the perception as to why one form of management style and work practice is superior and should supplant existing forms (North, 1990). Economic actors not only defend specific forms of management and work practices as means of achieving particular economic outcomes and performances (Marglin, 1991), but they also attempt to borrow from other societies what they consider to be "best practices."

This paper argues that forms of economic coordination and governance *cannot* easily be transferred from one society to another, for they are embedded in social systems of production distinctive to their particular society. Societies borrow selected principles of foreign management styles and work practices, but their effectiveness is generally limited. Economic performance is shaped by the entire social system of production in which firms are embedded and not simply by specific principles of particular management styles and work practices. Moreover, a society's social system of production tends to limit the kind of goods it can produce and with which it can compete successfully in international markets.

The chapter suggests, with empirical references to the Japanese, German, and American economies, that a society's social system of production is very path dependent and system specific. Because a society's modes of economic governance and coordination develop according to a particular logic and are system specific, the overall theme of the chapter is that there are serious limitations in the extent to which a society may mimic the forms of economic governance and performance of other societies. The focus of the chapter throughout is exclusively on manufacturing sectors.

SOCIAL SYSTEMS OF PRODUCTION: FURTHER CLARIFICATION AND TWO EXAMPLES

In recent years, some scholars (Florida and Kenney, 1991; Kenney and Florida, 1988, 1993; Oliver and Wilkinson, 1988) have assumed that the diffusion of particular forms of management styles and work practices across societies would lead to convergence in performance. However, the argument of this paper is that, even though British, French, and American firms may adopt certain aspects of Japanese management styles – e.g., just-in-time production complexes, self-managing teams, quality circles, the use of "statistical process controls" etc. – or some variant of the German vocational system, one should not conclude that their economies will be transformed. A nation's financial markets, educational system, industrial relations system, and other sociopolitical factors influence sectoral and national economic performance. In order to understand how and why a society's economy performs, it is necessary to understand its entire social system of production. If a society is to improve substantially the performance of its economy, it must do more than adopt some of the management and work practices of its foreign competitors. It must alter its entire social system of production.

In the history of modern capitalism, there is a logic by which institutions coalesce into a social system of production (Hollingsworth, 1991a, 1991b). This occurs – in part – because institutions are embedded in a culture in which their logic is symbolically grounded, organizationally structured, technically and materially constrained, politically defended, and historically shaped by specific rules and norms. Though institutions are constantly changing, there are sharp limits to the type and direction of

change that any particular institution can undergo because of its linkages
with other institutions. Thus, a society's business firms, educational system,
capital markets, industrial relations system, etc. can engage in serious restructuring only if the norms and rules, as well as most of the other institutions with which they are linked, also change.[1]

In any social system, there are pressures to have consistency in the rules
and norms across institutional sectors, though in any complex society, social systems are obviously imperfectly integrated. Indeed, the degree to
which the institutional norms and rules making up a social system of production are loosely or tightly coupled is a variable of considerable importance. In general, however, the institutions making up a social system of
production are interdependent, and changes in one institution generally result in changes in other institutions. Each institutional sphere is dependent
on the others for various types of resources, so there is interdependence
among the differing institutional spheres. Moreover, each society has its
norms, moral principles, rules and laws, recipes for action, as well as its
own idiosyncratic customs, traditions, and principles of justice (Burns and
Flam, 1987).

There are inherent obstacles to convergence among social systems of
production of different societies, for where a system is at any one point in
time is influenced by its initial state. Systems having quite different initial
states are unlikely to converge with one another's institutional practices. Existing institutional arrangements block certain institutional innovations
and facilitate others (Roland, 1990). Thus, the institutions making up a social system of production provide continuity, though institutional arrangements are always changing, but with a logic that is system specific. While
Williamson (1975, 1985) suggests that actors tend to choose the institutions that are most efficient, North (1990) is much closer to the mark in his
argument that most social institutions exist as a result of custom and habit
and are therefore inefficient. At any moment in time, the world tends to appear to its actors as very complex and uncertain. For this reason, actors often
engage in contradictory forms of behavior – pursuing different strategies as
hedges against what is viewed as a very uncertain world. And their hedging
and contradictory forms of behavior may lead to somewhat different societal
directions, but ones constrained by the institutional fabric within which the
actors are embedded.

Despite the emphasis on the logic of institutional continuity, this is not
an argument that systems change along some predetermined path. There are
critical turning points in the history of highly industrialized societies, but
the choices are limited by the existing institutional terrain. Being path dependent, a social system of production continues along a particular logic

until or unless a fundamental societal crisis intervenes (David, 1988; Durlauf, 1991; Hollingsworth, 1991a, 1991b; Krugman, 1991; Milgrom, Qian, and Roberts, 1991; Pred, 1966).

In the presentation that follows, the focus is on two social systems of production: the social system of mass standardized production and variants of a social system of flexible production. A major argument of the discussion is that at the core of each social system of production is a set of social institutions that are system specific and that are unlikely to diffuse to other societies. On the other hand, within a country's social system of production, there may be narrow dimensions of its management style, work organization, and policies and practices that are more mobile than others. Depending on the social system of production of a host society, these may be adopted from another system (for examples, see Ackroyd et al., 1988; Boyer, 1991; Cool and Lengnick-Hall, 1985; Freeman, 1982; Fucini and Fucini, 1990; Gordon, 1988; Graham 1988; Kujawa, 1980; Levine and Ohtsu, 1991; Oliver and Wilkinson, 1988; Shibagaki, Trevor, and Abo, 1989; Trevor, 1987, 1991; Turnball, 1988). But even though some dimensions of a society's social system of production are more susceptible of diffusing across societies than are other dimensions, all the component parts of a social system of production are socially constituted, contextually defined, and shaped by historical circumstances.

At this point, it is important to reemphasize a point made earlier in this volume. Some advanced industrial societies have more than one social system of production. But where this occurs, one tends to be dominant, and it usually imposes its flavor, constraints, and opportunities on other systems. In other words, the dominant system dictates the labor practices, finances, and the way that the state intervenes elsewhere in the society. Thus, over time, there tends to be some integration and/or diffusion of social systems of production within the same nation-state (Herrigel, 1995).

MASS STANDARDIZED SOCIAL SYSTEMS OF PRODUCTION

Until the 1960s, the model of mass production was widely held by American scholars to be the undisputed means of enhancing industrial efficiency. For at least three quarters of a century, most American industrial economists assumed that the most efficient means of reducing costs was by employing economies of scale and a standardized system of production. Mass production became the strategy for expanding a firm's market, and expanding markets became the means of minimizing costs. Many observers assumed that this was the direction in which industrial sectors were converging both within and across countries (Kerr et al., 1960).

Firms that successfully employed a mass production strategy had to engage in a particular form of industrial relations, use specific types of machinery, and relate in particular ways to other firms in the manufacturing process. Increasingly, mass producers took seriously Adam Smith's prescription that the most efficient way of organizing a factory was to routinize and differentiate workers' tasks down to the smallest detail. One way to break down manufacturing into ever more detailed operations was to employ specific purpose machinery which would focus on each manufacturing task along an assembly line. In much neoliberal thinking about mass production, employment was viewed as an impersonal economic exchange relationship, and machines, when it was profitable to do so, could easily be substituted for workers. Whatever labor was needed to work on assembly lines could be hired or dismissed on short notice. As machinery became more and more specialized, the skill and autonomy of individual workers often declined – although there was variation in the "deskilling" process from industry to industry and country to country.

Widespread adoption of mass production had major implications for the relationship between manufacturing firms and their suppliers. Because specific purpose machines operated in relatively stable markets, firms either engaged in backward integration or were in a strategic position to force their suppliers to invest in complementary supplies and equipment. Once firms announced their need for specific types of parts, suppliers had to produce at very low costs or lose their business. Over time, those firms that excelled in mass production tended to develop a hierarchical system of management, to adopt strategies of deskilling their employees, to install single-purpose, highly specialized machinery, and to engage in arm's-length dealings with suppliers and distributors based primarily on price. In the long run, the more a firm produced some standardized output, the more rigid the production process became – e.g., the more difficult it was for the firm to produce anything that deviated from the programmed capacity of its special purpose machines. On the other hand, such firms were extraordinarily flexible in dealing with the external labor market. As employees in firms engaged in standardized production had relatively low levels of skill, one worker could easily be exchanged for another. Management had little incentive to engage in long-term contracts with their workers or to invest in the skills of their employees.

This form of production was dependent on large, stable, and relatively well-defined markets for products that were essentially slow in their technological complexity and relatively low in their rate of technological change. Using transaction cost economics, some have argued that hierarchical structures were particularly well suited for mass production and distribution. When the transaction costs of working with external suppliers and distributors became too high, firms frequently resorted to a vertically integrated structure and assumed diverse functions in house (Chandler, 1962, 1977; Teece, 1988; Williamson, 1975, 1985).

Even in a country in which standardized mass production was the dominant technological paradigm, there were always industries that were organized differently (Sabel, 1988, 1991, 1992; Sabel and Zeitlin, 1985). Because heterogeneous markets existed for many products, many firms often competed with mass producers, sometimes by upgrading traditional skills and by producing carefully differentiated, high quality products. There is considerable historical literature replete with examples of mass and flexible producers existing in the same society (Friedman, 1988; Herrigel, 1989, 1993, 1995), although many observers viewed those who refused to engage in mass production to be "premodern" centers of production (Lamoreaux, 1985; Sabel and Zeitlin, 1985).

Not just any country could have a mass standardized production system as its dominant form of production. For such a social system to be dominant, firms had to be embedded in a particular environment, one with a particular type of industrial relations system, educational system, and financial markets, one in which the market mentality was very pervasive and civil society was weakly developed. Because firms engaged in mass standardized production required large and stable markets, they tended historically to succeed best in large societies. But the larger the spatial area in which this form of production was embedded, the greater the heterogeneity of interests of both labor and capital and thus the greater the difficulty of labor and management to organize effective associations..

Many historians have demonstrated how American schools historically were integrated into a social system of mass standardized production and how the education system was vocationalized (Hogan, 1982; Kantor and Tyack, 1982; Katz, 1971; Tyack, 1974). In such a system, schools for most of the labor force tended to emphasize the qualities and personality traits essential for performing semiskilled tasks: punctuality, obedience, regular and orderly work habits. Because labor markets in such a system were segmented, however, educational systems also tended to be segmented, but intricately linked with one another. Thus, such a system also had some schools for well-to-do children that emphasized student participation and less direct supervision by teachers and administrators (Bowles and Gintis, 1976). Hogan (1982: 163) argues that schools in a social system of mass production provide skills that are less technical than social and are less concerned with developing cognitive skills and judgments than attitudes and behavior appropriate to organizations and their labor process. Obviously, such an educational system is very useful for a social system of production that does not require a labor force with high technical skills or a high degree of work autonomy.

The historical development of capital markets, as part of an institutionalized social system of mass production, is very complex and will not be elaborated here. However, where social systems of mass standardized production have been highly institutionalized, the financial markets have also been highly developed. Large firms in such systems – in comparison with those in other societies – have tended to expand from retained earnings or to raise capital from the bond or equity markets, but less frequently from bank loans.

Once financial markets become highly institutionalized, securities become increasingly liquid. And the owners of such securities tend to sell their assets when they believe their investments are not properly managed. Since management embedded in such a system tends to be evaluated very much by the current price and earnings of the stocks and bonds of their companies, it has a high incentive to maximize short-term considerations at the expense of long-term strategy (Cox, 1986a, 1986b; Kotz, 1978; Navin and Sears, 1955; Zysman, 1983). This kind of emphasis on a short-term horizon limits the development of long-term stable relations between employers and employees – a prerequisite for a highly skilled and broadly trained workforce. Instead, the short-term maximization of profits means that firms in a social system of mass standardized production tend to be quick to lay off workers during an economic downturn, thus being heavily dependent on a lowly and narrowly skilled workforce.

A social system of mass standardized production is most likely to be dominant in a society in which the economy is weakly subordinated to religion, politics, and/or other social arrangements. Where the noneconomic aspects of society are weakly developed – e.g., a weak civil society – a market mentality tends to become pervasive. And the dominant institutional arrangements for coordinating a society's economy tend to be markets, corporate hierarchies, and a weakly structured regulatory state (Polanyi, 1957).

SOCIAL SYSTEMS OF FLEXIBLE PRODUCTION

For purposes of this discussion, flexible production is simply the inverse of mass production. It is the production of goods by means of general purpose resources rather than vice versa, a system of production which can flexibly adapt to different market demands. In systems in which flexible production is dominant, there is an ever-changing range of goods with customized designs to appeal to specialized tastes (Friedman, 1988; Herrigel, 1995; Kristensen, 1986; Sabel, 1987, 1991, 1992; Sabel and Zeitlin, 1985; Piore and Sabel, 1984; Streeck, 1987a, 1987b).

In the contemporary world, markets for many products are changing with great speed, and in those sectors where this is the case, it is less appropriate for firms to invest in product-specific machines and workers who are capable of doing only one thing. Production systems are closely linked to and influenced by available technology, and in numerous industries the emergence of microelectronic circuitry has done much to revolutionize systems of production, giving rise to what are widely called "economies of scope." The flexibility of microelectronic circuitry now permits large and small firms to introduce both quality and variety, in both small and large batches of production (Sorge and Streeck, 1988; Sorge et al., 1983; Streeck, 1987a). Because employees and general purpose machines in a flexible production system can be used for many different purposes, the flexibility of manufacturing systems is increasingly being defined by the extent to which its various parts can be combined and recombined and by the ease with which machinery and workers can be assigned to different tasks and products (Kristensen, 1986; Sabel, 1991, 1992). In contrast to mass standardized producers, flexible production requires workers who have high levels of skills and who can make changes on their own. This means that there is much less work supervision than in firms engaged in mass production. Because of the need to shift production strategies quickly, management in firms engaged in flexible production must be able to depend on employees to assume initiative, to integrate conception of tasks with execution, and to make specific deductions from general directives. Moreover, firms engaged in flexible production methods tend to become somewhat more specialized and less vertically integrated than firms engaged in mass production. As a result, such firms must be in close technical contact with other firms. In short, flexible producers require a highly skilled work force operating with minimal supervision, general-purpose machinery, and intense coordination-even frequent collaboration with other producers (Friedman, 1988; Hollingsworth and Streeck, 1993; Pyke, Becattini, and Sengenberger, 1991; Pyke and Sengenberger, 1992; for somewhat different, but very stimulating perspectives, see Pollart, 1991).

A key indicator to the development of a social system of flexible production in a society is its industrial relations system. Highly institutionalized social systems of flexible production require workers with broad levels of skills and some form of assurance that they will not be dismissed from their jobs. Indeed, job security tends to be necessary for employers to have sufficient incentives to make long-term investments in developing the skills of their workers.

To be most effective in employing technologies of flexible production, management must have a willingness to cooperate and have trusting relationships with their competitors, suppliers, customers, and workers (Sabel, 1990). But the degree to which these trust relationships can exist depends on the institutional environment in which firms are embedded (see Table 9-1 for characteristics of social systems of flexible production).

Social systems of mass standardized production tend to have firms embedded in environments that are impoverished in terms of collective forms of governance − e.g., trade unions, trade associations, employers' associations, etc. − and in societies in which the market mentality is pervasive.[2] But firms in social systems of flexible production are embedded in environments with highly developed institutional forms of a collective nature which promote long-term cooperation between labor and capital as well as between firms and suppliers. And the market mentality of the society is less pervasive. The collective nature of the environment also facilitates cooperation among competitors. The economic importance of institutional arrangements for rich and long-term relationships between labor and capital and among suppliers, customers, competitors, governments, universities, and/or banks is that such arrangements link together economic actors having relatively high levels of trust with each other, and having different knowledge bases − a form of coordination that is increasingly important as technology and knowledge become very complex and change very rapidly (Hollingsworth, 1991b; Hollingsworth and Streeck, 1993).

These comments may suggest that a social system of flexible production can exist on a voluntaristic, contractual basis − that is, economic actors simply have to structure their industrial relations system and their relations with their suppliers and customers in a prescribed way and a social system of flexible production will follow. However, the processes are far more complex. For a social system of flexible production to thrive, firms must be embedded in a *community, region,* or *country* in which many other firms share the same and/or complementary forms of production (Amin and Roberts, 1990). Firms that adhere to the principles of a social system of production over long periods of time tend to do so either because of communitarian obligations or because of some form of external coercion.

Moreover, for a social system of flexible production to sustain itself, firms must invest in a variety of redundant capacities. Such redundancies are likely to result only if firms are embedded in an environment in which associative organizations and/or the state require such investments. Firms act-

Table 9-1. A Typology of Social Systems of Production

Variables	Mass standardized production	Flexible production
Size and nature of the market	Large homogeneous markets, with competition based very much on price	Smaller markets; more heterogeneous tastes with competition based very much on quality
Technology of the product	Stable and slow to change; not highly complex. Products produced in large volume	Rapidly changing and highly complex; products produced in small batches
Organizational characteristics of firms		
Chain of production	Tendency for production to be vertically integrated	Vertical disintegration, with various types of obligational networks linking various actors together; subcontracting, cooperative contracting among small firms, joint ventures, and strategic alliances common
Work skills	Narrowly defined and very specific in nature	Well-trained, highly flexible, and broadly skilled workforce
Labor–management relations	Low trust between labor and management; poor communication but hierarchical in nature	Relatively high degree of trust
Internal labor market	Rigid	Flexible
Centralization	Very hierarchical and semiauthoritarian	Decentralized, consensual, and participatory type organization
Production equipment	Product-specific machines	General purpose machines
Work security	Relatively poor security except due to considerable class conflict	Long-term employment, relatively high job security
Investment in work skills by firm	Low	High
Conception of property rights	High degree of consciousness of property rights	Lower level of consciousness of property rights

Table 9-1 *(cont.)*

Variables	Mass standardized production	Flexible production
Environmental Structures		
Relationship with other firms	Highly conflictual, rather impoverished institutional environment	Highly cooperative relationships with suppliers, customers, and competitors in a very rich institutional environment
Collective action	Trade associations poorly developed and where existent are lacking in power to discipline members	Trade associations highly developed with capacity to govern industry and to discipline members
Modes of capital formation	Capital markets well developed; equities are highly liquid, frequently	Capital markets are less well developed, strong bank–firm links, extensive cross-firm ownership, long-term ownership of equities
Antitrust legislation	Designed to weaken cartels and various forms of collective action	More tolerance of various forms of collective action
Institutional training facilities	Public education emphasizing low levels of skills	Greater likelihood of strong apprenticeship programs linking vocational training and firms
Performance measures which get high priority in sectors	Wage inequality, lower quality products, innovativeness in new industries, conflictual labor–management relations	High wage equality, high quality products, innovativeness in product improvement, high social peace between labor and management
Type of civil society in which firms are embedded	Weakly developed	Highly developed
Degree of pervasiveness of market mentality of society	High	Low

ing voluntarily and primarily from a sense of a highly rational calculation of their investment needs are unlikely to develop such redundant capacities over the longer run. Manufacturing firms engaged in flexible forms of production require a workforce that is broadly and highly skilled, and capable of shifting from one task to another and of constantly learning new skills. But firms that are excessively rational in assessing their needs for skills are likely to proceed very cautiously in their skill investments; in such firms, accountants and cost benefit analysts are likely to insist that only those investments be made that will yield predictable rates of return. In a world of rapidly changing technologies and product markets, firms that invest *only* in those skills for which there is a demonstrated need are likely over time to have a less skilled workforce than they need. Moreover, firms that invest only in those skills that management is convinced they need, over time, run the risk of not being able to utilize the skills in which they have invested. With knowledge and technology becoming more complex and changing very rapidly, excessive rational economic thinking along the principles inherent in a social system of mass production may well result in poor economic performance. Thus, firms engaged in flexible production require excess or redundant investments in work skills, and can sustain this over time only if they are embedded in a social system of flexible production – which by definition has highly developed collective forms of behavior with the capacity to impose communitarian obligations among actors (for an excellent development of this argument for the German case, see Streeck, 1991b; also see Hollingsworth and Streeck, 1993).

Another redundant investment – one that is somewhat complementary – involves efforts to generate social peace. High quality and flexible production can persist only if there is social peace between labor and management. The maintenance of peace is costly, and it is impossible for cost analysts to demonstrate how much investment is needed in order to maintain a high level of social peace. Thus, just as highly rational managers are tempted to invest less in skills than will be needed over the longer term, so also they tend to underinvest in those things which lead to social peace. But for a firm to have a sufficient supply of social peace when needed, it must be willing to incur high investments in social peace when it does not appear to need it. In this sense, investment in and cultivation of social peace create a redundant resource which is exposed to the typical hazards of excessive rationality and short-term opportunism. Social peace as a redundant resource is more likely to be created as matter of legal or social obligation than as a rationally calculated economic interest (Hollingsworth and Streeck, 1993; Sorge and Streeck, 1988; Streeck, 1991b).

Investment in the redundant capacities of general skills and social peace tend to require long-term employment relationships. And while firms may occasionally develop such capacities based on *voluntarily* imposed decisions, such decisions tend to be less stable and less effective for the development of broad and high level skills and social peace than socially imposed or legally compulsory arrangements which originate from institutionalized obligations. Social systems of mass standardized production represent a social order based on contractual exchanges between utility-maximizing individuals (Williamson 1975, 1985), and most firms in such systems underinvest in the skills of their workers and in social peace. Social systems of flexible production require cooperative relations and communitarian obligations among firms, as well as collective inputs that firms would not experience based purely on a rational calculation of a firm's short-term economic interests (Hollingsworth, 1991a, 1991b; Streeck, 1991b).

In sum, societies with social systems of flexible production tend to have most – if not all – of the following characteristics:

- An industrial relations system that promotes continuous learning, broad skills, workforce participation in production decision making, and is perceived by employees to be fair and just.
- Less hierarchical and less compartmentalized arrangements within firms, thus enhancing communication and flexibility.
- A rigorous education and training system for labor and management, both within and outside of firms.
- Well-developed institutional arrangements which facilitate cooperation among competitors.
- Long-term stable relationships with high levels of communication and trust among suppliers and customers.
- A system of financing that permits firms to engage in long-term strategic planning.

All of these practices are mutually reinforcing. Because the institutional arrangements of each social system of flexible production are system-specific, they are not easily transferable from one society to another.

THE PATH DEPENDENCY OF SOCIAL SYSTEMS OF PRODUCTION

One gains some insight to the path dependency and distinctiveness of social systems of production by focusing on one historical process important in shaping a society's social system of production: the timing of its industrialization (Cole, 1978; Dore, 1987; Gerschenkron, 1962). Slow developers such as Britain and the United States had a long period of capital accumulation with numerous firms drawing workers from highly competitive labor markets. From such a tradition emerged the practices in the twentieth century of considerable job mobility from firm to firm, few constraints on the ability of employers to dismiss their workers, a tendency for employers to pay employees substantially different rates for different job tasks, and a practice of workers having narrow job assignments so that workers were easily substitutable. Relative to their size, these early developers had complex economies – e.g., many industries – coordinated by markets and corporate hierarchies. Their industries were *not* well embedded in an environment with such collective institutional arrangements as highly developed business associations, trade unions, or apprenticeship systems. In such an environment, there evolved over a long period of time a capitalist class with a high degree of consciousness about property rights; a workforce with a low degree of job security; a low degree of cooperative relations among competitors; a high degree of distrust and instability between firms and their suppliers; a high degree of distrust between labor and capital; and a political culture that emphasized a high degree of individualism. In such highly individualistic societies, the state was primarily regulatory in its function. Thus, there developed a social system of production with a low degree of communitarian obligations on the part of both capital and labor; an industrial relations system with low worker participation in managerial decisions, narrow job skills, and low levels of social peace; and a managerial style of decision making with a high degree of hyperrationality with heavy emphasis on short-term consequences (Elbaum and Lazonick, 1986; Hounshell, 1984; Whitely, 1991). Most of these characteristics are associated with a social system of mass standardized production and have persisted to the present day. Late developers – such as Sweden, Germany, and Japan – are toward the opposite end of the continuum on most of these characteristics, although these three countries vary in terms of their historical development and their social systems of production (for a discussion of regional variation within Germany, see Herrigel, 1995).

The way local, regional, and national economies are coordinated is the result of complex configurations of forces that seem to be deeply rooted in the histories of societies (Hollingsworth, 1991a, 1991b). Because the social processes which have resulted in social systems of flexible production are quite historically specific, the institutional arrangements that give support to such systems are not easily transferable from one country to another. As a result, it is unlikely that there will be rapid convergence in the way manufacturing sectors are coordinated across countries.

Thus far, the discussion has focused on why social systems of flexible production are more institutionalized in some societies than in others, without giving much consideration to the considerable variation that exists from country to country in such a social system. The discussion now focuses on two countries – Japan and Germany – the institutional configuration of which represents two contrasting examples of social systems of flexible production. The Japanese case is an example of a social system that emphasizes diversified quality *mass* production, while the German system emphasizes diversified quality production. Of course, there are other forms of social systems of flexible production in which the emphasis is less on large- and more on small-scale productions. Examples are the social systems of flexible production in parts of Northern Italy or Western Denmark, but for lack of space they are not discussed here. But it is in Germany and Japan that there are social systems of production that have been conducive to high and continued investment in human resources in large firms (Coriat, 1990).

The following discussion also includes the institutional configuration of the United States' social system of production as an example of a powerful economy that has historically been embedded in a social system of mass standardized production, and largely for that reason its economic actors find it very difficult to mimic the more effective practices and performance of their Japanese and German competitors. The analysis demonstrates with these three cases how a society's social system of production limits its capacity to compete in certain industrial sectors, but enhances its competitiveness in others.

LONG-TERM AND CONTINUOUS LEARNING: JAPANESE DIVERSIFIED QUALITY MASS PRODUCTION

In explaining the governance of Japanese manufacturing firms, one of the most important features, from which many others have been derived, is the distinctiveness of the Japanese capital markets. In both Japan and Germany, where industrialization occurred later and where mass markets have historically been much smaller than in the United Sates, firms have long been more dependent on outside financiers for capital – the large banks in Germany and the major financial groups (e.g., *zaibatsu, keiretsu*) in Japan (Aoki, 1988, 1990; Cox, 1986; Chandler, 1977: 499; Chandler and Daems, 1980: 6; Gerlach, 1989; Kocka, 1980). Historically, with the equity and bond markets poorly developed, it was quite common for Japanese firms – especially large firms – to rely on one lead bank for capital. Not only has that bank monitored the firm's operations very carefully, but it often has held equity in the firm, making the bank–firm relationship quite tight. In addition, there are large groups of business firms (e.g., Mitsubishi, Mitsui, Sumitomo), each having a major bank as its main lender. Not only is each group heavily dependent on a single bank, but within each group there is extensive interlocking stockholding, creating strong ties among firms within the group (Ballon and Tomita, 1988; Gerlach, 1989; Lincoln, 1980; Okimoto et al., 1984: 207–13).

In addition to the bank-centered groups of the *keiretsu,* there is a second form of industrial grouping, deriving from the subcontracting relationships between large firms and their suppliers. Like the *keiretsu* or bank-centered groups, these relationships are strengthened by mutual stockholding and interlocking directorships. In both types of institutional arrangements, this kind of mutual stockholding diversifies risk and buffers firms from the uncertainties of labor and product markets.

The role of these groups in channeling capital to firms has tended to lower the cost of capital relative to that in most western countries. The extensive cross-company pattern of stock ownership in Japan is an important reason why Japanese firms can forsake short-term profit maximization in favor of a strategy of long-term goals – a process very much in contrast with the pressures on American managers to maximize short-term gains. Moreover, the pattern of intercorporate stockholding encourages many long-term business relationships in Japan, which in turn reinforces ties of interdependence, exchange relations, and reciprocal trust among firms. These kinds of relationships have also led to low transaction costs among firms, high reliability of goods supplied from one firm to another, close coordination of delivery schedules, and meticulous attention to servicing (Abegglen and Stalk, 1985; Aoki, 1987, 1988, 1992; Dore, 1987; Lincoln and McBride, 1987; Okimoto and Rohlen, 1988: 266; Wallich and Wallich, 1976).

Having the option to develop long-term strategies, large Japanese firms have had the ability to develop the kind of long-term relations with their employees, on which investment in worker training and flexible specialization are built (Shirai, 1983). And because of their intercorporate ties, many large firms – particularly in steel, shipbuilding, and other heavy industries – have often shifted employees to other companies within their industrial group during economic downturns rather than dismissing their workers. Firms with long-term job security have the capacity to implement a seniority-based wage and promotion system, company welfare capitalism, consensus decision making, employee loyalty, job rotation and flexible labor assignments, and intensive in-firm instruction and on-the-job training (Aoki, 1988; Koike, 1983; O'Brien, 1993; Shigeyoshi, 1984; Stråth, 1993).

Across countries, there are also interesting linkages between labor markets and the system of training for management and labor. Whitley (1991) points out that where unitary educational systems exist – as in Japan and France – academic performance is the key to economic success (also see Hage, Garnier, and Fuller, 1988). Thus, schools provide a set of filters to select the most academically talented who are then guaranteed elite positions in industry and state. Such school systems have a poorly developed system for providing practical or vocational training. Thus, in Japan, business firms provide this type of training, and because of the existence of long-term job security, the training is high in firm-specific terms and not very generalizable to other organizations. This, of course, increases inflexibility in the external labor market.

When workers acquire most of their training, pursue their careers, and receive most of their benefits from a single firm, company unions rather than industrial unionism become quite common (Lincoln and Kalleberg, 1990; Lincoln and McBride, 1987; Shirai, 1983). Moreover, because large Japanese firms provide long-term job security, they do not classify jobs and occupations with the precision which the Americans do, thus adding greater flexibility to Japanese internal labor markets (Cole, 1979; Koike, 1988). Where employees have long-term job security, firms invest extraordinary resources in developing a distinctive firm culture and a set of practices designed to generate loyalty to and pride in the firm (Cole, 1992; Dore, 1973, 1987; Shimada, 1992; Whitley, 1992).

Japanese firms not only provide broad and high levels of skills within firms, but they emphasize job rotation in work teams. This results not only in considerable skill enhancement but also in teamwork and flexibility. Moreover, workers in teams operate as quality control over each other. And workers become accustomed to participating in solving problems, also in small groups. Rohlen (1992), Cole (1992), and Koike (1987) emphasize that this works successfully, for the Japanese have been socialized since grade school to pursue their own self-interests within small group processes. Another way of understanding the Japanese work process is to keep in mind the idea that the Japanese have long been socialized to integrate the obligations to the social group with one's own self-interest. In Japan, one learns to do this almost intuitively.

This form of industrial relations does not exist throughout Japan, as there are dualistic elements in the Japanese economy (Hashimoto and

Raisian, 1985; Levine and Ohtsu, 1991). Many Japanese employees – particularly women (Lebra, 1992) – are subject to layoffs, and wage levels in small firms are substantially less than in larger firms (Levine and Ohtsu, 1991). As the Japanese have had impressive rates of economic growth, however, even smaller firms have not laid off workers on the same scale as a number of western countries (Koike, 1983, 1988). Also, there is considerable evidence that small, fast-growing firms in high-tech sectors pay relatively high wages and provide long-term opportunities to their employees. Because of the existence of a business culture which emphasizes the appropriateness of long-term employment and a paternalistic attitude toward employees, the kind of dualism that is quite prevalent in the United States and other western economies is much less common in Japan, even in smaller firms that are not very profitable (Friedman, 1988; Kumon and Rosovsky, 1992; Lincoln and Kalleberg, 1990; Lincoln and McBride, 1987).

For some scholars, the distinctive features of the Japanese work organization – lifetime employment, seniority-based wage and promotion systems (e.g., *nenko*), welfarism, employee loyalty, consensus decision making, and participatory work structures – are part of a long tradition of corporate familism derived from Japanese feudalism. However, most present day scholars writing about the Japanese economy blend this cultural explanation with rationalist explanations (Cole, 1979; Dore, 1973, 1987; Lincoln and Kalleberg, 1990; Lincoln and McBride, 1987).

Each year, the profits of the firm are distributed to workers under a variable wage system, with a much smaller gap between the top executives and lowest starting wages than in the United States. Human resources are considered the most valuable asset of the firm, and decisions are diffused, consensual, and participatory. The compensation system is designed to maintain high overall morale of the workforce through a system of merit and seniority pay and bonuses based on the profits of the firm. In highly profitable years, a bonus can be as much as four or five months of regular salary (Ozaki, 1991: especially 23, 187).

This discussion of the Japanese institutional configuration would be incomplete without some mention of the Japanese state. Unlike the American case where the state is highly regulatory in nature (Campbell, Hollingsworth, and Lindberg, 1991; Hollingsworth and Lindberg, 1985), the Japanese state has been more involved in industrial development – though its role is less important today than in the 1950s. The Japanese state has developed many forms of protection to keep out foreign competition, it has fostered an environment for cooperation among fierce competitors, and it has channeled subsidies into targeted areas of research and development.

For many years, it adopted a set of macroeconomic policies designed to fuel economic growth with an undervalued yen vis-à-vis the dollar (Friedman, 1988; Johnson, 1982; Pempel, 1982; Samuels, 1987). However, some authors tend to overemphasize the role of the state in the Japanese economy (Anchordoguy, 1989; Brock, 1989). While the state does play an important role in helping firms to mobilize internal research resources, most Japanese research and development takes place within firms, and according to Kenney and Florida (1993: 58) "the Japanese state funds far less R & D than any other major capitalist economy, as measured on either a per capita or per unit of output basis." And the Japanese state has been quite unsuccessful in encouraging firms to mobilize internal resources when they have chosen not to do so.

Japan, like all other countries, does not have firms that compete and perform well in all industrial sectors. Indeed, Japan, like all other countries, has firms that succeed in some sectors, but not very well in others. By focusing attention on Japan, Germany, and the United States, it becomes quite obvious that why countries succeed in certain sectors depends less on such classic factor endowments as climate, natural resources, and land than on their national traditions, values, institutional arrangements, quality of labor and management, and the nature of capital markets.

In most societies, country specific traits are important in influencing which industry the nation's firms will be highly competitive in at a global level. Because of crowded living conditions and tight space constraints throughout the country, the Japanese have long concentrated on producing compact, portable, quiet, and multifunctional products. They have excelled in producing compact cars and trucks, small consumer electronic equipment (TV sets, copiers, radios, and video sets), motorcycles, machine tools, watches and clocks, and a number of business related products such as small computers, fans, pumps, and tools. Clustering of firms has benefitted from the long-term stable relationships that have existed between producers and suppliers and the *keiretsu* type institutional arrangement that has facilitated cooperation among complementary firms. As Porter observes, "With firms and their suppliers typically located close to each other, information flows freely, service is superb, and change is rapid. Larger firms sometimes have equity stakes in their suppliers, opening information further" (1990: 407). Because Japanese trade associations are highly developed and span a variety of suppliers, buyers, and related industries, they too have played an important role in developing cooperation among competing and complementary firms, as well as in facilitating the clustering of industries (Friedman, 1988; Levine, 1984; Miyamoto, 1988; Schneiberg and Hollingsworth, 1990).

The Japanese disadvantage in various national resources has ironically resulted in the development of several highly competitive industrial sectors. For example, the determination to overcome national disadvantages helped give rise to the Japanese steel and shipbuilding industries. In the case of steel, Japanese lack of raw materials and heavy dependence on foreign energy led to such intense innovation in acquisition of supplies and in development of highly efficient production processes that the Japanese emerged as one of the world's most competitive steel producers. Similarly, given Japan's remote location and its strong shipping needs both for exports and for the importation of oil and other raw materials, Japan developed one of the world's leading shipbuilding industries (O'Brien, 1993; Stråth, 1993).

Even though the Japanese have been enormously successful in improving upon existing products, they have been less successful in developing new products – primarily because of their particular institutional configuration. Their educational system emphasizes rote learning rather than creative synthesis or critical analysis. Their universities are structured to facilitate consensus decision making and group conformity. Moreover, the allocation of research funds within universities is poorly distributed on meritocratic criteria. The overall weakness of Japanese universities as research institutions is an important reason why the Japanese have lagged behind in industries involving chemistry, biotechnology, and other fields heavily dependent on basic science, and why the Japanese have won substantially fewer international prizes in the basic sciences than several much smaller European countries. Moreover, the poorly developed Japanese venture capital market has meant that there is little capital to assist entrepreneurs in bringing creative ideas to the marketplace. Among five advanced industrial societies, the number of new products developed by small firms was lowest in Japan. The way Japanese banks are tied into large groups also discourages investment in small start-up companies. And the fact that the most successful students in Japanese universities tend to enter large firms means that it is difficult for start-up firms to attract outstanding young talent. Most Japanese prefer long-term job security to the possibility of a personal fortune (Okimoto, 1986).

SOPHISTICATED INDUSTRIAL RELATIONS AND TRAINING: GERMAN DIVERSIFIED QUALITY SYSTEM OF PRODUCTION

Like Japan, German firms are not embedded in a strong neoliberal institutional environment. These two cases provide excellent evidence that societies are not converging along a common path of neoliberal modernization that was strongly predicted by American social science during the 1960s and 1970s. Rather, the two cases are strong testimony to the argument that firms in advanced capitalist societies are embedded in distinctive social systems of production which have emerged from different institutional trajectories. Nevertheless, a few scholars, focusing primarily on the West German society that emerged after World War II, have erroneously concluded that Germany has been "Americanized" (Berghahn, 1985). True, following World War II, stable parliamentary institutions were established, but most of the existing institutional arrangements in the German social system of production developed along a path of development that was established before World War I (Herrigel, 1995; Jaeger, 1988; Nocken, 1978; Winkler, 1974). A number of recent political economists argue that the German histories of banking, education, and corporatism are key parts of this path of development, resulting in what Katzenstein (1987) labels as a decentralized state in a highly centralized civil society.

In contrast to the Anglo-American economies, the German securities industries, as in Japan, have historically been less well developed, with the result that banks have long been much more important in supplying capital to firms than the equities and bond markets. Moreover, banks have also been important in exercising the stock voting rights of a substantial proportion of outstanding shares of the country's largest firms. Because banks have been so important in these two roles, bank officers have long served on the supervisory boards of hundreds of large companies and have even served as board chairmen of numerous firms. This type of long-term relationship between firms and banks has encouraged firms to be much more immune to the short-run fluctuations of the price of equities than their competitors in the United States and to take a long-term perspective concerning their industry needs (Cox, 1986a, 1986b; Deeg, 1992; Dyson, 1984; Esser, 1990; Kocka, 1980; Neuberger and Stokes, 1974; Tilly, 1976, 1982, 1986; Vittas, 1978; Zysman, 1983: 251–65). This capacity on the part of management has meant that German firms have had more incentive to engage in the long term development of products and have been less likely to lay off workers during a modest economic downturn, as has so often been the case with their American competitors who have been more constrained by short-run fluctuations in the financial markets.

Capitalist economies are very dynamic, and, as the relationships among German banks and business firms continue to evolve, some recent scholars (Deeg, 1992) argue that the historic importance of banks in coordinating the German economy is declining. This argument is based on the facts that (1) due to their retained earnings, many large German firms have been able to increase their independence from large banks (Welzk, 1986), and (2) savings banks and large regional banks (*Landesbanken*) have captured an increasing portion of the market of industrial lending which previously was dominated to a greater extent by three "big banks." While these trends have occurred, holdings by very large banks of shares in major firms and the cross-shareholdings among major firms still contribute to stability in the management of German firms and to the deterrence of hostile takeovers in contrast to the market and volatile pattern of ownership of large American firms (Vitols, 1995a, 1995b, 1995c, 1995d).

Another set of institutional arrangements which contribute to long-term strategic thinking within German firms is the country's industrial relations system. And the key to the German industrial relations system – and in my judgment much of the recent success of the German economy – is shaped by the highly developed centralized employer and business associations as well as trade unions. Peak association bargaining, mediated by the state, not only has played an important role in shaping distributional issues but also has played a role of great importance in influencing the quality and international competitiveness of German products. Employer associations and trade unions in Germany have had relatively encompassing and centralized organizational structures. The German Trade Union Federation (DGB Deutscher Gewerkschaftsbund) consists of 17 industrial unions which organize both blue and white collar workers. In 1987, approximately 39 percent of the employed workforce belonged to unions, though the proportion of manufacturing workers who were unionized was substantially higher. At the national level, employers are organized in the Federal Associations (BDA, the Bundesvereinigung Deutscher Arbeitgeberuerbände), a federation of 47 sectorial employer associations representing between 80 and 90 percent of private employers (Bunn, 1984; Markovits and Allen, 1984; Streeck, 1984b, 1991a).

Unions are responsible for collective bargaining and participation – through policies of codetermination – in corporate boardrooms, while elected work councils participate in organizing working conditions inside firms and ensuring that employment protection laws are obeyed by management. In the mid-1980s, among 480 of West Germany's largest companies – amounting to approximately half of the national output – workers and their representatives held approximately one half of the seats on the supervisory boards of firms. Collectively, these arrangements have been instrumental in reducing conflict between labor and management and in enhancing flexible production inside firms. The job security enjoyed by labor, under codetermination policies, has encouraged firms to invest in the long-term training of their labor force. When management has realized that it cannot easily dismiss workers in the event of economic adversity, it has had

CONTINUITIES AND CHANGES IN SSPs   287

an incentive to engage in the investment of employees with skills high and broad enough to adjust to complex and rapidly changing technologies and unstable markets. And in Germany, the rigidity imposed by strongly organized industrial unionism and works councils has encouraged firms to invest in more skills and social peace than management would otherwise have invested under flexible external market conditions, a process which has directly contributed to a diversified quality, flexible social system of production – the key to Germany's high level of competitiveness in the world economy.

Managers of many German firms found the system quite distasteful. They would like to have followed the practices of their American colleagues in the face of stiff international competitiveness by cutting wages and reducing the size of the workforce. Yet, because they were constrained by the system of codetermination (regulated at the plant level by the Works Constitution Act of 1972 and at the enterprise level by the Works Constitution Act of 1952, superseded in 1976) which resulted in a high wage system, German firms were forced – with little choice – to become engineering and high skill intensive, with diversified and high quality producers. With the rigidities that firms faced in dealing with job protection and high wages for their workers, it was highly rational for management to invest more in the training of their workforce than they would have been inclined to do were they simply following market signals. Almost unintentionally, German firms were pushed to develop one of the world's most skilled labor forces (Hollingsworth and Streeck, 1993; Streeck, 1984b, 1987b, 1991b).

However, the structure of the system has also led to a highly skilled labor force and high quality products in another way. The peak associations of employers and labor have resulted in an enterprise-based vocational training or apprenticeship program whereby young workers learn the theory behind their trade, the theoretical principles of related trades, as well as rich practical training for particular tasks. In the mid-1980s, approximately 60 percent of West German teenagers were engaged in such vocational training, which now tends to last approximately three and a half years. Employers' associations and unions have jointly developed different training programs directed to young people who, upon the completion of their training, go into more than 400 different occupations.

Since 1984, the number of training programs has been reduced to eighteen in order to provide a broader-based and less specialized curriculum, while at the same time the level of training has been substantially upgraded. Significantly, those who have gone through this form of apprenticeship training program have had lower rates of unemployment than young people in other countries with less developed training systems. Because of the rich theoretical training that is integrated into their apprenticeship, German workers have a high capacity to continue advancing their training (Hamilton, 1987; Streeck, 1991b; Streeck et al., 1987).

With a high level of worker training, German firms are less hierarchical than American firms – with workers more involved in both conceptualizing and executing projects. This, of course, has led to a strong emphasis on product quality, which in turn has increased opportunities for long-term close cooperation between assemblers and suppliers in controlling quality and in product research and development.

Streeck (1984a) and others (Shigeyoshi, 1984) have suggested that there is some similarity in the social systems of flexible production of West Germany and Japan, including a high degree of social peace, a workforce that is highly and broadly trained, a flexible labor market within firms, a relatively high level of worker autonomy, a financial system with close ties between large firms and banks, a high degree of stable and long-term relationships between assemblers and their suppliers: overall, a social system of production which results in very high quality products. Despite similarity in these characteristics, there are, of course, major differences in the social systems of production in the two countries. To mention but a few, the routes by which their systems evolved were very different. In Germany industrial unions have been highly developed, whereas in Japan the emphasis has been more on company unions. In Germany, both labor and business are politically well-entrenched in most levels of politics, whereas this is not at all the case with labor in Japan (Pempel and Tsunekawa, 1979). And in Germany, there is nothing resembling the *keiretsu* structure which is so prevalent among large Japanese firms. Moreover, the Germans tend to focus on the upscale, high-cost segments of many markets, whereas the Japanese – with their emphasis on large market share of various products – tend to be more concerned with low-priced, but high quality products. In Germany, the institutional arrangements underlying the rich development of skills have some continuity with corporate associations, which historically have strongly supported and sponsored vocational training. Vocational education has long been important as a precondition for access to certain sectors of the labor market in Germany, whereas historically Japan has had a much more limited public vocational training program.

In Germany, labor and employers' associations emerged to coordinate the class interests of the two sets of actors, and their strategies originally tended to focus very much on the demand rather than the supply side of the economy. And as they negotiated along class lines, the emphasis tended to concentrate more on distributional rather than on production issues. However, macro considerations rest on microlevel performance criteria. Paradoxically, the class mobilization of labor facilitated the codetermination policies in Germany, but over the long term, as German workers have more secure tenure at the firm level, they tend to become more attached and loyal to particular firms. Moreover, their participation on supervisory boards has led to labor's becoming more involved in production, supply side, and microlevel decisions. In the words of Streeck (1992: 100), the concerns of the workers are "shifting from distribution to production, from demand to supply management, and from macro- to the microlevel." In this sense, German industrial relations shifted during the 1980s from traditional issues of reconciling conflicting class interests of labor and capital to issues of integrating labor to the production strategies at the firm level. As the interests of labor shifted from the pursuit of class interests to the enhancement of the well-being of individual companies, there was increasing convergence in the interests of labor and management of individual firms. But as this happened, class solidarity weakened, the center of gravity of German politics shifted from the left toward the center, and the weakening of the welfare state became a distinct possibility. And while there was no likelihood that the German workers and managers would develop the same level of cooperation as existed between workers and managers in many large Japanese firms, there was less divergence in the industrial relations of the two systems as the concerns of German workers shifted to production, supply, and microlevel considerations from a primary emphasis on distributional concerns (for further elaboration, see Streeck, 1992).

The structure of the German political economy has influenced the industrial sectors in which the economy performs well. And like all other countries, Germany has excelled in competing in only particular industrial sectors – not all across the board: the production of machine tools, automobiles, and chemical products, as well as many traditional nineteenth-century industrial products. They have been especially successful in applying the latest microelectronic technology to the production of traditional products and to new production processes. On the other hand, the Germans have been less competitive in many newer industries, e.g., computers, semiconductors, and consumer electronics. In other words, the Germans have placed less emphasis on developing entirely new technologies and industries than in applying the latest technologies to the production of more traditional products. And it is the specific type of German industrial relations system (high job security, the high levels of qualification, and continuous training of German workers) which is conducive to the rapid diffusion of the latest technology to the production of more traditional but high quality products (Junne, 1989). In addition the strong engineering and technical background of senior management, the high levels of skill of the workforce, and a strong consumer demand for high-precision manufacturing processes have contributed to the development of various manufacturing sectors with very high quality products. These characteristics influence the particular product markets and niches in which the Germans are highly competitive.

At the global level many German manufacturing industries have competed extremely well on the basis of high performance product segments rather than costs. Despite Germany's relatively small population, during the 1980s, it was the world's largest exporter of manufactured goods – substantially ahead of both Japan and the United States. Approximately one half of the country's manufactured products were exported, while with automobiles, machine tools, and chemicals, it was in excess of 60 percent (Streeck, 1991a).

The German chemical industry is an excellent example of a sector whose success is based on the technical competence of its workforce. Moreover, this sector demonstrates that when an industry is highly successful in a country and is closely linked to complementary sectors in the same country, it tends to be involved in making up a cluster of industries. Thus, the Germans have a history of being strong in such complementary industries as synthetic fabrics, dyes, and plastics, as well as such related industries as the production of pumps, measuring instruments, plastics processing machinery, and even the construction of chemical plants.

In addition to chemically related sectors, the number of clusters in which German industries are highly competitive at a global level is considerable. Some of the most impressive are in steel (around Dortmund, Essen, and Dusseldorf), automotive industries (around Stuttgart, Munich, Ingolstadt, Neckarsulm, and Regensburg), machine tools (around Stuttgart), printing presses and printed materials (around Offenbach, Heidelberg, and Wurzburg), medical instruments (Tuttlingen), cutlery (Solingen), and machinery of many types. Significantly, German firms have been less successful in global competition in sectors involving consumer goods and services – in other words, in industries in which mass advertising and rapid development of new products are important (Chandler, 1990; Porter, 1990). As this discussion suggests, the key to the success of German industrial sectors results from the social configuration of a host of institutional arrangements, all complementing one another: the financial markets, the business associational and trade union structure, the system of training for labor and management, the industrial relations system, the structure of firms and their relationships with their suppliers and customers, and the role of the state in the German economy. All of these institutional arrangements are intertwined and are the outcomes of a unique path of development.

Germany's social system of production performed extraordinarily well during the 1970s and 1980s. However, it is facing a number of serious problems which are likely to influence its performance during the next decade. Because of space limitations, only two will be mentioned here.

First, as a result of the increasing intensity of international competitiveness and the overcapacity of industrial sectors, some sectors of the German economy will undoubtedly be faced with declining profits. This is already the case in the shipbuilding industry, certain segments in the steel industry, and more recently in the automobile industry. German labor costs have long been very high, but this was in large part offset by high skills and high productivity levels. But the high deutschmark vis-à-vis the dollar, combined with high production costs and the threats of reduced trade, have encouraged German firms in a number of industries to invest more of their production abroad (Mueller and Loveridge, 1995). The very high costs of German production – a consequence of the German social system of production – will over time place constraints on Germany's growth rates. There are a number of recent studies that demonstrate that for some years German foreign investment has contributed – on average – to an increase of at least 100,000 unemployed people annually (see articles in *German Brief* during the past three years).

Second, many German firms have performed extremely well in recent years because of their capacity to shift the latest technologies to traditional products and processes (see the discussions in Ergas, 1986; Junne, 1989; and Sabel et al., 1989). However, the speed with which technological innovation is occurring is increasing, and it is questionable – in the mind of this observer – whether the Germans can match the Japanese both in the quality of many products and in the speed with which the Japanese will be able to bring new products to international markets.

The social system of production within which firms are embedded is important in shaping the response of firms to the transformation that is occurring. But because of the *keiretsu* type system which is so prevalent in Japan, their firms in more traditional industries are closely linked with firms that are shaping the high technology, information intensive industries, which are defining the character of the emerging twenty-first century. Japanese firms – whether in traditional industries or in high-tech ones – are closely linked with state-of-the-art basic research and the industrial infrastructure which is rapidly shaping the new industrial revolution. The speed with which new and traditional industries can integrate the latest technology provides the Japanese the ability to pull away from their major competitors – Germany and the United States. Moreover, Japanese firms in the aggregate are spending a higher percentage of their resources on research and development than any other country.

But in Germany as in most other western countries, firms are not as effectively linked to others in so many different industries. And while Germany excels – by international standards – in the way that its firms are linked to its suppliers and distributors, its social system of production on this dimension is less effective than that of the Japanese, and, for this reason, the Japanese are likely to increase their share of international markets vis-à-vis many German firms.

SHORT-TERMISM AND INSTITUTIONAL INERTIA: THE DIFFICULT AMERICAN TRANSITION

The ability of the United States to move rapidly toward a social system of flexible production is very much limited by its prevailing practices of industrial relations, its education system, and its financial markets – in short, the constraints of its past social system of production. The type of industrial relations that facilitate diversified and high quality production strategies are those in which workers have broad levels of skills and some form of assurance that they will not be dismissed from their jobs. Indeed, job security or other arrangements which provide long-term employment tend to be necessary for employers to have incentives to make long-term investments in the skills of their workers. And while these types of incentive and skill systems have become quite widespread in the core of the Japanese and German economies, in the United States manufacturing employment has tended to be much more job-specific, workers have been less broadly trained, internal labor markets have been more rigid, and employers have had much less incentive to invest in their workers' skill development. Because the United States has had one of the world's most flexible external job markets, it has been much easier for American workers to leave jobs for other firms than is the case in countries where workers have long-term job security. This has also provided disincentives for American employers to invest in worker training.

The American industrial relations system is shaped in large part by the weakly developed business associations and trade unions. The large size and complexity of the American economy, combined with the racial, ethnic, and religious diversity of the working class have created substantial heterogeneity of interests among both labor and capital, making it difficult for each to engage in collective action. And the weak capacity of both capital and labor to organize collectively has placed severe limits on the ability of the United States to move more rapidly in developing a social system of flexible production.

Countries with firms tightly integrated into highly institutionalized systems of business associations (e.g., Japan and Germany) have rather rigid external labor markets but flexible internal labor markets. The United States, with weak associative structures, tends to have more flexible external labor markets but more rigid internal labor markets (Hollingsworth, 1991a, 1991b; Hollingsworth and Lindberg, 1985; Schneiberg and Hollingsworth, 1990).

The capital markets in the United States have also placed constraints on the development of broad employee skills by encouraging firms to engage in short-term maximization of profits. In the United States, the equity markets were highly institutionalized by the end of World War I, and managers of large firms have subsequently had low dependence on commercial banks for financing. Indeed, in recent years, the proportion of industrial funds contributed by commercial bank loans to American firms has been among the lowest in the world (Hollingsworth, 1991a, 1991b). By channeling investment capital into various industries, investment banks played an important role in transforming and stabilizing the railway, steel, copper, telephone, oil, and electrical product industries during the late nineteenth and early twentieth centuries. However, the Clayton Antitrust Act of 1914 made interlocking directorships among large banks and trusts illegal. Moreover, it forbade a corporation to acquire the stock of another if the acquisition reduced competition in the industry. In the longer term, the Clayton Act tended to reduce the ability of investment banks and firms to carry out a long-term strategy of promoting a community of interests among firms either in the same or in complementary industries. In addition, the American government in 1933 forced a sharp separation between commercial and investment banking. From that point on, investment banks lost much of their access to capital.

As a consequence, American nonfinancial corporations became dependent for raising capital on liquid financial markets rather than on banks. Increasingly, corporate managers became dependent on the whims and strategies of stockholders and bond owners. This resulted in an emphasis on a short-term time horizon for large firms which has limited the capacity of American management to develop long-term stable relations between employers and their employees – a prerequisite for a highly skilled and broadly trained work force and a flexible or diversified quality social system of production.

On the other hand, the structure of the financial markets does provide the Americans with an advantage in regard to the development of small new firms. Banks are generally reluctant to finance new firms, particularly those based on new technologies and new ideas, but the venture capital markets in America make considerable capital available for risky new ventures. However, those societies – e.g., Japan and Germany – that rely heavily on banks for capital tend to have poorly developed venture capital markets and relatively few start-up companies (Landau and Hatsopoulos, 1986; Reed and

Moreno, 1986). The Americans have often excelled in the development of new products and industries, but because of the particular social system of production of which American firms are a part, they often see their technological lead taken over by the Japanese, the Germans, the Swiss – or firms operating within a very different social system of production. On the other hand, there are negative consequences to innovativeness *a la* American style. Because of the flexible external labor markets in which American firms are embedded, there are frequent and unpredictable turnover among key personnel, disruption in research and development plans, unusually high salaries for research personnel, serious problems in protecting proprietary information, and high legal costs resulting from litigation over intellectual property rights. Over the long run, the Japanese strategy may prove to be more successful, for they are able to purchase or to build upon the successful technology that the Americans originally developed with their venture capital (Okimoto, 1986).

The flexibility of the external labor market and the innovativeness of new start-up firms are complemented by the system of American research universities. These universities not only emphasize intellectual entrepreneurship but, since professors at the leading American universities are not civil servants as in German and Japanese universities, American professors in many fields – e.g., biology, biochemistry, engineering, computer science, etc. – are business entrepreneurs as well, frequently having a synergistic relationship with business firms. And it is no accident that some of the most dynamic sectors of the American economy are located in close proximity to some of the leading American research universities. Moreover, the American state has also been involved in this synergy, by funding university research for the development of technology in advance of commercial markets. Thus, there have been dynamic networks involving university scientists, government agencies, as well as large and small firms in the early development of a large number of technologies and products – computers, semiconductors, nuclear power, microwave telecommunications, pharmaceuticals, etc. But once the knowledge base has been developed, the U.S. government has generally discontinued its participation in the networks, providing academic and business entrepreneurs the freedom to develop commercial applications for their creative activities. But having developed new products, firms generally find that the general level of technical literacy of the American labor force tends to lag behind that of their major foreign competitors, especially the Germans and the Japanese. This deficiency of American education is compounded by the institutional configuration of the American social system of production which provides few incentives for firms to invest in the development of broad skills for their workforce.

On the other hand, the American system of education is highly stratified, and *highly educated Americans* are socialized by their educational background to be creative as individuals, a trait that frequently gets translated into the development of new products. In contrast, the Japanese are socialized to be highly attentive to detail, to improve upon existing products, and to work effectively as part of a group. Whereas the Americans excel as individuals in communicating across different organizations, the Japanese excel in establishing horizontal feedback types of communication "from marketing to production and production to redesign," all within the same firm (Aoki, 1988: 247). In other words, the Japanese emphasis is clearly on group activity and the production phases of the industrial process, whereas the Americans have tended to be less creative in this area. This difference in where and how economic actors focus their energies in the two countries does much to explain why the Japanese have over the long run been so successful in commercially producing and marketing products that the Americans first developed.

Markets and hierarchies work well when firms are embedded in an institutional environment impoverished with collective forms of economic coordination. But the Japanese and German cases demonstrate that diversified quality forms of production work best when they are embedded in an environment with institutional arrangements which promote cooperation between producers and suppliers, and among competitors, especially an environment which facilitates the exchange of information among competitors. It requires firms to engage in collective behavior far in excess to what is needed for markets and hierarchies to function effectively and in excess of what single firms are likely to develop for themselves. Flexible and diversified quality production systems function best when they are embedded in an institutional environment with rich multilateral or collective dimensions: cooperative action on the part of competitors, rich training centers for workers and managers, and financial institutions willing to provide capital on a long-term basis.

Of course, a number of American industries have long been embedded in a dense collective environment, and it is these industries that perform extremely well globally. For example, American agriculture owes much of its twentieth century success to the way that agricultural producers have been embedded in a rich institutional environment that has provided cooperative activity among producers, the dissemination by the state of university-based knowledge to agricultural scientists, and financial assistance from a number of public and quasipublic institutions. Another sector with a long history of being embedded in a rich institutional environment is the American chemical industry. Since the turn of the century, chemical firms have been extensively involved in cooperative networks that have consisted of university-based scientists and from time to time, the federal government.

Like the Japanese and German cases, the successes and failures of most American manufacturing sectors at the global level also reflect certain national characteristics and historical traditions. Because of the low levels of skill of American labor in most manufacturing sectors and because American management has tended to be recruited from marketing, financial, and legal rather than engineering and production backgrounds, American manufacturing firms have been less successful in improving upon products once developed than their Japanese and German competitors. And because American consumers are less demanding of product quality than the Japanese and Germans, American firms – particularly in the consumer goods industries – have been more competitive in the production of low-cost standardized products which can be mass marketed and easily discarded. Also, in contrast to the German and Japanese, the Americans – particularly in many manufacturing industries – have been more willing to compromise on design, quality, and service and to compete in terms of price.

Relationships among producers and suppliers in the United States have been more opportunistic and based more on hard-nosed bargaining over prices than in Japan and Germany. This kind of intense bargaining over price has also had an adverse effect on the Americans' ability to sustain product quality and to achieve a high level of competitiveness in global markets. There are industries in which the technology is not very complex and does not change, and, given the large size of the American market, mass standardized production is still effective in such industrial sectors. For example, paper products, breakfast cereals, soft drinks, bug sprays, floor wax, deodorants, soaps, shaving cream, and hundreds of other products remain symbolic of the familiar hierarchical form of corporate America. However, even these industries are slowly shifting to other countries where the labor costs are much lower. On the other hand, some American sectors that are spin-offs from mass marketing strategies are relatively successful at the global level. For example, some of the world's most successful firms in the advertising, entertainment, and leisure industries are American. Finally, because of the heavy emphasis American managers place on the performance of their firms' prices on stock exchanges, there is heavy emphasis on the rate of return on investment as the key performance indicator. Thus, American firms, more than those in any other country, resort to acquisitions and mergers in order to influence quarterly and annual reports, but tend to underinvest in new plants, products, and skills, none of which improves the long-term competitive advantage of American firms at the global level.

PATH DEPENDENCY VERSUS CONVERGENCE OF SOCIAL SYSTEMS OF PRODUCTION

Whether or not a social system of production can sustain its particular performance standards depends not only on its intrinsic economic "rationality," but also on where it fits into a larger system. If a particular social system of production is immune from the competition of an alternative system, survival can be long-lasting. But if different social systems of production – with diverging criteria of good economic performance – meet in the world arena, the arbitrariness of nationally imposed constructed performance standards may be superseded by alternative performance criteria as a result of international competitiveness.

As Wallerstein (1980) and others (Chase-Dunn, 1989; Chirot and Hall, 1982) have demonstrated, the world economy is also socially constructed, just as are national economies. Even if different social systems of production are competing in the international arena, it is not always possible to determine which is more competitively effective at any moment in time. Hegemonic nation-states can shape, *within the short run,* the rules of trade that favor their industrial sectors and firms. But the history of hegemonic powers suggests that in the longer run, social systems of production, sustained largely by military and political power, eventually give way to more dynamic and competitive social systems of production (Gilpin, 1987; Kennedy, 1987; Keohane, 1984; Krasner, 1983; Lake, 1984). In our own day, as nation-states are increasingly integrated into a world economy, economic competition is likely to turn into competition over social systems of production. As a country's social system of production loses its international competitive advantage, its share of world output decreases – even if it is a hegemonic power. Such a country will slowly experience deindustrialization and/or will attempt to restructure its institutional arrangements and to readjust its performance preferences. But such a restructuring generally calls for a major redistribution of power within a society. Largely for this reason, societies have historically had limited capacity to construct a social system of production in the image of their major competitors.

But firms in lagging economies do attempt to mimic some of the management styles and work practices of their more successful competitors. We observe this in both the United Kingdom and the United States, where there has emerged the concept of "the Internationalization of Japanese Business" (Trevor, 1987). However, this phenomenon has been grossly exaggerated. Many who contend that there is an emerging Japanization of the world economy have not confronted the problem of what is distinctively Japanese. True, some Japanese practices are exported elsewhere. But much of our scholarship on Japanese firms in foreign settings demonstrates that they pragmatically adapt to foreign conditions rather than duplicate Japanese practices. As Levine and Ohtsu (1991) observe, Japanese companies in foreign settings generally find that they must contend with the foreign culture as well as the laws and rules of alien governments, foreign unions, and employers – all of which are at great variance with Japanese institutions. Of course, one may point to the joint venture between Toyota and General Motors in Fremont, California, as well as the cases of Honda and Nissan in the United States, as examples in which a number of Japanese management practices appear to have diffused to the American setting. But close examination of even these more extreme cases demonstrates a hybridization of Japanese and American practices. Nevertheless, this kind of hybridization has resulted in much more flexible patterns of production than were previously observed in the American automobile industry.

This, of course, raises the larger issue of joint ventures and strategic alliances taking place in advanced capitalist societies. In an era when the rate of technological change was relatively low, production processes in an industry were relatively standardized, and production runs were quite long, vertical integration was an appropriate strategy for firms that faced high uncertainties and small numbers in their interdependent relationships with other firms. However, when technology changes very rapidly and the costs of technology are very expensive, firms are less inclined to engage in vertical integration, and joint ventures and strategic alliances become more frequent – particularly among firms in different societies. Of course, the motives for this form of coordination are varied: the search for economies of scale, the need for market access, the sharing of risks, the need to have access to technology, and the need to pool know-how if no one firm has the capability to achieve its goals. Such projects have occurred in a variety of sectors, but especially in the pharmaceutical, computer, aerospace, nuclear energy, electronics, and automobile industries. Is the increasing frequency of this form of coordination leading to the convergence of national economies?

Undoubtedly, the increased frequency of joint ventures and strategic alliances does lead to some convergence in certain management styles and work practices among cooperating partners. However, the diffusion of these practices does not bring about convergence in social systems of production. Before World War II, foreign firms attempted to borrow certain principles of scientific management that had become widespread in the United States, but in general the American practices were greatly modified when implemented. Moreover, in making these modifications, foreign actors did so within the developmental trajectory of their own social systems of production. Similarly in our own day, selected principles of Japanese management styles and work practices diffuse to other countries, but they are selectively integrated into local institutional arrangements.

Each country's social system of production is a configuration of a host of institutional arrangements. Each system is constantly changing and is open to influence from other systems. And indeed many technologies and practices diffuse from one society to another, but the direction of change is constrained by the existing social system of production. Thus, the same technology may exist in numerous countries, but how it is employed varies from one institutional configuration to another.

One recent comparative study (Hollingsworth, Schmitter, and Streeck, 1993) has demonstrated that, across countries, clusters of industries develop along particular trajectories, each having its distinct microeconomic dynamics within which markets, corporate hierarchies, networks, associations, and governments operate. Because skills, management techniques, and modes of governance are embedded in distinctive social systems of production, they do not easily diffuse from one nation to another. As a result, variation across countries in social systems of production remains substantial, even if there is convergence at the global level in how selected industries (e.g., chemical, oil, large scale aircraft, etc.) are coordinated.

This variation remains substantial for there have been great differences in the path dependencies of countries. For more than a century, the German economy has explored a diversified quality social system of production (Herrigel, 1995), whereas since the 1950s, the Japanese have hybridized mass production along with diversified quality production. In both countries, specific institutional arrangements have allowed for the cohesiveness of their distinctive social systems of production. In contrast, the United States has been very much constrained by its earlier Fordist mass production system and its "short-termism" under the influence of its distinctive financial markets, weak unions and business associations, norms, rules, and recipes for action.

Under what circumstances may such distinctive trajectories be reversed? Because the contemporary tools of social science do not provide a clear answer, this is an important agenda for future research.

ENDNOTES

1. With this line of argument, we should reread Parsons and Smelser (1965), Smelser (1959), and Eisenstadt (1964, 1965, 1977). Indeed, this line of argument is also consistent with a more recent complex body of social theory. For example, DiMaggio and Powell (1983) argue that organizations are "isomorphic" vis-à-vis their environment and that they gradually assume the characteristics of the environment and organizations with which they interact. Similarly, many of

the "new institutionalists" in the discipline of sociology (Meyer and Scott, 1983; Granovetter, 1985; Zucker, 1987, 1988) contend that organizations conform to the prevailing social and cultural conditions of their environment and therefore have limited capacity to diffuse to other societies. However, the new institutionalists also argue that organizations can modify their environment (Pfeffer and Salancik, 1978; Young, 1988).

2. Historically, there were always examples of flexible production in societies where a social system of mass standardized production was dominant, and examples of standardized production occurred in societies in which flexible production was most common (Friedman, 1988; Herrigel, 1990; Sabel and Zeitlin, 1985).

BIBLIOGRAPHY

Abegglen, James C. and George Stalk, Jr. 1985. *Kaisha: The Japanese Corporation.* New York: Basic.

Ackroyd, S., G. Burell, M. Hughes, and A. Whitaker. 1988. "The Japanization of British Industry?" *Industrial Relations Journal.* 19: 11–23.

Amin, Ash and Kevin Roberts. 1990. "The Re-Emergence of Regional Economies? The Mythical Geography of Flexible Accumulation." *Society and Space.* 8 (March): 7–34.

Anchordoguy, Marie. 1989. *Computers, Inc.: Japan's Challenge to IBM.* Cambridge: Harvard East Asian Monograph.

Aoki, Masahiko. 1987. "The Japanese Firm in Transition." In Kozo Yamamura and Yasukichi Yasuba, eds. *The Political Economy of Japan*, vol. 1. Stanford: Stanford University Press. Pp. 263–88.

    1988. *Information, Incentives and Bargaining in the Japanese Economy.* Cambridge: Cambridge University Press.

    1990. "Toward an Economic Model of the Japanese Firm." *Journal of Economic Literature.* 28: 1–27.

    1992. "Decentralization-Centralization in Japanese Organization: a Duality Principle." In Shumpei Kumon and Henry Rosovsky, eds. *The Political Economy of Japan: Cultural and Social Dynamics*, III. Stanford: Stanford University Press. Pp. 142–69.

Ballon, Robert and Iwao Tomita. 1988. *The Financial Behavior of Japanese Corporations.* Tokyo: Kodansha International.

Berghahn, Volker. 1985. *Unternehmer und Politik in der Bundesrepublik.* Frankfurt: Suhrkamp.

Bowles, Samuel and Herbert Gintis. 1976. *Schooling in Capitalist America.* New York: Basic Books.

Boyer, Robert. 1991. "New Directions in Management Practices and Work Organization: General Principles and National Trajectories." Revised draft of paper presented at the OECD Conference on Technological Change as a Social Process, Helsinki, December 11–13, 1989.

Brock, Malcolm. 1989. *Biotechnology in Japan.* London: Routledge.

Bunn, R. F. 1984. "Employers Associations in the Federal Republic of Germany." In J. P. Windmuller and A. Gladstone, eds. *Employers Associations and Industrial Relations.* Oxford: Clarendon Press. Pp. 169–201.

Burns, Tom R. and Helena Flam. 1987. *The Shaping of Social Organization.* London and Beverly Hills: Sage Publications.

Campbell, John, J. Rogers Hollingsworth, and Leon Lindberg, eds. 1991. *The Governance of the American Economy.* Cambridge and New York: Cambridge University Press.

Carosso, Vincent P. 1970. *Investment Banking in America: A History.* Cambridge: Harvard University Press.

Chandler, Alfred D. 1962. *Strategy and Structure.* Cambridge: MIT Press.

1977. *The Visible Hand: The Managerial Revolution in American Business.* Cambridge: Harvard University Press.

1990. *Scale and Scope: The Dynamics of Industrial Capitalism.* Cambridge: Harvard University Press.

Chandler, Alfred D. and Herman Daems. 1980. *Managerial Hierarchies: Comparative Perspectives on the Rise of the Modern Industrial Enterprise.* Cambridge: Harvard University Press.

Chase-Dunn, Christopher. 1989. *Global Formation: Structures of the World Economy.* Cambridge: Basil Blackwell.

Chirot, Daniel and Thomas D. Hall. 1982. "World-System Theory." *Annual Review of Sociology.* 8: 81–106.

Cole, Robert E. 1978. "The Late-Developer Hypothesis: An Evaluation of Its Relevance for Japanese Employment Practices." *The Journal of Japanese Studies.* 4: 247–65.

1979. *Work, Mobility, and Participation.* Berkeley: University of California Press.

1991. "Some Cultural and Social Bases of Japanese Innovation: Small-Group Activities in Comparative Perspective." In Shumpei Kumon and Henry Rosovsky, eds. *The Political Economy of Japan: Cultural and Social Dynamics,* III. Stanford: Stanford University Press.

Cool, Karol and Cynthia A. Lengnick-Hall. 1985. "Second Thoughts on the Transferability of the Japanese Management Style." *Organization Studies.* 6: 1–22.

Coriat, Benjamin. 1990. "The Revitalization of Mass Production in the Computer Age." Unpublished paper presented at Conference on Pathways to Industrialization and Regional Development in the 1990s, Lake Arrow Head Conference Center, March 14–18, 1990.

Cox, Andrew. 1986a. "State, Finance and Industry in Comparative Perspective." In Andrew Cox, ed. *The State, Finance, and Industry.* New York: St. Martin's.

1986b. *The State, Finance, and Industry.* New York: St. Martin's.

David, Paul A. 1988. "Path-Dependence: Putting the Past in the Future of Economics." *IMSSS Technical Report.* No. 533 Stanford University.

Deeg, Richard E. 1992. "Banks and the State in Germany: The Critical Role of Subnational Institutions in Economic Governance." Ph.D. dissertation, MIT.

DiMaggio, Paul and Walter W. Powell. 1983. "The Iron Cage Revisited: Institutional Isomorphism and Collective Rationality in Organizational Fields." *American Sociological Review.* 48: 147–60.

Dore, Ronald. 1973. *British Factory, Japanese Factory: The Origins of Diversity in Industrial Relations.* Berkeley: University of California Press.

1987. *Taking Japan Seriously.* Stanford: Stanford University Press.

Durlauf, Steven N. 1991. "Path Dependence in Economics: The Invisible Hand in the Grip on the Past." *American Economics Association Papers and Proceedings.* 81: 70–74.

Dyson, Kenneth. 1984. "The State, Banks, and Industry. The West German Case." In Andrew Cox, ed. *State, Finance and Industry.* Brighton: Wheatsheaf.

Eisenstadt, Shmuel N. 1964. "Institutionalization and Change." *American Sociological Review.* 29 (April): 235–47.

1965. *Essay on Comparative Institutions.* New York: Wiley.

1977. "Convergence and Divergence of Modern and Modernizing Societies: Indications from the Analysis of Structuring Social Hierarchies in Middle Eastern Societies." *International Journal of Middle East Studies.* 8: 1–27.

Elbaum, Bernard and William Lazonick, eds. 1986. *The Decline of the British Economy.* Oxford: Clarendon Press.

Ergas, Henry. 1986. "Does Technology Policy Matter?" *CEPS Papers* No. 29. Brussels: Centre for European Policy Studies.

Esser, Josef. 1990. "Bank Power in West Germany Revisited." *West European Politics* 13: 17–32.

Esser, Josef and Wolfgang Fach. 1989. "Crisis Management 'Made in Germany': The Steel Industry." In Peter J. Katzenstein, ed. *Industry and Politics in West Germany.* Ithaca: Cornell University Press. Pp. 221–48.

Florida, Richard and Martin Kenney. 1991. "Transplanted Organizations: The Transfer of Japanese Industrial Organization to the U.S." *American Sociological Review.* 56: 381–98.

Freeman, Audrey. 1982. *Japanese Management of U.S. Work Forces.* New York: The Conference Board.

Friedman, David. 1988. *The Misunderstood Miracle: Industrial Development and Political Change in Japan.* Ithaca: Cornell University Press.

Fucini, Joseph J. and Suzy Fucini. 1990. *Working for the Japanese: Inside Mazda's American Auto Plant.* New York: Free Press.

Gerlach, Michael L. 1989. *Alliance and Social Organization of Japanese Business.* Berkeley: University of California Press.

Gerschenkron, Alexander. 1962. *Economic Backwardness in Historical Perspective.* Cambridge: Harvard University Press.

Gilpin, Robert. 1987. *The Political Economy of International Relations.* Princeton: Princeton University Press.

Gordon, Andrew. 1985. *The Evolution of Labor Relations in Japan: Heavy Industry, 1853–1955.* Cambridge: Harvard University Press.

Gordon, Donald Duncan. 1988. *Japanese Management in America and Britain.* Aldershot, U.K.: Avebury.

Graham, Gordon. 1988. "Japanization as Mythology." *Industrial Relations Journal.* 29: 69–75.

Granovetter, Mark. 1985. "Economic Action and Social Structure: The Problem of Embeddedness." *American Journal of Sociology.* 91: 481–510.

Hage, Jerald, Maurice Garnier, and Bruce Fuller. 1988. "The Active State, Investment in Human Capital, and Economic Growth: France 1825–1975." *American Sociological Review* 53: 824–37.

Hamilton, Stephen. 1987. "Apprenticeship as a Transition to Adulthood in West Germany." *American Journal of Education.* 95 (February): 314–45.

Hashimoto, M. and Raisian J. 1985. "Employment Tenure and Earnings Profiles in Japan and the United States." *American Economic Review.* 75: 721–35.

Herrigel, Gary. 1989. "Industrial Order and the Politics of Industrial Change: Mechanical Engineering." In Peter J. Katzenstein, ed. *Industry and Politics in West Germany: Toward the Third Republic.* Ithaca: Cornell University Press. Pp. 185–220.

——— 1993. "Industrial Order in the Machine Tool Industry: A Comparison of the United States and Germany." In J. Rogers Hollingsworth, Philippe Schmitter, and Wolfgang Streeck, eds. *Governing Capitalist Economies: Performance and Control of Economic Sectors.* New York: Oxford University Press. Pp. 97–128.

——— 1995. *Industrial Constructions: The Sources of German Industrial Power.* New York: Cambridge University Press.

Hogan, David. 1982. "Making It in America: Work, Education, and Social Structure." In Harvey Kantor and David B. Tyack, eds. *Work, Youth, and Schooling.* Stanford: Stanford University Press. Pp. 142–79.

Hollingsworth, J. Rogers 1991a. "Die Logik der Koordination des verabeitenden Gewerbes in Amerika." *Kolner Zeitschrift fur Soziologie und Sozial Psychologie.* 43 (March): 18–43.

——— 1991b. "The Logic of Coordinating American Manufacturing Sectors." In John Campbell, J. Rogers Hollingsworth, and Leon Lindberg, eds. *The Governance of the American Economy.* Cambridge and New York: Cambridge University Press. Pp. 35–73.

Hollingsworth, J. Rogers and Leon Lindberg. 1985. "The Role of Markets, Clans, Hierarchies, and Associative Behavior. In Philippe Schmitter and Wolfgang Streeck, eds. *Private Interest Government: Beyond Market and State.* London and Beverly Hills: Sage Publications. Pp. 221–54.

Hollingsworth, J. Rogers and Wolfgang Streeck. 1993. "Performance and Control of Economic Sectors." In J. Rogers Hollingsworth, Philippe Schmitter, and Wolfgang Streeck, eds. *Governing Capitalist Economies: Performance and Control of Economic Sectors.* New York: Oxford University Press. Chapter 11.

Hollingsworth, J. Rogers, Philippe Schmitter, and Wolfgang Streeck, eds. 1993. *Governing Capitalist Economies: Performance and Control of Economic Sectors.* New York: Oxford University Press.

Horn, N. and Jürgen Kocka, eds. *Recht and Entwicklung der Grossunternehmen im 19 Jahrhundert und fruehen 20 Jahrhundert.* Goettingen: Vanderhoek and Ruprecht.

Hounshell, David A. 1984. *From the American System to Mass Production, 1800–1932.* Baltimore: Johns Hopkins University Press.

Jaeger, Hans. 1988. *Geschichte der Wirtschaftsordnung in Deutschland.* Frankfurt: Suhrkamp.

Johnson, Chalmers. 1982. *MITI and the Japanese Miracle.* Stanford: Stanford University Press.

Junne, Gerd. 1989. "Competitiveness and the Impact of Change: Applications of 'High Technologies.'" In Peter J. Katzenstein, ed. *Industry and Politics in West Germany.* Ithaca: Cornell University Press. Pp. 249–74.

Kantor, Harvey and David B. Tyack, eds. 1982. *Work, Youth, and Schooling: Historical Perspectives on Vocationalism in American Education.* Stanford: Stanford University Press.

Katz, Michael. 1971. *Class, Bureaucracy and Schools.* New York: Praeger Publishers.

Katzenstein, Peter J. 1987. *Policy and Politics in West Germany: The Growth of a Semi-Sovereign State.* Philadelphia: Temple University Press.

Katzenstein, Peter J., ed. 1989. *Indusry and Politics in West Germany: Toward the Third Republic.* Ithaca: Cornell University Press.

Kennedy, Paul. 1987. "The Relative Decline of America." *The Atlantic.* 260: 29–38.

Kenney, Martin and Richard Florida. 1988. "Beyond Mass Production and the Labor Process in Japan." *Politics and Society.* 16: 121–58.

———. 1993. *Beyond Mass Production: The Japanese System and Its Transfer to the U.S.* New York: Oxford University Press.

Keohane, Robert. 1984. *After Hegemony: Cooperation and Discord in the World Political Economy.* Princeton: Princeton University Press.

Kern, Horst and Michael Schumann. 1987. "Limits of the Division of Labour: New Production and Employment Concepts in West German Industry." *Economic and Industrial Democracy.* 8: 152–70.

———. 1989. "New Concepts of Production in West German Plants." In Peter Katzenstein, ed. *Industry and Politics in West Germany.* Ithaca: Cornell University Press. Pp. 87–109.

Kerr, C., J. T. Dunlop, F. H. Harbison, and C. A. Myers. 1960. *Industrialism and Industrial Man: The Problems of Labor and Management in Economic Growth.* Cambridge: Harvard University Press.

Kocka, Jürgen. 1980. "The Rise of the Modern Industrial Enterprise in Germany." In Alfred Chandler and Herman Daems, eds. *Managing Hierarchies: Comparative Perspectives on the Rise of the Modern Industrial Enterprise.* Cambridge: Harvard University Press. Pp. 77–116.

Koike, Kazuo. 1983. "Internal Labor Markets: Workers in Large Firms." In Taishiro Shirai, ed. *Contemporary Industrial Relations in Japan.* Madison: University of Wisconsin Press. P. 29–62.

———. 1987. "Human Resource Management and Labor-Management Relations." In Kozo Yamamura and Yasukichi Yasuba, eds. *The Political Economy of Japan.* Stanford: Stanford University Press. Vol. 1: Pp. 289–330.

———. 1988. *Understanding Industrial Relations in Modern Japan.* London: Macmillan.

Kotz, David M. 1978. *Bank Control of Large Corporations in the United States.* Berkeley: University of California Press.

Krasner, Stephen D. 1983. *International Regimes.* Ithaca: Cornell University Press.

Kristensen, Peer Hull. 1986. *Industrial Models in the Melting Pot of History and Technological Projects and Organizational Changes.* Roskilde, Denmark: Institut for Samfun Dsokonomi.

Krugman, Paul. 1991. "History and Industry Location: The Case of the Manufacturing Belt." *American Economic Association Papers and Proceedings.* 81: 80–83.

Kujawa, Duane. 1980. *The Labor Relations of United States Multinationals Abroad: Comparative and Prospective Views.* Geneva: International Institute for Labor Studies, Research Series, No. 60.

Kumon, Shumpei and Henry Rosovsky, eds. 1992. *The Political Economy of Japan: Cultural and Social Dynamics,* III. Stanford: Stanford University Press.

Lake, David. 1984. "Beneath the Commerce of Nations: A Theory of International Economic Structures." *International Studies Quarterly.* 28: 143–70.

Lamoreaux, Naomi R. 1985. *The Great Merger Movement in American Business, 1895–1904.* Cambridge: Cambridge University Press.

Landau, Ralph and George N. Hatsopoulos. 1986. "Capital Formation in the United States and Japan." In Ralph Landau and Nathan Rosenberg, eds. *The Positive Sum Strategy.* Washington: National Academy Press. Pp. 583–606.

Lebra, Takie Sugiyama. 1992. "Gender and Culture in the Japanese Political Economy: Self-Portrayals of Prominent Businesswoman." In Shumpei Kumon and Henry Rosovsky, eds. *The Political Economy of Japan: Cultural and Social Dynamics,* III. Stanford: Stanford University Press. Pp. 364–419.

Levine, Solomon B. 1984. "Employers Associations in Japan." In John P. Windmuller and Alan Gladstone, eds. *Employers Associations and Industrial Relations: A Comparative Study.* Oxford: Oxford University Press. Pp. 318–56.

Levine, Solomon B. and Makoto Ohtsu. 1991. "Transplanting Japanese Labor Relations." *The Annals of the American Academy of Political and Social Science.* 513 (January): 102–16.

Lincoln, Edward J. 1980. "Financial Markets in Japan." *United States-Japan Trade Council Report,* No. 47. December 19.

Lincoln, James R. and Arne L. Kalleberg. 1990. *Culture, Control, and Commitment: A Study of Work Organization and Work Attitudes in the U.S. and Japan.* Cambridge: Cambridge University Press.

Lincoln, James R. and Kerry McBride. 1987. "Japanese Industrial Organization in Comparative Perspective." *Annual Review of Sociology.* 13: 289–312.

Marglin, Stephen A. 1991. "Understanding Capitalism: Control Versus Efficiency." In Bo Gustafsson, ed. *Power and Economic Institutions.* Aldershot, Hants, England: Edward Elgar. Pp. 225–52.

Markovits, A. S. and C. S. Allen. 1984. "Trade Unions and the Economic Crisis: The West German Case." In Peter Gourevitch et al. eds. *Unions and the Economic Crisis: Great Britain, West Germany, and Sweden.* London: George Allen and Unwin. Pp. 89–188.

Meyer, John W. and W. R. Scott. 1983. *Organizational Environments: Ritual and Rationality.* Beverly Hills: Sage Publications.

Milgrom, Paul, Yingyi Qian, and John Roberts. 1991. "Complementarities, Momentum, and the Evolution of Modern Manufacturing." *American Economic Association Papers and Proceedings.* 81: 84.

Miyamoto, Matao. 1988. "The Development of Business Associations in Pre-war Japan." In Hiroaki Yamazaki and Matao Miyamoto, eds. *Trade Associations in Business History.* Tokyo: Tokyo University Press. Pp. 1–45.

Mueller, Frank and Ray Loveridge. 1995. "The 'Second Industrial Divide'? The Role of the Large Firm in the Baden-Württemberg Model." *Industrial and Corporate Change.* 4(3): 555–82.

Navin, Thomas R. and Marian V. Sears. 1955. "The Rise of a Market for Industrial Securities, 1887–1902." *Business History Review.* 39: 105–38.

Neuberger, Hugh and Houston Stokes. 1974. "German Banks and German
        Growth, 1883–1913; An Empirical View." *Journal of Economic History.* 34:
        710–31.
Nocken, Ulrich. 1978. "Corporatism and Pluralism in German History." In Dirk
        Stegmann et al., eds. *Industrielle Gesellschaft und Politisches System.* Bonn:
        Verlag Neu Gesellschaft.
North, Douglass C. 1990. *Institutions, Institutional Change and Economic Performance.*
        Cambridge and New York: Cambridge University Press.
Oberbeck, Herbert and Martin Baethge. 1989. "Computer and Pinstripes: Finan-
        cial Institutions." In Peter J. Katzenstein, ed. *Industry and Politics in West
        Germany.* Ithaca: Cornell University Press. Pp. 275–303.
O'Brien, Patricia. 1993. "The Steel Industry of Japan and the United States." In J.
        Rogers Hollingsworth, Philippe Schmitter, and Wolfgang Streeck, eds.
        Governing Capitalist Economies: Performance and Control of Economic Sectors.
        New York: Oxford University Press. Pp. 43–71.
OECD. 1986. *Germany: OECD Economic Survey, 1985–1986.* Paris: OECD.
Okimoto, Daniel I. 1986. "The Japanese Challenge in High Technology." In Ralph
        Landau and Nathan Rosenberg, eds. *The Positive Sum Strategy.* Washing-
        ton, D.C.: National Academy Press. Pp. 541–67.
Okimoto, Daniel I. and Thomas P. Rohlen, eds. 1988. *Inside the Japanese System.*
        Stanford: Stanford University Press.
Okimoto, Daniel I. et al. 1984. *Competitive Edge: The Semiconductor Industry in the
        U.S. and Japan.* Stanford: Stanford University Press.
Oliver, Nick and Barry Wilkinson. 1988. *The Japanization of British Industry.* Ox-
        ford: Basil Blackwell.
Ozaki, Robert. 1991. *Human Capitalism: The Japanese Enterprise System as World
        Model.* New York: Penguin.
Parsons, Talcott and Neil J. Smelser. 1965. *Economy and Society.* New York: Free Press.
Pempel, T. J. 1982. *Policy and Politics in Japan: Creative Conservatism.* Philadelphia:
        Temple University Press.
Pempel, T. J. and K. Tsunekawa. 1979. "Corporatism without Labor? The Japanese
        Anomaly." In Philippe C. Schmitter and Gerhard Lehmbruch, eds. *Trends
        Toward Corporatist Intermediation.* Beverly Hills: Sage. Pp. 231–270.
Pfeffer, Jeffrey and Gerald Salancik. 1978. *The External Control of Organizations: A
        Resource Dependence Perspective.* New York: Harper & Row.
Piore, Michael J. and Charles F. Sabel. 1984. *The Second Industrial Divide: Possibili-
        ties for Prosperity.* New York: Basic Books.
Porter, Michael. 1990. *The Competitive Advantage of Nations.* New York: Free Press.
Pred, Allan. 1966. *The Spatial Dynamics of U.S. Urban-Industrial Growth,
        1800–1914.* Cambridge: MIT Press.
Pyke, F. and W. Sengenberger, eds. 1992. *Industrial Districts and Local Regeneration.*
        Geneva: International Institute for Labour Studies.
Pyke, F., G. Becattini, and W. Sengenberger. 1991. *Industrial Districts and Inter-
        firm Co-operation in Italy.* Geneva: International Institute for Labour
        Studies.
Polanyi, Karl. 1957. *The Great Transformation: The Political and Economic Origins of
        Our Time.* Boston: Beacon Press (originally published in 1944).
Pollert, Amna, ed. 1991. *Farewell to Flexibility?* Oxford: Blackwell.

Reed, John S. and Glen R. Moreno. 1986. "The Role of Large Banks in Financing Innovation." In Ralph Landau and Nathan Rosenberg, eds. *The Positive Sum Strategy.* Washington: National Academy Press. Pp. 453–66.

Rohlen, Thomas P. 1992. "Learning: The Mobilization of Knowledge in the Japanese Political Economy." In Shumpei Kumon and Henry Rosovsky, eds. *The Political Economy of Japan: Cultural and Social Dynamics,* III. Stanford: Stanford University Press. Pp. 321–63.

Roland, Gérard. 1990. "Gorbachev and the Common European Home: The Convergence Debate Revisited." *Kyklos.* 43: 385–409.

Sabel, Charles F. 1982. *Work and Politics.* Cambridge: Cambridge University Press.

———. 1987. "Changing Models of Economic Efficiency and Their Implications for Industrialization in the Third World." In Alejandro Foxley et al., eds. *Development, Democracy, and the Art of Trespassing.* Notre Dame: University of Notre Dame Press. Pp. 27–55.

———. 1988. "The Re-emergence of Regional Economies." In Paul Hirst and Jonathan Zeitlin, eds. *Reversing Industrial Decline.* Oxford: Berg. Pp. 17–70.

———. 1990. "Shades of Trust: The Construction and Destruction of Regional Economies." Paper presented before Technology and Competitiveness Conference, sponsored by the French Ministry for Research and Technology and OECD.

———. 1991. "Moebius-Strip Organizations and Open Labor Markets: Some Consequences of the Reintegration of Conception and Execution in a Volatile Economy." In Pierre Bourdieu and James S. Coleman, eds. *Social Theory for a Changing Society.* Boulder: Westview Press. Pp. 23–63.

———. 1992. "Studied Trust: Building New Forms of Co-operation in a Volatile Economy." In Frank Pyke and Werner Sengenberger, eds. *Industrial Districts and Local Economic Regeneration.* Geneva: International Institute for Labor Studies. Pp. 215–50.

Sabel, Charles F. and Jonathan Zeitlin. 1985. "Historical Alternatives to Mass Production: Politics, Markets, and Technology in Nineteenth Century Industrialization." *Past and Present.* 108 (August): 133–76.

Sabel, Charles F., Gary B. Herrigel, Richard Deeg, and Richard Kazis. 1989. "Regional Prosperities Compared: Massachusetts and Baden-Wurtemberg in the 1980s." *Economy and Society.* 18 (November): 374–404.

Samuels, Richard J. 1987. *The Business of the Japanese State.* Ithaca: Cornell University Press.

Schneiberg, Marc and J. Rogers Hollingsworth. 1990. "Can Transaction Cost Economics Explain Trade Associations?" In Masahiko Aoki, Bo Gustafsson, and Oliver E. Williamson, eds. *The Firm as a Nexus of Treaties.* London: Sage Publications. Pp. 320–46.

Shibagaki, Kazuo, Malcolm Trevor, and Tetsuo Abo, eds. 1989. *Japanese and European Management: Their International Adaptability.* Tokyo: University of Tokyo Press.

Shigeyoshi, Tokunaga, ed. 1984. *Industrial Relations in Transition: The Cases of Japan and the Federal Republic of Germany.* Tokyo: The University of Tokyo Press.

Shimada, Haruo. 1992. "Japan's Industrial Culture and Labor-Management Relations." In Shumpei Kumon and Henry Rosovsky, eds. *The Political Econo-*

my of Japan: Cultural and Social Dynamics, III. Stanford: Stanford University Press. Pp. 267–91.

Shirai, Tashiro, ed. 1983. *Contemporary Industrial Relations in Japan*. Madison: University of Wisconsin Press.

Smelser, Neil J. 1959. *Social Change in the Industrial Revolution*. London: Routledge and Kegan Paul.

Sorge, Arndt, G. Hartman, M. Warner, and I. Nicholas. 1983. *Microelectronics and Manpower in Manufacturing*. Aldershot, U.K.: Gower.

Sorge, Arndt and Wolfgang Streeck. 1988. "Industrial Relations and Technical Change: The Case for an Extended Perspective." In Richard Hyman and Wolfgang Streeck, eds. *New Technology and Industrial Relations*. New York and Oxford: Basil Blackwell. Pp. 19–47.

Sorge, Arndt and Malcolm Warner. 1986. *Comparative Factory Organization: An Anglo-German Comparison of Manufacturing, Management and Manpower.* Aldershot, U.K.: Gower.

Stråth, Bo. 1993. "The Shipbuilding Industries of Germany, Japan, and Sweden." In J. Rogers Hollingsworth, Philippe Schmitter, and Wolfgang Streeck, eds. *Governing Capitalist Economies: Performance and Control of Economic Sectors.* New York: Oxford University Press. Pp. 72–96.

Streeck, Wolfgang. 1984a. "Guaranteed Employment, Flexible Manpower Use, and Cooperative Manpower Management: A Trend Towards Convergence." In Tokunaga Shigeyoshi, ed. *Industrial Relations in Transition: The Cases of Japan and the Federal Republic of Germany.* Tokyo: The University of Tokyo Press. Pp. 81–116.

1984b. *Industrial Relations in West Germany. A Case Study of the Car Industry.* London: Heinemann.

1987a. "Industrial Relations and Industrial Change in the Motor Industry: An International View." *Economic and Industrial Democracy.* 8: 437–62.

1987b. "The Uncertainties of Management in the Management of Uncertainty: Employers, Labor Relations and Industrial Adjustment in the 1980s." *Work, Employment and Society.* 1: 281–308.

1989. "Successful Adjustment to Turbulent Markets: The Automobile Industry." In Peter J. Katzenstein, ed. *Industry and Politics in West Germany: Toward the Third Republic.* Ithaca: Cornell University Press. Pp. 113–84.

1991a. "The Federal Republic of Germany." In John Niland and Oliver Clarke, eds. *Agenda for Change: An International Analysis of Industrial Relations in Transition.* Sydney: Allen and Unwin. Pp. 53–89.

1991b. "On the Institutional Conditions of Diversified Quality Production." In Egon Matzner and Wolfgang Streeck, eds. *Beyond Keynesianism: The Socio-Economics of Production and Full Employment.* Aldershot, Hants, England: Edward Elgar. Pp. 21–61.

1992. *Social Institutions and Economic Performance: Studies of Industrial Relations in Advanced Capitalist Economies.* London and Newberry Park: Sage Productions.

Streeck, Wolfgang, et al. 1987 *The Role of Social Partners in Vocational Training and Further Training in the Federal Republic of Germany.* Berlin: European Centre for the Development of Vocational Training.

Tabb, William K. 1995.*The Postwar Japanese System: Cultural Economy and Economic Transformation.* New York: Oxford University Press.

Taylor, M. E. 1981. *Education and Work in the Federal Republic of Germany.* London: Anglo-German Foundation for the Study of Industrial Society.

Teece, David. 1988. "Technological Change and the Nature of the Firm." In Giovanni Dosi et al., eds. *Technical Change and Economic Theory.* London and New York: Pinter Publishers. Pp. 256–281.

Tilly, Richard. 1976. "German Banks, German Growth and Econometric History." *Journal of Economic History.* 36: 416–24.

———. 1982. "Mergers, External Growth and Finance in the Development of Large-Scale Enterprises in Germany, 1880–1913." *Journal of Economic History.* 42: 629–58.

———. 1986. "German Banking, 1850–1914: Development Assistance for the Strong." *Journal of European Economic History.* 15: 113–52.

Trevor, Malcolm, ed. 1987. *The Internationalization of Japanese Business: European and Japanese Perspectives.* Boulder: Westview Press.

Trevor, Malcolm. 1991. "The Overseas Strategies of Japanese Corporations." *The Annals of the American Academy of Political and Social Science.* Beverly Hills: Sage.

Turnball, Peter. 1988. "The Limits to Japanization – Just-in-time Labour Relations and the U.K. Automotive Industry." *New Technology, Work, and Employment.* 3: No. 1.

Tyack, David. 1974. *The One Best System: A History of American Urban Education.* Cambridge: Harvard University Press.

Vitols, Sigurt. 1995a. "German Banks and the Modernization of the Small Firm Sector: Long-Term Finance in Comparative Perspective." (Discussion Paper, Wissenschaftszentrum Berlin, FS-I-95-309).

———. 1995b. "Inflation versus Central Bank Independence? Banking Regulation and Financial Stability in the U.S. and Germany." (Discussion Paper, Wissenschaftszentrum Berlin, FS-I-95-312).

———. 1995c. "Corporate Governance versus Economic Governance: Banks and Industrial Restructuring in the U.S. and Germany." (Discussion Paper, Wissenschaftszentrum Berlin, FS-I-95-311).

———. 1995d. "Are German Banks Different?" (Discussion Paper, Wissenschaftszentrum Berlin, FS-I-95-308).

Vittas, Dimitri, et al. 1978. *The Role of Large Deposit Banks in the Financial Systems of Germany, France, Italy, the Netherlands, Switzerland, Sweden, Japan, and the United States.* London: Inter-Bank Research Organization.

Wallerstein, Immanuel. 1980. *The World System II.* New York: Academic Press.

Wallich, H. C. and M. I. Wallich. 1976. "Banking and Finance." In Hugh Patrick and Henry Rosovsky, eds. *Asia's New Giant: How the Japanese Economy Works.* Washington, D.C.: Brookings Institute. Pp. 249–316.

Welzk, Stefan. 1986. *Boom ohne Arbeitsplätze.* Cologne: Verlag Kipenheuer.

Whitley, Richard D., ed. 1992. *Business Systems in East Asia: Firms, Markets, and Societies.* London: Sage.

Williamson, Oliver E. 1975. *Markets and Hierarchies: Analysis and Antitrust Implications.* New York: Free Press.

1985. *The Economic Institutions of Capitalism.* New York: Free Press.

Winkler, H. A., ed. 1974. *Organiziertes Kapitalismus.* Goettingen: Vandenhoeck and Ruprecht.

Young, Ruth. 1988. "Is Population Ecology a Useful Paradigm for the Study of Organizations," *American Journal of Sociology.* 94.

Zucker, Lynne. 1987. "Institutional Theories of Organizations." *Annual Review of Sociology.* Palo Alto: Annual Reviews, Inc. 13: 443–63.

1988. *Institutional Patterns and Organizations.* Cambridge: Ballinger.

Zysman, John. 1983. *Governments, Markets, and Growth: Financial Systems and the Politics of Industrial Change.* Ithaca: Cornell University Press.

[17]

Financial History Review 4 (1997), pp. 7–29. Printed in the United Kingdom © 1997 Cambridge University Press.

Finance and industrial development.
Part 1: the United States and the United Kingdom[1]

WILLIAM LAZONICK

University of Massachusetts Lowell, University of Tokyo and INSEAD

and

MARY O'SULLIVAN

Harvard University and INSEAD

Over time, the innovation process, and the learning process that is its social substance, have become increasingly collective and cumulative and, hence, organisational.[2] The perspective on industrial development taken here identifies *organisational integration* and *financial commitment* as the social conditions permitting collective and cumulative learning to take place. Organisational integration describes the social relations that provide participants in a complex division of labour with the abilities and incentives to integrate their capabilities and efforts within organisations so that, potentially, they can generate organisational learning. Financial commitment describes the social relations that are the basis for a business organisation's continuing access to the financial resources required for sustaining the development and utilisation of productive resources. In combination, organisational integration and financial commitment provide social foundations for innovative business enterprise. In terms of inputs into the production process, organisational integration supplies knowledge while financial commitment supplies money. By contributing to the innovation process, however, these inputs are not commodities but reflect the social relations to the business organisation of those who supply knowledge and money.

The generation of innovation through organisational learning is inherently uncertain. The investment strategy resulting in a higher quality, lower cost product

[1] Funding for our research on industrial development and economic performance in the United States and Britain has been provided by the Committee on Industrial Theory and Assessment, University of Massachusetts, Lowell; STEP Group, Oslo; and the Jerome Levy Economics Institute of Bard College. We received helpful comments on previous versions of this paper from Bernard Elbaum, Leslie Hannah, Stephen Marglin and two anonymous referees of this journal.

[2] M. O'Sullivan, Innovation, industrial development, and corporate governance, Ph.D. thesis (Harvard University, 1996); and W. Lazonick and M. O'Sullivan, 'Organization, finance, and international competition', *Industrial and Corporate Change*, 5 (1996).

cannot be known in advance. Furthermore, what is learnt, as the innovation process evolves, changes the conception of the problems to be addressed, the possibilities for their solution and, therefore, the appropriate investment strategy for continued learning. Learning may make possible the attainment of ends previously considered impossible, although a restructuring of the learning process may be required to achieve them. In allocating resources to organisational learning, strategic decision-makers must know what the learning process is generating if they are to take account of opportunities for, and threats to, innovative success revealed by learning. In the innovation process, strategic decisions shape the direction and structure of learning, while the knowledge continually generated through learning can inform strategy. For such a dynamic interaction of strategy and learning to occur, strategists must be integrated into the network of social relations underlying the generation and transmission of organisational learning. If, instead, strategic control is exercised by decision-makers who are segmented from the process of organisational learning, the ongoing innovative success of the enterprise will be jeopardised because decision-makers will have neither the abilities nor incentives to promote that success.[3]

The financial commitment required to sustain organisational learning on a continuing basis means that strategic decision-makers must exercise 'organisational control' over the enterprise's revenues. In contrast, those who exercise 'market control' over enterprise revenues will favour financial liquidity, not financial commitment.[4] Placed in the perspective of the process of industrial development, the distinction between organisational control and market control has great practical importance for current debates over corporate governance and corporate employment. In all advanced economies, different groups are currently contending for control over the allocation of immense corporate revenues. When making their arguments for 'creating value for shareholders', proponents of market control rely on a theory that touts the market mechanism's efficacy for allocating resources to their 'best alternative uses'. But their theory offers no explanation of how the 'best alternative uses' come into being, or change over time.

The following analysis of the finance of industrial development draws on comparative-historical research with regard to Britain, Germany, Japan and the United States.[5] Of these four countries, Britain and the United States are currently regarded as the bastions of market control. Yet, as will be shown, market control over the allocation of corporate resources is a relatively new phenomenon in the industrial

---

[3] O'Sullivan, Innovation.

[4] ibid.; W. Lazonick, 'Controlling the market for corporate control', *Industrial and Corporate Change*, 1 (1992).

[5] See W. Lazonick and M. O'Sullivan, 'Big business and skill formation in the wealthiest nations: the organizational revolution in the twentieth century', in F. Amatori, A. D. Chandler Jr. and T. Hikino (eds), *Big Business and the Wealth of Nations* (Cambridge, Mass., 1996); Lazonick and O'Sullivan, 'Organization'; O'Sullivan, Innovation, chs 5–6; and W. Lazonick, *Business Organization and the Myth of the Market Economy* (Cambridge, 1990), chs 1–3.

history of the United States. Until the 1980s organisational control dominated, ensuring committed finance to American industry.

In the United States, the separation of stock ownership from strategic control during the first decades of the twentieth century entailed the transfer of strategic control from owner-entrepreneurs to salaried managers. This transition, characterised by organisational integration within the managerial structure and financial commitment on the basis of corporate retentions, provided the social foundations for the United States's rise to international industrial leadership. However, the period since 1950 has been marked by the over-extension of American corporate enterprise into diverse business activities, the challenges of more innovative industrial enterprises abroad, and the transformation of the power of stockholders in the United States. These developments eroded the effectiveness of organisational control in American corporations and created growing opportunities for the assertion of market control.

The British economy entered the twentieth century as the world industrial leader. Commentators often refer to an 'Anglo-American' (or 'Anglo-Saxon') model of corporate governance characterised by market control. We argue that, in contrast with the United States, the rise of market control in Britain from the 1950s was a more direct transition from proprietary control stemming from the previous limited exercise of organisational control. Given the relative failure of the 'managerial revolution' in Britain before 1950, market control of the allocation of corporate resources occurred earlier than in the United States. But, by the same token, the relative lack of sustained industrial development in the British economy meant that market control had less prior accumulations of productive resources than in the United States on which to live.

An understanding of the foundations of market control in the United States and Britain sheds considerable light on the problems of industrial development and international competition faced in these nations. The companion piece to this article, to appear in the next issue of *Financial History Review*, will look at two national economies – Germany and Japan – that have remained bastions of organisational control. Yet even in these nations, especially in Germany, the forces of market control are challenging organisational control. The comparative historical analysis of the rise of market control in the United States and Britain provides an essential foundation for assessing the evolution, and the implications for industrial performance, of such challenges to organisational control.

I

Compared with its own history, as well as the present situation in most advanced economies (with the particular exception of Britain), market control dominates the governance of big business in the United States. Manifesting market control are the high levels of financial distributions – both dividends and stock repurchases – of American non-financial corporations. Dividends as a proportion of corporate earnings – the pay-out ratio – rose from about 45 per cent during the 1960s and 1970s to over 60 per cent during the 1980s and 1990s. Stock repurchases increased even more dramatically to the extent that net equity issues became negative in many years during the 1980s. Stock repurchases were about 22 per cent of dividends in 1985 and about 47 per cent in 1989. Between 1990 and 1993 annual stock repurchases averaged about $33b., but in 1994 rose to nearly $70b. (33 per cent of dividends) and during the first nine months of 1995 were already greater than that amount.[6]

Throughout the 1980s, American corporations demonstrated a mounting predilection towards 'down-sizing', with professional, administrative and technical personnel, as well as blue-collar workers, being affected by the elimination of previously stable and remunerative jobs.[7] To justify their actions, corporate managers proclaimed that a corporation's prime, if not only, responsibility was to 'create value for shareholders'. For their success in 'maximising shareholder wealth', these strategic managers received ample, often exorbitant, personal rewards, whereas most other employees experienced lower earnings and less employment stability. This alignment of strategic managers with public stockholders is now typically regarded as a defining feature of the market-oriented system of corporate governance in the United States.

However, in historical perspective, market control over the allocation of American corporate resources stands out as a recent development. For most of the twentieth century public stockholders exercised little, if any, control over the allocation of corporate revenues. Ownership of corporate stock was separated from strategic control and accepted by public stockholders because of the liquidity of corporate equity traded on the stock market. This liquidity, in turn, stemmed from the market in industrial securities having arisen *as a result of* the growth of dominant enterprises during the last decades of the nineteenth century. These enterprises' successful development made possible the rise of a market in industrial securities, not vice versa. A market in industrial (as distinct from railroad and government) securities in the United States only came into existence at the turn of the century due to decisions to 'go public', made by a number of owner-controlled companies that had grown to commanding positions within their respective industries since the 1860s.[8]

After being founded on the basis of 'inside' capital provided by the entrepreneurs, their family members, friends and business associates, companies developed from new ventures into going concerns through the reinvestment of earnings to build a productive organisation. Both the possibility, and desirability, of a transfer of a

---

[6] 'Firms Ponder How Best to Use Their Cash', *Wall Street Journal*, 16 Oct. 1995, pp. A1, A9.

[7] W. Lazonick and M. O'Sullivan, 'Corporate employment and corporate governance: is prosperity sustainable in the United States?', Report to the Jerome Levy Economics Institute (Oct. 1996).

[8] T. Navin and M. Sears, 'Rise of a market in industrial securities', *Business History Review*, 29 (1955); and A. D. Chandler Jr, *The Visible Hand: The Managerial Revolution in American Business* (Cambridge, Mass., 1977).

FINANCE AND INDUSTRIAL DEVELOPMENT: PART I   II

company's ownership arose when the managerial organisation required to run the enterprise exceeded the capacity of a single person, or even a small group of partners. Ownership transfer particularly became a problem if original entrepreneurs and their backers were ready to retire, as occurred by the 1890s in the case of the post-Civil War generation of businessmen.[9] In most cases, the entrepreneur's family members were ill-suited to develop further a company that had relied on organisational learning for its competitive advantage.

The emergence of a market for industrial securities permitted original owners of highly successful enterprises to sell their firms (and often enabled them to retire from the industrial scene), while leaving intact the managerial organisations that had given such ventures their competitive advantages as going concerns. Unless managers were to assume ownership – a transfer that for most successful companies was generally beyond their collective means – the continued integration of strategy and learning within these undertakings required that stock ownership be separated from strategic control. During the 1890s and early 1900s, initial 'public' offerings made by Wall Street investment bankers went to relatively small circles of wealthy individuals (including companies' original owner-entrepreneurs and their families) and financial institutions – particularly insurance companies and the underwriting investment banks themselves. Of $6.2b. industrial common and preferred stock issued at the peak of the 'Great Merger Movement' between 1898 and 1902, 49 per cent was privately placed in exchange for the assets, or securities, of merged companies and another 45 per cent was issued by companies to their own stockholders as dividends, or for cash or for unknown purposes. Only six per cent was sold to the general public.[10]

To ensure an income from industrial securities possibly difficult to market, early portfolio investors favoured preferred stocks, or bonds, rather than common stocks. Indeed, in many initial offerings, common stocks were distributed as a bonus to purchasers of preferred stocks, or to the promoters and investment banks for their services.[11] As the industrial securities market developed, these stockholders were able to sell some of their holdings to the public. Over time, as the companies listed on the New York Stock Exchange (NYSE) continued to thrive, and as wealthy individuals and institutional investors disposed of some of their corporate stocks, stockholding became more dispersed. This decreased the threat of outside interference by substantial stockholders.[12] The sale of Liberty bonds during the First World War attracted the savings of a whole new tier of households into the securities markets. After the war, Wall Street captured much of these savings through sales of preferred stocks marketed as having the security of bonds.[13]

[9] Navin and Sears, 'Rise of a market', p. 108.
[10] R. L. Nelson, *Merger Movements in American Industry, 1895–1956* (Princeton, NJ, 1959), p. 94.
[11] J. T. Flynn, *Security Speculation: Its Economic Effects* (New York, 1934), p. 140.
[12] G. C. Means, 'The diffusion of stock ownership in the United States', *Quarterly Journal of Economics*, 44 (1930).
[13] V. P. Carosso, *Investment Banking in America* (Cambridge, Mass., 1970), p. 250; and United States Bureau of the Census, *Historical Statistics of the United States* (Washington, DC, 1976), pp. 1005–6.

During the 1920s, many leading industrial companies made their stock available for purchase by employees and, by 1928, there were more than 800,000 employee stockholders.[14] Companies also sold stock to customers, resulting in the addition of 1m. new stockholders between 1920 and 1928.[15] Furthermore, the marketing of stock itself became a highly developed business, with institutional forms of stock-holding, such as the investment trust, becoming popular amongst small-scale investors.[16] Stock splits also became a common way of making stocks more accessible to households further down the income scale.[17] As a result, whereas in 1900 there had been an estimated 4.4m. stockholders on the books of American corporations, holding an average of 140 $100 (par value) shares, by 1928 there were 18m. stockholders holding an average of 51 shares.[18] Moreover, the late 1920s stock market boom brought in new people, many of whom borrowed to buy stocks on margin in attempts to get rich quickly. In 1927 an unprecedented $1.7b. of new stock was issued, but that amount doubled over the next year and again during 1929. In the process, common stocks gained wide acceptance, with the proportion of common to preferred stocks issued rising from 67 per cent in 1927 to 300 per cent by 1929.[19]

As stockholding became increasingly dispersed, the possibility of any group of stockholders challenging the managerial control of corporate resources diminished. Although most stock, whether preferred or common, carried voting rights, dispersion of holdings made it difficult for any small group to use these rights to challenge managerial control. Furthermore, over the first decades of the twentieth century corporate managers had tended to dilute the power of preferred stockholders by granting common stockholders more votes per dollar of stock. This was because preferred stockholders – behaving more like creditors than speculators – tended to scrutinise managerial actions and performance more closely than common stockholders when dividend payments had been missed. Moreover, during the 1920s American corporations found that shareholder power could be diluted even more explicitly through the issue of non-voting stock.[20] Subsequently, when the NYSE required that listed stock carried voting rights, the result was not an increase in shareholder power but rather, by maintaining public confidence in the holding of corporate stock, the fostering of the further dispersion of stockholding, thus making it all the more difficult for a small group of stockholders to challenge managerial control.

In parallel, the evolution of corporation law from the nineteenth century

[14] Means, 'Diffusion of stock ownership', p. 568.
[15] ibid.
[16] Carosso, *Investment Banking*, ch. 14.
[17] A. S. Dewing, *A Study of Corporation Securities, and Their Nature and Uses in Finance* (New York, 1934), p. 98.
[18] A. A. Berle and G. C. Means, *The Modern Corporation and Private Property* (New York, 1932), p. 56.
[19] US Bureau of the Census, *Historical Statistics*, p. 1006.
[20] J. H. Sears, *The New Place of the Stockholder* (New York, 1929), pp. 90–1.

strengthened managers' right to exercise control. This was not because managers represented a 'special interest' group, but was part of a general process by which American laws of property supported developmental change, even if this conflicted with existing property rights.[21] The most important power accorded to corporate managers by statute and legal precedent was the determination of dividends.[22] In general, the law was reluctant to interfere with managerial discretion. Equally, public stockholders, whose main interest in holding corporate stock was liquidity, held back from challenging management. Companies listed on the NYSE – which quickly became the exchange of preference for all leading industrial enterprises – had established themselves as dominant enterprises in their particular industries with the capacity to generate regularly high levels of profits. Once public, these high levels of profits made possible continuous dividend payments, which convinced stockholders of their stocks' liquidity. By refusing to reduce dividends, except under the most dire circumstances, corporate managers ensured that their control over the allocation of corporate revenues would not be challenged by stockholders.[23]

Wall Street helped to create confidence in corporate stocks' liquidity by identifying, and actively promoting, companies which had already acquired productive bases that could generate consistent streams of profits. Ever more stringent requirements for listing on the NYSE built public confidence in the market, which, by bringing in new buyers of stocks, added further to the market's liquidity.[24] Public confidence was also bolstered from the 1910s by the securities ratings services of Moodys, and Standard and Poors, whose own businesses were based on their reputations for impartiality and credibility.[25] However, most important in establishing a highly liquid market in industrial stocks was the emergence from the late nineteenth century of a large number of dynamic industrial enterprises. These, through superior development and utilisation of productive resources, gained distinct competitive advantages during the era before a market in industrial securities existed. Such companies – many of which still maintain dominant market shares – made the United States by the 1920s the world's most powerful industrial nation.

The stock market did not serve as a source of funds for long-term business investment. When an enterprise went public, the stock market was the instrument by which stock ownership was separated from strategic control over internally generated corporate revenues. As owner-entrepreneurs of dominant going concerns retired, cash and securities in hand, they left investment decision-making under the

---

[21] M. Horwitz, *The Transformation of American Law, 1780–1860* (Cambridge, Mass., 1977); idem, *The Transformation of American Law: The Crisis of Legal Orthodoxy, 1870–1960* (New York, 1992); and M. J. Sklar, *The Corporate Reconstruction of America, 1890–1916: The Market, the Law and Politics* (Cambridge, 1988).

[22] J. W. Hurst, *The Legitimacy of the Business Corporation in the Law of the United States, 1780–1970* (Charlottesville, Va, 1970).

[23] Stevens, 'Stockholders' voting'.

[24] Hurst, *Legitimacy*; and see also R. Michie, *The London and New York Stock Exchanges, 1850–1914* (London, 1987).

[25] A. Belkaoui, *Industrial Bonds and the Rating Process* (Westport, Conn., 1983), pp. 10–11.

control of the most able, energetic and visionary of the career managers recruited during the previous decade. Often the purpose of ownership transfer was also to enable one company to acquire another. Typically, the acquiring company issued a further amount of its own stock for the existing stock of the company to be acquired, whose stock was then subsequently retired.[26] Following an acquisition, the acquiring company might have made substantial investments in the acquired company, but this was not financed by the issue of equity. Funds raised through public equity issues were also applied to restructuring corporate balance sheets – to pay off debt, build cash reserves or finance acquisitions – as was the practice during the late 1920s speculative boom. Companies then realised windfalls obtainable through equity sales to the public, who were willing to buy at prices wildly out of line with the long-run earning power of the underlying corporate assets.[27]

Throughout the twentieth century, corporate retentions (sometimes leveraged with money raised through issues of long-term bonds as opposed to equity) have been the main sources of funds for American business investment. In a sample of 84 large manufacturing corporations, over the period 1921–29 funds retained just equalled their total fixed capital expenditures.[28] More recently, during the period 1970–85, retained earnings were 67 per cent of the gross sources, and 86 per cent of net sources, of funds for non-financial corporations. For the same period, new equity issues represented 0.8 per cent of the gross sources and 1.1 per cent of the net sources of funds, for non-financial corporations.[29]

When companies issued stock for financing investment in new productive assets, usually it was in the form of preferred stocks, often with restricted voting rights. In terms of secure prospects of future returns, a preferred stock is much closer to a corporate bond than a common stock. For going concerns with the option to finance long-term investment on the basis of either stocks or bonds, the use of stocks is expensive. This is due not so much to the high transaction costs involved in equity financing, but rather because an attempt at equity financing signals to potential portfolio investors that corporate management is not confident about its company meeting a bond issue's debt-service requirements. For a company with access to bond financing instead to choose to issue equity would, therefore, be self-defeating.

Throughout most of the twentieth century, American public stockholders have made no direct contribution to decisions regarding the allocation of corporate revenues. Nor have they hired, fired, rewarded or punished the corporate managers who made these decisions. Ostensibly the board of directors represents stockholders' interests in these matters. But it is well known, historically, that the top managers of American corporations, not the stockholders, have chosen the boards of directors,

[26] A. R. Koch, *The Financing of Large Corporations, 1920–39* (New York, 1943).
[27] ibid., ch. 6.
[28] ibid., p. 81.
[29] See B. H. Hall, 'Corporate restructuring and investment horizons in the United States, 1976–1987', *Business History Review*, 68 (1994), p. 139.

and that it would be very expensive for stockholders to mount a proxy contest to replace top management.[30] In historical perspective, public stockholders' lack of control over industrial corporations' retained earnings has not been imposed by corporate managers or government regulators, as some have contended.[31] The market in industrial securities evolved in the United States to effect the separation of stock ownership from strategic control because it offered households liquidity while not requiring commitment. American households became willing to hold stocks in publicly-traded corporations only because their 'ownership' stakes did not entail any commitment of their time, effort or additional funds to ensure the success of companies. A general willingness to leave control over the allocation of corporate revenues with managers stemmed in part from the prior revenue-generating successes of publicly-listed corporations under managerial control, and in part from the limited liability protection that public stockholders enjoyed. But, more fundamentally, this abdication of control derived from the confidence of public stockholders in their investments being liquid and therefore saleable on the market at any time.

In American industrial development, the emergence of dominant enterprises gave rise to stock markets, not vice versa. Public investors' willingness to hold industrial stocks without the ability to exercise control over the allocation of corporate revenues meant that 'ownership' rights adhering to these stocks actually enhanced the control of corporate managers. During the 1920s and 1930s, and for many companies well beyond, with strategic managers integrated into the organisational learning processes of their enterprises, the financial commitment made possible by managerial control provided an essential foundation for the pursuit of innovative investment strategies.

Yet the very growth of the enterprise that the separation of ownership from control made possible also created conditions that, in the presence of the ideology that public stockholders are the true owners of the enterprise, tended to distance strategic managers from organisational learning. The separation of stock ownership from strategic control, as it occurred in the United States, encouraged both the continuous growth of industrial corporations and the centralisation of strategic control so that these companies grew larger and larger as unitary strategic entities. With their development through expansion, extension and diversification, these corporations often reaped 'cumulation advantages' by building on existing capabilities.[32] However, they also faced the 'cumulation disadvantages' of organisational segmentation which, although they are not inherent in, are more likely to occur with rapid and large-scale enterprise growth. Specifically, an enterprise's expansion within markets, across vertical activities and into new markets could lead to the separation of strategic managers from organisational learning processes – that is, strategic segmentation.

---

[30] J. Lorsch, with E. MacIver, *Pawns or Potentates: The Reality of America's Corporate Boards* (Boston, Mass., 1989).

[31] For example, M. Roe, *Strong Managers, Weak Owners* (Princeton, NJ, 1994).

[32] O'Sullivan, Innovation, ch. 4.

During the 1920s American industrial corporations undertook a wave of acquisitions for purposes of both vertical integration and diversification.[33] Unlike the turn-of-the-century merger movement that contributed to the rise of a market in industrial securities, acquisitions during the 1920s could make use of a highly liquid stock market. Stockholders of acquired firms were willing to accept the stock of acquiring corporations as payment for their equity holdings.

The growth of American industrial corporations slowed substantially during the 1930s, but major corporations kept largely intact their managerial organisations and expanded their research and development facilities.[34] Armed with these capabilities, companies, such as General Motors, General Electric, Westinghouse and Du Pont, received substantial government subsidies for research, development and expansion during the Second World War and became integral to the post-war military-industrial complex. Mergers and acquisitions once more became prominent during the 1950s. The 200 largest manufacturing corporations held 47 per cent of all United States corporate assets in 1947, 56 per cent in 1957 and 59 per cent in 1967.[35] Unless strategic decision-making could be effectively decentralised within these corporations, strategic segmentation was likely to arise.

In 1962 Alfred D. Chandler documented the emergence and diffusion of the multidivisional structure from the 1920s until the 1950s. By permitting administrative decentralisation, this organisational structure was supposed to permit the corporation to diversify into many new businesses without succumbing to strategic segmentation.[36] But Chandler's conceptualisation of the corporate head office as the realm of strategic decision-making, and the corporate divisions as the realms of operational control, already contemplated the segmentation between strategy and learning that during the 1940s and 1950s began to afflict some of the largest, and previously most successful, corporations.[37]

The 1960s conglomerate movement both reflected and exacerbated that segmentation. These mergers and acquisitions entailed conglomeration of lines of business lacking mutual technological or market relations. Between 1948 and 1955 only ten per cent of acquired assets were in the 'pure conglomerate' category, in 1964–71 35 per cent and in 1972–79 46 per cent. By the period 1972–79, horizontal or vertical acquisitions in the same line of business had fallen to 23 per cent of all assets acquired, down dramatically from 49 per cent in 1948–55. For the top 200 manufacturing companies ranked by sales, the mean number of lines of business rose from

---

[33] US Bureau of the Census, *Historical Statistics*, p. 914.

[34] D. Mowery, 'Industrial research, 1900–1950', in B. Elbaum and W. Lazonick (eds), *The Decline of the British Economy* (Oxford, 1986), pp. 191–2.

[35] G. Hay and C. Untiet, 'Statistical measurement of the conglomerate problem', in R. D. Blair and R. F. Lanzillotti (eds), *The Conglomerate Corporation: An Antitrust Law and Economics Symposium* (Cambridge, Mass., 1981), p. 165.

[36] A. D. Chandler Jr, *Strategy and Structure: Chapters in the History of the Industrial Enterprise* (Cambridge, Mass., 1962).

[37] O'Sullivan, Innovation, ch. 5.

4.8 in 1950 to 10.9 in 1975. Of the 148 companies of the 200 largest in 1950 that survived until 1975, the mean number of lines of business was 5.2 in 1950 and 9.7 in 1975. Among the best known conglomerates were Beatrice Foods (290 acqui-sitions between 1950 and 1978), W. R. Grace (186), International Telephone and Telegraph (163), Gulf and Western Industries (155), Textron (115), Litton Industries (99) and LTV (58).[38]

Propounding the ideology that a well-trained general manager could manage anything, the conglomerate movement glorified strategic segmentation. In acquiring companies and consolidating financial decision-making within the head office, the conglomerate typically stripped control from the strategic managers of the acquired businesses. Although these former top managers were frequently retained as divisional heads, subsequent failure to meet financial performance targets often led to their replacement by someone from the head office who had scant knowledge of the organisational learning required to compete effectively on product markets.[39]

Consequently, the 1960s conglomerate movement gave way during the 1970s to large-scale divestiture of businesses and, for the first time, the buying and selling of companies became a major financial business.[40] As Wall Street turned merger and acquisition activity into an end in itself, companies with low price-earnings ratios became targets for take-over because their acquisition produced a 'one-shot' increase in earnings per share of the conglomerate. These rises in earnings both profited stockholders and augmented the financial capacity of the conglomerate to make more acquisitions.[41]

By the late 1960s, conglomerate financing had graduated from cash to stock, and then to debt, with the debt-equity ratio in manufacturing rising from 0.48 in 1965 to 0.72 in 1970.[42] Then, during the 1970s and early 1980s, deconglomeration came to the fore with about one-third of the acquisitions made during the conglomerate movement being sold off, typically under conditions of financial duress.[43] In 1975 and 1976 divestitures were actually greater than announced mergers and acquisitions.[44] From the perspective of productive performance, divestitures had the potential for rectifying the problems of strategic segmentation that the conglom-erate movement had exacerbated. However, the failure of the conglomerate

---

[38] D. Ravenscraft and F.M. Scherer, *Mergers, Sell-Offs, and Economic Efficiency* (Washington, DC, 1987). pp. 30, 32, 38, 39.

[39] See M. Holland, *When the Machine Stopped: A Cautionary Tale from Industrial America* (Boston, Mass., 1984); and also W. Lazonick and J. West, 'Organizational integration and competitive advantage: explaining strategy and performance in American industry', *Industrial and Corporate Change*, 4 (1995), pp. 261–4.

[40] A. D. Chandler Jr, *Scale and Scope: The Dynamics of Industrial Capitalism* (Cambridge, Mass., 1990), p. 624.

[41] Editors, *Fortune: The Conglomerate Commotion* (New York, 1970).

[42] US Bureau of the Census, *Historical Statistics*, p. 928.

[43] Ravenscraft and Scherer, *Mergers*, p. 190.

[44] Merrill Lynch Advisory Services, *Mergerstat Review* (New York, 1994), p. 120.

movement also laid the foundations for the rise of a new financial instrument – the high-yield, or junk, bond. This failure further increased during the 1970s the incentive and ability for Wall Street to treat productive enterprises like financial assets. Far more than even the debt-financed conglomeration of the late 1960s, the use of junk bonds for buy-outs and take-overs enforced financial liquidity on industrial corporations, thus subjecting them to market control.

During the early 1970s, a portion of the debt incurred in the conglomerate movement, either to finance acquisitions or to fend them off, emerged as 'fallen angels'. These bonds had been issued as investment grade bonds but were now rated below investment grade.[45] In 1973, when their value stood at $8.2b., Michael Milken, an employee of the Wall Street firm of Drexel Burnham, began to convince institutional investors that they should hold these higher risk securities to obtain higher yields. He convinced enough; over the next few years he created a liquid market in 'junk' bonds.[46] In 1977 junk bonds had represented only 2.5 per cent of corporate bonds outstanding and in 1982 3.8 per cent but, by 1985, nine per cent of all corporate bonds were junk.[47] Underlying the increase in junk bonds from the late 1970s were new issues, a business that Milken's Los Angeles office of Drexel Burnham Lambert quickly turned into its own.[48] Whereas newly floated junk bonds totalled $8b. for the six years, 1977–82, with issues in the last year amounting to $2.7b., in 1983 the volume of junk bond issues leapt to $8b. and thereafter rose to a peak of $34.3b. in 1986.[49]

New issues of junk bonds provided the finance for divisional managers of a conglomerate enterprise to separate their division from its overall structure. By placing divisional managers in positions of strategic control, these buy-outs created the possibility for the reintegration of strategy and learning. But, with intensifying global competition, the disruptions to the organisational learning processes arising from conglomeration appear to have severely diminished the cumulation advantages inherent in the divisional buy-outs, once they had gained strategic independence.[50] There is evidence that the debt-service requirements of these divisional buy-outs resulted in significant cost-cutting.[51] With trimming the fat of day-to-day operations, many companies found that they also had to cut out the bone of developmental investment. The debt that financed the buy-outs rather than funding

---

[45] R. A. Taggart Jr, 'The growth of the "junk" bond market and its role in financing takeovers', in A. J. Auerbach (ed.), *Mergers and Acquisitions* (Chicago, 1988). p. 9; and C. Bruck, *The Predators' Ball: The Junk-Bond Raiders and the Man Who Staked Them* (New York, 1988), pp. 27, 37–8, 44.

[46] ibid., ch. 1.

[47] Taggart, 'Growth of the "junk" bond market', p. 9.

[48] ibid., p. 8; Bruck, *Predators' Ball*; and J. B. Stewart, *Den of Thieves* (New York, 1991).

[49] K. J. Perry and R. A. Taggart Jr, 'Development of the junk bond market and its role in portfolio management and corporate finance', in E. I. Altman (ed.), *The High-Yield Debt Market: Investment, Performance, and Economic Impact* (Homewood, Ill. 1990), p. 187.

[50] Holland, *When the Machine Stopped.*

[51] F. Lichtenberg and D. Siegel, 'The effects of leveraged buyouts on productivity and related aspects of firm behavior', *Journal of Financial Economics*, 27 (1990); and Hall, 'Corporate restructuring'.

investment in new productive assets only transferred claims over returns to existing assets. Yet with the difference that, by loading up a company with debt, a junk-bond-financed buy-out made it imperative for the enterprise to pay out earnings rather than retain them for new productive investment.

During the 1980s those who ran the Wall Street firms that made money from financing buy-outs were well aware of the advantages of debt service in enforcing liquidity on corporate management. They were also eager to portray the imposition of financial discipline on corporate managers as the solution to the poor performance of American industry. Frederick Joseph, Chief Executive Officer of Drexel Burnham Lambert during the Milken era, summed up the view from the Street:

Increased debt has important consequences for management. It reduces discretion in spending free cash flow. Instead of pouring free cash flow into perks or unproductive investments, management is forced to direct cash flow to debt service, effectively returning it to the investing public. 'Debt creation without retention of the proceeds of the issue enables managers to effectively bond their promise to pay our (sic) future cash flows,' notes Harvard economist Michael C. Jensen. 'Thus debt can be an effective substitute for dividends.'[52]

By 1990, when these words were published, the use of junk bonds had long since been transformed from financing divisional buy-outs to financing hostile take-overs of entire corporations. Corporate raiders of the 1980s were often hand-picked by Michael Milken to launch a take-over, which relied on his network of institutional · investors (including savings and loan companies) to buy the junk bonds that the acquired company would issue when it was taken over as the means to buy up the stock that allowed it be taken over! In 1986 there were 76 public company buy-outs – 20 per cent of all public take-overs – at a real average value (in 1988 dollars) of $303.3 m. The average real value of 47 company buy-outs in 1987, and 125 in 1988, was around $480m., about three times the average value of the divisional buy-outs during these years.[53]

The purpose of a high-value public-company buy-out, such as the much-publicised KKR take-over of RJR Nabisco, was, to use Michael Jensen's apt phrase, 'to disgorge the free cash flow' from companies that had allegedly 'matured'.[54] The attempt to transform committed finance into liquid finance sent stock prices up when the target was 'put in play', as did the speculative bidding that occurred as the possibility of take-over loomed near. To pay for the high cost of the take-over, and the high rates of interest incurred in junk-bond financing, divisions were sold off

[52] F. H. Joseph, 'A Wall Street view of the high-yield debt market and corporate leverage', in Altman, *High-Yield Debt Market*, pp. 123–4.

[53] M. C. Jensen, 'The eclipse of the public corporation', *Harvard Business Review*, 67 (1989), p. 65; and Merrill Lynch Advisory Services, *Mergerstat Review*, p. 95.

[54] Jensen, 'Eclipse of the public corporation'; and idem, 'The agency cost of free cash flow, corporate finance, and takeovers', *American Economic Review*, 76 (1986). See also B. Burrough and J. Helyar, *Barbarians at the Gate* (New York, 1990); G. Anders, *Merchants of Debt: KKR and the Mortgaging of American Business* (New York, 1992); M. Johnston, *Takeover: The New Wall Street Warriors* (New York, 1986); Stewart, *Den of Thieves*; and Bruck, *Predators' Ball*.

and the cash flow of the company was made as 'free' as possible from other claims –
such as those of long-time employees, suppliers and customers.[55]

What financial interests bent on financial liquidity count as free cash flow may be
resources that, with appropriate organisational integration, could be reinvested in
organisational learning. During the 1980s control over corporate revenues shifted
dramatically in favour of such financial interests. In addition to debt-enforced
liquidity, the decade saw a substantial increase in institutional investors' ability to
obtain high yields on corporate stock. Whereas households held 90 per cent of all
corporate equity in 1952, they had only 48 per cent in 1994 and undoubtedly
considerably less more recently as, during the first half of 1996, record sums – $50b.
dollars in January and February alone[56] – flowed into mutual funds to reap the
returns of the stock market boom. Collectivising the savings of households, pension
funds' share of outstanding corporate stocks increased by 25 percentage points, and
mutual funds by 10 percentage points, from 1952 to 1994. During the 1980s and
1990s, marked increases in dividend : profit payout ratios, combined with unprecedented corporate stock repurchases and corporate downsizing, supported the high
yields on corporate stock. In addition, with inflation defeated – largely because of
the much diminished power of the labour movement as well as the pressures of
foreign competition – real bond yields became markedly higher during the 1980s
and 1990s than previously.[57] Also pushing up bond yields were the deregulation of
financial markets from the late 1970s and the integration of the bond and stock
markets through institutional investors' investment portfolio strategies.

By the collective power of institutional investing, households – at least the 45 per
cent who have pension coverage[58] – can now put pressure on companies to raise
their stock yields and stock prices. During the 1960s mutual funds, with about 85
per cent of their assets in stocks, increased their control over outstanding stock to
over four per cent. They also played an important 'arbitrage' role in the conglomeration movement by buying up large blocks of stock that were rumoured to be in
play to sell to corporate raiders at higher prices.[59] In 1975 institutional investors,
faced by inflation and low securities yields, pressured Wall Street to end fixed
commissions on trading. This set the stage for a major increase in the volume of
trading through the churning of investment portfolios and intensified the shift
of Wall Street from investment banking to securities trading.[60] The participation of

---

[55] A. Shleifer and L. H. Summers, 'Breach of trust in hostile takeovers', in A. J. Auerbach (ed.),
Corporate Takeovers: Causes and Consequences (Chicago, 1988).

[56] E. Wyatt, 'Money keeps pouring into market funds', *New York Times*, 7 Mar. 1996.

[57] United States Congress, *Economic Report of the President, 1996* (Washington, DC, 1996), pp. 343, 360.

[58] T. Ghilarducci, *Labor's Capital: The Economics and Politics of Private Pensions* (Cambridge, Mass.,
1992), p. 3.

[59] Editors. *Fortune: Conglomerate*, p. 142.

[60] R. H. K. Vietor, 'Regulation-defined financial markets: fragmentation and integration in financial
services', in S. L. Hayes III (ed.), *Wall Street and Regulation* (Boston, Mass., 1987), pp. 42–5;
K. Auletta, *Greed and Glory on Wall Street* (New York, 1986); and T. Carrington, *The Year They Sold
Wall Street* (Boston, Mass., 1985).

institutional investors made it possible for Milken to create the junk-bond market during the 1970s and to use it to launch hostile take-overs during the 1980s.

By the mid-1980s institutional investors could have a direct effect on corporations. The top managers of American companies have been increasingly open – and amply rewarded for acceding – to institutional investors' demands. In the aftermath of the October 1987 stock market crash, major institutional investors began to engage in 'relational' investment to get companies to take actions that would increase the value of their stockholdings.[61] As a result, the Standard & Poor's stock price index only declined by seven per cent in 1988, bounced back by well over 21 per cent in 1989 and over the 1990s scarcely looked back. In promoting market control rather than organisational control, the revolutions in production and finance of the 1970s have drastically undermined the social conditions during the 1980s and 1990s for innovation and industrial development in the United States.

II

During the interwar period, when managerial control was well established in American business corporations, proprietary control – the integration of ownership and control in the person of the owner-entrepreneur and his progeny – was the dominant feature of British industry.[62] Proprietary control had characterised the governance of industry in all major capitalist economies over the nineteenth century. But Britain had dominated the world economy without the systematic education and training of technical specialists and administrative personnel who could be integrated into innovative managerial organisations.[63] In combination with proprietary control over the allocation of enterprise revenues, the British economy had built its international competitive advantage during the nineteenth century on the basis of ample supplies of locally concentrated craft skill.[64] Within the staple industries, the persistence of craft control over the development and utilisation of technology had acted as a constraint upon individual enterprises becoming dominant within their manufacturing branch.

The increasing importance of managerial organisation in American industry induced leading industrialists, as well as philanthropic foundations created from industrial wealth, to organise and finance the transformation of higher education to generate a supply of graduates able and willing to pursue careers as 'organization

---

[61] See, for example, M. Blair, *Ownership and Control: Rethinking Corporate Governance for the Twenty-First Century* (Washington, DC, 1995), ch. 5.

[62] See R. Church, 'The family firm in industrial capitalism: international perspectives on hypotheses and history', *Business History*, 35 (1993).

[63] Elbaum and Lazonick, *Decline of the British Economy*.

[64] K. Burgess, *The Origins of British Industrial Relations* (London, 1975); E. Hobsbawm, *Workers: Worlds of Labor* (New York, 1984); Elbaum and Lazonick, *Decline of the British Economy*; R. Harrison and J. Zeitlin (eds), *Divisions of Labour: Skilled Workers and Technological Change in Nineteenth Century England* (Brighton, 1985); and W. Lazonick, *Competitive Advantage on the Shop Floor* (Cambridge, Mass., 1990).

men'.[65] By the 1890s the land-grant college system had become integral to the American economy's industrial development. The success of land-grant colleges, such as MIT, Cornell, and Purdue, pressured elite private institutions to allocate resources to research and teaching that supported industrial development.[66] In Britain no such educational transformation occurred even during the first half of the twentieth century.[67] Although a few companies, such as Unilever and Imperial Chemical Industries, built world-class managerial organisations,[68] Britain's leading industrialists placed no pressure upon the higher education system to serve the personnel requirements of a managerial revolution.

Amongst British businessmen, large accumulations of wealth and substantial political power were in the hands of financiers based in the City of London, rather than industrialists.[69] Using upper-class educational institutions as means of entry, and marriages as instruments of merger, wealthy financiers joined with the old landowning elite (many of whom had grown recently wealthy through rising land values) to form a new aristocracy. The bases of wealth in financial activities were social connections and acquired reputations, not industrial innovation. Hence the importance to ultimate economic success of social contacts and standing, developed at the top educational institutions – Oxford and Cambridge as well as public schools such as Eton and Harrow.[70] The aristocracy that controlled these elite institutions had no need for an educational system that developed technologists. In Britain's rise to international industrial dominance, technological knowledge and experience had generally been possessed by skilled workers who had acquired it on the shop floor. Therefore, the British elite positively resisted the notion that a concern with technology had any place in an upper-class education. Those who aspired to be members of this elite wanted education to set them apart from the lower orders, not to bring them in closer contact with them. Thus they valued the study of science as a branch of higher knowledge, but had little interest in its application to industry.

[65] D. Noble, *America by Design* (New York, 1977).

[66] L. Ferleger and W. Lazonick, 'The managerial revolution and the developmental state: the case of US agriculture', *Business and Economic History*, 2nd ser., 22 (1993); and idem, 'Higher education for innovation: land-grant colleges and the managerial revolution', *Business and Economic History*, 2nd ser., 23 (1994).

[67] See W. Lazonick, 'Strategy, structure, and management development in the United States and Britain', in K. Kobayashi and M. Morikawa (eds), *Development of Managerial Enterprise* (Tokyo, 1986).

[68] W. Reader, *Imperial Chemical Industries*, 2 vols (Oxford, 1970 and 1975); and C. Wilson, *The History of Unilever* (Cambridge, 1968).

[69] W. D. Rubenstein, 'Wealth, elites, and the class structure of modern Britain', *Past and Present*, 76 (1977); idem, 'The Victorian middle classes: wealth, occupation, and geography', *Economic History Review*, 2nd ser., 30 (1977); Y. Cassis, 'Bankers in English society in the late nineteenth century', *Economic History Review*, 2nd ser., 38 (1985); M. Daunton, '"Gentlemanly capitalism" and British industry, 1820–1914', *Past and Present*, 122 (1989); and idem, 'Financial elites and British society, 1880–1950', in Y. Cassis (ed.), *Finance and Financiers in European History, 1880–1960* (Cambridge, 1992).

[70] Lazonick, 'Strategy, structure and management development', pp. 119–34.

In the late nineteenth century, British industrialists generally had middle-class, or even working-class, origins, with their roots in the Midlands, the North, or abroad.[71] The most successful, who could contemplate joining the upper class, did not challenge the anti-industry bias of the elite educational system. Rather, they sought to elevate their social standing by distancing themselves from the social foundations of their industrial success. They typically located their head offices in London and sent their sons to be educated at the top public schools and, if possible, at Oxbridge. Seeking to partake of aristocratic culture to serve their aspirations for upward mobility, they did not want to transform the nation's premier educational institutions into servants of industry. Successful industrialists wanted to become 'gentlemen' rather than 'players'.[72]

For successful industrialists, control over an established industrial enterprise remained the foundation of their material wealth. They brought in their sons and sons-in-law to manage their businesses, so perpetuating the integration of family ownership and control. The larger owner-controlled firms that, because of enterprise expansion or a dearth of qualified family members, had to recruit top managers from outside the family gave highest preference to young men with a classical Oxbridge education.[73] Thus those who came to control British industrial enterprises during the first half of the twentieth century were not well equipped or well positioned to lead their firms in the pursuit of technological innovation. Even in high-technology companies, the persistence of proprietary control typically fostered strategic segmentation. Increasingly from 1900, many technical specialists, employed by science-based enterprises, came from the newly established provincial universities that tried to cater to the educational needs of technologists and, for that reason alone, the British upper classes viewed these institutions of higher learning as inferior.[74] With top management recruited through family connections and from the elite educational system, these university-educated technologists could not aspire, over the course of their careers, to climb through the enterprise structure into positions of strategic control.[75]

These barriers to social mobility within the enterprise reduced the commitment of technical specialists to organisational goals and enhanced the attractiveness of inter-firm mobility as the route to career progress. Such prospects of employee exit, in turn, reduced the incentive for top managers to invest in the productive capabilities of these employees. The persistence of proprietary control, therefore, meant that leading British industrial enterprises effectively segmented strategy from

[71] Rubenstein, 'Victorian middle classes'; and D. J. Jeremy, 'Anatomy of the British business elite, 1860–1980', *Business History*, 26 (1984).

[72] D. C. Coleman, 'Gentlemen and players,' *Economic History Review*, 2nd ser., 26 (1973).

[73] Cambridge University Appointments Board, *University Education and Business* (Cambridge, 1945), pp. 39–40; and Acton Society Trust, *Management Succession* (London, 1956), pp. 28–9.

[74] M. Sanderson, 'The English civic universities and the "industrial spirit", 1870–1914', *Historical Research*, 61 (1988).

[75] Lazonick, 'Strategy, structure, and management development', pp. 119–34.

learning, thus seriously impeding the development and utilisation of technology in these companies.

The objectives and activities of British financial institutions during the first half of the twentieth century reflected these characteristics of industrial enterprises. The British counterparts to Wall Street investment banks were the merchant banks that dominated the City and made it a world financial centre. Merchant banks such as Barings, Hambros, Lazards, Rothschilds and Schroders were much more dependent on international business than Wall Street.[76] Their lack of involvement in financing domestic industry reflected the general absence of dominant industrial enterprises in the British economy.[77] Underwriting equity issues of dominant American enterprises enabled Wall Street to transform the NYSE into a highly liquid market for high-quality industrial securities, thus facilitating the separation of ownership from control. The City played no equivalent role in transforming the London Stock Exchange.[78] In the United States the stock market was used primarily to transfer ownership of existing assets, whereas in Britain it was commonly used to finance investments in new assets. Around the turn of the century, provincial stock exchanges, close to the centres of industrial activity, were often better positioned than the London Stock Exchange to provide such services.[79] However, increasingly during the first decades of the twentieth century, industrial enterprises that were seeking substantial amounts of external finance looked to the wealth accumulations in London, with a listing on the London Stock Exchange being critical for a flotation's success.[80] Both companies and stockholders favoured preferred over ordinary (common) stock (shares).[81] Compared with the NYSE, the relatively lax listing provisions of the London Stock Exchange did little to instil public confidence in the liquidity of quoted companies.[82] Missing, as a result, was a basic condition – the liquidity of investment portfolios – for the separation of ownership and control.

The persistence of proprietary control meant that the prime form of debt

[76] M. Edelstein, *Overseas Investment in the Age of High Imperialism, 1850–1914* (New York, 1982); S. Chapman, *The Rise of Merchant Banking* (London, 1984); S. Pollard, 'Capital exports: harmful or beneficial', *Economic History Review*, 38 (1985); Daunton, '"Gentlemanly capitalism" and British industry'; W. A. Thomas, *The Finance of British Industry, 1918–1976* (London, 1978), p. 48; and P. L. Cottrell, *Industrial Finance, 1830–1914: The Finance and Organization of English Manufacturing Industry* (London, 1980), pp. 181–2.

[77] Thomas, *Finance of British Industry*, chs 3 and 7; M. Best and J. Humphries, 'The City and industrial decline', in Elbaum and Lazonick, *Decline of the British Economy*; and Y. Cassis, 'British finance: success and controversy', in J. J. Van Helten and Y. Cassis (eds), *Capitalism in a Mature Economy: Financial Institutions, Capital Exports, and British Industry, 1870–1939* (Aldershot, 1990).

[78] Michie, *London and New York Stock Exchanges*.

[79] J. B. Jefferys, *Business Organisation in Great Britain, 1856–1914* (New York, 1977), p. 371; and see also Cottrell, *Industrial Finance*, ch. 5.

[80] A. E. Harrison, 'Joint-stock company flotation in the cycle, motor vehicle and related industries, 1882–1914', *Business History*, 23 (1981); and R. C. Michie, 'The Stock Exchange and the British economy, 1870–1939,' in Van Helten and Cassis, *Capitalism in a Mature Economy*.

[81] Thomas, *Finance of British Industry*, ch. 2.

[82] Michie, *London and New York Stock Exchanges*; and Cottrell, *Industrial Finance*, pp. 184–90.

financing for industrial enterprises was the commercial bank overdraft, an ostensibly short-term financial instrument, generally subject to annual review. Firms with successful records of profits and debt service could renew and extend overdrafts, so that what was supposed to be a provision for working capital became in effect part of the enterprise's fixed capital.[83] But, for the commercial banks, the advantage of the overdraft was that it provided them with an ever-ready instrument of market control. During the 1920s, bank advances to the staple industries were placed in jeopardy when these industries – especially textiles, steel and shipbuilding – began to lose their dominant international positions.[84] Many firms in these branches of manufacturing were particularly vulnerable because of speculative recapitalisations after the First World War.[85] Often involving the merger of an unquoted firm with a quoted company, these recapitalisations began to loosen the grip of proprietary control. To rescue the bank's bad and doubtful loans, the Bank of England initiated during the late 1920s industry-wide rationalisations that compelled debt-ridden firms to amalgamate into larger enterprises under centralised managerial control. To effect these amalgamations, owners of the constituent firms, as well as debtors, were issued ordinary shares in the new company, weakening and in many cases severing the integration of ownership and control. These forced amalgamations did not, however, entail managerial reorganisation to transform the productive capabilities of enterprises.[86] Instead of creating the social foundations for organisational control, these bank-led amalgamations left substantial sectors of industry ever more vulnerable to the forces of market control.

During the interwar period, in industries of the second industrial revolution (including electrical engineering and chemicals), proprietary firms within the same industry amalgamated for the purpose of controlling product prices through issuing stock in the new company. Such merger activity was particularly marked in the periods 1919–20 and 1927–29.[87] Within the amalgamated structure, however, the constituent businesses typically maintained their proprietary independence, thus impeding the use of the amalgamation to rationalise product lines and engage in cooperative activities such as research and marketing.[88]

---

[83] Cottrell, *Industrial Finance*, ch. 7; Thomas, *Finance of British Industry*, ch. 7; D. M. Ross, 'The clearing banks and industry – new perspectives on the inter-war years,' in Van Helten and Cassis, *Capitalism in a Mature Economy*; and see also A. E. Harrison, 'F. Hopper & Co.: the problems of capital supply in the cycle manufacturing industry, 1891–1914', *Business History*, 24 (1982).

[84] Ross, 'Clearing banks'; and M. Collins, *Banks and Industrial Finance in Britain, 1800–1939* (Cambridge, 1995), ch. 6.

[85] S. Tolliday, 'Steel and rationalization policies, 1918–1950', in Elbaum and Lazonick, *Decline of the British Economy*; J. H. Bamberg, 'The rationalisation of the British cotton industry in the interwar years', *Textile History*, 19 (1988).

[86] L. Hannah, *The Rise of the Corporate Economy* (Baltimore, 2nd ed., 1983), ch. 3.

[87] ibid., p. 93.

[88] A. D. Chandler Jr, 'The growth of the transnational industrial firm in the United States and the United Kingdom: a comparative analysis', *Economic History Review*, 2nd ser., 33 (1980); and Hannah, *Rise of the Corporate Economy*, ch. 7.

Over time, as private stockholders in these amalgamations sold their stakes on the market, stock ownership became divorced from strategic control, but without leaving in place managerial organisations to shape innovative investment strategies. By the 1940s and 1950s many firms that had remained proprietary took advantage of a growing demand by portfolio investors for corporate equities and liquidated their holdings by issuing ordinary stock to the public.[89]

During the second half of the 1950s, a merger and acquisition movement resulted in a marked concentration of British industry. The 100 largest companies increased their control of assets of all companies quoted on the London Stock Exchange from 56 per cent in 1954 to 66 per cent in 1964 and to 73 per cent in 1968.[90] Amalgamations were particularly evident in industries, such as food and drink, that used well-known and stable technologies but in which brand-name recognition permitted enterprises to attain dominant market shares.[91] In this merger and acquisition wave, the 'hostile takeover' appeared for the first time on a significant scale amongst any of the advanced economies.[92] The attempt by strategic managers to make their companies less attractive targets through reductions in liquid assets was one cause of an increase in the corporate pay-out ratio from 30 per cent in 1958–59 to 37 per cent in 1961–62.[93]

Institutional investors were among the participants in the market for corporate control from the late 1950s. Until the 1950s, the vast majority of pension funds had invested in fixed-rate securities. By the late 1950s, pension fund management had been professionalised, with vigorous competition among the institutional investors to attract more customers.[94] But portfolio management of pension funds only began to exert a major influence on corporate financial policy and corporate stock yields in the deregulated financial environment of the 1980s. During the first half of the 1980s the value of British pension funds increased from 15 per cent to 28 per cent of GDP, compared with an increase from 23 per cent to 29 per cent in the United States. In both Germany and Japan, this figure was about five per cent in 1985.[95] Coming into the era of financial deregulation of the 1980s, the congenital weaknesses of British corporate enterprises meant that, by international comparison, organisational control had never attained a firm foundation. During the 1980s,

[89] Thomas, *Finance of British Industry*, ch. 6.

[90] A. Singh, 'Take-overs, economic natural selection and the theory of the firm: evidence from the postwar United Kingdom experience', *Economic Journal*, 85 (1975). p. 499.

[91] ibid.; and Chandler, *Scale and Scope*, ch. 9.

[92] See L. Hannah, 'Takeover bids in Britain before 1950: an exercise in business "pre-history"', *Business History*, 15 (1974); J. F. Wright, 'The capital market and the finance of industry', in G. D. N. Worswick and P. H. Ady (eds), *The British Economy in the Nineteen-Fifties* (Oxford, 1962); and Singh, 'Take-Overs'.

[93] Thomas, *Finance of British Industry*, pp. 236, 240–1.

[94] L. Hannah, *Inventing Retirement: The Development of Occupational Pensions in Britain* (Cambridge, 1986), ch. 5.

[95] T. Ghilarducci, 'International pension funds and capital markets', photocopy (AFL-CIO, Washington, DC, 1994).

international competition and capital movements, combined with the quest for higher yields on portfolio investments, created pressures to weaken organisational control in all of the advanced economies. In Britain, perhaps even more so than in the United States, the deregulated financial environment of the 1980s advanced the power of market control. Dividends and stock prices soared, as did the salaries of top managers of industrial enterprises, who cooperated with the forces of market control.[96]

III

The finance of industrial development cannot be understood in the absence of an explanation of the sources of industrial development. Recently, proponents of market control have pointed, with justification, to managerial abuse and ill-informed allocations of corporate resources as the rationale for 'creating value for shareholders' through dividend payments, stock repurchases, and workforce down-sizings.[97] Problems of corporate governance are real. Especially in the United States, but also in Britain, top corporate executives are grossly overpaid relative to other employees in their organisations and to their top management counterparts in other advanced economies.[98] And over the past few decades, under a system in which strategic decision-making has increasingly been concentrated at the top of large enterprises, American and British corporations have, in many industries in which they used to be world leaders, lost substantial market shares.

The proponents of market control define the source of the problem as 'agency costs' that, with stock ownership separated from managerial control, take the form of 'managerial discretion'. They then assume that managerial discretion can only take the forms of managerial perquisites and unproductive investments – resources that managers allocate to advance their own selfish interests. The solution is the 'market for corporate control' that pressures incumbent managers to 'create value for shareholders' or else lose their positions of allocative control.

What the proponents of market control see as a solution to the dissipation of resources by management, we see as part of the problem. Strategic managers need to have discretion if investments in developing and utilising productive resources are to be made that result in sustained competitive advantage for their enterprises and sustainable prosperity for the economy. But who these decision-makers are, how they make their decisions, and whom they seek to benefit have profound impacts on whether these companies invest for the future or live off the past.

The comparative historical evidence shows that the problem for innovation and industrial development is not that strategic managers have discretion, but that they have become too segmented from the organisations in which the development and

---

[96] J. Charkham, *Keeping Good Company: A Study of Corporate Governance in Five Countries* (Oxford, 1994), ch. 6.

[97] Jensen, 'Eclipse of public corporation'.

[98] G. Crystal, *In Search of Excess: The Overcompensation of American Executives* (New York, 1991).

utilisation of productive resources occurs. The market for corporate control tends
to exacerbate this strategic segmentation. In the presence of a powerful market for
corporate control, the use of stock-based rewards aligns the interests of strategic
managers with public stockholders, making it all the more certain that the
integration of strategy and learning will not occur.[99] Once the importance of
organisational learning to the development and utilisation of productive resources is
recognised, one cannot avoid the fact that the most important investments that an
innovative enterprise makes are in human resources, not physical resources.
Although, in common parlance, business executives will say that their human assets
are their companies' most valuable assets, in corporate law and in accounting
practice, human capabilities are not treated as corporate assets because people cannot
be owned. Investments in human resources are counted as *expenses*, as are the
returns to human resources that take the forms of higher incomes, better benefits
and more stable employment. The conventional concept of property on which
these accounting practices are based, however, ignores the collective assets and
collective returns that are the essential realities of innovative enterprise.[100]

The problem of corporate governance and industrial development is not resolved
by simply advocating, as has recently been done in both the United States and
Britain, that industrial corporations be run for other 'stakeholders' – especially
employees – besides stockholders.[101] The danger is that different groups, who can
lay claim to shares of corporate revenues, will, as has increasingly been the case of
stockholders in the United States and Britain, extract corporate revenues, whether
or not their contributions to the generation of these revenues makes these returns
possible on a sustainable basis. The result of the creation of a 'stakeholder society'
might be to increase the propensity for major industrial enterprises and the economy
in which they operate to live off the past rather than invest for the future.

The comparative-historical evidence on the United States and Britain shows the
importance of collective organisation, and the integration of strategic decision-
makers into this organisation, for successful industrial development. In the United
States during the first half of the century this collective organisation took the form
of the 'managerial revolution' – a transformation in business organisation that
provides a major explanation for the industrial success of the United States compared
with Britain during this century. Even then, by the late twentieth century, organisational integration in the United States has itself fallen short of internationally
competitive standards. As we shall argue in a subsequent contribution to *Financial
History Review* on the finance of industrial development in Japan and Germany, the
weakness of American industry in international competition is that organisational
integration has not been extended to broader groups of people both within

---

[99] Lazonick, 'Controlling the market', pp. 461–6.
[100] O'Sullivan, Innovation, ch.7.
[101] R. B. Reich, 'How to avoid these layoffs?', *New York Times*, 4 Jan. 1996, A13; and 'Shareholder
values', *The Economist*, 10 Feb. 1996, p. 15.

and across industrial enterprises to meet the evolving requirements of industrial innovation.

The ideology that the 'shareholder' is the 'principal' for whom the industrial corporation is run helps to ensure that such organisational transformations will not take place. This ideology places a premium on economic performance that reaps the benefits of prior investments in productive capabilities while ignoring the new investments in organisational learning that can potentially generate greater returns for more people in the future.

[18]

Financial History Review 4 (1997), pp. 117–138. Printed in the United Kingdom © 1997 Cambridge University Press.

Finance and industrial development

Part II: Japan and Germany[1]

WILLIAM LAZONICK

University of Massachusetts Lowell, University of Tokyo and INSEAD

and

MARY O'SULLIVAN

INSEAD

Industrial development requires financial commitment to permit the development and utilisation of productive resources. At the level of the industrial enterprise, financial commitment is needed to allocate resources to developmental investment strategies, including processes of organisational learning. The extent and duration of financial commitment must be sufficient to enable the enterprise to generate products that are of sufficiently high quality, but at a low cost, to reap returns that can sustain it as an organisation. The need for organisation to develop and utilise productive resources means that the allocation of an enterprise's financial resources must be subject to some form of 'organisational control'.

In a previous contribution, we analysed the evolution of 'market control', and the concomitant shift from financial commitment to financial liquidity, in the allocation of corporate resources in the United States and the United Kingdom.[2] Given current pressures for a shift from organisational control to market control in many other advanced economies, in this companion piece we provide a comparative-historical perspective on the foundations of organisational control in the governance of industrial corporations in Japan and Germany.

---

[1] Discussions with T. Abe, E. Daito, K. Ishii, K. Kobayashi, H. Miyajima, T. Okazaki, K. Sugihara, A. Takatsuki, N. Tamaki, H. Takeda, K. Wada and T. Yuzawa helped focus the research for this paper. R. Dore, S. Marglin and two anonymous referees offered useful comments on earlier drafts. The Faculty of Economics, University of Tokyo, provided excellent research facilities while the Committee on Industrial Theory and Assessment, University of Massachusetts Lowell, STEP Group, Oslo, and the Jerome Levy Economics Institute of Bard College provided funding.

[2] 'Finance and industrial development. Part I: the United States and the United Kingdom', *Financial History Review*, 4, 1 (1997), pp. 7–29.

I

In contrast to the ascendancy of market control in the United States, organisational control remains the rule in Japan. The institutions that currently support organisational control – namely, lifetime employment and cross-shareholding – are post-1945 developments. But an evolution towards organisational control can be traced back to the Meiji period (1868–1912) when, with family and joint stock ownership, salaried managers began to acquire positions of strategic decision-making power in major industrial enterprises.

During the 1870s, the restoration government sought to foster industrial development by importing Western machinery and specialists to launch a number of state-owned mines, shipyards and factories.[3] Beginning in 1880, the government started privatising its enterprises. Some of these assets were acquired by family-owned concerns, such as Mitsui, Mitsubishi and Sumitomo, that quickly emerged as the nation's major zaibatsu [financial cliques].[4] In addition, through their growing trading activities, the zaibatsu acquired substantial interests in other manufacturing enterprises during the late nineteenth century. Over time, the zaibatsu often became the dominant stockholders in industrial enterprises and transformed them into affiliates. For example, during the early 1900s, Kanegafuchi Cotton Spinning and Oji Paper became Mitsui affiliates when Mitsui Bank increased its holdings of these companies' stocks. Mitsui also acquired Shibaura Engineering Works, which later became part of Toshiba, when the company defaulted on its bank loans.[5]

However, the zaibatsu were not involved in promoting new manufacturing ventures. In industries, such as cotton spinning and paper manufacturing, that required both considerable capital and imported technical expertise, new ventures were started as joint stock companies, with the zaibatsu often taking participations as part of a network of investors.[6] Resources were raised by the sale of shares on an instalment basis. Only a portion – often just one-sixth of the value of the stocks – was paid-up at the outset, with the rest remaining on call as required by the company. In this way, dividend payments – typically ten per cent of paid-up capital – were kept to a minimum while a commitment of capital infusions was secured for the longer term. With many early flotations, investors had to be given strong incentives, such as guaranteed dividends of the order of eight to ten per cent.[7]

Among early investors were former daimyo and samurai who converted into

[3] T. Smith, *Political Change and Industrial Development in Japan* (Stanford, 1955).
[4] H. Morikawa, *Zaibatsu* (Tokyo, 1992), ch. 1.
[5] ibid., p. 59.
[6] K. Nakagawa, 'The "learning industrial revolution" and business management', in T. Yui and K. Nakagawa (eds), *Japanese Management in Historical Perspective* (Tokyo, 1989), pp. 1–25.
[7] J. Hirschmeier, *The Origins of Entrepreneurship in Meiji Japan* (Cambridge, 1964), p. 158; S. Yonekawa, 'Flotation booms in the cotton spinning industry, 1870–1890', *Business History Review*, 61 (1987); K. Ishii, 'Japan', in R. Cameron and V. Bovykin (eds), *International Banking, 1870–1914* (New York, 1991), pp. 223–6; J. Roberts, *Mitsui* (New York, 1973), pp. 118, 122; and J. Hirschmeier and T. Yui, *The Development of Japanese Business* (London, 2nd ed, 1981), pp. 112–13.

stockholdings bonds that they had received from the Meiji government as compensation for the loss of feudal tax revenues.[8] These debt issues were absorbed by the note-issuing national banks, established between 1873 and 1882. Increasingly, however, investors were wealthy merchants and landlords. Generally, in railway and cotton-textile companies, stockholders numbered between 100 and 500, with a few major holders usually playing the most active roles in launching and directing such enterprises.[9]

In many cases, individual investors would buy stock in a new venture with funds borrowed from a bank, that were secured by the new stock issues.[10] Bank loans thus indirectly capitalised business enterprises. Investors had an immediate interest in the success of a venture because they, not the company, were obliged to repay the loans. In addition, investors often had to take out additional bank loans to pay calls when companies required more capital. Much of this financing came from the increasingly powerful commercial banks. The first 'ordinary' (as distinct from 'national') bank was Mitsui Bank, founded in 1876, with government funds accounting for half of its initial deposits (and one-third of all Japanese bank deposits).[11] In 1907, the five largest banks held 21 per cent of all bank deposits and made 17 per cent of all bank loans.[12] Four of these were businesses of the four leading zaibatsu: Mitsui, Sumitomo, Mitsubishi and Yasuda. The other, Dai'ichi Bank, second in deposits and loans to Mitsui, had been established as the first national bank in 1873. After the founding of the Bank of Japan in 1882, however, Dai'ichi and other surviving national banks were transformed into 'regular' commercial banks.

In 1890, in the aftermath of a joint stock flotation boom, many borrowers could neither meet payments on their stock-backed loans nor secure further credit. The Bank of Japan discounted these loans for a number of specially designated companies. Subsequently, an extension of Bank of Japan loans – 'special discounting facilities' – became a means for financing industrial development with stock as collateral. Until 1917, most eligible companies were banks which were, in turn, making loans to industrial concerns. Thereafter, however, the Bank of Japan increased its direct lending to creditworthy industrial enterprises, especially major cotton-textile companies.[13]

The practice of providing bank loans on collateral comprising corporate stock meant that financial institutions, including the Bank of Japan, had an interest in the

[8] A. Fraser, 'Hachisuka Mochiaka (1846–1918)', in Yui and Nakagawa, *Japanese Management*; and K. Sakurai, *Financial Aspects of the Economic Development of Japan, 1868–1958* (Tokyo, 1964), p. 25.

[9] Hirschmeier and Yui, *Development of Japanese Business*, p. 112.

[10] Sakurai, *Financial Aspects*, pp. 31, 116, 132–3.

[11] Morikawa, *Zaibatsu*, p. 10.

[12] Japan Business History Institute, *The Mitsui Bank* (Tokyo, 1976), p. 67; and Sakurai, *Financial Aspects*, p. 51.

[13] N. Tamaki, *Japanese Banking* (Cambridge, 1995), pp. 67, 79, 116; and Sakurai, *Financial Aspects*, p. 282.

emergence of well-functioning stock exchanges that, when the need arose, would increase the liquidity of this collateral.[14] When the Tokyo and Osaka Stock Exchanges were founded as profit-making joint stock companies in 1878, most trading was in rice and bean futures. Over the ensuing decades, trading in securities was often fictitious, with no exchange of stock certificates occurring at settlement while among the most widely traded stocks were equities in the stock exchanges themselves. Only from the mid-1890s, following booms in the promotion of railway and cotton-spinning companies, was corporate stock listed and actively traded on the Tokyo and Osaka exchanges. By about 1910, Tokyo definitively surpassed Osaka to become the dominant market.[15]

By 1900, however, the most important sources of financial commitment were the major zaibatsu, which were financing their own principal subsidiaries from retained earnings. The zaibatsu banks also lent to 'outside' businesses, some of which became zaibatsu affiliates. In expanding their loan business, the most powerful banks were able to borrow at special rates from the Bank of Japan, while smaller banks borrowed from the major banks. Through borrowing from the Bank of Japan, the commercial banks were enabled to make loans to industrial enterprises at levels well above those permitted by their own liabilities. By 1902, however, Mitsui Bank, through holding deposits from the zaibatsu's constituent companies, was able to reduce its Bank of Japan borrowings to zero. Similarly, Sumitomo Bank reduced its Bank of Japan borrowings from 55 per cent of its loans in 1895 to zero a decade later.[16]

Playing supporting roles in financing industrial development were special government banks, such as the Hypothec Bank (founded in 1895), which provided long-term finance for small-scale enterprise, and the Industrial Bank of Japan (IBJ) (1902), which became the key financial institution for Japan's advance into Manchuria. Subsequently, IBJ was called upon by the Finance Ministry to mobilise emergency loans for the collapsing Tokyo and Osaka Stock Exchanges in 1916, to provide loans for investments in China in 1917 and 1918, and to support the sagging shipping and shipbuilding industries during the early 1920s. In addition, over the 1920s, IBJ combined with the leading zaibatsu banks to support the securities markets and provide assistance to a wide variety of troubled, but important, industries. During the late 1930s, IBJ played a leading role in financing new 'national policy firms' engaged in military production and, at the end of 1941, IBJ was the 'main bank' in 82 of 121 loan syndicates for such financing among commercial banks.[17]

This financial system was further supported by funds from the postal savings system, which drew small savings from rural areas not serviced by private commer-

---

[14] T. Adams, *Japanese Securities Markets* (Tokyo, 1953), p. 29; and Tamaki, *Japanese Banking*, p. 136.
[15] ibid., ch. 1 and p. 108.
[16] Morikawa, *Zaibatsu*, pp. 79, 96, 161–9; and Sakurai, *Financial Aspects*, p. 58.
[17] Tamaki, *Japanese Banking*, pp. 98–9, 101, 122–3, 145–6; and J. Teranishi, 'Financial sector reform after the war', in J. Teranishi and Y. Kosai (eds), *The Japanese Experience of Economic Reforms* (Houndmills, 1993), pp. 160–1.

cial banks. By 1900 the postal savings system held 10 per cent of all banking deposits and, by 1919, almost 13 per cent. Controlled by the Deposit Bureau of the Ministry of Finance, these funds could be used strategically to support government policies for industrial development and imperial expansion during the interwar period.[18]

But, whatever the direct role of the state in financing investment projects and shaping national investment strategies, by the interwar period the investment strategies of the zaibatsu were the driving force of Japanese industrial development. Beginning with Mitsui in 1909, the zaibatsus' growth led them to transform their main trading, banking, mining and shipping businesses into subsidiaries. To fund expansion within Japan's rapid industrial expansion during and immediately after the First World War, many subsidiaries were reorganised as joint stock companies that offered limited numbers of shares to non-family members, mainly company employees and close business associates.[19]

During the 1920s, the leading zaibatsu – typically consisting of a holding company, main subsidiaries and affiliated enterprises – emerged as, according to Morikawa, 'probably the largest business empires in the world'. In addition, during the first decades of the century, a number of new family-owned zaibatsu, such as Kuhara and Suzuki, expanded rapidly and, over the interwar period, there emerged a number of 'newly risen' [shinkô] zaibatsu, such as Nissan, Nichitsu and Mori, that financed their expansion through public stock issues.[20]

As these systems of industrial finance evolved from the late nineteenth century until the Second World War, so did the loci of control over the allocation of resources within Japanese enterprises. During the Meiji era, in the zaibatsu structure, control was often shared among related families, with the Japanese practice of legally adopting an energetic and talented manager as the son of the owner-entrepreneur facilitating the maintenance and extension of family links. In the case of new ventures begun as limited liability joint stock enterprises, control was shared among a number of significant stockholders, often with no familial links. The identity of these active stockholders, however, was by no means left to the market. From the mid-1870s, networks of investors evolved to make joint commitments of their financial resources to banks, railways and manufacturing concerns.

The key figure in creating these networks of committed joint stock investors was Shibusawa Eiichi. Leaving a high position in the Ministry of Finance in 1873, Shibusawa took the lead in founding Dai'ichi National Bank, in which major merchant houses, including Mitsui, were its main investors. He took the entrepreneurial initiative to start Oji Paper in 1875 and the Osaka Spinning Mill in 1883, the first large-scale cotton-textile company, the success of which sparked a mill-building boom. Over 43 years, Shibusawa helped organise some 250 new industrial and commercial concerns and was involved with over 500 enterprises. He remained

[18] Teranishi, 'Financial sector reform', p. 134; and R. Goldsmith, *The Financial Development of Japan, 1868–1977* (New Haven, 1983), pp. 86–7.

[19] ibid., pp. 161, 193–4.

[20] Morikawa, *Zaibatsu*, p. 119 and ch. 5.

president of Dai'ichi Bank for his entire business career, acted as an adviser to Mitsui and was chairman or president of up to 15 companies at a time while serving on the board of directors of many other companies. In 1880 he became the chairman of the newly-established Association of Banks and, in 1890, organised and then headed the Tokyo Chamber of Commerce.[21]

These activities helped to make the developmental strategies of government and business complementary, and created a network of wealthy individuals who united to finance industrial development. Shibusawa also quickly learned that success required not only committed finance but also technical expertise. During its initial years Oji Paper suffered from a lack of technical expertise. Therefore, in 1879 Shibusawa sent his nephew, Okawa Heizaburô, to study paper manufacturing technology abroad and he returned to become the key company employee during the 1880s and 1890s. Also in 1879, in anticipation of entering the cotton-textile industry, Shibusawa instructed Yamanobe Takeo, then reading economics at the University of London, first to shift his studies toward technology and thereafter to spend time in a modern Lancashire cotton-textile mill. Yamanobe returned in 1880 and became a central figure in the pioneering Osaka Cotton Mill.[22]

Meanwhile, to foster indigenous learning, during the first half of the 1870s private and public interests set up educational institutions such as Keio University, the Institute of Technology (later part of Tokyo Imperial University) and the Commercial Law School (which became Hitotsubashi University). Business enterprises eagerly recruited graduates of these institutions and, also, often incurred considerable expense in sending these employees abroad for varying lengths of time to acquire greater industrial experience.[23] Over time, these salaried managers became increasingly powerful relative to owners as strategic decision-makers. In joint stock companies unaffiliated with the zaibatsu, stockholding diffused during the first two decades of this century with large stockholders becoming less active on company boards. Even within the zaibatsu holding companies, the need for industrial experience meant that salaried managers often exercised strategic control.[24] As an exception that proves the rule, Hirschmeier and Yui have argued that 'one of the main reasons why Yasuda zaibatsu did not diversify significantly was Yasuda Zenjiro's one-man rule and his neglect of training capable top managers'.[25]

---

[21] Hirschmeier, *Origins of Entrepreneurship*, pp. 188–9; and E. Abe, 'Shibusawa, Eiichi (1840–1931)', in M. Warner (ed.), *International Encyclopedia of Business and Management* (London, 1996).

[22] Morikawa, *Zaibatsu*, pp. 62–3; Hirschmeier and Yui, *Development of Japanese Business*, p. 106; and Nakagawa, 'Learning industrial revolution', pp. 2–3.

[23] S. Yonekawa, 'University graduates in Japanese enterprises before the Second World War', *Business History*, 26 (1984); R. Iwauchi, 'The growth of white-collar employment in relation to the educational system', and H. Uchida, 'Comment', both in Yui and Nakagawa, *Japanese Management*; and Hirschmeier and Yui, *Development of Japanese Business*, pp. 154, 166.

[24] H. Morikawa, 'The increasing power of salaried managers in Japan's large corporations', in W. Wray (ed.), *Managing Industrial Enterprise* (Cambridge, 1989); and Morikawa, *Zaibatsu*, pp. 218–19.

[25] Hirschmeier and Yui, *Development of Japanese Business*, p. 154.

Whatever the locus of control over the allocation of enterprise resources, during the interwar period the overall development strategy of the economy became increasingly dominated by the investment requirements of militarisation and imperial expansion. The nation's productive capabilities and investment power became ever more concentrated within a relatively small number of zaibatsu, old and new. When, following the Second World War, the results of prewar militarism were defeat and devastation, both the Allied Occupation and the Japanese people held the zaibatsu families and their top managers largely to blame. The dissolution of the zaibatsu met with little resistance.

Under the Supreme Commander for the Allied Powers (SCAP), ownership of the stock of 30 zaibatsu holding companies, including Mitsui, Mitsubishi, Sumitomo and Yasuda, were transferred to the Holding Company Liquidation Commission (HCLC) to be redistributed to the public. Another 53 companies went through reorganisations so that they ceased to be holding companies. In addition, hundreds of affiliated zaibatsu companies were classified as 'restricted concerns' and, under the supervision of HCLC, ordered to dispose of their stocks. Holding companies became illegal and a five per cent limitation was placed on the amount of stock that one company could hold in another.[26] Previously central to Japan's industrial development, the zaibatsu were 'completely broken up'.[27] Two-fifths of all industrial securities went through the liquidation process. Given priority to buy stock, employees often did so with money borrowed from their companies. Next in line were residents of localities where the companies had production facilities while the remainder was put on the market for sale. The stock markets had been closed in 1945, so initial transfers were traded over-the-counter. Reopened in 1949, the stock markets operated as non-profit organisations that forbade blatantly speculative business such as futures trading.[28]

The zaibatsu dissolution process significantly diffused stockholding. But the reorganisation of ownership and control of corporations over the decade went much deeper. The forced resignation of some 5,000 executives between 1945 and 1948, which lowered the average age of top managers from 60 to 50, created opportunities for 'third-rank executives', so-called because they were plucked from the ranks of middle management to take leadership positions.[29] Commenting on these changes in stockholding and corporate control, Kosai has argued that 'nowhere was the separation of management and ownership more thoroughgoing than in post-war Japan'.[30]

---

[26] T. Adams and I. Hoshii, *A Financial History of the New Japan* (Tokyo, 1972), pp. 23–5; T. Bisson, *Zaibatsu Dissolution in Japan* (Westport, 1976); and E. Hadley, *Antitrust in Japan* (Berkeley, 1970).

[27] Adams and Hoshii, *Financial History*, p. 25.

[28] ibid., p. 26.

[29] H. Morikawa, 'Japan: increasing organizational capabilities of large industrial enterprises, 1880s–1980s', in A. Chandler, F. Amatori and T. Hikino (eds), *Big Business and the Wealth of Nations* (Cambridge, 1997).

[30] Y. Kosai, *The Era of High-Speed Growth* (Tokyo, 1986), p. 26.

During the late 1940s, however, the transformation of corporate control threatened to go much further. Dire economic conditions and SCAP democratisation
initiatives gave rise to a militant labour movement of white-collar (technical and
administrative) and blue-collar (operative) employees that wanted to take over idle
factories and put them into operation. In 1950, under economic conditions deliberately rendered more severe by the Occupation's anti-inflationary 'Dodge line',
companies, such as Toyota, Toshiba and Hitachi, sacked militant workers and
offered enterprise unionism to those remaining. Another opportunity for companies
to expel militants and introduce enterprise unionism came during the post-Korean
War recession of 1953.[31]

'Lifetime employment' was an entrenched institution by the mid-1950s – the
prime achievement of enterprise unionism – and was a system that gave white-
collar and blue-collar workers employment security to retirement at 55 or 60.
Foremen and supervisors were union members, as were all university-educated
personnel for at least the initial ten years of their employment before they made the
official transition into 'management'. Union officials, who were company
employees, held regularly scheduled conferences with management at different
levels of the enterprise to resolve issues concerning remuneration, work conditions,
work organisation, inter-departmental and inter-company transfers and production.[32] From the mid-1950s to the mid-1970s, only an estimated 35 per cent of
the participants in the labour force belonged to enterprise unions, but that proportion included virtually all male employees of the major enterprises central to
Japan's remarkable rise to industrial power. Through vertical keiretsu [enterprise
groups], moreover, the success of these dominant enterprises created high levels of
employment security even in those subsidiaries where enterprise unions were not
established.[33]

The Japanese system of organisational control was, and remains, an intensely
hierarchical structure, with ultimate strategic decision-making being the prerogative
of an executive board of top managers. This executive board is, however, made up
almost entirely of active insiders, most of whom have spent their entire careers with
the enterprise group.

Protecting this structure of organisational control in the postwar period has been
the system of cross-shareholding. Companies are willing to own other companies'
stock, despite low dividend yields and understandings that the shares are not to be
sold on the market. The cross-shareholding movement emerged during the early

[31] J. Moore, *Japanese Workers and the Struggle for Power, 1945–1947* (Madison, 1983); A. Gordon,
The Evolution of Labor Relations in Japan (Cambridge, 1985), pt 3; N. Hiwatari, Japanese corporate
governance reexamined, paper prepared for Conference on Employees and Corporate Governance,
Columbia University Law School, 22 Nov. 1996; and M. Cusumano, *The Japanese Automobile
Industry* (Cambridge, 1985).
[32] K. Shimokawa, *The Japanese Automobile Industry* (London, 1994), ch. 3.
[33] W. Lazonick, 'Cooperative employment relations in manufacturing and Japanese economic
growth', in J. Schor and J.-I. You (eds), *Capital, the State, and Labour* (Aldershot, 1995).

1950s to ensure that these industrial corporations would have the requisite financial commitment to re-equip their plants and retrain their workers.

Old zaibatsu relationships provided an initial foundation for cross-shareholding. After the zaibatsu dissolution, many of the former zaibatsu companies looked to the former zaibatsu banks, now known as 'main banks', to take the lead in providing loans. With the end of Allied occupation in 1952, these companies reformed themselves into kigyo shudan, or horizontal enterprise groups. The most powerful groups, Mitsui, Mitsubishi and Sumitomo, resumed the use of the traditional zaibatsu names. 'President's clubs' emerged at which the heads of these companies within a group met on a regular basis.

The main banks did not provide all the financing that the industrial enterprises in their groups required. Rather, their demonstrated commitment of financial resources to such companies provided a signal to other major banks, outside the particular enterprise group, that the financing of these industrial companies should be supported. During the early 1960s, three other leading banks – Fuji, Sanwa and Dai'ichi – also formalised their main bank relations with a growing number of companies to form the remainder of the six major kigyo shudan that exist in Japan today.[34]

The evolution of the main bank system and the cross-shareholding movement went hand in hand. To ensure that outsiders could not use stock ownership to gain access to company revenues needed for internal finance and to service bank loans, the banks and the industrial companies, within and across enterprise groups, took equities off the market by holding each other's shares. Increasingly, business relations among companies, be they industrial or financial, became cemented by cross-shareholding arrangements. Over time, an intricate web of cross-shareholding emerged. By 1955 cross-shareholding was at 25 per cent of outstanding stocks listed on the Tokyo Stock Exchange and, by 1960, at about 40 per cent. After declining slightly during the early 1960s, cross-shareholding gradually increased to over 60 per cent in the mid-1970s, largely as a response to Japan's increasing exposure to international capital markets. The current level of cross-shareholding is about 65 per cent.[35]

Besides the absorption of stock already outstanding on the market, the overall level of cross-shareholding during the 1950s and 1960s was increased by offering existing stockholders rights issues at par and stock dividends, as well as by distributing shares at par or free to other businesses. Only during the early 1970s did Japanese companies start to issue new shares at market prices, a practice that expanded considerably when the stock market was booming in the late 1980s. Even then,

---

[34] Mitsubishi Economic Research Institute, *Mitsui-Mitsubishi-Sumitomo* (Tokyo, 1955), p. 17; Hadley, *Antitrust*, ch. 1; and Morikawa, 'Increasing organizational capabilities'.

[35] J. Hodder and A. Tschoegl, 'Corporate finance in Japan', in S. Takagi (ed.), *Japanese Capital Markets* (Oxford, 1993), p. 150.

Japanese companies balanced market offerings with stock distributions to stable shareholders to maintain the level of cross-shareholding.[36]

Cross-shareholding enabled Japanese companies to limit cash dividends and retain earnings. During the 1950s, Japanese companies paid five yen on 50¥ par value shares and, thereafter, restricted nominal dividend increases. The dividend yield on corporate stock, valued at stock market prices, averaged seven per cent in 1955 but declined steadily over the ensuing decades to around four per cent during the 1960s, two per cent during the 1970s and under one per cent in the 1980s and 1990s.[37]

Meanwhile, during the 1950s and 1960s, companies' capital requirements far outran their internal sources of funds and they turned to the banks for what the Japanese call 'indirect finance'. Over the 1960s, bank borrowing by non-financial corporations was about 45 per cent of total funding sources, compared with about 15 per cent in the United States and Britain, and 21 per cent in Germany. By 1980, the aggregate debt-equity ratio for Japanese manufacturing corporations was 4 : 1, four times the ratio in the United States.[38] Such high levels of bank borrowing were only possible in a system in which the recognised role of the major city banks, the main banks of industrial companies, was to commit finance to industrial development. Supporting this financial commitment was the Bank of Japan, which, in a highly regulated environment, lent at low rates to the city banks so that they could, in turn, engage in 'overlending' funds to industrial enterprises.[39]

Just as before 1939, during the 'high-growth era' the state played an important supporting role in ensuring financial commitment to industry. For example, during the early 1950s, IBJ was reorganised as a non-governmental joint stock company that, after initially being supported by the Trust Fund (formerly the Deposit Bureau) of the Ministry of Finance, became integral to the main bank system. But, with the marked shift of enterprise strategies towards consumer markets rather than military demand, corporate enterprises rather than the state became even more important in allocating resources to industrial development. Critical to providing financial commitment for industrial development were lifetime employment and cross-shareholding, the institutional foundations of organisational control.

II

Like their Japanese counterparts, in recent decades the access of large German companies to committed finance for industrial development has proved to be more

---

[36] ibid., p. 154; Japan Securities Research Institute, *Securities Markets in Japan, 1986* (Tokyo, 1986), ch. 2; and idem, *Securities Markets in Japan, 1996* (Tokyo, 1996), p. 43.

[37] Tokyo Stock Exchange, *Fact Book, 1996* (Tokyo, 1996), p. 108.

[38] M. Aoki, H. Patrick and P. Sheard, 'The Japanese main bank system', in M. Aoki and H. Patrick (eds), *The Japanese Main Bank System* (Oxford, 1994), p. 37; and Hodder and Tschoegl, 'Corporate finance', p. 134.

[39] Y. Suzuki (ed.), *The Japanese Financial System* (Oxford, 1987).

enduring than in the United States. Throughout the postwar period, leading German industrial enterprises have financed their investments primarily with internal funds. The control of most of their voting shares by other German industrial enterprises and large German banks has helped to insulate incumbent management from public stockholders in search of high dividends and stock prices. A market for corporate control has yet to emerge in Germany.

The persistence of organisational control in German industry makes its mode of corporate governance much closer to that of Japan than the United States. In comparative perspective, however, the evolution to organisational control that Germany experienced over the course of this century renders its industrial enterprises currently more susceptible to market control than Japanese. In particular, alongside high wage costs, there is a movement in favour of financial liquidity in the German banking sector – a sector that historians of German industrial develop-ment have long viewed as a bastion of 'patient capital'.

In comparative perspective, the relationship between the Berlin credit banks or 'great banks' [Grossbanken] and major industrial enterprises is one of the most distinctive features of German industrialisation during the last decades of the nineteenth century. Especially after unification in 1871, these banks – A. Schaafhausen'scher Bankverein, Disconto-Gesellschaft, Darmstädter Bank and Berliner Handelsgesellschaft, established prior to unification, and Deutsche Bank, Commerz- und Disconto-Bank, Dresdner Bank and Nationalbank für Deutschland set up in the decade after it – acted as venture capitalists by providing financial commitment to developmental investments. In servicing the demands of industry, the banks advanced capital through current account arrangements that operated like a combined deposit account and line of credit.[40] In 1883, credit advanced by these banks through current accounts comprised 51 per cent of credit extended by the Grossbanken; in 1913 73 per cent.[41]

The Grossbanken initially set up technical departments and, later, trustee [Treuhand] societies to help them evaluate the organisational and technological capabilities of the companies that they financed. To remain close to strategic decision-making, they secured seats on the Aufsichtsräte [supervisory boards] of their client companies. The Grossbanken that came to dominate industrial finance during the 1880s and 1890s were those that played this venture capital role for the mining, machinery and electrical industries.

When these ventures became going concerns, the banks floated shares to enable these companies to repay bank loans.[42] These issues began the process through

---

[40] J. Riesser, *The German Great Banks* (Washington, 1931 edn), p. 266; and P. Barrett Whale, *Joint-Stock Banking in Germany* (London, 1930), pp. 37–8.

[41] E. Eistert and J. Ringel, 'Die Finanzierung des Wirtschaftlichen Wachstums durch die Banken', in W. Hoffmann (ed.), *Untersuchungen zum Wachstum der deutschen Wirtschaft* (Tübingen, 1971), p. 156.

[42] Riesser, *German Great Banks*, p. 368; Barrett Whale, *Joint-Stock Banking*, pp. 37–52; and H. Pohl, 'Forms and phases of industry finance up to the Second World War', *German Yearbook of Business History* (1984), pp. 80–1.

which ownership became separated from control in a number of leading industrial enterprises. The banks first took the securities on their own books and then distributed them when they deemed conditions favourable.[43] After flotations, the banks maintained a continuing relationship with joint stock companies [Aktiengesellschaft or AG] but generally ceased to finance their investments. Even for companies that had relied heavily on bank finance in their first stages and maintained current account links with the banks, retained earnings became the foundation of their continued growth as going concerns.[44]

The Grossbanken also provided financial commitment to proprietary enterprises in which the founding families had already financed the transition from new ventures to going concerns. In some cases, bank financing became important only when what had been a going concern found itself in financial distress.[45] In such cases, the Grossbanken sometimes used their influence to insist that the enterprise reorganise as an Aktiengesellschaft.[46] To the extent that these 'bail-outs' proved successful, as in bank-financed ventures, the industrial enterprises in question came to rely increasingly on retained earnings as a source of investment finance.[47]

In providing these financial services, the Grossbanken had a strong interest in institutional arrangements that bolstered financial commitment to industrial enterprises. The Grossbanken derived their revenues not only from current account transactions but also from their securities' businesses. Between 1885 and 1908 these contributed almost 25 per cent of the credit banks' gross profits. Industrial securities were an important component of this business – such shares accounted for 25 to 30

[43] Barrett Whale, *Joint-Stock Banking*, pp. 446–8; W. Feldenkirchen, 'Banking and economic growth', in W. Lee (ed.), *German Industry and German Industrialisation* (London, 1991), p. 131; and R. Tilly, 'An overview on the role of the large German banks up to 1914', in Y. Cassis (ed.), *Finance and Financiers in European history, 1880–1960* (Cambridge, 1992), p. 104.

[44] Pohl, 'Forms and phases'; Feldenkirchen, 'Banking and economic growth'; idem, 'The banks and the steel industry in the Ruhr', *German Yearbook of Business History* (1981); idem, 'Capital raised and its use by mechanical engineering firms in the nineteenth and early twentieth centuries', *German Yearbook of Business History* (1983); idem, 'Zur Finanzierung von Grossunternehmen in der chemischen und elektrotechnischen Industrie Deutschlands vor dem Ersten Weltkrieg', in R. Tilly (ed.), *Beitrage zur quantitativen vergleichenden Unternehmensgeschichte* (Stuttgart, 1985); W. G. Hoffmann, F. Grumbach and H. Hesse, *Das Wachstum der deutschen Wirtschaft seit der Mitte des 19 Jahrunderts* (Berlin, 1965), p. 273; R. Rettig, Investitions- und Finanzierungsverhalten deutscher Grossunternehmen, 1880–1911, Ph.D. thesis (University of Munster, 1978); R. Tilly, 'German banking, 1850–1914', *Journal of European Economic History*, 15 (1986); and V. Wellhöner, *Grossbanken und Grossindustrie im Kaiserreich* (Gottingen, 1989).

[45] ibid., pp. 97, 107, 121, 125–34; 155–7, 171–3, 217; and Feldenkirchen, 'Banking and economic growth', pp. 126–7.

[46] J. Kocka, 'Family and bureaucracy in German industrial management', *Business History Review*, 45 (1971), pp. 147–8; L. Gall, G. Feldman, H. James, C.-L. Holtfrerich and H. Buschgen, *The Deutsche Bank, 1870–1995* (London, 1995), pp. 37–45; and J. Edwards and S. Ogilvie, 'Universal banks and German industrialisation', *Economic History Review*, 49 (1996), pp. 439–40.

[47] Feldenkirchen, 'Banking and economic growth', p. 128.

per cent, and bonds seven to 12 per cent, of the market value of securities issued in Germany during the early 1900s.[48]

The Grossbanken took pains to build their reputations as issuers of high-quality securities. Known as Emissionskredit, this reputation facilitated flotations of their own and their clients' securities. A bank's current account relationship with an industrial enterprise gave it access to information for evaluating the enterprise's strength and, thus, its potential attractiveness to portfolio investors.[49] Their Emissionskredit was so valuable to the banks that they were inclined to repurchase shares that they had issued if there was a subsequent decline in stock prices.[50]

The Grossbanken placed securities with investors in their own deposit networks (a process in which Deutsche Bank took the lead), and worked hard to ensure that their depositors were content with the quality of their portfolios. Their success in building far-reaching networks of deposit branches allowed the Grossbanken to expand greatly their capacity to float securities.[51] Within these networks, the banks deliberately sought out those investors who would be stable stockholders. To attract them, the banks encouraged industrial companies to maintain stable dividends while recognising the need of industrial managers to retain earnings for reinvestment.[52]

The proxy voting system, or Depotstimmrecht, gave the Grossbanken significant influence over the allocation of corporate resources. It permitted banks to vote shares owned by bank customers who had placed them in trustee deposit accounts. Then, as now, the predominance of bearer shares gave the banks the right to vote securities that they held on deposit.[53] Further inducing the widespread deposit of shares was an exemption for shares held in trustee accounts from a stamp tax imposed by Bismarck on their transfer.[54] By encouraging stable shareholding and by coordinating the exchange of shares among their own customers, the Grossbanken largely usurped the business of the German stock exchanges.[55]

By creating a market in industrial shares and controlling the proxy votes as trustees of these shares, the Grossbanken contributed to the separation of ownership of stock from control over the allocation of corporate resources. As Germany's leading industrial enterprises evolved, the banks inevitably had to share control with

[48] Riesser, *German Great Banks*, pp. 334–6, 359–63, 465.
[49] ibid., pp. 5–6, 368; and Barrett Whale, *Joint-Stock Banking*, p. 121.
[50] Riesser, *German Great Banks*, pp. 247, 356.
[51] ibid., pp. 9–10, 608.
[52] W. Hoffmann, 'Die unverteilten Gewinne der Kapitalgesellschaften in Deutschland, 1871–1957', *Zeitschrift für die gesamte Staatswissenschaft*, 115 (1959); and Pohl, 'Forms and phases', p. 81.
[53] Riesser, *German Great Banks*, pp. 608–11; and Barrett Whale, *Joint-Stock Banking*, p. 54.
[54] Riesser, *German Great Banks*, pp. 324, 618–22.
[55] R. Hilferding, *Finance Capital* (London, 1981), pp. 107–50; Riesser, *German Great Banks*, pp. 370, 618–22; R. Tilly, 'Mergers, external growth, and finance in the development of large-scale enterprise in Germany, 1880–1913', *Journal of Economic History*, 42 (1982); and N. Reich, 'Auswirkungen der deutschen Aktienrechtsform von 1884 auf die Konzentration der deutschen Wirtschaft', in J. Kocka and N. Horn (eds), *Recht und Entwicklung der Grossunternehmen im 19. und frühen 20. Jahrhundert* (Gottingen, 1979).

salaried managers within industrial enterprises on whose administrative and technical experience they had to rely.[56] In many of the most successful companies by 1900, the autonomy of industrial managers in strategic decision-making had increased as the practice of maintaining an exclusive relationship with one bank, or Hausbank, had lost ground to multi-bank links. Some of these multiple financial linkages developed through mergers; others reflected the deliberate attempts of financially strong companies to restrict the influence of any one bank. More generally, leading industrial enterprises' high profitability led to enormous competition among banks to provide financial services to these companies.[57]

In a number of leading German enterprises, families rather than the Grossbanken ensured financial commitment. At companies like Siemens, Krupp, Deutscher Kaiser (Thyssen), Rheinische Stahlwerke (Wolff), Hörder Verein and Stollwerck, the founders and owners retained the majority of capital and laid down their firms' strategies.[58] In many of these family-owned or -controlled companies, the propensity to retain earnings would seem, in some cases, to have been heightened by the desire to·avoid bank influence.[59] In all of these companies, in contrast with the persistence of proprietary capitalism in Britain,[60] the key to the successful investment of retained earnings was the building of integrated organisations of salaried technical and administrative personnel.[61]

The financial independence of leading industrial enterprises was strengthened further after the First World War. Expansion for war production, subsequent military defeat, the loss of international markets and the victors' demands for reparations had a crippling effect on the German economy. Yet enterprises that before 1914 had invested in successful organisations entered the Weimar Republic in relatively powerful positions. They had been accorded preferential treatment in the award of contracts by wartime military procurement offices. The large profits realised from those contracts, as well as their already substantial accumulated earnings, provided

[56] J. Kocka, 'The rise of the modern industrial enterprise in Germany', in A. Chandler and Herman Daems (eds), *Managerial Hierarchies* (Cambridge, 1980), p. 92; idem, 'Entrepreneurs and managers in German industrialisation', in P. Mathias and M. Postan (eds), *Cambridge Economic History of Europe*, 7, pt 1 (Cambridge, 1973); and Barrett Whale, *Joint-Stock Banking*, pp. 55–65.

[57] ibid., pp. 55–7; Edwards and Ogilvie, 'Universal banks', p. 440; Feldenkirchen, 'Banking and economic growth', p. 133; Kocka, 'Rise of modern industrial enterprise', pp. 89–98; Pohl, 'Forms and phases', p. 82; and Wellhöner, *Grossbanken*, pp. 236–47.

[58] J. Brockstedt, 'Family enterprise and the rise of large-scale enterprise in Germany, 1871–1914', in A. Okochi and S. Yasuoka (eds), *Family Business in the Era of Industrial Growth* (Tokyo, 1984), pp. 237–67; Kocka, 'Family and bureaucracy'; idem, 'Entrepreneurs and managers', pp. 578–89; and H. Pohl, 'On the history of organisation and management in large German enterprises since the nineteenth century', *German Yearbook of Business History* (1982), pp. 439–71.

[59] Feldenkirchen, 'Banking and economic growth', p. 127.

[60] Lazonick and O'Sullivan, 'Finance and industrial development'.

[61] Kocka, 'Rise of modern industrial enterprise'; A. Chandler, *Scale and Scope* (Cambridge, 1990), pp. 393–587; Brockstedt, 'Family enterprise'; and Pohl, 'History of organisation'.

investment funds or at least a capacity to borrow from abroad at a time when the rest of industry was financially constrained.[62]

In the flight into fixed assets induced by the unprecedented inflation during the early Weimar years, many of these powerful enterprises converted their access to finance into an enormous expansion of their productive capacity. They also used these resources to take participations in other enterprises, thus creating industrial concerns [Konzerne]. These were organisations in which a holding company held long-term shareholdings in a number of member firms that maintained their legal identities but combined some of their resources and coordinated certain dimensions of their activities. The holding office's task was to encourage an integration of the financial and investment strategies of these companies.[63]

Many of the amalgamations were financially motivated and resulted in the creation of huge empires whose productive activities were unrelated or distantly related.[64] Some collapsed or ran into serious financial difficulties with the end of the inflation and the stabilisation of the currency in 1924/25.[65] Industrial combinations gained new justification in the aftermath of monetary stabilisation as the Rationalisierung (literally, rationalisation) of industry, undertaken by major enterprises to control capacity and output, gained momentum.[66] The process of building these structures created a dense web of interlocking shareholdings and directorates among companies. As a result, there was a substantial increase in the size of securities portfolios maintained by industrial corporations: from ten per cent of net assets in 1913 to 30 per cent in the 1920s and 35–40 per cent in the 1930s.[67] By 1927 nearly all of the top 100 German companies were Konzerne.[68]

The postwar inflation, the profitability of financial transactions associated with conglomeration and rationalisation as well as increasing competition from savings, cooperative and foreign banks shifted the Grossbanken's business interests.[69] Financial liquidity – the generation of high returns from existing assets – became relatively more attractive during the 1920s than financial commitment, the provision of services promoting industrial development. To cope with inflation, many of the Grossbanken turned from their traditional credit businesses to speculation in securi-

---

[62] H. Turner, *German Big Business and the Rise of Hitler* (Oxford, 1985), pp. 10–11; and Pohl, 'Forms and phases', p. 85.

[63] R. Liefmann, *Cartels, Concerns and Trusts* (New York, 1977), pp. 225–32.

[64] ibid., p. 249; and Pohl, 'Forms and phases', pp. 86–7.

[65] Liefmann, *Cartels*, pp. 259–61; and W. Feldenkirchen, 'Concentration in German industry, 1870–1939', in H. Pohl and W. Treue (eds), *The Concentration Process in the Entrepreneurial Economy Since the Late Nineteenth Century* (Stuttgart, 1988), pp. 126–7.

[66] H. Levy, *Industrial Germany* (Cambridge, 1935), pp. 9, 10, 206–7.

[67] Tilly, 'Mergers, external growth, and finance', p. 160.

[68] H. Siegrist, 'Deutsche Grossunternehmung vom späten 19 Jahrhundert bis zur Weimarer Republik', *Geschichte und Gesellschaft*, 6 (1980), p. 87.

[69] T. Balderston, 'German banking between the wars', *Business History Review*, 65 (1991); and G. Feldman, 'Banks and banking in Germany after the First World War', in Cassis, *Finance and Financiers*.

ties and foreign exchange. The Grossbanken made substantial paper profits during the inflation and greatly increased their dividends. They also extended their business activities by buying up provincial banks at a relatively low cost.[70]

The acceptance of the Dawes Plan and the return to gold restored international confidence in the German economy, with high interest rates attracting considerable capital imports, especially from the United States. The Grossbanken, meanwhile, had lost a substantial proportion of their deposits because of the inflation.[71] Their securities' business suffered as the domestic capital market languished following stabilisation. Leading industrial enterprises increasingly bypassed the Grossbanken by raising money through foreign flotations underwritten by foreign banks.[72] The Grossbanken also faced increased competition from other domestic banks, in particular the deregulated savings banks. From the late 1920s, in the face of falling profit margins, the Grossbanken financed riskier businesses, thus setting the stage for the 1931 German banking crisis.

Meanwhile, within industry, conglomeration and rationalisation resulted in an overcentralisation of strategic control.[73] Increasingly, control was managerial rather than familial as dominant enterprises combined and bought out smaller companies. When the Nazis rose to power, the highly concentrated industrial sector provided ready foundations for its coordination with the Third Reich to mobilise the economy for war.[74]

Under the Nazi militarisation programme, financial commitment became paramount. The Nazis permitted profits to grow even as they controlled wages through a tight incomes policy. By 1938 profits were 105 per cent higher than they had been in 1928 whereas total wages were three per cent lower.[75] To ensure that profits would be invested in productive capacity, the Nazis passed a Company Law in 1937 that formally recognised the separation of ownership and control that had already largely taken place in industry. This Act strengthened the position of incumbent managers against what were described as 'the mass of irresponsible shareholders who largely lacked the necessary insight into the position of business'.[76] The Nazis also introduced a number of legal and taxation provisions that restricted dividend distributions and favoured the retention of earnings. From 1933 to 1938 retained profits on lucrative government contracts financed well over 60 per cent of the increase in industrial capital with the rest coming from intercorporate stock issues. The Nazis also strengthened the linkages among companies through their policy of enforced

[70] A. Weber, *Depositbanken und Spekulationsbanken: Ein Vergleich deutschen und englischen Bankwesens* (Munich, 1938), p. 147; Barrett Whale, *Joint-Stock Banking*, p. 238; and Feldman, 'Banks and banking', pp. 246–7.

[71] C.-L. Holtfrerich, *The German Inflation, 1914–1923* (Berlin, 1986), pp. 271–8.

[72] Balderston, 'German banking', p. 572.

[73] Levy, *Industrial Germany*, pp. 10, 227; and Pohl, 'History of organisation', pp. 113–21.

[74] D. Abraham, *The Collapse of the Weimar Republic* (Princeton, 1981); and Turner. *German Big Business*.

[75] Hoffmann et al., *Das Wachstum*, pp. 506–9.

[76] F. Neumann, *Behemoth* (New York, 1944), p. 288.

cartelisation followed by their system of main committees and industrial rings.[77] Especially during the early 1940s, they transformed the economy's traditional sectors by forcing many smaller enterprises to integrate their industrial operations with those of the larger combines, which, through stockholdings, often assumed formal control.[78]

Immediately after the war, in reaction to the abuse of the concentrated power of managers during the Nazi period, there was considerable political support for integrating workers into the governance process in industrial enterprises. Although falling far short of its ambitions, the postwar movement for industrial democracy made some progress in attaining codetermination [Mitbestimmung] at the level of the Aufsichtsrat in enterprises.[79] Passed only under the threat of a major strike, the Codetermination Act of 1951 mandated parity of representation for workers on the supervisory boards of all coal, iron, and steel companies [Montanmitbestimmung], although, in other industries, workers were denied equal representation. The Works Councils Act of 1952 obligated enterprises with more than 500 employees to reserve only one-third of the supervisory board seats for employee representatives. The Codetermination Act of 1976, however, decreed that all companies with more than 2,000 employees increase employee representation on their supervisory boards from one-third to one-half of the seats. Even then, in the event of a tied vote, a double vote was granted to the chairman of the board, who was required by law to be a shareholder, thus tilting the balance of control of the supervisory board firmly against employees.[80]

Notwithstanding the restrictions on the control that employees can exercise through supervisory board participation, in historical and comparative perspective, codetermination has extended organisational control in industry beyond the narrow confines of managerial control. In the postwar economy, an institutional basis for organisational control has also emerged through works councils at the plant level. The Works Constitution Act of 1952 mandated the formation of works councils [Betriebsräte], comprising representatives of blue-collar and white-collar workers, with the purpose of giving labour the right to participate in, and receive information about, the management of the shop floor.

In contrast to the codetermination of supervisory boards, the works councils were a conservative initiative, designed to some extent to curb the excesses of unaccountable managerial control. But, in being granted exclusive domain over labour representation at the plant level, they were made formally independent of

---

[77] Pohl, 'Forms and phases', p. 91; and Neumann, *Behemoth*, p. 593.

[78] F. McKitrick, The stabilization of the Mittelstand: artisans in Germany from National Socialism to the Federal Republic, 1939–1953, Ph.D. thesis (Columbia University, 1994).

[79] A. Markovits, *The Politics of the West German Trade Unions* (Cambridge, 1986); and W. Müller-Jentsch, 'Germany', in J. Rogers and W. Streeck (eds), *Works Councils* (Chicago, 1995).

[80] W. Streeck, 'Codetermination', in B. Wilperte and A. Sorge (eds), *International Yearbook of Organizational Democracy* (1984); and T. Raiser, 'The theory of enterprise law in the Federal Republic of Germany', *American Journal of Comparative Law*, 36 (1988).

the unions. Intended to serve as a counterweight to the unions' political power, the role of works councils was to cooperate with management for 'the benefit of the employees and of the establishment'.[81] Fearing that they would transform labour representation into a system of 'yellow' or enterprise unions that would ultimately undermine labour's political power, the unions stridently opposed the introduction of works councils.[82] Notwithstanding their initial objections, however, the unions established close links with works councils so that by the early 1970s more than 80 per cent of works councillors were union representatives.[83]

Compared with the governance structures that existed until 1939, the works councils, in combination with codetermination on the supervisory boards, have been central to a shift away from uncontested managerial control towards contested organisational control. Sustaining organisational control in the Federal Republic of Germany (FRG) has been the organisational integration of managers and workers into collective and cumulative learning processes that have generated innovation and international competitive advantage.[84]

Especially in comparison with post-1945 organisational control in Japan, organisational control in Germany has been contested because prime vestiges of prewar managerial control – namely, bank-enterprise relations and inter-company share-holding networks – remain strong. Most of the major German industrial enterprises on which the post-1945 economy has relied to undertake industrial investment are those that became dominant before 1939. With defeat, the declared intention of the Allied Occupation forces, particularly American, was to break up the concentration of economic power in industry and banking and replace it with market control. But the onset of the Cold War, and the perceived importance of the West German economy as a bulwark against Soviet power, undermined the commitment to this path. Despite the dissolution of industrial trusts, such as I. G. Farben, the constituent companies often re-emerged as dominant autonomous enterprises and established financial links with one another.

In general, inter-company links remained extremely strong within the post-1945 economy; in 1960 non-financial enterprises accounted for just under 36 per cent of total assets held in the form of shares, making them by far the largest stockholder group. Although strictly comparable figures are not available, the level of inter-company stockholding would seem to have at least been maintained; in 1984 non-financial enterprises held just over 36 per cent of shares issued by enterprises.[85]

---

[81] Works Constitution Act, s2(1).

[82] Markovits, *Politics of West German Trade Unions*, pp. 61–83; H. Wiedemann, 'Codetermination by workers in German enterprises', *American Journal of Comparative Law*, 28 (1980); and Müller-Jentsch, 'Germany', p. 54.

[83] K. Thelen, *Union of Parts* (Ithaca, 1992), p. 80; and Müller-Jentsch, 'Germany', p. 57.

[84] W. Lazonick and M. O'Sullivan, 'Organization, finance and international competition', *Industrial and Corporate Change*, 5 (1996).

[85] J. Edwards and K. Fischer, *Banks, Finance, and Investment in Germany* (Cambridge, 1994), pp. 180, 182.

Although much less important as a stockholding group than non-financial enterprises, banks and insurance companies also held significant equity participations in corporations during the postwar period – around eight to ten per cent in 1984.[86] A study of bank holdings in 74 large enterprises in 1974/75 showed that Deutsche Bank, Dresdner Bank and Commerzbank collectively accounted for two-thirds of bank participations and were, thus, among the most influential stockholders in the economy. The most important stockholder, however, appears to be Allianz AG, the FRG's largest insurance company.[87]

In 1973 companies in which the share of the largest stockholder was at least 25 per cent accounted for more than 70 per cent of the market value of the equity capital of listed AGs.[88] But a high proportion of major stockholders are themselves companies. A study of the 300 largest industrial enterprises in 1972 showed that, classified in terms of direct ownership, 'owner-controlled' companies accounted for 75 per cent of the sample's aggregate turnover. In contrast, when categorised in terms of ultimate ownership, manager-controlled firms accounted for the majority of total turnover (65 per cent) and owner-controlled firms for only 35 per cent.[89]

The striking difference between direct and ultimate ownership largely stems from the most important companies in the inter-company shareholding networks being among the most widely held in Germany. But even these have, over the postwar period, been insulated from market control. Most domestic shares are held on deposit by the private banking sector and the vast majority are deposited with the 'Big Three' banks.[90] The banks exercise proxy voting rights for these shares, subject to certain requirements for stockholder approval. In 1974 banks controlled an average of 57 per cent of the total votes, of which only seven per cent came from the banks' own stockholdings. The remainder were proxy votes that the banks exercised on behalf of their depositors. In the ten largest AGs by turnover, the banks controlled a total of 67 per cent of the votes compared with 43 per cent for the AGs ranked from 51 to 100.[91] The big banks are themselves among the most diffusely held AGs and the proxy voting system allows them to control each other's shareholders' meetings. In 1986 Deutsche Bank controlled 47 per cent, Dresdner Bank 47 per cent, and Commerzbank 35 per cent, of their own votes and, in combination, they exercised 60 to 64 per cent of the votes of each bank.[92]

[86] ibid.
[87] Gessler Commission, 'Grunsatzfragen der Kreditwirtschaft', *Scheifenreihe des Bundesministerium der Finanzen*, 28 (1979), p. 467; and E. Owen Smith, *The German Economy* (London, 1994), p. 338.
[88] B. Iber, 'Zur Entwicklung der Aktionarsstruktur in der Bundesrepublik Deutschland, 1963–1983', *Zeitschrift für Betriebswirtschaft*, 55 (1985), p. 1111.
[89] Edwards and Fischer, *Banks, Finance and Investment*, p. 188; and G. Schreyogg and H. Steinmann, 'Zur Trennung von Eigentum und Verfugungsgewalt', *Zeitschrift für Betriebswirtschaft*, 51 (1981).
[90] Smith, *German Economy*, p. 359.
[91] Monopolkommission, *Hauptgutachten II* (Baden-Baden, 1978), p. 199.
[92] A. Gottschalk, 'Der Stimmrechtseinfluss der Banken in den Aktionarsversammlungen von Grossunternehmen', *WSI Mitteilungen*, 5 (1988).

The proxy voting system gives banks a preponderant influence on decisions taken at shareholder meetings, including election of supervisory boards, of diffusely-held companies. In 1974 banks were directly represented on the supervisory boards of 75 of the largest 100 AGs, with 179 seats in total being occupied by the banks – 102 by the big banks and 55 by Deutsche Bank alone.[93]

In using this power, the postwar banks appear to have acquiesced in the system that bolstered organisational control for the sake of industrial development. With some exceptions, they were content to leave strategic control in the hands of industrial managers so long as they made decisions that seemed to advance the competitive position of their enterprises.[94] In the highly regulated financial system within which the big banks were accorded the scope to develop strong positions in a number of attractive market segments, they had stronger incentives to support organisational control in the corporate economy than to confront it. They had a significant interest in the continued success of the FRG's leading industrial enterprises since they represented a lucrative source of revenues for their short-term lending, export financing and corporate financial services businesses.[95]

The access of the major industrial enterprises to internally generated funds undermines the notion that uncontested bank control of industry was a systematic feature of the postwar West German economy.[96] As had been the case before the war, soon after internal funds became the predominant source of investment finance for the major industrial enterprises.[97] As early as the 1950s, internally-generated funds financed more than 75 per cent of net investment. Focused on the reconstruction of their own organisations and asset bases, the limited funds that the banks had available to lend to industry tended to be short-term loans. Sometimes companies used these funds for long-term purposes, but the banks attempted to limit this behaviour to control their maturity risk. The long-term finance provided by the banking system was ultimately funded from the Marshall Counterpart Fund and channelled to the banks by the Kreditanstalt für Wiederaufbau [Reconstruction Loan Corporation].[98] The banks bore the credit risks of the loans that they made out of these monies – loans that were primarily directed towards bottleneck investments in the economy.[99]

Internal finance remained important throughout the entire period from 1950 to 1989. To the extent that large companies have sought access to external finance, the preferred source was bank loans rather than equity or bond issues, with long-term

[93] Monopolkommission, *Hauptgutachten*.
[94] K. Dyson, 'The state, banks and industry', in A. Cox (ed.), *State, Finance and Industry* (Brighton, 1986), p. 139.
[95] Gall et al., *Deutsche Bank*, pp. 610–56.
[96] Dyson, 'State, banks and industry'; J. Esser, 'Bank power in West Germany revised', *West European Politics*, 13 (1990), pp. 17–32; and Edwards and Fischer, *Banks, Finance and Investment*, pp. 228–40.
[97] H. Wallich, *Mainsprings of the German Revival* (New Haven, 1955), p. 166.
[98] A. Shonfield, *Modern Capitalism* (Oxford, 1965), p. 276.
[99] ibid., p. 279; and W. Abelshauser, 'West German economic recovery, 1945–1951', *The Three Banks Review*, 135 (1982).

debt accounting for 12 per cent of the net sources of investment finance and equity issues a tiny 1.5 per cent.[100] In the period 1971 and 1985, internal funds comprised 88 per cent of the net sources of investment finance for large manufacturing AGs and long-term loans less than two per cent, compared with 73 per cent and 14 per cent in the case of producing enterprises.[101] German enterprises – large firms as well as the producing sector as a whole – are as reliant and, if anything, more reliant on internal funds as a source of investment finance than their counterparts in other advanced industrial economies.[102]

Codetermination of supervisory boards, works councils, inter-company share-holding and the banks' relationships with industry as shareholders and in exercising depositors' proxies make it very difficult to pinpoint exactly where control has resided in major German enterprises in the postwar decades. But, whatever the variations in corporate control across particular enterprises, these institutions ensured that control over the allocation of corporate resources was an organisational phenomenon in the FRG in the postwar period. Market control may well, as we will suggest in the conclusion, be looming on the horizon for industry but, into the 1990s, it has been a relatively unknown phenomenon in postwar Germany.

III

During the 1990s, in both Japan and Germany, organisational control remains intact. Major industrial enterprises maintain control over the allocation of corporate revenues and returns, and the institutions of corporate governance enable workers as well as managers to influence the resource-allocation process. The persistence of organisational control in these two national economies is in marked contrast to the evolution to market control in both the United States and Britain.[103] The roots of organisational control in both Japan and Germany since 1945 can be found in the rise of managerial control in major industrial enterprises during the half-century before the war as well as the elaboration of the Japanese and German banking systems to support financial commitment.

Nevertheless, in the aftermath of defeat in 1945, the transformation to organisational control was much more thoroughgoing in Japan than in Germany. The strategy and structure of the Japanese banking system had been and remained much more explicitly devoted to providing financial commitment for industrial development. Similarly, Japanese labour had been and remained much more tied to the fate of particular enterprises.

[100] Edwards and Fischer, *Banks, Finance and Investment*, pp. 49–70.
[101] ibid., p. 127.
[102] C. Mayer and I. Alexander, 'Banks and securities markets', *Journal of the Japanese and International Economies*, 4 (1990); B. Hall, 'Corporate restructuring and investment horizons in the United States, 1976–1987', *Business History Review*, 68 (1994); and J. Corbett, 'The financing of industry, 1970–1989', *Journal of the Japanese and International Economies*, 10 (1996).
[103] Lazonick and O'Sullivan, 'Finance and industrial development'.

During the 1990s, however, even within Japan, there are interests who, for the sake of financial liquidity, would favour a transition from organisational control to market control. The 1980s saw a considerable reduction in the role of Japanese banks in supporting financial commitment, as highly successful industrial enterprises used retained earnings and stock issues to amortise debt. To secure their own futures, Japanese banks are likely to become more engaged in providing financial services that promote financial liquidity. In addition, as manifested in rising government deficits, the nation faces a major challenge in financing the retirement of an ageing population. The apparent success of market control in augmenting the returns to savers in the United States and Britain may become increasingly attractive to the Japanese.

In contrast to their Japanese counterparts, German labour and German finance have pursued their interests through organisations that have had more autonomy from the strategies and structures of industrial enterprises. During the 1990s, Germany has faced severe competitive challenges, particularly from the Japanese, in many of the high-quality industrial markets in which its enterprises were previously unrivalled. But German labour has been loath to give up the high wages and low working hours that enterprises had been able to afford before their industrial dominance was challenged. For their part, especially in the postwar era, the business activities of German banks were much more diversified beyond industrial finance than the activities of Japanese financial institutions. Given the business opportunities available in the global economy, the competitive challenges facing German industry and the reluctance of labour to renegotiate wages and work hours, German banks have an interest in viewing the revenues and assets of German industrial enterprises as sources of financial liquidity rather than financial commitment. Should German labour and German finance insist on pursuing their own independent strategies in extracting returns from industrial enterprises, German corporate governance may well dissipate into a 'stakeholder economy' that undermines the foundations of organisational control.[104]

---

[104] M. O'Sullivan, 'Sustainable prosperity, corporate governance, and innovation in Europe', in J. Smith and J. Michie (eds), *Innovation, Cooperation and Growth* (Oxford, forthcoming).

[19]

Cambridge Journal of Economics 1998, 22, 117–136

Do employment and income security cause unemployment? A comparative study of the US and the E-4

Robert Buchele and Jens Christiansen*

High unemployment in Europe has led many economists and policy-makers to praise rapid job creation and low unemployment in the US and to credit its relatively unregulated labour markets for this success. We question the implication that Europe should adopt US-style labour market deregulation and flexibility. A detailed examination of the US and E-4 (French, German, Italian, and UK) data reveals almost no difference in unemployment rates for 'prime-age' males but large ones for other demographic groups both within and among all countries (and not just between the US and the E-4). We also assess the impact of various employment regulations, wage-setting institutions, and income security policies on E-4 unemployment. We conclude that the evidence is mixed, and, more importantly, that the same institutions which may raise unemployment in Europe are also contributing to its more rapid earnings growth and greater earnings equality relative to the US. Thus, European labour market deregulation would at best be a very mixed blessing.

1. Introduction

A spectre is haunting Europe—the spectre of unemployment. The drastic deterioration in European employment performance over the past three-and-a-half decades is amply demonstrated by the average unemployment rate of the four largest European economies (the E-4): France, Germany, Italy, and the UK. Unemployment in these countries has quadrupled since the early 1960s and doubled over the past two decades. What makes this development even more haunting is the fact that no reversal of the trend is in sight.

Labour economists and politicians concerned about high unemployment in Europe often look to the achievements of comparatively unregulated US labour markets: rapid job creation and relatively low unemployment. This paper calls into question the implication that US-style labour market flexibility is the answer for Europe. The paper is divided into two parts: first, we examine the employment/unemployment performance of the E-4 and the US, considering various alternative measures of joblessness. Second, we evaluate the role of widely varying labour market institutions and regulations in shaping equally widely varying labour market outcomes among these countries.

Manuscript received 10 February 1997; final version received 4 July 1997.

* Smith College and Mount Holyoke College, respectively. We should like to thank Francesca Bettio, Sam Rosenberg, and an anonymous referee for very detailed and helpful comments on an earlier version of this paper.

118   R. Buchele and J. Christiansen

2. Joblessness: a closer look at the record

In this section, we argue that: (1) differences between US and European unemployment performance in the 1980s and 1990s are not as great as commonly believed; (2) important differences *among* European countries are often overlooked in comparisons *between* the US and Europe; and (3) within countries, unemployment rates vary markedly across age-gender categories, with generally lower rates (and smaller US–European differences) for 'prime-age' (i.e., 25–54-year-old) males than for other groups.[1]

2.1. Unemployment rates

Table 1 presents average unemployment rates for the E-4 and the US for selected periods from the early 1960s to the present. A comparison of alternative OECD measures shows rates based on 'commonly used definitions' in Part (a) that are somewhat lower for Italy and the UK than the 'standardised' rates in Part (b) and almost identical for France and the US.[2] The biggest difference between Part (a) and Part (b)—the unemployment rates for Germany in the last period—is due to the differential treatment of eastern Germany after unification. These alternative unemployment estimates suggest that if unification had not occurred, there might have been little change in Germany's average unemployment between 1980–87 and 1988–96.[3] The US Bureau of Labor Statistics publishes international labour force statistics, applying US concepts. Except for Italy, average unemployment rates based on this concept are similar to the OECD standardised rates. Therefore, only Italy's unemployment rate, according to US definitions, is reported in Part (c) of Table 1.[4]

The performance of the E-4 is summarised (for comparison to the US) in the last rows of Parts (a) and (b) of Table 1. By either definition, E-4 unemployment was about two percentage points below the US in the 1960s and 1970s and about three percentage points above the US in the late 1980s to mid-1990s period. This reversal in the relative unemployment performance of the US vs. the E-4, along with much higher long-term unemployment in Europe, is widely cited as evidence of the relative success of the United States' 'unregulated' labour markets compared to Europe's 'overregulated' labour markets.

Table 2 breaks down the overall unemployment rates by age and gender for the periods 1980–87 and 1988–95. What stands out here is the great variation across age-gender groups within countries and across countries within age-gender groups. Thus, we identify

---

[1] They also vary strongly between regions (particularly in the case of Italy and the UK), but we do not deal with that variation in this paper.

[2] The term 'commonly used definitions' means that these are 'the most commonly cited' and 'frequently published' unemployment statistics (OECD, *Economic Outlook*, no. 57, 1995, p. A77), not that they are based on a common (or uniform) definition of unemployment. The OECD standardised rates are designed to improve comparability across countries (see OECD, 1985; OECD, *Employment Outlook*, 1987, ch. 5).

[3] Part (a) shows a 1·4 percentage point increase in unemployment in Germany between 1980–87 and 1988–96. Part (b), which excludes eastern Germany, shows no change between the two periods. Neither table represents Germany's employment performance in the 1990s entirely fairly relative to the earlier periods. On the one hand, the rise in unemployment shown in Part (a) is largely a consequence of competitive shocks in the former East German economy after unification. On the other hand, the unchanged unemployment shown in Part (b) does mask a rise in unemployment that would have occurred in the absence of the initial stimulus that unification provided to the former West German economy.

[4] Until 1993, Italy included the 'inactive unemployed' in its unemployment count. The BLS excludes anyone who has not actively looked for work during the past 30 days, so the adjustment to the US concept significantly reduces the Italian rates. See Sorrentino (1993, 1995).

Do employment and income security cause unemployment?   119

Table 1. *Unemployment rates (%)*

(a) Rates based on commonly used definitions (OECD)

	1974–79	1980–87	1988–96
France	4·5	8.8	10·7
Germany*	3·0	6·7	8.1
Italy	6·4	8.0	10·3
United Kingdom	4·1	9·5	8.1
United States	6·8	7·8	6·1
E-4	4·5	8.7	9·3

*All figures (unless otherwise indicated) are for western Germany up to (and including) 1990 and for unified Germany since 1991.
Source: OECD, *Economic Outlook*, no. 60, December 1996, Annex Table 21.

(b) Standardised rates (OECD) (%)

	1961–73	1974–79	1980–87	1988–96
France	1·9	4·5	8.9	10·7
Germany#	0·8	3·2	5·9	5·9
Italy	4·7	6·6	9·1	10·9
United Kingdom	2·8	5·0	10·5	8.7
United States	4·8	6·7	7·6	6·1
E-4	2·6	4·8	8.6	8.8

#For western Germany only.
Sources: First two columns: Maddison, 1991, Table C.6.(b). Last two columns: OECD, *Economic Outlook*, no. 60, December 1996, Annex Table 22 (with World Wide Web Update for 1996) and OECD, *Economic Surveys, Germany*, 1996, Table M.

(c) Rates based on approximations of US Concepts (BLS) (%)

	1975–79	1980–87	1988–96
Italy	4·0	6·0	9·2

Source: US Department of Labor, Bureau of Labor Statistics, *Monthly Labor Review*, December 1990, Table 49, and April 1996, Table 47.

specific 'pockets' of high or low unemployment in particular countries: except in Germany, youth unemployment is much higher than adult unemployment. In France and Italy, female unemployment is much higher than male unemployment. Prime-age male unemployment is relatively low everywhere, being significantly above 6% only in France (last period) and the UK. We conclude from this quick look at the data that it is incorrect to generalise about 'Europe's unemployment problem' relative to the US. Rather, high unemployment is a problem confronting particular demographic groups in specific countries. Ranking these five countries by their unemployment rates for each of the 12 age-gender categories in Table 2, the US ranks lowest in four (three of those concern women), while Germany has the lowest youth unemployment, and Italy does best for older workers.

120   R. Buchele and J. Christiansen

Table 2. *Unemployment rates (OECD, commonly used definitions) by age group (%)*

(a) Men

	1980–87			1988–95		
	15–24 yrs	25–54 yrs	55–64 yrs	15–24 yrs	25–54 yrs	55–64 yrs
France	16·2	5·0	6·2	18.3	7·3	7·0
Germany	7·9	5·2	8.4	6·4**	5·4**	9·4**
Italy	25·6	3·2	1·8	27·7	5·7	2·8
United Kingdom	19·0*	9·5*	10·3*	16·0	8.1	10·2
United States	15·3	6·1	4·5	13·0	5·1	4·3
E-4	17·2	5·7	6·7	17·1	6·6	7·4

(b) Women

	1980–87			1988–95		
	15–24 yrs	25–54 yrs	55–64 yrs	15–24 yrs	25–54 yrs	55–64 yrs
France	26·7	8.5	7·1	27·1	11·5	7·8
Germany	9·3	7·0	9·0	7·1**	8·4**	12·9**
Italy	37·1	9·9	4·0	37·8	13·4	4·2
United Kingdom	16·3*	9·4*	6·6*	11·2	6·5	5·1
United States	13·7	8.7	6·7	11·6	5·0	3·4
E-4	22·4	8.7	6·7	20·8	10·0	7·5

*Rates are for the years 1984–87 only. **Rates are for the years 1988–94.
Source: OECD, *Labour Force Statistics 1974–94*, 1996.

2.2. Some broader measures of unemployment

Given the conceptual ambiguities about who is unemployed and differences among countries in how those ambiguities are resolved (e.g., the treatment of discouraged and part-time workers), it may be useful to compare countries' *non-employment* rates. Non-employment includes everyone without a job, thereby avoiding the distinction between unemployment and inactivity (or being out of the labour force).[1] For the countries in our sample there is only one demographic group for which there is no socially or culturally legitimate reason to be non-employed: prime-age males. Youths may be in school, older workers may be retired, women may be at home with children (with husbands who earn enough to support their family with one job). Only for prime-age males can we claim that a lower non-employment rate is unambiguously better than a higher one.

Average non-employment rates for prime-age and older males are reported for the periods 1980–87 and 1988–95 in Table 3. In the 1980–87 period, the US had the second highest prime-age male non-employment rate among our five countries. But while its non-employment rate remained almost constant (and the UK's fell slightly) between 1980–87 and 1988–95, France, Italy, and Germany's all rose substantially. However, even in the later period, both France and Italy still had lower prime-age male non-employment rates than the US, and so did western Germany (figure not reported).

Non-employment among 55–64-year-old men in the 1988–95 period varies from below 40% in the US and Italy to almost 60% in France. These differences largely reflect differences among countries in opportunities for older job losers to choose early

[1] Even here, some ambiguity remains in the case of involuntary part-time employment. In Germany, for example, workers with part-time jobs who would like full-time work are counted as unemployed (Abraham and Houseman, 1993, p. 48, fn.).

Do employment and income security cause unemployment?   121

Table 3. *Male non-employment rates (%)*

	1980–87		1988–95	
	25–54 yrs	55–64 yrs	25–54 yrs	55–64 yrs
France	8.8	47·9	11·7	58.6
Germany	10·6	42·2	12·0**	49·8**
Italy	7·1	32·5	11·3	38.9
United Kingdom	13·9*	38.5*	13·6	40·8
United States	11·8	33·9	11·9	36·1
E-4	10·1	40·3	12·2	47·0

* Rates are for 1984–87 only. **Rates are for 1988–94 only. The non-employment rate is the ratio of the non-employed (inactive and unemployed) to the total population.
Source: Calculations by authors from data in OECD, *Labour Force Statistics 1974–94*, 1996.

retirement. In France, for instance, early retirement 'bridging pensions' appeared in the 1970s, and the normal age of entitlement to a public pension was reduced from 65 to 60 in 1983 (OECD, *Employment Outlook*, 1992, p. 208). In Germany, in the mid-1980s, the duration of unemployment benefits was gradually increased to as much as 32 months for those aged 54 and above, and the obligation of those aged 58 and over to register themselves as active job-seekers in order to receive benefits was removed. Those aged 57 1/2 or older at the time of job loss retain the right to an unemployment allowance until they reach 65, when they become eligible for a public pension (OECD, *Employment Outlook*, 1992, p. 212). In Italy, the normal retirement age is 60, and (since 1982) workers who lose jobs due to economic crisis or industrial reorganisation can retire at aged 55 and 50, respectively, at as much as 72% of previous pay (Blöndal and Pearson, Tables 5 and 6). Further evidence that high non-employment rates for this age group do not necessarily imply greater hardship is found in the proportion of out-of-the-labour-force 55–64-year-old males who have formally retired: roughly 80% for France and 90% for Germany vs. 50% for the US and only 30% for the UK (OECD, *Employment Outlook*, 1988, p. 67). Clearly, older men's non-employment rates are influenced by the availability of retirement benefits. They probably also depend on the availability of jobs. The welfare implications of the non-employment rate for this age group is therefore ambiguous—we cannot assume, as we do for prime-age males, that a lower non-employment rate is better than a higher one.

Table 4 adjusts the prime-age male non-employment rates (averages over 1992–93) by the rate of incarceration of 25–54-year-old males.[1] Because incarceration rates are almost six times higher in the US than they are in Europe, the very small European advantage in prime-age male non-employment widens into a significant difference when the prison population is included in the non-employment rate. In summary, the large 1988–95 prime-age male *un*employment gap in favour of the US (5·1% vs. 6·6% in Table 2a, or almost 30%), shrinks to an insignificant *non*-employment gap (11·9% vs. 12·2% in Table 3, or 3%) and reverses itself for 1992/93 in favour of the European countries (14·6% vs. 13·0% in Table 4, column 3, or 12%), when the non-employment rates are adjusted to include the incarcerated population.

[1] Our adjustment assumes that aggregate employment would not increase if fewer people were incarcerated. The idea of adjusting unemployment data by the incarceration rate is suggested by Freeman (1995). An extensive search for international data on incarceration rates turned up a single source which provided rates only for the period 1992–93: Mauer (1995).

122   R. Buchele and J. Christiansen

Table 4. *Male non-employment rates, 25–54 years old, adjusted for incarcerated population (%)*

	(1) 1992–93 average	(2) Incarceration rate 1992–93	(3) Adjusted non-employment rate
France	12·2	0·28	12·4
Germany	11·5	0·27	11·7
Italy	11·5	0·27	11·7
United Kingdom	15·8	0·31	16·1
United States	13·1	1·71	14·6
E-4	12·8	0·28	13·0

(1) Non-employment rates are calculated as described in Table 3.
(2) Incarceration rates are estimates of the number of 25–54-year-old males who are incarcerated expressed as a percentage of their number in the population.
(3) The adjusted rate adds the incarcerated population to both the numerator and denominator of the non-employment rate.
Sources for incarceration rates: Mauer, 1995, Table 1; and *Statistical Abstract of the United States*, 1996, Table 350.

Table 5. *Augmented (BLS 'U-7' type) unemployment rates, 1993 (%)*

	Women	Men	
		(1)	(2)
France	17·7	10·9	11·2
Germany	10·5	7·0	7·3
Italy	21·9	8.5	8.8
United Kingdom	10·5	14·0	14·3
United States	10·4	10·1	11·7
E-4	15·2	10·1	10·4

Note: For women and for men (column 1) the BLS U-7 type unemployment rate is the official rate augmented by discouraged workers and half the involuntarily part-time employed. In column (2), the U-7 unemployment rate for men is further adjusted by the number of incarcerated 16–64-year-old males, expressed as a percentage of the labour force (reported in Table 6, column 3).
Source: OECD, *Employment Outlook*, 1995, Tables 2.18 and 6.

Finally, we consider two widely cited alternative measures of unemployment: the BLS 'U-7' type unemployment rate (based on the US Bureau of Labor Statistics adjustment that includes discouraged workers and involuntarily part-time employed workers) and the long-term (one year or more) unemployment rate. The 1993 U-7 rates are reported in Table 5, where, for men, they are augmented by male incarceration rates.[1] By the U-7 measure, female unemployment is nearly 50% higher in the E-4 than it is in the US (15·2% vs. 10·4%), but male unemployment is the same (10·1%) and adjusted male unemployment is 11% lower (10·4% vs. 11·7%).

Male long-term unemployment rates, adjusted for discouraged labour force dropouts

[1] In none of these countries is the female incarceration rate high enough to warrant a comparable adjustment.

Table 6. *Male long-term unemployment rates, adjusted for discouraged worker and incarceration rates, 1993 (%)*

	(1) LTUR	(2) DWR	(3) IR	(4) adjusted LTUR
France	2·9	0·1	0·29	3·3
Germany	2·4	—*	0·28	2·7
Italy	4·3	0·9**	0·28	5·4
United Kingdom	5·8	0·5	0·32	6·6
United States	1·0	0·8	1·82	3·5
E-4	3·9	0·5	0·29	4·5

(1) Long-term unemployment rate (those unemployed for one year or more as a percentage of the labour force). See OECD, *Employment Outlook*, 1995, Table 1·8.

(2) Discouraged worker rate (those who say they would like to work but are not currently looking for work because they believe that no suitable job is available, expressed as a percentage of the labour force). See OECD, *Employment Outlook*, 1995, Table 2.1.

(3) Incarceration rate (incarcerated males aged 16–64 as a percentage of the male labour force).

(4) The adjusted long-term unemployment rate is the sum of the long-term unemployed, discouraged workers and the incarcerated, divided by the sum of the labour force, discouraged workers and the incarcerated.

* In Germany the unemployment rate is estimated from the registered unemployed, and individuals need not be actively seeking work to be registered. ** The DWR for Italy is for 1991.

and the incarcerated, are reported in Table 6. The first column of Table 6 shows that the E-4 have much higher long-term rates than the US (nearly four times higher on average). After adjusting these rates for labour force dropout and incarceration rates (columns 2 and 3), this gap narrows to one percentage point (4·5% vs. 3·5%). Thus, two-thirds of the highly publicised difference between US and European male long-term unemployment rates is eliminated if we include discouraged and incarcerated males with the long-term unemployed.[1]

3. The role of labour market institutions and regulations

In this section, we address the argument that European labour market institutions and regulations are the cause of rising European joblessness. We consider the impact of three different kinds of labour market institutions: (1) employment protection laws; (2) wage-setting institutions; and (3) unemployment insurance and other income support programmes. We find that the evidence is mixed, and, more importantly, that the same institutions which may contribute to the E-4's unemployment problems (*vis à vis* the US) also appear to contribute to the relative success of the E-4 in earnings growth and greater earnings equality.

3.1. Employment protection

It is often argued that employment protection laws are a major cause of high European unemployment. In theory, the net effect of protective legislation and norms is ambiguous. Generally, one would expect employment protection to reduce lay-offs and discharges and therefore the flow into (and level of) unemployment. At the same time, however,

[1] We acknowledge that this could involve an 'overadjustment' of the data. Some discouraged workers and some prison inmates may have been employed within the last year.

124   R. Buchele and J. Christiansen

employment protection may reduce hiring by employers who fear being unable to reduce their workforce in the future. The net effect of employment protection on unemployment then becomes an empirical question.

There is a clear consensus among economists that, at least through the mid-1980s, Italy had the most highly regulated labour market in Europe in terms of legal restrictions on firing. Some observers argued that dismissals, whether individual or collective, were 'practically impossible'. In the former case, only criminal acts seemed to justify termination of employment; in the latter case, unions were able to delay any lay-off by 25–40 days and in most cases, they would 'occupy a plant until an agreement [was] negotiated' (Emerson, 1988, pp. 808, 810). Nevertheless, according to two employer surveys conducted in 1985 and 1989, the perceived impact of regulatory restraints on hiring and firing decreased in the last half of the 1980s (Mosley, 1994, p. 68). However, Italy further strengthened employment protection in 1990 by extending unfair dismissal regulations dating from the 1960s to previously exempt small firms (Mosley, 1994, p. 66).

German law requires two to three months' notice for individual and collective dismissals, and they have to be approved by the relevant works council. Collective dismissals require an additional one-month notification of the Labour Office, which may be extended another month. The Employment Promotion Act of 1985 lowered some barriers to lay-offs and made it easier for employers to hire workers on fixed-term contracts (Abraham and Houseman, 1994, p. 64; Mosley, 1994, p. 66). Employers, however, did not register any change in their perception of the stringency of restrictions in the last half of the 1980s (Mosley, 1994, p. 68).

In France, dismissed workers are entitled to retraining at public training facilities. For collective dismissals, employers originally had to consult works councils and request the authorisation of the Labour Office. This latter rule was abolished after the change in government in 1986 (Emerson, 1988). After another change in government in 1989, however, employment protection was increased again, and the role of public authorities strengthened. In 1993, official approval of obligatory social plans was introduced for collective redundancies (Mosley, 1994, p. 66). Legislation with respect to temporary work contracts varied in much the same manner as dismissal rules.

The UK is the E-4 country with the most consistent trend towards deregulation since 1979. In the area of employment protection, this has primarily taken the form of an extension of the qualifying period for unfair dismissal coverage from 26 to 105 weeks of continuous employment. Rules about collective redundancies were not affected. Temporary contracts have never been regulated in the UK (Mosley, 1994, p. 67). The previously cited employer survey showed UK employers as least likely among a sample of 12 European countries to perceive significant constraints on their freedom to hire and fire workers. As Mosley (1994, p. 70) notes, however, despite the UK's laxity, the risk of involuntary termination (from either dismissals or termination of fixed-term contracts) is relatively low.

The basic legal status of employees in the US is described by the doctrine of 'employment-at-will', in which employees can be dismissed without notice or compensation for any reason (Edwards, 1993). This doctrine has been challenged in state courts, and some states have passed laws requiring 'just cause' for dismissals. In 1988, a law requiring 60 days advance notice for plant closings and mass lay-offs was enacted, but compliance has not been effectively enforced.

The *OECD Jobs Study* (OECD, 1994) presents the results of a number of studies that attempt to quantify the 'strictness' of employment protection in 21 OECD countries

Do employment and income security cause unemployment?   125

(among them Grubb and Wells, 1993; OECD *Employment Outlook*, 1993; Bertola, 1990; Emerson, 1988). These studies evaluate procedural inconveniences and delays, months of advance notice and severance pay mandated by law, and difficulties in justifying individual dismissals of workers on regular contracts. They also assess protections for workers on fixed-term contracts and report surveyed employers' opinions on the seriousness of obstacles to dismissing employees on both regular and fixed-term contracts. The *OECD Jobs Study* develops country rankings based on these various criteria and combines them, along with Bertola's (1990) widely cited ranking, into a single consensus ranking of countries on strictness of employment protection legislation. Although the process is qualitative and somewhat subjective, it provides an unambiguous ranking of the five countries of our study. At the one extreme is the US which imposes almost no constraints on individual dismissals, except that they should not be based on sex, race, or age. Among the European countries, the UK imposes the least constraints on employers' ability to adjust the size of their work force. At the other extreme, all observers seem to agree, is Italy, with relatively strict protective laws and practices.[1] France and Germany fall between the UK and Italy and quite near each other, whether the focus is on severance and notification rules or on employers' perception of the bureaucratic burdens connected with dismissals.

What is much more ambiguous is the net impact of employment protection on overall unemployment. Lazear (1990) found that higher severance pay raises non-employment and unemployment rates. However, Addison and Grosso (1996), after correcting errors in his data, find the negative effects of severance pay to be negligible and the effects of advance notice 'to be associated with broadly favorable outcomes' (p. 585).

The *OECD Jobs Study* (Table 6.9) does show that various employment/population ratios are negatively correlated (and self-employment positively correlated) with employment protection indices, but it concedes that a deregulation strategy presents 'both opportunities for stimulating job creation and risks of increasing employment instability if fixed-term contracts grow to a considerable proportion' (p. 80). Similarly, Layard, Nickell, and Jackman (1991) conclude that 'on balance, employment protection laws are probably bad for employment since they strengthen insider power and encourage the payment of efficiency wages to motivate workers who cannot be threatened with dismissal. But...the evidence on adverse employment effects is not strong enough to warrant a total abandonment of the practice' (p. 108).

Other observers express even more serious doubts about the link between employment protection and unemployment. Just as Flanagan (1987, p. 211) calls the effect of restrictions on employment 'ambiguous and probably small', Bentolila and Bertola (1990, pp. 381–82) find that 'firing costs do not have large effects on *hiring* decisions, nor do high firing costs reduce the *average* level of employment'.

For the five countries in our study, we note mixed evidence of a link between employment protection and unemployment. While it is true that Italy, the country with the strictest rules of protection, has—by several measures—the highest unemployment, it is also the case that unemployment in the UK—and particularly long-term unemployment—is relatively high, despite the fact that employment protection in the UK is weak in comparison with the other European countries.

There is another reason for scepticism about employment protection being a primary

---

[1] In fact, among the 21 countries ranked by the *OECD Jobs Study*, the US is ranked least restrictive and Italy most restrictive.

126   R. Buchele and J. Christiansen

Table 7. *Job creation and destruction: average annual rates as a percentage of total employment*

	(1) Gross job gains	(2) Gross job losses	(3) Net change (1) – (2)	(4) Job turnover (1) + (2)
France				
1984–89	13·9	12·8	1·2	26·7
1989–92	13·7	13·9	–0·2	27·6
Germany				
1983–90	9·0	7·5	1·5	16·5
Italy				
1984–89	12·7	10·6	2·2	23·3
1989–92	11·8	11·9	–0·1	23·7
United Kingdom				
1987–89	9·0	5·1	3·9	14·1
1989–91	8.0	6·4	1·6	14·4
United States				
1984–88	13·2	10·0	3·2	23·2
1989–91	12·6	11·1	1·4	23·7

Note: Gross job gains are the sum of employment gains in all establishments reporting a net increase in employment, and gross job losses are the sum of employment declines in all establishments reporting a net decrease in employment. Job gains and losses which do not result in net employment changes for the establishment are therefore not counted. This implies that true gross job gains and losses are even higher than reported in the table.

Source: OECD, *Jobs Study: Evidence and Explanation, Part I*, 1994, Table 1.8.

cause of unemployment. Economists' basic criticism of restrictions on firing is that they reduce employment flexibility—the ability to adjust employment to current levels of demand. The *direct, observable* impact on labour market behaviour should therefore be to reduce worker flows into and out of jobs and gross rates of job creation and destruction. There are limited data on this question, but what is available clearly refutes the stereotype of 'sclerotic' European labour markets. Thus, Table 7 shows no systematic pattern among these countries in job turnover, with rates around 25% per year for France, Italy, and the US and around 15% per year for the UK and Germany. Likewise, Table 8 shows that in 1987 hiring and separation rates were similar in France, Germany, and the US.[1] Based on its analysis of worker flows between employment, unemployment, and non-participation, the CEPR monograph *Unemployment: Choices for Europe* (1995) states that in Europe more 'worker turnover is in the form of direct job-to-job movements, whereas in the US most worker turnover is via unemployment or non-participation' (p. 11). We conclude, along with the authors of this monograph, that 'there is *no* obvious transatlantic difference in hiring, separation and worker turnover rates' (p. 11).

Finally, we note that restricted employment-level flexibility, where it does exist, may be offset by enhanced 'internal flexibility'—the ability of employers to reassign broadly trained, functionally flexible workers to a relatively wide variety of jobs in response to changes in product markets or technology (Rosenberg, 1989). This 'tradeoff' between external vs. internal flexibility has been particularly emphasised in discussions of Japanese

[1] CEPR (1995, pp. 19–20) offers some speculation about why the rates for the UK are so much lower than those for the other countries, suggesting that this is due to exceptional circumstances and differences between the UK and the other countries in how the data are constructed.

Do employment and income security cause unemployment?   127

Table 8. *Employment inflows and outflows, 1987*

	(1) Inflows (hiring as a % of employment)	(2) Outflows (separations as a % of employment)
France	28.9	30·7
Germany	22·3	21·5
United Kingdom	6·6	6·6
United States	25·3	26·5

Source: Burda and Wyplosz, 1994, Table 1. Calculations by authors.

employment relations, but it is also observed in Europe, especially in Germany (Sengenberger, 1992).

3.2. Wage-setting institutions

It is a basic tenet of neoclassical economics that the more responsive wages are to 'market forces', the smaller the effect of unfavourable shifts in labour demand on employment. Wage-setting institutions that inhibit downward wage flexibility and/or reduce relative wage flexibility also reduce employment (growth) and increase unemployment.[1] The list of usual suspects includes unions, collective bargaining, statutory minimum wages, and wages councils. Before examining these factors, we summarise recent developments in levels and distributions of earnings.

3.2.1. Trends in earnings. Table 9 reports trends in the earnings distributions of our five countries between 1973 and 1990. It shows that in all countries the earnings of men at the 90th percentile gained relative to the median (although the gain was negligible in France). For women this holds only for the UK and the US. In Italy, and to a lesser extent in Germany and France, men and women at the 10th percentile also gained relative to the median, but in the US and UK they lost ground. The largest increase in earnings inequality between 1979 and 1990 occurred in the US (where the ratio of the 90th to the 10th percentile increased by 20% for men and 22% for women), followed by the UK (where it increased by 16% and 18% respectively). The starkest statistics in this table are the exceptionally low ratios of the 10th percentile to median earnings in the US and their deterioration between 1979 and 1990 for both men and women.

Table 10 examines the changes in the real earnings of males at the 90th, 50th, and 10th percentiles that produced the changes in the earnings distributions reported in the preceding table. These data show widely differing rates of growth of real earnings. For the 1970s, France reported significant earnings growth, while the US saw much smaller increases. In the 1980s, earnings rose relatively strongly for most workers in Germany and the UK and somewhat less in France and Italy.[2] In the US, median earnings fell for men, and earnings at the 10th percentile declined for both men and women. These data also show that the rise in earnings inequality in the UK (Table 9) was due primarily to rapid

---

[1] The *OECD Jobs Studies* (1994, Chart 5.1) provides evidence that OECD countries in which wage dispersion increased the most during the 1980s also experienced the fastest employment growth.

[2] Italy is a unique case, with strong earnings gains for men at the top and the bottom, and negligible gains for the median. This suggests that mean earnings for men rose substantially, even though the median did not.

128   **R. Buchele and J. Christiansen**

Table 9. *Trends in earnings dispersions*

	Men				Women			
	1973	1979	1990	Avg. annual % change since 1979	1973	1979	1990	Avg. annual % change since 1979
France								
Ratio 90th/50th percentile:	2·00	2·05	2·11[a]	0·2	1·72	1·69	1·69[a]	0
Ratio 10th/50th percentile:	0·62	0·62	0·66	0·5	0·65	0·65	0·67	0·3
Germany								
Ratio 90th/50th percentile:	—	1·47	1·65	1·1	—	1·59[b]	1·58	-0·1
Ratio 10th/50th percentile:	—	0·67	0·71	1·1	—	0·59	0·66	1·0
Italy								
Ratio 90th/50th percentile:	—	1·37	1·56[c]	1·6	—	1·29	1·29[c]	0
Ratio 10th/50th percentile:	—	0·67	0·75	2·0	—	0·54	0·64	2·2
United Kingdom								
Ratio 90th/50th percentile:	—	1·84[d]	1·99[a]	1·3	—	1·77[d]	1·93[a]	1·5
Ratio 10th/50th percentile:	—	0·63	0·59	-1·3	—	0·67	0·62	-1·3
United States								
Ratio 90th/50th percentile:	1·93[e]	1·93	2·14[f]	1·0	1·97[e]	1·96	2·15[f]	0·9
Ratio 10th/50th percentile:	0·41	0·41	0·38	-0·8	0·47	0·49	0·44	-1·1

Notes: [a] Data for 1991, [b] for 1981, [c] for 1987, [d] for 1985, [e] for 1975, [f] for 1989.
Source: OECD, *Employment Outlook*, 1993, Table 5.2.

Do employment and income security cause unemployment?   129

Table 10. *Average annual rates of change in real earnings at the 90th, 50th, and 10th percentile (%)*

	Men		Women	
	1973–79	1979–90	1973–79	1979–90
France[a]				
90th percentile	2·4	1·1	3·2	1·2
50th percentile	1·8	0·6	3·4	1·1
10th percentile	2·0	0·6	3·0	0·7
Germany[b]				
90th percentile	—	3·7	—	4·7
50th percentile	—	3·5	—	4·6
10th percentile	—	4·2	—	7·4
Italy[c]				
90th percentile	—	2·2	—	1·6
50th percentile	—	0·5	—	1·7
10th percentile	—	2·0	—	3·9
United Kingdom[d]				
90th percentile	—	3·4	—	4·2
50th percentile	—	2·2	—	3·0
10th percentile	—	1·2	—	2·0
United States[e]				
90th percentile	0·5	0·4	1·0	1·7
50th percentile	0·5	−0·6	1·3	0·7
10th percentile	0·5	−1·4	2·7	−0·4

Notes:[a] Second period is 1979–87. [b] Second period is 1983–88. [c] Second period is 1979–87. [d] Second period is 1983–92. [e] Second period is 1985–91.
Source: OECD, *Employment Outlook*, 1993, Table 5.3.

earnings growth at the top, while the increase in inequality in the US resulted from a combination of a fall in earnings at the bottom and a rise of those at the top.

We have documented broadly divergent earnings trends among this group of major industrialised countries. These national economies operate in the same world economy, facing similar patterns of demand and with access to similar technology, yet in Germany low-wage workers' earnings grew rapidly, while they increased slowly in France, Italy, and the UK, and even fell in the US. In some countries, the earnings distribution became radically more unequal (the UK and the US), while in others it changed little. We now turn to a discussion of the wage-setting institutions in these countries which have given rise to these divergent records.

3.2.2. Unionisation and collective bargaining coverage. To the extent that unions raise workers' bargaining power *vis à vis* employers, they would be able to raise the average wage level. Collective bargaining also likely reduces short-run aggregate wage flexibility (since wages are contractually fixed) and relative wage flexibility (since collective bargaining introduces a kind of 'moral inertia' into the determination of pay scales and relative wages). We therefore expect that, over the long run (and given the rate of growth of labour productivity), countries where union strength and collective bargaining coverage have declined the most will have experienced the smallest wage gains (especially lower and middle level wages) and the biggest increases in earnings inequality.

Tables 11 and 12 report trends among our countries in unionisation and collective

130   R. Buchele and J. Christiansen

Table 11. *Union membership as a percentage of wage and salary earners*

	1960	1970	1975	1980	1985	1990
France	19	22	23	19	16	10
Germany	35	33	37	37	37	33
Italy	25	36	47	49	42	39
United Kingdom	44	45	48	51	46	39
United States	32	28	23	23	18	16

Sources: Visser, 1988, Table 2 for the E-4 in 1960; Kaufman, 1989, Appendix Table 8 for the US in 1960 and 1970; OECD, *Employment Outlook*, 1991, Table 4.1 for 1970–85 (except the US in 1970); OECD, *Employment Outlook*, 1994, Table 5.7 for 1990.

Table 12. *Collective bargaining coverage (covered employees as a percentage of all employees with bargaining rights) (%)* ·

	1980	1985	1990
France	85[a]	92	—
Germany	91	91	90[d]
Italy	—	>75	—
United Kingdom	70[b]	64	47
United States	26	20	18

Notes: [a] Data for 1981; [b] for 1978; [c] exact year unspecified; [d] for 1992.
Sources: OECD, *Employment Outlook*, 1994, Table 5.8 (except Italy).
For Italy: Layard, Nickell and Jackman, 1991, Table 6, p. 52.

bargaining coverage.[1] In the four European countries, the share of employees covered by collective bargaining is substantially higher than the share that belongs to unions. The reason is that in much of Europe collectively bargained wage settlements for an industry or sector are automatically extended to non-union workers in the sector. This happens where employers who are members of their sector's employers' association are obliged to follow the agreement reached between their association and the union (as in Germany and Italy), or where wage settlements are extended by statute to other firms that are not members of an employers' association (as in France).

Union density fell in the US throughout the period 1960–90. It either rose or held steady in all four European countries between 1960 and 1980 and then fell (fairly sharply everywhere except in Germany) between 1980 and 1990. In the US, where collective bargaining coverage does not extend significantly beyond union memberships, there was a parallel drop in coverage. In the UK, which saw 'a collapse in multi-employer bargaining in the late 1980s' (Milner, 1995, p. 87), collective bargaining coverage fell by 33% while union density fell by 24% between 1980 and 1990. Milner concludes from his historical study of collective bargaining coverage in the UK, that 'coverage is lower now than at any point since the Second World War and that 'the gap between collective bargaining coverage and union density has narrowed to an unprecedented degree'. In the three

[1] While the union density rates (Table 11) for 1960 are from a different source than those for 1970 and later, the estimates for 1960 are comparable to those for later years (i.e., the series 'splice' well). The figure for collective bargaining coverage (Table 12) for Italy is a 'ball park' estimate and not as reliable as the other estimates in the table.

Do employment and income security cause unemployment?   131

continental European countries, collective bargaining coverage appears to have held up in the 1980s, despite significant declines in union density in France and Italy. We also note that Germany's collective bargaining system is ranked by most observers as the most centralised and corporatist of the E-4 (see comparative rankings in Dell'Aringa and Lodovici, 1992). The US is, of course, at the opposite end of these rankings.

What effect did these developments have on earnings trends? In the US, which experienced a 30% drop in union density and a corresponding drop in collective bargaining coverage in the 1980s, median wages stagnated, lower-paid workers' wages fell, and the wage distribution became much more unequal (as seen in Tables 10 and 9). Similarly, in the UK, where union density and collective bargaining coverage fell, the earnings distribution became sharply more unequal. However, despite the UK's weak productivity growth (Gordon, 1995, Table 3) and declining union strength in the 1980s, median earnings rose strongly, and even 10th percentile earnings increased.[1] In Germany, which experienced the least erosion of union density, earnings at all levels rose faster than in any other country, with especially strong gains at the bottom.[2]

3.2.3. Minimum wages. The five countries in this study represent three different approaches to setting minimum wages (see Bazen and Benhayoun, 1992; Dolado, *et al.*, 1996; OECD, 1994, Table 4.5): national statutory minimums as in France and the US;[3] sectoral collective bargaining agreements setting many different minimum rates for different jobs as in Germany and Italy; and minimum wages set for low-wage industries by unions and trade groups, such as the UK's (recently abolished) Wages Councils.

Minimum wage protection suffered divergent fates in these countries. In France, the minimum wage remained fairly steady from the mid-1970s to the late 1980s at around 50% of average earnings, while in the US it fell from around 45% to 35% (OECD, 1994, Chart 5.14). In Germany and Italy, the minimum wage for the vast majority of workers is the base wage set by the sectoral collective bargaining process which remained important through the 1980s. In the UK, the number and influence of the Wages Councils which 'probably never covered more than 15% of workers' (Bamber and Lansbury, 1993, p. 40), declined throughout the 1980s. Workers under the age of 21 were removed from coverage in 1986, and in 1993, the last 26 Wages Councils were abolished.

Trends in the earnings distributions shown in Table 9 suggest that minimum wage provisions have an important influence on the degree of earnings inequality. In the three countries where minimum wage institutions survived the 1980s (France, Germany, and Italy), earnings at the 10th percentile actually rose relatively to those at the 50th percentile. In the two countries where minimum wage protection eroded (the UK and the US), they fell relative to the median.

Both union collective bargaining priorities and minimum wage legislation serve to prevent wages at the bottom of the wage distribution from falling (not just absolutely, but also relatively to the median wage). In countries where collective bargaining coverage

---

[1] It is possible that the apparent rise of 10th percentile earnings is a statistical artifact resulting from the especially high concentration of job loss among low-paid workers in the UK (see Schmitt, 1994, p. 188). Their departure shifts some workers who were formerly in the second earnings decile down into the bottom decile so that, even if these workers' earnings are actually falling, earnings observed at the 10th percentile can be higher in 1990 than they were in 1979.

[2] We note in passing that this observation is inconsistent with either the corporatist or the Calmfors and Drifill hypothesis that the centralisation of bargaining promotes wage restraint.

[3] In France, the statutory minimum can be improved by sectoral agreements which can be extended by the authorities. In the US, the states can (and do) set minima above the Federal standard.

132   R. Buchele and J. Christiansen

has remained high and/or statutory, minimum wages have not been eroded, wages at the 10th percentile have risen along with wages at the median and 90th percentile. Where collective bargaining coverage and/or minimum wage protections have been eroded, wages at the 10th percentile have fallen—either absolutely (in the US) or relatively (in the UK). And it is only in these two countries that unemployment has fallen over the last two time periods in our study (1980–87 and 1988–96). These associations between wage trends at the bottom of the wage distribution, on the one hand, and unemployment trends, on the other, appear to suggest a trade-off between job growth and the growth of earnings of low-paid workers.

3.3. Unemployment insurance and income support

It is widely accepted that the unemployment rate is affected by the availability and generosity of unemployment benefits. Theory suggests that availability of unemployment benefits can raise the unemployment rate both directly (raising the reservation wage of the unemployed, thereby prolonging the job search and the average duration of a spell of unemployment) and indirectly (reducing the 'cost of job loss', thereby increasing labour's bargaining power, raising wages, and reducing employment). The practical policy issue is not whether unemployment insurance raises unemployment, but rather how large this effect is and how can it be minimised without undermining the safety net function of unemployment insurance.[1]

There are two basic principles governing how unemployment compensation is determined:[2] (1) the *insurance* principle, in which eligibility depends on previous work experience and benefits are set in relation to previous earnings for a limited duration (Italy and the US being the purist examples); and (2) the *social welfare* principle, in which eligibility is means tested and the emphasis is on guaranteeing a minimum level of income for a longer duration (the UK since 1981). Some countries have developed schemes based on a combination of both principles, with generally more welfare-oriented unemployment assistance (UA) kicking in when unemployment insurance (UI) benefits are exhausted. (France and Germany are examples, except that in Germany UA benefits remain wage-related, and there is a third—guaranteed minimum income—scheme for those who are not adequately covered by UI and UA.)

Three parameters determine the generosity and impact of these unemployment compensation schemes: the benefit *level* (usually measured as a percentage of previous earnings replaced), the *duration* of benefits (the length of time a person can receive benefits) and the *coverage* (the percentage of the unemployed who receive benefits). Coverage depends on eligibility requirements and on duration of benefits. Initial replacement rates and coverage for our five countries are reported in Table 13. Replacement rates are relatively high (and stable) in France and Germany and relatively low in Italy. They have been fairly stable (at about one-third of previous earnings) in the US, and they have declined precipitously in the UK since the early 1970s. Coverage, on the other hand, in 1991 was relatively high in Germany and the UK, low in Italy, and intermediate in France and the US.

Benefit duration varies from six months (in Italy and the US) to potentially unlimited duration in the other countries (as workers who exhaust their unemployment insurance benefits segue into unemployment assistance and more general income support

---

[1] The more important issue is not the effect of unemployment insurance on the official unemployment rate, but rather on the level and the growth of employment, a question we do not address in this paper.

[2] This discussion is based primarily on Reissert and Schmid (1994).

Do employment and income security cause unemployment?   133

Table 13. *Initial unemployment insurance replacement rates (1961–91) and coverage (1991) (%)*

	1961	1971	1981	1991	Coverage
France	60	58	55	57	44
Germany*	42	42	40	40	64
Italy	22	10	4	15	19
United Kingdom	27	47	39	24	62
United States	33	32	35	31	34

Note: The replacement rate is the gross benefit income in the first three months of unemployment as a percentage of average gross earnings for a 40-year-old unemployed worker with a dependent spouse and no children.

*Since unemployment benefits are not taxed in Germany, the gross replacement rate understates its generosity. Most studies (e.g., OECD, *Employment Outlook*, 1991, Table 7.2; Burtless, 1987) put Germany's replacement rates at the same level as France's.

Sources: Replacement rates: Blöndal and Pearson, 1995, Table 2. Coverage: OECD, *Jobs Study*, 1994, Table 8.4.

Table 14. *Summary measure of unemployment benefit entitlements (%)*

	1961	1971	1981	1991
France	25	24	31	37
Germany	30	29	29	28
Italy	4	2	1	3
United Kingdom	24	25	24	18
United States	17	11	15	11

Note: The index is a simple average of replacement rates for beneficiaries in three family circumstances (single, dependent spouse, working spouse) by two earnings levels (average and two-thirds average earnings) by three durations (the first, second and third, and fourth and fifth years). This index appears to understate Germany's benefit levels for the reason noted in Table 13.

Source: Blöndal and Pearson, 1995, Table 4.

programmes). Benefit replacement rates and duration have been combined into a summary measure of overall benefit generosity by the OECD (see OECD, 1994, Ch. 8; Blöndal and Pearson, 1995). The index—shown in Table 14—averages benefit replacement rates over a five-year period for workers in three different family circumstances and two earnings levels. By this measure, long-term income support for the unemployed (in 1991) is most generous in France and Germany, less generous (and decreasing) in the UK and the US, and negligible in Italy. Comparing this ranking with the ranking of these country's long-term unemployment rates (LTURs) in Table 6 (which shows Italy and the UK to have by far the highest LTURs both before and after our adjustment) fails to establish any correlation between the level and duration of income support programmes for the unemployed and the incidence of long-term unemployment.[1]

[1] It is probably more appropriate to address this issue using the incidence of long-term unemployment among the unemployed (the percentage of the unemployed who have been jobless for 12 months or more) rather than the LTUR, since the level and duration of benefits are more likely to affect how long someone who becomes unemployed remains unemployed than it is to affect their likelihood of being unemployed. In fact, using this measure (reported in OECD, 1995, Table R) does not change our country ranking on long-term unemployment or our conclusion.

134   **R. Buchele and J. Christiansen**

Table 15. *Replacement rates for early retirement and disability schemes, 1993 (%)*

	Early retirement	Disability
France	65	41
Germany	63	56
Italy	72	77
United Kingdom	—	36
United States	—	24

Note: Early retirement figures are the average for the case of a single person and a married person with a dependent spouse and are for the most generous scheme that permits retirement more than five years before the normal retirement date. Disability figures are the average for a single and married person with average earnings, who is 40 years old and fully incapacitated.
Source: Blöndal and Pearson, 1995, Tables 5 and 8.

Blöndal and Pearson (1995) make the important point that in many countries more working-age people without jobs receive *non-employment* benefits than receive unemployment benefits, particularly early retirement and invalidity (or disability) benefits. They argue that there is likely to be some degree of substitution between non-employment benefits and unemployment benefits, since governments, employers, and job losers may all have reasons to prefer a transition to early retirement or disability rather than to unemployment. A rough indication of the level of non-employment benefits is provided in Table 15. These benefits are at least as generous as unemployment benefits in most of our countries and more generous in Italy. These data probably go a long way towards accounting for the relatively high *non-employment* rates of 55–64-year-old males in France and Germany (Table 3) and the very low *un*employment rate for older males in Italy (Table 2).

4. Conclusion

We have examined a number of institutional factors in order to determine whether labour market rigidities can be judged the main culprit for the overall increase in unemployment over the past 35 years and for the dramatic differences in unemployment rates among the five countries under review. We conclude that these institutional factors change in a pattern that is much too varied and erratic both within and among these countries to account for the general rise in unemployment. We believe that further research should pursue the suggestions of several analysts that the overall upward trend in unemployment rates is related to a global decline in the growth of aggregate demand throughout the advanced industrialised economies.[1] The effects of this slowdown, however, are mediated by the specific labour market institutions and policies of each country. Thus, for the E-4 they manifest themselves in relatively poor employment performance and for the US in relatively poor earnings and productivity performance (Buchele and Christiansen, 1995; Freeman, 1994). We caution, however, that commonly cited differences in unemployment rates are exaggerated, and that it is not at all clear that US-style employment

---

[1] This argument is explored by Eatwell (1995) and Michie and Wilkinson (1994), among others.

and earnings 'flexibility' yield employment gains that are worth the price that Americans pay in inequality and slow earnings growth.

Bibliography

Abraham, K. G. and Houseman, S. N. 1994. Does employment protection inhibit labor market flexibility? in Blank, R. (ed.), *Social Protection versus Economic Flexibility*, Chicago, University of Chicago Press

Addison, J. and Grosso, J. 1996. Job security provisions and employment: revised estimates, *Industrial Relations*, vol. 35, no. 4, October, 585–603

Bamber, G. J. and Lansbury, R. D. 1993. *International and Comparative Industrial Relations*, 2nd edn, London, Allen and Unwin

Bazen, S. and Benhayoun, G. 1992. Low pay and wage regulation in the European Community, *British Journal of Industrial Relations*, December, 623–38

Bentolila, S. and Bertola, G. 1990. Firing costs and labour demand: how bad is Eurosclerosis? *Review of Economic Studies*, vol. 57, 381–402

Bertola, G. 1990. Job security, employment, and wages, *European Economic Review*, vol. 34, 851–86

Blöndal, S. and Pearson, M. 1995. Unemployment and other non-employment benefits, *Oxford Review of Economic Policy*, vol. 11, no. 1, 136–69

Buchele, R. and Christiansen, J. 1995. Productivity, real wages, and worker rights: a cross national comparison, *Labour: Review of Labour Economics and Industrial Relations*, Autumn, 405–23

Buechtemann, C. F. (ed.) 1993. *Employment Security and Labor Market Behavior: Interdisciplinary Approaches and International Evidence*, New York, ILR Press

Burda, M. and Wyplosz, C. 1994. Gross worker and job flows in Europe, *European Economic Review*, vol. 38, no. 6, 1287–315

Burtless, G. 1987. Jobless pay and high European unemployment, in Lawrence, R. Z. and Schultze, C. L. (eds), *Barriers to European Growth: A Transatlantic View*, Washington DC, The Brookings Institution

Calmfors, L and Driffill, J. 1988. Centralization of wage bargaining, *Economic Policy*, April

Centre for Economic Policy Research. 1995. *Unemployment: Choices for Europe*, London, CEPR

Dell'Aringa, C. and Lodovici, M. S. 1992. Industrial relations and economic performance, in Treu, T. (ed.), *Participation in Public Policy-Making. The Role of Trade Unions and Employers Associations*, Berlin, de Gruyter

Dolado, J. *et al.* 1996. The economic impact of minimum wages in Europe, *Economic Policy*, no. 23, 319–72

Eatwell, J. 1995. 'Disguised Unemployment: the G7 Experience', Discussion Paper no. 106, United Nations Conference on Trade and Development

Edwards, R. 1993. *Rights at Work*, Washington DC, The Brookings Institution

Emerson M. 1988. Regulation or deregulation of the labour market: policy regimes for the recruitment and dismissal of employees in the industrialised countries, *European Economic Review*, vol. 32, no. 4, 775–817

Flanagan, R. J. 1987. Labor market behavior and European economic growth, in Lawrence, R. Z. and Schultze, C. L. (eds), *Barriers to European Growth: A Transatlantic View*, Washington DC, The Brookings Institution

Freeman, R. B. 1995. The limits of wage flexibility to curing unemployment, *Oxford Review of Economic Policy*, vol. 11, no. 1, 63–72

Freeman, R. B. 1994. How labor fares in advanced countries, in Freeman, R. B. (ed.), *Working Under Different Rules*, New York, Russell Sage

Gordon, R. J. 1995. 'Is There a Tradeoff Between Unemployment and Productivity Growth?' NBER Working Paper no. 5081

Grubb, D. and Wells, W. 1993. Employment regulation and patterns of work in EC Countries, *OECD Economic Studies*, no. 21, 7–58

Kaufman, B. E. 1989. *The Economics of Labor Markets and Labor Relations*, Chicago, The Dryden Press

Layard, R., Nickell, S., and Jackman, R. 1991. *Unemployment: Macroeconomic Performance and the Labour Market*, Oxford, Oxford University Press

136   R. Buchele and J. Christiansen

Lazear, E. P. 1990. Job security provisions and employment, *The Quarterly Journal of Economics*, vol, 105, no.3, 699–726

Maddison, A. 1991. *Dynamic Forces in Capitalist Development: A Long-run Comparative View*, Oxford, Oxford University Press

Martin, J. 1994. The extent of high unemployment in OECD countries, in *Reducing Unemployment: Current Issues and Policy Options*, The Federal Reserve Bank of Kansas City

Mauer, M. 1995. The international use of incarceration, *The Prison Journal*, March, 113–23

Michie, J. and Wilkinson, F. 1994. The growth of unemployment in the 1980s, in Michie, J. and Grieve Smith, J. (eds), *Unemployment in Europe*, London, Academic Press

Milner, S. 1995. The coverage of collective pay-setting institutions in Britain, 1895–1990, *British Journal of Industrial Relations*, March, 69–91

Mosley, H. 1994. Employment protection and labor force adjustment in EC countries, in Schmid, G. (ed.), *Labor Market Institutions in Europe: A Socioeconomic Evaluation of Performance*, Armonk, NY, M. E. Sharpe

OECD various years. *Economic Outlook*, Paris, OECD

OECD various years. *Employment Outlook*, Paris, OECD

OECD various years. *Labour Force Statistics*, Paris, OECD

OECD 1994. *The OECD Jobs Study: Evidence and Explanations: Parts I and II*, Paris, OECD

OECD 1985. *Standardised Unemployment Rates*, Paris, OECD

OECD 1996, *Economics Surveys, Germany*, Paris, OECD

Reissert, B. and Schmid, G. 1994. Unemployment compensation and active labor market policy, in Schmid, G. (ed.), *Labor Market Institutions in Europe*, Armonk, NY, M. E. Sharpe

Rosenberg, S. 1989. From segmentation to flexibility, *Labour and Society*, vol. 14, no. 4, October

Schmitt, J. 1994. The changing structure of male earnings in Britain, 1974–1988, pp. 177–264 in Freeman, R. and Katz, L. (eds), *Differences and Changes in Wage Structures*, Chicago, University of Chicago Press

Sengenberger, W. 1992. Revisiting the legal and institutional framework for employment security: an international comparative perspective, pp. 150–182 in Koshiro, K. (ed.), *Employment Security and Labor Market Flexibility*, Detroit, Wayne State University Press

Sorrentino, C. 1993. International comparisons of unemployment indicators, *Monthly Labor Review*, March, 3–24

Sorrentino, C. 1995. International unemployment indicators, 1983–93, *Monthly Labor Review*, August, 31–50

US Bureau of the Census various years. *Statistical Abstract*, Washington DC, GPO

US Department of Labor, Bureau of Labor Statistics (various years). *Monthly Labor Review*

Visser, J. 1988. Trade unionism in Western Europe: present situation and prospects, *Labour and Society*, vol. 13, no. 2, April

[20]

RONALD DORE

WILL GLOBAL CAPITALISM BE

ANGLO-SAXON CAPITALISM?

W ITH THE END of the military and ideological confrontation of the Cold War, people have come to notice that state vs. market is not the only important dimension along which national economic systems differ: it was not central planning that differentiated the capitalist systems of Germany and Japan from those of Britain and America. But from the beginning of the 'types of capitalism' debates of the 1990s, there was one implicit question: as open national economies merge into a single world economic system, how far will the global diffusion of the Anglo-Saxon form of capitalism go? Will there still be room for rather different forms of capitalism to survive in countries like Japan and Germany?[1]

We tend now to forget that Anglo-Saxon capitalism has not always assumed its current thorough-going, neo-liberal form. A quarter of a century ago, most people in Britain accepted 'mixed economy' as a reasonable characterization of the world they lived in, and as on the whole a sensible set of arrangements: it was not only a question of a mixture of public ownership (in coal and steel as well as in utilities) and private industry. 'Mixed economy' also acknowledged that people worked for a mixture of motives, some more for personal profit, some more for public service. It seemed much in keeping with the spirit of the mid 1970s for the Social Science Research Council,[2] as it then was, to set up a panel to produce a report on the Social Responsibility of Industry, and for the report to assume that those who managed corporations should also have mixed motives, mixed objectives, not just that of profit maximization. They should acknowledge that they had obligations not only to their shareholders, but also to those who would later become known as their stakeholders. There was a flurry of interest—another approach to dethroning the bottom line—in the idea of reworking the national accounts to produce a calculation of Net National Welfare whereby policing, pollution control and prisons would count as disvalues and carry a negative sign, not a positive one as in the calculation of GDP.[3]

One other personal memory symbolizes the assumptions of the time— Richard Titmuss, arguing in the LSE Academic Board that university teachers should not be paid supplementary fees for acting as examiners. They were paid a decent salary to do a job, and had a duty to do all that the job required. He lost the argument. The consensus was that people do, indeed, work for a mixture of motives; that for academics—as for others in the public service—duty, public spirit, a sense of responsibility to students and to the discipline, together with the enthusiasm generated by intellectual curiosity and the competition for renown, ought to be the overwhelmingly dominant motivators. But a little extra cash can also help to carry one through the more boring parts of the job.

The shift in that pragmatic consensus over the last twenty years has been remarkable. From the notion of a little bit of extra cash as a useful, marginal incentive, to the belief that cash, and the fear of being deprived of it, are the only reliable means of stopping people (in the economists' jargon) from shirking—becoming lazy time-servers. Both the main British parties now share the belief that only competition for private profits can bring a reliable train service, cheap electricity, safe nuclear fuel or 'efficient' prisons. Performance-related pay has been enforced

---

[1] A revised version of a lecture given at the London School of Economics, May 2000, to mark the publication of the author's *Stockmarket Capitalism, Welfare Capitalism: Japan and Germany versus the Anglo-Saxons*, Oxford 2000. Many people in Britain and America who have neither Angles nor Saxons among their ancestors object to the term 'Anglo-Saxon'; but it has become established in the literature of comparative capitalisms, thanks to the lead initially given by Michel Albert (*Capitalisme contre capitalisme*, Paris 1991). The similarity of Canadian, Australian and New Zealand patterns to the British and American ones provides some justification for the phrase.

[2] As Britain's Economic and Social Research Council was known, before its chairman headed off the threat of budget cuts by accepting, as a quid pro quo, Keith Joseph's view that there was nothing social about economics and not much genuine science, either.

[3] Amartya Sen, a member of the panel who showed some interest in the idea, went on to develop the Human Development Index for the UNDP.

throughout the public service. The academic marketplace grows ever more like an auction for prize bulls. And in industry, there is ever heavier reliance on stock-options, rather than a fixed salary, as the form of executive remuneration.

The popularity of stock-options for directors and senior executives has a double significance. Not only does it reflect the dominant view about why people work rather than shirk, it also serves to align the private interest of the manager agent with that of his shareholder principal, and so reinforces the shift to shareholder-sovereignty in business philosophies that has been going on over the last twenty years. The talk about the social responsibility of corporations—so-called stakeholder theories, popular in business schools twenty years ago—has all but disappeared from such institutions. And the economists have proffered their legitimating blessings. I recall George Akerlof devoting an LSE public lecture to explaining—indeed, proving with algebra—that if what you wanted was to do good, you would get more good done the Rockefeller way, by single-minded maximization and donating your superior profits to charity, than by diluting your profit drive in order to be nice to your employees or suppliers. There is no need for such exhortations today, for that has become the dominating consensus: maximizing shareholder-value is exactly what management should be about. While every consulting firm has its own definition of shareholder-value, and its own pet formula for calculating it, almost everyone agrees that it is the dominant, touchstone objective. Treating your employees, your customers or your suppliers decently is fine, provided it can be shown—and only if it can be shown—to count on the bottom line, to increase earnings or raise the share-price.

Global trends

Anglo-Saxon capitalism itself, then, is an evolving set of institutions, not a constant; and it has evolved into something rather different today from what it was twenty years ago.[4] As for the source of these changes, it has become fashionable, in the last five years, to attribute almost everything that happens to the processes of globalization. It is true that globalization had something to do with it. The growth of international

---

[4] R. Dore, W. Lazonick and M. O'Sullivan, 'Varieties of Capitalism in the Twentieth Century', *Oxford Review of Economic Policy*, vol. 15, no. 4, 1999.

trade and investment made it administratively almost impossible to maintain foreign-exchange controls, and this not only greatly narrowed the scope for nation-state economic policy-making, but also had other reverberating consequences—among them, the growing dominance of American financial institutions in world financial markets. It was mostly Frenchmen who were advising Elf Aquitaine and Total in their take-over battle, and Germans advising Mannesmann, but they were doing so as employees of American investment banks, working to American methods and criteria. To organizational dominance is added American cultural hegemony, nowhere more apparent than in the economics profession, as the hot topics—principal-agent theory, for instance—of Chicago and Berkeley become the hot topics of Milan, Osaka or Madrid. At the political level, too, it is manifest in the way that institutional practices spread from the United States to Britain, Europe and Japan—whether it be the liberalization of stockbroking fees or the introduction of working families' tax credit.

Political zeal

But these aspects of globalization are far from the whole story. It was not because Englishmen were going abroad for their mortgages in droves that control over building society interest rates was abolished in Britain in the 1980s—with the result that, as we have recently seen, raising interest rates across the board (and thereby increasing the financing and exporting problems of manufacturers) came to be the only way of cooling off the housing market. That bit of deregulation happened because the Thatcher government had a strong belief in the sovereign virtues of competition. Demutualization of building societies and the unlocking of shareholder-value naturally followed. And so with many of the other changes that have contributed to making the stock-market ever more central to the British economy, and shareholder-value the central concern of management. They have precious little to do with the constraints of globalization and a lot to do with shifts in ideology, and with the expression of ideology in economic policies. The growth of private savings, with the cutback in basic pensions and the withering away of SERPS, had to do with the Thatcher government's belief that the welfare state was a vicious breeder of dependency. The movement of private savings from fixed-interest vehicles to equity (encouraged by tax concessions—the Personal Equity Plans, now revamped as Individual Savings Accounts) had to do with that government's faith in the stock-market as the most efficient means of allocating capital and improving national competitiveness. Similarly, globalization had little effect on the shift of corporate pensions from defined-benefit to what are euphemistically called 'defined-contribution' (i.e., *un*defined-benefit) forms, and the increased investment of pension funds in equities. Behind all these ideological shifts, of course, there lay structural power-shifts, too. The decline of trade unions was one element of this, as it was of the whole process of reinforcing the sovereignty of shareholders at other stakeholders' expense.

Internal evolution

There is an argument that, while not perhaps a consequence of globalization, these changes do have a kind of inevitability about them. They are not just the product of arbitrary—and reversible—shifts of ideology, but the consequence of internal evolutionary change, brought about by the material, social and technological advances within all industrial societies. The characterizations of such internal evolution are multiple: greater institutional complexity, the expansion of individual choice that comes with greater affluence, increasing social mobility, the erosion of deference—a continuation, if you like, of the processes of rationalization Max Weber identified, described in Schiller's phrase about the demagicking, disenchantment, demystification of the world. In the nineteenth century, men and women learned to do without the need to invoke, or acknowledge, an arbitrary divine authority. In the twentieth century, with bigger bank accounts, birth control, more sophisticated education, they learned—by marketizing and securitizing everything, and writing cast-iron contracts—to do without the support of (or obligations to) such human collectivities as nations, or even to other individual human beings.

In an image that links both globalization and the internal evolution of societies, Lawrence Summers has graphically characterized the structural change:

> In a world without courts, one lends money to one's brother-in-law and relies on one's wife's parents to enforce the agreement. In a world without borders, arms-length formal contracts—of which securitization is only the most canonical example—become ever more critical to innovation and growth. So, too, do the means of reliably enforcing them.[5]

---

[5] American Academy of Arts and Sciences, *Bulletin*, Spring 2000. Summers goes on to say that, since Americans don't trust each other anyway and are used to going to the law at the drop of a hat, they have a competitive edge in global finance.

The *Economist* recently made much the same argument about the Westernization of the business empires of the Chinese diaspora, originally built on ethnic networks, now increasingly using 'signatures on contracts' rather than 'handshakes and trust'. But it added one important element to the explanation—the diffusion of ideology. The sons of the founding entrepreneurs were now taking over after a 'thorough training'— some might call it brainwashing—at American business schools.[6]

In the light of these two sets of arguments—globalization, and inevitable systemic evolution—what is likely to happen in Japan and Germany? Are we likely to see a rerun of the changes that have taken place in Britain and America over the last twenty years? Still, in spite of a decade or more of accelerating globalization, both societies are less marketized than Britain was even in the corporatist 1970s. They remain economies in which the stock-market plays a much less central role, and the state a larger one; in which the financial sector is less dominant, and manufacturing industry correspondingly more important; in which engineers tend to have the edge over accountants, and the doctrine of the supremacy of shareholder-value is still a much weaker element in determining company goals.

The case of Japan

To start with Japan, since it is the society I know best. What does it mean to say that it is a much less marketized society than Britain ever was in the 1970s (or, indeed, ever has been, in the last century)? Firstly, labour-markets. For executive talent, there simply is no labour-market in Japan: no headhunters, luring managerial supermen with attractive packages of options, pensions and bonuses, apart from those—and in the financial sector, this has become a by no means insignificant exception—working for the growing number of foreign firms. The boards of the major Japanese corporations consist of the top managers, mostly appointed after a lifetime of working for the firm. The president, appointed from among them, earns the top grade of the incremental salary-structure on which he started, forty years earlier, when he was recruited as a raw graduate—a grade only a few percentage points above his previous wage.[7] After four years, the president will have the major say in appoint-

---

[6] *Economist*, 29 April 2000, p. 77.
[7] As was the case in the British Civil Service, before it started recruiting permanent secretaries from the market.

ing his successor and then move on, to become the chairman. After another four years, he will give over the chairmanship and become a senior advisor.

There is more movement from firm to firm lower down the scale, especially in the service sector, and somewhat more influence of market forces—the supply and demand for skills—on levels of pay; but even in small firms there is a strong propensity towards long tenures, with wage adjustments depending primarily on the firm's ability to afford them. In larger firms, with enterprise unions, even manual workers have an employment system similar to that of their managers: an unwritten, but effective, guarantee of employment to retirement, to be broken only by generous early-retirement packages. They also have a similar internal promotion system, combining seniority with performance criteria. Economists—uncomfortable if they cannot see markets everywhere— like to say that Japanese firms have *internal* labour-markets. But an internal labour-*market* usually implies that, although the competition for vacancies is confined to existing employees, there is still competition, followed, when an appointment is made, by a process of recontracting— bargaining the appropriate wage for the job. This is not what happens in Japan. People are posted by the personnel department from one job to another, in much the same way as happens in the British army or diplomatic corps. If their salary changes, it does so in accordance with the rules of the pay-system. The so-called internal labour-market is internal all right; but not really a market.

The employees of a Matsushita or a Sharp thus have a sense of a relationship with their firm comparable to a soldier's sense of regimental loyalty. The board members—typically, there will be many: some 15 per cent of male employees aged between fifty and fifty-four are on their firms' boards—are more likely to see themselves as the elders of an enterprise community than as the agents of shareholder principals. They are at the top of the hierarchy of employees, but they are still employees; servants, whose only master is 'the company'—a transcendental entity, with a history, a personality, a reputation and, if they do their job, a future. This conception is a long way from that of the firm as a network of contracts. One indicator of difference: in the annual wage-negotiations (still called the 'spring offensive', a legacy of the days when they really were an expression of class warfare), a manager who talks down the union's demand from 4 to 2 per cent knows that, as a result, his own pay will probably only go up by 2 per cent, too. Again, this is much closer to civil service pay negotiations than to wage-bargaining in British private industry.

One important reason why managers have such little sense of themselves as agents of shareholder principals—despite the fact that their law gives shareholders powers over the firm comparable to English ones—lies in the Japanese cross-shareholding system. More than half the equity of Japanese firms is held by 'stable shareholders'—the banks who float the firm's loans, the insurance companies who broker their insurance, and other companies with whom the firm trades or has joint ventures—often (as with the banks) on a reciprocal basis: Hitachi owns several million Nissan shares, and *vice versa*. In other words, the bulk of shares are still locked up in what one might call 'relational', as opposed to, in Summers's phrase, 'arms-length' and 'contractual' shareholding patterns, with the stable shareholders also providing a safe guarantee against hostile takeovers. Share prices are set through the trading of a relatively small proportion of the shares, by securities companies, individual speculators and, increasingly in recent years, by foreign pension and mutual funds, who now hold some 14 per cent of equity.

Once again, and in a very important sense: less market. The Japanese stock-market is not a place where you can buy and sell control over companies. Agreed mergers do take place; but a deep-seated cultural antipathy towards the idea of buying and selling what are still seen as communities is here reinforced by the knowledge that stable shareholders will rally to the defence, if anyone attempts a takeover.

Muted competition

This, then—the nature of the firm, and the self-perceptions and objectives of managers—is a crucial feature making Japan significantly less marketist than Britain, for instance. Let me quickly mention three other salient features that distinguish the Japanese economy. Firstly, the long-term patterns of inter-firm cooperation—between main banks and client firms, for instance, or automobile companies and their suppliers—which can survive considerable changes in market conditions. Secondly, the balance between cooperation and competition, which characterizes market competitors everywhere, is tilted here much more strongly towards cooperation, largely through the powerful industry associations.

And thirdly, the strong role of government, both in development—the winner-picking, selective subsidies, promotion of research clubs, and so on—and, just as importantly, as a sort of umpire, resolving distributional conflicts of interest, largely through negotiations with the industry associations, in something of the same spirit as the army of industry regulators in Britain, but with much of the regulation in Japan being through informal 'administrative guidance'—relational regulation, one might call it.

Note how widely applicable that word 'relational' is in describing the Japanese economy. 'Relational banking' as opposed to arm's-length, contractual banking, is a familiar term, as is 'relational trading' with suppliers. Employment patterns might equally be described as relational. That wide applicability of the term gives a clue to the sense in which Japanese economic institutions hang together as a system—through what one might call motivational consistency. Similar behavioural dispositions are called for in a variety of situations: the acceptance, first of all, of certain basic obligations, imposed on one as a member of Japanese society; and then the willingness to take on further obligations, by entering into long-term commitments that seriously limit one's options—one's ability to shift, for example, to another employer, another supplier, another bank. There is a pervasive tendency, to borrow the useful terms of Arthur Okun, to turn auction markets into customer ones.[8]

There is a second mechanism that makes these institutions hang together as a system—institutional interlock, institutional complementarity. Lifetime employment would not last for very long if there were no cross-shareholding system suppressing takeovers, so that managers had to worry about being undervalued in the stock-market and so give absolute priority to making profits, downsizing rapidly when it was necessary to do so.

Stagnation

It was this system, of course, which, up until the 1990s, received so much praise, so much discussion in America's business schools, as the secret of Japan's success. Its capacity for long-term investment and cooperative synergies were said to be responsible for growth rates (4 to 5 per cent in the 1980s) double those of the short-termist, ruthlessly com-

---

[8] Arthur Okun, *Prices and Quantities, A macroeconomic analysis*, Washington 1981.

petitive Anglo-Saxon economies. 'Every American weakness', wrote an American banker, was seen

> to mirror a Japanese strength: the twelve-year-old schoolboy in necktie and short pants doing college-level maths, the modestly paid company executive pouring funds into research and development, clean, crime- and pothole-free city streets, gleaming bullet-trains and world-class factories, high savings rates, and the sober brilliance of MOF bureaucrats.[9]

That same banker, addressing a Japanese business lunch more recently:

> Only when we see less well-performing Japanese companies taken over by real owners can we expect to see a thorough purging of excess capacity. Only when the Tokyo Stock Market becomes a genuine stock market, with shares that represent real ownership of corporate assets changing hands, can we find out what Japanese companies are actually worth. And only when owners capture the residual returns of business can we expect them to shoulder the full risks of bankruptcy.[10]

Such talk has gone down well in Japan since the late 1990s. As the Prime Minister Yoshihiko Mori said in his acceptance speech in the Diet recently: 'The system and the ways of thinking which, for fifty years, have supported Japan's astonishing development, have now become inappropriate for the world we live in', and must be reformed.[11] As to how they should be reformed, the slogans that have dominated the debate—deregulation, greater disclosure and transparency, better returns on equity, global standards, rethinking lifetime employment—have not been very explicit; nor was the Prime Minister's speech. Yet the spur to the broad consensus on reform is clear: while the United States—about whose deficiencies the Japanese used to be so patronizing—is booming ahead, Japan is stagnating.

Why is it stagnating? My potted history of the 1990s goes like this. The bursting of the late 1980s asset bubble, and the collapse of real-estate and stock-market prices, left Japanese banks with a debt overhang of massive proportions and this, together with the strong negative-wealth effect on consumers, brought an initial severe recession. The banks'

---

[9] R. Taggart Murphy, *The Weight of the Yen*, New York 1996.
[10] R. Taggart Murphy, 'Tinkering or reform? The deregulation of Japan's financial system', Hotel Okura, The Tokyo Report, June 1997.
[11] *Nihon Keizai Shimbun*, 20 April 2000.

strategy was to trade through and conceal their technical insolvency until the economy began to pick up, and they could write off their bad debts against profits. (A standard banking strategy, practised by the American banks in the 1980s and by the Crédit Lyonnais more recently; though, as M. Trichet and the Japanese Ministry of Finance have subsequently found, collusion in the cosmetic accounting necessary can get you into trouble.) By the middle of the 1990s, thanks to some heavy Keynesian reflation packages, it seemed that the strategy was working. The economy did indeed begin to pick up, with a growth rate of 5.5 per cent in 1996. The next year, in a premature burst of fiscal prudence, the Ministry of Finance tried to wind down what was already thought to be an alarming public debt by raising social security charges and the sales tax. The consequent dampening of consumer spending coincided with the Asian crisis, bringing a fresh blow to exports and to the banks. A couple of major financial institutions were allowed to fail, and the sense of gloom and insecurity brought another major fall in investment and consumer spending.

The banking crisis has more or less been solved (with public money), but the problems of confidence and demand-deficiency remain. Exports continue to do well, in spite of an overvalued exchange rate. The second-biggest carmaker—so badly managed financially that it had to sell a controlling stake to Renault—continues to run what is reputedly Europe's most efficient auto-plant, in Sunderland. Industrial research flourishes—the number of patents registered annually in the United States by Japanese firms grew by over 50 per cent during the 1990s. It is domestic demand that is the problem. At first it was a matter of anxious consumers, saving too much and spending too little; more recently, spending has been further hit by a rise in unemployment and cuts in bonuses—hence, reduced purchasing power. Pessimists and optimists are still arguing over whether it has or hasn't bottomed out, and still finding indices to bolster either case. The downward spiral could steepen if the marketeer advocates of 'blood-on-the-floor' restructuring have their way. Even if they do not (and there were quite fierce reactions when Standard and Poor downgraded Toyota's bond rating for not being serious about axing jobs), there is enough such talk to keep anxieties high, consumer demand constrained and investment plans cautious, in spite of some recovery in profits.

Meanwhile, the American boom goes from strength to strength. Buoyant Americans consume between 4 and 5 per cent more than they produce, while anxious Japanese consume between 2 and 3 per cent less than they produce, and send their savings across the Pacific to help support the consumer debt that sustains the American boom. Hegemons and their citizens do well in this strange world.

Reform movement

That gloom and loss of self-confidence are the central factors in the general consensus on the need for fundamental change seems beyond doubt. Japanese opinion has reverted, after the self-congratulatory mood of the late 1980s, to what has been a consistent stance since 1870—namely, acknowledgement of the need to catch up with what are still often called, in a five-character cliché, the 'advanced countries of Europe and America'; although today it is almost exclusively America that reformers have in mind. Much is known and written in Japan about the horrors of American society, about its inequalities, and the excesses of American boardroom salaries; nevertheless, as far as com-petitiveness is concerned, America is the model. The exemplars of self-reliant entrepreneurship are to be found in Silicon Valley, of bold and effective risk-taking in American venture capitalists, of effective and honest corporate governance in American corporations, of 'trans-parency' in financial transactions on the American stock-exchange, of consumer protection in American courts. Once, Japanese businessmen used to be sent to get their MBAs at American business schools for 'know thine enemy' purposes, and came back to their firms as loyal par-ticipants in a consciously different system. Nowadays, more of them either go under their own steam or else desert their sponsoring firm to return as 'consultants', teaching how to maximize shareholder-value. It is economists with PhDs from Chicago and MIT, nowadays, who make the running on government committees.

The reformers have concentrated on two main goals. One is deregula-tion: more competition, consumer sovereignty, a reduction of the power of the industry associations (in cahoots with the bureaucrats), the end of what was called the 'convoy system' of mutual support in banking, the opening up of sectors like insurance to foreign firms. The second is the transformation of Japanese corporations into proper capitalist firms, both through raising profit-levels, and heightening managers' concern with shareholder-value, by changes in corporate governance; and—as a means to that end of greater efficiency—through instituting far more flexible labour-market practices: an end to lifetime employment, and a revolution in pay-systems, to reward performance rather than seniority.

Recall the initial distinction of the forces for change: global markets and cultural globalization on the one hand (in this case, the force of the American model) and internal, evolutionary development on the other. There are two trends of long-term internal change in Japanese society which lend the reformers support. The first is a development towards greater heterogeneity and individualism. A symptomatic quote from a lawyer, criticizing a book from the 1980s which had praised the Japanese system as being not plain capitalism but 'human-capital-ism':

> Is human-capital-ism really so good for humans? In the truly *modern* labour contract, a worker sells his work; he doesn't sell his soul, his commitment. The employee-sovereign firm requires Japanese to spend their whole lives, from birth to retirement, in enforced competition, first to enter the firm, then for advancement within it. For that they have to sacrifice freedom and individuality, human feeling and creativity. They have no time for cultural pursuits, for playing a useful role in the family or community. They are offered spiritual poverty in return for material riches.[12]

The second major internal change has been the growing wealth of the middle and upper-middle strata. The managers and the chattering classes of the media and the universities in the 1960s were hard up, saving desperately to get out of employer-owned housing and into a home of their own before they were fifty. Today, a much larger proportion have sizeable financial assets: the 'more power to the shareholder' slogan has greater appeal.

There is also a reasonable argument from necessity, on two counts. Firstly, the globalization of financial markets means that Japanese firms will be starved of capital if they do not offer rates of return comparable with those in countries that use capital most efficiently—although this argument is weakened, as far as long-term capital is concerned, by the

---

[12] Nakajima Shuzo, *Kabushiki no mochiai to kaishaho (Cross-shareholding and company law)*, Tokyo 1990. The book is a printing, with afterthought comments, of a 1977 Masters thesis. The foil for his arguments is Itami Hiroyuki, *Jimpon-shugi kigyo (The human-capital-ist enterprise)*, Tokyo 1987.

remarkable volatility of yen exchange-rates. Secondly, higher profits and dividend levels may be the only way to cope with demographic change. Two mechanisms are involved. First, in an ageing society such as Japan's, the pressure to make savings profitable will increase. Secondly, one of the things that has, hitherto, made them tolerably profitable was population growth, driving a steady increase in land prices which, in turn, helped to produce a steady increase in share prices (steady and gradual, that is, until the late 1980s bubble). The capital gains in the stock-market, as much asset inflation as real-asset accumulation, provided respectable rates of return in spite of dividend yields rarely exceeding 1 per cent—the abysmal level that America is only just reaching, at the peak of its stock-exchange bubble. Absent these capital gains, with the ending of the population growth that ultimately sustained them, and profits and dividend levels must rise or nobody will save, and the life insurance companies will all go down the drain.

Actual change?

Yet, for all the talk, actual system change has been marginal. After volumes of reports on corporate governance, not much has happened. Some firms have sliced their boards in two and brought in one or two outside directors to their strategy board, but without any clear representative role for shareholders. Six years ago, only a handful of company presidents or chairmen made the rounds of fund managers in London and New York; now they go in droves but still, the number of Japanese firms with as much as 40 per cent of their capital in foreign hands, much less Mannesmann's 60 per cent, is tiny. Almost every firm has gone over to what it calls a 'merit' pay and promotion system, less geared to seniority, but even in Nissan, under vigorous Renault management, the age of the latest board appointments has dropped only to 46 and 47, from the traditional 51 and 52-year-olds. And the pay spread which, for managers in their forties, used to lie between about 30 per cent above and 20 per cent below the median—i.e., the median for lifetime employees of the same age, on the same career-track—has, in most firms, widened only by a few percentage points. There is much talk of the cross-shareholding system unwinding, but it does not yet show up appreciably in the statistics, and looks much more like the emergency adjustment of balance-sheets by firms in trouble than a bold rejection of the system. The law has been changed to allow directors and senior managers to be paid with stock-options but, in the two hundred or so firms that have adopted the scheme, such payments have been symbolic rather than constituting a substantial part of directors' emoluments.

Deregulation has broken up a number of cosy arrangements that gave producers a comfortable life at the consumer's expense but, except in a few industries like domestic airlines and gasoline distribution, its impact has been limited. Lifetime employment has been, as they say, 're-thought', but it is still bankruptcies and voluntary early retirement that are adding to the unemployment rolls, not redundancy dismissals. Labour legislation has enlarged the scope of agency despatch and other, non-standard forms of employment, but the numbers involved are still small. There is much talk—standard OECD talk—about rolling back the welfare state, but the pay-as-you-go pension scheme, which provides pensions by redistributing labour income (rather than relying, as most British pensions do, on the capital share of GNP) is still alive and well, and has recently been revamped in a way that should see it through the worst period of ageing effects. At the same time, a new and compulsory old people's long-term-care insurance scheme has been launched, which should have beneficial employment side effects. In April 2000, when Sasebo Shipbuilding applied for protection from creditors in order to restructure, the list of diversification start-ups it was planning (in order to absorb its former workers) included a long-term-care provider agency. The banks are finally going to get a tax-privileged equity-saving scheme, modelled on the American 401(K) plans; but 87 per cent of the great pool of ten-year-deposit post-office savings that came due in April 2000 went back into post-office accounts.

It does seem, too, that the reformers' control over the ideological airspace may be weakening, with the ending of the Japanese banking crisis, and with doubts increasing as to the sustainability of the American boom. One straw in the wind was the contribution by Miyauchi Yoshihiko, president of the financial-lease firm, Orix, to a recent *Asahi Shimbun* symposium. Well known as a leading shareholder-value man—and two years ago, chairman of a business committee on corporate governance whose report was greeted with great enthusiasm (some think, originally inspired by) the California Public Employees' Retirement Scheme, or CalPERS, America's leading pension fund—Miyauchi spoke of coming

> to have doubts about shareholder capitalism. I'm forever sending out the message that the kind of shareholders we want are those interested in medium and long-term growth. But if it's medium and long-term growth

you are interested in, then what you are talking about is what is often spoken of as the Japanese vice—namely, concern for stakeholders.[13]

It is just, he concluded, that Japanese have hitherto not acknowledged the centrality of shareholders among the stakeholders.

Germany: statutory restraint

Capitalism in Germany deviates from the marketist model in much the same way as it does in Japan: more regulation in restraint of competition; a dense associational life, producing important public goods such as the training system; and, above all, firms run more for the benefit of their employees than for their shareholders. The debates about competition and deregulation, about shareholder-value, about the welfare state, are very similar, too. There are, however, important differences.

First, the cultural gap between Germany and America is far smaller than that between America and Japan. As one consequence of this, German executives are much more likely to be fluent, English-speaking participants in an international labour-market—Ron Sommer, of Deutsche Telecom, used to run an American company, for instance. Far more German executives are thoroughly at home in an Anglo-Saxon business environment. At the start of the Vodafone–Mannesmann takeover battle, both Blair and Schröder might have talked as if it were a contest between two different cultural systems; but Klaus Esser of Mannesmann played the defence strictly on a 'We can provide the best deal for shareholders' basis, without appeal to cultural traditions or national autonomy. It is unlikely that the president of Sony, say, for all his frequent speeches about shareholder-value, and the firm's determinedly cultivated image as a global rather than a Japanese company, would ever have done the same. Integration into Europe, of course, also provides an important extra dimension to debates on institutional reform in Germany— particularly those regarding financial regulation, competition policy and corporate governance—with Brussels pushing predominantly in a marketist, Anglo-Saxon direction.

There is a third, crucial difference. The Japanese community firm rests on communitarian traditions. Its structure is governed not by

---

[13] *Asahi Shimbun*, 12 April 2000.

statute but by convention, supported only peripherally by case law. In Germany, by contrast, the employee-favouring stakeholder system rests not on convention but on law. Through the twin systems of codetermination—through works councils in the firm, and the legal support for bargained wage-contracts between industrial unions and employers' associations—the system balances the legal rights of employees against those of shareholders. It does so in a way that acknowledges a starting-point of class antagonism, and makes an awareness of the zero-sum elements of the employment relation much more salient. In Japan, those who advocate 'more attention to shareholders' only rarely admit that this might mean less attention to employees; in Germany, the battle between reformers and defenders of the employee-favouring firm is clearly joined and fought in class terms—business interests versus the workers and their unions. The survival of the Japanese system depends in part upon the inertia of cultural reproduction and the continuing dominance of a communitarian managerial ethic of benevolent responsibility. In Germany, it depends on the continuing strength of trade unions. Which is likely to erode faster?

Relative survival power

Three factors, at least, suggest that it is the Japanese system that has the greater chance of resisting incorporation into American-led global capitalism along Anglo-Saxon lines, and of carrying into the age of high technology an economic structure with a dense web of obligation-loaded 'relational' transactions, with much of its business done in customer, not auction, markets. First and foremost, there is the sense of cultural, and racial, distinctness. That *this* is Japanese, and *that* American, can become a far more potent argument for preserving the *this* than such calls in Germany would be. German social cohesion may have drawn on informal, socially rooted obligations, which its legal-rational bureaucratic traditions enabled it to 'constitutionalize' in law. But if that legal structure does not continue to be rooted in some kind of 'spirit' of community, the web of obligation can much more easily be 'deconstitutionalized'.

A second factor, intricately interlinked, that makes Japan a more likely resister to global Anglo-Saxon capitalism is that its corporatism, to use the term loosely, has been more 'holistic'. That is to say, it has depended more on all the compromising parties sharing some sense that they have to 'think for the nation', and less on a simple horse-traded class compromise between opposing interests in a zero-sum game. This is apparent in the annual wage-round debates in Japan, in which both sides attach a great deal of weight to their interpretation of the needs of the national macroeconomy. In Germany, by contrast, the attempt at true concertation—of the kind that worked, and still works, in the Netherlands and Austria—failed. Inflation control depended on how the unions and employers accepted the discipline—or the threat—of unilateral action by the Bundesbank. Schröder's present problems with his 'Alliance for Jobs' spring, in large measure, from the unions' insistence on retaining their self-defined mission of maximizing the interests of their members, rather than attempting to move beyond and 'think for the nation'.

One does not have to go back to medieval feudal traditions to explain the difference between the two countries in this propensity for 'holistic' corporatist thinking, even if such deeper roots are not to be ruled out. It is enough to hark back to the 1920s. Japan, too, had its militant unions, who had to face not only employers but also the police, and the violence of hired thugs: people were killed. But the violence was on nothing like the scale seen in Germany—or even in America, for that matter. Nor was the shaping of the post-war institutions profoundly influenced, as the German unions were, by returning exiles with vivid memories of that brutality. The tiny handful of Japanese exiles coming back from China and Russia were vastly outnumbered, in the post-war unions, by people who had earlier made their compromises in the Patriotic Labour Front, into which the pre-war organizations had been incorporated. That history still counts. It means there is greater scope in Japan for propagating the notion that there is a national, rather than just a class interest, in preserving established structures and organizations, and protecting them against the pressures of global markets, global firms and US-dominated global institutions.

One final reason why Japan might put up a stiffer resistance to Anglo-Saxon capitalism than Germany is because of its neighbours. There are many similarities between Japan and Korea, in terms of employment institutions, business practices and views of the state's role in the economy, and in the debates currently under way over how far 'Americanization' should be allowed to go. China's state-owned enterprises, for all their diminishing contribution to GNP, are still norm-setters, and their employee-favouring orientation is not in doubt—any more than China's nationalistic propensity to resist American 'corruption' of its Confucian socialist soul. Both of these countries are still some way from Japan's industrial maturity, still growing at a fast rate. In another few decades, the weight of East Asia in the whole world economy could seriously eclipse that of the United States and of Europe, with profound consequences for capitalist development. At present, the Japanese are in no mood to think of preserving their institutions because of some valued quality of 'Asian-ness'—still synonymous, for the vast majority, with backwardness, in contrast to American modernity. That may not always be so, particularly if the new Cold War which seems to be shaping up between China and America really takes hold, as it might well do if the Pentagon perceives China to have serious rival potential in missile and anti-missile defence technology. The interconnexions between the 'soft' power of cultural hegemony, and the 'hard' power of military might, have fascinated political scientists for centuries. The multiple modes in which both kinds of power may now be influencing the shape of economic institutions in the non-hegemons are no less complex and fascinating.

Name Index